WILLIAM PITT

AND

THE GREAT WAR

Emery Walker Ph. sc.

William Pitt, in later life
From a painting by Hoppner

WILLIAM PITT

AND

THE GREAT WAR

BY

J. HOLLAND ROSE, LITT.D.

England and France have held in their hands the fate of the
world, especially that of European civilization. How much harm
we have done one another : how much good we might have done !
—*Napoleon to Colonel Wilks*, 20*th April* 1816.

GREENWOOD PRESS, PUBLISHERS
WESTPORT, CONNECTICUT

Originally published in 1911
by G. Bell and Sons, Ltd., London

Reprinted from an original copy in the collections
of the Brooklyn Public Library

First Greenwood Reprinting 1971

Library of Congress Catalogue Card Number 71-110862

SBN 8371-4533-3

Printed in the United States of America

PREFACE

IN the former volume, entitled "William Pitt and National Revival," I sought to trace the career of Pitt the Younger up to the year 1791. Until then he was occupied almost entirely with attempts to repair the evils arising out of the old order of things. Retrenchment and Reform were his first watchwords; and though in the year 1785 he failed in his efforts to renovate the life of Parliament and to improve the fiscal relations with Ireland, yet his domestic policy in the main achieved a surprising success. Scarcely less eminent, though far less known, were his services in the sphere of diplomacy. In the year 1783, when he became First Lord of the Treasury and Chancellor of the Exchequer, nearly half of the British Empire was torn away, and the remainder seemed to be at the mercy of the allied Houses of Bourbon. France, enjoying the alliance of Spain and Austria and the diplomatic wooings of Catharine II and Frederick the Great, gave the law to Europe.

By the year 1790 all had changed. In 1787 Pitt supported Frederick William II of Prussia in overthrowing French supremacy in the Dutch Netherlands; and a year later he framed with those two States an alliance which not only dictated terms to Austria at the Congress of Reichenbach but also compelled her to forego her farreaching schemes on the lower Danube, and to restore the *status quo* in Central Europe and in her Belgian provinces. British policy triumphed over that of Spain in the Nootka Sound dispute of the year 1790, thereby securing for the Empire the coast of what is now British Columbia; it also saved Sweden from a position of acute danger; and Pitt cherished the hope of forming a league of the smaller States, including the Dutch Republic, Denmark, Sweden, Poland, and, if possible, Turkey, which, with support from Great Britain and Prussia, would withstand the almost revolutionary schemes of the Russian and Austrian Courts.

These larger aims were unattainable. The duplicity of the Court of Berlin, the triumphs of the Russian arms on the Danube, and changes in the general diplomatic situation, enabled Catharine II to foil the efforts of Pitt in 1791. She worked her will on the Turks and not long after on the Poles; Sweden came to an understanding with her; and Prussia, slighting the British alliance, drew near to the new Hapsburg Sovereign, Leopold II. In fact, the events of the French Revolution in the year 1791 served to focus attention more and more upon Paris; and monarchs who had thought of little but the conquest or partition of weaker States now talked of a crusade to restore order at Paris, with Gustavus III of Sweden as the new Cœur de Lion. This occidentation of diplomacy became pronounced at the time of the attempted escape of Louis XVI and Marie Antoinette to the eastern frontier at Midsummer 1791. Their capture at Varennes and their ignominious return to Paris are in several respects the central event of the French Revolution. The incident aroused both democrats and royalists to a fury which foredoomed to failure all attempts at compromise between the old order and the new. The fierceness of the strife in France incited monarchists in all lands to importunate demands for the extirpation of "the French plague"; and hence were set in motion forces which Pitt vainly strove to curb. War soon broke out in Central Europe. His endeavours to localize it were fruitless; and thenceforth his chief task was to bring to an honourable close a conflict which he had not sought. It is therefore fitting that this study of the latter, less felicitous, but equally glorious part of his career should begin with a survey of the situation in Great Britain and on the Continent at the time of the incident at Varennes which opened a new chapter in the history of Europe.

In the present volume I have sought to narrate faithfully and as fully as is possible the story of the dispute with France, the chief episodes of the war, and the varied influences which it exerted upon political developments in these islands, including the early Radical movement, the Irish Rebellion of 1798, and other events which brought about the Union of the British and Irish Parliaments, the break up of the great national party at Westminster in 1801, and the collapse of the strength of Pitt early in the course of the struggle with the concentrated might of Napoleon.

That mighty drama dwarfs the actors. Even the French Emperor could not sustain the rôle which he aspired to play, and, failing to discern the signs of the times, was whirled aside by the forces which he claimed to control. Is it surprising that Pitt, more slightly endowed by nature, and beset by the many limitations which hampered the advisers of George III, should have sunk beneath burdens such as no other English statesman has been called upon to bear? The success or failure of such a career is, however, to be measured by the final success or failure of his policy; and in this respect, as I have shown, the victor in the Great War was not Napoleon but Pitt.

To that high enterprise he consecrated all the powers of his being. His public life is everything; his private life, unfortunately, counts for little. The materials for reconstructing it are meagre. I have been able here and there to throw new light on his friendships, difficulties, trials, and, in particular, on the love episode of the year 1797. But in the main the story of the life of Pitt must soar high above the club and the *salon* to

. . . the toppling heights of Duty scaled.

Again I must express my hearty thanks to those who have generously placed at my disposal new materials of great value, especially to His Grace the Duke of Portland, the Earl of Harrowby, Earl Stanhope, E. G. Pretyman, Esq., M.P., and A. M. Broadley, Esq.; also to the Rev. William Hunt, D.Litt., and Colonel E. M. Lloyd, late R.E., for valuable advice tendered during the correction of the proofs, and to Mr. Hubert Hall of H.M. Public Record Office for assistance during my researches there. I am also indebted to Lord Auckland and to Messrs. Longmans for permission to reproduce the miniature of the Hon. Miss Eden which appeared in Lord Ashbourne's "Pitt, Some Chapters of his Life and Times," and to Mr. and Mrs. Doulton for permission to my daughter to make the sketch of Bowling Green House, the last residence of Pitt, which is reproduced near the end of this volume. In the preface to the former volume I expressed my acknowledgements to recent works bearing on this subject; and I need only add that numerous new letters of George III, Pitt, Grenville, Burke, Canning, etc., which could only be referred to here, will be published in a work entitled "Pitt and Napoleon Miscellanies," including also essays and notes.

J. H. R.

MARCH 1911.

CONTENTS

CHAP.   PAGE

I. ROYALISTS AND RADICALS 1

II. BEFORE THE STORM 29

III. PEACE OR WAR? 57

IV. THE RUPTURE WITH FRANCE 85

V. THE FLEMISH CAMPAIGN (1793) . . . 118

VI. TOULON 143

VII. THE BRITISH JACOBINS 164

VIII. PITT AND THE ALLIES (1794-5) 195

IX. THE WEST INDIES 219

X. SPAIN AND HAYTI 230

XI. THE CAPE OF GOOD HOPE: CORSICA: QUIBERON 250

XII. PITT AS WAR MINISTER (1793-8) . . . 265

XIII. DEARTH AND DISCONTENT 282

XIV. THE YEARS OF STRAIN (1796-7) . . . 299

XV. NATIONAL REVIVAL 321

XVI. THE IRISH REBELLION 339

XVII. THE SECOND COALITION 365

XVIII. THE UNION 389

XIX. THE UNION (CONTINUED) 411

XX. RESIGNATION 431

XXI. PITT AND HIS FRIENDS (1794-1805) . . . 454

XXII. ADDINGTON OR PITT? 483

XXIII. PITT AND NAPOLEON 505

XXIV. THE LAST STRUGGLE 534

EPILOGUE 559

STATISTICS OF THE YEARS 1792-1801 . . . 571

INDEX 573

LIST OF ILLUSTRATIONS

TO FACE
PAGE

WILLIAM PITT, IN LATER LIFE. (From a painting by
Hoppner in the National Portrait Gallery).

Frontispiece

THE HOUSE OF COMMONS IN 1793. (From a painting in
the National Portrait Gallery by K. A. Hickel) . 164

THE HON. ELEANOR EDEN. (From a miniature) . . 300

HENRY DUNDAS, FIRST VISCOUNT MELVILLE. (From a
painting by Sir T. Lawrence) 484

BOWLING GREEN HOUSE, PUTNEY HEATH. (From a
pencil sketch by Elsie H. Rose). 554

ERRATA

Page 180, *ad fin., for* "Hamilton, Rowan" *read* "Hamilton Rowan."
  „   311, line 1, *for* "formerly" *read* "brother of."
  „   311, line 2, *for* "Lord Hood" *read* "Sir Alexander Hood."
  „   551, line 11 from end, *for* "6th" *read* "4th."

ABBREVIATIONS OF THE TITLES OF THE CHIEF WORKS REFERRED TO IN THIS VOLUME

ANN. REG. = " Annual Register."

ASHBOURNE = " Pitt: some Chapters of his Life and Times," by the Rt. Hon. Lord Ashbourne. 1898.

AUCKLAND JOURNALS = " The Journal and Corresp. of William, Lord Auckland." 4 vols. 1861.

BEAUFORT P. = " MSS. of the Duke of Beaufort," etc. (Hist. MSS. Comm.). 1891.

B.M. ADD. MSS. = Additional Manuscripts of the British Museum.

BUCKINGHAM P. = " Mems. of the Court and Cabinets of George III," by the Duke of Buckingham. 2 vols. 1853.

CAMPBELL. = " Lives of the Lord Chancellors," by Lord Campbell. 8 vols. 1845-69.

CASTLEREAGH CORRESP. = " Mems. and Corresp. of Viscount Castlereagh." 8 vols. 1848-53.

CHEVENING MSS. = Manuscripts of Earl Stanhope, preserved at Chevening.

CUNNINGHAM = " Growth of Eng. Industry and Commerce (Modern Times)," by Dr. W. Cunningham. 1892.

DROPMORE P. = " The Manuscripts of J. B. Fortescue, Esq., preserved at Dropmore " (Hist. MSS. Comm.). 7 vols. 1892-1910.

FORTESCUE = " The History of the British Army," by the Hon. J. W. Fortescue. vol. iv.

HÄUSSER = " Deutsche Geschichte (1786-1804)," by L. Häusser. 4 vols. 1861-3.

HOLLAND = " Memoirs of the Whig Party," by Lord Holland. 2 vols. 1852.

JESSE = " Mems. of the Life and Reign of George III," by J. H. Jesse. 3 vols. 1867.

LECKY = " Hist. of England in the Eighteenth Century," by W. E. H. Lecky. 8 vols. Fifth edit. 1891-1904.

MALMESBURY DIARIES = " Diaries and Corresp. of the First Earl of Malmesbury." 4 vols. 1844.

PARL. HIST. = " History of the Parliamentary Debates " (after 1804 continued in Hansard).

PELLEW = " Life and Corresp. of the first Viscount Sidmouth," by Rev. C. Pellew. 3 vols. 1847.

PITT MSS. = Pitt MSS., preserved at H.M. Public Record Office.

PORRITT = "The Unreformed House of Commons," by E. Porritt, 2 vols. 1909.

PRETYMAN MSS. = MSS. of E. G. Pretyman, Esq., M.P., preserved at Orwell Park.

ROSE G., " DIARIES " = " Diaries and Corresp. of Rt. Hon. G. Rose." 2 vols. 1860.

ROSE, "NAPOLEON" = "Life of Napoleon," by J. H. Rose. 2 vols. 1909.

ROSE, "THIRD COALITION " = "Select Despatches . . . relating to the Formation of the Third Coalition (1804-5)," ed. by J. H. Rose (Royal Historical Soc., 1904).

RUTLAND P. = " MSS. of the Duke of Rutland " (Hist. MSS. Comm.). 3 vols. 1894.

RUVILLE = "William Pitt, Earl of Chatham," by A. von Ruville (Eng. transl.). 3 vols. 1907.

SOREL = " L'Europe et la Révolution française," par A. Sorel. Pts. II, III. 1889, 1897.

STANHOPE = " Life of . . . William Pitt," by Earl Stanhope. 4 vols. 3rd edition. 1867.

SYBEL = "Geschichte der Revolutionzeit (1789-1800)," von H. von Sybel. Eng. translation. 4 vols. 1867-9.

VIVENOT = " Quellen zur Geschichte der deutschen Kaiserpolitik Œsterreichs . . ." von A. von Vivenot. 1873.

WRAXALL = "Memoirs of Sir N. W. Wraxall " (1772-84), edited by H. B. Wheatley. 5 vols. 1884.

WILLIAM PITT

AND

THE GREAT WAR

WILLIAM PITT AND THE GREAT WAR

CHAPTER I

ROYALISTS AND RADICALS[1]

Détruire l'anarchie française, c'est se préparer une gloire immortelle.—
CATHARINE II, 1791.

The pretended Rights of Man, which have made this havoc, cannot be the rights of the people. For to be a people and to have these rights are incompatible. The one supposes the presence, the other the absence, of a state of civil society.—BURKE, *Appeal from the New to the Old Whigs*.

A constitution is the property of a nation and not of those who exercise the Government.—T. PAINE, *Rights of Man*, part ii.

IN the midst of a maze of events there may sometimes be found one which serves as a clue, revealing hidden paths, connecting ways which seem far apart, and leading to a clear issue. Such was the attempted flight of Louis XVI and Marie Antoinette to the eastern frontier of France at midsummer 1791, which may be termed the central event of the French Revolution, at least in its first phases. The aim of joining the armed bands of *émigrés* and the forces held in readiness by Austria was so obvious as to dispel the myth of "a patriot King" misled for a time by evil counsellors. True, the moderates, from sheer alarm, still sought to save the monarchy, and for a time with surprising success. But bolder men, possessed both of insight and humour,

---

[1] I am perfectly aware that the term "Radical" (in its first form, "Radical Reformer") does not appear until a few years later; but I use it here and in the following chapters because there is no other word which expresses the same meaning.

perceived the futility of all such efforts to hold down on the throne the father of his people lest he should again run away. In this perception the young Republican party found its genesis and its inspiration. In truth, the attempted flight of the King was a death-blow to the moderate party, into which the lamented leader, Mirabeau, had sought to infuse some of his masterful energy. Thenceforth, the future belonged either to the Jacobins or to the out and out royalists.

These last saw the horizon brighten in the East. Louis XVI being under constraint in Paris, their leaders were the French Princes, the Comte de Provence (afterwards Louis XVIII) and the Comte d'Artois (Charles X). Around them at Coblentz there clustered angry swarms of French nobles, gentlemen, and orthodox priests, whose zeal was reckoned by the earliness of the date at which they had "emigrated." For many months the agents of these *émigrés* had vainly urged the Chanceries of the Continent to a royalist crusade against the French rebels; and it seemed appropriate that Gustavus III of Sweden should be their only convert. Now of a sudden their demands appeared, instinct with statecraft; and courtiers everywhere exclaimed that "the French pest" must be stamped out. In that thought lay in germ a quarter of a century of war.

Already the Prussian and Austrian Governments had vaguely discussed the need of a joint intervention in France. In fact this subject formed one of the pretexts for the missions of the Prussian envoy, Bischoffswerder, to the Emperor Leopold in February and June 1791.[1] As was shown at the close of the former volume, "William Pitt and National Revival," neither Court took the matter seriously, the Eastern Question being then their chief concern. But the flight to Varennes, which Leopold had helped to arrange, imposed on him the duty of avenging the ensuing insults to his sister. He prepared to do so with a degree of caution highly characteristic of him. He refused to move until he knew the disposition of the Powers, especially of England. From Padua, where the news of the capture of Louis at Varennes reached him, he wrote an autograph letter to George III, dated 6th July, urging him to join in a general demand for the liberation of the King and Queen of France. He also invited the monarchs of Europe to launch a Declaration, that they regarded the cause of Louis

---

[1] See Vivenot, i, 176-81; Beer, "Leopold II, Franz II, und Catharina," 140 *et seq.*; Clapham, "Causes of the War of 1792," ch. iv.

as their own, and in the last resort to put down a usurpation of power which it behoved all Governments to repress.[1]

The reply of George, dated St. James's, 23rd July, bears the imprint of the cool and cautious personality of Pitt and Grenville, who in this matter may be counted as one. The King avowed his sympathy with the French Royal Family and his interest in the present proposals, but declared that his attitude must depend on his relations to other Powers. He therefore cherished the hope that the Emperor would consult the welfare of the whole of Europe by aiding in the work of pacification between Austria and Turkey now proceeding at Sistova. So soon as those negotiations were completed, he would instruct his Ministers to consider the best means of cementing a union between the Allies and the Emperor.[2]

Leopold must have gnashed his teeth on reading this reply, which beat him at his own game of *finesse*. He had used the difficulties of England as a means of escaping from the pledges plighted at the Conference of Reichenbach in July 1790. Pitt and Grenville retorted by ironically refusing all help until he fulfilled those pledges. As we have seen, they succeeded; and the pacification in the East, as also in Belgium, was the result.

Equally chilling was the conduct of Pitt towards the *émigrés*. The French Princes at Coblentz had sent over the former French Minister, Calonne, "to solicit from His Majesty an assurance of his neutrality in the event . . . of an attempt being made by the Emperor and other Powers in support of the royal party in France." Pitt and Grenville refused to receive Calonne, and sent to the Comte d'Artois a letter expressing sympathy with the situation of the King and Queen of France, but declining to give any promise as to the line of conduct which the British Government might pursue.[3]

No less vague were the terms in which George III replied to a letter of the King of Sweden. Gustavus had for some little

---

[1] B.M. Add. MSS., 34438; Vivenot, i, 185, 186. "He [the Emperor] was extremely agitated when he gave me the letter for the King" (Elgin to Grenville, 7th July, in "Dropmore P.," ii, 126).

[2] B.M. Add. MSS., 34438.

[3] *Ibid.* Grenville to Ewart, 26th July. Calonne for some little time resided at Wimbledon House. His letters to Pitt show that he met with frequent rebuffs; but he had one interview with him early in June 1790. I have found no details of it.

time been at Aix-la-Chapelle in the hope of leading a royalist crusade into France as a sequel to the expected escape of Louis XVI and Marie Antoinette. As readers of Carlyle will remember, the Swedish noble, Count Fersen, chivalrously helped their flight towards Metz; and deep was the chagrin of Gustavus and his squire on hearing the news from Varennes. They longed to strike at once. But how could they strike while Leopold, Catharine, and Frederick William declared that everything must depend on the action of England? The following significant sentence in Fersen's diary shows the feeling prevalent at Brussels, as elsewhere, respecting England: "We must know if that Power regards the continuation of anarchy in France as more advantageous than order."[1] Fersen had imbibed this notion at Brussels from Count Mercy d'Argenteau, the Austrian Minister, whose letters often harp on this string. Thus on 7th March 1791 he writes: "The worst obstacles for the King of France will always come from England, which wishes to prolong the horrors in France and ruin her." A little later he avers that the only way to save the French monarchy is by a civil war, "and England (unless won over) will support the popular party."[2]

In order to win Pitt over to the cause of neutrality from which he never intended to swerve, Gustavus and Fersen persuaded an Englishman named Crawford to proceed to London with letters for George III and Pitt, dated 22nd July.[3] To the King he described the danger to all Governments which must ensue if the French revolted with impunity. He therefore begged to know speedily whether His Majesty would accord full liberty "to the Princes of Germany and to those, who, owing to the long disance, can only arrive by sea."[4] Evidently, then, Gustavus feared lest England might stop the fleet in which he intended to convey Swedish and Russian troops to the coast of Normandy for a dash at Paris. The answer of George soothed these fears, and

---

[1] "Diary and Corresp. of Fersen," 121.

[2] Arneth, "Marie Antoinette, Joseph II, und Leopold II," 148, 152.

[3] Mr. Nisbet Bain (*op. cit.*, ii, 129) accuses Pitt and his colleagues of waiving aside a proposed visit of Gustavus III to London, because "they had no desire to meet face to face a monarch they had already twice deceived." Mr. Bain must refer to the charges (invented at St. Petersburg) that Pitt had egged Gustavus on to war against Russia, and then deserted him. In the former volume (chapters xxi-iii) I proved the falsity of those charges. It would be more correct to say that Gustavus deserted England.

[4] B.M. Add. MSS., 34438.

that of Pitt, dated August 1791, was a model of courtly complaisance.

Compared with the shrewd balancings of the Emperor Leopold and the cold neutrality of Pitt, the policy of Frederick William II of Prussia seemed for a time to be instinct with generosity. Despite the fears of his counsellors that a *rapprochement* to Austria would involve Prussia in the ruin which the friendship of the Hapsburgs had brought on France, the King turned eagerly towards Vienna; and on 25th July Kaunitz and Bischoffswerder signed a preliminary treaty of alliance mutually guaranteeing their territories, and agreeing to further the aims of the Emperor respecting France. Frederick William was on fire for the royalist crusade. He even assured Baron Rolle, the agent of the French princes, that something would be done in that season.[1] Pitt and Grenville disapproved the action of Prussia in signing this compact, impairing as it did the validity of the Anglo-Prussian alliance of the year 1788; but Frederick William peevishly asserted his right to make what treaties he thought good, and remarked that he was now quits with England for the bad turns she had played him.[2] On their side, the British Ministers, by way of marking their disapproval of the warlike counsels of Berlin and Vienna, decided not to send an envoy to Pilnitz, the summer abode of the Elector of Saxony, where a conference was arranged between Leopold and Frederick William.

As is well known, the Comte d'Artois and Calonne now cherished lofty hopes of decisive action by all the monarchs against the French rebels. But Leopold, with his usual caution, repelled alike the solicitations of Artois and the warlike counsels of Frederick William, the result of their deliberations being the famous Declaration of Pilnitz (27th August). In it they expressed the hope that all the sovereigns of Europe

will not refuse to employ, in conjunction with their said Majesties, the most efficient means in proportion to their resources, to place the King of France in a position to establish with the most absolute freedom, the foundations of a monarchical form of government, which shall at once be in harmony with the rights of sovereigns and promote the welfare of the French nation. In that case [*alors et dans ce cas*] their

---

[1] Martens, v, 236-9; "F. O.," Prussia, 22. Ewart to Grenville, 4th August.

[2] On 15th August Prussia renounced her alliance with Turkey (Vivenot, i, 225).

said Majesties, the Emperor and the King of Prussia, are resolved to
act promptly and in common accord with the forces necessary to attain
the desired common end.

Obviously, the gist of the whole Declaration lay in the words
alors et dans ce cas. If they be emphasized, they destroy the
force of the document; for a union of all the monarchs was an
impossibility, it being well known that England would not, and
Sardinia, and Naples (probably also Spain) could not, take up
arms. In fact, on that very evening Leopold wrote to Kaunitz
that he had not in the least committed himself.—"*Alors et dans
ce cas* is with me the law and the prophets. If England fails us,
the case is non-existent." Further, when the Comte d'Artois,
two days later, urged the Emperor to give effect to the Declaration by ordering his troops to march westwards, he sent a sharp
retort, asserted that he would not go beyond the Declaration,
and forbade the French Princes to do so.[1]

To the good sense and insight of Grenville and Pitt, the
Pilnitz Declaration was one of the *comédies augustes* of history,
as Mallet du Pan termed it. Grenville saw that Leopold would
stay his hand until England chose to act, meanwhile alleging
her neutrality as an excuse for doing nothing.[2] Thus, the resolve
of Catharine to give nothing but fair words being already sur-
mised, the *émigrés* found to their annoyance that Pitt's passivity
clogged their efforts—the chief reason why they shrilly upbraided
him for his insular egotism. Certainly his attitude was far from
romantic; but surely, after the sharp lesson which he had received
from the House of Commons in the spring of 1791 during the
dispute with Russia, caution was needful; and he probably discerned a truth hidden from the *émigrés*, that an invasion of France
for the rescue of the King and Queen would seal their doom and
increase the welter in that unhappy land.

Pitt and Grenville spent the middle of September at Weymouth in attendance on George III; and we can imagine their
satisfaction at the prospect of universal peace and prosperity.
Pitt consoled himself for the not very creditable end to the
Russian negotiation by reflecting that our revenue was steadily
rising. "We are already £178,000 gainers in this quarter," he
wrote to George Rose on 10th August.[3] In fact, the cyclonic

[1] Sybel, bk. ii, ch. vi; Vivenot, i, 235, 243.
[2] "Dropmore P.," ii, 192.   [3] G. Rose, "Diaries," i, 111.

disturbances of the past few years now gave place to a lull. The Russo-Turkish War had virtually ended; Catharine and Gustavus were on friendly terms; the ferment in the Hapsburg dominions had died down, except in Brabant; the Poles were working their new constitution well; and, but for Jacobin propaganda in Italy and the Rhineland, the outlook was serene.

At this time, too, there seemed a chance of a reconciliation between Louis XVI and his people. On 14th September he accepted the new democratic constitution, a step which filled France with rejoicing and furnished the desired excuse for Leopold to remain passive. Kaunitz, who had consistently opposed intervention in France, now asserted that Louis had voluntarily accepted the constitution. The action of Louis and Marie Antoinette was in reality forced. Amidst the Queen's expressions of contempt for the French Princes at Coblentz, the suppressed fire of her fury against her captors flashes forth in this sentence written to Mercy d'Argenteau (28th August)—"The only question for us is to lull them to sleep and inspire them with confidence so as to trick them the better afterwards."— And again (12th September)—"My God! Must I, with this blood in my veins, pass my days among such beings as these, and in such an age as this?" Leopold must have known her real feelings; but he chose to abide by the official language of Louis, and to advise the Powers to accept the new situation.[1]

This peaceful turn of affairs sorely troubled the French Princes and Burke. In August and September 1791 his son Richard was at Coblentz, and informed his father of the consternation of the *émigrés* on hearing that the Emperor declined to draw the sword. Burke himself was equally agitated, and on or about 24th September had a long interview with Pitt and Grenville, at the house of the latter. We gather from Burke's " Letters on the Conduct of our Domestic Parties," that it was the first time he had met Pitt in private; and the meeting must have been somewhat awkward. After dining, with Grenville as host, the three men conferred together till eleven o'clock, discussing the whole situation " very calmly " (says Burke); but we can fancy the tumult of feelings in the breast of the old man when he found both Ministers firm as adamant against intervention in France. " They are certainly right as to their general

---

[1] Arneth, 206, 210; Vivenot, i, 270.

inclinations," he wrote to his son, "perfectly so, I have not a shadow of doubt; but at the same time they are cold and dead as to any attempt whatsoever to give them effect." The heat of the Irish royalist failed to kindle a spark of feeling in the two cousins. He found that their "deadness" proceeded from a rooted distrust of the Emperor Leopold, and from a conviction that Britain had nothing to fear from Jacobinical propaganda. Above all they believed that the present was not the time for action, especially as the imminence of bankruptcy in France would discredit the new Legislative Assembly, and render an invasion easier in the near future.

Are we to infer from this that Pitt and his cousin looked forward to a time when the monarchs could invade France with safety? Such an inference would be rash. It is more probable that they here found an excuse for postponing their decision and a means of calming an insistent visitor. Certainly they impressed Burke with a belief in their sincere but secret sympathy with the royalist cause. The three men also agreed in suspecting Leopold, though Burke tried to prove that his treachery was not premeditated, but sprang from "some complexional inconstancy." Pitt and Grenville, knowing the doggedness with which the Emperor pushed towards his goal, amidst many a shift and turn, evidently were not convinced.

At this time they had special reasons for distrusting Leopold and his advisers. The Austrian Government had received a letter, dated Dresden, 27th August (the day of the Declaration of Pilnitz), stating that England promised to remain neutral only on condition that the Emperor would not withdraw any troops from his Belgic lands, as they were needed to uphold the arrangements of which she was a guarantee. This extraordinary statement grew out of a remark of Grenville to the Austrian Ambassador in London, that, in view of the unrest in the Netherlands, it might be well not to leave them without troops.[1] The mis-statement was not only accepted at Vienna, but was forwarded to various Courts, the final version being that England might attack Austria if she withdrew her troops from Flanders, and that therefore Leopold could not draw the sword against

[1] Burke ("Corresp.," iii, 308, 342, 346) shows that Mercy d'Argenteau, after his brief mission to London, spread the slander. Pitt and Grenville said nothing decisive to him on this or any other topic. Kaunitz partly adopted the charge. (See Vivenot, i, 272.)

France until his army on the Turkish borders arrived in Swabia. Some were found who believed this odd *farrago*; but those who watched the calculating balance of Hapsburg policy saw in it one more excuse for a masterly inactivity.

Still less were our Ministers inclined to unite with Catharine in the universal royalist league then under discussion at St. Petersburg. The Czarina having charged her ambassador, Vorontzoff, to find out the sentiments of Pitt and Grenville on this subject, he replied that England would persevere in the strict neutrality which she had all along observed, " and that, with respect to the measures of active intervention which other Powers might have in contemplation, it was His Majesty's determination not to take any part either in supporting or in opposing them." Now Russia, like Austria and Spain, had decided not to act unless England joined the concert;[1] and this waiting on the action of a Power which had already declared its resolve to do nothing enables us to test the sincerity of the continental monarchs. As for the Czarina, her royalist fervour expended itself in deposing the busts of democrats, in ordering the French Minister to remain away from Court, and in condemning any Russian who had dealings with him to be publicly flogged. Moreover, while thus drilling her own subjects, the quondam friend of Diderot kept her eyes fixed upon Warsaw. The shrewdest diplomatist of the age had already divined her aims, which he thus trenchantly summed up: " The Empress only waits to see Austria and Prussia committed in France, to overturn everything in Poland."[2] Kaunitz lived on to see his cynical prophecy fulfilled to the letter.

The reader will have noticed with some surprise the statement of Burke that Pitt and Grenville had not the slightest fear of the spread of French principles in England. As we know, Burke vehemently maintained the contrary, averring that the French plague, unless crushed at Paris, would infect the world. In his survey of the European States he admitted that we were less liable to infection than Germany, Holland, and Italy, owing to the excellence of our constitution; but he feared that our nearness to France, and our zeal for liberty, would expose us to

[1] " F. O.," Russia, 22. Grenville to Whitworth, 27th October, and W. to G., 14th October 1791.
[2] Larivière, " Cath. II et la Rév. franç.," 88-90, 110-17.

some danger. Why he should have cherished these fears is hard to say; for to him the French Revolution was "a wild attempt to methodize anarchy," "a foul, impious, monstrous thing, wholly out of the course of moral nature."[1] Surely if British and French principles were so utterly different, we were in no more danger of infection from the Jacobins than of catching swine fever.

This was virtually the view of Pitt and Grenville; for there were no premonitory symptoms of infection, but much the reverse. Londoners showed the utmost joy at the first news of the escape of the King and Queen from Paris, and were equally depressed by the news from Varennes. As we shall presently see, it was with shouts of "Long live the King," "Church and State," "Down with the Dissenters," "No Olivers," "Down with the Rump," "No false Rights of Man," that the rabble of Birmingham wrecked and burnt the houses of Dr. Priestley and other prominent Nonconformists of that town. Only by slow degrees did this loyal enthusiasm give place to opinions which in course of time came to be called Radical. It may be well to trace briefly the fluctuations of public opinion, to which the career of Pitt stands in vital relation.

The growth of discontent in Great Britain may be ascribed to definite evils in the body politic, and it seems to have arisen only secondarily from French propaganda. The first question which kindled the fire of resentment was that of the civic and political disabilities still imposed on Nonconformists by the Corporation and Test Acts of the reign of Charles II. Pitt's decision in the session of 1787 to uphold those Acts ensured the rejection of Beaufoy's motion for their repeal of 176 votes to 98; but undeterred by his defeat, Beaufoy brought the matter before the House on 8th May 1789, and, despite the opposition of Pitt, secured 102 votes against 122. The Prime Minister's chief argument was that if Dissenters were admitted to civic rights they might use their power to overthrow the Church Establishment.[2] Clearly the opinion of the House was drifting away from him on that question; and it is a proof of his growing indifference to questions of Reform that now, four days after the assembly of the States-General of France at Versailles, he should have held to views so repugnant to the spirit of the age.

[1] Burke's "Works," iii, 8, 369 (Bohn edit.).
[2] "Parl. Hist.," xxviii, 1-41.

Thenceforth that question could not be debated solely on its own merits. The attacks made by the French National Assembly on the Church of France, particularly the confiscation of its tithes and landed property, soon aroused heated feelings in this country, though on a subject of a wholly different kind. The result was that, while Dissenters peacefully agitated for permission to act as citizens, they were represented as endeavouring to despoil the Church, after the fashion of Talleyrand and Mirabeau. A work by a Manchester merchant, Thomas Walker, reveals the influence of this question on the political activities of the time. The Nonconformists of that town and county hoped to gain a majority in next session or in the following Parliament, while the High Churchmen, to the cry of " The Church in Danger," declared the two Acts of Charles II to be the bulwarks of the constitution.[1] This cry was everywhere taken up, with the result that in the Parliament elected in 1790 the Tories gained ground. Consequently, even the able advocacy of Fox on behalf of religious liberty failed to save Beaufoy's motion from a crushing defeat. Pitt spoke against the proposal and carried the House with him by 294 votes to 105. This vote illustrates the baleful influence exerted by the French Revolution on the cause of Reform in these islands.

A second example soon occurred. Only three days later Flood brought forward a motion for Parliamentary Reform which the wildest of alarmists could not call revolutionary. He proposed to add to the House of Commons one hundred members, elected by the resident householders of the counties, those areas being far less corrupt than the towns; and he suggested that, if the total number of members were deemed excessive, fifty seats in the smallest boroughs might be declared vacant. This proposal differed but little from that of Pitt in the session of 1785, which aimed at disfranchising thirty-six decayed boroughs and apportioning their seventy-two members to the larger counties, as also to London and Westminster. In a speech which might have been made by Pitt in pre-Revolution times Flood declared that the events in France showed the need of a timely repair of outworn institutions.

This was as a red rag to Windham, a prominent recruit from the Whigs, who now used all the artifices of rhetoric to terrify his

---

[1] T. Walker, " Review of . . . political events in Manchester (1789-1794)."

hearers. He besought them in turn not to repair their house in the hurricane season, not to imitate the valetudinarian of the " Spectator," who read medical books until he discovered he had every symptom of the gout except the pain. These fallacious similes captivated the squires; and Pitt himself complimented the orator on his ingenious arguments. For himself, he declared his desire of Reform to be as zealous as ever; but he "could see no utility in any gentleman's bringing forward such a motion as the present at that moment," and feared that the cause might thereby suffer disgrace and lose ground. Fox, on the other hand, ridiculed all thought of panic on account of the French Revolution, but he admitted that the majority both in Parliament and the nation did not want Reform. Grenville, Wilberforce, and Burke opposed the motion, while even Duncombe declined to vote for it at present. It was accordingly adjourned *sine die*.[1]

Disappointment at the course of these debates served to band Nonconformists and reformers in a close alliance. Hitherto they had alike supported Pitt and the royal prerogative, especially at the time of the Regency struggle. In May 1789, when Pitt opposed the Nonconformist claims, Dr. Priestley wrote that Fox would regain his popularity with Dissenters, while Pitt would lose ground.[2] Now, when the doors of the franchise and of civic privilege were fast barred, resentment and indignation began to arouse the groups of the unprivileged left outside. The news that Frenchmen had framed a Departmental System, in which all privileges had vanished, and all men were citizens, with equal rights in the making of laws and local regulations, worked potently in England, furthering the growth of an institution little known in this country, the political club. As the Jacobins had adapted the English idea of a club to political uses, so now the early Radicals re-adapted it to English needs. "The Manchester Constitutional Society "[3] was founded by

[1] T. Walker, " Review of . . . political events in Manchester (1789-1794)," 452-79. I cannot agree with Mr. J. R. le B. Hammond ("Fox," 76) that Pitt now spoke as the avowed enemy of parliamentary reform. Indeed, he never spoke in that sense, but opposed it as inopportune.

[2] Rutt, " Mems. of Priestly," ii, 25. As is well known, Burke's " Reflections on the Fr. Rev.," was in part an answer to Dr. Price's sermon of 4th November 1789 in the Old Jewry chapel, to the Society for celebrating the Revolution of 1688.

[3] It was more of a club than the branches of the " Society for Con-

Walker and others in October 1790, in order to oppose a
" Church and King Club," which High Churchmen had started
in March, after the news of the triumph of their principles in
Parliament. The Manchester reformers struck the key-note of
the coming age by asserting in their programme that in every
community the authority of the governors must be derived
from the consent of the governed, and that the welfare of the
people was the true aim of Government. They further declared
that honours and rewards were due only for services rendered
to the State; that all officials, without exception, were responsible to the people; that "actions only, not opinions, are the
proper objects of civil jurisdictions"; that no law is fairly made
except by a majority of the people; and that the people of
Great Britain were not fully and fairly represented in Parliament.[1]

The Church and King Club, on the contrary, reprobated all
change in "one of the most beautiful systems of government
that the combined efforts of human wisdom has [sic] ever yet
been able to accomplish." The issue between the two parties
was thus sharply outlined. The Tories of Manchester gloried
in a state of things which shut out about half of their fellow-
citizens from civic rights and their whole community from any
direct share in the making of laws. In their eyes the Church
and the monarchy were in danger if Nonconformists became
citizens, and if a score of Cornish villages yielded up their legislative powers to Manchester, Leeds, Birmingham, and other hives
of industry.

Scotland also began to awake. The torpor of that keen and
intellectual people, under a system of misrepresentation which
assigned to them forty-five members and forty-four to Cornwall,
is incomprehensible, unless we may ascribe it to the waning of
all enthusiasm after the "forty-five" and to the supremacy of
material interests so characteristic of the age. In any case, this
political apathy was now to end; and here, too, as in the case
of England, Government applied the spur.

On 10th May 1791 Sir Gilbert Elliot (afterwards Earl of
Minto) brought forward a motion in Parliament for the repeal
of the Test Act, so far as it concerned Scotland. He voiced a

stitutional Information," which did good work in 1780-4, but expired in 1784
owing to the disgust of reformers at the Fox-North Coalition—so Place
asserts (B.M. Add. MSS., 27808).
[1] T. Walker, *op. cit.*, 18, 19.

petition of the General Assembly of the Church of Scotland, and declared that the Presbyterians felt the grievance of being excluded from civic offices unless they perverted. On wider grounds also he appealed against this petty form of persecution, which might make men hypocrites but never sincere converts. Henry Dundas and his nephew, Robert Dundas (Lord Advocate for Scotland), opposed the motion, mainly because it would infringe the terms of the Act of Union; but Henry added the curious argument that, if Scottish Presbyterians were relieved from the Test Act, then the English Dissenters would have been "unjustly, harshly, and cruelly used." Pitt avowed himself "not a violent friend, but a firm and steady friend" of the Test Act, as being essential to the security of the Church and therefore of the civil establishment of the country. Accordingly, Elliot's motion was defeated by 149 votes to 62.[1] It is curious that, a month earlier, the House had agreed to a Bill granting slightly wider toleration to "Catholic Dissenters."[2]

While Pitt was thus strengthening the old buttresses of Church and State, the son of a Quaker had subjected the whole fabric to a battery of violent rhetoric. It is scarcely too much to call Thomas Paine the Rousseau of English democracy. For, if his arguments lacked the novelty of those of the Genevese thinker (and even they were far from original), they equalled them in effectiveness, and excelled them in practicability. "The Rights of Man" (Part I) may be termed an insular version of the "Contrat Social," with this difference, that the English writer pointed the way to changes which were far from visionary, while the Genevese seer outlined a polity fit only for a Swiss canton peopled by philosophers. Paine had had the advantage of close contact with men and affairs in both hemispheres. Not even Cobbett, his literary successor, passed through more varied experiences. Born in 1737 at Thetford in Norfolk, Paine divided his early life between stay-making, excise work, the vending of tobacco, and a seafaring life. His keen eyes, lofty brow, prominent nose, proclaimed him a thinker and fighter, and therefore, in that age, a rebel. What more natural than that he, a foe to authority and hater of oppression, should go to America to help on the cause of Washington? There at last he discovered his true vocation. His broadsides struck home. "Rebellious staymaker, unkempt,"

[1] "Parl. Hist.," xxix, 488-510.   [2] *Ibid.*, 113-9.

says Carlyle, "who feels that he, a single needleman, did by his
'Common Sense' pamphlet, free America; that he can, and will
free all this world; perhaps even the other." Tom Paine, indeed,
had the rare gift of voicing tersely and stridently the dumb desires of the masses Further, a sojourn in France before and
during the early part of the Revolution enabled him to frame a
crushing retort to Burke's "Reflections." The result was Part I
of the "Rights of Man," which he flung off at the "Angel" in
Islington in February 1791.[1]

The general aims of the pamphlet are now as little open to
question as the famous Declaration which he sought to vindicate. Paine trenchantly attacked Burke's claim that no people,
not even our own, had an inherent right to choose its own ruler,
and that the Revolution Settlement of 1688 was binding for
ever. Paine, on the contrary, asserted that "every age and
generation must be as free to act for itself *in all cases* as the
ages and generations that preceded it. The vanity and presumption of governing beyond the grave is the most ridiculous
and insolent of all tyrannies." Further, on the general question
at issue, Paine remarked: "That men should take up arms, and
spend their lives and fortunes, *not* to maintain their rights, but
to maintain they have *not* rights, is an entirely new species of
discovery and suited to the paradoxical genius of Mr. Burke."
In reply to the noble passage: "The age of chivalry is gone . . .,"
Paine shrewdly says: "In the rhapsody of his imagination he
has discovered a world of windmills, and his sorrows are that
there are no Quixotes to attack them."

After thus exposing the weak points of the royalist case, Paine
proceeded to defend the mob, firstly, because the aristocratic
plots against the French Revolution were really formidable (a
very disputable thesis), and secondly, because the mob in all old
countries is the outcome of their unfair and brutal system of
government. "It is by distortedly exalting some men," he says,
"that others are distortedly debased, till the whole is out of
nature. A vast mass of mankind are degradedly thrown into
the background of the human picture, to bring forward with
greater glare the puppet show of State and aristocracy." Here
was obviously the Junius of democracy, for whom the only
effective answer was the gag and gyve. Indeed, Burke in his

[1] M. D. Conway, "Life of T. Paine," i, 284.

"Appeal from the New to the Old Whigs" suggested that the
proper refutation was by means of "criminal justice."[1]

Pitt's opinions at this time on French and English democracy tend towards a moderate and reforming royalism—witness his comment on Burke's " Reflections," that the writer would
have done well to extol the English constitution rather than to
attack the French.[2] In this remark we may detect his preference
for construction over destruction, for the allaying, rather than the
exciting, of passion. Nevertheless the one-sidedness of the English constitution made for unrest. So soon as one bold voice
clearly contrasted those defects with the inspiring precepts of
the French Rights of Man, there was an end to political apathy.
A proof of this was furnished by the number of replies called
forth by Burke's " Reflections." They numbered thirty-eight.[3]
Apart from that of Paine, the "Vindiciae Gallicae" of Sir
James Mackintosh made the most impression, especially the
last chapter, wherein he declared that the conspiracy of the
monarchs to crush the liberties of France would recoil on their
own heads.

Fear of the alleged royalist league quickened the sympathy of
Britons with the French reformers; while the sympathy of friends
of order with Louis XVI and Marie Antoinette after the Varennes
incident deepened their apprehension of all change. Thus were
called into play all the feelings which most deeply move mankind
—love of our richly storied past and its embodiment, the English
constitution; while on the other hand no small part of our people
harboured resentment against the narrow franchise and class
legislation at home, and felt a growing fear that the nascent
freedom of Frenchmen might expire under the heel of the
military Powers of Central Europe. Accordingly clubs and
societies grew apace, and many of them helped on the circula-
lation of cheap editions of Paine's pamphlet.

The result of this clash of opinion was seen in the added
keenness of party strife and in the disturbances of 14th July
1791. The occasion of these last was the celebration by a subscription dinner of the second anniversary of the fall of the

---

[1] Burke's Works, iii, 76 (Bohn edit.).
[2] *Ibid.*, iii, 12. So, too, on 30th August 1791 Priestley wrote that Pitt had
shown himself unfavourable to their cause (Rutt, " Life of Priestley," ii, 145).
[3] Prior, " Life of Burke," 322, who states very incorrectly that not one of
them has survived.

Bastille. Both at Manchester and Birmingham the announcement of this insular and inoffensive function aroused strong feelings either of envy or of opposition. The Tories of Manchester resolved that, if the local Constitutional Club chose to dine on that day it should be at their peril. The populace was urged to pull down the hotel on their heads, "as the brains of every man who dined there would be much improved by being mingled with bricks and mortar." Thomas Walker's control of the local constables sufficed to thwart this pleasantry.

But on that day the forces of reaction broke loose at Birmingham. In the Midland capital political feeling ran as high as at Manchester. The best known of the reformers was Dr. Priestley, a Unitarian minister, whose researches in physical science had gained him a world-wide reputation and a fellowship in the Royal Society. He and many other reformers proposed to feast in public in honour of the French national festival. Unfortunately, the annoyance of the loyalists at this proposal was inflamed by a recent sermon of Priestley on the death of Dr. Price and by the circulation of a seditious handbill. Dr. Keir, a Churchman who was to preside at the dinner, did not prove to the satisfaction of all that this was a trick of the enemy. Public opinion was also excited by the discovery of the words "This barn to let" chalked on some of the churches of the town; and charges were bandied to and fro that this was the work of the Dissenters, or of the most virulent of their opponents.

What is certain is that these *hors d'œuvres* endangered the rest of the *menu*. The dinner-committee, however, struggled manfully with their difficulties. They had a Churchman in the chair, and Priestley was not present. The loyalty of the diners also received due scenic warrant in the work of a local artist. The dining-hall of the hotel was "decorated with three emblematical pieces of sculpture, mixed with painting in a new style of composition. The central was a finely executed medallion of His Majesty, surrounded with a Glory, on each side of which was an alabaster obelisk, one exhibiting Gallic Liberty breaking the bonds of Despotism, and the other representing British Liberty in its present enjoyment." The terms in which the fourteen toasts were proposed breathed of the same flamboyant loyalty, the only one open to criticism being the following: " The Prince of Wales! May he have the wisdom to prefer the glory of being the chief of an entire [*sic*] free people to that of being only the splendid fountain of corruption."[1]

The dinner passed with only occasional rounds of hissing from the loyalists outside. But, as the evening wore on and the speeches inside still continued, the crowd became restive. Stone-throwing began and was not discouraged by the two magistrates, the Rev. Dr. Spencer and John Carles, who had now arrived. In fact, the clergyman with an oath praised a lad who said that Priestley ought to be ducked; Carles also promised the rabble drink; and when a local humourist asked for permission to knock the dust out of Priestley's wig, the champions of order burst out laughing. A witness at the trial averred that he saw an attorney, John Brook, go among the mob and point towards Priestley's chapel. However that may be, the rabble moved off thither and speedily wrecked it. His residence at Fair Hill was next demolished, his library and scientific instruments being burnt or smashed. This was but the prelude to organized attacks on the houses of the leading Nonconformists, whether they had been at the dinner or not. The resulting riots soon involved in ruin a large part of the town. Prominent Churchmen who sought to end these disgraceful scenes suffered both in person and property. A word of remonstrance sufficed to turn into new channels the tide of hatred and greed; for, as happened in the Gordon riots of 1780, rascality speedily rushed in to seize the spoils.

The usually dull archives of the Home Office yield proof of the terror that reigned in the Midland capital. A Mr. Garbett wrote to Dundas on 17th July that the wrecking still went on, that the Nonconformists were in the utmost dread and misery, and all people looked for help from outside to stay the pillage. As for himself, though he was not a "marked man," his hand trembled at the scenes he had witnessed. There can be little doubt that the magistrates from the first acted with culpable weakness, as Whitbread proved in the House of Commons, for they did not enrol special constables until the rioters had got the upper hand. Dundas, as Home Secretary, seems to have done his duty. The news of the riot of the 14th reached him at 10 a.m. on the 15th (Friday); and he at once sent post haste to Nottingham, ordering the immediate despatch of the 15th Dragoons.

---

[1] "H. O.," Geo. III (Domestic), 19.

By dint of a forced march of fifty-six miles the horsemen reached Birmingham on the evening of that same day (Sunday); but two days more elapsed before drunken blackmailers ceased to molest Hagley, Halesowen, and other villages. Few persons lost their lives, except about a dozen of the pillagers who lay helpless with drink in the cellars of houses which their more zealous comrades had given over to the flames.[1]

The verdict of Grenville was as follows: "I do not admire riots in favour of Government much more than riots against it." That of his less cautious brother, the Marquis of Buckingham, is as follows: "I am not sorry for this *excess, excessive as it has been.*" That of Pitt is not recorded. He did not speak during the debate on this subject on 21st May 1792; but the rejection of Whitbread's motion for an inquiry by 189 votes to 46 implies unanimity on the Ministerial side.[2]

In the winter of 1791-2 various incidents occurred which further excited public opinion. On 17th February 1792 appeared the second part of Paine's " Rights of Man." He started from the assumption that the birth of a democratic State in America would herald the advent of Revolutions not only in France, but in all lands; and that British and Hessians would live to bless the day when they were defeated by the soldiers of Washington. He then proceeded to arraign all Governments of the old type, and asserted that constitutions ought to be the natural outcome of the collective activities of the whole people. There was nothing mysterious about Government, if Courts had not hidden away the patent fact that it dealt primarily with the making and administering of laws. We are apt to be impressed by these remarks until we contrast them with the majestic period wherein Burke depicts human society as a venerable and mysterious whole bequeathed by the wisdom of our forefathers. An admirer of Burke cannot but quote the passage in full: " Our political system is placed in a just correspondence and symmetry with the order of the world, and with the mode of existence decreed to a permanent body composed of transitory

---

[1] *Ibid.* As late as 9th August a proclamation was posted about Birmingham: " The friends of the good cause are requested to meet us at Revolution Place to-morrow night at 11 o'clock in order to fix upon those persons who are to be the future objects of our malice." Of course this was but an incitation to plunder. See Massey, iii, 462-6, on the Birmingham riots.

[2] " Dropmore P.," ii, 133, 136; " Parl. Hist.," xxix, 1464.

parts; wherein by the disposition of a stupendous wisdom, moulding together the great mysterious incorporation of the human race, the whole, at one time, is never old, or middle-aged, or young, but in a condition of unchangeable constancy, moves on through the varied tenour of perpetual decay, fall, renovation and progression. Thus, by preserving the method of nature in the conduct of the State, in what we improve we are never wholly new; in what we retain we are never wholly obsolete." [1]

This is a majestic conception. But, after all, the practical question at issue is—how much of the old shall we retain and how much must be discarded? Unfortunately for himself and his cause, Burke was now urging his countrymen to support two military Powers in their effort to compel the French people to revert to institutions which were alike obsolete and detested. Is it surprising that Paine, utterly lacking all sense of reverence for the past, should brand this conduct as treasonable to the imperious needs of the present? Viewing monarchy as represented by Versailles or Carlton House, and aristocracy by the intrigues of Coblentz and the orgies of Brooks's Club, he gave short shrift to both forms of Government. Monarchy he pronounced more or less despotic; and under aristocracy (he says) the interests of the whole body necessarily suffer; democracy alone secures the rule of the general will; and this can be thoroughly secured only in a democratic republic. He then attacks the English constitution as unjust and extravagant, claiming that the formation of a close alliance between England, France, and America would enable the expenses of government (Army, Navy, and Civil List inclusive) to be reduced to a million and a half a year.

With regard to the means of raising revenue, Paine sketched a plan of progressive taxation on incomes, ranging from 3d. in the pound on incomes less than £500 to punitive proportions after £10,000 was reached; while in his Spartan arithmetic great wealth appeared so dire a misfortune that he rid the possessors of the whole of incomes of £23,000 and upwards. As for Pitt's financial reforms, he laughed them to scorn. He also accused him of throwing over the fair promises that marked his early career, of advertising for enemies abroad, while at home he toadied to the Court. "The defect lies in the system. . . .

---

[1] Burke "Reflections on the Fr. Rev.," 39 (Mr. Payne's edit.).

Prop it as you please, it continually sinks into Court government, and ever will." Finally he urged a limitation of armaments,
and prophesied that wars would cease when nations had their
freely elected Conventions. The cynic will remember with satisfaction that, two months later, began the war between France
and Austria, which developed into the most tremendous series
of wars recorded in history.

The republican and levelling doctrines frankly advocated in
Paine's second pamphlet made a greater sensation than the first
part had done; and Fox, who approved the former production,
sternly reprobated the latter. It is possible that Government
sought to stop its publication; for Chapman, the publisher, to
whom Paine first applied, offered him £1,000 for the manuscript,
and yet very soon afterwards declared it to be too dangerous for
him to print.[1] Certainly the work soon quickened the tone of
political thought. Already the London Society for promoting
Constitutional Information, which had died of inanition in 1784,
had come to life again before the close of the year 1791. And
at the end of that year a determined man, Thomas Hardy,
a poor shoemaker of Westminster, set to work to interest his
comrades in politics. He assembled four men at an ale-house,
and they agreed to take action. At their second meeting, on
25th January 1792, they mustered eight strong, and resolved to
start "The London Corresponding Society for the Reform of
Parliamentary Representation." Its finances were scarcely on a
par with its title: they consisted of eightpence, the first weekly
subscription. But the idea proved infectious; and amidst the
heat engendered by Paine's second pamphlet, the number of
members rose to forty-one.[2] The first manifesto of the Society,
dated 2nd April, claimed political liberty as the birthright of
man, declared the British nation to be misrepresented by its Parliament, and, while repudiating all disorderly methods, demanded
a thorough reform of that body.

So far as I have been able to discover, this was the first
political club started by English working-men at that time. But
now the men of Sheffield also organized themselves. Their
" Association " began in an assembly of five or six mechanics,
who discussed "the enormous high price of provisions" and

[1] Conway, *op. cit.*, ii, 330. The printer and publisher were prosecuted
later on, as well as Paine, who fled to France.
[2] "Mem. of T. Hardy," by himself (Lond., 1832).

"the waste and lavish [*sic*] of the public property by place-men, pensioners, luxury and debauchery,—sources of the griev-ous burthens under which the nation groans." The practical character of their lamentations attracted many working men, with the result that they resolved to reprint and circulate 1,600 copies of Paine's "Rights of Man" (Part I), at sixpence a copy. On 15th January 1792 they wrote up to the "London Society for Constitutional Information" to plan co-operation with them.

At first the ideas of the Sheffield Association were somewhat parochial. But the need of common action all over the Kingdom was taking shape in several minds, and when Scotland awoke to political activity (as will appear in Chapter VII) the idea of a General Convention took firm root and led to remarkable developments. For the present, the chief work of these clubs was the circulation of Paine's volumes (even in Welsh, Gaelic, and Erse) at the price of sixpence or even less. They also dis-tributed "The Catechism of the French Constitution" (of 1791), drawn up by Christie, a Scot domiciled at Paris, which set forth the beauties of that child of many hopes. Less objectionable was a pamphlet—"The Rights of Men and the Duties of Men." For the most part, however, their literature was acridly repub-lican in tone and of a levelling tendency. Thus, for the first time since the brief attempt of the Cromwellian Levellers, the rich and the poor began to group themselves in hostile camps, at the strident tones of Paine's cry for a graduated Income Tax. Is it surprising that the sight of the free institutions of France and of the forced economy of the Court of the Tuileries should lead our workers to question the utility of the State-paid debaucheries of Carlton House, and of the whole system of patronage and pen-sions? Burke and Pitt had pruned away a few of the worst ex-crescences; but now they saw with dismay the whole of the body politic subjected to remorseless criticism by those whose duty was to toil and not to think or question.

This was a new departure in eighteenth-century England. Hitherto working men had taken only a fleeting and fitful inter-est in politics. How should they do so in days when newspapers were very dear, and their contents had only the remotest bear-ing on the life of the masses? The London mob had bawled and rioted for "Wilkes and Liberty," but mainly from personal motives and love of horse-play. Now, however, all was changed; and artisans were willing to sacrifice their time and their pence

to learn and teach a political catechism, and spread the writings
of Paine. Consequently the new Radical Clubs differed widely
from the short-lived County Associations of 1780 which charged
a substantial fee for membership. Moreover, these Associations
expired in the years 1783-4, owing to the disgust at Fox's
Coalition with Lord North. We are therefore justified in declaring that English democracy entered on a new lease of life,
and did not, as has been asserted,[1] merely continue the movement of 1780. The earlier efforts had been wholly insular in
character; they aimed at staying the tide of corruption; their
methods were in the main academic, and certainly never affected
the great mass of the people. Now reformers were moved by
a wider enthusiasm for the rights of humanity, and sought not
merely to abolish pocket boroughs and sinecures, but to level
up the poor and level down the wealthy. It was this aspect of
Paine's teaching that excited men to a frenzy of reprobation or
of hope.

A certain continuity of tradition and method is observable in
a club, called The Friends of the People, which was founded at
Freemasons' Tavern in April 1792, with a subscription of five
guineas a year. The members included Cartwright, Erskine,
Lord Edward Fitzgerald, Philip Francis, Charles Grey, Lambton,
the Earl of Lauderdale, Mackintosh, Sheridan, Whitbread, and
some sixty others; but Fox refused to join. Their profession of faith was more moderate than that of Hardy's Club; it
emphasized the need of avoiding innovation and of restoring
the constitution to its original purity.[2] This was in the spirit
of the Associations of 1780; but the new club was far less
characteristic of the times than the clubs of working men described above.

The appearance of Paine's " Rights of Man " (Part II), the
founding of these societies, and the outbreak of war between
France and Austria in April 1792 made a deep impression on
Pitt. He opposed a notice of a motion of Reform for the follow-

---

[1] Leslie Stephen, "The Eng. Utilitarians," i, 121. I fully admit that the
Chartist leaders in 1838 went back to the Westminster programme of 1780.
See "The Life and Struggles of William Lovett"; but the spirit and methods
of the new agitation were wholly different. On this topic I feel compelled to
differ from Mr. J. L. le B. Hammond ("Fox," ch. v, *ad init.*).   Mr. C. B. R.
Kent ("The English Radicals," 156) states the case correctly.

[2] "Parl. Hist.," xxix, 1303-9.

ing session, brought forward by Grey on 30th April. While
affirming his continued interest in that subject, Pitt deprecated
its introduction at that time as involving the risk of anarchy.

My object [he continued] always has been, and is now more particularly so, to give permanence to that which we actually enjoy rather than
remove subsisting grievances. . . . I once thought, and still think, upon
the point of the representation of the Commons, that, if some mode
could be adopted by which the people could have any additional
security for a continuance of the blessings which they now enjoy, it
would be an improvement in the constitution of this country. That was
the extent of my object. Further I never wished to go; and if this can be
obtained without the risk of losing what we have, I should think it wise
to make the experiment. When I say this, it is not because I believe
there is any existing grievance in this country that is felt at this hour.

At the end of the American War (he continued) when bankruptcy seemed imminent, he believed Reform to be necessary in
order to restore public confidence and remedy certain notorious
grievances. Even then very many moderate men opposed his
efforts as involving danger to the State. How much more would
they deprecate sweeping proposals which rightly aroused general
apprehension? He then censured the action of certain members
of the House in joining an Association (the " Friends of the
People ") which was supported by those who aimed at the overthrowing of hereditary monarchy, titles of nobility, and all ideas
of subordination. He would oppose all proposals for Reform
rather than run the risk of changes so sweeping.—" All, all may
be lost by an indiscreet attempt upon the subject." Clearly, Pitt
was about to join the ranks of the alarmists. But members
generally were of his opinion. In vain did Fox, Erskine, Grey,
and Sheridan deprecate the attempt to confuse moderate Reform
with reckless innovation. Burke illogically but effectively
dragged in the French spectre, and Windham declared that
the public mind here, as in other lands, was in such a state that
the slightest scratch might produce a mortal wound.

The gulf between Pitt and the reformers now became impass-
able. His speech of 10th May against any relaxation of the
penal laws against Unitarians is a curious blend of bigotry
and panic. Eleven days later a stringent proclamation was issued
against all who wrote, printed, and dispersed " divers wicked and
seditious writings." It ordered all magistrates to search out the

authors and abettors of them, and to take steps for preventing disorder. It also inculcated "a due submission to the laws, and a just confidence in the integrity and wisdom of Parliament." Anything less calculated to beget such a confidence than this proclamation, threatening alike to reformers and levellers, can scarcely be conceived. On 25th May Grey opposed it in an acrid speech; he inveighed against Pitt as an apostate, who never kept his word, and always intended to delude Parliament and people. The sting of the speech lay, not in these reckless charges, but in the citing of Pitt's opinions as expressed in a resolution passed at the Thatched House Tavern in May 1782, which declared that without Parliamentary Reform neither the liberty of the nation nor the permanence of a virtuous administration was secure. Pitt's reply, however, convinced all those whose minds were open to conviction. He proved to demonstration that he had never approved of universal suffrage; yet that was now the goal aimed at by Paine and the Societies founded on the basis of the Rights of Man. The speech of Dundas also showed that the writings of Paine, and the founding of clubs with those ends in view, had led to the present action of the Cabinet.

Undoubtedly those clubs had behaved in a provocative manner. Apart from their correspondence with the Jacobins Club (which will be described later), they advocated aims which then seemed utterly subversive of order. Thus, early in May 1792, the Sheffield Society declared their object to be "a radical Reform of the country, as soon as prudence and discretion would permit, and established on that system which is consistent with the Rights of Man." Further, the hope is expressed that not only the neighbouring towns and villages, most of which were forming similar societies, but also the whole country would be "united in the same cause, which cannot fail of being the case wherever the most excellent works of Thomas Paine find reception."[1]

Now, this banding together of societies and clubs pointed the way to the forming of a National Convention which would truly represent the whole nation. In judging the action of Pitt and his colleagues at this crisis, we must remember that they had before them the alarming example of the Jacobins Club of

---

[1] "Application of Barruel's 'Memoirs of Jacobinism' to the Secret Societies of Ireland and Great Britain," 32-3.

Paris, which had gained enormous power by its network of affiliated clubs. This body again was modelled on the various societies of the Illuminati in Germany, whose organizer, Weishaupt, summed up his contention in the words: "All their union shall be carried on by the correspondence and visits of the brethren. If we can gain but that point, we shall have succeeded in all we want."[1] This is why the name Corresponding Society stank in the nostrils of all rulers. It implied a parasitic organization which, if allowed to grow, would strangle the established Government. Signs were not wanting that this was the aim of the new Radical Clubs. Thus the delegates of the United Constitutional Societies who met at Norwich drew up on 24th March 1792 resolutions expressing satisfaction at the rapid growth of those bodies, already numbering some hundreds, "which by delegates preserve a mutual intercourse." . . . "To Mr. Thomas Paine our thanks are specially due for his first and second parts of the ' Rights of Man '; and we sincerely wish that he may live to see his labours crowned with success in the general diffusion of liberty and happiness among mankind." . . . "We . . . earnestly entreat our brethren to increase in their Associations in order to form one grand and extensive Union of all the friends of liberty."[2] It is not surprising that this plan of a National Convention of levellers produced something like a panic among the well-to-do; and it is futile to assert that men who avowed their belief in the subversive teaching of Part II of Paine's book were concerned merely with the Reform of Parliament. They put that object in their public manifestoes; but, like many of the Chartists of a later date, their ultimate aim was the redistribution of wealth; and this it was which brought on them the unflinching opposition of Pitt.

Nevertheless even these considerations do not justify him in opposing the reformers root and branch. The greatest statesman is he who distinguishes between the real grievances of a suffering people and the visionary or dangerous schemes which they beget in ill-balanced brains. To oppose moderate reformers as well as extremists is both unjust and unwise. It confounds together the would-be healers and the enemies of the existing order. Furthermore, an indiscriminate attack tends to close the ranks

[1] "Application of Barruel's ' Memoirs of Jacobinism ' to the Secret Societies of Ireland and Great Britain," Introduction, p. x.
[2] "H. O.," Geo. III (Domestic), 20.

in a solid phalanx, and it should be the aim of a tactician first to seek to loosen those ranks.

Finally, we cannot forget that Pitt had had it in his power to redress the most obvious of the grievances which kept large masses of his countrymen outside the pale of political rights and civic privilege. Those grievances were made known to him temperately in the years 1787, 1789, and 1790; but he refused to amend them, and gradually drifted to the side of the alarmists and reactionaries. Who is the wiser guide at such a time? He who sets to work betimes to cure certain ills which are producing irritation in the body politic? Or he who looks on the irritation as a sign that nothing should be done? The lessons of history and the experience of everyday life plead for timely cure and warn against a nervous postponement. Doubtless Pitt would have found it difficult to persuade some of his followers to apply the knife in the session of 1791 or 1792. But in the Parliament elected in 1790 his position was better assured, his temper more imperious, than in that of 1785, which needed much tactful management. The fact, then, must be faced that he declined to run the risk of the curative operation, even at a time when there were no serious symptoms in the patient and little or no risk for the surgeon.

The reason which he assigned for his refusal claims careful notice. It was that his earlier proposals (those of 1782-5) had aimed at national security; while those of the present would tend to insecurity. Possibly in the month of April 1792 this argument had some validity; though up to that time all the violence had been on the Tory side. But the plea does not excuse Pitt for not taking action in the year 1790. That was the period when the earlier apathy of the nation to Reform was giving way to interest, and interest had not yet grown into excitement. Still less had loyalty waned under the repressive measures whereby he now proposed to give it vigour.

Thus, Pitt missed a great opportunity, perhaps the greatest of his career. What it means is clear to us, who know that the cause of Reform passed under a cloud for the space of thirty-eight years. It is of course unfair to censure him and his friends for lacking a prophetic vision of the long woes that were to come. Most of the blame lavished upon him arises from forgetfulness of the fact that he was not a seer mounted on some political Pisgah, but a pioneer struggling through an unexplored jungle. Nevertheless, as the duty of a pioneer is not merely to hew a path, but also to note the lie of the land and the signs of the weather, we must admit that Pitt did not possess the highest instincts of his craft. He cannot be ranked with Julius Caesar, Charlemagne, Alfred the Great, Edward I, or Burleigh, still less with those giants of his own age, Napoleon and Stein; for these men boldly grappled with the elements of unrest or disloyalty, and by wise legislation wrought them into the fabric of the State. Probably the lack of response to his reforming efforts in the year 1785 ingrained in him the conviction that Britons would always be loyal if their burdens were lessened and their comforts increased; and now in 1792 he looked on the remissions of taxation (described in the following chapter) as a panacea against discontent. Under normal conditions that would have been the case. It was not so now, because new ideas were in the air, and these forbade a bovine acceptance of abundant fodder. In truth, Pitt had not that gift without which the highest abilities and the most strenuous endeavours will at novel crises be at fault—a sympathetic insight into the needs and aspirations of the people. His analytical powers enabled him to detect the follies of the royalist crusaders; but he lacked those higher powers of synthesis which alone could discern the nascent strength of Democracy.

CHAPTER II

BEFORE THE STORM

I find it to be a very general notion, at least in the Assembly, that if France can preserve a neutrality with England, she will be able to cope with all the rest of Europe united.—GOWER TO GRENVILLE, *22nd April* 1792.

INDIRECT evidence as to the intentions of a statesman is often more convincing than his official assertions. The world always suspects the latter; and many politicians have found it expedient to adopt the ironical device practised frequently with success by Bismarck on his Austrian colleagues at Frankfurt, that of telling the truth. Fortunately the English party game has nearly always been kept up with sportsmanlike fair play; and Pitt himself was so scrupulously truthful that we are rarely in doubt as to his opinions, save when he veiled them by ministerial reserve. Nevertheless, on the all-important subject of his attitude towards Revolutionary France, it is satisfactory to have indirect proofs of his desire to maintain a strict, if not friendly, neutrality. This proof lies in his handling of the nation's armaments and finances.

The debate on the Army Estimates on 15th February 1792 is of interest in more respects than one. The news of the definitive signature of peace between Russia and Turkey by the Treaty of Jassy, put an end to the last fears of a resumption of war in the East; and, as the prospects were equally pacific in the West, the Ministry carried out slight reductions in the land forces. These were fixed in the year 1785 at seventy-three regiments of 410 men each, divided into eight companies, with two companies *en second*. In 1789 the number of companies per regiment was fixed at ten, without any companies *en second*. Now the Secretary at War, Sir Charles Yonge, proposed further reductions, which, with those of 1789, would lessen each regiment by seventy privates, and save the country the sum of £51,000. No diminution was proposed in the number of officers;

and this gave Fox a handle for an attack. He said that the natural plan would be to reduce the number of regiments to sixty-four. Instead of that, the number of seventy regiments was retained, and new corps were now proposed for the East Indies, one for the West Indies, and one for Canada, chiefly to be used for pioneer work and clearance of woods. General Burgoyne and Fox protested against the keeping up of skeleton regiments, the latter adding the caustic comment that the plan was "the least in point of saving and the greatest in point of patronage."[1]

The practices prevalent in that age give colour to the charge. On the other hand, professional men have defended a system which kept up the *cadres* of regiments in time of peace, as providing a body of trained officers and privates, which in time of war could be filled out by recruits. Of course it is far inferior to the plan of a reserve of trained men; but that plan had not yet been hammered out by Scharnhorst, under the stress of the Napoleonic domination in Prussia. As to the reduction of seven men per company, now proposed, it may have been due partly to political reasons. Several reports in the Home Office and War Office archives prove that discontent was rife among the troops, especially in the northern districts, on account of insufficient pay and the progress of Radical propaganda among them. The reduction may have afforded the means of sifting out the ringleaders.

Retrenchment, if not Reform, was the order of the day. Pitt discerned the important fact that a recovery in the finance and trade of the country must be encouraged through a series of years to produce a marked effect. For then the application of capital to industry, and the increase in production and revenue can proceed at the rate of compound interest. Already his hopes, for which he was indebted to the "Wealth of Nations,"[2] had been largely realized. The Report of the Select Committee of the House of Commons presented in May 1791 showed the following growth in the ordinary revenue (exclusive of the Land and Malt Taxes):

1786	£11,867,055
1787	12,923,134
1788	13,007,642
1789	13,433,068
1790	14,072,978

[1] "Parl. Hist.," xxix, 810-15.   [2] *Ibid.*, 834.

During those five years the sum of £4,750,000 had been allotted to the Sinking Fund for the payment of the National Debt; and a further sum of £674,592, accruing from the interest of stock and expired annuities, had gone towards the same object —a crushing retort to the taunts of Fox and Sheridan, that the Sinking Fund was a mere pretence. On the whole the sum of £5,424,592 had been paid off from the National Debt in five years. It is therefore not surprising that three per cent. Consols, which were down at fifty-four when Pitt took office at the end of 1783, touched ninety in the year 1791. The hopes and fears of the year 1792 find expression in the fact that in March they stood at ninety-seven, and in December dropped to seventy-four.

For the present Pitt entertained the highest hopes. In his Budget Speech of 17th February he declared the revenue to be in so flourishing a state that he could grant relief to the taxpayers. In the year 1791 the permanent taxes had yielded £14,132,000; and those on land and malt brought the total up to £16,690,000; but he proposed to take £16,212,000 as the probable revenue for the following year. The expenditure would be lessened by £104,000 on the navy (2,000 seamen being discharged), and about £50,000 on the army ; £36,000 would also be saved by the non-renewal of the subsidy for Hessian troops. There were, however, additions, due to the establishment of the Government of Upper Canada, and the portions allotted to the Duke of York (on the occasion of his marriage with a Prussian princess) and the Duke of Clarence. The expenditure would, therefore, stand at £15,811,000; but, taking the average of four years, he reckoned the probable surplus at no more than £401,000. On the other hand, he anticipated no new expenses except for the fortification of posts in the West Indies and the completion of forts for the further protection of the home dockyards. On the whole, then, he reckoned that he had £600,000 to spare ; and of this amount he proposed to allocate £400,000 to the reduction of the National Debt and the repeal of the extra duty on malt, an impost much disliked by farmers. He also announced a remission of permanent taxes to the extent of £200,000, namely, on female servants, carts, and waggons, and that of three shillings on each house having less than seven windows. These were burdens that had undoubtedly affected the poor. Further, he hoped to add the sum of £200,000 every year to the Sinking Fund, and he pointed out that, at this rate of payment, that fund would amount to £4,000,000 per annum in the space of fifteen years, after which time the interest might be applied to the relief of the nation's burdens.

Then, rising high above the level of facts and figures, he ventured on this remarkable prophecy:

I am not, indeed, presumptuous enough to suppose that, when I name fifteen years, I am not naming a period in which events may arise which human foresight cannot reach, and which may baffle all our conjectures. We must not count with certainty on a continuance of our present prosperity during such an interval; but unquestionably there never was a time in the history of this country, when, from the situation of Europe, we might more reasonably expect fifteen years of peace than at the present moment.

Imagination pictures what might possibly have been the outcome of events if Great Britain and France had continued to exert on one another the peaceful and mutually beneficent influence which Pitt had sought to bring about. In that case, we can imagine the reformed French monarchy, or a Republic of the type longed for by Mme. Roland, permeating the thought and action of neighbouring States, until the cause of Parliamentary Reform in England, and the cognate efforts for civic and religious liberty on the Continent achieved a lasting triumph. That Pitt cherished these hopes is seen not only in his eloquent words, but in the efforts which he put forth to open up the world to commerce. The year 1792 ought to be remembered, not only for the outbreak of war and the horrors of the September massacres at Paris, but also for the attempt to inaugurate friendly relations with China. Pitt set great store by the embassy which he at this time sent out to Pekin under the lead of Lord Macartney. In happier times this enterprise might have served to link East and West in friendly intercourse; and Europe, weary of barren strifes, would have known no other rivalries than those of peace.

Alas: this is but a mirage. As it fades away, we discern an arid waste. War broke out between France and Austria within two months of this sanguine utterance. It soon embroiled France and England in mortal strife. All hope of retrenchment and Reform was crushed. The National Debt rose by leaps and bounds, and the Sinking Fund proved to be a snare. Taxation became an ever-grinding evil, until the poor, whose lot Pitt hoped to lighten, looked on him as the harshest of taskmasters, the puppet of kings, and the paymaster of the Continental Coalition. The spring of the year 1807 found England burdened beyond endurance, the Third Coalition stricken to death by the blows of Napoleon, while Pitt had fourteen months previously succumbed to heart-breaking toils and woes.

Before adverting to the complications with France which were thenceforth to absorb his energies, I must refer to some incidents of the session and summer of the year 1792.

One of the most noteworthy enactments was Fox's Libel Bill. In May 1791 that statesman had proposed to the House of Commons to subject cases of libel to the award of juries, not of judges. Pitt warmly approved the measure, maintaining that, far from protecting libellers, it would have the contrary effect. The Bill passed the Commons on 31st May; but owing to dilatory and factious procedure in the Lords, it was held over until the year 1792. Thanks to the noble plea for liberty urged by the venerable Earl Camden, it passed on 21st May.[1] It is matter of congratulation that Great Britain gained this new safeguard for freedom of speech before she encountered the storms of the revolutionary era.

There is little else to chronicle except two occurrences which displayed the power and the foresight of Pitt. They were the fall of Thurlow and the endeavour of the Prime Minister to form a working alliance with the Old Whigs. The former of these events greatly impressed the contemporaries of Pitt, who likened the ejected Chancellor to Lucifer or to a Titan blasted by Jove's thunderbolt. In this age we find it difficult to account for the prestige of Thurlow. His legal learning was far from profound, his speeches were more ponderous than powerful, and his attacks were bludgeon blows rather than home thrusts. Of the lighter graces and social gifts he had scant store. Indeed, his private life displayed no redeeming feature. Everyone disliked him, but very many feared him, mainly, perhaps, because of his facility for intrigue, his power of bullying, and his great influence at Court. As we have seen, the conciliatory efforts of the monarch had hitherto averted a rupture between Pitt and Thurlow. But not even the favour of George III could render the crabbed old Chancellor endurable. His spitefulness had increased since Pitt's

---

[1] "Parl. Hist.," xxix, 551-602, 1404-31.

nomination of Pepper Arden to the Mastership of the Rolls; and he showed his spleen by obstructing Government measures in the House of Lords. In April 1792 he flouted Pitt's efforts on behalf of the abolition of the Slave Trade; and on 15th May he ridiculed his proposal that to every new State loan a Sinking Fund should necessarily be appended. The Commons had passed this measure; but in the Lords Thurlow spoke contemptuously of the proposal; and his influence, if not his arguments, brought the Government majority down to six.

Pitt was furious. Despite a letter from Windsor urging the need of forbearance in the interests of the public service, he resolved to end this intolerable situation. Respectfully but firmly he begged the King to decide between him and Thurlow. The result was a foregone conclusion. Having to choose between an overbearing Chancellor, and a Prime Minister whose tact, firmness, and transcendent abilities formed the keystone of the political fabric, the King instructed Dundas to request Thurlow to deliver up the Great Seal.[1] For the convenience of public business, his resignation was deferred to the end of the session, which came at the middle of June. The Great Seal was then placed in commission until January 1793 when Lord Loughborough, formerly a follower of the Prince of Wales and Fox, became Lord Chancellor.

The dismissal of Thurlow is interesting on general as well as constitutional grounds. It marks an important step in the evolution of the Cabinet. Thenceforth the will of the Prime Minister was held to be paramount whenever any one of his colleagues openly and sharply differed from him. Thus the authority of the Prime Minister became more clearly defined. Not even the favour of the Sovereign could thenceforth uphold a Minister who openly opposed and scorned the head of the Cabinet. The recognition of this fact has undoubtedly conduced to the amenity of parliamentary life; for etiquette has imposed on Ministers the observance of outward signs of deference to their chief, and (save a few times in the breezy careers of Canning and Palmerston) dissensions have been confined to the council chamber.

As to Thurlow's feelings, they appear in his frank admission to Sir John Scott, the future Chancellor, Lord Eldon: " I did not think that the King would have parted with me so easily. As

---

[1] Stanhope, ii, 148-50, and App., xv.

to that other man [Pitt], he has done to me just what I should
have done to him if I could."[1] It is not often that a plotter
shows his hand so clearly; and we must admire Pitt's discern-
ment no less than his firmness at this crisis. Would that he had
found a more faithful successor. Possibly some suspicion as to
Loughborough's powers of intrigue led Pitt to make cautious
advances to that promising lawyer, Sir John Scott. To his
honour, be it said, Scott at once declared that he must cease to
be Solicitor-General, as he had received much assistance from
Thurlow. In vain did Pitt expostulate with him. At last he
persuaded him to consult Thurlow, who advised him to do
nothing so foolish, seeing that Pitt would be compelled at some
future time to confer the Great Seal upon him. With this parting gleam of insight and kindliness, the morose figure of Thurlow vanishes.

More than once in the session of 1792 rumours were afloat as
to a reconstruction of the Cabinet. Early in that year, when the
debates on the Russian armament somewhat shook Pitt's position, it was stated that the King desired to get rid of him.
Gillray heard of the story, and visualized it with his usual skill.
He represented the Marquis of Lansdowne ("Malagrida") as
driving at full speed to St. James's Palace, heralded by the dove
of peace, while Fox, Sheridan, etc., hang on behind and cry
out, "Stop; stop; take us in." Pitt and Dundas are seen leaving
the palace. The rumour gains in credibility from a Memorandum of the Marquis; but it is doubtful whether George ever
thought seriously of giving up Pitt, still less of seeking support
from the discredited and unpopular Lansdowne, whose views on
the French Revolution were utterly opposed to those of the
King. Probably the King put questions to him merely with the
view of gratifying his own curiosity and exciting unreal hopes.
Certainly Pitt scoffed at the idea of resignation. On 3rd March
he referred to the rumour, in a letter to the Earl of Westmorland, merely to dismiss it as ridiculous.[2]

Far more important were the negotiations that began in May—
June 1792. Pitt paved the way for a union with the Old Whigs
by consulting the opinions of the Duke of Portland and other
leading Whigs, assembled at Burlington House, respecting the

[1] Twiss, "Life of Lord Eldon," ch. x.
[2] Fitzmaurice, "Shelburne," iii, 500-4; Salomon, "Pitt," 596. The King
later on teased the Duke of Leeds by a more compromising overture.

proclamation against seditious writings. They suggested a few alterations in his draft and he adopted them. Fox alone declared against the whole scheme, and afterwards hotly opposed it in the House of Commons. This step having shown the cleavage in the Whig party, Dundas and Loughborough sought to effect a union of the Portland Whigs with the Government. The Duke of Portland strongly approved of it. Even Fox welcomed the proposal, but only on the understanding that the Whigs joined the Ministry on fair and even terms, sharing equally in the patronage. The Duke further suggested that Pitt should give up the Treasury and allow a neutral man like the Duke of Leeds to take that office. We can picture the upward tilt of the nose with which Pitt received this proposal.

Lord Malmesbury, who was present at this discussion of the Whig leaders on 13th June, himself saw great difficulties in such a plan, as also from the opposition of the King and the Prince of Wales. On the next day Loughborough met Pitt at Dundas's house, and reported him to be favourable to the idea of a coalition. Pitt further said that the King and the Queen would welcome it, except in so far as it concerned Fox, whose conduct in Parliament during the last few months had given great offence. Pitt further declared that he did not remember a single word in all the disputes with Fox which could prevent him honourably and consistently acting with him. He added that it might be difficult to give him the Foreign Office at once, but he could certainly have it in a few months' time. On 16th June Malmesbury saw Fox at Burlington House, and found him in an unusually acrid and suspicious mood, from the notion that the whole affair was a plot of Pitt to break up the Whig party. Beside which, Fox said that it was idle to expect Pitt to admit the Whig leaders on an equal footing. Malmesbury, however, maintained that, if Fox and the Duke were agreed, they would lead the whole of their party with them, at which remark Fox became silent and embarrassed.

Pitt, on the other hand, was very open to Loughborough, and expressed a wish to form a strong and united Ministry which could face the difficulties of the time. The chief obstacle to a coalition, he said, was Fox's support of French principles, which must preclude his taking the Foreign Office immediately. The remark is noteworthy as implying Pitt's expectation that either Fox might tone down his opinions, or the Revolution might abate its violence. Further, when Loughborough reminded him of the ardour of his advocacy of the Abolitionist cause, he replied that some concession must be made on that head, as the King strongly objected to the way in which it was pushed on by addresses and petitions, a method which he himself disliked. Further, he freely admitted that the "national Aristocracy" of the country must have its due weight and power.[1] These confessions (assuming that Loughborough reported them correctly) prepare us for the half right turn which now becomes the trend of Pitt's political career. In order to further the formation of a truly national party, he was willing, if necessary, to postpone the cause of the slaves and of Parliamentary Reform until the advent of calmer times.

At this stage of the discussions, then, Pitt was willing to meet the Whigs half way. But the chief difficulty lay, not with Fox and his friends, but with the King. When Pitt mentioned the proposal to him, there came the characteristic reply: "Anything complimentary to them, but no power."[2] How was it possible to harmonize this resolve with that of Fox, that the Whigs must have an equality of power? Grenville was a further obstacle. How could that stiff and ambitious man give up the Foreign Office to Fox, whose principles he detested? We hear little of Grenville in these days, probably because of his marriage to Lady Ann Pitt, daughter of Lord Camelford. But certainly he would not have tolerated a half Whig Cabinet.

It is therefore strange that the proposals were ever renewed. Renewed, however, they were, in the second week of July. Loughborough having spread the impression that Pitt desired their renewal, Leeds was again pushed to the front, it being suggested that he might be First Lord of the Treasury. Finally, on 14th August, the King granted him a private interview at Windsor, but stated that nothing had been said on the subject for a long time, and that it had never been seriously considered, it being impossible for Pitt to give up the Treasury and act as *Commis* to the Whig leaders. This statement should have lessened the Duke's astonishment at hearing from Pitt on 22nd August that there had been no thought of any change in the Government.[3] This assertion seems to belie Pitt's reputation for truthfulness. But it is noteworthy that Grenville scarcely refers to the dis-

---

[1] "Malmesbury Diaries," ii, 454-64.   [2] "Leeds Mem.," 188.
[3] *Ibid.*, 194.

cussions on this subject, deeply though it concerned him. Further, Rose, who was in close touch with Ministers, wrote to Auckland on 13th July that he had heard only through the newspapers of the "negotiations for a sort of Coalition," and that he knew there had been none; that Dundas had conferred with Loughborough, but there had been no negotiation.[1]

Now the proneness of these two men to scheming and intrigue is well known; and it seems probable that they so skilfully pulled the wires at Burlington House as to quicken the appetites of the Whig leaders. Dundas may have acted with a view to breaking up the Whig party, and Loughborough in order to bring about a general shuffle of the cards favourable to himself. Malmesbury and others, whose desires or interests lay in a union of the Portland Whigs with Pitt, furthered the scheme, and gave full credence to Loughborough's reports. But we may doubt whether Pitt took the affair seriously after the crushing declaration of the King: "Anything complimentary to them, but no power." The last blow to the scheme was dealt by Pitt in an interview with Loughborough, so we may infer from the following letter from George III to the former:

Weymouth, *August* 20, 1792.[2]

I cannot but think Mr. Pitt has judged right in seeing Lord Loughborough, as that will convince him, however [whoever?] were parties to the proposal brought by the Duke of Leeds, that the scheme can never succeed: that the Duke of Portland was equally concerned with the former appeared clearly from his letters. . . .

The King, then, looked on the whole affair as a Whig plot; and Pitt, whatever his feelings were at first, finally frowned upon the proposal. Doubtless, in an official sense, there was justification for his remark to the Duke of Leeds, that the coalition had never been in contemplation; for the matter seems never to have come before the Cabinet. But as a statement between man and man it leaves something to be desired on the score of accuracy. Annoyance at the very exalted position marked out for the Duke, whose capacity Pitt rated decidedly low, may have led him to belittle the whole affair; for signs of constraint and annoyance are obvious in his other answers to his late colleague. There, then, we must leave this question, involved in something

[1] "Auckland Journals," ii, 417, 418.   [2] Pitt MSS., 103.

of mystery.[1] We shall not be far wrong in concluding that Pitt wished for the formation of a national Ministry, and that the plan failed, partly from the resolve of Fox never to play second to Pitt; and still more from the personal way in which the King regarded the suggestion.

The King meanwhile had marked his sense of the value of Pitt's services by pressing on him the honourable position of Warden of the Cinque Ports, with a stipend of £3,000 a year, intimating at the same time that he would not hear of his declining it (6th August).[2] It is a proof of the spotless purity of Pitt's reputation that not a single libel or gibe appeared in the Press on his acceptance of this almost honorary post.[3]

One brilliant recruit to the Whig ranks was now won over to the national cause, of which Pitt was seen to be the incarnation. Already at Eton and Oxford George Canning had shown the versatility of his genius and the precocious maturity of his eloquence. When his Oxford friend, Jenkinson (the future Earl of Liverpool) made a sensational *début* in the House on the Tory side, Sheridan remarked that the Whigs would soon provide an antidote in the person of young Canning. Great, then, was their annoyance when the prodigy showed signs of breaking away from the society of the Crewes and Sheridan, in order to ally himself with Pitt. So little is known respecting the youth of Canning that the motives which prompted his breach with Sheridan are involved in uncertainty. It is clear, however, from his own confession that, after some discussion with Orde, he himself made the first offer of allegiance to Pitt in a letter of 26th July 1792. He then informed the Prime Minister that, though on terms of friendship with eminent members of the Opposition, he was "in no way bound to them by any personal or political obligation," and was therefore entirely free to choose his own party; that he was ambitious of being connected with Pitt, but lacked the means to win an election, and yet refused to be brought in by any individual—a reference, seemingly, to an offer made to him by the Duke of Portland. In reply, Pitt proposed an interview at Downing Street on Wednesday, 15th August.[4]

[1] I accept, with some qualification, Mr. Oscar Browning's explanation, that Lord Loughborough had exaggerated the accounts of his interviews with Pitt and the Whig leaders (see "Leeds Mem.," 197, note).
[2] Stanhope, ii, 160.   [3] "Bland Burges P.," 208.
[4] Stanhope, "Miscellanies," ii, 57-63. Letter of Canning to W. Sturges

At noon on that day the two men first met. We can picture them as they faced one another in the formal surroundings of the Prime Minister's study. Pitt, at this time thirty-three years of age, had lost some of the slimness of youth, but his figure was bony, angular, and somewhat awkward. His face was as yet scarcely marked by the slight Bacchic blotches which told of carouses with Dundas at Wimbledon. Months and years of triumph (apart from the Russian defeat) had stiffened his confidence and pride; but the fateful shadow of the French Revolution must have struck a chill to his being, especially then, on the arrival of news of the pitiable surrender of Louis XVI and Marie Antoinette, and the shooting down of the Swiss Guards at the Tuileries. No royalist could look on the future without inward shuddering; and both these men were ardent royalists. We know from Canning's confession that it was the starting of the club, the Friends of the People, in April 1792, which disgusted him with the forward section of the Whigs; and their subsequent action completed the breach. Pitt's endeavour to form a national Administration must have gained a new significance from the terrible news from Paris. We may be sure, then, that the youth of twenty-two years gazed with eager interest on the stately form before him as at the embodiment of political wisdom, purity, and patriotism.

They shook hands. Then for a time they ambled coyly around the subject at issue, and talked of " France and Jenkinson, and other equally important concerns." Indeed Pitt seems to have been as nervous and awkward as the novice. At length he plunged into business. " It is your wish, I believe, Mr. Canning (and I am sure it is mine), to come in, etc." On Canning bowing assent, Pitt remarked that it was not easy to find an inexpensive seat, and commented on his expressed desire not to tie himself to any borough-owner. Whereupon the young aspirant, with more pride than tact, threw in the remark that he would not like to be personally beholden to such an one, for instance, as Lord Lonsdale (who first brought Pitt into Parliament). The

Bourne, 3rd September 1792. This interview is not referred to by Mr. H. W. V. Temperley ("Canning," ch. ii), Mr. Sichel ("Sheridan"), Captain Bagot ("Canning and his Friends"), or E. Festing ("Frere and his Friends"). In "Pitt and Napoleon Miscellanies" I shall publish new letters of Canning. One, dated 15th March 1793, declines an offer of Portland to bring him into Parliament.

Prime Minister seemed not to notice the *gaucherie*, and stated that the Treasury had only six seats at its disposal, but could arrange matters with " proprietors of burgage-tenures." Thereupon Canning broke in more deftly. In that case, he said, it must be made clear that he bound himself to follow, not the borough-owner, but the Prime Minister. Here he more than recovered lost ground, if indeed he had lost any. Pitt expressed his sense of the compliment, and said that this could be managed, unless the young member came to differ absolutely from his patron. Canning then frankly confessed his inability to follow Pitt in maintaining the Test Act. Equally frank and cordial was the reply, that he (Pitt) did not claim exact agreement, especially on " speculative subjects," but only " a general good disposition towards Government," which might be strengthened by frequent contact.

Such was the course of this memorable interview. It sealed for ever the allegiance of the youth to his self-chosen leader. He had prepared Sheridan, and through him Fox and Bouverie, for this change of front. The openness, the charm, the self-effacing patriotism of the Minister thenceforth drew him as by an irresistible magnet. The brilliance and joviality of Fox and Sheridan counted as nothing against the national impulse which the master now set in motion and the pupil was destined to carry to further lengths. There was a natural sympathy between these men both in aim and temperament. It is a sign of the greatness of Pitt that from the outset he laid the spell of his genius irrevocably upon Canning.

Deferring to the next chapter a study of the democratic movement in Great Britain, we now turn our attention to the relations of Pitt to France, a topic which thenceforth dominates his life story and the destinies of mankind.

In the month of January 1792, there arrived in London an envoy charged with important proposals from the French Government. It was Talleyrand, ex-bishop of Autun. Pitt had become acquainted with him during his residence at Rheims in the summer of 1783; but the circumstances of the case now forbade anything more than passing intercourse with that most charming of talkers and subtlest of diplomatists. Talleyrand, having been a member of the first, or Constituent, Assembly, was prevented by the constitution of September 1791 from holding any office for two years after that date. Therefore his visit to London was ostensibly on private affairs. The Duc de Biron was the envoy, and Talleyrand merely his adviser. He was instructed to seek "to maintain and strengthen the good understanding which exists between the two Kingdoms."[1]

This was only the official pretext for the mission, the secret aim of which was to win the friendship, if not the alliance, of England in case of a Franco-Austrian war. In the early days of January 1792 the constitutional Ministry, holding office, though not power, at Paris, seemed to be working for a rupture with the Hapsburgs, partly in order to please the Jacobins, and partly to escape the ever increasing difficulties of its position. The earlier causes of dispute do not concern us here. As we have seen, the Emperor Leopold was far from desirous of war; but the provocative attitude of the Legislative Assembly at Paris and the humiliations of his sister, Marie Antoinette, aroused his resentment; and, early in January, he was heard to say "that if the French madmen were determined to force him into a war, they should find that the pacific Leopold knew how to wage it with the greatest vigour, and would oblige them to pay its expenses in something more solid than assignats." Our ambassador, Sir Robert Keith, was, however, convinced that this outburst and the westward march of troops were but "empty parade."[2]

On the other hand Earl Gower, British ambassador at Paris, reported that the Ministry, the Assembly, and the Jacobins Club (with the exception of Robespierre and his clique) desired war.[3] In truth, there seemed little risk in a struggle with the exhausted Hapsburg States, provided that they had support neither from Prussia nor from England. De Ségur therefore set out for Berlin, and Talleyrand for London, to secure the friendly neutrality or support of those Governments. The latter envoy was specially suited for his mission, as he carried on the traditions of Mirabeau, who in the closing months of his life urged the need of an Anglo-French *entente*.[4]

Talleyrand and Biron reached London on 24th January 1792. Before reaching the capital they read in the English papers that they had arrived there, and had been very coldly received by Pitt—a specimen of the arts by which the French *émigrés* in

[1] Pallain, "La Mission de Talleyrand à Londres," 41.
[2] Keith's "Mems.," ii, 494. Keith to Grenville, 14th January 1792.
[3] "Gower's Despatches," 142, 143, 145, 149.   [4] Pallain, pp. xv-xviii.

London sought to embitter the relations between the two lands. Talleyrand had the good fortune to occupy a seat in the Strangers' Gallery at the opening of Parliament close to two ardent royalists, Cazalès and Lally-Tollendal. What must have been their feelings on hearing in the King's speech the statement of his friendly relations to the other Powers and his resolve to reduce the army and navy?

Already Pitt had seen Talleyrand. He reminded him in a friendly way of their meeting at Rheims, remarked on the unofficial character of the ex-bishop's " mission," but expressed his willingness to discuss French affairs, about which he even showed "curiosity." Grenville afterwards spoke to the envoy in the same courteous but non-committal manner. Talleyrand was, however, charmed. He wrote to Delessart, the Foreign Minister at Paris: " Your best ground is England; . . . Believe me the rumours current in France about the disposition of England towards us are false." [1] He urged the need of showing a bold front; for "it is with a fleet that you must speak to England."

Talleyrand throughout showed the sagacity which earned him fame in diplomacy. He was not depressed by the King's frigid reception of him at St. James's on 1st February, or by the Queen refusing even to notice him. Even the escapades of Biron did not dash his hopes. That envoy ran up debts and bargained about horses *avec un nommé Tattersall, qui tient dans sa main tous les chevaux d'Angleterre*, until he was arrested for debt and immured in a " sponging house," whence the appeals of the ex-bishop failed to rescue him. As Biron had come with an official order to buy horses with a view to the impending war with Austria, we may infer that his arrest was the work of some keen-witted *émigré*.

Even this, however, was better than the fortunes of Ségur, who found himself openly flouted both by King and courtiers at Berlin. For Frederick William was still bent on a vigorous policy. On 7th February his Ministers signed with Prince Reuss, the Austrian envoy, a secret treaty of defensive alliance, mainly for the settlement of French affairs, but also with a side glance at Poland. The Prussian Ministers probably hoped for a peaceful but profitable settlement, which would leave them free for a decisive intervention in the Polish troubles now coming to

[1] Pallain, 56, 57.

a crisis; but Frederick William was in a more warlike mood, and longed to overthrow the "rebels" in France. Ségur's mission to Berlin was therefore an utter failure. That of Talleyrand, on the other hand, achieved its purpose, mainly because Pitt and Grenville never had any other desire than to remain strictly neutral. It was therefore superfluous for Talleyrand to hint delicately at the desirability of the friendship of France for England, in view of the war with Tippoo Sahib in India, and the increasing ferment in Ireland.[1]

On 1st March Grenville again assured him of the earnest desire of the British Government to see the end of the troubles in France, and declared that Pitt and he had been deeply wounded by the oft-repeated insinuations that they had sought to foment them. All such charges were absurd; for "a commercial people stands only to gain by the freedom of all those who surround it." We may reasonably conclude that these were the words of Pitt; for they recall that noble passage of the "Wealth of Nations": "A nation that would enrich itself by trade is certainly most likely to do so when its neighbours are all rich, industrious, and commercial nations."[2] For the rest, Grenville defied the calumniators of England to adduce a single proof in support of their slanders, and requested Talleyrand to remain some time in England for the purpose of observing public opinion. He warned him, however, that the Cabinet could not give an answer to his main proposal.

More than this Talleyrand could scarcely expect. He had already divined the important secret that the Cabinet was divided on this subject, the King, Thurlow, and Camden being hostile to France, while Pitt, Grenville, and Dundas were friendly. When Talleyrand ventured to ascribe those sentiments to Pitt and Grenville, the latter did not deny it, and he at once echoed the desire expressed by the envoy for the conclusion of an Anglo-French alliance. That the greater part of the British people would have welcomed such a compact admits of no doubt. On the walls were often chalked the words: "No war with the French." Talleyrand advised the Foreign Minister, Delessart, to send immediately to London a fully accredited ambassador; for the talk often was: "We have an ambassador at Paris. Why have not you one here?" Nevertheless, a despatch of Grenville

---

[1] Pallain, 106, 107.   [2] "Wealth of Nations," bk. iv, ch. iii.

to Gower, on 9th March, shows that Pitt and he keenly felt the
need of caution. They therefore enjoined complete silence on
Gower. In truth, Grenville's expressions, quoted above, were
merely the outcome of the good will which he and Pitt felt
towards France. But these words from the two powerful Ministers
meant safety for France on her coasts, whatever might betide
her on the Meuse and the Rhine.

On the day when Grenville spoke these words of peace, two
events occurred which portended war. Leopold II died; and
an irritating despatch, which he and Kaunitz had recently sent
to Paris, was read out to the Legislative Assembly. Thereafter a rupture was inevitable. Francis II, who now ascended
the throne of his father, was a shy, proud, delicate youth of
twenty-four years, having only a superficial knowledge of public
affairs, scarcely known to the Ministers, and endowed with a
narrow pedantic nature which was to be the bane of his people.
He lacked alike the sagacity, the foresight, and the suppleness
of Leopold. Further, though his inexperience should have inspired him with a dread of war for his storm-tossed States, yet
that same misfortune subjected him to the advice of the veteran
Chancellor, Kaunitz. That crabbed old man advised the maintenance of a stiff attitude towards France; and this, in her present temper, entailed war.

The last despatch from Vienna to Paris contained strongly
worded advice to the French Government and Assembly to
adopt a less provocative attitude, to withdraw its troops from
the northern frontier, and, above all, to rid itself of the factious
minority which controlled its counsels. If Leopold had hoped
to intimidate France or to strengthen the peace-party at Paris,
he made the greatest mistake of his reign. The war party at
once gained the ascendancy, decreed the arrest of Delessart for
his tame reply to Vienna, and broke up the constitutional
Ministry. Their successors were mainly Girondins. The most
noteworthy are Roland, who took the Home Office; Clavière,
Finance; and Dumouriez, Foreign Affairs. The last was a man
of great energy and resource. A soldier by training, and with a
dash of the adventurer in his nature, he now leapt to the front,
and astonished France by his zeal and activity. He was not
devoid of prudence; for, as appears from Gower's despatch
of 30th March, he persuaded the Assembly to postpone action
until an answer arrived to his last despatch to Vienna. Gower

found from conversation with Dumouriez that a rupture must ensue if a satisfactory reply did not arrive by 15th April.[1] Four days later, as no answer came, the Council of Ministers decided on war; and on the next day Louis formally proposed it to the Assembly, which assented with acclamation.

Secondary causes helped on the rupture. Frederick William encouraged the young Emperor to draw the sword, and led him to expect Alsace and Lorraine as his share of the spoil, the duchies of Jülich and Berg falling to Prussia. Catharine also fanned the crusading zeal at Berlin and Vienna in the hope of having "more elbow-room," obviously in Poland.[2] Further, the news from Madrid and Stockholm indisposed the French Assembly to endure any dictation from Vienna. At the end of February Floridablanca fell from power at Madrid, and his successor, Aranda, showed a peaceful front. And, on 16th March Gustavus of Sweden was assassinated by Anckarström, a tool of the revengeful nobles. This loss was severely felt. The royalist crusade now had no Tancred, only an uninspiring Duke of Brunswick.

Though France took the final step of declaring war, it is now known that Austria had done much to provoke it and nothing to prevent it. The young Emperor refused to withdraw a word of the provocative despatch; and in his letter to Thugut at Brussels, he declared he was weary of the state of things in France and had decided to act and put an end to it; "that he should march his troops at once, and the French must be amused for two months until the troops arrived; then, whether the French attacked him or not, he should attack them."[3] Keith also wrote from Vienna to Grenville on 2nd May, that the French declaration of war had come in the nick of time to furnish the Hapsburgs with the opportunity of throwing the odium of the war upon France.[4] Other proofs might be cited; and it seems certain that, if France had not thrown down the gauntlet, both the German Powers would have attacked her in the early summer of 1792. Pitt and Grenville, looking on at these conflicting schemes, formed the perfectly correct surmise that both sides were bent on war, and that little or nothing could be done to avert it.

We must now trace the policy of Pitt somewhat closely. The

---

[1] "Gower's Despatches," 165, 171.   [2] Sorel, ii, 216.
[3] Fersen, "Diary" (Eng. edit.), 255.
[4] Clapham, "Causes of the War of 1792," 231.

question at issue is, whether he favoured the royalist or the democratic cause, and was responsible for the ensuing friction between
England and France, which culminated in the long and disastrous
strifes of 1793-1801.

Dumouriez, as we have seen, threw down the gauntlet to
Austria in the hope of securing the neutrality of Prussia and
the friendship of England. Accordingly he decided to send
Talleyrand on a second mission to London. That skilful diplomat had recently returned to Paris; and the Foreign Minister
drew up, perhaps in concert with him, a Memoir entitled " Reflections on a Negotiation with England in case of War," which
provided the text for Talleyrand's discourse to Pitt and Grenville. The gist of it is that Talleyrand must convince the British
Government of the need of a French attack on the Belgic provinces of Austria as the sole means of safety. For, while offensive
in appearance, it is in reality defensive. France does not intend
to keep those provinces; and, even if her conquest of them
brings about the collapse of the Stadholder's power in Holland,
England will do well not to intervene in favour of the Orange
régime. For what good can the Island Power gain by war with
France? She may take the French colonies; but that will mean
a tiresome struggle with the revolted negroes in the West Indies.
France, meanwhile, with her new-born strength, will conquer
Central Europe and then throw her energy into her fleet. The
better course, then, for England will be to remain neutral, even
if Holland be revolutionized, and the estuary of the Scheldt be
thrown open to all nations. Or, still better, England may help
France to keep in check the King of Prussia and the Prince of
Orange. In that case the two free Powers will march hand in
hand and " become the arbiters of peace or war for the whole
world."

This remarkable pronouncement claims attention for several
reasons. Firstly, it proves that Dumouriez and Talleyrand believed their sole chance of safety to lie in the conquest of
Austria's Belgic provinces, where a cognate people would receive
them with open arms. That is to say, they desired war with
Austria, and they did not dread the prospect of war with Prussia,
provided that England remained neutral and friendly. Pitt and
Grenville were well aware of this from Gower's despatches. Our
ambassador had warned them that France recked little of a war
with the whole of Europe, provided that England held aloof.

Secondly, this fact disposes of the subsequent charge of Fox against Pitt, that he ought to have sided with France in 1792 and thereby to have prevented the attack of the German Powers. For, as we have seen, it was she who took the irrevocable step of declaring war on Austria; and further, the details given above prove that all that Frenchmen expected from Pitt was neutrality. By remaining neutral, while the French overran Belgium, Pitt was favouring the French plans more than any British statesman had done since the time of James II. Thirdly, we notice in the closing sentences of these Reflections signs of that extraordinary self-confidence which led Girondins and Jacobins to face without flinching even the prospect of war with England.

What was Pitt's conduct at this crisis? He knew enough of the politics of Berlin and Vienna to see that those Courts would almost certainly make war on France. He adopted therefore the line of conduct which prudence and love of peace dictated, a strict neutrality. But he refused to proclaim it to the world, as it would encourage France to attack Austria. At the same time Grenville let it be known that Austria must not be deprived of her Belgic lands, which England had assured to her, firstly by the Treaty of Utrecht (1713), and quite recently by the Reichenbach Convention. As Grenville phrased it— "The Pays Bas form the chain which unites England to the Continent, and the central knot of our relations to Austria and Russia. It would be broken if they belonged to France." Talleyrand and Dumouriez knew this perfectly well, and prudently declared that France had no intention of keeping those lands. Would that the Jacobins and Napoleon had shown the same wise self-restraint! It was their resolve to dominate the Netherlands which brought them into irreconcilable opposition to Pitt and his successors down to the year 1814.

Statesmanlike though the aims of Dumouriez were, they suffered not a little in their exposition. Talleyrand, the brain of the policy, was not its mouthpiece. In the French embassy at Portman Square he figured merely as adviser to the French ambassador, the *ci-devant* Marquis de Chauvelin, a vain and showy young man, devoid of the qualities of insight, tact, and patience in which the ex-bishop of Autun excelled his contemporaries. Had this sage counsellor remained in London to the end of the year, things might have gone very differently. The instructions issued to Chauvelin contain ideas similar to those outlined above; but they lay stress on the utility of a French alliance for England, in order to thwart the aims of a greedy Coalition and to ensure her own internal tranquillity, which, it is hinted, France can easily ruffle. Talleyrand is also charged to offer to cede the small but valuable island, Tobago, which we lost in 1783, provided that the British Government guaranteed a French loan of £3,000,000 or £4,000,000, to be raised in London; and he is to suggest that, if the two Powers acted together, they could revolutionize Spanish America and control the world.[1]

Our curiosity is aroused as to the reception which Pitt and Grenville gave to these schemes. It is not certain, however, that Chauvelin and Talleyrand showed their hand completely; for events told against them from the outset. Chauvelin bore with him an autograph letter from Louis XVI to George III, couched in the friendliest terms, and expressing the hope of closer relations between the two peoples.[2] But before he could present it to the King at St. James's, it appeared in the Paris papers. This breach of etiquette created a bad impression; for it seemed that the letter was merely a bid for an alliance between the two peoples. It is quite possible that Dumouriez, with his natural impulsiveness, allowed it to gain currency in order to identify Louis XVI with French democracy, and that in its turn with public opinion in England. Further, we now know that Marie Antoinette, in her resolve to paralyse the policy and the defensive power of France, wrote at once to Fersen at Brussels that her consort's letter was very far from speaking his real sentiments.[3] This news, when passed on to London, must have made it clear that the two envoys represented the Girondin Ministry, but not the King of France. Then again tidings soon arrived of the disgraceful flight of the French troops on the Belgian frontier, the new levies, at sight of the Austrian horse, rushing back to Lille in wild disorder and there murdering their General, Theobald Dillon. George III and Grenville wrote of this event in terms of disgust and contempt.[4] It is therefore not surprising that the reception of Chauvelin was far from promis-

---

[1] On the Tobago proposal see "Dropmore P.," ii, 260.
[2] Pallain, 215-9. The original is in Pitt MSS., 333.
[3] Fersen, "Diary" (Eng. edit.), 316, 319.
[4] "Dropmore P.," ii, 267. See, too, further details in "Dumouriez and the Defence of England against Napoleon," by J. H. Rose and A. M. Broadley.

ing; and Talleyrand doubtless felt that the time was not ripe for discussing an Anglo-French *entente* for the control of the world.

In fact, the envoys were received coolly from the outset. The outbreak of war on the Continent had caused almost a panic in the City. The Funds dropped sharply, and Pitt ordered an official denial to sinister reports of a forthcoming raid by the press-gang. A little later he assured a deputation of merchants that England would hold strictly aloof from the war. Chauvelin reported these facts to his Government along with the assurance that the Cabinet had definitely resolved on neutrality. How he came to know of that decision is a mystery; and it is scarcely less odd that a copy of his despatch reporting it should be in the Pitt Papers.[1] On the whole, then, France had good reason to be satisfied with Pitt. Austria, on the other hand, disliked his conduct. Kaunitz, with his usual acerbity, gave out that England was secretly hostile to the House of Hapsburg; and Keith, finding his position increasingly awkward, begged for his recall.

The first sign of friction between England and France arose out of the King's proclamation against seditious writings, which we noticed in the last chapter. Chauvelin complained of some of its phrases, and stated that France waged war for national safety, not for aggrandizement. Grenville thereupon loftily remarked that Chauvelin had no right to express an opinion on a question which concerned solely the King's Government and Parliament. The British reply irritated by its curt correctness.

Equally unfortunate were some incidents in the ensuing debates on this topic. Some members emphasized their loyalty by adverting tartly to the connections of Thomas Paine and English reformers with the French Jacobins. On 31st May the Duke of Richmond charged that writer with being an emissary from abroad, because he had advised the destruction of the British navy.[2] There is no such passage in the "Rights of Man"; and the Duke must have read with the distorting lens of fear or hatred the suggestion that, if England, France, and the United States were allied, a very small navy would be needed, costing not more than half a million a year.[3] But this incident is typical of the prejudice that was growing against France. Grenville in

Pitt MSS., 333. Chauvelin to Dumouriez, 28th April.
[2] "Parl. Hist.," xxix, 1522.   [3] "Rights of Man," pt. ii, ch. v.

the same debate declared that the Corresponding Societies avowed their connection with foreign clubs and were engaged in circulating pamphlets. The conclusion was obvious, that close relations with France must be avoided. As to the feeling of the Royal Family, it was manifested in an effusively loyal speech by the Prince of Wales, his first speech at Westminster. In it he marked his entire severance from Fox on this question.

Grenville's complaisance to the French envoys was perhaps little more than a blind to mask his contempt for them and their principles. On 19th June he wrote to Auckland respecting the "ignorance and absurdity of the French mission," but suggested that the picking a quarrel with France would only help the English Jacobins to introduce French notions. Even if this mission were got rid of, some one else might come who might make even more mischief. These expressions refer to the connections which Chauvelin and Talleyrand had formed with the Opposition. As Bland Burges remarked: "Talleyrand is intimate with Paine, Horne Tooke, Lord Lansdowne, and a few more of that stamp, and is generally scouted by every one else." George III's words were equally contemptuous and marked his resolve to have as little as possible to do with France.[1] Pitt did not state his opinions on this topic; but he probably held those of Grenville.

The prejudices of the King and the resolves of the two chief Ministers proved fatal to an ardent appeal which came from Paris in the middle of June. As the attitude of the Court of Berlin became more and more warlike, Dumouriez put forth one more effort to gain the friendly mediation of England and thus assure peace with Prussia. Chauvelin, swallowing his annoyance at Grenville's recent note, pointed out that Austria was making great efforts to induce Prussia, Holland, and the lesser German States to join her in the war against liberty. The designs of the monarchs against Poland were notorious; and it was clear that a vast conspiracy was being hatched against the free States of the Continent. Would not England, then, endeavour to stop the formation of this reactionary league?

The occasion was, indeed, highly important. It is conceivable that, if British influence had been powerful at Berlin, a spirited declaration would have had some effect at that Court. Unfor-

---

[1] " Dropmore P.," ii, 282 ; " Auckland Journals," ii, 410.

tunately our influence had sunk to zero since the Oczakoff fiasco of 1791. Moreover, the Prussian Government had by that time decided to break with France. Her envoys were dismissed from Berlin in the first week of June, and it is probable that Pitt and Grenville by 18th June knew of the warlike resolve of the Prussian Government. In any case, after a delay of twenty days, they sent once more a reply to Chauvelin's request, affirming the earnest desire of His Majesty to contribute to the restoration of peace, but re-asserting his decision in favour of unswerving neutrality. On 24th July Prussia declared war against France, and three days later the Duke of Brunswick issued the famous manifesto to the French people which thrilled the French people with indignation against the hapless sovereigns at the Tuileries whom it was designed to protect.[1]

The outbreak of war on the Rhine and Meuse was an event of incalculable importance. As we have seen, Pitt discouraged the bellicose tendencies of the *émigrés* and of the Austrian and Prussian Courts. But the passions of the time ran too high to admit of the continuance of peace; and State after State was soon to be drawn into the devouring vortex of strife. Strange to say the first to suffer from the outbreak of hostilities was Poland. That Republic entered on a new lease of life in the spring of the year 1791. The constitution adopted with enthusiasm on 3rd May substituted an hereditary for an elective monarchy, and otherwise strengthened the fabric of that almost anarchic State. Social and civic reforms promised also to call its burghers and serfs to a life of activity or comfort. But the change at once aroused keen dislike at St. Petersburg and Berlin. Prussian statesmen resented any improvement in the condition of their nominal ally, and declared that, if Russia gained a strong position on the Euxine, Prussia and Austria must secure indemnities at the expense of Poland.

The Czarina soon succeeded in heading them in that direction. After the signature of the Peace of Jassy with the Turks early in January 1792, she began openly to encourage the factious efforts of Polish malcontents. The troubles at Paris also enabled her to engage the Courts of Vienna and Berlin

---

[1] "Ann. Reg." (1792), 178-82, 225-32; Sorel, ii, 445-54; Heidrich, pt. ii, ch. ii. I fully agree with Dr. Salomon ("Pitt," 537) as to the sincerity of Pitt's desire for neutrality.

in a western crusade on which she bestowed her richest blessing, her own inmost desires meanwhile finding expression
in the following confidential utterance: " I am breaking my head
to make the Cabinets of Vienna and Berlin intervene in the
affairs of France. I wish to see them plunged into some very
complicated question in order to have my own hands free." [1]
Though her old opponent, Kaunitz, fathomed her intentions,
she partly succeeded in persuading the Austrian and Prussian
Ministers that their mission clearly was to stamp out Jacobinism
at Paris, while Providence reserved for her the duty of extirpat-
ing its offshoots at Warsaw. In the Viennese Court, where the
value of a regenerated Poland as a buffer State was duly appreciated, there were some qualms as to the spoliation of that unoffending State; but Prussian politicians, in their eagerness for
the Polish districts, Danzig and Thorn, harboured few scruples
as to betraying the cause of their allies at Warsaw.

Little by little the outlines of a scheme were sketched between
Austria and Prussia for securing indemnities for the expenses
of the war against France; and it was arranged that Prussia
should acquire the coveted lands on the lower Vistula; also
Anspach and Baireuth; Austria was to effect the long-desired
Belgic-Bavarian exchange, besides gaining parts of Alsace; and
it was understood that Russia would annex the Polish Ukraine
and work her will in the rest of Poland. The Polish part of the
scheme was, however, stiffly opposed by Kaunitz; and in the
sequel the old Chancellor ended his long and distinguished career
by way of protest against a change of front which he deemed
unwise and disgraceful.[2]

Early in May everything was ready for the restoration of
anarchy in Poland. Catharine ordered her troops to enter its
borders; and the factious Polish nobles whom she had sheltered
during the winter returned to their land and formed a " Confederation " at Targowicz on 14th May for the purpose of undoing
the reforms of 1791. Daniel Hailes, our envoy at Warsaw, kept
Grenville fully informed of this affair. On 16th June he reported
Austria's desertion of Poland, the brutal refusal of the Court of
Berlin to accord help to its ally, the heroic efforts of Kosciusko

[1] Sybel, ii, 142.
[2] For the discussions between the three Powers on Poland see Heidrich,
165-219; and Salomon, " Das Politische System des jüngeren Pitt und die
zweite Teilung Polens" (Berlin, 1895).

and the Polish levies to resist the Russian armies, and the despair of the patriots of Warsaw, adding the cynical comment that at Warsaw patriotism was only a cloak for private interest, and that the new constitution was generally regarded as the death-blow to Polish independence.[1] Whether he added these words to please Grenville, who had always discouraged the Polish cause,[2] is not easy to say; but the statement cannot be reconciled with Hailes's earlier enthusiasm for that well-meant effort.

On all sides the Polish patriots now found indifference or hostility. The Elector of Saxony (their King-elect) gave them cold words; and Catharine demanded the restoration of the old constitution of which she was a guarantor. King Stanislaus, a prey to deep despondency, saw the defence collapse on all sides, and at the close of June the Russians drew near to Warsaw. Many of the Polish reformers fled to Leipzig and there prepared to appeal to Europe against this forcible suppression of a truly national constitution.

Amidst these scenes Hailes was replaced by Colonel Gardiner, who received from Grenville the following instructions, dated 4th August 1792. He informed him that Hailes had last year been charged "to confine himself to such assurances of His Majesty's good wishes as could be given without committing H.M. to any particular line of conduct with respect to any troubles that might arise on the subject [of the Polish Revolution]. The event has unhappily but too well justified their reserve; and the present situation is such as to leave little hope that the tranquillity of that unfortunate land can be restored without its falling again into the most entire dependence on the power of Russia, even if no further dismemberment of territory should take place." Grenville then stated that Prussia's conduct was due to fear of a strong Government in Poland; but the present alternative (a Russian occupation) would probably be worse for her. He added these sentences: "No intervention of the Maritime Powers [England and Holland] could be service-able to Poland, at least not without a much greater exertion and expense than the importance to their separate interests could possibly justify. . . . You are to be very careful not to do any-thing which could hold out ill-grounded expectations of support from this country."

[1] "F. O.," Poland, 6. Hailes to Grenville, 16th and 27th June 1792.
[2] "Dropmore P.," ii, 142; see, too, ii, 279.

In these words Grenville passed sentence of death upon Poland. On this important subject he must have acted with the consent of Pitt; but the opinion of the latter is unknown. It would seem that after the weak treatment of the Oczakoff crisis by Parliament, he gave up all hope of saving either Turkey or Poland. If that was impracticable in the spring of 1791, how much more so in August 1792, when French affairs claimed far closer attention? It is worth noticing that several of the Foxites (not Fox himself, for he was still intent on a Russian alliance),[1] now revised their opinion about Catharine II and inveighed against her for trampling on the liberties of Poland. Did they now discover the folly of their conduct in previously encouraging her?

In despair of help from England, some of the patriots of Warsaw turned towards France. But this added to their misfortunes. It gave the schemers of Berlin the longed-for excuse of intervening by force under the pretext that they must stamp out " the French evil " from States bordering on their own. On hearing of the advance of three Prussian columns, Catharine threw her whole weight into Polish affairs.

So closely did the fortunes of Poland intertwine themselves with those of France. The outbreak of the Franco-Austrian war meant ruin for the reformers at Warsaw. Had Austria held to her former resolve, to prevent the triumph of Russia or Prussia in Poland, it is possible that Pitt and Grenville would have decided to support her. As it was, they maintained their cautious and timid neutrality. The reports of Hailes were explicit enough to show that another partition was at hand; but, so far as I can discover, they lifted not a finger to prevent it. The excess of Pitt's caution at this crisis enables us to gauge the magnitude of the disaster to the Polish cause involved by his surrender to the Czarina in the spring and summer of 1791. By a wonderful display of skill and audacity she emerged triumphant from all her difficulties, and now, while egging on the German Powers to war with France, planted her heel on the liberties of Poland. Her conquest was easy and profitable. The restoration of order at Paris proved to be fraught with unexpected dangers, and the German sovereigns scarcely set their hands to the task before they discovered that they were her dupes. If

---

[1] " Mems. of Fox," iii, 18.

the French war worked disaster at Warsaw, the prospect of a partition of Poland undoubtedly helped to lessen the pressure on France during the campaign of Valmy. Hope of further spoils in 1794-5 distracted the aims of the Allies; and Pitt was destined to see the efforts of the monarchical league in the West weaken and die away under the magnetic influence of the eastern problem. Well would it have been for him if he could have upheld Poland in 1791. By so doing he would have removed the cause of bitter dissensions between the Houses of Romanoff, Hapsburg, and Hohenzollern. As will appear in due course, Revolutionary France achieved her marvellous triumphs partly by the prowess of her sons, but still more owing to the intrigues and feuds which clogged the efforts of the Allies and baffled the constructive powers of Pitt.

CHAPTER III

PEACE OR WAR?

It seems absolutely impossible to hesitate as to supporting our Ally [Holland] in case of necessity, and the explicit declaration of our sentiments is the most likely way to prevent the case occurring.—PITT TO LORD STAFFORD, 13th November 1792.

ONE of the first requisites for the study of a period whose outlines are well known, is to bar out the insidious notion that the course of events was inevitable. Nine persons out of ten have recourse to that easy but fallacious way of explaining events. The whole war, they say, or think, was inevitable. It was fated that the Duke of Brunswick should issue his threatening manifesto to the Parisians if violence were offered to Louis XVI; that they should resent the threat, rise in revolt, and dethrone the King, and thereafter massacre royalists in the prisons. The innate vigour of the democratic cause further required that the French should stand their ground at Valmy and win a pitched battle at Jemappes, that victory leading to an exaltation of soul in which the French Republicans pushed on their claims in such a way as to bring England into the field. History, when written in this way, is a symmetrical mosaic; and the human mind loves patterns.

But events are not neatly chiselled; they do not fall into geometrical groups, however much the memory, for its own ease, seeks to arrange them thus. Their edges are jagged; and the slightest jar might have sent them in different ways. To recur to the events in question: the Duke of Brunswick objected to issuing the manifesto, and only owing to the weariness or weakness of old age, yielded to the insistence of the *émigrés* at his headquarters: the insurrection at Paris came about doubtfully and fitfully; the issue on 10th August hung mainly on the personal bearing of the King; the massacres were the work of

57

an insignificant minority, which the vast mass regarded with sheer stupefaction; and even the proclamation of the French Republic by the National Convention on 21st September was not without many searchings of heart.[1]

Meanwhile Pitt and Grenville had not the slightest inkling as to the trend of events. The latter on 13th July 1792 wrote thus to Earl Gower at Paris: " My speculations are that the first entrance of the foreign troops [into France] will be followed by negotiations; but how they are to end, or what possibility there is to establish any form of government, or any order in France, is far beyond any conjectures I can form." [2] This uncertainty is illuminating. It shows that Pitt and Grenville were not far-seeing schemers bent on undermining the liberties of France and Britain by a war on which they had long resolved, but fallible mortals, unable to see a handbreadth through the turmoil, but cherishing the hope that somehow all would soon become clear. As to British policy during the summer of 1792, it may be classed as masterly inactivity or nervous passivity, according to the standpoint of the critic. In one case alone did Pitt and Grenville take a step displeasing to the French Government, namely, by recalling Gower from the embassy at Paris; and this was due to the fall of the French monarchy on 10th August, and to the danger attending the residence of a noble in Paris. Only by a display of firmness did Gower and his secretary, Lindsay, succeed in obtaining passports from the new Foreign Minister, Lebrun.[3]

That follower of Dumouriez had as colleagues the former Girondin Ministers, Clavière, Roland, and Servan. Besides them were Monge (the physicist) for the Navy, and Danton for Justice, the latter a far from reassuring choice, as he was known to be largely responsible for the massacres in the prisons of Paris early in September. Little is known about the publicist, Lebrun, on whom now rested the duty of negotiating with England, Spain, Holland, etc. It is one of the astonishing facts of this time that unknown men leaped to the front at Paris, directed affairs to momentous issues, and then sank into obscurity or perished. The Genevese Clavière started assignats and managed revolutionary finance; Servan controlled the War Office for some months with much ability, and then fell; Pétion, Santerre, the

---

[1] Aulard, " La Rév. Franç.," 270-2.   [2] " Dropmore P.," ii, 291.
[3] " Bland Burges P.," 207, 211.

popular Paris brewer, and an ex-hawker, Hanriot, were suc-
cessively rulers of Paris for a brief space.

But of all the puzzles of this time Lebrun is perhaps the chief.
In his thirtieth year he was Foreign Minister of France, when
she broke with England, Holland, Spain, and the Empire. He
is believed by many (*e.g.*, by W. A. Miles, who knew him well)
to be largely responsible for those wars. Yet who was this
Lebrun? Before the Revolution he had to leave France for his
advanced opinions, and took refuge at Liége, where Miles found
him toiling for a scanty pittance at journalistic hack-work.
Suffering much at the hands of the Austrians in 1790, he fled
back to Paris, joined the Girondins, wrote for them, made himself useful to Dumouriez during his tenure of the Foreign Office,
and, not long after his resignation, stepped into his shoes and
appropriated his policy. In order to finish with him here, we
may note that he voted for the death of Louis XVI, and, as
President of the Executive Council at that time, signed the
order for the execution. He and other Girondins were driven
from power on 2nd June 1793 (when Hanriot's brazen voice
decided the fate of the Girondins) and he was guillotined on
23rd December of that year, for the alleged crime of conspiring to
place Philippe Egalité on the throne. Mme. Roland, who helped
Lebrun to rise to power, limns his portrait in these sharp outlines: " He passed for a wise man, because he showed no kind
of *élan*; and for a clever man, because he was a fairly good
clerk; but he possessed neither activity, intellect, nor force of
character." The want of *élan* seems to be a term relative merely
to the characteristics of the Girondins, who, whatever they lacked,
had that Gallic quality in rich measure.

Chauvelin, the French ambassador in London, is another of
these revolutionary rockets. Only in fiction and the drama does
he stand forth at all clearly to the eye. History knows him
not, except that he had been a marquis, then took up with the
Girondins, finally shot up among the Jacobins and made much
noise by his intrigues and despatches. With all his showiness
and vanity he had enough shrewdness to suit his language at
the French embassy in Portman Square to the Jacobin jargon
of the times. After the September massacres the only hope for
an aristocratic envoy was to figure as an irreproachable patriot.
Chauvelin's dealings with the English malcontents therefore became more and more pronounced; for indeed they served both

as a life insurance and as a means of annoying Pitt and Grenville in return for their refusal to recognize him as the ambassador of the new Republic. Londoners in general sided with the
Ministry and snubbed the French envoys. Dumont describes
their annoyance, during a visit to Ranelagh, at being received
everywhere with the audible whisper, " Here comes the French
embassy "; whereupon faces were turned away and a wide space
was left around them.[1]

Such, then, were the men on whom largely rested the future
of Europe. Lebrun mistook fussiness for activity. At a time
when tact and dignity prescribed a diminution of the staff at
Portman Square, he sent two almost untried men, Noël and, a
little later, Benoît, to help Chauvelin to mark time. Talleyrand also gained permission to return to London as *adjoint*
to Chauvelin, which, it appears, was the only safe means of
escaping from Paris. Chauvelin speedily quarrelled with him.
But the doings of the French embassy concern us little for the
present, as Pitt and Grenville paid no • attention to the offers,
similar to those made in April, which Lebrun charged his envoys to make for an Anglo-French alliance. It is not surprising, after the September massacres, that Ministers should
hold sternly aloof from the French envoys; but we may note
that Miles considered their attitude most unwise. He further
remarked that the proud reserve of Grenville was almost offensive.[2] We made the acquaintance of Miles as British agent
at Paris in 1790 and noted his consequential airs. In 1792 they
were full blown.

The opinions of George III and Pitt on the events of that
bloody harvest-time in Paris are very little known. The King's
letters from Weymouth to Pitt in August—September are few
and brief. On 16th September, after the arrival of news of
the massacres, he writes to say that his decision respecting the
Prince of Wales's debts is irrevocable. After that there is a long
silence. Pitt's reserve is equally impenetrable. We know, however, from the letters of Burke that the conduct of Ministers
deeply disappointed him. Writing to Grenville on 19th September he says that the crisis exceeds in gravity any that is
recorded in history; and he adds these curious words: " I know
it is the opinion of His Majesty's Ministers that the new [French]

---

[1] Dumont, "Souvenirs"; Bulwer Lytton, "Hist. Characters" (Talleyrand).
[2] W. A. Miles, " Corresp.," i, 349-51; Sorel, iii, 18-20.

principles may be encouraged, and even triumph over every interior and exterior resistance, and may even overturn other States
as they have that of France, without any sort of danger of their
extending in their consequences to this Kingdom."[1] Can we
have a clearer testimony to the calm but rigid resolve with
which Pitt and his colleague clung to neutrality? On the following day (the day of the Battle of Valmy) Pitt frigidly
declined the request of the Austrian and Neapolitan ambas-
sadors, that the British Government would exclude from its
territories all those who should be guilty of an attack on the
French royal family. On 21st September Grenville issued a
guarded statement on this subject to the *corps diplomatique*; but
it was far from meeting the desires of the royalists.[2]

Reticence is a virtue over-developed in an aristocracy—"that
austere domination," as Burke terms it. The virtue is slow in
taking root among democracies. The early Radical clubs of
Great Britain regarded it as their cherished privilege to
state their opinions on foreign affairs with Athenian loquacity;
and the months of October and November 1792, when we
vainly seek to know the inner feelings of Pitt, are enlivened by
resolutions expressing joy at the downfall of tyrants, and fervent
beliefs in the advent of a fraternal millennium, the first fruits of
which were the election of Paine as deputy for Calais to the
National Convention.

In the dealings of nations, as of individuals, feelings often
count for more than interests. This was the case in the last four
months of the year 1792, when the subjects in dispute bulked
small in comparison with the passions and prejudices which
magnified and distorted them. The psychology of the time
therefore demands no less attention than its diplomacy. Its first
weeks were darkened by news of the September massacres.
Even now the details of that cowardly crime arouse horror : and
surely no part of Carlyle's epic sinks so low as that in which
he seeks to compare that loathsome butchery with the bloodshed of a battlefield.[3] No such special pleading was attempted
by leaders of thought of that period. On 10th September Romilly, a friend of human progress, wrote to Dumont:
" How could we ever be so deceived in the character of the
French nation as to think them capable of liberty? . . . One

---

[1] Burke, " Corresp.," iv, 7.   [2] Sorel, iii, 139.
[3] Carlyle, " Fr. Rev.," iii, bk. i, ch. vi.

might as well think of establishing a republic of tigers in some forest of Africa." To which the collaborator of Mirabeau replied: "Let us burn all our books; let us cease to think and dream of the best system of legislation, since men make so diabolical a use of every truth and every principle."[1] These feelings were general among Frenchmen. Buzot stated that the loss of morality, with all its attendant evils, dated from the September massacres.

It seems strange that the democratic cause made headway in England after this fell event. Probably its details were but dimly known to the poor, who were at this time the victims of a bad harvest and severe dearth. The months of September and October were marked by heavy and persistent rains. The Marquis of Buckingham on 23rd September wrote at Stowe to his brother, Lord Grenville, that he was living amidst a vortex of mud, clay, and water such as was never known before—the result of six weeks of unsettled weather, which must impair the harvest and increase the difficulty of maintaining order.[2] Certainly the stars in their courses fought against the *ancien régime*. The rains which made a receptive seed-bed for the writings of Paine also hampered the progress of Brunswick towards the Argonne, crowded his hospitals with invalids, and in part induced that inglorious retreat. As the storms lasted far into the autumn, disaffection increased apace.

The results serve to enliven the dull tones of our Home Office archives. There one reads of bread riots and meal riots so far back as May 1792, in which stalls are overturned and despoiled; also of more persistent agitation in the factory towns of the North. Liverpool leads off with a dock-strike that is with difficulty ended. Then the colliers of Wigan stop work and seek to persuade all their comrades to follow their example. Most threatening of all is the situation at Manchester and Sheffield. There, in addition to disorder among the townsfolk, disaffection gains ground among the troops sent to keep order. This again is traceable to the dearness of food, for which the scanty pay of the trooper by no means suffices. Here, then, is the opportunity for the apostle of discontent judiciously to offer a cheap edition of the "Rights of Man," on which fare the troop becomes half-mutinous and sends in a petition for higher pay. This the per-

[1] "Mems. of Romilly," i, 351, 352. [2] "Dropmore P.," ii, 318.

plexed authorities do not grant, but build barracks, a proceeding eyed askance by publicans and patriots as the beginning of military rule.[1]

The South of England, too, is beset by fears of a novel kind. After the overthrow of the French monarchy on 10th August fugitives from France come fast to the coasts of Kent and Sussex. The flights become thicker day by day up to the end of that fell month of September. Orthodox priests, always in disguise, form the bulk of the new arrivals. As many as 700 of them land at Eastbourne, and strain the hospitality of that little town. About as many reach Portsmouth and Gosport, to the perplexity of the authorities. When assured that they are staunch royalists and not apostles of Revolution, the commander allots shelter in the barracks at Forton, where for the present they exist on two pence a day each. Plymouth, which receives fewer of them, frowns on the newcomers as politically suspect and economically ruinous. The mayor assures Dundas that, if more priests arrive, or are sent there, they will be driven away by the townsfolk for fear of dearth of corn. In Jersey the food question eclipses all others; for 2,000 priests (so it is said) land there, until all ideas of hospitality are cast to the winds and the refugees are threatened with expulsion. Only in the vast obscurantism of London is there safety for these exiles. A subscription list is started on their behalf; the King offers the royal house at Winchester for the overplus at Portsmouth: and by degrees the scared throngs huddle down into the dire poverty and uneasy rest that are to be their lot for many a year.[2]

Strange adventures befell many of the French nobles in their escape. The Duc de Liancourt, commanding the troops at Rouen, was fain to flee to the coast, hire a deckless craft, and conceal himself under faggots. In that manner he put to sea and finally made the opposite coast at Hastings. There, still nervous, he made his way to the nearest inn, and, to proclaim his insularity, called for porter. The beverage was too much for him, and he retired to his room in a state of unconscious passivity. On his awaking, the strange surroundings seemed those of a French lock-up; but as he crept down to make his escape, the mugs caught his eye; and their brightness con-

[1] " H. O.," Geo. III (Domestic), 19, 20.
[2] *Ibid.* In all, 3,772 French refugees landed in September 1792 (" Ann. Reg." 39). The first subscription for them realized £1,468. Burke gave £20.

vinced him that he was in England. Such was his story, told to the family at Bury, where Fanny Burney was staying. Several of the wealthier French refugees settled at Richmond, and there found Horace Walpole as charmer and friend. But the most distinguished group was that at Juniper Hall, near Dorking, where finally Mme. de Staël and Talleyrand enlivened the dull days and long drives with unfailing stores of wit. We shall later on make the acquaintance of the French *émigrés* in a more active and bellicose mood.

Such, then, was the mental condition of our folk. Depressed by rain and dear food, beset by stories of plotters from Paris, or harrowed by the tales of misery of the French *émigrés*, Britons came to look on France as a land peopled by demons, who sought to involve other lands in the ruin to which they had reduced their own. In this state of nervousness and excitement little was needed to bring about a furious reaction on behalf of Church and King.

The follies of English democrats helped on this reaction. Whispers went about of strange and threatening orders of arms at Birmingham. A correspondent at the midland capital informed Dundas at the end of September that a Dr. Maxwell, of York, had ordered 20,000 daggers, which were to be 12 inches in the blade and 5¼ inches in the handle. The informant convinced the manufacturer that he must apprise the Home Secretary of this order and send him a specimen of the weapon. Probably it was the same which Burke melodramatically cast down on the floor of the House of Commons during his speech of 28th December. The dimensions exactly tally with those named by the biographer of Lord Eldon, who retained that dagger, though Bland Burges also put in a claim to have possessed it. The scepticism which one feels about this prodigious order of daggers, which others give as 3,000, is somewhat lessened by finding another letter, of 2nd October 1792, addressed to Dundas by James Maxwell of York, who stated that he highly disapproved of the "French" opinions of his younger brother (specimens of whose letters he enclosed), and had just given him £500 so as to dissuade him from going to Manchester to stir up discontent there.[1] This unbrotherly

[1] "H. O.," Geo. III (Domestic), 21; Twiss, "Life of Lord Eldon," i, 218; "Bland Burges P.," 203. Our agent, Munro, on 17th December 1792 reported from Paris: "Dr. Maxwell has at last obtained a company in the French

conduct condemns the elder Maxwell, but his information to some extent corroborated that which came from Birmingham. The whole affair may have been merely a device to frighten Ministers; but report says that Pitt took it seriously and ascribed to him the singular statement that Ministers soon might not have a hand to act with or a tongue to speak with.[1]

Certainly there was a good deal of discontent in the manufacturing towns, but it is not easy to say whether it resulted more from dear food or from political reasons. At Stockport a new club styled " The Friends of universal Peace and the Rights of Man," issued and circulated a manifesto asserting their right to inquire into political affairs:

It is our labour that supports monarchy, aristocracy, and the priesthood. . . . We are not the "swinish multitude" that Mr. Burke speaks of. A majority of the House of Commons is returned by less than 6,000 voters; whereas, if the representation were equal (and we sincerely hope that it shortly will be), nearly that number will elect every single member. Not one-twentieth part of the commoners of Great Britain are electors. . . . We have a National Debt of more than £270,000,000, and pay £17,000,000 a year in taxes. More than one fourth of our incomes goes in taxes.[2]

The Radical clubs also showed a desire to pry into foreign affairs; witness the following letter from Thomas Hardy to Dr. Adams, Secretary of the London Society for Constitutional Information:

No. 9 Piccadilly (London), *Sept.* 21 1792.[3]

The London Corresponding Society having taken the resolution of transmitting to the French National Convention an address . . . to assure that suffering nation that we sympathize with them in their misfortunes; that we view their exertions with admiration; that we wish to give them all such contenance [*sic*] and support as individuals unsupported and oppressed themselves can afford; and that, should those in power here dare (in violation of the nation's pledged faith of neutrality and in opposition to the well-known sentiments of the people at large) to join the German band of despots united against Liberty, we disclaim all concurrence therein, and will to a man exert every justifiable means

---

service, and I understand is soon to leave this to join the army" (Gower's "Despatches," 260). Mr. Elgar has not been able to trace him afterwards.

[1] Massey, iv, 45. This was said to be spoken to Bland Burges; but the papers of the latter (p. 204) contain no reference to it.

[2] "H. O.," Geo. III (Domestic), 21.   [3] *Ibid.*

for counteracting their machinations against the freedom and happiness
of mankind.

I am ordered by the Committee to acquaint the Society for Constitutional Information therewith, in order to be favoured with their opinions
thereon, and in hopes that, if they approve the idea and recommend its
adoption to the different societies, the publication of such a respectable
number of *real* names will greatly check the hostile measures which
might otherwise be put in execution.

On 5th October the Society for Constitutional Information
agreed to the plan, and ordered the drafting of a joint address to
the French Convention. By this time the news of the successful stand of the French troops against the Allies at Valmy and
the subsequent retreat of the latter greatly encouraged the English democrats; and a more militant tone appears in their
addresses. Thus in that meeting of 5th October a letter was
read from Joel Barlow containing these sentences: " A great
Revolution in the management of the affairs of nations is doubtless soon to be expected through all Europe; and in the progress of mankind towards this attainment it is greatly to be
desired that the convictions to be acquired from rational discussion should precede and preclude those which must result from
physical exertion."

Why " precede and preclude "? The two expressions are incompatible. It seems that some more moderate member must
have added the latter word as a sop to the authorities. In any
case the last words of the sentence were clearly intended as a
threat. On 26th October, John Frost being in the chair, the
same Society framed the following resolution:

That the Secretary do procure correct copies of the Manifesto published by the late General Burgoyne while in America, of the first
Manifesto lately published by the Duke of Brunswick in France, of the
last Royal Proclamation against writings and meetings in England, and
of the Emperor's recent proclamation at Brussels on the same subject;
in order that these four pieces may be printed fairly together on one
sheet of paper, and be transmitted by this Society to all the associated
Societies in Great Britain.[1]

It was then resolved to publish this resolution in the " Argus,"
" Morning   Chronicle," [2] " Star," " Morning   Post," " English

[1] " H. O.," Geo. III (Domestic), 21.

[2] Miles (" Corresp.," 333) states that the editors of the " Argus" and

Chronicle," "World," and "Courier." These papers supported
the democratic cause. In order to counteract their influence Pitt
and his colleagues about this time helped to start two newspapers, "The Sun" and "The True Briton," the advent of which
was much rèsented by Mr. Walter of "The Times," after his
support of the Government.[1] Apparently these papers were of a
more popular type, and heralded the advent of a cheap and
sensational royalism. Sheridan wittily advised that the motto of
"The Sun" should be, not merely the beginning, but the whole
of the passage:

> Solem quis dicere falsum
> Audeat? Ille etiam caecos instare tumultus
> Saepe monet, fraudemque, et operta tumescere bella.[2]

The combined address from several patriotic (*i.e.* reform)
societies, arranged for by Thomas Hardy, was not read at the
bar of the French Convention until 7th November. It set forth
that the five thousand signatories indignantly stepped forth to
rescue their country from the opprobrium thrown upon it by the
base conduct of the Government. In vain did Ministers seek to
overawe the timid and mislead the credulous: for Knowledge
and Reason were making great strides in England, so that
Britons now looked on Frenchmen only as "citizens of the
world, children of the common Father," not as enemies to be
assassinated "at the command of weak or ambitious Kings, or
of corrupt Ministers." Their real enemies were the destructive
aristocracy, "the bane of all the countries of the earth. You
have acted wisely in banishing it from France." They (the
signatories) could not take up arms to help France, because the
Government had pledged the national faith that it would remain
neutral. The Elector of Hanover had joined his troops to those
of traitors and robbers; "but the King of England will do well
to remember that England is not Hanover; should he forget
this, we will not forget it. . . . We ardently wish a Triple Alliance, not of crowned heads, but of the people of America,
France, and Great Britain will give liberty to Europe and peace

"Morning Chronicle" were regularly paid by the French Embassy and were
often there.
  [1] "Bland Burges P.," 227-9.
  [2] Virgil, "Georgics," i, 463-5. "Who would dare call the sun a liar? In
truth, he often warns of the approach of hidden seditions and of the swellings
of treachery and strifes yet unseen."

to the world." The address was signed by Margarot and Hardy. It and other addresses were reported verbatim by our *chargé d'affaires*, Munro, to the Foreign Office.[1]

The democratic ferment in England speedily aroused a decided opposition. Macaulay probably does not much exaggerate when he says that out of twenty well-to-do persons nineteen were ardently loyal and firmly anti-Jacobin. The month of November saw the formation of an "Ante [*sic*]-Levelling Society, for supporting the Civil Power in suppressing Tumults and maintaining the constitutional Government of this Country in King, Lords, and Commons." Its programme leaves much to be desired in the matter of style, but nothing in respect to loyalty.[2] The club was founded by Reeves and others. Hardy notes in his memoirs that it soon began to do much harm to the Corresponding Society.

Far aloof from this turmoil stands the solitary and inscrutable figure of Pitt. At this time he was leading, almost with ostentation, the life of a country gentleman, dividing his time between Holwood and Walmer Castle. Very few of his letters of this period survive. Writing from Walmer on 16th October to Grenville, he makes merely a verbal alteration in an important despatch on which the latter consulted him. Indeed he left the conduct of foreign affairs to Grenville far more fully than he had done to the Duke of Leeds. I have found no draft of a despatch written wholly by Pitt at the time, or indeed at the crisis that followed. There is, however, a significant phrase in his letter to Grenville, that, if the French retained Savoy, this would bring about a new order of things.[3] For the most part Pitt at this time gave himself up to rest and recreation at Walmer Castle. The charm of the sea and of the Downs seems to have laid hold on him; for General Smith, writing to Lord Auckland from Walmer, says that Pitt is soon in love with the King's present and gladly spends there all the time he can spare. Lord and Lady Chatham were with him and encouraged his passion for that retired spot. A little later he had a flying visit from one who was to become a devoted friend, the brilliant and versatile Earl of Mornington. Coming over from Ramsgate and lunching at Walmer, he found that Pitt had so far taken up with country sports as to follow the hounds in chase of "a basketted hare."

---

[1] "F. O.," France, 40.   [2] "H. O.," Geo. III (Domestic), 22.
[3] "Dropmore P.," ii, 322.

Apart from the bad harvest and the spectre of want which crept over the country, Pitt found little to alarm him at this time. In preparation for the opening of Parliament, he distributed to each of his friends six printed copies of his speech on the abatement of the Spanish armament taxes, for the purpose of circulation in the country.[1] Clearly he thought that the proposed economies in the public services would salve the prevailing discontent. At the close of October the French agent, Noël, reported to Lebrun that Pitt was not arming, and was still inclined to hold aloof from French affairs.[2] In fact, so late as 6th November, Grenville wrote to Auckland that on all grounds non-intervention in continental affairs is the best policy for Great Britain.[3]

But now a time drew near when anger was to expel calculation; when the impulses of the populace flung aside the counsels of statesmen, and the friends of universal peace helped to loose the dogs of war. This new phase in the life of Europe opened up when the dense columns of Dumouriez drove the thin lines of Austria from a strong position at Jemappes (6th November). Mons opened its gates on the following day; and the other towns of Belgium speedily followed suit, the French receiving a hearty welcome everywhere. The conquest of the Belgic Provinces puffed up the French with boundless pride mingled with contempt for the old Governments; and these feelings awakened a formidable response in these islands. The news of the conquest of the Pays Bas by the *sansculottes*, received with bewilderment and disgust in Piccadilly, aroused wild hopes among the weavers of Spitalfields. "The activity and insolence of the French emissaries and their allies in this country have certainly increased much with Dumouriez's success," so wrote Grenville to Auckland on 26th November.

In these days we smile at the notion of foreign agents influencing public opinion; but it seems certain that Chauvelin and his staff made persistent efforts to fan the embers of discontent into a flame.[4] Lord Sheffield declared that even the

---

[1] "Auckland Journals," ii, 449, 455; "Dropmore P.," ii, 324.
[2] Sorel, iii, 143.   [3] "Auckland Journals," ii, 465.
[4] On 24th November Noël wrote from London to Lebrun: "Tous les symptômes annoncent que les mouvements révolutionnaires ne peuvent être éloignés." Quoted by Sorel, iii, 214. See, too, Ernouf's "Maret," p. 84.

neighbourhood of Sheffield Park, near Lewes, was thoroughly worked by French emissaries; but it is not unlikely that land-lord nervousness transfigured some wretched refugees, on their way from the coast, into Jacobinical envoys. Certainly the town which gave him his title was in a dangerous state. An officer stationed there describes the joy of the men of Sheffield in cele-brating Dumouriez' victory. They roasted an ox whole, de-voured it, and then formed a procession, 10,000 strong, behind the French tricolour and a picture which represented Dundas stabbing Liberty and Burke treading down "the swinish multi-tude." He states that they were enrolled in Corresponding Societies, had bought firearms, and were seeking to corrupt the soldiery.[1]

Derby seems to have been equally fervid, if we may judge by the address which on 20th November went from its branch of the Society for Constitutional Information to the French National Convention, couched in these terms. " It was reserved for the Gallic Republic to break the accursed knot which has leagued Kings for ages past against the rest of the world. Reason and Philosophy are making great strides; and precedent and hereditary notions go fast to decline. By teaching mankind that they are all equal in rights, you have dedicated a glorious edifice to Liberty, which must hereafter prove the dungeon of tyrants and the asylum of the oppressed."[2]

Still more seditious was the action of the London Correspond-ing Society. On 28th November Joel Barlow and John Frost, deputed by that body, presented an address to the French Con-vention, congratulating it on the triumphs of liberty, and assured Frenchmen that innumerable societies and clubs were springing up in England. " After the example given by France," they said, " Revolutions will become easy. Reason is about to make rapid progress; and it would not be extraordinary if in a much less space of time than can be imagined, the French should send addresses of congratulation to a National Convention of Eng-land." They then informed the French deputies that 1,000 pairs of shoes had come from the Society as a gift to the soldiers of liberty, and the gift would be repeated weekly for the next six

---

[1] "Auckland Journals," ii, 481. Tomline, iii, 458, 459. Burke's unfortunate phrase in the " Reflections": " Learning will be cast into the mire and trodden down under the hoofs of a swinish multitude."

[2] B.M. Place MSS., vol. entitled " Libel, Sedition, Treason, Persecution."

weeks. They also presented an address which ended thus: "Other nations will soon follow your steps in this career of improvement, and, rising from their lethargy, will arm themselves for the purpose of claiming the Rights of Man with that all-powerful voice which man cannot resist." Next came a deputation from the English and Irish residents in Paris, which assured the French deputies that a majority of the British people desired to copy their example, and that the old Governments would soon survive merely as a memory. The three addresses aroused immense enthusiasm, and a decree was passed for their printing and circulation.[1]

These ecstatic praises of the Convention sounded oddly, as that body had just been discussing a petition from several Parisians who had lately been imprisoned without knowing why or by whom. And the Belfast address of congratulation on the progress of religious liberty was followed by the complaints of two members of the Convention that they had been half drowned at Chartres for a profession of atheism.[2] But undoubtedly these addresses by British Radicals caused exultation on both sides of the Channel. Frenchmen believed that our people were about to overthrow the Cabinet;[3] while the visitors returned home to trumpet forth the triumphs of Reason and the doom of Tyranny.

Certainly the action of the French Convention seemed to assume the speedy advent of a Jacobinical millennium. To the eye of faith the headlong flight of the Austrians from Belgium opened up boundless vistas of conquest, or rather, of fraternization with liberated serfs. Consequently the month from 16th November to 15th December witnessed the issue of four defiantly propagandist decrees. That of 16th November enjoined on French generals the pursuit of the Austrians on to any territory where they might find refuge—obviously a threat to the German and Dutch States near at hand. On the same day the French deputies decreed freedom of navigation on the estuary of the River Scheldt within the Dutch territory, which that people had strictly controlled since the Treaty of Münster (1648). In this connection it is well to remember that the right of the Dutch to

---

[1] "Moniteur," 29th November 1792.

[2] "Residence in France in 1792-5," by an English Lady, i, 190-2.

[3] Auckland says ("Journals," ii, 473) he has seen Paris bulletins and letters which counted absolutely on a revolt in England.

exclude foreigners from that estuary had been recognized by France in five treaties signed with Great Britain since the Peace of Utrecht. Further, by the Anglo-Dutch alliance of the year 1788, we had covenanted to uphold the rights of the Dutch in this and other respects. Thus, the French Republic was taking upon itself to rescind a well-established right of the Dutch Republic.

There is, however, another side to this question. The law of Nature, as distinct from the law of nations, forbade the barring of a navigable river to the commerce of aliens; and in this particular case the exclusive privileges retained by the Dutch had almost strangled the trade of Antwerp. Visitors describe the desolate aspect of the quays and streets in a city which was clearly designed to be one of the great marts of the world. Of this gospel of Nature, as set forth by Rousseau, the French were the interpreters; but they would have done well to appeal to Holland and Great Britain to abrogate this odious privilege, adding also the assurance, formerly given by Dumouriez, that Belgium would never become French.

Unfortunately the disinterested character of the crusade for liberty was now belied by two additional decrees which created the worst possible impression. On 19th November the French Convention declared its resolve to "grant fraternity and assistance to all people who wish to recover their liberty," and further ordered its generals to give effect to this decree. Eight days later it rescinded the former resolution, that France would make no conquests, by ordering the incorporation of Savoy in the French Republic. The priest Grégoire was equal to the task of proving that this involved no contradiction of the former principle, because the Savoyards wished to join France and Nature herself had proclaimed the desirability of union. By the same patriotic logic France could rightfully absorb all parts of the Continent where Jacobins abounded and natural frontiers were lacking.

These decrees brought about an entirely new situation. The annexation of Savoy furnished a practical commentary on the airy proposals announced on 16th and 19th November; but these alone were sufficient to cause Pitt and Grenville the deepest concern. On the 27th the latter wrote to Auckland at The Hague in terms which show his conviction that France meant to revolutionize the Dutch Republic, and also, if possible, Great Britain. Respecting the decrees of the 16th and 19th he wrote:

" The whole is a concerted plan to drive us to extremities, with a view of producing an impression in the interior of the country." [1] That is, he believed the Convention to be set on forcing England either to declare war, or to give way disgracefully; and in either case the result would be an increase of seditious feeling in these islands. This continued to be his view. For on 4th December, after reading the seditious addresses of the English societies to the Convention, he wrote again to Auckland that the French evidently relied on the malcontents both in England and Holland to paralyse the Governments; and, he added, " This is above all others a reason for firmness in the present moment, and for resisting, while the power of resistance is yet in our hands. For the success of their unfounded claims would not only give rise to new pretensions, but would give them additional influence." [2] Pitt's views were the same, though he stated them more firmly and not as an alarmist. On 9th December he wrote to the Earl of Westmorland, Lord Lieutenant of Ireland, that the gross disregard of treaties shown of late by France, her encouragement of the spirit of revolt in all lands, and her public reception of addresses from English societies, " full of treasonable sentiments," compelled the Government, though very reluctantly, to add to the armed forces. He added these words: " I am clear that the circumstances require vigour and decision both at home and abroad. And the spirit of the country seems within these last ten days to have taken so favourable a turn that I think we may look with great confidence to the event." [3] Thus Pitt and Grenville equally felt the need of firmness in resisting the French decrees, partly because of their aggressive and illegal nature, but also because surrender would inflate the spirits of British malcontents.

Current events served to strengthen this opinion. France had hitherto won all the points of the game by sheer audacity. Everywhere she had attacked, and everywhere she had found unexpected weakness. Custine's army had extorted a forced loan from Frankfurt. Dumouriez was threatening Aix-la-Chapelle on the east, and the Dutch on the north. The spirit which animated the French Foreign Office appears in the letter which Lebrun, its chief, wrote to Dumouriez on 22nd November: " To the glory of having freed the Belgian Catholics, I hope you will

[1] " Dropmore P.," ii, 344. Grenville to Auckland, 27th November.
[2] *Ibid.*, 351-2.   [3] Salomon, " Pitt," 599.

join that of delivering their Batavian brothers from the yoke of the Stadholder."[1] There can be no doubt that the general laid his plans for that purpose, though he also sent pacific overtures to Auckland at The Hague.[2]

To crown the indignation of royalists, there came the tidings that on 3rd December the French Convention decreed the trial of Louis XVI for high treason against the nation. The news aroused furious resentment; but it is noteworthy that Pitt and Grenville rarely, if ever, referred to this event; and that, before it was known, they had declared the impossibility of avoiding a rupture with the French Government if it persisted in adhering to the November decrees. On this question the final court of appeal is the despatches and letters of our Ministers. An examination of them discloses the reasons for their firmness. On 13th November, when the evacuation of Brussels by the Austrians was known, Ministers assured the Dutch Government that they would oppose a French invasion of Holland. They charged Auckland to declare that His Majesty had "no hesitation as to the propriety of his assisting the Dutch Republic as circumstances might require, against any attempt on the part of any other Power to invade its dominions or to disturb its Government." This declaration was to be published in order to discourage the plots of the Dutch "Patriots," and to warn the French Government and its general of the danger of a hostile advance. Auckland replied on 16th November: "It is impossible to convey to Your Lordships an adequate sense of the impression made by this voluntary declaration of His Majesty's sentiments and intentions respecting the Republic on the occasion of the present crisis. The generosity of this measure, which in a few hours was generally known, and which to-morrow will be circulated on the Continent in the newspapers of the Republic, is acknowledged by everyone." The Prince of Orange at once wrote to thank the King for this proof of his friendship, and added the suggestion that the anchoring of a British squadron in the Downs would, more than anything else, tend to "hold in check our enemies."[3]

Pitt and Grenville did not comply with this last request; and

---

[1] Rojas, "Miranda dans la Rév. Franç.," 3-4.

[2] "Dropmore P.," ii, 339, 341, 343; "Auckland Journals," ii, 471; Lecky, vi, 70-4.

[3] "F. O.," Holland, 20.

the British declaration itself came just two days too late to give pause to the National Convention, before it published the decree on the opening of the Scheldt. Possibly in the days of telegraphs the warning would have been flashed from The Hague to Paris in time. As it was, both Powers publicly committed themselves on the same day to opposite courses of action from which pride or conviction forbade them to recede. So narrow sometimes is the space that at first divides the paths leading towards peace and war.

The concern of Pitt and Grenville at the French conquest of Belgium appears in their instructions to Stratton, our *chargé d'affaires* at Vienna, to confer with the Austrian Chancellor, Cobenzl, on the threatening situation, setting forth the desire of George III to contribute to the tranquillity of all the States of Europe. In his reply of 22nd December Cobenzl declared that Austria and Prussia must have indemnities for their expenses in the war, the restoration of monarchy at Paris being another essential to a settlement.[1] These statements were most discouraging: the former pointed to a speedy partition of Poland; and the forcible restoration of the Bourbons was at this time wholly repugnant to the feelings of Pitt.

Meanwhile the prospect of war with France had become far more threatening. The decree of 16th November on the Scheldt, and that of 19th November on helping foreign malcontents, were a direct defiance to all neighbouring States, and especially to Great Britain and Holland. In the latter country the Patriots were, as in 1787, actively helped from Paris, and threatened the existence of the Orange *régime*, of which we were the guarantors. Moreover, the opening of the Scheldt was a serious blow to Dutch commerce. Sir James Harris, writing from The Hague in December 1784, when this very question brought Joseph II to the brink of war with Holland, quoted the declaration of the Grand Pensionary, that the Dutch ought to spend their last florin " rather than submit to so destructive and humiliating a measure as the opening of the Scheldt."[2] The effusive thanks of the Dutch when the Court of Versailles opposed the demand of Joseph II, shows that they looked on the control of that estuary as vital to their interests. This question was brought to an issue on 23rd November, when French

[1] " F. O.," Austria, 31, 32. See, too, Vivenot, ii, 446, 447.
[2] " Malmesbury Diaries," ii, 89, 90.

gunboats entered the Scheldt, and, despite the fire of the Dutch guardship, made their way up the river in order to assist in the reduction of the citadel of Antwerp. The senior captain of the gunboats announced that he did this by order of Dumouriez. On 8th December seven French ships sailed up to that city, the first since the Treaty of Münster.

The affair of the Scheldt was not the only cause of alarm. The Dutch authorities managed to get a copy of a secret letter (dated 20th November) from Dumouriez to Maulde, French envoy at The Hague, in which he assured him that he would do his best to keep him in that post (despite the ill will of the Paris Government); for he had much need of him for certain negotiations. He added these words: "I count on carrying liberty to the Batavians (Dutch) as I have done to the Belgians; also that the Revolution will take place in Holland so that things will return to the state they were in 1788." The Dutch Government gave a copy of this letter to Auckland, who forwarded it to Grenville on 23rd November. It reached Whitehall three days later. Curiously enough, Grenville did not hear of the French decree for the opening of the Scheldt until 26th November. But on that day he wrote to Auckland a despatch which shows his conviction that France meant to force us into war, and that the chief question for Great Britain and Holland now was—when should hostilities begin? Clearly, then, Grenville, and probably Pitt, regarded a rupture with France as unavoidable, unless she revoked the aggressive decrees. Nevertheless they decided to send a special envoy to Paris, and drew up rough drafts undated and addressed to some person unnamed, bidding him make careful inquiries into the state of affairs at that capital.

We cannot wonder that Pitt took a gloomy view of things; for on 24th November a "moderate" member of the French Convention proposed an addition to the decree of 19th November (offering help to malcontents in other States), so as to limit it to nations with which France was at war. This proposal— obviously designed to soothe the apprehensions of Pitt—displeased the "patriotic" majority, which disposed of it by carrying the "previous question." After this the decree of 19th November could no longer be treated as a meaningless effervescence of Gallic enthusiasm; and, when taken with the disloyal addresses presented by certain English clubs on 28th November, its reaffirmation produced the worst possible impression.

On the 29th, Nagel, the Dutch envoy in London, proffered a formal appeal for help, in addition to requests which he had made to Grenville a few days before. He further begged him to order the assembling of a squadron at the Downs, or at Gravesend, so as to assist the Dutch speedily, if need arose.[1] Meanwhile our allies (as usually happens with small States in presence of danger) sought to temporize; and herein, as also in the caution of Pitt and Grenville, lay the reason why war did not break out at once. No one can peruse the despatches of our Ministers without seeing that they considered war inevitable, unless the French retracted the obnoxious decrees. It is well to notice that at this time the question of the trial of Louis XVI had not come up for consideration. The dispute turned solely on the frontier rights of the Dutch, which Pitt and his colleagues believed to be violated by France, and which we were in honour bound to vindicate.

On 1st December, then, came the first of those precautionary measures which not seldom precipitate the conflict they are designed to avert. The Cabinet issued a royal proclamation, calling out part of the militia. Ministers took this step partly as a retort to the seditious addresses of English Radical clubs to the French Convention,[2] partly in order to repress tumults. There had been rioting in a few towns, and the reports from Scotland were alarming. On 22nd November Dundas, writing to Pitt from Melville Castle, N.B., stated that sedition had spread rapidly of late in Scotland, and he estimated that five regiments would be needed to hold down Dundee, Perth, and Montrose. He added that the clergy of the Established Church and their following were loyal, the others far otherwise.[3]

Still worse was the news from Ireland. Early in 1792 the Dublin Parliament repealed one or two of the most odious statutes against Roman Catholics; but later in the year contumeliously rejected their petition for the franchise. Conse-

---

[1] "Malmesbury Diaries," ii, 89, 90. This despatch, and the letter of the Prince of Orange referred to above, correct the statement of Mr. Browning ("Varennes," etc., 191) and Mr. Hammond ("Fox," 257), that the Dutch did not call upon us for help. This was asserted by Lord Lansdowne on 21st December, but his information was unofficial and is refuted by that given above.

[2] Marsh, "Politics of Great Britain and France," i, 260-2. The militia were not called out in Surrey, Herts, Berks, and Bucks ("Dropmore P.," ii, 348).

[3] Pretyman MSS.

quently the mass of Irishmen was ready to join the Society of United Irishmen, a formidable association founded in Ulster in 1791 by Wolfe Tone. This able young lawyer, fired with zeal for the French Revolution, conceived the statesmanlike notion of banding together both Presbyterians and Catholics in a national movement against the exclusive and dominant English caste. The conduct of the Dublin Parliament made his dream a reality. At once the ultra-Protestant traders of the North clasped hands with the Catholic gentry and peasants of the Centre and South. This unheard-of union was destined to lead Pitt on to a legislative experiment which will concern us later. Here we may notice that the clubs of Irish malcontents proceeded to act on a plan already mooted in the English societies, that of sending delegates to form a National Convention in Dublin. The aim was to constitute a body far more national than the corrupt Protestant clique that sat in Parliament, and, after overawing that body, to sunder the connection with England. The precedent set by the Ulster Volunteers in their meeting at Dungannon in 1782 warranted the hope of an even completer triumph than was then secured. The correspondence that passed between Pitt and the Lord-Lieutenant, Westmorland, reveals the concern which they felt at the news. Pitt advised the early meeting of the Dublin Parliament, the proposal of concessions sufficient to allay discontent, and a determined resistance to all attempts at intimidation. He also suggested the keeping a close watch on the importation of arms, and levying a Militia if it were practicable.[1] In reply Westmorland stated (1st December) that the manifesto of a meeting of United Irishmen in Dublin was most threatening, and that the " French mania " was spreading everywhere. He added: " Belfast is, as always, noisy and republican; but not above 200 or 300 Volunteers are there." [2] It seems probable that the embodying of the Militia in Great Britain was partly with the view of enabling a few regular regiments to proceed to Ireland.

While taking these precautionary measures, Pitt and Grenville adopted a tone far from unfriendly to the French envoy. Earlier in the autumn Grenville refused to see Chauvelin on the ground

[1] Pitt to Westmorland, 14th October and 18th November 1792, in Salomon, " Pitt " (App.); " Dropmore P.," ii, 318, 320-3, 328, 330, 333, 336; " Mems. of Lord Ed. Fitzgerald," 155-60.
[2] Pretyman MSS.

that the French Government which sent him no longer existed. But after some *pourparlers* he consented to receive him on 29th November. With his usual *hauteur* he prepared to teach the ex-Marquis his place from the outset. He placed for him a stiff small chair; but the envoy quickly repelled the slight and vindicated the honour of the Republic by occupying the largest arm-chair available. After this preliminary skirmish things went more smoothly; but only the briefest summary of their conversation can be given here. Chauvelin assured Grenville of the desire of France to respect the neutrality of the Dutch, though they had fired on two French vessels entering the Scheldt. The opening of that river, he said, was a right decreed by Nature, and confirmed to France by the conquest of Brabant—a point which he pressed Grenville to concede. He then charged England with unfriendly conduct in other respects. In reply Grenville said that he welcomed this informal explanation, but he declined to give any assurance on the Scheldt affair. If (said he) France and England were not on good terms, it was not the fault of the latter Power, which had consistently remained neutral but declined to allow the rights of its Allies to be violated.[1]

Equally firm, though more affable, was the behaviour of Pitt in an interview of 2nd December with a Frenchman who was destined to become Foreign Minister under Napoleon. Maret, the future Duc de Bassano, at this time made a very informal *début* on the stage of diplomacy. Despite many statements to the contrary it is certain that he had no official position in England. He came here merely in order to look after the affairs of the Duke of Orleans, especially to bring back his daughter, who had for some time resided in Suffolk with Mme. de Genlis and "Pamela." Maret's own words to Miles are decisive on this point: "I was not a secret agent; I had no authority to treat, nor had I any mission; and in declaring this to Mr. Pitt and to you I said nothing but the truth."[2] With characteristic mendacity Lebrun afterwards informed the Convention that Maret was a secret agent and that Pitt had requested an interview with him. The interview came about owing to the exertions of William Smith, M.P., a well-intentioned Whig, who hoped much from an

---

[1] "F. O.," France, 40. For Grenville's account of the interview, see "Pitt and Napoleon Miscellanies."

[2] Miles, "Correspondence," ii, 46; see, too, Ernouf, "Maret," 89, 95. This corrects the mis-statement of Lecky (vi, 94) on this topic.

informal conversation between Pitt and one of the head clerks of the French Foreign Office. Chauvelin viewed it with jealousy, it being his aim to represent Maret as an emissary to the British and Irish malcontents.[1] Pitt, when he granted the interview, cannot have known of this, or of the design of Lebrun ultimately to foist Maret into the place of Morgues at the French Embassy. Accordingly he welcomed Maret cordially. No tactical skirmish about chairs took place, and Maret afterwards declared that the great Minister behaved affably throughout, brightening his converse at times by a smile. As the personality of the two statesmen and the gravity of the crisis invest this interview with unique interest, Pitt's account of it, which is in the Pretyman MSS., must be given almost in full.

He [Maret] expressed his regret at the distant and suspicious terms on which England and France appeared to stand, his readiness to give me any *éclaircissement* he could, and his belief that the present French Government would be very glad if means could be found by private agents, with no official character, to set on foot a friendly explanation.

I told him that, if they were desirous of such an explanation, it seemed to me much to be wished under the critical circumstances; as we might by conversing freely learn whether it was possible to avoid those extremities which we should very much regret but which seemed from what we saw of the conduct and designs of France to be fast approaching; and I then mentioned to him distinctly that the resolution announced respecting the Scheldt was considered as proof of an intention to proceed to a rupture with Holland; that a rupture with Holland on this ground or any other injurious to their rights, must also lead to an immediate rupture with this country; and that altho' we should deeply regret the event and were really desirous of preserving, if possible, the neutrality to which we had hitherto adhered, we were fully determined, if the case arose, to give our utmost support to our ally.

His answer was that he hoped nothing of the sort would happen; that he believed there was no design of proceeding to hostilities against Holland; and that it was much the wish of the French Government to be on good terms with this country; that they wished to *ménager l'Angleterre*, and therefore to *ménager l'Hollande*; that these were the sentiments of M. le Brun when he left Paris about 3 weeks ago; that he believed them to be those of M. Dumouriez; and that, from the despatches of M. Chauvelin, which he had seen while here, he believed they continued to be those of the *Conseil Exécutif*; that he thought a confidential explanation on this subject very desirable; and would either

[1] Ernouf, "Maret," 90.

go to Paris or write to M. le Brun, to state what had passed in our conversation, and that he was persuaded they would be disposed to [send?] some other person here to enter privately into negotiations upon it. He afterwards dropped an idea that some difficulty might perhaps arise from the *Conseil Exécutif* feeling itself pressed by the weight of public opinion to propose to us to receive some person here in a formal character. To this I observed that the circumstances would by no means admit of any formal communication, and that they would certainly see the necessity of avoiding the difficulties which must arise from such a proposal, if they were sincere in wishing an explanation with a view to remove obstacles.

Towards the end of the conversation, on his repeating his belief that it would be the wish of the French Government to have such an explanation and to remove, if possible, the grounds of misunderstanding, I remarked to him that, if this was really desired, there was another point which must be attended to—that he must have seen the impression made here by the decree in France avowing a design of endeavouring to extend their principles of government by raising disturbances in other countries; that, while this was professed or attempted, and till we had full security on this point, no explanation could answer its purpose, and that such a conduct must be considered as an act of hostility to neutral nations. He answered that he knew the impression which this circumstance produced, and had seen the decree I mentioned with consternation; that he believed it passed only in a moment of fermentation and went beyond what was intended; that it could be meant only against nations at war, and was considered as one way of carrying on war against them; that he believed it was not conformable to the sentiments of the *Conseil Exécutif*, and that they might possibly find means to revise it. To this I said that, whatever were the sentiments of the *Conseil Exécutif*, the decree, as it stood, might justly be considered by any neutral nation as an act of hostility. He concluded by saying that he would immediately send to M. le Brun an account of what had passed, which he hoped might lead to happy consequences.

Maret prefaced his report of this interview by assuring Lebrun that Pitt was decidedly in favour of peace, and in fact dreaded war more than the Whig aristocrats; but, he added, Lord Hawkesbury and the majority of Ministers were for war— a somewhat doubtful statement. Maret's description of the interview is graphic but far from complete. He reported Pitt's gracious effort to minimize the difficulties of form arising from the lapse of official relations between France and England. But (he wrote) the Minister's brow darkened at the mention of the names of Noël and Chauvelin; and he finally suggested that Maret should be the accredited French agent at London.[1]

Pitt's account does not name these personal details, and it lays more stress on the difficulties caused by the French decrees opening the Scheldt and offering help to malcontents. We must further remember that Maret's words of warning to his compatriots on the latter subject were suppressed in the version published at Paris, which therefore gave the impression that Pitt was not deeply moved by recent events. This *suppressio veri* partly accounts for the persistence of the French deputies in their resolves, which prevented the friendly explanations undoubtedly desired by Pitt and Maret.

Bad news also came in from The Hague, to the effect that the French were demanding a passage through the Dutch fortress of Maestricht. These tidings caused the worst impression. Grenville wrote in reply to Auckland on 4th December. " The conduct of the French in all their late proceedings appears to His Majesty's servants to indicate a fixed and settled design of hostility against this country and the [Dutch] Republic." Equally threatening were " their almost undisguised attempts now making to excite insurrection here and in Holland." Consequently His Majesty had decided to arm in self defence, and he hoped that the Dutch would firmly repel all attempts derogatory to their neutrality. The King (he added), while taking these precautionary measures, would not omit such steps as might lead to friendly explanations with France through the private agents of that Government; but no ambassador would be received.[2] Pitt and Grenville set little store by the soothing explanations of Dumouriez and his friend, Maulde, who had made overtures to Auckland which met with a guarded but not unfavourable response. On their renewal, Auckland received them coldly, remarking that the whole situation was changed by the late violent decrees of the French Convention. At that time, too, the friendly Maulde was recalled and replaced by Tainville, " a professed Jacobin with brutal manners and evident indiscretion." [3] Thus faded away the last faint hopes in that quarter.

---

[1] " Ann. Reg." (1792), 190-3; Ernouf, " Maret," 94-8.

[2] " F. O.," Holland, 41; B.M. Add. MSS., 34446. Grenville to Auckland, 4th December.

[3] " F. O.," Holland, 42. Auckland to Grenville, 7th and 8th December 1792. See, too, Miles, " Correspondence," i, 382 ; Sorel, iii, 224.

Equally sombre was the outlook at Paris. The pacific reports sent by Maret and Maulde from London and The Hague were before the French Ministers at their meeting on 5th December. They had also the benefit of a lucid and suggestive *Mémoire* sent by Talleyrand from London a week earlier, setting forth the desirability of a friendly understanding between the two free peoples, who, advancing hand in hand, might give liberty to backward peoples (especially Spanish America), and draw thence boundless benefits. It was the plan which Dumouriez and he had drawn up in the spring of that year. Probably the Executive Council took no notice of it; for certain papers found in the iron chest at the Tuileries cast doubts on the purity of Talleyrand's patriotism. Further, as Pache, Minister at War, hated Dumouriez, personal bias told strongly against the moderate proposals coming from London and The Hague. Nevertheless the Executive Council now decided to defer for the present the invasion of Holland, meanwhile chasing the Austrians beyond the Rhine, and fortifying Antwerp. The last step was declared not to infringe the principles of the Republic, "which oppose the spirit of conquest."

Obviously there was nothing to prevent the same liberal adaptation of these principles to Belgium as Grégoire had proposed for the welfare of the Savoyards. A few deputations of the liberated people, asking for union with France, would enable some equally skilful dialectician to discover that Belgium was naturally a part of the Republic. For the present, however, the Belgians sent a deputation to demand unconditional independence ; and it taxed the ingenuity even of Barrère, then President of the Convention, to waive aside that request, with airy phrases as to the alliance of the two peoples emanating from the hands of Nature herself (4th December).[1]

Pitt cannot have heard of the French Cabinet's decision of 5th December, but he must have read of the ambiguous treatment of the Belgians at the bar of the Convention the day previously. It had long been a maxim at Whitehall that the Pays Bas must never go to France. To prevent such a disaster England had poured forth blood and treasure for more than a century. Pitt's resolve two years before, to maintain Austrian authority in those provinces, had deeply offended Prussia. Now he

[1] Sorel, iii, 204, 224.

and Grenville turned to the Court of Vienna, and on 7th December made friendly overtures to Stadion, Austrian ambassador at London.[1] Thus, the French menace ended the long period of estrangement between Great Britain and Austria, though, as will duly appear, mutual confidence took root very slowly.

On 9th December Lebrun sent off an important despatch to Chauvelin. With respect to the decree of 19th November, it stated that France would never demean herself by assisting rioters, but would respond to the "general will" of a people that desired to break its chains. Further, France could not reverse her decision concerning the Scheldt. She would not revolutionize Holland, but she expected Great Britain not to intervene in support of a constitution which the Dutch considered "vicious and destructive of their interests." Finally, the French Government could not recognize the guarantees of the Dutch constitution undertaken by England and Prussia in 1788.[2] On the same day Lebrun sent a message to Maret, who was still in London, adverting in ironical terms to the military preparations in England, at which the French would feel no alarm, and insinuating that the doctrines of liberty were making rapid progress there. As to negotiations, the only bases on which they could proceed were the recognition of the Republic, and the refusal of the French Cabinet to treat except by a fully accredited envoy.

On receipt of this letter on the 14th, Maret at once showed it to Miles, who urged him to request an immediate interview with the Prime Minister. This was accorded, and at 8 p.m. of that day, Maret met Pitt again. I have found no account of this interview. All we know is that it was short and depressing. Maret had to impart the unwelcome news that all the communications to the French Government must pass through the hands of Chauvelin—a personal triumph for that envoy. Pitt on his side declined to give any answer on the subject of Maret's communication, or on that of receiving Chauvelin.[3] We can imagine that under that stiff and cold exterior the Prime Minister concealed deep agitation; for the determination of the French rigidly to adhere to their decrees, to force Chauvelin upon the British Government, and to require the recognition of the French Republic, meant war.

[1] Vivenot, ii, 393.   [2] Sorel, iii, 225, 226.
[3] Miles, "Corresp.," i, 388, 389.

CHAPTER IV

THE RUPTURE WITH FRANCE

La guerre aux rois était la conséquence naturelle du procès fait au roi de France; la propagande conquérante devait être liée au régicide.—SOREL.

THE opening of Parliament on 13th December 1792 took place amidst circumstances that were depressing to friends of peace. Affairs were gyrating in a vicious circle. Diplomacy, as we have seen, had come to a deadlock; but more threatening even than the dispute between Pitt and Lebrun were the rising passions of the two peoples. The republican ferment at Paris had worked all the more strongly since 20th November, the date of the discovery of the iron chest containing proofs of the anti-national intrigues of the King and Queen. Hence the decree (3rd December) for the trial of Louis XVI at the bar of the Convention with its inevitable sequel, the heating of royalist passion in all neighbouring lands. It is one of the many mishaps of the revolutionary movement that its enthusiasm finally aroused an opposite enthusiasm, its fury begot fury, and thus set in a series of cyclones which scarcely spent their force even at Waterloo.

An essentially philosophic movement at the outset, the French Revolution was now guided by demagogues and adventurers, whose only hope of keeping erect lay in constant and convulsive efforts forwards. Worst symptom of all, its armies already bade fair to play the part of the Praetorians of the later Roman Empire. Nothing is more singular at this time than the fear of the troops. Amidst the distress prevalent at Paris, much apprehension was felt at the return of the armies of Custine and Dumouriez. In part, of course, this uneasiness arose from a suspicion that these men, especially the latter, might take up the *rôle* of Monk and save Louis. But a member of the French Convention assured Miles that the disbanding of those tumultuary forces would bring on a social crisis.

War, [he wrote on 9th December] is to a certain extent inevitable, not so much for the purpose of opening the Scheldt, for that is rather a pretext in order to animate the people and preserve their enthusiasm, but to get rid of 300,000 armed vagabonds, who can never be allowed to return without evident risk to the Convention and Executive Council. . . . It is her opinion [Madame Roland's] and mine that we cannot make peace with the Emperor without danger to the Republic, and that it would be hazardous to recall an army, flushed with victory and impatient to gather fresh laurels, into the heart of a country whose commerce and manufactures have lost their activity, and which would leave the disbanded multitude without resources or employment.[1]

These words are noteworthy; for they show that prudential or party motives led some at least of the Girondins, formerly friends of England, to desire an extension of the war.

In England, too, the war spirit was rising. The traditional loyalty of the land had been strengthened by the tactful behaviour of George III since Pitt's accession to power. These feelings warmed to a steady glow at the time of the King's illness in 1788-9; and now the trial of Louis XVI, albeit on grounds which Britons could not understand, seemed an act of contemptible cruelty. To bring Louis from Versailles to Paris, to load him with indignities at the Tuileries, to stop his despairing bolt for freedom, to compass his downfall, to attack him in his palace and massacre his defenders, to depose him, and now to try him for his life for the crime of helping on his would-be deliverers, appeared to a nation of sportsmen a series of odious outrages on the laws of fair play. The action of certain Radical Clubs in sending addresses of congratulation to the National Convention also aroused deep disgust; and (as Bland Burges wrote to Auckland on 18th December) Loyal Associations sprang up on all sides.[2] A typical address was sent by the Dover Association to Pitt, as Lord Warden, on 19th December, asking for permission to take arms in defence of King and Constitution against invaders from without or levellers within.[3] The example was widely followed; and thus, as usually happens in this land, the puny preparations of Government were helped on by the eager exertions of the people.

The revulsion in public opinion early in December was so

[1] Miles, "Corresp.," i, 385-7.   [2] B.M. Add. MSS., 34446.
[3] Pitt MSS., 245. Published in "Napoleon and the Invasion of England," by H. E. Wheeler and A. M. Broadley, ii, App.

marked as to impress even Chauvelin. He warned Lebrun that
within a month the English had so changed as scarcely to be
recognizable; but he added: " Pitt seems to have killed public
opinion in England." A conversation which Sheridan had with
him on 7th December ought to have disproved this fable. The
Whig orator sternly reprobated the French decree of 19th
November, offering aid to malcontents, and stated that the Opposition desired peace with France, but not if she attacked
Holland. Nine-tenths of the people would resent any attempt
to interfere with England or her Allies.

This patriotic utterance of Sheridan expressed the feelings
of a large part of the Whig Opposition. Parliament on 13th
December showed marked approval of the King's Speech, which,
while affirming his peaceful intentions, asserted his resolve to
strengthen the forces. Lansdowne and Stanhope struck a few
jarring notes; but in the Commons the Opposition was almost
paralysed by a split between the New and Old Whigs. At a
meeting of the party, held on 11th December at Burlington
House, the majority decided to support the Government. Indeed Parliament would probably have presented a united front
but for the action of Lansdowne, Stanhope, and Fox. Much
depended on the conduct of the great orator at this crisis.
A warning uttered by him to French Republicans might have
had the most salutary effect. Unfortunately his conduct was
such as to impair the unity of English sentiment and thereby to
encourage the delusions of the men in power at Paris. In the
meeting on 11th December he asserted that there was no fear
of a revolt (in which he was doubtless correct) and that the
calling out of the Militia was a mere trick, which he would
strenuously oppose. He admitted that we must support the
Dutch if they were attacked, and disapproved of the French
decree respecting the Scheldt, but strongly deprecated war on
that account. On the 12th he threw caution to the winds, and
stated with an oath that there was no address that Pitt could
frame on which he would not propose an amendment and divide
the House.[1] This is party spirit run mad; but it was in that
spirit that Fox went to the House on the 13th.

There he made one of his finest flights of oratory. None of
his speeches excels it in beauty of diction and matchless energy

_____
[1] " Malmesbury Diaries," ii, 475.

of thought. Most forcible was the passage in which he derided
the ministerial maxim that the canon of English laws and
liberties was complete; that we might thenceforth stand still,
and call upon a wondering world to admire it as a model of
human perfection. Even more biting were his taunts at Ministers
for seeking to stamp out the discontent which their injustice and
violence had created.

You have gone upon the principles of slavery in all your proceedings;
you neglect in your conduct the foundation of all legitimate government, the rights of the people; and, setting up this bugbear, you spread
a panic for the very purpose of sanctifying this infringement, while
again the very infringement engenders the evil which you dread. One
extreme naturally leads to another. Those who dread republicanism fly
for shelter to the Crown. Those who desire Reform and are calumniated
are driven by despair to republicanism. And this is the evil that I
dread. These are the extremes into which these violent agitations hurry
the people, to the decrease of that middle order of men who shudder as
much at republicanism on the one hand as they do at despotism on the
other.[1]

He then taunted Ministers with abandoning Poland and not
opposing the coalition of Austria and Prussia, and asserted
that the Cabinet refused to negotiate with France because she
was a Republic, and her Ministers had not been anointed with
the holy oil of Rheims. The weakest part of the speech was
that which dealt with the existing crisis. For of what use was
it to point out where Ministers had gone astray months and
years before, if he did not now mark out for them a practicable
course? In truth, though the prince of debaters, Fox lacked
self-restraint, balance of judgement, and practical sagacity. The
sole important issue was the encouraging of the peace party at
Paris, with a view to the revocation of the aggressive decrees of
the Convention. In private, Fox had admitted that they were
wholly indefensible; and yet, in order to snatch an oratorical
triumph, he fired off a diatribe which could not but stiffen the
necks of the French Jacobins. At such a crisis the true statesman merges the partisan in the patriot and says not a word to
weaken his own Government and hearten its opponents. To
this height of self-denial Fox rarely rose; and the judgement
alike of his fellows and of posterity has pronounced this speech
a masterpiece of partisan invective and of political fatuity.

[1] "Parl. Hist.," xxx, 19-21.

For how was it possible to recognize the French Republic until it had withdrawn its threats to existing Governments? Pitt had reason to believe that a firm protest against the aggressive decrees of November was the only means of averting an overturn of international law. He took the proper means of protesting against them, and his protest was disregarded. In such a case, to recognize a revolutionary Government which had just proclaimed its sympathy with malcontents and its resolve to dictate terms to our Dutch allies, would have been a sign of weakness. There was but one chance of peace, namely, that Parliament should give so overwhelming a support to Pitt and Grenville as to convince the tyros at Paris that they had to do, not with a clique, but a nation. This unanimity the efforts of Fox impaired. Some of his friends voted with him from a sense of personal regard; but the greater number passed over to the Government or did not vote. Consequently the Foxites mustered 50 votes against 290.

Equally inopportune was his motion of 15th December, for sending a Minister to Paris to treat with that Government. His knowledge of all that went on at the French Embassy in Portman Square was so exact (witness his repetition publicly on the 13th of the very words of one of Lebrun's despatches to Chauvelin),[1] that he must have known of the informal communications between Pitt and Maret, and of the arrival on the 14th of despatches from Paris, which negatived the requests of the Prime Minister. Doubtless it was this last circumstance which curtailed and weakened Fox's second speech. Grey, Erskine, and Whitbread vigorously supported the motion; but there was a general feeling that the despatch of an ambassador to Paris would be a weak acquiescence in the French claims. The motion was therefore negatived. Pitt was not present at these first debates, not having yet been re-elected by the University of Cambridge after his recent acceptance of the Lord Wardenship of the Cinque Ports. The defence of the Government therefore devolved chiefly upon Dundas, Windham, and Burke—a significant conjunction of names. On 16th December Burke for the first time took his seat on the Treasury Bench.

A national party might now have been formed but for the inaction of the Duke of Portland. During the meetings at his

---

[1] Miles ("Corresp.," i, 391), who also asserts that Sheridan echoed words used by the French agent, Noël.

mansion, Burlington House, he evinced strong disapproval of
the views of Fox; and, as official leader of the Whigs, he had it
in his power to bring nearly the whole of the party over to the
Government side. From this course, which would have placed
country above party, the Duke shrank; and his followers were
left to sort themselves at will. There was a general expectation
that Portland would publicly declare against Fox; but friendship
or timidity held him tongue-tied. Malmesbury sought to waken
him from his "trance," but in vain.[1] He lay under "the wand
of the magician" (Pitt's phrase for the witchery that Fox exerted),
even when so staunch a Whig as Sir Gilbert Elliot saw that the
wizard's enchantments were working infinite mischief.[2]

Owing to the wrong-headedness of Fox and the timidity of
Portland, Pitt's triumph in the Commons was not decisive enough
to tear the veil away from the eyes of the French Jacobins.
Nothing short of unanimity at Westminster could have worked
that miracle. Surely not even that novice in diplomacy, Lebrun,
would have threatened to appeal from the British Government
to the British nation, had he not believed the Government to be
without support.

This delusion appears in the memorable decree of 15th December. The French Convention thereby asserts its resolve to
revolutionize all countries where its armies are or shall come.
It will recognize no institutions alien to the principles of Liberty,
Equality, and Fraternity. All feudal dues, customs, and privileges
are to be annulled, and the liberated people will meet in primary
assemblies to organize an Administration. Arrangements will
be made for defraying the expenses of the liberating army, and
for maintaining it while it remains.[3] Finally France declares
that she will treat as an enemy the people which refuses to
accept Liberty and Equality, and tolerates its prince and
privileged castes. The decree is at once followed by a proclamation drawn up for the benefit of the subject peoples whom it
may concern. Finally, the Convention decides that the course
of rivers must everywhere be free, and directs its generals to
enforce that principle with respect to the Scheldt.

In view of this stern reiteration of the right to overturn all

[1] "Malmesbury Diaries," ii, 478-81.
[2] "Life and Letters of Earl Minto," ii, 82.
[3] Chuquet, "Jemappes," 196-7, shows that the urgent needs of the army
in Belgium were the *raison d'être* of the decree.

Governments that conflict with revolutionary principles, it is impossible to consider the decree of 19th November, offering assistance to malcontent peoples, as a meaningless display of emotion. Subsequent events threw a sinister light on it. The annexation of Savoy on 27th November was not a convincing proof of altruism; and the refusal of the Executive Council, on 8th and 9th December, to reconsider its decision on the Scheldt, marked a firm resolve to carry out French policy in the Pays Bas, even if it led to war with England. Now there came, as a damning corollary, the decree of 15th December, which flung defiance at all Governments of the old type. Like Mohammed, Lebrun stood forth with the "Contrat Social" in one hand, the sword in the other, and bade the world take its choice.

For England there could be no doubt. Pitt and Grenville had decided that the only chance of peace lay in offering a firm front to every act of aggression. In this they had general support. Fox might choose to distort facts by declaring that Ministers were about to plunge the country into war on a matter of form [1] (the refusal to treat officially with the French Republic); but everyone knew that the first aggressive action was that of France, directed against the Anglo-Dutch alliance. The firmness of Ministers gained them support in unexpected quarters. On 20th December, when they asked for a vote for 25,000 seamen, including 5,000 marines, Sheridan heartily declared that he would have supported a vote for 40,000 seamen if that number had been deemed necessary. He also made a suggestion that the British Parliament or people should appeal to the generous instincts of Frenchmen to spare the life of Louis XVI. The proposal came somewhat oddly in a debate for increasing our forces against France; and it brought up Burke in one of his most acrid moods. Such an appeal, he said, was futile, for Louis was in the custody of assassins who were both accusers and judges: his death was inevitable. Sheridan and Fox heartily reprobated this recklessly vindictive language.

Pitt then pointed out that on 17th August George III had expressed an earnest desire for the safety of Louis and the Royal Family of France in terms which were then read out. The same was the desire of every Briton; and the sentiments now expressed in that House would be heard and noted at Paris. If any more

---

[1] "Dropmore F.," ii, 359-62; "Parl. Hist.," xxx, 126.

formal measure were to be adopted, he suggested the entering a protest in the Journals of the House; but any public representation, he said, must be couched in terms of indignation which must tend to defeat its own object. With this method of procedure Fox and Sheridan expressed their entire concurrence.[1] It is therefore a malicious falsehood to say that Pitt opposed their suggestion.[2] Burke certainly did so, and in the worst possible taste; but Pitt carried it out so far as was deemed desirable. If Sheridan and Fox wished for a public appeal, it was for them to set it on foot.

I must here notice the vague and misleading statements in Godoy's Memoirs (written a generation later) that Spain made strenuous efforts to save the life of Louis XVI and opened " an unlimited credit " at Paris with the view of bribing members of the Convention to secure his acquittal. Further, that he, Godoy, secretly approached Pitt in order to secure his financial aid, which that statesman obstinately refused.[3] The story does not hang well together; for if Spain had already opened an unlimited credit at Paris, why did she want pecuniary help from Pitt? Further, the opening of unlimited credit, presumably with a Parisian bank, did not consort well with the secret methods which were essential to the success of the plan.

In order to probe this matter to the bottom, I have examined the British Foreign Office archives relating to Spain for the months of December and January. They are detailed and apparently complete. F. J. Jackson, our *chargé d'affaires* at Madrid, wrote to Lord Grenville every three or four days, as the relations of the two States had been far from cordial owing to friction caused by the cession of Nootka Sound, Captain Vancouver having been employed to settle the boundaries and fix a neutral zone between the two Empires. Grenville also wrote three times to Jackson to express his apprehension that the timidity and poverty of Spain would cause her to yield to the French Republic in the matter of some demonstrations on the frontier. But there is no word implying that Spain requested help from England, either pecuniary or diplomatic, in order to

[1] " Parl. Hist.," xxx, 137-46.
[2] " Mems. tirés des Papiers d'un homme d'Etat," ii, 100. This false assertion was adopted by Malouet (" Méms.," ii, 201), whence it has been copied largely, without examination of the debate itself.
[3] Godoy, " Mems.," i, ch. vi.

save Louis. Early in January Charles IV made such an appeal
to the French Convention, but it was treated with contemptuous
indifference. At that time the Courts of London and Madrid
were beginning to draw closer together in order to withstand
the demands of France; but nothing passed between them
officially respecting the saving of Louis. Now, where the life of
a King was at stake, any communication must have been official,
and if it were made through the Spanish ambassador in London,
Grenville would certainly have referred to it in his despatches
to Madrid.[1] We may therefore dismiss Godoy's story as a cruel
and baseless slander, due to the spiteful desire of a discredited
politician to drag down a great name nearer to his own level.

It is also worth noting that Malouet, who was then in close
touch with Grenville on San Domingo affairs, does not mention
in his Memoirs any attempt to involve the Cabinet in a scheme
for bribing the Convention—an action which the French exiles
in England and Holland were perfectly able to carry out themselves had they been so minded. The only document bearing
on this question is a Memorial drawn up on 7th December by
Malouet, Lally-Tollendal, and Gillier, stating their horror at the
King's trial, and their belief that his life might be spared if
George III and the British Government issued a Declaration
stating their lively interest in Louis XVI and his family, their
resolve for ever to refuse an asylum to all regicides, and to cut
off all supplies of food from France if the crime were committed.[2]
The Memorial was probably presented to Lord Grenville; but
its inutility, or danger, in the proud and exacting mood then
prevalent at Paris, is obvious. The confidential reports sent by
" M. S." from Paris to Lord Grenville do not refer to any such
overture to the Cabinet.[3]

Lastly, there is the curious fact that the ex-abbé Noël, one of
Chauvelin's "advisers," came to Miles late on 18th December,
and affected much concern at the prospect of the execution
of Louis. He then suggested that Pitt should confer with a
M. Talon, residing in Sloane Street, who had immense resources
and stood well with all parties in France, in order to devise some
means for saving the life of that monarch. When Miles asked
Noël how Pitt was to assist in this laudable project, no answer
was forthcoming. We must commend Noël's prudence; for he

[1] " F. O.," Spain," 25, 26.   [2] " F. O.," France, 40.
[3] " F. O.," France, 40, 41.

had already stated that Talon was under impeachment in France. How a man accused of treason could help his King, save by secretly using some of his immense resources to bribe the deputies, is no more apparent to us than it was to Miles. In fact he detected a snare in this effort to associate Pitt with a wealthy French exile in what must evidently be merely an affair of bribery. He therefore declined to bring the matter before Pitt, whereupon Noël betrayed signs of satisfaction at finding that the Minister really was neutral on French internal affairs.[1] This little episode should open the eyes of detractors of Pitt to the extraordinary difficulty of his position. Of one thing we may be certain. The readiest way of assuring the doom of the hapless monarch was to take up some one of the silly or guileful schemes then mooted for pressing the British Government to take sides in the trial. Pitt's rigorous neutrality was the best means of helping the advocates of Louis in their uphill fight with the hostile Convention.

Reverting to events at Westminster, we note that Ministers, on 21st December, introduced into the Upper House an Aliens Bill for subjecting to supervision the many thousands of foreigners who had flocked to these shores. The debates on this measure showed some approach to unanimity, though Lansdowne and Lauderdale in the Lords, and Fox in the Commons opposed it as a breach of the hospitable traditions of this land. On the 28th Burke spoke in its support with his usual passion, flinging down a Birmingham dagger as a sign of the French

---

[1] Miles, "Corresp.," i, 398-400. Unfortunately, Lord Acton ("Lects. on the French Rev.," 253) accepted the stories against Pitt. He states that Danton secretly offered to save Louis for £40,000; that Lansdowne, Sheridan, and Fox urged Pitt to interpose; and that Pitt informed Maret that he did not do so because the execution of Louis would ruin the Whigs. I must reply that Lord Fitzmaurice assures me there is no sign that the first Lord Lansdowne urged Pitt to bribe the Convention, though in the debate of 21st December 1792 he suggested the sending an ambassador to Paris to improve the relations of the two lands, and assuage the hostility to Louis. Further, Danton could scarcely have made that offer; for he left Paris for Belgium on 1st December, and did not return till 14th January, after which he was engrossed in the last illness of his wife. Danton's name was dragged into the affair probably by mistake for Dannon (see Belloc, "Danton," 200). Lastly, as Maret left London on 19th December, and did not return until 30th January, he did not see Pitt at the crucial time of the trial. And would Pitt have made so damaging a remark to a Frenchman? Is it not obviously a Whig slander?

fraternity now introduced into these happy islands.[1] After a few alterations in committee, the Bill passed on the last day of the year.

Meanwhile, on 18th December, Lebrun had sent to the Convention a report on the negotiations, which was not adapted to soften the passions of the time, being merely a piece of parliamentary declamation; but, as declamation rather than reason held sway at Paris, some of its phrases must be quoted. After citing with approval passages from the recent speech of Fox, Lebrun referred to the eager interest taken by the British nation in the triumphs of the French arms. " But," he continued, " these glorious events have a quite contrary effect upon the English Minister. In a moment, the dread and jealousy of our victories, the entreaties of cowardly rebels [the French *émigrés*], the vile intrigues of hostile Courts, and the secret suspicions that the numerous addresses from all parts of England excited, determined him to more decisive military preparations and to an immediate assembling of Parliament." Lebrun then accused Pitt of seeking to stir up public opinion against France, and of exciting, " by the most corrupt means, distrusts, doubts, and disorders." A still more extraordinary charge followed, namely, that Pitt and Grenville, while refusing to acknowledge the French diplomatic agents, had " requested to see them confidentially, to hold communications with them, and to grant them secret conferences." [2] Lebrun then referred in contemptuous terms to the British naval preparations, and stated that he had firmly maintained the decree respecting the Scheldt. He then affirmed the reasonableness of the decree of 19th November; and scouted the notion that France harboured designs against Holland. In answer to this last he had said in effect: " That it was much to be wished that the British Ministry had never meddled more with the internal government of that Republic than we ourselves wish to meddle." Finally, if these disputes led to a rupture, " the war will be only the war of the British Minister against us; and we will not fail to make a solemn appeal to the English nation." . . . " In short, we will leave it to the English nation to judge between us, and the issue of this contest may lead to consequences which he [Pitt] did not expect."

[1] " Parl. Hist.," xxx, 189. See ch. iii of this work.
[2] See ch. iii for a refutation of this.

In the sordid annals of party strife this report of Lebrun holds a high place. In order to furbish up the dulled prestige of the Gironde he sought to excite national animosity, and to revive the former hatred of the name of Pitt. What could be more criminal than to sneer at the smallness of England's naval preparations? What more false than to charge Pitt and Grenville with secretly begging for interviews with agents whom outwardly they scorned? It is by acts like these that nations are set by the ears; and generally they are at one another's throats before the lie can be exposed. Lebrun's report was received with loud applause. No one questioned the accuracy of its details; and these blind followers of a blind guide unanimously voted that it should be printed and widely circulated. On 20th December Lebrun sent a copy of it to Chauvelin, along with instructions which lost none of their emphasis in the note drawn up at Portman Square. He forwarded another copy of the report to Noël, with this significant explanation: "This document will keep you in touch with the ideas of this country and will show you that I scarcely have this affair in my hands any longer." [1]

This admission is illuminating. The trial of Louis XVI had, as the men of the Mountain foresaw, placed the Girondin Ministry and its followers in a most embarrassing position. Many of them inclined to mercy or to compromises which found little favour with the populace. Accordingly, the procedure at the trial, as also the final verdict, turned largely on the desperate efforts of the Jacobins to discredit their rivals, who sought by all means to keep their foothold in the revolutionary torrent. One of the most obvious devices was to represent the Executive Council as the champion of ultra-democratic ideas as against envious and reactionary England. If this notion gained currency, Lebrun and his colleagues might hope still to ride on the crest of the wave.

Historical students will remember another occasion when a tottering Ministry sought to keep pace with public opinion at Paris. The Duc de Gramont on 12th July 1870 instructed the French ambassador, Benedetti, to insist on obtaining from King William of Prussia an immediate answer to a demand that was certain to arouse angry feelings; and he sent to Benedetti the

---

[1] Sorel, iii, 241. So, too, Gouverneur Morris, then in Paris, thought the French Ministers, despite their bluster, wished to avoid war "if the people will let them." (Quoted by Lecky, vi, 114.)

explanation that public opinion was *outflanking* the Ministry, and that "the effervescence of spirits is such that we do not know whether we shall succeed in mastering it." Thus, twice within eighty years France was hurried towards the brink of the precipice because her Foreign Minister could not control an effervescence of spirits which he himself had helped to excite.

Lebrun's missives of 20th December bore fruit seven days later in Chauvelin's despatch to Grenville. As this document has often been printed, only a brief summary need be given here. The French envoy insisted that the conduct of France towards England had throughout been correct and conciliatory; but the Executive Council had long observed with concern the unfriendliness of the British Ministers, and now pressed its envoy to demand definitely whether they held the position of a neutral or an enemy. The only possible cause of enmity could be a misinterpretation of the decree of 19th November, which obviously applied merely to peoples that demanded the fraternal aid of Frenchmen. As France wished to respect the independence of England and her allies, she would not attack the Dutch. The opening of the Scheldt, however, was a question decided irrevocably by reason and justice, besides being a matter of small moment; and the British Ministers could not venture to make it a cause of war. If they did, they would not be supported by the British people. Chauvelin then demanded an official reply, and expressed the hope that the British Cabinet would not engage in a war for which it alone would be responsible and to which the people would not accord its support.[1]

What Pitt and Grenville thought of Chauvelin's last effort on behalf of peace will best appear in Grenville's despatch of 28th December to Auckland at The Hague:

The tone and language of Chauvelin's note of the 27th appear calculated to accelerate a rupture, and the same conclusion seems to follow from the circumstance of M. Maret's having informed Mr. Pitt that it was not intended by the *Conseil Exécutif* to charge any private agent with any commission of the nature which he had himself suggested in his first conference. I have some reason to believe that it is now intended to bring forward immediately in Holland the same question of receiving formal and official communication from the *Conseil Exécutif*. I trust that the answer will be conformable to opinions entertained here;

[1] "Parl. Hist.," xxx, 250-3; "Ann. Reg." (1793), 114-16.

and, with the view of avoiding as far as possible, any difference, however slight, in the expression of our sentiments, I shall lose no time in sending to Your Excellency the copy of the answer to M. Chauvelin when it is settled.

I cannot conclude this dispatch without again urging Your Excellency to press in the strongest manner possible upon the Dutch Ministers the necessity of immediately bringing forward their whole force. It is evident that the present intentions of France are those of aggression. Whichever of the Allies is first attacked, there can be no doubt under the present circumstances, but that they must make common cause in order to render the calamity of war short, if it is unavoidable. And if the state of the preparations of the Republic is found inadequate to the emergency, the attack will certainly be first made there where least resistance is expected. Every circumstance therefore, of interest and dignity require [*sic*] that no exertion of which the Republic can be made capable, should be spared at such a moment as the present.[1]

Evidently Grenville looked on Chauvelin's note as an ultimatum; and it is noteworthy that Pitt on 28th December refused to see Chauvelin. Our Dutch Allies, however, were by no means ready. The separate Admiralties of the Dutch Provinces had not enough men to equip, still less to man, their ships; and almost their only defence lay in a British squadron which set sail for Flushing on or about 29th December.[2]

For the present, then, Pitt and Grenville contented themselves with sending a stiff rejoinder to Chauvelin's note. Grenville reminded him that he had no official character in this country since the fall of the French monarchy, and that the sinister meaning of the decree of 19th November, as shown in the public reception given at Paris to the promoters of sedition in this country, was in no wise cleared away by his recent declaration, which still claimed the right to encourage disloyalty. With regard to the Scheldt question, Grenville declared again that it was of the highest importance both in point of fact and of principle; of fact, because the action of France pre-supposed her sovereignty of the Low Countries; of principle, because, if passed over, it would give her the right to abrogate treaties at her will. The desire of England to preserve strict neutrality in French affairs was universally acknowledged, and he (Chauvelin) had not urged a single circumstance in disproof of it. But, England (continued Grenville) "will never see with indifference that

<hr>

[1] B.M. Add. MSS., 34446.   [2] *Ibid.*, and "Dropmore P.," ii, 361.

France shall make herself, either directly or indirectly, sovereign of the Low Countries, or general arbitress of the rights and liberties of Europe. If France is really desirous of maintaining friendship and peace with England, she must show herself disposed to renounce her views of aggression and aggrandisement, and to confine herself within her own territory, without insulting other Governments, without disturbing their tranquillity, without violating their rights."[1]

This stern rebuke to the flippant claim of the French Ministers to settle the affairs of neighbouring States in accord with their own principles has often been ascribed to Pitt himself. This is doubtful. I can find no proof that he intervened directly in the affairs of the Foreign Office after the accession of Grenville, as he had done in the days of the Duke of Leeds. Perhaps the austere personality of Grenville forbade any intervention; or it may be that the two cousins were in so complete an agreement on principles that Pitt left all details to the Foreign Minister. Certain it is that he himself remained almost passive at this time; and all the acts were the acts of Grenville. It was well known that the two men were in close touch. " I consider his lordship the same as Mr. Pitt," wrote Miles to Aust.[2]

More important is the question—What were the aims of the British Government for the settlement of Europe? Fortunately, we are able to answer this without a shadow of doubt. For on 29th December Grenville sent off a despatch to Whitworth at St. Petersburg referring to an effusive offer of alliance from Catharine II. Through Vorontzoff, her envoy at London, she expressed her admiration of the generous conduct of George III, and her earnest desire to help him in restoring order to Europe by means of a concert of the Powers, which might be formed at London. At the same time she found means to instruct her partisans in the British Parliament to relax their efforts against the Ministry.[3] Pitt and Grenville were not dazzled by these proposals. The latter generously declared to Auckland that he did not believe the Opposition to be influenced by unpatriotic motives; and he doubted the sincerity of Catharine's offer.[4] Nevertheless, in view of the imminence of a French attack on Holland, Grenville decided to encourage the Czarina to form a league of the

[1] " Parl. Hist.," xxx, 253-6; "Ann. Reg." (1793), 116-9.
[2] " Miles, "Corresp.," i, 351.   [3] " Dropmore P.," ii, 363.
[4] B.M. Add. MSS., 34446.

Powers; but the instructions which he sent on 29th December
to Whitworth set forth aims very different from hers. He suggested that the Powers not yet at war should invite the French
people to accept the following terms:

The withdrawing of their arms within the limits of the French territory:
the abandoning their conquests; the rescinding any acts injurious to
the sovereignty or rights of any other nations; and the giving, in some
public and unequivocal manner, a pledge of their intention no longer to
foment troubles and to excite disturbances against their own Governments. In return for these stipulations the different Powers of Europe
who should be parties to this measure might engage to abandon all
measures or views of hostility against France or interference in their
internal affairs, and to maintain a correspondence or intercourse of
amity with the existing powers in that country with whom such a treaty
may be concluded. [If, however, France refuses to give these pledges,
then the Powers will take] active measures to obtain the ends in view,
and it may be considered whether, in such a case, they might not
reasonably look to some indemnity for the expenses and hazards to
which they would necessarily be exposed.[1]

From this remarkable pronouncement it appears that Pitt
and Grenville harboured no hostility to the French Republic
as such, provided that it acted on the principles which it professed up to the end of October 1792. The ensuing acts of
aggression and propagandism they unflinchingly opposed, but
in the hope that the combined remonstrances of all the Powers
would induce the French leaders to withdraw their untenable claims. Above all, the British Cabinet did not refuse
eventually to recognize the new state of things at Paris, a point
of view very far removed from the flaming royalism of
Catharine II and Burke. Whether a concert of the Powers could
have been formed on these moderate terms is very doubtful.
What is certain is that Pitt and Grenville saw in it the chief
hope of peace, and that they did not desire to force royalty on
reluctant France. For them the war, if it came, was not a war
of opinion—Monarchy *versus* Republic. It was a struggle to
preserve the Balance of Power, which in all ages our statesmen
had seen to be incompatible with the sovereignty of France in
the Low Countries. That danger averted, they were content to
let France settle her own affairs, if she behaved with the like
tolerance towards her neighbours.

[1] B.M. Add. MSS., 34446. Grenville to Whitworth, 29th December.

Unhappily, these pacific and enlightened views were not accompanied by conciliatory manners. It was the bane of Pitt, and still more of Grenville, that their innate reserve often cooled their friends and heated their opponents.[1] In the case of so vain and touchy a man as Chauvelin a little affability would have gone a long way; and this was especially desirable, as he had enough support at Paris to thwart the attempt to replace him by some envoy less disliked at St. James's. Nevertheless, they persisted in their resolve not to recognize him officially; and the Executive Council made it a point of honour to force him on the British Court. Personal questions therefore told against a peaceful settlement. Even at the end of the year 1792 it was not wholly impossible, provided that the questions in dispute were treated with open-mindedness and a desire to understand the point of view of the opponent.

Undoubtedly it was for the French Government to take the first steps towards reconciliation by retracting or toning down the decrees of 16th and 19th November and 15th December, which had brought about the crisis. Further, the Convention ought to have seen through and thwarted the attempt of Lebrun to regain popularity by insulting Pitt in the report of 18th December. Had that body been less intent on the party manœuvres centring in the trial of Louis XVI, it would assuredly not have furthered the insidious designs of that Minister. It might have offered to recall Chauvelin, and to substitute Maret, a man known to be a *persona grata* to Pitt. Finally, in view of the large concourse of Frenchmen now in London, reckoned at 15,000, the Executive Council would have done well to say nothing about the passing of the Aliens Bill, obviously a precautionary measure called for by the emergency.[2]

The French Ministers took exactly the contrary course. On 30th December they decided that Chauvelin should demand the withdrawal of that measure, as contrary to the treaty of 1786; failing this, France would declare that compact at an end. They also began to prepare for an invasion of England, on a plan which came before them on 28th December; and on the last day of the year, Monge, Minister for the Navy, issued a circular letter to Friends of Liberty and Equality in the seaports. It contained passages to the following effect:

------

[1] Miles, " Corresp.," i, 441.   [2] *Ibid.*, i, 439.

The English Government is arming, and the King of Spain, encouraged by this, is preparing to attack us. These two tyrannical Powers, after persecuting the patriots on their own territories, think no doubt that they will be able to influence the judgment to be pronounced on the traitor, Louis. They hope to frighten us; but no! a people which has made itself free, a people which has driven out of the bosom of France, and as far as the distant borders of the Rhine, the terrible army of the Prussians and Austrians—the people of France will not suffer laws to be dictated to them by any tyrant. The King and his Parliament mean to make war upon us. Will the English republicans suffer it? Already these free men show their discontent and the repugnance which they have to bear arms against their brothers, the French. Well! We will fly to their succour. We will make a descent in the island. We will lodge there 50,000 caps of Liberty. We will plant there the sacred tree, and we will stretch out our arms to our republican brethren. The tyranny of their Government will soon be destroyed.

What did the famous mathematician think of this effusion in the heyday of the Empire, when he became Count of Pelusium with a Westphalian estate bringing in 200,000 francs a year? A collection of the frank confessions of the *ci-devant* Jacobins would form an entertaining volume.

Not the least piquant of them would be the criticisms of a Breton captain, Kersaint, on the bellicose speech which he launched at the Convention on 1st January 1793. Admitting that Pitt really wanted peace, while Fox only desired to abase his rival, he averred that the Prime Minister would try to arrest France in her rapid career of land conquest either by a naval war or by an armed mediation. War, said Kersaint, must result, were it only from the perplexities of Pitt and the hatred of George III for the French Republic. France, then, must threaten to free the Scottish and Irish nations which England had so long oppressed. The Republic could appeal with telling effect to the English sailors not to fight against the champions of the Rights of Man. Further, France need not fear the British Empire; for it is vulnerable in every sea, on all the continental markets, while France stands four-square, rooted in her fertile soil. Let them, then, attack the sources of British wealth which are easily assailable. " The credit of England rests upon fictitious wealth, the real riches of that people are scattered everywhere. . . . Asia, Portugal and Spain are the best markets for English products. . . . We must attack Lisbon and the Brazils, and carry an auxiliary army to Tippoo Sultan." As for Spain (continued Kersaint) she could be paralysed by the revolutionizing of Spanish America—the suggestion of Miranda to Dumouriez. In fact, Frenchmen need not fear war with all Governments. Open enmity was better than neutrality. This war would "regulate the destiny of nations and found the liberty of the world." Accordingly he proposed to offer to England either war or an alliance; to equip thirty sail of the line and twenty-four frigates; and to form a Committee of General Defence. The Convention assented to this last and referred the other questions to it.

Thus opened the terrible year, 1793. The circular letter of Monge and the speech of Kersaint furnished the weather-gauge for the future. In them we detect the mental exaltation, the boundless daring, the overwrought conviction of their neighbours' weakness, which were to carry Frenchmen up to bewildering heights of glory and overwhelm them in final disaster. We behold in awful perspective the conquest of Holland, Italy, and Central Europe, the Irish Rebellion, the Egyptian Expedition, the war on British commerce, culminating in the Continental System, with its ensuing campaigns in Spain and Russia, and the downfall of Napoleon. All this and more can be seen dimly, as in a crystal globe, in that fateful phrase of Kersaint—"The credit of England rests upon fictitious wealth."

Turning to the last details that preceded the declaration of war, we notice that on 7th January Chauvelin, acting on the order of Lebrun, sent in a sharp protest against the Aliens Bill as an infraction of Pitt's Treaty of Commerce of 1786. On one count Chauvelin certainly had a right to complain; for, strange to say, the Act was put in operation against Talleyrand, nominally his adviser, and the champion of the Anglo-French *entente*. The ex-Bishop of Autun penned an eloquent protest, which apparently had some effect, for he was not expelled until March 1794.[1] Far more incisive was Chauvelin's complaint. We can imagine his feelings when Grenville curtly declined to receive it.[2] At the same time Grenville refused to discuss or explain the stoppage of certain cargoes of grain destined for French ports.

---

[1] I published it in the "Eng. Hist. Rev." for April 1906; see, too, Fitzmaurice, "Shelburne," iii, 515. Bulwer Lytton, "Hist. Characters" (Talleyrand), wrongly states that he was at once expelled.

[2] "Ann. Reg.," 122-5; "Parl. Hist.," xxx, 259-61; Miles, "Corresp.," ii, 4.

His private correspondence with Auckland shows that this measure was due to the fear that the French would store the corn for the use of the army that was threatening Holland. That motive of course could not be disclosed to Chauvelin; and Grenville declined to explain it at all until the resolutions arrived at in Paris were clearly set forth.

On Sunday, 13th January, Chauvelin received from Lebrun a long despatch, drawn up in less provoking terms than the last. He sought an informal interview with Grenville, which was imdiately granted. Grenville's hitherto unpublished account of the interview may be quoted in full, as it enables us to see the *nuances* of the situation:

Jan. 13, 1793.[1]

M. Chauvelin as soon as he came into my room began by stating that he was desirous of explaining that all his steps subsequent to the date of my letter of Dec. 31 had been taken in consequence of positive instructions from the *Conseil Exécutif*, given before they had received that letter. That they had seen in that letter one thing which had been satisfactory to them, notwithstanding the other things of which they might complain—this was the assurance which enabled them to reject the idea entertained by some persons in France of its being the intention of the Government here to declare war at all events. Under this assurance they had authorized him to give to their answer a form which was not liable to the exceptions which had before been taken. He then gave me the despatch from M. Le Brun. When I had read it I told him only that the circumstances were too critical for me to say anything as to its contents except to refer him to the answer which I should be [*sic*] to give to it.

He then said that there was one other point which he was desirous of mentioning. That one of the difficulties of the present situation of the two Countries was the want of a proper channel of communication. That he himself, from having no access to the King's Ministers, was frequently unable to give accounts of their real views and intentions. That he was therefore to desire the permission to see me often *sous la même forme* that he had now come [*sic*].

I told him that this was a point on which I was unwilling to take upon myself personally to give him an answer; but that he should have one; and in order to avoid mistakes I repeated to him the phrase, that his request was to see me *sous la même forme*. He said "yes," and that this was conceived to be a means of arriving sooner at the object of his

---

[1] " F. O.," France, 41.

being allowed to present to the King the *lettres de créance* with which he was charged. As he did not express this quite distinctly, I asked him again whether I understood him right; that his present request was only to communicate under the form in which he now came. He again assented to this, but in doing it threw out that he had *almost* had direct orders from the *Conseil Exécutif* to apply for permission to present his letters. He however expressly assented to my statement that the other was at present his only request.

Nothing else material passed, except justifications of himself from the imputation of treating on public business with some persons in this country with whom he had connections of private friendship and intercourse, and complaints of the manner in which he was treated in the newspapers. To neither of these points I said anything.[1]

It is not surprising that Grenville asked for time to consult his colleagues (probably also the King) before returning an answer to Lebrun's missive; for, though unobjectionable in form, it re-affirmed the French claims and justified all the proceedings of that Government. Lebrun accused the Pitt Cabinet of raising difficulties of form and of discovering hostile intentions where none existed. While repudiating the notion of annexing Belgium, he firmly adhered to the Scheldt decree. France, he declared, would respond to all appeals which emanated from the general will of a nation, and he even asserted that she could treat only with a Government which "is deemed the organ of the general will of the nation governed." If her efforts for peace failed, she would fight England with regret but without fear.[2]

In effect, then, this despatch held out no hope of a reconciliation. There came with it, however, a long and rambling letter from Maret to Miles, which was intended partly to threaten, partly to cajole the Ministry. In its more dulcet passages the hope was set forth that the Scheldt affair could be settled, and even that Chauvelin might be replaced by the estimable Barthélemy. Miles, highly elated, hurried to the Foreign Office on that momentous Sunday, 13th January, and found that a Cabinet

---

[1] Whether Chauvelin was guilty of any worse offence than entertaining at his house the editors of Opposition newspapers (Miles, "Corresp.," i, 440) is not proven. Maret admitted to Miles that some scoundrels were sowing sedition in England; but he added the not very comforting assurance that, in that case, they would cease to be Frenchmen. Miles evidently believed those intrigues to be the work of French emissaries. (*Ibid.,* 450, 451).

[2] "Parl. Hist.," xxx, 262-6; "Ann. Reg.," 119-22.

meeting was proceeding. Pitt came out and cordially received Maret's note. He returned to the Cabinet meeting (at which, strange to say, Burke was present) but came out again " furious, freighted with the bile of the whole Cabinet," and forbade Miles to have any dealings with the French Executive Council.[1]

How are we to explain this change from affability to anger? The impressionable Miles believed that in that hour Pitt capitulated to Burke and became a man of war. The reader who takes the trouble to compare Lebrun's note with that of Maret will probably come to another conclusion, namely, that the latter seems very like a device to throw the British Ministry off its guard. The terms of the two notes are widely divergent; and, in such a case, Pitt naturally accepted that of Lebrun and scouted that of Maret, as of a busybody or an intriguer. Grenville objected to this double-dealing;[2] and probably the presence of Burke at the Cabinet meeting sharpened the demand for its cessation.

Another explanation of Pitt's fury is possible. Grenville and he may have received news of the warlike preparations going on in the French seaports and on the Dutch borders. I have found no proof of this; but it is certain that by this time they must have had before them the inflammatory appeal of Monge to French and English Jacobins as well as the boastful tirade of Kersaint to the Convention. Having these proofs of the warlike ardour of the French and of their reliance on British reformers, how could Pitt and Grenville look on the philanthropic professions of Maret as anything but a snare, and Miles as his dupe? Miles had ever been officious. Clearly the time had come to stop his fussy advances to an unofficial agent, which Lebrun might once more ascribe to Pitt's secret fear of France.

It would be interesting to discover how far Pitt and Grenville were at this time aware of the secret designs of the French Executive Council. On this topic I have found no definite evidence. It is very unlikely that on 13th January they knew of the aggressive plans which the Executive Council had formed three days before. But it is certain that such plans were set on foot on 10th January. On that day the Executive Council drew up secret orders for Generals Dumouriez and Miranda. The former was then at Paris concerting plans for the next

---

[1] Miles, " Corresp.," ii, 28-36, 42. See, too, Sorel, iii, 258, on Maret's letter.
[2] " Dropmore P.," ii, 366; but see Miles, " Corresp.," ii, 43, 44.

campaign, not for the purpose of saving Louis XVI, as he afterwards stated. Whether he fanned the warlike ardour of the
Executive Council will perhaps never be known. But undoubtedly on 10th January the Executive Council bade him
order his lieutenant, Miranda, to prepare for the invasion of
Dutch Flanders and Walcheren within twelve days. Furnaces
were to be supplied to the French gun-vessels in the Scheldt
so as to beat off the frigates, whether English or Dutch is not
stated.[1]

Why did not Miranda carry out this plan? Merely because
he had neither stores nor food [2]—a fact which justifies the British
Government in placing an embargo on the corn intended for
France. Undoubtedly if he had had supplies, Miranda would have
seized the lands at the mouth of the Scheldt, and cut off the
retreat of the Stadholder to his place of refuge, Walcheren. It
will further be observed that these orders were given at Paris
three days after the despatch of Lebrun's and Maret's notes to
London. The design apparently was to amuse England until a
deadly blow could be struck at the Dutch. Auckland, writing
on the 11th at The Hague, expressed to Grenville the hope that
war might be avoided, or, if that were impossible, that the
rupture should be postponed until the Austrians and Prussians
had re-crossed the Rhine. The preparations of the Dutch were
going on with the usual slowness.[3] Evidently the French Government counted on their traditional inertia and on the malcontents in Great Britain and Ireland. The private letters of
Maret, that *soi-disant* friend of peace, breathe full assurance of
victory.[4]

Grenville of course sent no answer to the last missive of
Maret; but to Lebrun he replied, on 18th January, that his
explanations were wholly unsatisfactory, as they maintained the
right of the Executive Council to annul treaties at will. Until
satisfaction were granted for the aggressions on His Majesty's
ally, he would continue to take all measures needful for their
common safety. The terms of this reply were doubtless due to
the last news received from Paris. On 12th January the arch-
intriguer, Brissot, had fired off at the Convention a warlike
harangue in which he depicted the British Ministry as helpless

---

[1] "Corresp. du Gén. Miranda avec le Gén. Dumouriez ... depuis janvier
1793," 3-8. See "Dropmore P.," ii, 371, on Dumouriez' plan.
[2] *Ibid.*, 8.   [3] "Dropmore P.," ii, 365.   [4] Miles, ii, 36.

in the midst of a discontented populace and without a friend in the world. France could therefore easily arouse Ireland and Scotland to revolt, besides carrying liberty to India.[1] On the following day the Convention ordered the equipment of 30 sail-of-the-line and 20 frigates, and the construction of 25 sail-of-the-line and 20 frigates.

On his side Chauvelin saw the rupture to be imminent. In forwarding Grenville's despatch to Lebrun on the 19th he described his situation in London as intolerable, and added that no alternative but war was left. His assistant, Reinhard, ended a letter of that day to Miles with the words "*M. Chauvelin leaves.*" That resolve must have been strengthened by Grenville's haughty note of the 20th, stating that no special means could be taken to protect his couriers and that he must rank "among the general mass of foreigners resident in England." On the same day Grenville informed Sir James Murray, who had gone on a special mission to the Prussian headquarters, that war was likely to break out, as France "insists on terms entirely inconsistent with the Government of this country and His Majesty's dignity and honour." His Majesty is strenuously making preparations and hopes to concert plans with Prussia and Austria.[2]

Such was the state of affairs on 21st January, when Louis XVI laid his head on the block in the Place de la Révolution. The news of this tragedy reached London late in the afternoon of the 23rd; and the horror which it aroused led to a demand at the Haymarket that the farce should be put off. On the advice of the Cabinet George III now intervened. At a Court held on the morrow at the Queen's House (on the site of Buckingham Palace) an order was issued that Chauvelin, as the envoy deputed by Louis XVI, should leave the country on or before 1st February. But on or before 25th January, that is, before the news of this mandate can have reached Paris, Lebrun had decided to recall the French mission from London. On 25th January he wrote to Monsieur Greenville [*sic*] stating that, as his plenipotentiary, Chauvelin, had orders to return to Paris, Maret would proceed to London to look after the papers at the French Embassy. This statement merits attention; for it shows that Chauvelin's departure was hastened only a day

---

[1] "Gower's Despatches," 278.   [2] B.M. Add. MSS., 34447.

or two by the King's command;[1] and further it refutes the oft-
repeated assertion that Maret came charged with offers of peace
to which Pitt and Grenville paid no heed.

It will be well to examine this latter question somewhat
closely. In order to understand the situation at Paris, we must
remember that Dumouriez was at that time hesitating between
an attack on Holland and a pacific mission to England. On
23rd January, while at Paris, he wrote two very significant
letters, one to Miranda, the other to Auckland. In the former
he states: " The Executive Council . . . has thought of sending me
as special ambassador to England to make that country decide
definitely for peace or war. Consequently *an order has been given
for our ambassador, Chauvelin, to return.* To-morrow they will
send a secret agent [Maret], very well known to Mr. Pitt and
Mr. Fox, to ask the two parties (that is to say the whole nation)
for a safe-conduct for me and an assurance that I shall be
welcome. As I have to ask for *yes* or *no*, like Cato at Carthage,
this mission will not last more than eight days." Pending the
reply to the first question (says Dumouriez) he will set out for
Dunkirk, Bruges, and Antwerp. His second letter, of the same
date, is to Auckland at The Hague, stating that he knows him to
be desirous of peace, as he himself is. Can they not have an
interview on the Dutch frontier, near Antwerp, where he will be
on 30th January?[2]

Now it is clear from Grenville's and Auckland's correspondence that Ministers paid some heed to the offer of Dumouriez.
Nothing came of it owing to the arrival of news of the French
declaration of war; but the proposal was at least considered.[3]
There is not a line to show that Pitt and Grenville took Maret's
so-called "mission" at all seriously. For, in the first place, he
had no powers, no authority to do anything more than collect
the papers of the embassy. He himself gave out to Miles
that he came on a "pacific mission," but he carefully refrained

[1] "F. O.," France, 41. The order to Chauvelin must have been given
earlier, probably on 22nd January, as will be seen by Dumouriez' letter to
Miranda soon to be quoted. George III's order of 24th January (endorsed
by Pitt) for Chauvelin's expulsion cannot have the importance which Mr.
J. L. le B. Hammond ("Fox," 262-3) assigns to it. See "Pitt and Napoleon
Miscellanies" for Lebrun's letter to Grenville.
[2] Published in "Dumouriez, etc.," 159, 160, by J. H. Rose and A. M.
Broadley, from B.M. Add. MSS., 34447.
[3] Lecky, vi, 119-22.

from telling even him what it was.[1] His biographer, Ernouf, has invested his journey to London with some importance by declaring that on 22nd January he (Maret) drew up and sent off a "despatch" to Chauvelin, stating that the French Executive Council desired peace, and that he was coming as *chargé d'affaires* to the French Embassy in London. This missive (whether signed by Lebrun is not stated) met Chauvelin on his way from London to Dover; but it produced no change whatever in his plans. He proceeded on his way to Paris, passing Maret in the night near Abbeville. To assign much importance to his "despatch" is to overrate both his errand and his position at Paris. Maret was only one of the head clerks at the French Foreign Office and had no right to sign official despatches. If he really was charged by Lebrun to tender the olive-branch, why was not that despatch sent to London in a form and manner which would procure credence and have some effect? Again, if Maret came to restore peace, why did he not at once produce his powers? The question was infinitely important and undeniably urgent. Instead of taking decisive action, as any well-wisher of mankind must have done at so awful a crisis, he declined to enter into particulars, and, on the plea that Chauvelin was ordered to Paris (which he himself knew before he left that city) waited for further instructions—which never came. Finally he confessed to Miles that he came to prepare the way for Dumouriez and to discover whether that general would be assured of personal safety if he came to England.

Parturiunt montes, nascetur ridiculus mus.

Such must have been the thought of Miles, when he heard this singular admission. For what trust could be placed in Dumouriez, whose conquest of Belgium—the source of the present difficulties—had by no means sated his desire for its natural sequel, the conquest of Holland? That Maret had credentials of some kind may be admitted; for he showed them to Miles and claimed to be *chargé d'affaires*; but, as Miles found his powers to be "extremely limited,"[2] we may doubt whether they extended beyond the collection and transport of the archives of Portman Square. If he had any authority to treat with our Government, it is curious that he refrained from

[1] Miles, "Corresp.," ii, 55.
[2] Miles, "Conduct of France towards Gt. Britain," 108; "Corresp.," ii, 62.

doing so merely on the ground of Chauvelin's departure. "Apprehensive that this event might derange what had been agreed upon, he despatched a messenger with a letter to Lebrun stating that *under the present circumstances, he should not think himself authorized to communicate with the British Ministers without fresh instructions.*"[1] Notwithstanding the urgency of the case, he received not a line, not even a newspaper, from Paris during his stay in London. In fact, the *soi-disant* "*chargé d'affaires*" of France knew so little of the real state of affairs that he assured Miles of the desire of his countrymen to give up Nice, Mainz, Worms, the Rhineland, the Scheldt, and the Low Countries[2]—at the very time (31st January) when Danton carried unanimously a decree annexing the Low Countries to the French Republic.

The explanation of the silence of Maret and the ambiguous conduct of Dumouriez may be found in the Memoirs of the latter. He states that a proposal came up in the French Executive Council at Paris on 22nd January to send him to London; but it was negatived by three votes to two. Nevertheless, he arranged with the minority (Lebrun and Garat) that he should go to Antwerp and have *pourparlers* with Auckland preparatory to a mission to England, while Maret returned to London to pave the way for him.[3] The scheme was a private venture, proposed by Dumouriez, and favoured only by the minority of the Council. In such a case neither Dumouriez nor Maret could be invested with official functions; and it was only a last despairing effort for peace that led Maret to pose as a *chargé d'affaires* and write to Paris for "fresh instructions." This praiseworthy device did not altogether impose even on Miles, who clearly was puzzled by the air of mystery that his friend assumed.

In view of the facts now set forth, can we blame Pitt and Grenville for declining to treat with Maret? He brought with him no proof that he had any other function than that of taking over the archives of the French embassy. Grenville stated to Auckland that Maret's presence caused much dabbling in the funds, and that his presence was most undesirable if Dumouriez really intended to treat for peace. Pitt afterwards assured the

[1] Miles, "Conduct of France towards Great Britain," 108.
[2] Miles, "Corresp.," ii, 62.
[3] Dumouriez, "Méms.," ii, 128-31 (edit. of 1794).

House of Commons that Maret had not made the smallest communication to Ministers.[1] Evidently they looked on him as an unofficial emissary, to which level Chauvelin had persistently endeavoured to degrade him.

Finally, on 4th February, Grenville ordered Maret to leave the country. By this time news had arrived from Paris that France had laid an embargo on British ships in her ports; and this portended more serious news. By that time the die was cast. On 31st January Danton carried the Convention with him in a fiery speech, crowned with that gigantic phrase—" Let us fling down to the Kings the head of a King as gage of battle"; then, in defiance of the well-known facts of the case, he urged the deputies to decree an act of political union with the Belgians, who were already one at heart with them. On the following day the Convention confirmed this aggressive action by unanimously decreeing war against Great Britain and Holland. By so doing the deputies of France merely endorsed the decision formed by the Executive Council on 10th January.

The outbreak of war between France and England is an event so fraught with momentous issues to Pitt, to the two Powers, and to the whole world, that I have striven to set forth as fully as possible every incident, every misunderstanding, every collision of interests or feelings, that brought it to pass. No episode in the development of the nations of Europe is so tragic as this. That two peoples should, within the space of nine months, abjure their friendly relations and furiously grapple in a life and death struggle over questions of secondary importance leads the dazed beholder at first to grope after the old Greek idea of ἄτη or Nemesis. In reality the case does not call for supernatural agency. The story is pitiably human, if the student will but master its complex details. It may be well to close our study with a few general observations, though they almost necessarily involve the risk of over-statement.

Firstly, the position of absolute neutrality which Pitt took up from the beginning of the troubles in France was extremely

---

[1] "Parl. Hist.," xxx, 350. Fox admitted (p. 371) that Maret did not think himself authorized to negotiate. See, too, Bland Burges in "Auckland Journals," ii, 493. I cannot agree with Mr. Oscar Browning ("Varennes, etc.," 198), and Mr. J. L. le B. Hammond ("Fox," 258) as to the importance of Maret's "mission." Lecky (vi, 126) also overrates it, in my judgement.

difficult to maintain amidst the rising passions of the year 1792. The Franco-Austrian war soon led to a situation in which the future conduct of the neutral aroused far more suspicion, and scarcely less hatred, than that of the enemy himself. When brains reeled with rage against tyrants; when cheeks flushed at the thought of the woes of Marie Antoinette, correct neutrality seemed inhuman. In an age that vibrated to the appeals of Madame Roland and Burke, cold passivity aroused doubt or contempt. Yet it is certain that Pitt and Grenville clung to that position, even when its difficulties increased ten-fold with the fall of the monarchy and the September massacres. Lebrun, on coming into office after the former of those events, was careful to inform his countrymen that the withdrawal of the British ambassador was not an unfriendly act, and that England was making no preparations for war. Later on he chose to represent Pitt's conduct as persistently unfriendly; but his earlier words prove the contrary.

Again, was it practicable (as Fox claimed) for Pitt to forbid Austria and Prussia to coalesce against France? Probably it was not possible, without bringing Russia and Sweden into the field on the royalist side. In the excited state of men's minds, an act so annoying as that of armed mediation would have widened the circle of war; and, as we have seen, it was the belief of Pitt and Grenville, in August—September 1792, that the continental war might probably end from the inability of the combatants to continue it. No one at that time foresaw the easy conquest of Savoy and the Low Countries by the French troops. In one of the few references to foreign affairs in Pitt's letters of the month following, we find him stating that if France conquers and keeps Savoy, a new situation will arise.[1] But he remained passive while the French drove the Sardinian troops from Savoy; and his whole conduct at this time moved Burke to indignation, if not despair. So late as 6th November Grenville expressed to Auckland his firm belief in the policy of strict neutrality.[2]

What was it, then, that blighted these hopes? The answer must be that the French victory of Jemappes (6th November) and the phenomenally easy conquest of the Austrian Netherlands speedily brought about a new and most threatening situation.

---

[1] "Dropmore P.," ii, 322.   [2] "Auckland Journals," ii, 465.

It has been usual to say, with Goethe, that Valmy was the
birth of a new age. Far more truly may we say so of Jemappes
and its immediate results. That decisive triumph and the welcome accorded by the liberated Belgians opened up vistas of
beneficent triumph that set the brain of France in a whirl.
Hence the decrees of 16th November—15th December, which
tear to pieces the old diplomacy, and apply to astonished
Europe the gospel of Rousseau. In place of musty treaties there
will be Social Contracts; instead of States there will be nations
that will speak straight to one another's heart. They do speak:
English Radical Clubs speak to the heart of France, the Convention; and Grégoire, President of that body, makes answer
that if the rulers of England threaten the delegates and their
comrades, Frenchmen will cross the Straits and fly to their help
—" Come, generous Britons," he cries, " let us all confederate for
the welfare of Humanity." [1] In the new age, then, political life
will be a series of *tableaux* from the gospel of Rousseau. To
the true believer there can be no compromise. Relics of old-
world customs, such as the closing of the Scheldt by the Dutch,
must vanish. Here, as elsewhere, Nature will infallibly guide
men aright.

It was the application of these principles to our ally, the
Dutch Republic, which Pitt refused to accept, especially as their
corollary made for the aggrandisement of France. In his eyes
international law imposed stringent obligations, which no one
State, or nation, had the right to revoke. Old world theories of
life, when rudely assailed at Paris, moved their champions to an
enthusiasm scarcely less keen than that of the Jacobins. Britons
who fraternized with the new hierophants were counted traitors
to their King. Moreover, by a most unfortunate coincidence, the
British Government publicly announced its resolve to support
the Dutch Republic on the very day when the French Convention passed the first of its subversive decrees. Thus, national
pride came sharply into conflict. Neither side could give way
without seeming to betray alike its principles and its honour.

Personal questions played a baneful part in embittering the
feud. Pitt and Grenville shrouded themselves in their insular and
innate austerity. They judged the English Radical clubs too
harshly; they ascribed to those who congratulated the Conven-

---

[1] " Moniteur," 29th November 1792.

tion on 28th November treasonable aims which can scarcely have arisen in England when the addresses were drawn up. Apart from frothy republican talk, which should have been treated with quiet contempt, those congratulations contained no sign of consciousness that France was about to challenge us to conflict. We may admit that Frost and Barlow showed great tactlessness in presenting those addresses when friction between the two nations had already begun; for the incident, besides stiffening the necks of Frenchmen, gave the Reform movement an appearance of disloyalty to England which worked infinite harm. Nevertheless, on reviewing these questions, we see that Pitt treated the foolish ebullitions of youth as though they implied malice.

Surely, too, he, and still more Grenville, were unwise in placing Chauvelin under a political and social ban, which naturally led him to consort with the bitterest enemies of Government in order to annoy Ministers here and please his employers at Paris. A touchy and sensitive nature like Chauvelin's is usually open to the soothing influences of flattery. Grenville, however, drove him to open enmity, which finally wreaked its revenge;[1] for it was Chauvelin's report on the readiness of Britons to revolt which finally decided the Convention to declare war on 1st February. We may also inquire why the Court of St. James's did not make clear the course of conduct which it proposed to take in the future respecting France.[2] As outlined in the despatch of 29th December to Whitworth, it formed the basis of a practicable compromise. If it could be stated confidentially to Russia, Austria, and Prussia, why not to France? Probably the objections of George III to the faintest sign of recognition of the French Republic[3] account for the fact that these enlightened intentions remained, down to the year 1800, secret except to those Powers. But statesmen err when they bury their good intentions in the secrecy of archives and allow public opinion to sympathize with the enemy. Here was Pitt's most serious blunder. At the outset of the struggle, and throughout its

[1] Maret stated that " M. Chauvelin had shamefully deceived the Executive Council, and that nothing but misrepresentations and falsehoods had marked his despatches since he lost all hope of remaining in this country" (Miles, "Corresp.," ii, 62).

[2] Wilberforce urged this ("Life," ii, 13).

[3] "Dropmore P.," ii, 339, 351, 378.

course, he scorned those tactful arts and melodramatic ways
which win over waverers and inspire the fainthearted. Here he
showed himself not a son of Chatham, but a Grenville. The
results of this frigidity were disastrous. All Frenchmen and
many Britons believed that he went out of his way to assail a
peaceful Republic in order to crush liberty abroad and at home.
History has exposed the falseness of the slander; but a statesman ought not to owe his vindication to research in archives.
He needs whole-hearted support in the present more than justification by students.

In this respect Pitt showed less of worldly wisdom than the
journalists and barristers who leaped to power at Paris. Their
chief source of strength lay in skilful appeals to popular passion.
In reality their case was untenable before any calm and judicial
tribunal. But the France of that age was anything but calm
and judicial. It lived on enthusiasm and sensation; and the
Girondins and Jacobins fed it almost to repletion. Unfortunately
Danton, the only man who combined strength with some insight
into statecraft, was away in Belgium while the crisis developed;
and the conduct of affairs rested mainly with Lebrun and his
envoy Chauvelin. It is only fair to remember that they were
thirty and twenty-seven years of age respectively, and had had
just four months and eight months of official experience. In
such a case pity must blend with censure. The frightful loss
of experienced men and the giddy preference for new-comers
were among the most fatal characteristics of the revolutionary
movement. Needing natures that were able, yet self-restrained,
bold, but cautiously bold, it now found as leaders calculating
fanatics like Robespierre, headstrong orators and wire-pullers
like the Girondin leaders, or lucky journalists like Lebrun. To
play to the gallery was his first instinct; and the tottering fortunes of the Gironde made it almost a necessity. Hence his
refusal and that of his colleagues to draw back a hair's breadth
from the unjustifiable position which they had taken up. Behind
them loomed the September massacres, fatal to two Foreign
Ministers of France; before them shone the splendours of a
liberating crusade. We can scarcely blame men so ardent, so
hard pressed.

But there are some rules of the game which even the most
irresponsible of Ministers must observe. Here both Chauvelin
and Lebrun went fatally astray. Chauvelin's *pique* at the inter-

view which Pitt had with Maret on 2nd December led him flag-
rantly to misrepresent that incident, and Lebrun, as we have
seen, reported it to the Convention in such a way as to impute
to Pitt a discreditable and cowardly intrigue. This is the
climax of malice. An envoy and a Minister who scatter such
insinuations are the most reckless of firebrands. By this conduct
both Lebrun and Chauvelin inflamed the passions of their
countrymen. In truth, it was passion, not policy, that made the
war. The charges which they brought against England were of
secondary importance—her demand for the revocation of the
decrees concerning the Scheldt and the encouragement offered
to malcontents, together with her stoppage of corn ships lading
for France, and her Aliens Bill. Such were the pretexts for the
recall of Chauvelin, which, as we have seen, was decided at Paris
before the Court of St. James's determined to dismiss him.

Another fact comes out clearly from a survey of the evidence
given above, namely, that the execution of Louis XVI was in no
sense the cause of the war. The question turned essentially on the
conduct of France towards our Dutch Allies. Before Louis was
put on his trial Pitt and Grenville had decided that the French
must retract their aggressive decree against Holland, backed up
as it was by a claim to support malcontents in any land. Failing
this, war would have ensued, even if Louis had not been condemned to death. The tragedy of 21st January made no difference to the issue; for, as we have seen, the French Government
by 10th January decided to push on its plans against the Dutch
Republic. It is also impossible to attach any importance to the
vague offers of Dumouriez and Maret, at which Lebrun connived
probably so as to be able to say, without committing himself
in the least, that he had done all he could for peace.

We may therefore conclude that the wealth and defenceless-
ness of the Dutch Netherlands lured on the enthusiasts and
intriguers of Paris to an enterprise the terrible results of which
were unsuspected by them. Nothing is more remarkable than
the full assurance of victory which breathes in the letters of
Dumouriez, the despatches of Lebrun, and the speeches of the
French deputies. Experienced statesmen were soon to stand
aghast at the triumph of the Republican arms; but it fell short
of the hopes of the French politicians. In this boundless self-
confidence, sublime were it not so disastrous, is to be found the
chief cause of war in 1793.

CHAPTER V

THE FLEMISH CAMPAIGN (1793)

The war is not only unavoidable, but, under the circumstances of the case, absolutely necessary to the existence of Great Britain and Europe.—PITT, Speech of 11th March, 1793.

I N this chapter and the following, dealing with phases of the Great War, the narrative may seem at times to diverge far from the life of Pitt. But, in truth, his career now depended upon the issue of this gigantic strife. Therefore an account merely of his domestic concerns, of the debates at Westminster, or even of British and Irish affairs, would be a one-sided and superficial sketch. For in reality his destiny, together with that of Great Britain and of Europe at large, turned upon the events that unfolded themselves in Flanders and the Rhineland, at Toulon and Quiberon, in Hayti, Corsica, and Egypt. As these in their turn were potently influenced by the policy pursued at Paris, Vienna, Berlin, and Madrid, we must take a survey, wide but minute, sometimes to all appearance diffuse, yet in reality vitally related to the main theme. In order to simplify the narrative, I have sought to disentangle the strands of war policy and to follow them severally, connecting them, however, in the chapter entitled " Pitt as War Minister," which will sum up the results of these studies on the period 1793-8.

If proof be needed that Pitt entered upon the French war with regret, it may be found in the fact that on 5th February he and Grenville empowered Auckland to discuss the pacific overtures of Dumouriez. Grenville, it is true, saw in this move merely a device to gain time;[1] and we may detect in the British reply the sanguine nature of the Prime Minister. But his hopes ended on 8th February, when news arrived of the declaration of war by the French Convention against Great Britain and Hol-

---

[1] " Dropmore P.," ii, 377.

land. Thereupon Pitt entered into the struggle without a shadow of doubt.[1] For him it was always a struggle to prevent the domination of the Netherlands by France; and we may note, as a sign of the continuity of that policy, that on it largely depended the rupture with Napoleon in 1803. Pitt summed up the object of the war in the word " security." In his view, as in that of his successor, Castlereagh, national security was wholly incompatible with the possession of Holland, or even the Belgic Provinces, by France.

In taking this practical view of the crisis Pitt differed sharply from George III and Burke. They looked on the struggle as one for the restoration of monarchy. The King on 9th February wrote to Grenville that he hoped the war would be the " means of restoring some degree of order to that unprincipled country," and Burke flung into an unquotable phrase his anger that the war should turn on the question of the Scheldt.[2] For the present the aggressive conduct of France welded together these two wings of the royalist party; but events were soon to reveal the fundamental difference of view. Indeed, it coloured all their opinions about the struggle. Wilberforce reports Pitt as saying that the war would be a short war, and certainly ended in one or two campaigns. " No, Sir," retorted Burke, " it will be a long war and a dangerous war, but it must be undertaken."[3] In his eyes the struggle was one between two irreconcilable principles— democracy and monarchy. Certainly the effort to force 25,000,000 Frenchmen back into the well-worn grooves was stupendous. Further, the great Irishman, with the idealism and chivalry which invest his nature with so much charm, urged the Allies to abjure all thought of indemnifying themselves at the expense of France, and to declare their sole aim to be the destruction of anarchy and the restoration of monarchy, a course of action which would range on their side a large number of Frenchmen and avert all risk of identifying that nation with the regicide Republic. The new letters of Burke suggest the advantages of

[1] " Parl. Hist.," xxx, 565.
[2] " Dropmore P.," ii, 378; Prior, " Burke," 368.
[3] " Life of Wilberforce," ii, 11. Note the statement of George Rose to Auckland (8th February, 1793): " Our revenue goes on gloriously. The year ending 5th January shows £300,000 more than the year preceding. . . . We may suffer in some respects; but we must crush the miscreants "(B.M. Add. MSS., 34448).

such a declaration and most justly censure the Allies for avowing their intention of taking land from France. The old man
saw clearly that by so doing they banded Frenchmen together
for a national effort. In the following pages the thoughtful reader
will notice the disastrous effects of this blunder. Here Burke
stood on strong ground; and Pitt was far from guiltless.

On the general question, however, whether the war should be
for the restoration of monarchy or the attainment of security,
Pitt's position is unassailable. For the mere suspicion that the
Allies intended to impose Louis XVII on France condemned
monarchy in the eyes of patriotic Frenchmen. Only amidst the
exhaustion following on the Napoleonic wars could an intensely
patriotic people accept a king at the sword's point. In the first
glow of democratic ardour absolute destruction seemed preferable to so craven a surrender. While, then, we join Burke in
censuring the procedure of the Allies, we must pronounce his
advice fatal to the cause which he wished to commend. Further,
his was a counsel of perfection to Austria, England, and the Dutch
Republic. Deeming themselves attacked by France, they were
determined to gain security from the reckless schemes of
aggrandizing philanthropy now in favour at Paris; and, viewing the matter impartially, we must admit that they were
right. The French having been the aggressors, the three States
justly demanded security at that weak point in the European
system, the Flemish border. Further, as Pitt limited his aims to
the expulsion of the French from the Low Countries, he might
reasonably hope for a speedy peace, the task which he set
before himself being far smaller than that of forcing a king back
on the French nation.[1] Ultimately the stiffneckedness of Napoleon brought all the Powers to the latter solution; but no one in
1793 could foresee the monstrous claim for " the natural frontiers "
—the Rhine, Alps, Pyrenees, and Ocean—which prolonged the
struggle to the year 1814.

Pitt's optimism will appear not unnatural, if we review the
general situation early in the year 1793. The political atmo-

---

[1] "F. O.," Austria, 32 (Stratton to Grenville, 22nd December, 1792).
Cobenzl, Austrian Chancellor, assured Stratton that Francis II would require
from France "l'établissement d'une constitution quelconque fondée sur les
bases les plus essentiels du gouvernement monarchique."
  In view of these considerations I cannot endorse Lecky's censure (vi, 134)
on Pitt's " blindness " as to the character of the war.

sphere was disturbed by two cyclones, one in the west, the other in the east, of Europe. That which centred in the French Revolution seemed to have reached its maximum intensity; and skilled observers augured from the execution of Louis XVI a relapse into savage but almost helpless anarchy. The recent successes of the French in the Rhineland and Brabant were rightly ascribed to the supineness of Prussia and Austria; and already the armies of Custine and Dumouriez were in sore straits. The plunder of the liberated peoples by the troops and by commissioners sent to carry out the decrees of fraternity had led to sharp reprisals all along the straggling front from Mainz to Bruges; and now Danton's decree of 31st January, annexing the Belgic provinces to France, exasperated that people.

Further, the men in power at Paris had as yet shown no organizing capacity. The administration of the War Department by "papa" Pache had been a masterpiece of imbecile knavery which infuriated Dumouriez and his half-starving troops. We have heard much of the blunders of British Ministers in this war; but even at their worst they never sank to the depths revealed in the correspondence of Dumouriez with Pache. In truth, both Powers began the war very badly; but France repaired her faults far more quickly, chiefly because the young democracy soon came to award the guillotine for incompetent conduct over which the nepotism of Whitehall spread a decent cloak. The discovery by the Jacobins of the law of the survival of the fittest served to array the military genius of France against Court favourites or the dull products of the system of seniority.

For the present, the misery of the French troops, the immense extent of their lines, and the singular ingratitude of the liberated peoples, promised a speedy reversal of the campaign of 1792. For the re-conquest of Belgium, the Allies now had ready on or near the Rhine 55,000 Austrians under the Duke of Coburg. On their right were 11,000 Prussians, under Frederick of Brunswick-Oels, and 13,000 Hanoverians, destined for Guelderland. These last were to be paid by the Maritime Powers. In reserve were 33,000 Prussians, under Hohenlohe-Kirchberg. For the invasion of Eastern France, Frederick William of Prussia marshalled, near Frankfurt, a force of 42,000 of his own troops, together with 14,000 other Germans. Further south was General Wurmser with 24,000 Austrians. And this was not all. The Holy Roman Empire promised a force of 120,000, whenever its Translucencies, Bishops, Abbesses, and Knights could muster them; and further east there loomed the hosts of Russia. If these forces had been used straightforwardly, France must have been overborne.[1]

But the half of them were not used at all. Before the campaign opened, the eastern cyclone drew to itself the energies which ostensibly were directed against France. Just one week before the execution of Louis XVI, five Prussian columns crossed the borders of Poland. This act aroused a furious outcry, especially as Frederick William preluded it by a manifesto hypocritically dwelling upon the danger of allowing Jacobinism to take root in Poland. Fears of Prussian and Muscovite rapacity had induced Pitt and Grenville to seek disclaimers of partition at Berlin and St. Petersburg. Assurances enough were forthcoming. On 29th January 1793 Markoff sought to convince Whitworth that no partition was intended.[2] But in view of the entire passivity of Pitt on the Polish Question since his surrender to Catharine in 1791 the two Powers laid their plans for the act of robbery which took place a few months later.[3]

In this they had the rather doubtful acquiescence of Austria, provided that they furthered the Belgic-Bavarian exchange so long favoured at Vienna and resisted at Berlin. As we have seen, Pitt strongly opposed the exchange; but, early in February 1793, Grenville and he heard that the Emperor Francis II hoped to facilitate the transference of the Elector of Bavaria from Munich to Brussels by adding Lille and Valenciennes to his new dominion.[4] These tidings led them to adopt a decision which was largely to influence the course of the war. They resolved to commit Austria deeply to war with France by favouring the acquisition of Lille and Valenciennes by the Hapsburgs provided that they retained Belgium. This, however, was far from the wishes of that Court, which longed for parts of Alsace and Lorraine, and viewed Belgium merely as a sop to be flung to the Elector of Bavaria.[5]

---

[1] Sir James Murray, our envoy at Frankfurt, was assured on 1st February that 138,419 Austrians were ready for the campaign.

[2] B.M. Add. MSS., 34448.

[3] See Martens, v, 530-5, for the Russo-Prussian treaty of 13th July 1793.

[4] Murray to Grenville, 19th January 1793; see "Pitt and Napoleon Miscellanies," which also contain the new letters of Burke referred to above.

[5] Vivenot, ii, 498-506.

Was there ever a more singular game of cross-purposes? Austria pursued the war with France chiefly with the object of gaining Bavaria and parts of Eastern France, Belgium (with Lille and Valenciennes) being allotted to the Elector uprooted at Munich. Prussia and Russia promised to abet this scheme as a set-off to their prospective plunder of Poland; but, obviously, after securing their booty in the summer of 1793, they had no interest in aggrandizing the House of Hapsburg. Further, England entered on the Flemish campaign with motives widely different from those of Austria. Pitt and Grenville sought to plant her more firmly at Brussels by girdling her with the fortresses of French Flanders; but she sought to recover Belgium only to fling it to the Elector. Finally neither Russia nor the German Powers cared an iota about the security of Holland. Their eyes were fixed on Warsaw or Munich. In truth, despite all their protestations as to the need of re-establishing the French monarchy, they were mainly bent on continuing the territorial scrambles of former years. The two aims were utterly incompatible.

In comparison with the motives prompting the actions of States, treaties are of secondary importance. Nevertheless (to finish with these wearisome details) we may note that on 25th March Grenville and Vorontzoff signed at Downing Street a treaty of alliance whereby Russia promised, firstly, to use her forces, along with those of England, against France; secondly, to prevent neutrals from helping France indirectly (a clause which involved the lapse of the principles of the Armed Neutrality), and thirdly, to grant to England a favourable commercial treaty.[1] Agreement with Prussia and Austria was more difficult, but at last, on 14th July and 30th August, compacts were signed with them for military aid in return for subsidies; and in the spring and summer of 1793 Grenville arranged similar conventions with Sardinia, Hesse-Cassel, Spain, and Naples. In this haphazard manner did these States agree to war against France. Their aims being as diverse as their methods were disjointed, the term "First Coalition" applied to this league is almost a misnomer.

Before describing the first campaign of the war it will be well briefly to survey the armed forces of the Crown and the organization for war. Firstly, we must remember that Pitt had devoted

---

[1] Martens, v, 438-42.

great attention to the navy and to the fortification of Portsmouth and Plymouth. Despite the hostile vote of the House of Commons in 1785, he had succeeded in finding money enough to enable the Duke of Richmond to place those dockyard towns beyond reach of a *coup de main*; and to Pitt may be ascribed the unquestioned superiority of Britain at sea. Of the 113 sail-of-the-line then available, about 90 could soon be placed in commission, that is, so soon as the press-gang provided the larger part of the *personnel*.

The state of the army was far less satisfactory. Never, in all probability, since the ignominious times of Charles II, had it been in so weak a condition relatively to the Continental Powers. In the Budget of 1792 Pitt asked merely for 17,013 men as guards and garrisons in these islands; and he reduced even that scanty force to 13,701 men for the next six months. The regiments were in some cases little more than skeletons, but with a fairly full complement of officers. Nominally the army consisted of eighty-one battalions; but of these the West Indies claimed as many as nineteen. India needed nine; and on the whole only twenty-eight line regiments, together with the Guards and the cavalry, remained for the defence of Great Britain and Ireland. Efforts were made in December 1792 to bring in recruits, but with little effect. The defence of London, the dockyard towns, and other important posts, depended of course partly on the militia; 19,000 of that useful force were embodied early in February. But as the authorities forbore to compel men to serve in person, there was a rush for substitutes, which naturally told against recruiting for the Line.[1] Volunteer Associations were also relied on for local defence, and for overawing the malcontent or disorderly elements in the populace. The safety of the coasts and therefore of the capital rested primarily with the navy; and for England the war promised to be almost entirely a naval war.

Equally chaotic was the administration for war. Some time in February 1793 Dundas sent to Pitt a Memorandum respecting a new arrangement of offices which had been mooted in the Cabinet. The need of some change may be judged by the fact that Dundas was Secretary for Home Affairs (down to July 1794), First Commissioner for India (that is, virtually, Secretary for India), and Treasurer of the Navy, besides drawing glory and

[1] Hon. J. W. Fortescue, " Hist. of the British Army," iv, 77-83.

profit from his airy duties of Groom of the Stole. What changes had been proposed does not appear; but Dundas expressed himself as follows: " First: That I should remain precisely as I am while the war continues, provided the arrangement takes place respecting the Groom of the Stole to Lord Chatham, together with all the consequent changes in other offices. This in my judgment is by much the best for the public service, and ought to supersede all other individual wishes." Failing this patriotic arrangement, Dundas requested that he should have the first claim for the Privy Seal for Scotland, provided that Lord Chatham did not take the Stole. He (Dundas) would give up the latter but retain his office at the India Board and the Navy. Or, thirdly, if he received the Privy Seal for Scotland, he would give up his other offices except that at the India Board. This last plan would involve a large reduction of income, but he preferred it to the others except the two previously named.[1]

Nevertheless no change of any importance took place. Dundas continued to be a portly pluralist, utterly unable to overtake the work of three important offices, with the conduct of the war often superadded; and Chatham remained at the Admiralty until the close of 1794, to the annoyance of all champions of efficiency. In the course of that year Pitt urged the need of strengthening both the Admiralty and War Departments; but, as we shall see, Dundas strongly objected to the creation of a Secretary of State for War, because his duties would overlap those of the other Departments, and important decisions must be formed by the Cabinet as a whole.[2] I shall touch on this question more fully in Chapter XII, but mention it here as a sign of the mental cloudiness which led British Ministers for the first eighteen months of the war to plod along with the most haphazard arrangements known even to that age. The contrast between the boyish irresponsibility of military management in England and the terrible concentration of power in the hands of Carnot at Paris, after July 1793, goes far to explain the disasters to the Union Jack after the first few months of the war.

The triumph of the French Republic and its transformation into a military Empire cannot be understood until we probe the inner weakness of the First Coalition and realize the unpreparedness of Great Britain. Moreover, as the Allies believed that

<hr>

[1] Pretyman MSS.   [2] Chevening MSS.

France would speedily succumb, the allocation of the spoil claimed their attention more than preparations for the hunt. The unexpected vigour of the French might have undeceived them. While Coburg was leisurely preparing to drive the levies of Dumouriez from the district between Verviers and Aix-la-Chapelle, the latter laid his plans for a dash into the almost unprotected Dutch Netherlands, where he hoped to find precious spoils and valuable munitions of war.[1] Breaking up therefore from Antwerp on 16th February, the Republicans quickly advanced towards the estuary known as the Hollandsdiep, while two other columns marched on Breda and Bergen-op-Zoom. As Dumouriez had foreseen, the torpor of the Stadholder's forces was as marked as the eagerness of the Dutch Patriots to welcome the invaders. Breda fell on 26th February; but he failed to cross the Hollandsdiep, for there the Sea Power intervened.

On 15th February Auckland begged that the Duke of York might be sent over with a few battalions. The Ministry at once answered the appeal. On 20th February seven battalions of the British Guards were paraded at Whitehall; the Duke of York announced that the first three would go to Holland, and asked for volunteers from the other four. The whole line stepped forward. Huddled on to small transports, the little force reached the Dutch estuaries in time to thwart the efforts of Dumouriez. Their arrival heartened the defenders of the Hollandsdiep, and held the French at bay. Meanwhile Coburg had bestirred himself, and, marching on Miranda's vanguard on the River Roer, threw it back in utter rout. Dumouriez, falling back hastily to succour his lieutenant, encountered the Austrian force at Neerwinden, where the unsteadiness of the Republican levies enabled Coburg and his brilliant lieutenant, the Archduke Charles, to win a decisive triumph (18th March). A great part of the French levies melted away. The Belgians rose against the retreating bands; and in a few days that land was lost to France. The failure of Dumouriez to turn his army against the Convention, and his flight to the Austrian outposts, need not be described here.[2] Suffice it to say that the northern frontier of France lay open to attack.

[1] Murray reported to Grenville on 10th and 18th February that the Allies at Frankfurt were disturbed by news of the negotiation with Dumouriez. See too, Vivenot, ii, 489.

[2] "Dropmore P.," ii, 377-81; "Dumouriez," by J. H. Rose and A. M. Broadley, 162-75.

An advance in force in the month of April or May might have ended the war.

But, as we have seen, the Allies were too jealous and too distrustful to act with the necessary vigour. Austria refused to recognize the Prussian scheme for the Partition of Poland; and the North German Power retaliated by withholding its contingent from the support of Coburg.[1] That commander, finding himself duped by the Prussians, pressed the British and Dutch Governments to send him succour. To this he had some claim; for it was the Austrian victory at Neerwinden which saved Holland from the French; and the best method of protecting that land was to capture the northern fortresses of France. The Dutch army numbered on paper 50,000 men; 13,500 Hanoverians were marching towards Guelderland; 8,000 Hessians were entering the British service. In such a case it would have been disgraceful not to assist Coburg in completing his triumph. Thus, as often happens with British expeditions, the scope of the Duke of York's operations now greatly widened. His original instructions of 23rd February ordered him not to move more than twenty-four hours away from Helvoetsluys. On 19th March, as the danger lessened, the War Office gave him leave to advance, moving on the right of Coburg's army towards Antwerp and Ghent.[2]

The news of Neerwinden led George III to adopt even more vigorous measures. True, he disliked Coburg's pressing demand for help, seeing that no treaty of alliance was formed; but he permitted the forward move on Ghent, and formulated a still bolder scheme, that the British, Hanoverians, and Dutch should advance to besiege Dunkirk; for the capture of that place would enable a siege-train to be brought easily to the Austrians for the leaguer of Lille and Valenciennes.[3] To Grenville he expressed the hope that these measures would speedily end the war.[4]

The letter is important as showing the great influence of the

---

[1] " F. O.," Austria, 32, Morton Eden to Grenville, 30th March.

[2] "War Office " 6, (7); 23rd February, to Duke of York; B.M. Add. MSS 34448, Grenville to Auckland, 23rd February; Calvert, "Campaigns in Flanders and Holland," chs. i, ii.

[3] This letter (for which see "Pitt and Napoleon Miscellanies") corrects Mr. Fortescue's statement (iv, 125) that Ministers alone were responsible for the Dunkirk scheme. George III was morally responsible for it.

[4] "Dropmore P.," ii, 387.

King on military affairs. It must be remembered that Pitt,
Grenville, and Dundas (the three leading members of the
Cabinet) had no knowledge of these questions, while that
shadowy personage, Sir George Yonge, Secretary at War, had
no seat in the Cabinet. A more unsatisfactory state of things
cannot be conceived. It tended to subject questions of military
policy to that influential trio, which in its turn was swayed by

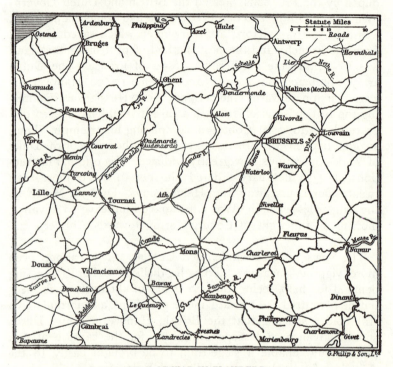

SEAT OF WAR IN FLANDERS

the will of the King. According to constitutional custom, the
Cabinet was collectively responsible for questions of war policy;
but it is difficult to say how far Ministers were individually
responsible. Pitt and Grenville certainly influenced the decisions
arrived at; Dundas drew up and signed the chief military despatches; but the wishes of George III had great weight.

In fact, questions of war policy turned largely on motives
other than military. The resolve of the King and his Ministers to share in the invasion of France sprang not only from

feelings of military honour, but also from the exigencies of diplomacy. By the middle of March it was clear that Russia and Prussia would acquire unexpectedly extensive tracts of Polish land. Francis II vented his spleen at this rebuff on his Chancellor, Philip Cobenzl, who was virtually disgraced, while a clever but unprincipled schemer, Thugut, took his place.[1] Another unwelcome surprise was in store. The Emperor had hoped to find in the Belgic-Bavarian exchange " compensation " for the presumedly moderate gains of his rivals in Poland. But to this plan, as we have seen, George III and his Ministers stoutly demurred; and Grenville held out the prospect of the acquisition of Lille and Valenciennes in order once more to lay that disquieting spectre. As it also alarmed some of the German princes, whose help was needed against France, the Court of Vienna saw this vision fade away until Thugut hit upon the design of conquering Alsace, and finding there the means of effecting the longed-for exchange. Pitt and Grenville, however, clung to the policy of rooting Austria firmly at Brussels, with Lille and Valenciennes as her outworks, and this involved the effort of winning those two fortresses for the Hapsburgs. Thugut suggested that, if Austria could not secure French Flanders, she must find compensation elsewhere; and he declined to satisfy Eden's curiosity on this threatening word.[2] It therefore behoved us to strengthen Austria's stroke at French Flanders, especially as she now acquiesced in the British contention, that the Allies should neither interfere with the form of Government in France nor recognize the Comte de Provence as Regent.[3]

The British Government, however, moved forward its troops into Flanders reluctantly, firstly, because it wanted to use them in the West Indies,[4] and also discerned the preference of Frederick William for a Polish to a Flemish campaign. That monarch and his generals left the Austrians to bear the brunt of everything on the banks of the Rhine, and also in Brabant. His

[1] " F. O.," Austria, 33, Eden to Grenville, 27th and 28th March, 10th April; Vivenot, ii, 541; Häusser, i, 483.

[2] *Ibid.*, Eden to Grenville, 15th April. This probably refers to Alsace; but it may possibly hint at a partition of Venice which had been mooted at Vienna before. A slice of Piedmont was also desired (Eden to Grenville, 8th June).

[3] *Ibid.*, Eden to Grenville, 30th March.

[4] The West India expedition was again and again deferred in favour of that to la Vendée or Toulon (Vivenot, iii, 383).

manner of setting about the siege of Mainz was a masterpiece of politic delay, in which amorous dalliance played its part.[1] When complaints came from his Allies, he hotly retorted that Coburg had sent him only 5,000 troops from the northern army instead of the 15,000 that were promised. The Austrians replied with no less warmth that Coburg needed those 10,000 men because he had had no succour from the Prussian force supporting him. The result was that the Duke of York's corps was thrust into the part which the Prussian contingent ought to have taken. Accordingly Pitt and some of his colleagues deemed it preferable, now that Holland was safe, to withdraw the British troops with a view to a series of expeditions against the coasts and colonies of France. This problem called for a clear and decided solution. Nowhere do we so much lament the secrecy of Cabinet discussions as on these questions—should the meagre forces of Britain be used on maritime expeditions (their normal function in war), or form a petty division in the crusade of two great Military Powers; or, worst of all, should they be parcelled out in both kinds of warfare?

All that we know is that George III, on 29th March, strongly advocated the siege of Dunkirk, in the hope that the capture of that seaport would assist the Austrians in reducing the fortresses of French Flanders, and thus put an end to the war. On the other hand, the Duke of Richmond counselled the withdrawal of the British force for use against the coasts and colonies of France; and his two letters to Pitt, dated Goodwood, 3rd and 5th April, show that Pitt inclined to that opinion. The question was important in view of a forthcoming conference of the allied commanders and envoys at Antwerp. The letters are too long for quotation. In that of 3rd April the duke declares that Ministers must soon decide whether to persevere in Flanders or in maritime expeditions. "To attempt both is to do neither well." For himself, he would much prefer to attack Cherbourg, Brest, l'Orient, Rochefort, Nantes and Bordeaux; but he fears that the ardour of the Duke of York will lead him into an extensive campaign in Flanders.

In the second and longer letter, Richmond warns Pitt that, if he prefers to attack the ports and colonies of France (especially the West Indies), he ought at once to warn the envoys of the

---

[1] Sybel, iii, 38-40; Häusser, i, 488, 489.

Allies at Antwerp (who were about to discuss the plan of campaign), that we could not long afford succour to them, and trusted that after six weeks they could do without it, or, at least, would need it only to a very slight extent. If, he continues, Coburg and the Prussians demur to this, we must reply that England was at first no party to the war, and entered into it only for the defence of the Dutch; that participation in a continental campaign is so unpopular and ruinous, that we may be compelled to desist from it; that by means of naval expeditions we can help the common cause steadily and effectively; and that we are in no position to act on the Continent because " our army, cavalry and infantry, consists almost wholly of recruits, no part of which (men or horses) have been raised two months, and the greater part of which are at this moment only raising." Further, if we clearly warn the Allies of our resolve to withdraw our troops, they cannot complain of it. Pitt should therefore instruct Lord Auckland to give clear expression to these ideas. Coburg will then probably argue as to the extreme importance of clinching the successes already won, and will therefore urge the Duke of York to besiege Dunkirk, Graveline, and St. Omer, with a view to drawing him on finally towards Paris. But any such proceeding is to be resisted. The German Powers will dismember France; but we, having little military weight, shall probably gain next to nothing. Far more advantageous will be our action elsewhere, e.g., in the seizure of Cherbourg, Toulon, etc. Richmond ends by requesting of Pitt the favour of an interview.[1]

Either the interview did not take place, or the duke's arguments failed to lower the sanguine spirits of the Prime Minister to the level of prudence. All the letters of Pitt at that time exude confidence from every line. He hopes that Dumouriez will succeed in overthrowing the regicides at Paris. The backwardness of the Prussians in supporting Coburg does not deter him from ordering to Flanders all the available British and mercenary troops, in order to besiege Dunkirk, and otherwise help the Imperialists. As if this is not enough, on or just before 1st April he treats with Malouet, the French envoy from Hayti, for the transfer of that colony to the British Crown; he writes hopefully of finding a force large enough to make an attempt on the French coast; and a little later Grenville men-

---

[1] Pretyman MSS. I have published the letter of 5th April 1793 almost in full in the " Eng. Hist. Rev." for April 1910.

tions a Mediterranean campaign. The King, too, in referring to a recent offer of peace from Paris, writes that the bounds of "that dangerous and faithless nation" must be greatly circumscribed before such a proposal can be entertained.[1]

Thus France is to be attacked in Flanders, on the north or north-west coast, on the Mediterranean coast and in Corsica, as well as the West Indies, by an army which musters scarcely 20,000 effectives. In this confidence, which wells forth into five distinct schemes, is to be found the cause for the Jacobin triumphs which shattered the First Coalition.

Austria and Prussia were equally puffed up with unreal hopes. At the conference at Antwerp in the second week of April occurred the first of the many blunders which helped to rally Frenchmen around the tricolour. Coburg's promise, in a recent proclamation to Dumouriez and the French nation, that the Allies would not make conquests at the expense of France, was warmly disavowed at the first sitting. Accordingly, a few days later, Coburg issued a second proclamation, announcing the end of the armistice and omitting all reference to his disinterested views. The change of tone speedily convinced the French people of the imminence of schemes of partition. This it was, quite as much as Jacobin fanaticism, which banded Frenchmen enthusiastically in the defence of the Republic. Patriotism strengthened the enthusiasm for liberty, and nerved twenty-five million Frenchmen with a resolve to fling back the sacrilegious invaders.

About this time the French Government sent pacific proposals to London, which met with no very encouraging reception, Pitt and Grenville probably regarding them as a means of sowing discord among the Allies, of worming out their plans, or of gaining time for the French preparations. It is indeed difficult to believe that they had any other object. After the defection of Dumouriez and his Staff, France was in a desperate state, and her rulers naturally sought to gain a brief respite. Grenville therefore replied that if France really desired to end the war which she had forced upon England, definite proposals might be sent to the British headquarters in the Netherlands.[2] None was sent.

Meanwhile, the jealousies of the German Powers, the delay of

---

[1] "Dropmore P.," ii, 388-93, 399.

[2] "F. O.," France, 42. I cannot agree with Sorel (iii, 405) in taking the French overtures seriously.

Austria in coming to terms with England, and the refusal of Coburg to define his plan of campaign, paralysed the actions of the Allies and saved France. As for the British force, it was too weak to act independently; and yet the pride of George III forbade its fusion in Coburg's army.[1] By the third week of April the Duke of York had with him 4,200 British infantry, 2,300 horsemen, besides 13,000 Hanoverians (clamorous for more pay), and 15,000 Dutch troops of poor quality and doubtful fidelity; 8,000 hired Hessians had not yet arrived.[2] Yet the King and his Ministers persisted in hoping for the conquest of French Flanders. The War Office despatch of 16th April specified as the chief aim of the war the re-conquest of the Low Countries by Austria, "with such extended and safe frontier as may secure the tranquillity and independence of Holland." But Pitt and his colleagues, far from concentrating on Flanders, continued to toy with expeditions to Brittany, Provence, Corsica, and the West Indies.

At first they pressed Coburg to consent to the deviation of the British force towards Dunkirk; and only on his urgent protest was that ex-centric move given up until Valenciennes should have fallen. The Austrian contention was undoubtedly right, as the British Government grudgingly admitted. The Duke of York's force therefore moved along with that of Coburg towards that fortress and showed great gallantry in compelling the French to evacuate the supporting camp of Famars (23rd May). Early in June the siege of Valenciennes began in earnest. A British officer described the defence of the French as "obstinate but not spirited." They made no sorties, and Custine's army of 40,000 men, which should have sought to raise the siege, did not attack, probably owing to the unsteadiness and apathy of his troops.[3] This lack of energy cost him his life; for on 10th July he was ordered back to Paris and soon went to the guillotine.

At that time the Jacobins were in a state of mind in which fury and despair struggled for the mastery. The outlook was as gloomy as before Valmy in September 1792. Bad news poured in from all sides. The Girondins, after the collapse of their power on 2nd June, appealed to the Departments, and two thirds of France seemed about to support them against the tyranny of the capital. Had not the Jacobins developed an organizing

---

[1] "W. O.," 6 (10), Dundas to Murray (now secretary to the Duke of York).
[2] Calvert, 80.   [3] Calvert, ch. iii; Fortescue, iv, 111.

power immeasurably superior to that of the moderates, the royalists, and the Allies, the rule of that desperate minority must speedily have been swept away. On 12th July the Parisian Government declared itself at war with the moderates, who now had the upper hand at Lyons and in neighbouring districts. On that same day Condé (a small fortress north of Valenciennes) opened its gates. On 22nd July Mainz surrendered to the King of Prussia; and six days later the Austrian and British standards were hoisted on the ramparts of Valenciennes.

This event raised to its climax the fury of the Jacobins; and on 9th August the Convention passed with acclamation a decree declaring Pitt to be an enemy of the human race. This singular manifestation of Gallic effervescence came about in the following way. The Committee of Public Safety having presented a report on the scarcity of corn and bread, the Convention was electrified by the doleful recital. In the ensuing debate stories are told of men disguised as women who practise insidious devices among the *queues* at the bakers' shops. At once the Convention decrees that men acting thus while in disguise shall be deemed worthy of death. A deputy named Garnier then suggests that as this is clearly a device of the infamous Pitt to increase disorder, it shall be declared lawful to murder him. Couthon, for once speaking the language of moderation, objects to this proposal as unworthy of the Republic, and moves that Pitt be declared an enemy of the human race. This is at once approved as worthy of the humanity and dignity of the Convention. The decree, then, was obviously a device for shelving the stupid and bloodthirsty motion of Garnier. The whole discussion may be compared with Pitt's declaration to the House of Commons on 12th February 1793, that the war, though undoubtedly provoked by France, would never be waged by England for motives of vengeance, but merely for the attainment of security.

Why at this time the name of Pitt should have driven the Parisian legislators half frantic is not easy to see. Up to that time the exploits of the small British force at Famars and Valenciennes had been no more than creditable; and it was not till the end of the month that the news of the entry of Admiral Hood's fleet into Toulon threw Paris into a frenzy. The decree of 9th August therefore has merely a psychological interest. When tyrants thundered at the gates of the Republic, France needed some names the mere sound of which sufficed to drive her sons to arms. In 1792 it was Brunswick or Condé. When they ceased to be effective, the populace found others first in Coburg and finally in Pitt. Other names waxed and waned; but that of the son of Chatham stood fixed in a dull haze of hatred. Thus, by a singular irony, the very man who in 1786 had branded with folly those Englishmen who declared France to be our natural enemy, was now by her banned as the enemy of the human race. And such he remains for the great majority of Frenchmen. The hasty and fortuitous phrase of Couthon, which was designed to save him from the assassin's knife, will doubtless be the permanent catchword, irremovable by research and explanation.

The ravings of the French Convention would soon have ended, had not a great organizer now appeared. On 17th August 1793 Carnot entered the Committee of Public Safety, and thenceforth wielded its limitless powers for purposes of national defence. He was an officer of engineers, and had eagerly studied the principles of strategy. Throwing himself with ardour into the Revolution, he became a member of the National Assembly, and now was charged with the supervision of the War Department. At the War Committee he had the help of officers scarcely less able. Among them Mallet du Pan, in an interesting survey of French administrators, names D'Arçon as largely contributing to the French triumphs at Dunkirk and Maubeuge. He calls him a soul on fire and full of resource.[1] But the brain and will of this Committee was Carnot. His application to work for some twelve or fourteen hours a day, his hold on masses of details, and his burning patriotism, enabled him to inflame, control, and energize Frenchmen until they became a nation in arms. Moreover, Carnot had the invaluable gift of selecting the best commanders. True, the Frenchman was not hampered by a monarch who regarded the army as his own, nor by clogging claims of seniority. The "organizer of victory" had before him a clear field and no favour.

The most urgent danger for the Republic soon proved to be not in Flanders, but in Brittany and la Vendée. There *la petite noblesse* and the peasantry still lived on friendly terms. They were alike shocked by the expulsion of the orthodox priests and the murder of the King. Summoned by the Republic to arms in the spring of 1793, they rushed to arms against her. In la Vendée,

---

[1] " Dropmore P.," iii, 493.

the densely wooded district south of the lower Loire, everything favoured the defence. The hardy peasants were ably led by that born leader of men, the chivalrous Marquis de Larochejaquelein, who had inspired the men of his neighbourhood with the words: "If I advance, follow me; if I retreat, slay me; if I fall, avenge me." With him was his cousin, Lescure, not less brave, but of a cooler and more calculating temper. The ardently Catholic peasantry of the west furnished as leaders a carter, Cathelineau, of rare ability and generosity of character, and Stofflet, a game-keeper, of stern and vindictive stamp. Nerved by fanatical hatred against the atheists and regicides of Paris, these levies of the west proved more than a match for all the National Guards, whole columns of whom they lured into the depths of the Bocage and cut down to the last man. As Victor Hugo has finely said: "It was a war of the town against the forest." At first the forest-dwellers threatened to overrun the towns. On 11th June they took Saumur, a town on the Loire, after a desperate fight, and sought to open communication with the coast and the British fleet by seizing Nantes. This attempt, however, failed; and it is generally admitted that they erred in not marching on Paris after their first successes. After gaining a sure base of operations, they should have strained every nerve in order to strike at the heart. And if distance and lack of supplies and equipment shortened their reach, they might at least have carried the war into the rich central provinces, on which the capital subsisted.

But the mistake of these poor peasants was venial when compared with those of the Allies. On the capture of Mainz, Condé, and Valenciennes, the Prussian, Austrian, and British commanders did not enforce an unconditional surrender, but offered to allow the garrisons to march out with the honours of war on condition of not serving against them for a year. A better example of shirking present problems at the cost of enhanced difficulties in the future cannot be imagined. By this improvident lenity the Allies enabled the regicides to hurl fully 25,000 trained troops against the royalists of the West and deal them terrible blows. In September and October the Republicans gained considerable successes, especially at Cholet. Soon the Vendéan War became little more than a guerilla strife, which Pitt fed by means of arms and stores, but not in the energetic manner desired by Burke and Windham.

These ardent royalists constantly pressed him to help the men of Poitou and Brittany, but had to deplore the wearisome delays which then clogged all military and naval operations. Most bitterly did Burke write to Windham, early in November 1793, that Ministers were so eager in seeking to win indemnities from France that they had hardened the national resistance of that nation, and meanwhile had not sent a single shipload of stores to the brave men of Poitou. Of course it was less easy than Burke imagined to get stores across a sea not yet fully commanded by the British fleet, and through inlets and harbours closely watched by the enemy. But the inaction of a force entrusted to the Earl of Moira for the support of the French royalists is certainly discreditable to him and to Ministers. Among them the Duke of Richmond, Master of Ordnance, distinguished himself by his incapacity and his ridiculous orders. Another obvious misfit was Lord Chatham at the Admiralty. But how can we explain the inactivity of four regiments in the Channel Islands all the summer? Surely they could have seized St. Malo or the Quiberon Peninsula.[1] Such a diversion would have been highly effective. For the Bretons and Vendéans, when supplied with arms, could have marched eastwards and roused the royalists of Normandy, Maine, and Touraine. With so potent a foe near to Paris, must not the regicides have been overborne by Coburg in Flanders? Everything tends to show that the Republicans feared the royalists of the West more than the Austrians in the North. But, as will appear in a later chapter, Pitt and Dundas decided to throw their strength into the West Indies. On 26th November 1793, Sir John Jervis sailed for that deadly bourne with 7,000 troops.

Events were soon to reveal the seriousness of this mistake. It was far more important to strike at Paris through Brittany than to occupy even the richest of the French West Indies. For a triumphant advance of the Bretons and Vendéans must not only have lessened the material resources of the Republic but also have deprived its defenders of one of their chief advantages. Hitherto the Republicans had been better massed together, while their assailants were spread over wide spaces. It is a well-known principle in war that an army operating on an inner arc, or what are termed interior lines, has a great advantage over forces spread over the outer circumference. The Allies

[1] " Dropmore P.," ii, 436.

then held the Pyrenees, the Maritime Alps, the Rhine, and most of Flanders, Brittany, and parts of the South. The defenders, possessing the central provinces, could mass their units far more quickly and choose the point on that outer curve against which they would aim their blow.

This principle was thoroughly understood by Carnot. Near the centre of the circle he massed the levies that were to save the Republic, and, confiding them to zealots who were resolved to conquer or die, he soon had on foot armies which, however contemptible as units, were formidable from their weight and their enthusiasm. As in mechanics the mass multiplied by the speed gives the effective force, so in the campaign of 1793 the *levée en masse* multiplied by enthusiasm and impelled by the brain power of Carnot begot a momentum which, when brought to bear on light, scattered, and almost stationary bodies, proved to be irresistible. For while Carnot trusted to concentration, the Allies either sank into inertia, or made ex-centric movements which ultimately played into their opponents' hands. The Prussians, after taking Mainz, did little more than rest on their laurels, their only move being towards Luxemburg. Coburg was inclined to follow their example on the ground that an advance to Paris would unite all the French parties against him, while the siege of the remaining fortresses in the North would allow anarchy to run riot at the centre.[1] The argument is a good example of political *finesse* applied to a military problem, with disastrous results. Coburg therefore set about the siege of Quesnoy.

Certainly he could urge in excuse that the British Government now insisted on the resumption of its favourite plan, the capture of that nest of privateers, Dunkirk. On receipt of the news of the surrender of Valenciennes, an order was sent to the Duke of York to begin the siege of that once important stronghold, and capture it for Great Britain, though it might be allowed finally to fall to the Emperor as one of his new Barrier fortresses, provided that we gained indemnities in other parts of the world. French and German historians, with their usual bias against Great Britain, have assumed that she had resolved to keep Dunkirk. The contrary is proved by the despatches of Dundas to Murray, and by a letter of Sir Gilbert Elliot whom Pitt appointed commissioner to regulate affairs at Dunkirk. Writing to Lady

---

[1] Sybel, iii, 136, 137.

Elliot on 10th September Sir Gilbert says: "No further conquests are to be made in that quarter in the name of Great
Britain, nor is it intended to retain Dunkirk after the peace." [1]
A speedy capture of Dunkirk was evidently expected, for the
same despatch ordered that the Hessian corps, some 8,000
strong, then with the Duke, must be held in readiness to depart
to some other destination.[2] This referred either to the expedition in the Mediterranean (soon to be noticed) or to another,
also in course of preparation, against Brittany. The Duke of
York disapproved of the divergence towards Dunkirk, and the
withdrawal of troops from his command.[3]

We here touch upon the weak side of Pitt's war policy. His
aims at first had been merely to defend England from invasion,
and to use the fleet and as many troops as could well be spared,
to threaten various points along the coast of France and to capture her colonies. From these comparatively simple aims he
had been drawn aside into a continental campaign, owing to the
desirability of re-establishing Austria firmly in the Pays Bas.
That is to say, a political aim drew him away from the simple
and effective plan of a maritime and colonial war. Or rather it
would be more correct to say that he tried to carry on a limited
continental campaign as well as the coast expeditions which
promised to paralyse the activities of large numbers of
Frenchmen.

Accordingly, Pitt and his colleagues, instead of concentrating
their activities on Flanders, prepared also to harass the coasts
and colonies of France, and to withdraw part of the Duke of
York's force for service in the Mediterranean or the West Indies.
Instructions to this effect annoyed both the duke and Coburg.
Most reluctantly did the latter consent to the divergence of the
British towards Dunkirk; but, as he had already decided to
spend the rest of the campaign in reducing the border fortresses,
the division of forces had none of those appalling results which
Alison and others have detected. The duke's corps, then, turned
off to the right, and, after gaining some successes over bodies of
the French, set about the siege of Dunkirk. If his siege train
had arrived in time, the town would probably soon have sur-

---

[1] "Mems. of Sir G. Elliot (Earl of Minto)," ii, 159.
[2] "W. O.," 6 (10), 1st August, to Sir J. Murray, which corrects the statement in Sybel (iii, 140), that England meant to keep Dunkirk.
[3] "Malmesbury Diaries," iii, 18.

rendered. But now Carnot was able to utilize some of the forces raised in the *levée en masse*. By the beginning of September the French relieving army amounted to 45,000 men under General Houchard; while the Hessians and Hanoverians covering the siege operations did not exceed 9,000 men. These made a most obstinate and skilful defence in the village of Bambeke, and thereafter at Hondschoote; but the inequality of force was too great; and they were outflanked and driven back towards Furnes and Nieuport with the loss of 2,600 men (6th to 8th September). The garrison also attacked the besiegers and received much assistance from French gunboats moored near the shore. It was an unfortunate circumstance that a storm on 1st September had compelled a British frigate and a sloop to leave their moorings. Even so, the duke's force beat back their assailants into the town. But the defeat of the covering army at Hondschoote placed it between the French, the walls of Dunkirk, and the sea. Only by a speedy retreat could he save his men; and at midnight he drew off, leaving behind 32 siege guns and large quantities of stores.[1]

At once there arose an outcry against our naval and transport authorities for not sending a squadron to cover the right flank of the Duke of York opposite Dunkirk. Elliot reports that the duke violently censured Richmond, head of the Ordnance Department, and Chatham, First Lord of the Admiralty, the latter of whom was universally allowed to be incompetent. Elliot adds: "I have seen Dundas and Pitt since the bad news. Dundas seems much dismayed. Pitt tried to carry it off better."[2] Certainly the delay in sending ships and stores was discreditable to all concerned. But the decisive action was that of Hondschoote, six miles distant from the coast, and that reverse was due to the inability of Coburg to spare the reinforcements which Murray pressed him to send. On its side the French Government was ill satisfied with the success at Hondschoote. Censuring Houchard for not pressing his advantage to the utmost and capturing the duke's whole army, it replaced him by his young and energetic subaltern, an ex-draper named Jourdan, who was destined to become one of Napoleon's marshals, while Houchard speedily went to the guillotine. By these drastic methods France found leaders who could conquer. For them the inspiring thought was—victory or the guillotine.

[1] Calvert, 119-21.   [2] "Mems. of Sir G. Elliot," ii, 160.

The news of the failure at Dunkirk shattered Pitt's hope of a speedy end to the war. That he faced the prospect of a second campaign with his usual buoyancy appears from some notes which bear the date 16th September [1793] and are headed: "Force to be employed in Flanders, or on the coast of France in the Channel and the Ocean." He proposes to increase 9 regiments at home to 800 men apiece, to raise 8 new regiments; and these, along with Guards and troops from Ireland would number at least 20,000. He also hoped that at least 20,000 more Austrians and about 25,000 Bavarians would be available for Flanders, raising the total force in that quarter to 175,000 men.[1] These roseate views are apt to provoke derision; but we must remember that not until the close of the year 1793 did the Republic put forth her full strength and beat back her enemies at all points.

It would be tedious to follow in detail the rest of Coburg's operations in Flanders. Early in September he took Quesnoy, and then drew together his forces for the capture of the intrenched camp at Maubeuge. In this he seemed about to succeed, when Jourdan's relieving force of 60,000 men, handled by Carnot, drove the Austrians back at Wattignies with much loss, and thus saved the garrison at Maubeuge, now in dire straits. On that day, 16th October, the head of Marie Antoinette fell at Paris.

As for the Duke of York's army, after remaining in a sorry plight near Ostend, it moved forward to Quesnoy to prolong Coburg's right; but the retreat of the main body involved his retirement towards Ostend, near which town he routed some detachments of French. For a time the Allies gained a few advantages and recovered lost ground. But the Republicans more than made up for occasional losses by pouring troops into Flanders; and, moving under cover of their fortresses, they often dealt heavy blows. In quality the Austrians and British far surpassed the raw levies of France; but these, having the advantage in number and position, could take the offensive along a wide ill-defended front. Wherever Coburg and the Duke of York attacked, they gained an advantage, soon to be lost in face of the gathering masses of the enemy. As Coburg pointed out, France sent forth another horde to take the place of one which

[1] Pitt MSS., 196.

perished or melted away; and the Allies rarely had the chance of taking the offensive. By this last statement he passed sentence against himself. An able commander, even with inferior forces, will mass them so as to strike with effect. Pitt and Grenville continually pressed him to form some plan of action in conjunction with the Duke of York; but to this he as persistently demurred.[1] Is it surprising that Pitt demanded the removal of Coburg?

The Rhenish campaign, in which Austria took more interest, also languished owing to the sluggishness of the Duke of Brunswick. This, in its turn, resulted from political reasons. Frederick William, in spite of his treaty obligations to England, refused to move forward until she guaranteed his late gains in Poland and made further advances of money. Then, too, he felt no interest in Austria's proposed acquisition of parts of Alsace and Lorraine. Pitt and Grenville despatched Lord Yarmouth to the King's headquarters to make a formal protest against the proposed withdrawal of the Prussian army. Finally, Frederick William gave the order to advance, but too late to gain the results which prompt and vigorous co-operation with the Austrians should have achieved.[2] In short, the course of events in 1793 affords the classic example of the collapse of vast and imposing efforts owing to division of interests and the intrusion of jealousies and intrigues. Pitt and Grenville did their best to keep the Coalition united and active; but a Power which granted only limited help could not impart that unity of design without which great enterprises come to naught.

---

[1] Vivenot, iii, 352, 353.

[2] *Ibid.*, 320, 321, 339, 379, 380; "Dropmore P.," ii, 470, 536. In the last passage Yarmouth accuses the King of Prussia of deliberately thwarting the action of the Austrian army under Wurmser.

CHAPTER VI

TOULON

Delay leads impotent and snail-paced beggary:
Then fiery expedition be my wing,
Jove's Mercury, and herald for a King.
—SHAKESPEARE, *King Richard III*, act iv, sc. 3.

THE enterprise destined to develop into the occupation of Toulon arose out of the negotiations for alliance with Austria, Sardinia, and Naples. By the first of these England pledged herself to send a considerable fleet into the Mediterranean, as an effective help to the military operations then going on in the Maritime Alps and the Genoese Riviera. Indeed, the Court of Vienna made this almost a *sine quâ non* of its alliance. On its side the British Government gained assurances of military aid from Sardinia and Naples, the former of those States agreeing to furnish 20,000 troops in return for the annual subsidy of £200,000.

Here, then, were the foundations of a Mediterranean policy on which Pitt and his colleagues began to build in the years 1793-4, with the singular and unforeseen results at Toulon and in Corsica. Everything favoured some such design. The French marine was enfeebled by mutiny, and, as the spring of 1793 merged into summer, there came ominous signs of revolt in the South against the Jacobin faction supreme at Paris. Accordingly Grenville urged the Hapsburg Court, in return for British help in Flanders, to assist an expedition of the Allies to the coast of Provence. The conduct of the Austrian Chancellor, Thugut, was characteristic. Far from strengthening the Imperial forces in Italy, he prepared to withdraw some of them for the Rhenish campaign, now that a British fleet spread its covering wings over the Kingdom of Sardinia.[1]

[1] " F. O.," Austria, 33, Grenville to Eden, 11th June; Eden to Grenville, 26th June.

143

Nevertheless the British Ministers persevered with their scheme; but whether they at first aimed at Corsica or Toulon is uncertain.[1] Certain it is that Pitt on 19th July proposed to detach three line regiments from the Duke of York's force in Flanders and send them to the Mediterranean along with one brigade of the Hessian corps and a body of Würtembergers. He pointed out that the naval superiority of Hood and the Spanish fleet in that sea would enable us to strike a telling blow at Provence if we were helped by Sardinians, Neapolitans, and Austrians from the Milanese. He admitted the strength of the arguments in favour of our land forces acting together on one point; but he added: "What I now mention seems to offer a fair chance of doing something material in the South [of France], and, if we distress the enemy on more sides than one, while their internal distraction continues, it seems hardly possible that they can long oppose any effectual resistance."[2]

Pitt wrote thus at the time when Mainz and Valenciennes were on the point of surrender, and the Bretons, together with nearly the whole of the South of France, were in open revolt against the regicide Republic. Equally characteristic of his sanguine temperament is his Memorandum of 23rd August 1793 as to the allied forces which ought to be available for service against France in June 1794, namely, 30,000 in Flanders, while 50,000 marched thence on Paris; 50,000 to attack Brest, and as many more to attack Toulon.[3]

It so chanced that on that very day the ardour of the Provençaux brought about a very different situation. The arrival of Hood's fleet encouraged the moderates to send two Commissioners, representing the two coast Departments, to seek help from the British fleet. Thereupon on his flagship, the "Victory," Hood drew up a public Declaration that, if the ships-of-war in Toulon and Marseilles were unrigged and the French Royal standard hoisted, he would take those cities under his protection, respect private property and, on the conclusion of peace, restore the warships to the French monarchy. He then sent to a Spanish squadron, under Langara, cruising off the coast of Roussillon, with a request for help. That officer soon had the

---

[1] "Dropmore P.," ii, 392, 399, 407, 412. Spain hoped to find her "indemnity" in Corsica. See too Fortescue, iv, 116, 117.

[2] See "Eng. Hist. Rev." for October 1909, p. 748.

[3] Pitt MSS., 196.

promise of 2,000 Spanish troops, to be detached from the army invading that province. The Jacobin forces under Carteaux having crushed the moderates in Marseilles, Hood made for Toulon, though as yet the Spanish ships were not in sight. He cast anchor in the outer roadstead on 27th August, and landed 1,500 men near Fort Lamalgue, east of the town. In the afternoon fifteen Spanish ships arrived, and on the next day landed 1,000 men. On the 28th Hood also issued a proclamation to the effect that he would hold Toulon in trust only for Louis XVII until peace should be restored to France.[1] To this the Toulonese assented; the opposition of some of their sailors and troops soon collapsed; and a detachment of Carteaux' force was easily dislodged from a strong position near Ollioules, north-west of the town (31st August). Toulon therefore seemed a sure gain for the royalist cause.

Yet Pitt and his colleagues were careful not to identify themselves with that cause. Hood, having implied in his Toulon proclamation that one of the objects of Great Britain was the restoration of the French monarchy, Ministers warned him that "the true ground of the war was to repel an unjust and unprovoked aggression against His Majesty, and his Allies, and the rest of Europe, which had been evidently threatened and endangered by the conduct of France." True, in the course of the struggle England had supported the French Royalists, and might find it prudent, especially in view of the events at Toulon, to assist in restoring monarchy. "But," adds Lord Chatham, "it is to be considered as arising out of the circumstances and founded on the considerations which I have stated, and not as making part of the object for which His Majesty originally took up arms."[2] This gentle rebuke to Hood (an impetuous and opinionated officer), clearly shows the attitude of the Cabinet towards that problem. For Great Britain the re-establishment of monarchy was not an affair of principle, but solely of expediency. It is also noteworthy that the inhabitants of Toulon retained the tricolour flag, thus signifying their adhesion to constitutional royalism as established in 1791.

The fortunes of the Republic now appeared desperate; and the Allies would certainly have triumphed had they put forth a tithe of the energy developed by the Jacobins at Paris. With

---

[1] "H. O.," Adm. Medit., 1793.   [2] *Ibid.*

ordinarily good management on the part of Austria, Sardinia, and Naples, Toulon might have become the centre of a great royalist movement in the South. That was certainly the expectation of Pitt; and Langara, the Spanish admiral at Toulon, expressed to his Government the hope that the war would soon end with honour.[1]

No one at first realized the difficulties of the enterprise. The ramparts of Toulon were extensive; and the outlying forts, from Lamalgue on the east to Mount Faron on the north, and the works on the west and south-west, spread over a circumference of fully fifteen miles. Then again the French royalist committee in Toulon was somewhat suspicious of the Allies. In truth a blight seemed to settle on the royalist cause when it handed over to foreigners one of the cherished citadels of France. Loyalty to Louis XVII now spelt treason to the nation. The crisis is interesting because it set sharply against one another the principles of monarchy and nationality; and the sequel proved that the national idea, though still far from mature even in France, had more potency than royalism. A keen-sighted observer had very forcibly warned the Marseillais against delivering their city into the hands of the Spaniards, a crime which must ruin their efforts. Such was the judgement of Bonaparte in that curious pamphlet " Le Souper de Beaucaire."

Other invisible agencies, those of time and space, told against the Allies. Despatches sent by Hood were at least eleven days in reaching their destination, and often far longer. Consequently, the plans framed at home were always belated. The first tidings (received on 7th September) found the Cabinet half committed to another enterprise, that in the West Indies, which Pitt very reluctantly postponed owing to the drain of troops to Flanders and Toulon. A further disadvantage was that disputes between the British and Spanish commanders at Toulon were known at Whitehall long after they had come to a head; and the final reports of the sore straits of the garrison led to the despatch to Cork of orders for the sailing of reinforcements five days after the evacuation began at Toulon.

In these brisk and giddy-paced times it is difficult to realize the difficulties which then beset British commanders warring in the Mediterranean against an enemy who could send news to

[1] " F. O.," Spain, 28. St. Helens to Grenville, 4th and 11th September.

Paris in three days. Now the telegraph has annihilated space; but then, as in the campaigns of Francis I against Charles V, the compactness of France and her central position told enormously in her favour. The defence of Toulon was practicable, provided that adequate reinforcements arrived in time. As will soon appear, Pitt urged the despatch of strong reinforcements from Ireland; and, but for delays due to the want of transports, things might have gone very differently at Toulon. He also expected Austria to send succours if only as a means of protecting her Italian possessions. In truth, if the Hapsburgs had discerned the signs of the times, they would have taken steps to defend the Milanese at Toulon. They were destined to rue their folly.

Further, on 14th September, despite bad news from Dunkirk, Dundas issued orders that 4,000 Hessians, serving under the Duke of York, must be withdrawn in order to strengthen the garrison at Toulon, their place being taken by others hired at Cassel. On 28th September Dundas added that the artillery sent for Dunkirk would be withdrawn from Flanders as it was urgently needed at Toulon. Thus these two expeditions competed together, and produced a dislocation of plans and ordering of troops to and fro, which told against success in either quarter. By 27th October Ministers definitely decided that Toulon, or la Vendée, was a better fulcrum for their scanty forces than Flanders.[1] Even so, with all these dislocations of the Flemish plans, Pitt and Dundas relied too much upon Austria; and all too late found out that she was a broken reed. The Sardinians, also, lacking due support from the Court of Vienna, were afraid to denude their borders and therefore sent an inadequate contingent, despite the fact that they had promised to place 20,000 troops at the disposal of England free from all expense.

Far different was the procedure of the French. Carnot determined to retake Lyons and Toulon, even if the efforts against Spain and Sardinia had to be relaxed. Further, on the 16th of September there arrived at the Republican army west of Toulon the incarnation of warlike energy and skill. At the bidding of the Commissioners of the Convention, Napoleon Bonaparte had come from the arsenal at Marseilles to assist the few artillerymen then before Toulon. On the 17th he was placed in command

[1] "W. O.," 6 (10). See Fortescue (iv, pt. i, chs. vi, vii) for criticisms of these measures.

of their insignificant siege artillery, and forthwith from the slopes two miles west of the town he opened fire on the nearest ships. It is incorrect to claim for him the origination of the plan of sinking the fleet by a fire from the height behind l'Eguilette; for three days earlier the Commissioners of the Convention had written that they would secure a position whence the allied fleet could be sunk by red-hot cannon-balls; and there was no point but the high ground behind Fort l'Eguilette which dominated both the inner and the outer harbours.[1] But it may freely be granted that Bonaparte clinched the arguments in favour of this course and brought to bear on it that masterful energy which assures triumph. It was the first occasion on which he crossed the path of Pitt; and here, as always, he had the advantage of a central position, and of wielding a compact and homogeneous force against discordant Allies.

The worst difficulty confronting the defenders of Toulon remains to be noted. There the Sea Power is at the mercy of the Land Power. To attempt to defend that city at the head of its land-locked harbour, dominated by promontories, was to court disaster unless the fleet had an army to protect it. In such a case a fleet is a source of danger rather than of safety. Its true function is to act where it can, either directly or indirectly, command the land. It operates with most effect against low and exposed coasts. St. Jean d'Acre affords, perhaps, the best example of a town at the mercy of a fleet. Portsmouth, Sydney, Brest, and Toulon cannot be held by an enemy unless he brings forces sufficient to hold the neighbouring heights. In occupying Toulon, the Sea Power was virtually putting its head into the lion's jaw. Only by degrees did the authorities at home understand this all-important fact. For some time it was veiled from Pitt; and, as we shall see, the Austrian Chancellor, Thugut, never did understand it. To those who were on the spot, the need of occupying the promontory behind l'Eguilette was apparent; and on 21st September Lord Mulgrave and Rear-Admiral Gravina led a force to seize the very height on which Bonaparte's will had already fastened. The Allies crowned it with a temporary work dignified by the name of Fort Mulgrave. The fortunes

[1] The arguments of Mr. Spenser Wilkinson in "Owens College Essays," do not convince me that Napoleon alone devised that plan. Chuquet's conclusion ("Toulon," 176), "Bonaparte partageait l'avis des représentants," seems to me thoroughly sound. So, too, Cottin, "Toulon et les Anglais," ch. xi.

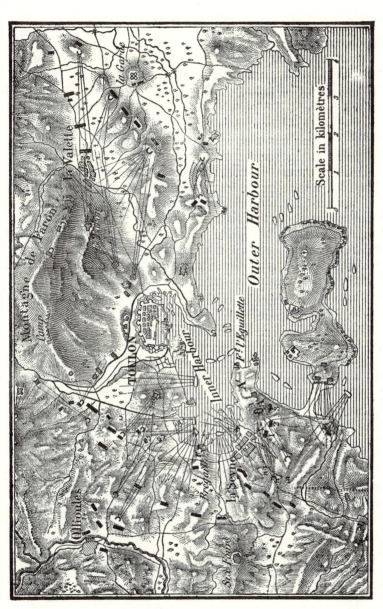

THE SIEGE OF TOULON, 1793, from "L'Histoire de France depuis la Révolution de 1789," by Emmanuel Toulougeon. Paris, An. XII. [1803].

A. Fort Mulgrave. A'. Promontory of L'Eguillette. 1 and 2. Batteries. 3. Battery "Hommes sans Peur." The black and shaded rectangles are the Republican and Allied positions respectively.

of Toulon turned on the possession of all the heights commanding the harbour, but especially of this one.

Even before the arrival of Bonaparte the difficulties of defence
were very great. A British naval officer wrote on the 14th to
Lord St. Helens, British ambassador at Madrid, that the situation of the little garrison was very critical owing to daily attacks
from the 5,000 French at Ollioules and the same number on the
eastern side. The Allies, he added, could not wholly trust the
French royalists serving with them, and they were glad to send
away on four French sail-of-the-line some 6,000 French sailors
who had bargained to be landed on the Biscay coast. Having
only 1,570 British and 3,460 Spaniards, they could scarcely man
the ramparts and forts, several of which, especially those on
Mount Faron, were not nearly ready. The houses of the town
were far too near to the ramparts; but the Allies dared not
demolish them until reinforcements arrived. Fortunately the
Spanish Admiral, Gravina, was alert, intelligent, and trustworthy; and Piedmontese were known to be advancing over
the Maritime Alps into the county of Nice. Part of Hood's
fleet was engaged in intercepting the supplies and stores destined for the Republicans.[1]

The letter brings out vividly the perils of the garrison, which
must have evacuated Toulon had not reinforcements speedily
arrived. On 26th September Hood wrote that the Allies were
kept in perpetual alarm by the French batteries, which must be
kept under at all risks, until more troops arrived.[2] Fortunately
the foresight of Pitt and Grenville had provided the means of
backing up operations in the Mediterranean. Apart from the
treaty with Sardinia, there was a compact with Naples, whereby
that Court promised a force of 6,000 men and 12 warships, the
naval expenses being borne by England.[3] By 5th October 1,350

---

[1] "F. O.," Spain, 28.

[2] "H. O." (Adm. Medit., 1793). Nevertheless Hood sent off a small
squadron to offer help to Paoli in Corsica, but with very disappointing results.
On 7th October he writes: "Paoli is a composition of art and deceipt [sic]."
He also dwells on the hostile conduct of Genoa and Tuscany.

[3] Martens, v, 473-83. In "H. O.," Secrs. of State, 4, is a despatch of
General Acton of 30th October 1793 to Sir W. Hamilton, stating that when
transports reach Naples, they will take off 1,200 more troops for Toulon,
making a total of 6,300. But ships and supplies of food were wanting. The
troops must be commanded by a Neapolitan, Marshal Fortiquerri, whom
Hood had censured for incompetence!

Sardinian and 4,000 Neapolitan troops arrived, thus enabling
the garrison to hold up against the ever increasing forces of the
Republicans. On the other hand, the fall of Lyons on 9th
October set free large numbers who were available for service at
Toulon. Consequently the troops and seamen of the Allies were
persistently overworked, so that Hood was constrained to hire
1,500 Maltese seamen, to take the place of those serving the
batteries. At first only 750 British troops could be spared from
Gibraltar; but by the end of October, when further help was at
hand, the allied forces (rank and file) stood as follows:

British	2,114
French Royalists	1,542
Spaniards.	6,840
Neapolitans	4,832
Sardinians	1,584
	16,912

So exacting was the service, and so unhealthy the season (it
cost Bonaparte a sharp attack of malarial fever), that the number fit for duty did not exceed 12,000.

It is interesting to compare these figures with the estimate
of Pitt which is in the Pitt MSS. (No. 196).

September 16.

Force which it is supposed may be collected at Toulon by the end
of October or early in November:

Rank and File.

British Marines	1,500
„ flank companies from Gibraltar	600
„ „ „ „ Ireland	2,000 [1]
„ Two battalions from Flanders (to be replaced by detachments from the Guards)	1,200
„ Cavalry from Ireland	900
Hessians from Flanders (to be replaced by the additional corps ordered)	5,000
Spanish (suppose)	3,000
Neapolitan	6,000
Sardinian	9,000
Austrian	5,000
Total . .	33,200
	[sic—really 34,200.]

[1] On 15th September Pitt wrote to the Earl of Westmorland, Viceroy of

This Force may be estimated (allowing for some deduction) at 30,000 men. To this may possibly be added some Force from Corsica, and probably early in the spring, an additional body of 11,000 Sardinians, perhaps also of 10,000 Austrians, and some troops of Baden from hence. Possibly also a body of Swiss, and in the course of the next summer (if the expedition to the West Indies is successful) about 4,000 or 5,000 British on their return from the Islands. If 10,000, or 12,000, Swiss can be secured, it seems not unreasonable to expect that, by the beginning of next year, there may be an army in the South of France of near 60,000 men.

Pitt, then, regarded Toulon as the base of operations in the South of France so extensive as to deal a decisive blow at the Republic. The scheme was surely due to the influence of Bacchus rather than of Mars. For how was it possible to spare 6,200 men from the Duke of York's force, then hard pressed after its retreat from Dunkirk? The estimate of the Sardinian contingent was based on the treaty obligations of that Power rather than on probable performance; while that for the Spaniards is strangely beneath the mark. How boyishly hopeful also to suppose that the British forces destined for the future conquest of Corsica could spare a contingent for service in Provence in the spring of 1794, and that the nervous little Court of Turin would send an *additional* body of 11,000 men far into France. Thus early in Pitt's strategic combinations we can detect the vitiating flaw. He did not know men, and therefore he did not know Cabinets. He believed them to be acting according to his own high standard of public duty and magnanimous endeavour. Consequently he never allowed for the calculating meanness which shifted the burdens on to other shoulders.

The one factor on which he had a right to count was the despatch of a respectable force of Austrians from the Milanese by way of Genoa. The Austrian Governor of Milan promised to

Ireland, asking him to send the flank companies (the best men) of the regiments then in Ireland. Westmorland agreed on 18th September, but said they could not sail in less than three weeks. As the crisis at Toulon deepened, Pitt, about the middle of November, begged the Lord Lieutenant to send the 35th, 41st, and 42nd regiments from Ireland to Toulon. On 20th November Westmorland agreed (though pointing out the danger of an Irish rising). On the 30th he said the two latter regiments were ready to sail from Cork whenever the transports should arrive; but the delays in the arrival and sailing of transports had always been serious—a prophetic remark (Pitt MSS., 331).

send 5,000 men; but not a man ever stirred.[1] Hood did not
hear this disappointing news till 24th November.[2] He at once
sent off to London an urgent request for succour; and orders
were given *on 23rd December* (the day after the arrival of the
news) for three regiments to sail from Cork for his relief. Thus
it came about that 12,000 Allies were left unsupported at Toulon
to bear the brunt of attacks of some 40,000 Frenchmen now
directed by a genius. O'Hara, who took over the command on
his arrival on 27th October, at once gave a verdict consonant
with his pessimistic character. Hood wrote on the morrow to
Dundas : " General O'Hara has just been with me and alarmed
me much. He says our posts are not tenable and that we are
in a dangerous situation for lack of troops that can be relied
upon. And, what is very unpleasant, is the conduct of the
Spaniards, who are striving for power here." On 11th November O'Hara reported that, in the absence of engineer officers, the
forts had been injudiciously constructed; that their garrisons
began to suffer from exposure to the bleak weather; that the
broken and wooded country greatly favoured the advance of
the enemy, and hampered all efforts to dislodge him; that the
Spaniards and Sardinians had no artillery, tools, or camp equip-
ments; and that the only means of securing Toulon was to have
an army capable of taking the field.[3] Hood and he therefore
counted the hours for the arrival of 5,000 Austrians from Genoa,
and of troops from England.

The difficulties of the Allies were enhanced by the disputes
which soon arose between the British and Spaniards as to the
command of the garrison. The tactful Gravina having been
badly wounded in driving the French from Mount Faron, Langara put in a claim that his successor should be commander-in-

---

[1] " Dropmore P.," ii, 471. Thugut took no interest whatever in Toulon
(see Vivenot, iii, 324, 327, 362, 363). Other proofs follow (pp. 381, 384) of the
pressing demands which Grenville, also Mr. Trevor at Turin, made for the
fulfilment of the Emperor's promise. Some difficulties supervened as to the
provisioning of the 5,000 Austrian troops on the march and the place of embarkation; but these were far from insuperable. Clearly the operating cause
was Thugut's conviction that there was at Toulon a number of troops " excéd-
ant ce que toute place quelconque peut exiger pour sa défense " (*ibid.*, 385).

[2] " H. O." (Adm. Medit., 1793), Hood to Dundas, 24th November.

[3] *Ibid.* O'Hara to Hood. This reached London on 8th December; but,
as we have seen, Ministers up to 22nd December continued to rely on the
arrival of the Austrians as providing a sufficient reinforcement.

chief of the allied forces (23rd October). To this Hood stoutly
demurred, on the ground that he received Toulon in trust before
the Spaniards appeared; and, though it was true that the Spanish troops outnumbered the British, yet the command of the
Neapolitan and Sardinian contingents belonged of right to the
subsidizing Power. He therefore claimed the supreme command
for General O'Hara. This matter caused much annoyance at
Madrid, where that rankling sore, Nootka Sound, was still kept
open by the all-powerful Minister, Alcudia. Hood's testiness
increased the friction at Toulon. The Spaniards were justified
in claiming equality at that fortress; for only by their arrival
did the position become tenable; and the joint proclamations of
Hood and Langara formed a tacit admission of that equality.
But Pitt early resolved to take a firm stand on this subject. On
17th October, in discussing the instructions for Sir Gilbert
Elliot, the British Commissioner designated for Toulon, he declared that we must appoint him governor of that town in consequence of its surrender to us.[1]

Pitt kept up this stiff attitude, and on 30th November stated
to St. Helens that, as Toulon surrendered to Hood alone
(Langara having declined to share in the original enterprise)
England must appoint the commander-in-chief, especially as she
could not transfer to a Spaniard the command of her subsidized
Allies. The despatch concluded thus: " His Majesty has in no
case any view upon that place different from that which has
been avowed in his name—that at the conclusion of peace that
port should be restored to the crown of France and that in the
interval it should serve in His Majesty's hands as a means of
carrying on the war and as a pledge of indemnity to him and
his Allies, including the Crown of Spain, whose claim to indemnity His Majesty has so distinctly avowed." [2]

These words were added because the French Royalists and the
Spaniards asserted that England's high-handed conduct at
Toulon arose from her resolve to make of it a second Gibraltar.
The insinuation struck home then, and has been widely repeated.[3]
But, on the first receipt of the news of the gain of Toulon,
Grenville declared explicitly to the Austrian Court " that what-

[1] " Dropmore P.," ii, 447; " Mems. of Sir G. Elliot," ii, 190, et seq.
[2] " F. O.," Spain, 28.
[3] Even by M. Cottin in his works, " Toulon et les Anglais," " L'Angleterre
et les Princes."

ever indemnification is to be acquired by this country must be looked for in the foreign settlements and colonies of France."[1] As we shall see in later chapters, Corsica and the French West Indies were the acquisitions aimed at by the Pitt Ministry.

Some colour was given to this charge by the refusal of the British Government to allow the Comte de Provence, the *soi-disant* Regent of France, to proceed to Toulon. Grenville even instructed Francis Drake, our envoy at Genoa, to prevent him embarking at that port. At first sight this conduct seems indefensible, especially as the Court of Madrid favoured the Prince's scheme. It must be remembered, however, that the British Government had consistently refused to acknowledge the Prince as Regent, and was now exceedingly annoyed with him for announcing his resolve to go to Toulon, without first applying for permission to George III.[2] This violation of etiquette prejudiced his case from the outset. Further, the Royalists of Toulon had declared for Louis XVII, and a majority of them throughout France opposed the claim of "Monsieur" to the Regency. The constitution of 1791 gave him no such right on his own initiative; and, as Toulon stood for that constitution, not for the "pure" royalism which he now championed, his arrival would place the garrison "at the discretion of wild and hot-headed emigrants and expose them to the reproaches and discontents of the Regent's Court."[3] Besides, what could the Regent of France do in Toulon, a town closely besieged and in danger of being taken? His dignity and influence would be far better maintained by remaining at large than by proceeding thither.[4]

Finally, the two princes had given no assurance or promise that they would recognize the claims of the Allies to indemnities from France for the expenses of the war.[5] On this last matter the *émigrés* were beginning to raise shrill protests at London; and it was certainly wise to come to some understanding with

[1] "F. O.," Austria, 34. Grenville to Eden, 7th September. So in his letter of 4th October to Pitt he refers to "such other towns or districts [in S. France] as may become objects of indemnity." See, too, "Dropmore P.," ii, 412, 438; Vivenot, iii, 326.

[2] "Dropmore P.," iii, 487.   [3] "H. O.," 455, *ad fin.*

[4] "Malmesbury Diaries," iii, 33.

[5] "F. O.," Spain, 28. Grenville to St. Helens, 22nd October 1793. Cottin omits this despatch, which is essential to the understanding of British policy. See for further details C. J. Fox, "Bonaparte at the Siege of Toulon," bk. ii, ch. ii.

the princes on this point before they were put in possession of Provence. Pitt and Grenville were not made of the same stuff as the Ministers in power in 1815, who demanded no return for the sacrifices of blood and treasure in the Waterloo campaign. None the less, it is certain that Pitt and his cousin had no thought of keeping either Dunkirk or Toulon, save as a pledge for the acquisition of some of the French West Indies and Corsica.[1] This was hinted at plainly in the British Declaration issued at Toulon on 20th November:

That altho' at the conclusion of peace, we shall think ourselves entitled to stipulate such terms as may afford just security to ourselves and our Allies, and a reasonable indemnification for the risks and expenses of a war in which, without any provocation on our part, we have been compelled to engage, yet that, for our part our views of indemnification can only have relation to places not on the Continent of Europe.

After this explicit statement, there ought to have been no bickerings about British aggrandisement at Toulon. Some of the hot-heads in that town (echoed by Fox later on at Westminster) chose to consider the Declaration as an infraction of Hood's promise that he would hold Toulon merely in trust for Louis XVII. The difference, however was not vital. Pitt and Grenville intended to hold Toulon merely as a pledge that the British claims to an indemnity elsewhere would be satisfied. Spain had most cause for annoyance with the Declaration, inasmuch as she, though having a superior number of troops in that town, was neither allowed to consider it as a pledge for her future indemnities, nor to share in its government. It was confided to three Commissioners—Sir Gilbert Elliot, Hood, and O'Hara, Elliot being virtually Governor.

In one other matter the Courts of St. James and of Madrid were at variance. The latter urged the need of speedily removing the French warships from Toulon to a Spanish port, or of making preparations for burning them. Whereas Pitt, who regarded Toulon, not as a windfall, but as a base of operations for a campaign in Provence, maintained that such conduct must

[1] "F. O.," Spain, 28. On 30th November Grenville instructed St. Helens to express regret that Spain seemed to retract her wish, previously expressed, that Corsica should go to England; and also to advise that Spain should take her indemnity from France on the Pyrenean frontier.

blight their prospects. With phenomenal stupidity, Langara allowed his secret instructions on this topic to leak out, thereby rousing the rage of the Toulonese and the contempt of his British colleagues. The Duke of Alcudia (better known as Godoy) expressed sincere regret for this *bêtise*. But the mischief was done. The French royalists thenceforth figured as traitors who had let in a band of thieves intent only on the seizure of the French warships.

As if this were not enough, Hood quarrelled with our military officers, with results highly exasperating to our land forces.[1] These last did not shine during the siege. True, in the sortie of 29th November they captured a battery recently erected north of Malbosquet; but, their eagerness exceeding their discipline, they rushed on, despite orders to remain in the battery, like a pack of hounds after a fox (wrote Hood);[2] whereupon the French rushed upon them, driving them back with heavy loss. O'Hara, while striving to retrieve the day, was wounded and captured. His mantle of gloom devolved upon Major-General David Dundas, a desponding officer, who had recently requested leave to return on furlough on the ground of ill health and inability to cope with the work. This general's letters to his ever confident relative, Henry Dundas, at Whitehall, were always in a minor key. In his eyes the Spanish troops were "everything that is bad"; half of the Toulonese were hostile to the Allies; and the latter were heavily handicapped by having to defend their own fleets. There was some truth in this; but the whining tone of the letters, due to ill health, drew from the Minister a stinging retort, to the effect that the occupation of Toulon had taken Ministers wholly by surprise; that they had done their best to comply with the new demands for troops, and expected their general not to look at his own difficulties alone, but to remember those of the enemy and endeavour to beat him.[3]

This was the spirit in which Hood faced the problem. Even at the close of November, when all hope of the arrival of the 5,000 Austrians was past, he refused to listen to David Dundas's advice for the evacuation of Toulon; and surely this pertinacity was consonant with the traditions of the British navy, and of the

---

[1] Fortescue, iv, 172.   [2] "H. O.," Adm. Medit., 1793.

[3] "H. O.," Mil., 455. Fortescue (iv, 175) vehemently censures Henry Dundas, but I think without sufficient ground. The letters of David Dundas called for reproof. See Mr. Oscar Browning's "Youth of Napoleon" (App. iv).

army in its better days; but out of this question arose a feud between army and navy which developed in Corsica with disastrous results. Ministers strove to send all the succour available. But they did not hear until 22nd December that the 5,000 Austrians were being withheld. Henry Dundas's letter of the 28th also breathes deep concern at the news that Sir R. Boyd had not forwarded from Gibraltar the reinforcements ordered thence. Further, it appears from an official estimate drawn up at Whitehall on 18th December, that the troops already at or ordered to Toulon were believed to be as follows: British, 2,828; Spanish, 4,147; Sardinians, 2,162; Neapolitans, 8,600. Dundas also included the 1,100 British troops ordered from Gibraltar (where at that time there was no chance of an attack), and 2,361 men under directions to sail from Cork, but which could not stir owing to the non-arrival of the transports.[1] The resulting total of 21,198 is, of course, merely a sign of Henry Dundas's optimism. But obviously Ministers were unaware of the acute crisis at Toulon at the time of its surrender. In the age of telegraphy, that disaster would have been averted. The delays of the Austrians, and the muddles at Gibraltar and Cork, would have been known betimes.

Strange to say, there was at that time lying at anchor at Spithead a force under Lord Moira's command, destined for Brittany, but held back for various causes, which would probably have turned the balance at Toulon, had Ministers known of the dire need of reinforcements. It is mortifying to read the letters of Pitt and the Marquis of Buckingham early in December, complaining that Moira's force is strangely inactive.[2] Still more startling is it to read the hurried order of 23rd December (six days after the loss of Toulon), that the 40th regiment, then unexpectedly detained at Cork, though detached for service with Lord Moira, should set sail at once for the French stronghold along with the other regiments also detained at Cork.[3] What might not have happened, had those troops set sail for Toulon before the close of November?

Hero-worshippers will probably maintain that, even if Toulon had been held harmoniously by all the troops which the imagination of Pitt and Dundas conjured up, nevertheless the genius and

[1] Pitt MSS., 331; "H. O.," Mil., 455.
[2] "Dropmore P.," ii, 476, 477; "Mems. of Sir G. Elliot," ii, 198.
[3] Admiralty. Out Letters, xiii.

daring of the little Corsican would have prevailed. This view is tenable; but the prosaic mind, which notes the venturesome extension of Bonaparte's batteries in November—December, until they presented their right flanks to the cliffs and their rear to the open sea, though at too high a level to be cannonaded, will probably conclude that, if Hood and Langara had had a force of 20,000 men, they could have driven the French from those works. As it was, the Allies, not having enough men, stood on the defensive all along their very extensive front, and were overpowered at Fort Mulgrave, which was some miles away from the city. Its garrison of 700 men (British, Spanish, and a few Neapolitans) was assailed in the stormy night of 16th-17th December by 7,000 of the best of the Republican troops. The ensuing conflict will best be understood from the hitherto unpublished account given by the commander-in-chief. After describing the heavy cannonade from three French batteries against Fort Mulgrave, he continues thus:

H.M.S. "Victory," Hières Bay, Dec. 21, 1793.[1]

. . . The works suffered much. The number of men killed and wounded was considerable. The weather was rainy and the consequent fatigue great. At 2 a.m. of the 17th, the enemy, who had every advantage in assembling and suddenly advancing, attacked the fort in great force. Although no part of this temporary post was such as could well resist determined troops, yet for a considerable time it was defended; but, on the enemy entering on the Spanish side, the British quarter, commanded by Captain Conolly of the 18th regiment, could not be much longer maintained, notwithstanding several gallant efforts were made for that purpose. It was therefore at last carried, and the remains of the garrison of 700 men retired towards the shore of Balaguier, under the protection of the other posts established on those heights, and which continued to be faintly attacked by the enemy. As this position of Balaguier was a most essential one for the preservation of the harbour, and as we had no communication with it but by water, 2,200 men had been placed there for some time past. On the night preceding the attack, 300 more men had been sent over, and on the morning of the 17th, 400 were embarked still further to support it.

When the firing at Balaguier ceased, we remained in anxious suspense as to the event, till a little before daylight, when a new scene opened by an attack on all our posts on Mt. Pharon. The enemy were repulsed on the east side, where was our principal force of about 700 men, commanded by a most distinguished officer, the Piedmontese Colonel, de Jermagnan, whose loss we deeply lament; but on the back of the mountain—near 1,800 feet high, steep, rocky, deemed almost inaccessible, and which we had laboured much to make so—they found means once more to penetrate between our posts, which occupied an extent of above two miles, guarded by about 450 men; and in a very short space of time we saw that with great numbers they crowned all that side of the mountain which overlooks the town.

In this despatch David Dundas proclaimed his own incompetence. For some time it had been obvious that the Republicans were about to attack Fort Mulgrave, which everybody knew to be essential to the defence of the fleet. Yet he took no steps to strengthen this "temporary post" so that it might resist a determined attack. He also entrusted one half of the battery to the Spaniards whom he had declared to be "everything that is bad." On his own showing, as many as 2,500 allied troops were near at hand on the Balaguier or Eguilette heights to act as supports, before Bonaparte's attack began; and 400 more were sent thither soon afterwards. A spirited attack by those troops on the victors at Fort Mulgrave on its blind side might have retrieved the day; but a panic seized part of the supports, whom Sidney Smith describes as rushing like swine towards the sea though the enemy was only in a condition to attack "faintly." Hood was furious at this spiritless acceptance of defeat; and in his despatch to Whitehall censured the troops for not making a timely effort;[1] but as David Dundas had all along opined that the place was untenable, he decided to hold a council of war. It registered the wishes of the desponding chief. The officers decided that it was impossible either to retake the two positions lost, or to establish a post on the outer, or Cepet, peninsula, capable of protecting the roadstead from the cross fires which the French would pour in from the Balaguier and Cape Brun promontories.

During the next three days the evacuation took place amidst scenes of misery for the royalist refugees that baffle the imagination. As many as 14,877 were crowded on board the British ships, together with some 8,000 troops. At the same time Captains Sidney Smith, Hare, and Edge, with a picked body of men burnt or otherwise damaged 27 French warships left in the har-

---

[1] "H. O.," Adm. Medit., 1794.

bour, while 18 were brought away by the Allies. Eleven of the twenty-seven were not seriously injured by the fire, and they afterwards flew the tricolour. But the loss of 34 warships and nearly all the masts and other valuable stores was a blow from which the French navy did not recover until Bonaparte before his Egyptian expedition breathed his own matchless vigour into the administration. In ships and stores, then, France suffered far more heavily than the Allies. Their losses elude the inquiries of the statistician. They consisted in the utter discredit of the royalist cause throughout France, the resentment that ever follows on clumsy or disloyal co-operation, and the revelation of the hollowness of the imposing fabric of the First Coalition. In the south of France four nations failed to hold a single fortress which her own sons had placed in their power.

The Nemesis which waits upon weakness and vacillation has rarely appeared in more mocking guise than at the close of the year 1793 About the time when Toulon surrendered, the Austrian Government finally came to the determination to despatch thither the 5,000 men which it had formerly promised to send. Grenville received this news from Eden in the first days of 1794, shortly after the surrender of the fortress was known. Thereupon he penned these bitter words: " If the first promise had been fulfilled agreeably to the expectation which His Majesty was justified in forming, the assistance of such a body of disciplined troops would have sufficed to ensure the defence of that important post; and the injury which the common cause has sustained on this occasion can be ascribed only to the tardiness and indecision which so strongly characterize the Austrian Government." [1] Most tactfully he bade Eden refrain from reproaches on this occasion and to use it merely as an argument for throwing greater vigour into the next campaign.

Events pointed the moral far more strongly than Eden could do. As by a lightning flash, the purblind politicians of Vienna could now discern the storm-wrack drifting upon them. The weakness of the Piedmontese army, their own unpreparedness in the Milanese, the friendliness of Genoa to France, and the Jacobinical ferment in all parts of Italy, portended a speedy irruption of the Republicans into an almost defenceless land where they were sure of a welcome from the now awakened populace.

---

[1] " F. O.," Austria, 36. Grenville to Eden, 3rd January 1794.

So long as Toulon held out, Piedmont and Milan were safe.
Now, the slackness of Austria enabled her future destroyer to
place his foot on the first rung of the ladder of fame, and
prompted those mighty plans for the conquest of the Italian
States which were to ensure her overthrow and his supremacy.

Well might Eden dwell on the consternation prevalent at
Vienna early in 1794. For, along with news of the loss of
Toulon, tidings of defeat and retreat came from the Rhineland.
Able and vigorous young generals, Hoche and Pichegru, had
beaten back Austrians and Prussians from the hills around
Wörth and Weissenburg; so that the Allies fell back with heavy
losses towards the Rhine. Thus, on the whole, the efforts of
Austria, Great Britain, Prussia, Holland, and some of the smaller
German States had availed merely to capture four fortresses,
Mainz, Condé, Valenciennes, and Quesnoy. It is not surprising
that public opinion in England, even in loyal circles, became
clamorous against the conduct of the war.[1]

Not the least of the misfortunes attending the Toulon episode
was that the logic of events, and also the growing savagery of
the Reign of Terror, edged Pitt away from his standpoint of
complete neutrality as to the future government of France.
How could the ally of the Toulonese Royalists profess indifference on that topic? On 5th October he wrote as follows to
Grenville respecting the powers to be granted to Sir Gilbert
Elliot at Toulon:

I do not see that we can go on secure grounds if we treat with any
separate districts or bodies of men [in France] who stop short of some
declaration in favour of monarchy: nor do I see any way so likely to
unite considerable numbers in one vigorous effort as by specifying
monarchy as the only system in the re-establishment of which we are
disposed to concur. This idea by no means precludes us from treating
with any other form of regular Government, if, in the end, any other
should be solidly established; but it holds out monarchy as the only
one from which we expect any good, and in favour of which we are
disposed to enter into concert.[2]

These words are remarkable. Clearly, in Pitt's view of things,
" security " for England and Holland was the paramount aim;
but he was beginning to feel that the Republican groups which
scrambled to power at Paris over the headless trunks of their

[1] Pellew, " Sidmouth," i, 112.   [2] " Dropmore P.," ii, 438.

enemies, could offer no adequate security. When the Revolution began to solidify, as it seemed about to do in 1795-7, he was willing to treat with its chiefs; but already he was feeling the horns of the dilemma, which may be described in words adapted from Talleyrand's famous *mot* of the year 1814: "Either the Bourbons or the Republic: everything else is an intrigue." The Toulon episode, more than anything else, bound France to the regicide cause, and Pitt, albeit unwillingly, to the irreconcilable Royalists. Thus the event which brought Bonaparte to the front, shattered the aim of the Prime Minister to effect merely the restoration of the Balance of Power.

CHAPTER VII

THE BRITISH JACOBINS

The much better way doubtless will be, in this wavering condition of our affairs, to defer the changing or circumscribing of our Senate more than may be done with ease till the Commonwealth be thoroughly settled in peace and safety.—MILTON, *A Free Commonwealth.*

> But cease, ye fleecing Senators
> Your country to undo,
> Or know, we British *sans-culottes*
> Hereafter may fleece you.
> THELWALL, *A Shearing Song.*

THE outbreak of hostilities often tends to embitter the strife of parties. Those who oppose war find abundant cause for criticism in the conduct of Ministers, who in their turn perforce adopt measures alien to the traditions of Westminster. A system founded on compromise cannot suddenly take on the ways of a military State; and efforts in this direction generally produce more friction than activity. At such times John Bull, flurried and angry, short-sighted but opinionated, bewildered but dogged as ever, is a sight to move the gods to laughter and his counsellors to despair.

The events of the session of 1793 illustrate my meaning. In view of the notorious sympathy of the Radical Clubs with France, Pitt proposed a Bill against Traitorous Correspondence with the enemy. Both he and Burke proved that the measure, far from being an insidious attack on the liberties of the subject, merely aimed at enforcing " the police of war." Nevertheless, it passed only by a majority of one—a warning to the Ministry not to proceed further in that doubtful course (9th April 1793). Pitt had the full support of the House in opposing Grey's motion for Parliamentary Reform, which was thrown out by 282 votes to 41. The war spirit also appeared in a sharp rebuff given to Wilberforce and the Abolitionists on 14th May. The institution

THE HOUSE OF COMMONS IN 1793

(FROM A PAINTING BY H. A. HICKEL IN THE NATIONAL PORTRAIT GALLERY)

of a Board of Agriculture (which Hussey, Sheridan, and Fox opposed as a piece of jobbery) and the renewal of the Charter of the East India Company were the chief practical results of that session. But the barrenness of the session, the passing of the Traitorous Correspondence Bill, and the hardships connected with the balloting for the militia stirred the Radical Clubs to redoubled energy; so that home affairs for two or three years centred in their propaganda and in Pitt's repressive efforts. The development of a keen political consciousness in the masses is a subject of so much interest that I may be pardoned for dwelling on it somewhat fully, with the aid of new materials drawn from the Home Office Archives.

There we see the causes of unrest. Hunger, hatred of the militia laws, chafing against restraints entailed by the war, all conduce to discontent. The newly awakened Caliban is also a prey to suspicion. He hates foreigners. Yet, either as refugees or prisoners, they swarm along the south coast (there were for a time 5,000 prisoners in Winchester). Fishermen are tempted to help in their escape, and a mariner of Emsworth is arraigned for treason on this count. Even so far west as Bodmin the prisoners are numerous and threatening. They convince many of the townsfolk that England would be better off as a Republic; and two patriotic ladies in fear and horror inform Lord Mount Edgcumbe anonymously that Frenchmen cut a mark round the neck of King George on all coins. The vicar of Ringmer, near Lewes, reports that the smugglers of the Sussex coast carry on a regular intercourse with France. In the Isle of Wight even the French royalists, who are there awaiting the despatch of Lord Moira's long-deferred expedition to Brittany, figure as murderous Jacobins. In Bath, too, the mayor, Mr. Harington, is troubled by the influx of Gallic artists and dancing-masters, especially as they mix in all the "routs," and dare even there to whisper treason against King George. Another report comes that a French usher in a large school near London—was it Harrow?—has converted several of the boys to republicanism. Clearly, these are cases for the Aliens Act.

Even Britons, untainted by Gallic connections, are suspect. At Billingsgate a soldier swears that he was set upon at night because he wore the uniform of "a d——d tyrant"; and other evidence proves that the service was unpopular for political reasons as well as the poor pay. Farmers are plied by emissaries of the clubs as they come in to market. Complaints come to Dundas that farmers and shippers on the coasts of Lancashire and Cumberland sell corn to "the natural enemy."

The discontent takes colour from its surroundings. At Pocklington in Yorkshire the villagers threaten to burn the magistrates in their houses in revenge for the conviction of poachers. The rowdies of Olney in Bucks. (formerly a sore trial to Cowper and John Newton) terrorize the neighbourhood. Everywhere the high price of corn produces irritation. The tinworkers of North Cornwall march in force to Padstow to prevent the exportation of corn from that little harbour; otherwise they are law-abiding, though a magistrate warns Dundas that local malcontents are setting them against the Government. Multiply these typical cases a thousand fold, and it will be seen that the old rural system is strained to breaking point. The amenities of the rule of the squires are now paid back, and that, too, at a time when England needs one mind, one heart, one soul. At and near Sheffield serious riots break out owing to the enclosures of common-fields and wastes, the houses of the agricultural "reformers" being burnt or wrecked. On the whole, however, I have found fewer references to enclosures than might be expected.[1]

As generally happens in times of excitement, the towns are the first to voice the dumb or muttering hatreds of the villages. Parisians led the Revolution in France, though its causes lay thickest and deepest in the rural districts. Not until Paris "stormed" its castle did the villagers attack theirs. So, too, in the muffled repetition of the revolutionary music which England sounds forth, the towns buzz, while the country supplies but a dull ground-tone. Dearness of food and scarcity of work were the chief causes of discontent. The spokesmen for the Spitalfields weavers, who number 14,000, sent up a temperate petition setting forth their distress; but, as is often the case in London, their thoughts turned not to politics, but to practical means of cure. They stated that the trade in velvets, brocades, and rich silks would be absolutely ruined unless steps were taken to revive the fashion in these fabrics. In Liverpool there were far other grievances. There, as in all seaports, the tyranny of the press-gang was sharply resented; and, early in November 1793, the populace clamoured for the election of a "liberty-loving mayor,"

---

[1] See "The Complaints of the Poor People of England," by G. Dyer, B.A. (late of Emmanuel College, Camb., 1793).

Mr. Tarleton, who promised to keep the press-gang out of the town.[1]

In general the malcontents urged their case most pointedly in towns and villages, where branches of the Radical Societies had taken root. These Societies or clubs continued to grow in number and influence through the year 1793, the typical club being now concerned, not with faro, but with the "Rights of Man." Some of the Reform Clubs sought to moderate the Gallicizing zeal of the extreme wing. Thus, the "Friends of the People," whose subscription of two and a half guineas was some guarantee for moderation, formally expressed their disapproval of Paine's works and all Republican agencies—a futile declaration ; for his "Rights of Man" was the very life-blood of the new clubs. Working men had shown little or no interest in the earlier motions for Reform. The Associations of the years 1780-5 had lapsed ; and it was clearly the joint influence of the French Revolution and Paine's productions which led to the remarkable awakening of the year 1792.

Besides the London Corresponding Society, started (as we saw in Chapter III) by Thomas Hardy early in that year, there was another formidable organization, the Society for Constitutional Information, founded in London at the close of 1791. It, too, was concerned with much more than the Reform of Parliament; for on 18th May 1792 it recommended the publication in a cheap form of Paine's "Rights of Man"; and on 21st November it appointed a Committee for Foreign Correspondence. A little later were adopted some of the phrases used in the French Convention, and St. André, Roland, and Barrere were admitted to membership. It does not appear that either this Society, or Hardy's, corresponded with France after the declaration of war; for the Parliamentary Committee of Secrecy, charged in 1794 to report on seditious proceedings would, if it were possible, have fastened on so compromising an act. Its members belonged to a higher class than those of Hardy's Society; for they included Romney the painter, Holcroft the dramatist, Horne Tooke, the humorous *littérateur*, and Thelwall, the ablest lecturer of the day.[2] That these men had advanced far beyond the standpoint of the Whiggish " Friends

---

[1] "H. O.," Geo. III (Domestic), 27, 28.

[2] E. Smith, "The English Jacobins," 111-3; C. Cestre, "John Thelwall," ch. ii.

of the People," appears from a letter from one of the Norwich
Radical Clubs to the London Corresponding Society:

> The Friends of the People mean only a partial Reform, because they
> leave out words expressing the Duke of Richmond's plan and talk only
> of a Reform; while the Manchester people seem to intimate, by ad-
> dressing Mr. Paine, as though they were intent upon Republican prin-
> ciples only. Now, to come closer to the main question, it is only
> desired to know whether the generality of the Societies mean to rest
> satisfied with the Duke of Richmond's plan only, or whether it is their
> private design to rip up monarchy by the roots and place democracy in
> its stead.[1]

These Societies seem to have put forth no definite programme.
Their defenders claimed that they adhered to the Westminster
programme of 1780, championed by Fox and the Duke of Richmond. But Fox strongly disapproved of their aims, and even
refused to present their petition for annual parliaments and
universal suffrage.[2] In truth, the actions of these bodies belied
their words. They largely devoted their funds and their energies
to the circulation in a cheap form of the works of Paine,
200,000 copies being sold in 1793,[3] and still more in the following year. The Societies also adopted methods of organization
similar to those of the French Jacobins Club, and advocated the
assembly of a representative Convention. Every sixteen members
of the London Corresponding Society could form a division; and
the divisions, by the process of swarming-off, rapidly extended the
organization. They also sent delegates who conferred on matters
of importance, either locally or at headquarters; and the head
delegation finally claimed to represent very large numbers in
London and affiliated centres. In the conduct of details Spartan
self-restraint was everywhere manifest. Members were urged to
be brief in their remarks and business-like in their methods.
Officials must give a solemn promise not to skulk, or make off,
owing to persecution; and members were warned that noisy
declamation was not a proof of zeal but might be a cloak for
treachery. Above the chairman's seat was suspended a card with

---

[1] "Report of the Committee of Secrecy," May 1794. The Duke of Richmond's plan was the Westminster programme of 1780, which became the
"six points" of the Charter of 1838.

[2] See Fox's letter of 2nd May 1793 to Hardy in "State Trials," xxiv, 791.

[3] M. Conway, "Life of T. Paine," i, 346.

the words—"Beware of Orators." One would like to have witnessed the proceedings of these dully earnest men.

Both in the provinces and in London, reformers of the old type sought to curb the more dangerous of these developments, especially correspondence with the Jacobins' Club at Paris. Thus, the Manchester Constitutional Society having published its address of congratulation to that body, together with the reply of Carras, a member, George Lloyd, entered a formal protest in these terms: "We are not a Republican Society; but from such connection and correspondence we shall involve ourselves in the imputation of Republicanism." He added that their aim was solely the Reform of Parliament, and with that foreigners had no concern whatever.[1] Nevertheless the Society kept up its foreign correspondence, and received addresses from Jacobin Clubs in France.

Another threatening symptom was the attempt to excite discontent among the soldiery. There being then very few barracks, the men were quartered on the public houses; and several petitions were sent to Whitehall by publicans (sometimes even by Corporations), pointing out the many inconveniences of this custom. Thus in the autumn of 1793 the publicans of Winchester complained that they had had to lodge as many as 5,000 men during their passage through that city, besides the Bucks. regiment stationed there, and they begged that barracks might be built. The authorities paid the more heed to these petitions because local malcontents "got at" the soldiery in the taverns, and brought home to them their grievances, namely, poor pay, insufficient allowance for food at its enhanced prices, and the severities of discipline exercised by "effeminate puppies" drawn from aristocratic circles. In particular they circulated a pamphlet—"The Soldiers' Friend: or Considerations on the late pretended Augmentation of the Subsistence of the Private Soldiers"—pointing out the close connection between the officers and "the ruling faction," which "ever must exist while we suffer ourselves to be governed by a faction."

When the war with France unexpectedly lengthened out, the Ministry decided to erect new barracks, accommodating 34,000 men, at a total expense of about £1,400,000. In the debate of 8th April 1796, Fox and General Smith savagely

[1] In the Place MSS. (Brit. Mus.), vol. entitled "Libel, Sedition, Treason, Persecution"—a valuable collection.

assailed this proceeding as fatal to English liberty. "Good God!" exclaimed Smith, "is every town to be made a citadel and every village converted into a garrison?" Windham had little difficulty in showing that the old barracks were in general badly situated, and not adapted for cavalry. Buildings for the use of 5,400 horsemen were now erected; and on the whole question he asserted that the men would live more cheaply, and would contract less vicious habits than when lodged in inns. Above all, they would be removed from the sedition-mongers, who now plied them with doctrines destructive alike of loyalty and military discipline. Windham then quoted a phrase from Molière's "Médecin malgré lui": "If I cannot make him dumb, I will make you deaf."[1] The inference was that the inability of the Cabinet to silence malcontents involved the expenditure of £1,400,000 partly in order to stop the ears of the soldiery.

Lord Bacon, in his pregnant aphorisms upon sedition, does not venture on a definition of that indefinable term. Where, indeed, shall one draw the line between justifiable discontent and the inciting of men to lawless and violent acts? We shall notice presently the claim of a Scottish judge that an agitator may have good and upright intentions, and yet, if his words and acts lead to general discontent, he is guilty of sedition and perhaps of high treason. At the other extreme of thought stands the born malcontent. He is generally an idealist, having a keen sense of the miseries of mankind and very imperfect notions as to the difficulty of peacefully and permanently ending them. In times of political excitement the statesman has to deal with large bands of zealots nerved by these irreconcilable principles. It was the misfortune of Pitt that he sought to hold together a nation rent asunder by the doctrines of Burke and Paine. Compromise was out of the question; and yet a British states-man cannot govern unless the majority of the people is ready for compromise. His position becomes untenable if, while upholding the throne, he infuriates all friends of progress; if, when he seeks to remove abuses, he is dubbed a traitor to King, Church, and Constitution. And yet, to abandon his post because of these difficulties is not only cowardly, but also an act of disloyalty alike to King and people.

As the political thermometer rose towards fever point through the years 1792-3, Government kept closer watch upon the politi-

[1] "Parl. Hist.," xxxii, 929-44.

cal Societies; but for a long time Pitt took no action against them. It seems probable that, if they had confined themselves to their professed programme (that of the Westminster Reformers of 1780) he would have remained passive. He did not prosecute those which in November 1792 congratulated the French Convention on the triumph of its arms in Belgium and the advent of a Gallic millennium. What, then, were the developments which met with his stern opposition?

But, firstly, we must ask the question, Why did not Pitt, in view of the unswerving loyalty of the great majority of Britons, rely on the good sense and weight of that mass to overbear the Jacobinical minority? It is much to be regretted that he did not take that more intelligent and more courageous course. But the events of the French Revolution seemed to show the need of early taking decided measures against a resolute and desperate group. At half a dozen crises in the years 1789-92 firm action would have crushed the anarchic forces in Paris, Lyons, and Marseilles; but, for lack of a strong guiding hand, those forces broke loose, with results which all genuine friends of liberty have ever since deplored. It is perfectly certain that, if Mirabeau had had a free hand, he would have used coercive measures by the side of which those of Pitt's so-called "Reign of Terror" would have been but as a pop-gun to a cannon. Besides, to taunt Pitt with falseness to his principles of the years 1782-5 is to ignore the patent facts that he advocated very moderate changes in the representation. The Reform movement virtually collapsed in 1785. That which now borrowed its watchwords was in the main a Republican and levelling agency. The creed of the Radicals of 1793 was summed up, not in the academic programme of the Friends of the People, the lineal heir to the earlier Associations, but in Part II of Paine's "Rights of Man."

Here, surely, are the reasons for Pitt's repressive policy. He entered on it regretfully, but he felt no sense of inconsistency in his change of attitude towards Reform. The times had wholly changed; and that movement changed with them. As Macaulay has well pointed out, Pitt never declared that, under no circumstances, would he favour a moderate Reform of Parliament. But he did declare that in his view Reform was at present highly perilous; and he resolutely set himself to the task of coercing those men and those agencies who advocated it in dangerous forms and by lawless methods.

The first prosecution that need be noticed here was directed against Paine for the seditious utterances in the "Rights of Man," particularly in Part II. The Attorney-General made out a formidable indictment, whereupon Paine, then a member of the French National Convention, informed him that the prosecution might as well be directed against the man in the moon, and that the liberties of the people of England were in reality on their trial. After this impertinence the sentence went against Paine by default, and that, too, despite a skilful speech by Erskine (December 1792). The aim of Government of course was to warn those who were circulating Paine's works that their conduct was seditious and that they did so at their peril.

The Home Office Archives show that in very many cases the warning was disregarded, and several prosecutions ensued, with varying results. Still more frequent were the cases of cursing the King, sometimes in obscene terms. To these we need pay no heed. Frequently the offence was committed in taverns by democrats in a state of mental exaltation. To this exciting cause we may probably ascribe the folly of John Frost, the attorney with whom Pitt had some dealings during the Reform agitation of 1782. He was now charged with exclaiming excitedly: "I am for equality"; and, when challenged as to the meaning of his words, he added: "There ought to be no Kings." In this connection it should be remembered that Frost and Barlow had on 28th November 1792 presented to the French National Convention the most mischievous of all the addresses sent by Radical Clubs to that body. It ended with the statement that other nations would soon imitate France (that is by overthrowing the monarchy) and would "arm themselves for the purpose of claiming the Rights of Man."[1] This piece of bravado must have told against Frost at the trial; for it proved that amidst his potations at the tavern he spoke his real mind. Erskine did his best to defend Frost by quoting Pitt's letters to him of May 1782, on the subject of Reform.[2] The device was clever; but obviously Pitt's association with Frost for strictly constitutional purposes in 1782 could not excuse the seditious language of the latter under wholly different conditions eleven years later. Frost was condemned to six months' imprisonment in Newgate

[1] "Collection of Addresses . . . to the National Convention of France" (Debrett, 1793), 14.
[2] "Speeches of Lord Erskine," 293.

and was struck off the roll of attorneys.[1] Other noteworthy trials ensued, notably that of the "Morning Chronicle" newspaper, which ended in an acquittal; but it will be well now to turn to the important developments taking place north of the Tweed.

Scotland had now thrown off the trance under which she had lain since 1745 ; and her chief towns bade fair to outbid London, Leeds, Sheffield, and Norwich as centres of democratic activity. There was every reason why she should awake. She had very little influence in Parliament. She returned 45 members as against Cornwall's 44; while the total number of persons entitled to vote for the fifteen representatives of the Scottish burghs was 1,303,[2] a number smaller than that of the electors of the city of Westminster. This singular system was defended chiefly on the ground of the turbulence of the national character. Even in 1831 a Scottish member declared that Scots could never assemble without drawing blood; and one of their champions, Lord Cockburn, made the quaint admission: " The Scots are bad mobbers. They are too serious at it. They never joke, and they throw stones." It did not occur to that generation that the cure for this bloodthirsty seriousness was frequent public meetings, not no meetings at all. That a high-spirited people should so long have remained in political childhood seems incredible, until we remember that a borough election like that of Westminster was absolutely unknown in the whole course of Scottish history. Further, it was notorious that the 45 Scottish members were the most obedient group of placemen in the House of Commons; and their docility had increased under the bountiful sway of Henry Dundas, whose control of patronage sufficed to keep the Caledonian squad close to heel.

This political apathy was now to end. The men of Edinburgh, Glasgow, and Dundee began to discuss the " Rights of Man," and to follow the lead given by the London Corresponding Society. Thus, on 3rd October 1792, Lieutenant-Colonel William Dalrymple presided over the first meeting of " The Associated Friends of the Constitution and of the People," held at Glasgow. Resolutions were passed in favour of an equal representation of the people in Parliament, shorter Parliaments, and co-operation

---

[1] " State Trials," xxii, 471-522.   [2] Porritt, ii, 128.

with "the Friends of the People" in London. The entrance and annual subscriptions were fixed at sixpence and one shilling. Thomas Muir of Huntershill, an able young advocate, was appointed Vice-President. Other Societies were soon formed, and on 11th December there assembled at Edinburgh a General Convention of Delegates from the Societies of the Friends of the People throughout Scotland. Its proceedings were orderly, beginning and ending with prayer. Resolutions were passed deprecating violence whether in language or action; and the presence either of Lord Daer or Colonel Dalrymple in the chair showed that some, at least, of the gentry were for Reform. This was exceptional. A little later the gentlemen of several towns and counties asserted their loyalty in flamboyant petitions; and the farmers of Dalkeith district at their meeting added to their loyal toasts the following: " May we have no fox in our fold or greys (wild oats) in our corn."[1] Sir Kenneth Mackenzie on 3rd January 1793 informed William Pulteney that in the North the towns were thoroughly loyal, with the exception of Perth and Dundee, where certain ministers and writers led the people astray.[2]

Nevertheless, the authorities, notably the Lord Advocate, Robert Dundas, took alarm; and on 2nd January 1793 Thomas Muir was brought before the deputy-sheriff of Midlothian. Muir was a man of highly interesting personality. The son of a Glasgow tradesman, he had shown marked abilities at school and at the University, whence, owing to his advanced opinions, he was forced to migrate to Edinburgh. There, in his twenty-seventh year, he soon became a leader of the Scottish Reformers, his sincerity, eloquence, and enthusiasm everywhere arousing keen interest. Had his good sense been equal to his abilities, he might have gone far; but events soon showed him to be tactless and headstrong. He went far beyond the rest of the delegates assembled at Edinburgh, namely, in bringing forward, despite the reluctance of the Convention, an Address from the Society of United Irishmen in Dublin. Their conduct much alarmed the authorities at Dublin Castle, who adopted stringent precautions. Muir should therefore have seen, what his colleagues did see, that any plan of co-operation was certain to irritate Government. Nevertheless he persisted in bringing before the

---

[1] " H. O.," Scotland, 7.   [2] *Ibid.*

Convention the Irish Address, which strongly pointed out the need of common action in the struggle for Reform and urged both peoples to persevere "until we have planted the flag of freedom on the summit, and are at once victorious and secure." Further, the authorities accused Muir of circulating Paine's writings and other pamphlets, including "A Dialogue between the Governors and the Governed," which contained such sentences as these: "The law is the general will—a new order." "Nations cannot revolt; tyrants are the only rebels." "We will live without tyrants, without impostors (priests)."[1] The writings were probably seditious in their tendency;[2] but the evidence that he circulated them was of the flimsiest character.[3]

Unfortunately, Muir left the country, though in no clandestine manner, while legal proceedings were pending. After a short stay in London he proceeded to Paris, in order (as he said at his trial) to try to persuade the French democrats to spare the life of Louis XVI. The credibility of this statement is lessened by the fact that he arrived in Paris only the evening before the King's execution and remained there long after that tragedy.[4] A letter from a Scot in Paris, James Smith, to a friend in Glasgow, which the postal authorities opened, stated that the writer met Muir in a *café* of the Palais Royal; that Muir did not hear of his indictment till the evening of 8th February, and would return to face his trial, though he was loth to leave France, as he had made "valuable and dear connections." "Mr. Christie advised me," adds the writer, "to make some little proficiency in the language before I begin to think of beginning to do anything."[5] Now, as a clique of Britons in Paris had not long before drunk the toast of "The coming Convention of Great Britain and Ireland," Government naturally connected the efforts of Muir with this republican propaganda. His next doings increased this suspicion. He left France on an American ship which

---

[1] "State Trials," xxiii, 118-26.

[2] I differ here from Lord Cockburn, "Examination of the Trials for Sedition in Scotland," i, 147.

[3] *Ibid.*, i, 162-5; "State Trials," xxiii, 146-8, 160.

[4] P. Mackenzie, "Life of Muir," does not state the reason for Muir's visit to Paris.

[5] "H. O.," Scotland, 8. Dunlop, Lord Provost of Glasgow, sent it to Robert Dundas on 12th March 1793. For this William Christie, who translated the French Constitution of 1791 into English, see Alger, "Englishmen in the French Revolution," 78, 98.

landed him at Belfast; he stayed there a few days, and landed at Stranraer on 31st July, only to be arrested, along with his books and papers, and sent to Edinburgh.

The ensuing trial, held on 30th and 31st August, aroused intense interest, owing to the eloquence of Muir and the unscrupulous zeal of the Scottish authorities in ensuring his conviction. They packed the jury with men who belonged to a loyal Association; and it is said that the Lord Justice Clerk, McQueen of Braxfield, welcomed one of them with the words: "Come awa', Maister Horner, come awa', and help us to hang ane of thae daamed scoondrels." The trial itself bristled with irregularities; and Muir, who rejected the proffered help of Erskine and conducted his own defence, fastened on them so effectively, that at the conclusion of his final speech the Court resounded with applause. All was in vain. The jury found him guilty, whereupon the Court of Justiciary pronounced sentence of transportation for fourteen years.[1]

Admiration of the virtues and courage of Muir must not blind us to the fact that his conduct had been most provocative. His visit to Paris, on the scarcely credible pretext that he went thither to save the King's life, his connection with the United Irishmen, and his stay in Belfast, told against him. Robert Dundas, in informing his uncle, Henry Dundas, of his arrest, added: "I have little doubt that, tho' he avows his intention of coming home to have been a view to stand trial, [that] he is an emissary from France or the disaffected in Ireland."[2] The Scot who first advocated common action with the Irish malcontents should have paid good heed to his steps. Muir did not do so. Accordingly, though the direct evidence at the trial told in his favour, the circumstantial evidence weighed heavily against him.[3] At such a time men's actions count for more than their words. It was the visit to Paris and the dealings with the United Irishmen, far more than biassed witnesses and the bullying of Braxfield, which led to the condemnation of this talented youth. For his

[1] See Campbell, "Lives of the Lord Chancellors," vii, 273, note, and viii, 143-5, for criticisms on the judges: also Cockburn, *op. cit.*, i, 147-80; "Life of Romilly," i, 23.

[2] "H. O.," Scotland, 8. Letter of 2nd August 1793. Dundas further stated that Muir had several Irish handbills on him.

[3] Curiously enough, Lord Cockburn paid no heed to this in his otherwise able examination of the case.

arrest occurred at the time when terror was the order of the day at Paris, and when the issue of an inflammatory address at Dundee spread panic in official circles.

Before adverting to this matter, we may note that Muir settled down by no means unhappily at Sydney, and bought a farm which he named Huntershill, after his birthplace. It is now a suburb of Sydney. A letter from the infant settlement, published in the " Gentleman's Magazine " of March 1797, describes him and the other Scottish " martyrs "—Skirving, Margarot, and Gerrald—as treated indulgently by the authorities, who allotted to them convicts to till their lands. Shortly afterwards Muir escaped, and, after exciting experiences, in which he was wounded, made his way to France. In Paris, early in 1798, he published some articles on the United Irishmen, which Wolfe Tone and other Irish patriots deemed most harmful to their cause. They therefore remonstrated with him, but received the reply that he knew Ireland as well as they did, and had the confidence of the United Irishmen as much as they had. Wolfe Tone says of him: " Of all the vain obstinate blockheads that ever I met I never saw his equal." [1] Fortunately for his associates, Muir retired into the provinces and died in the year 1799.

Dundee played a leading part in the democratic agitation. Its population, consisting largely of poor weavers, suffered severely in the year 1793 from dearness of food and scarcity of fuel. On this mass of needy operatives the doctrines of Paine fell like a spark on tinder. Dundee became the chief focus of discontent in Scotland. A Tree of Liberty was planted in Belmont Grounds; bread riots were of frequent occurrence; and Dundas was burnt in effigy. In the Home Office Archives is a statement that a local tradesman named Wyllie generously supplied the waistcoat and breeches: " they was of satin." [2] In July 1793 there appeared an " Address to the People," dated " Berean Meeting House, Dundee," which painted the Government in the darkest colours, and contained these assertions: " You are plunged into war by a wicked Ministry and a compliant Parliament, who seem careless and unconcerned for your interest, the end and design of which is almost too horrid to relate, the destruction of a whole people merely because they will be free. . . . Your treasure is wasting fast: the blood of your brethren is pouring out, and all this to form chains for a free people and eventually

[1] T. Wolfe Tone, "Autobiography," ii, 285.   [2] "H. O.," Scotland, 7.

to rivet them on yourselves." On 1st August 1793 a Government agent found the MS. from which this placard was printed in the house of a liquor-seller in Edinburgh. It was in the writing of a minister, Palmer: so were two letters referring to it.[1] Robert Dundas therefore sent to have Palmer arrested. In mentioning this fact to Henry Dundas, he added that Palmer was "the most dangerous rebel in Scotland." It transpired in the course of the trial that the address was originally written by a weaver named Mealmaker, and that Palmer re-wrote it, toning down some expressions which he thought too strong. Mealmaker was a witness at the trial, but was not allowed directly to incriminate himself. The authorities preferred to strike at Palmer, a man of parts, educated at Eton and Cambridge, who latterly had officiated as Unitarian Minister at Montrose and Dundee. Doubtless these facts as well as his association with the Scottish Friends of Liberty brought on him a sentence of five years' transportation.[2]

If the authorities hoped to crush the Scottish movement by these severities they were disappointed; for it throve on them. A spy, "J. B.," who regularly supplied Robert Dundas with reports about the Edinburgh club, wrote on 14th September 1793 that the sentence on Palmer had given new life to the Association; for, after a time of decline in the early summer, more than 200 now attended its meetings. On 28th October he stated that nearly all the Scottish clubs had revived. Dunlop, Lord Provost of Glasgow, also declared that discontent made progress every day; that the soldiery were corrupted, and that there was an urgent need of barracks.[3] Indignation also ran high at London. Evan Nepean wrote to Robert Dundas: "There is a devil of a stir here about Muir and Palmer." Braxfield's address to the jury was thus parodied in the "Morning Chronicle" of 4th March 1794:

> I am bound by the law, while I sit in this place,
> To say in plain terms what I think of this case.
> My opinion is this, and you're bound to pursue it,
> The defendants are guilty, and I'll make them rue it.

---

[1] "H. O.," Scotland, 8. W. Scot to R. Dundas, 1st August.
[2] See the "Narrative of the Sufferings of T. F. Palmer and W. Skirving" (1794), and "Monthly Mag.," xvii, 83-5, for Palmer's adventures. He died of dysentery in 1799.
[3] "H. O.," Scotland, 9.

Nevertheless, as another Convention had met at Edinburgh, Robert Dundas wrote to his uncle on 2nd November 1793 strongly deprecating any mitigation of the sentences. It was therefore in vain that the Earl of Lauderdale, Grey, and Sheridan interviewed the Home Secretary and pointed out that the offence of " leasing-making," or verbal sedition, was punishable in Scots law only with banishment, not with forcible detention at the Antipodes.[1] Henry Dundas informed his nephew on 16th November that he would refer the whole question back to the Court of Justiciary, and if it defended the verdict " scientifically " and in full detail, he would " carry the sentence into execution and meet the clamour in Parliament without any kind of dismay."[2] Braxfield and his colleagues defended their conduct in an exhaustive treatise on " leasing-making," which the curious may read in the Home Office Archives.

What was the attitude of Pitt towards these events? Ultimately he was responsible for these unjust and vindictive sentences; and it is a poor excuse to urge that he gave Dundas a free hand in Scottish affairs. Still, it is unquestionable that the initiative lay with the two Dundases. If any Englishman exerted influence on the sentences it was the Lord Chancellor, Loughborough.[3] He treated with contempt the motion of Earl Stanhope on 31st January 1794 for an examination into the case of Muir, when the Earl found himself in the position which he so much coveted— a minority of one. On the cases of Muir and Palmer coming before the Commons (10th March), Pitt upheld the Scottish Court of Justiciary in what was perhaps the worst speech of his whole career. He defended even the careful selection of jurymen hostile to Muir on the curious plea that though they were declared loyalists, yet they might be impartial as jurymen. He further denied that there had been any miscarriage of justice, or that the sentence on the " daring delinquents " needed revision. And these excuses for biassed and vindictive sentences were urged after Fox had uttered a noble and manly plea for justice, not for mercy. Grey bitterly declared that Muir was to be sent for fourteen years to Sydney for the offence of pleading for Reform, which Pitt and the Duke of Richmond advocated twelve

[1] Their Memorial to Henry Dundas is in " H. O.," Geo. III (Domestic), 27. They did not claim that he was innocent, merely that the punishment was excessive and unjust.

[2] " Arniston Mems.," 240.   [3] Campbell, op. cit., viii, 145, 147.

years before. They sat in the King's Cabinet: Muir was sent to
herd with felons. This taunt flew wide of the mark. Pitt in his
motions for Reform had always made it clear that, while desirous
of "a moderate and substantial Reform," he utterly repudiated
universal suffrage. If those were his views in 1782-5, how could
he accept the Radical programme now that it included the absurd demand for annual Parliaments? None the less Pitt was
answerable for the action of the Home Minister in referring
the sentences back to the judges who inflicted them—a course
of conduct at once cowardly and farcical. Pitt's speech also
proves him to have known of the irregularities that disgraced the
trials. But he, a lawyer, condoned them and applauded the
harsh and vindictive sentences. In short, he acted as an alarmist,
not as a dispenser of justice.

It is easy for us now to descant on the virtues of moderation.
But how many men would have held on an even course when the
guillotine worked its fell work in France, when the Goddess of
Reason was enthroned in Notre Dame, and when Jacobinism
seemed about to sweep over the Continent? Here, as at so many
points, France proved to be the worst foe to ordered liberty.
Robespierre and Hébert were the men who assured the doom
of Muir and Palmer. A trivial incident will suffice to illustrate the
alarm of Englishmen at the assembly of a British Convention.
In December 1793 Drane, the mayor of Reading, reported to
his neighbour Addington (Speaker of the House of Commons)
that the "infamous Tom Paine" and a member of the French
Convention had been overheard conversing in French in a public-
house. Their talk turned on a proposed visit to the British
Convention then sitting in Edinburgh. At once Addington sent
for a warrant from the Home Office, while the mayor urged his
informant to hunt the miscreants down. The machinery of the
law was set in motion. A search was instituted; the warrant
came down from Whitehall; and not until the sum of fourteen
guineas had gone to the informant for his patriotic exertions did
the authorities discover that they had been hoaxed.[1]

The Edinburgh Convention, consisting of delegates of forty-
five Reform Societies, seems to have pursued dully decorous
methods until 6th November, when citizens Hamilton, Rowan,
and Simon Butler came to represent Ireland; Joseph Gerrald

---

[1] "H. O.," Geo. III (Domestic), 27.

and Maurice Margarot were the delegates from the London Corresponding Society; and Sinclair and York from the Society for Constitutional Information which met at the Crown and Anchor. A Convention of English Societies assembled at London about the same time, and deputed the four delegates to join the Edinburgh body and form a British Convention.[1] Accordingly, on 19th November, it took the title, " British Convention of Delegates of the People, associated to obtain Universal Suffrage and Annual Parliaments." The statement of Margarot, that the London police sought to prevent his journey to Edinburgh, should have been a warning to members to measure their words well. Unfortunately, Margarot, a vain hot-headed fellow, at once began to boast of the importance of the Radical Societies; though fluctuating in number, they were numerous in London; there were thirty of them in Norwich; and in the Sheffield district their members numbered 50,000. " If," he added, " we could get a Convention of England and Scotland called, we might represent six or seven hundred thousand males, which is a majority of all the adults of the Kingdom; and the Ministry would not dare to refuse our rights."[2] Butler then declared that Belfast was in a state of veiled rebellion; Gerrald, the ablest and best educated of the delegates, also scoffed at the old party system, and said, " party is ever a bird of prey, and the people their banquet." On 19th November a delegate from Sheffield, M. C. Brown, moved that the next British Convention should meet near the borders of England and Scotland. Thereupon Gerrald proposed that York should be chosen, despite its ecclesiastical surroundings; for (said he), " as the Saviour of the world was often found in the company of sinners, let us go there for the same gracious purpose, to convert to repentance."[3]

All this was but the prelude to more serious work. On 26th-28th November the Convention declared it to be the duty of citizens to resist any law, similar to that lately passed in Dublin, for preventing the assembly of a Convention in Great Britain; and the delegates resolved to prepare to summon a Convention if the following emergencies should arise—an invasion, the landing of Hanoverian troops, the passing of a Con-

---

[1] For the instructions see E. Smith, "The Story of the English Jacobins," 87.
[2] " State Trials," xxiii, 414.
[3] J. Gerrald had published a pamphlet, "A Convention the only Means of saving us from Ruin" (1793). It is in the British Museum.

vention Act, or the suspension of the Habeas Corpus Act. These
defiant resolutions were proposed by Sinclair; and, as he afterwards became a Government informer, they were probably
intended to lure the Convention away from its proper business
into seditious ways. However that may be, the delegates
solemnly assented to these resolutions.

Scotsmen will notice alike with pride and indignation that the
delegates of the Societies north of the Tweed adhered to their
main purpose, Parliamentary Reform, until, under the lead of
the men of London, Sheffield, and Dublin, debates became
almost Parisian in vehemence. As reported in the " Edinburgh
Gazetteer" of 3rd December, they gave Robert Dundas the
wished-for handle of attack. Then and there he decided to disperse the Convention, so he informed Henry Dundas in the
following letter of 6th December: " Last Tuesday's '[Edinburgh]
Gazetteer,' containing a further account of the proceedings of
the Convention appeared to the Solicitor and me so strong that
we agreed to take notice of them. The proper warrants were
accordingly made, and early yesterday morning put in execution
against Margarot, Gerrald, Callender, Skirving, and one or two
others, and with such effect that we have secured all their
Minutes and papers. Their conduct has excited universal detestation." [1] The expulsion took place quite peaceably. The
Lord Provost informed the delegates that it was not their meeting, but their publications, that led him to intervene. The Chairman, Paterson, thereupon "skulked off"; but Brown, the Sheffield
delegate, took the chair, and declared that he would not quit it
save under compulsion. The Lord Provost and constables then
pulled him down; and the meeting was adjourned. Events ran
the same course on the morrow, save that the chairman, Gerrald,
was allowed to wind up the proceedings with prayer before he
was pulled down. Thus ended the first British Convention.

The natural sequel was a trial of the leaders, Sinclair, Margarot, Gerrald, and Skirving. Sinclair turned informer, whereupon his indictment was allowed to lapse. The others were
charged with attending the meetings of the Convention which,
" under the pretence of procuring a Reform of Parliament,
were evidently of a dangerous and destructive tendency," modelled on those of the French Convention and with the like aims

[1] " H. O.," Scotland, 9.

in view. The charge was held to be proven, and they were severally sentenced to transportation for fourteen years. The cases
aroused keen interest, in part owing to the novel claims put
forward by the prosecutor and endorsed by the Judges. The
Lord Advocate argued that these men, in claiming to represent
a majority of the people, were in reality planning a revolt; and
Lord Justice Clerk finally declared that the crime of sedition
consisted "in endeavouring to create a dissatisfaction in the
country, which nobody can tell where it will end. It will very
naturally end in overt rebellion; if it has that tendency, though
not in the mind of the parties at the time, yet, if they have been
guilty of poisoning the minds of the lieges, I apprehend that that
will constitute the crime of sedition to all intents and purposes."[1]

To find a parallel to this monstrous claim, that sedition may
be unintentional and may consist in some action which the Government judges by its results, one would have to hark back to the
days of Judge Jeffreys, whom indeed McQueen of Braxfield resembled in ferocity, cunning, and effrontery. The insolence of
Margarot at the bar to some extent excused the chief judge for
the exhibition of the same conduct on the bench. But in the
case of Gerrald, an English gentleman of refined character and
faultless demeanour, the brutalities of Braxfield aroused universal
loathing. In one respect Gerrald committed an imprudence. He
appeared in the dock, not in a wig, but displaying a shock of
dishevelled hair, a sign of French and republican sympathies
which seemed a defiance to the Court. Nevertheless, his speech
in his own defence moved to its depths the mind of a young
poet who had tramped all the way from Glasgow in the bleak
March weather in order to hear the trial. At the end of the
speech young Campbell turned to his neighbour, a humble
tradesman, and said: "By heavens, Sir, that is a great man";
to which there came the reply: "Yes, Sir, he is not only a great
man himself, but he makes every other man feel great who
listens to him."

In truth, the Scottish trials were a moral defeat for Pitt and
his colleagues. Sympathy with the prisoners and detestation of
the judges aroused a general outcry, which became furious when
Braxfield declared that he had no idea that his sentence of transportation involved servitude and hard labour.[2] The assertion im-

[1] "State Trials," xxiii, 766.   [2] "Auckland Journals," iii, 205.

plies an incredible ignorance in the man who had packed the juries and sought to get his victims hanged. It may be regarded as a cunning and cowardly attempt to shift part of the odium on to the Government. Certainly the prestige of the Cabinet now fell to zero. Ministers were held responsible for Braxfield's wanton vagaries, and were accused of luring English democrats into the meshes of the Scottish law. This last charge is absurd. As we have seen, the London police sought to stop Margarot, Sinclair, and Gerrald from going to Edinburgh. It was their presence and that of the Irishmen which gave to the Convention almost a national character, and placed it in rivalry to Parliament. Their speeches were by far the most provocative. Finally, as the letter quoted above shows, the initiative in arresting the delegates was taken by Robert Dundas and the Scottish Solicitor-General. On 11th December Henry Dundas wrote to his nephew: "You get great credit here [London] for your attack on the Convention."[1]

Far different was the comment of the London Corresponding Society. On 20th January 1794 that body convened a great meeting which passed protests against the war, the expulsion of the British Convention, and the arrest of delegates. It also resolved that the general committee should sit permanently throughout the ensuing session. Further, that if the Government attacked the liberties of the people in the ways described above, the committee should call "a General Convention of the People for taking such measures under their consideration."[2] Equally threatening were the resolutions of the Constitutional Society of London.[3] Pitt resolved to take up the gauntlet flung down by these two powerful Societies. On 24th February 1794 Eaton, a publisher of Newgate Street, was tried for publishing in his periodical pamphlet, "Politics for the People: or Hogswash," a little parable with which that witty lecturer, Thelwall, had delighted a debating society. He told how a gamecock, resplendent with ermine-spotted breast, and crown or cockscomb, lorded it greedily over all the fowls of the farmyard.[4] The parallel to George III was sufficiently close to agitate the official mind; but the jury gave an open verdict, which implied that the King was not hinted at.

[1] "Arniston Mems.," 242.   [2] E. Smith, "The Eng. Jacobins," 93-7.
[3] See "Report of the Committee of Secrecy" (17th May 1794).
[4] C. Cestre, "John Thelwall," 77.

The next prosecution, that of Thomas Walker, of Manchester, and six others broke down in a way highly discreditable to the authorities. Walker's services to the cause of Reform had, as we have seen, been conspicuous alike in energy and moderation, and his enemies in the Church and King Club made great exertions in order to procure a conviction. The archives of the Home Office throw a sinister light on their methods. A magistrate of Manchester, the Rev. John Griffith, informed the Home Secretary that Booth, a man who was imprisoned in June 1793 for seditious practices, made a declaration against Thomas Walker and McCullum, members of the local Constitutional Society. According to Booth, McCullum had said: "Petitioning Parliament be d—d. You may as well petition the devil to reform himself. The only way is for each Society to send a number of delegates to a certain place, and there declare themselves the Representatives of the People and support themselves as such." Thomas Walker had also said that each member must have a musket, for they would soon want them.[1] But it transpired in the trial of Walker, McCullum, and others that Griffith had let Booth see that he wanted to incriminate Walker. He not only offered Booth his pardon for such evidence, but left him alone with Dunn, a malicious perjurer, the falsity of whose charges against Walker was convincingly demonstrated.[2] The case proves how far an unscrupulous magistrate could succeed in getting charges trumped up against an innocent man who opposed him in politics. Doubtless in other cases personal spite, or the desire of a reward, led to the offer of false charges; and the student who peruses the Home Office archives needs to remember the Greek caution, μέμνησθ' ἀπιστεῖν, as much as if he were perusing French Memoirs.

It is therefore with much doubt that one reads the declaration of a Sheffield magistrate, in May 1794, that there was in that town " a most horrid conspiracy against State and Church under the pretence of Reform." A vast number of pikes and spears had been made and " cats " to throw in the road to lame the horses. 2nd July was fixed for the storming of the barracks and

---

[1] " H. O.," Geo. III (Domestic), 30.
[2] " State Trials," xxiii, 1055-1166. For technical reasons this statement of Booth could not be given at Walker's trial. Besides Walker's Constitutional Society, there were two others, the Reformation and Patriotic Societies, founded in March and April 1792.

town. " It is a mercy the plot is discovered. I am to be all night in the search." More detailed is the deposition of a magistrate of Sheffield, James Wilkinson, that a democrat named Widdison had made several pikes and sold twelve to Gales, a well-known Jacobinical printer. Further, that a witness, William Green, swore that a man named Jackson had employed him and others to make spear-heads ; they made twelve dozen or more in two days, and the heads were sent to the lodgings of Hill and Jackson. Wilkinson wrote for instructions how to deal with these men; also for a warrant to arrest Gales. On 20th May Dundas sent down warrants for the arrest of Gales, W. Camage, H. Yorke (*alias* Redhead), W. Broomhead, R. Moody, and T. Humphreys; he also issued a warrant against Williams, a gun-engraver, of the Tower, in London.[1]

In Birmingham, as we have seen the two magistrates, Carles and Spencer, were out and out loyalists; and, as they wrote to Dundas on 23rd May 1794 that there was not enough evidence to warrant a search for arms, we may infer that the Midland capital caused the authorities less concern than rebellious Sheffield. But even at Birmingham, with its traditions of exuberant loyalty, there were grounds for concern. John Brook, the mayor, informed Dundas that there were many malcontents in the neighbourhood, especially at Dudley.

Turning to the East, we find signs that Norwich seethed with discontent. From that city had come the first suggestion of a General Convention of the People. On 5th March 1793 one of the thirty Societies of Norwich wrote up to the London Corresponding Society advocating that step, which Hardy and his colleagues approved "so soon as the great body of the people shall be courageous and virtuous enough to join us in the attempt." I have found no proof that either at Norwich or in London these Societies used illegal methods. The seditious placards posted up at Norwich may have been the work of some fanatic or of an *agent provocateur*. But it is very doubtful whether the holding of a People's Convention in the manner proposed was not an act of defiance to Parliament, and therefore seditious. Individual members certainly came within the ban of the law. Thus, Dundas received tidings that two members of Hardy's Society, named Stone and Meakins, were circulating

[1] See E. Smith, " The Eng. Jacobins," ch. vi, for the meetings at Sheffield and the part played by Yorke.

seditious writings in Essex. When arrested they had with them one or two military books, copies of the revolutionary song, *Ça ira*, and similar papers;[1] but this fact does not incriminate the Society at large. In fact, the reports as to the purchase of arms and secret drillings are not very convincing. To take a few instances: information was sent to the Home Office that a man named Kitchen had sixty pikes in his house in George Street, near York Buildings; also that men were drilled secretly at the house of Spence, a seller of seditious pamphlets in the Little Turnstile, Holborn, and at that of Shelmerdine, a small trades-man of Southwark; the arms in the last case were bought from Williams, of the Tower, with a sum of £10 contributed by " a desperate tailor of China Walk, Lambeth."[2] Did patriotism or private spite or greed of money incite these reports? Drawings of pikes and spear-heads also diversified the report of the Secret Committee of the Lords appointed to investigate seditious proceedings, and probably convinced lovers of realism that plots actually existed.

More alarming in reality were the preparations for a General Convention of the People. The authorities knew that plans were actually on foot for sending delegates to form such a body. On 27th March 1794 the London Corresponding Society consulted the sister club on this question; and in due course delegates from the two Societies passed resolutions in favour of the scheme. Hardy thereupon sent a printed letter round to similar bodies, probably early in the month of April 1794. It ran thus:

Notwithstanding the unparalleled audacity of a corrupt and over-bearing faction which at present tramples on the rights and liberties of our people, our meetings cannot, in England, be interrupted without the previous adoption of a Convention Bill[3]—a measure it is our duty to anticipate. . . . Let us then form another British Convention. We have a central situation in our view, which we believe would be most convenient for the whole island, but which we forbear to mention . . . till we have the answers of the Societies with which we are in correspondence. Let us have your answer, then, by the 20th at farthest,

---

[1] " H. O.," Geo. III (Domestic), 31.

[2] *Ibid.*, 27, 29. Spence purveyed " Pigs' Meat," while Eaton sold " Hogs' Wash." The titles are a take-off of Burke's phrase "the swinish multitude."

[3] *I.e.*, similar to the one passed in Dublin against a People's Convention.

earlier if possible, whether you approve of the measure and how many delegates you can send, with the number also, if possible, of your Societies.

PS. We have appointed a Secret Committee on this. Will you do the same?[1]

In order to further the scheme, the London Corresponding Society held a meeting on 14th April at Chalk Farm, when an ardent appeal was read from Hardy to resist the encroachments on liberty recently made by " apostate reformers "—a fling at Pitt. " Are they alone," he asked, " to judge of the fit time for Reform? " The meeting then thanked Earl Stanhope for his manly and successful opposition to the attempt to bring Hanoverian and Hessian troops into England; it also condemned the late rapid advances of despotism and the arming one part of the people against the other. Finally it declared that in cases of necessity the safety of the people was the only law. We may here note that a few Hanoverian and Hessian battalions had been landed in Hampshire, as a temporary measure, previous to their transference to other ships. This occasioned some clamour at Westminster, Grey, Fox, Sheridan and others claiming that the liberties of England were in the direst danger. Pitt refused to accept a Bill of Indemnity for his action, and the House supported him by a great majority.[2]

The other reference at the Chalk Farm meeting was to the proposal to sanction the subscriptions to the Volunteer forces now being raised in various counties.[3] At the outset this noble movement had in view the defence of the constitution no less than of the land; and this doubtless accounts for the fact that Coke, Mingay, and other Norfolk Whigs struggled desperately and successfully to break up a county meeting held at Norwich for this purpose on 12th April, shouting down even so able a speaker as Windham. In general, however, these meetings were an immense success. That at Aylesbury realized £5,851 for a county corps; and one at Epsom, for Surrey, brought in nearly double as much.[4] Most noteworthy of all these meetings was one of 19th April 1794 at Birmingham, where loyal sentiments crystalized in a rhetorical jewel of rare lustre. The "Loyal

[1] " Report of the Parl. Comm. of Secrecy" (17th May 1794).
[2] "Parl. Hist.," xxx, 1363-91; xxxi, 1-27.   [3] *Ibid.*, xxxi, 97-121.
[4] " Morning Chronicle " for April 1794.

True Blues " of Birmingham, in view of the threats of the French
" to insult the chalky cliffs of Albion and to plant in this island
their accursed tree of liberty, more baneful in its effects than
the poisonous tree of Java which desolates the country and cor-
rupts the winds of heaven," resolved to quit the field of argument
and to take arms as a Military Association. For nothing could
be so effective as "the decided and awful plan of the whole
Nation rising in a mass of Volunteers, determined to dispute
every inch of ground with their daring aggressors and to spill
the last drop of their blood in defence of their religion and their
laws." They beg Edward Carver to command them; they will
choose their uniform, will arrange themselves as grenadiers and
light infantry; and, "to preserve the *coup d'œil*, the whole corps
will be arranged with the strictest attention to the height of the
members."[1] Possibly the Royalists of Birmingham may have
known of the hint conveyed in Hardy's letter, that the National
Convention should assemble in some convenient centre, a phrase
which seemed to point to their town, which, indeed, the Chartists
chose for that purpose in 1839.

In view of the fervent loyalty manifested on all sides, Ministers might surely have trusted to the majority to control the
restless minority. Auckland expressed the general opinion when
he said that the country in the proportion of ten to one was
sound and loyal.[2] As the majority was armed, while the malcontents had but small stores of pikes, there was little cause for
fear, though in the minority were some desperate men. In particular, Richard Davison, a prominent member of the Sheffield
Constitutional Society, recommended the clubs of London and
Norwich to buy consignments of pikes in order to resist the
" newly-armed minions of the bare-faced aristocracy of the present Administration "; and it afterwards appeared that he could
sell them at twenty pence each.[3] This letter was sent off on
24th April, 1794, seventeen days after the holding of a mass
meeting on Castle Hill, Sheffield, at which the chairman, Henry
Yorke (*alias* Redhead), declared that, when the sun of Reason
shone in its fullest meridian, the people would turn out the 558
gentlemen from Westminster. The meeting resolved that, as the
people ought to demand universal suffrage as a right, and not
petition for it as a favour, they would never again petition the

---

[1] "H. O.," Geo. III (Domestic), 30.   [2] "Auckland Journals," iii, 213.
[3] "State Trials," xxiv, 588, 600, 601.

House of Commons on this subject.[1] Contemptuous epithets were now constantly hurled at Parliament. On 2nd May, that genial toper, Horne Tooke, of Wimbledon, declared at a dinner of the Constitutional Society in London that Parliament was a scoundrel sink of corruption, and that the scoundrel Opposition joined the scoundrel Government in order to destroy the rights of Englishmen. In order to add weight to his epithets he called the company to witness to his complete sobriety.[2]

Pitt and his colleagues now decided to strike at the leaders who were planning a British Convention. Of these the most formidable was the Secretary of the London Corresponding Society. Accordingly, early on 12th May, some Bow Street officers made their way into Hardy's shop, No. 9, Piccadilly, arrested him, seized his papers, ransacking the room where Mrs. Hardy was in bed. The shock to her nerves was such as to bring on premature child-birth with fatal results. On the same day a royal message came to Parliament announcing that the efforts of certain Societies to summon a Convention in defiance of Parliament had led him to order the seizure of their books and papers. Those of the Corresponding and Constitutional Societies were brought, sealed up, to the House of Commons on the morrow, whereupon Pitt moved for the appointment of a secret committee to examine them. He himself, Dundas, and nineteen other members soon drew up the Report. When presented on 16th May, it contained a statement of all the threatening symptoms of the time, and so far ignored the legal efforts of those Societies as to form a very alarming diagnosis.[3]

The fears of Ministers were further aroused by the contents of a letter from the Rev. Jeremiah Joyce (tutor of Earl Stanhope's son) to Horne Tooke, which the Post Office had seized. It announced the arrest of citizen Hardy, and ended thus: "Query: is it possible to get ready by Thursday?"[4] Some effort of the imagination was needed to figure the Silenus of the literary world as a plotter against the lives of Ministers. But they now decided to arrest him and the Reverend Jeremiah, as well as Bonney, Richter, and Kyd, also members of the Constitutional

[1] "State Trials," xxiv, 626.   [2] E. Smith, "Eng. Jacobins," 116.
[3] "Parl. Hist.," xxxi, 475-97.
[4] "Life of Horne Tooke," ii, 119. It was afterwards absurdly said that Dundas, Horne Tooke's neighbour at Wimbledon, had had the letter filched from his house. Both of them lived on the west side of the "green."

Society, besides Camage and one or two other democrats of Sheffield. Davison, the would-be seller of pikes, had fled betimes.

These were the circumstances which induced Pitt to propose the suspension of the Habeas Corpus Act (16th May). The Report of the Secret Committee having been read, he proceeded to exaggerate the import of the more threatening parts of the evidence, and to convince the House that these Societies, which had congratulated the French Convention, and still aped its methods, were plotting to set up an authority openly hostile to Parliament. With all the force of his oratory he pictured the state of things that must ensue—"an enormous torrent of insurrection, which would sweep away all the barriers of government, law and religion, and leave our country a naked waste for usurped authority to range in, uncontrolled and unresisted." Despite the warning of Fox that the remedy now proposed was worse than the evil which it sought to avert; despite the pleas of Grey and Sheridan against indecent haste in hurrying on this arbitrary measure, it was forced through every stage in the Commons at that single sitting; finally, at half-past three in the morning, the numbers of the Whig protestors sank to 13, while the Ministerialists still mustered 108 strong.[1]

This collapse of the Opposition was due to a sharp cleavage in its ranks on the vital issues now at stake. As has already appeared, Pitt had consulted the Duke of Portland and his immediate followers on subjects affecting public order. Some of the Old Whigs, notably Windham, served on the Committee of Secrecy; and the evidence there forthcoming led them to propose a general support of Government both in its war policy and the maintenance of order. Those eager Royalists, Burke and Windham, took the lead in proposing an alliance with the Ministry The question arose whether the Old Whigs should support from outside or actually coalesce with the Ministry, taking their fair share of power. Burke strongly advised the latter course as the only means of assuring continued and strenuous support. This opened a sluice gate of correspondence, resulting in important changes in the Cabinet. I shall refer to this matter later, merely noting here that the Duke of Portland took over from Dundas the Home Office, which was thenceforth limited to British and Irish affairs, Dundas becoming Secretary of State for War, and

[1] "Parl. Hist.," xxxi, 497-505.

Windham Secretary at War. The changes were most opportune; for they strengthened the administrative machine and served to build up a national party strong enough to cope with the growing difficulties of the time. Thenceforth there was no danger of the overthrow of the Ministry. Further, the panic pervading all parts of England in May 1794 was soon allayed by the news of Howe's victory, termed " the glorious First of June"; while in July the fall of Robespierre caused a general sense of relief. In view of these events, Pitt would have done well to relax his efforts against the British Jacobins. He held on his way and encountered sharp rebuffs. The trial of Hardy and others in October dragged on to a great length; and, after hearing an enormous mass of evidence (some of which proved the posses- sion of arms by democrats) the jury returned a verdict of Not Guilty. This result, due to the masterly defence by Erskine and Gibbs, aroused a tumult of joy in the vast crowd out- side such as London had rarely seen. Hardy afterwards as- serted that, in case of a conviction, Government had decided to arrest about 800 more persons.[1] This is mere hearsay; but it has been fastened upon by those who seek to father upon Pitt the design of reviving the days of Strafford and " Thorough." A fortnight previously Watt, once a government informer, was convicted at Edinburgh of a treasonable plot to set the city on fire, sack the banks, and attack the castle. Before he went to execution he confessed his guilt.[2]

This was the only conviction obtained by Government. The trial of Horne Tooke ran a course unfavourable to Ministers, the evidence for the prosecution being flimsy in the extreme. Pitt himself was called to the witness-box, and when closely cross-questioned by Erskine as to his former connection with the Reform cause, admitted that he was present at a meeting at the Duke of Richmond's residence, at which delegates from county Reform Associations were present. The admission exposed him to the charge of inconsistency in the eyes of those who looked only at the surface of things. In reality, those who met at the Duke of Richmond's house had nothing in common with the democratic clubs which proposed to override the will of Parliament by a National Convention. Yet, as the superficial

---

[1] "Life of T. Hardy," 42; "State Trials," xxiv, 717, 729, 762, etc. The evidence fills 1,207 pages.

[2] *Ibid.*, 1-200.

view gains a ready assent, the fame of Pitt now underwent an eclipse. Never again did he hear the whole-hearted acclaim which greeted him in the years 1784-90. The roar of delight which went up at the news of the acquittal of Horne Tooke was a sign of the advent of a new era, in whose aspirations Pitt had no part.

The prosecutions against Bonney, Joyce, Kyd, and Holcroft were now dropped. The charge against Thelwall was pressed home, but resulted in another defeat for Government. Thus, except in the case of Watt, no proof was forthcoming of treasonable designs, though the apprehension of Davison of Sheffield might perhaps have led to discoveries of that nature. In the main, then, Pitt and his colleagues failed to justify the harsh measure of suspending the Habeas Corpus Act; and the failure of the State prosecutions led to a marked increase of the membership and activity of the London Corresponding Society, with results which will appear later.

Nevertheless, Pitt's conduct is far from indefensible with regard to the main point at issue, the meeting of a National Convention. In view of the projects of some of the wilder spirits at London, Sheffield, Norwich, and Edinburgh, it is presumptuous to charge him with causelessly seeking to bring about a "Reign of Terror." He was face to face with developments which might easily have become dangerous; and, with the example of Paris before him, he not unnaturally took what he thought to be the safer course, that of stopping them at the outset. Indeed, we may question whether Fox, had he been in power, would have allowed the assembling of a National Convention, pledged to press upon Parliament measures which he reprobated.

It is when we come to details that Pitt is open to the charge of acting with undue severity. Considering the proved loyalty of the great mass of the people, what need was there to inaugurate a system of arbitrary arrests? After all, England was not France. Here no systematic assault had been made on the institutions in Church and State. The constitution had suffered dilapidation, but it was storm-proof, and the garrison was strongly entrenched. Moreover, the democrats for the most part urged their case without any of the appeals to violence which wrought havoc in France. There the mob delighted to hurry a suspect to *la lanterne* and to parade heads on pikes. Here the mass meeting at Chalk Farm, or on Castle Hill, Sheffield, ended with loss neither of life nor of property. So far as I have found, not one life was taken by the people in the course of this agitation—a fact which speaks volumes for their religious sense, their self-restraint even amidst deep poverty, and, in general, their obedience to law even when they deemed it oppressive. The hero of the year 1794 is not William Pitt, but the British nation.

CHAPTER VIII

PITT AND THE ALLIES (1794-5)

The main object of His Majesty is the keeping together by influence and weight this great Confederation by which alone the designs of France can be resisted, and which, if left to itself, would be too likely to fall to pieces from the jarring interests of the Powers engaged in it.—GRENVILLE TO MALMESBURY, 21st April 1794.

The disgraceful failure of every military operation His Prussian Majesty has undertaken since the year 1791 has destroyed the reputation of the Prussian army; and the duplicity and versatility of his Cabinet put an end to all confidence and good faith.—MALMESBURY TO GRENVILLE, 20th September 1794.

AS in parliamentary life, so too in the wider spheres of diplomacy and warfare, a Coalition very rarely holds together under a succession of sharp blows. This is inherent in the nature of things. A complex or heterogeneous substance is easily split up by strokes which leave a homogeneous body intact. Rocks of volcanic origin defy the hammer under which conglomerates crumble away; and when these last are hurled against granite or flint, they splinter at once. Well might Shakespeare speak through the mouth of Ulysses these wise words on the divisions of the Greeks before Troy:

> Look how many Grecian tents do stand
> Hollow upon this plain, so many hollow factions.
> . . . .
> Troy in our weakness stands, not in her strength.[1]

Pitt and his colleagues were under no illusion as to the weakness of the first Coalition against France. They well knew the incurable jealousies of the Houses of Hapsburg and Hohenzollern, the utter weakness of the Holy Roman Empire, the

---

[1] "Troilus and Cressida," act i, sc. 3.

poverty or torpor of Spain, Sardinia, and Naples, the potent distractions produced by the recent partition of Poland, and the Machiavellian scheme of the Empress Catharine II to busy the Central Powers in French affairs so that she might have a free hand at Warsaw. All this and much more stood revealed to them. But they grounded their hopes of success on two important considerations; first, that the finances of France were exhausted; secondly, that the rule of the Jacobins, fertile in forced loans, forced service, and guillotining, must speedily collapse. On the subject of French finance there are many notes in the Pitt Papers, which show that Pitt believed an utter breakdown to be imminent. Grenville, too, at the close of October 1793, stated that France had lost at least 200,000 soldiers, while more than 50,000 were in hospital. The repugnance to military service was universal, and the deficit for the month of August alone was close on £17,000,000.[1]

Above all, Pitt and Grenville believed the French Government to be incompetent as well as exasperatingly cruel. In their eyes Jacobins were sworn foes to all that made government possible. The mistake was natural. The English Ministers knew little of what was going on in France, and therefore failed to understand that the desperadoes now in power at Paris were wielding a centralized despotism, compared with which that of Louis XIV was child's play. As to the Phœnix-like survival of French credit, it is inexplicable even to those who have witnessed the wonders wrought by Thiers in 1870-3. All that can be said is that the Jacobins killed the goose that laid the golden egg, and yet the golden eggs were laid. Let him who understands the miracle of revolutionary finance cast the first stone at Pitt.

The Prime Minister also erred when he believed the French social structure to be breaking up. Here again the miscalculation was perfectly natural in an age which regarded kings, nobles, and bishops as the fixed stars of a universe otherwise diversified only by a dim Milky Way. The French were the first to dispel these notions. In truth the strength of the young giant bore witness to the potency of the new and as yet allied forces—Democracy and Nationality. In 1792 Democracy girded itself eagerly against the semi-feudal Powers, Austria and

---

[1] "Dropmore P.," ii, 452.

Prussia; but the strength latent in the French people appeared only in the next year when, on the accession of England, Spain, and the Empire to the Coalition, plans were discussed of detaching Alsace, Lorraine, Roussillon, and Flanders.[1] To these sacrilegious schemes the French patriots opposed the dogma of Rousseau —the indivisibility of the general will. " Perish 25,000,000 Frenchmen rather than the Republic one and indivisible." This perfervid, if illogical, exclamation of a Commissioner of the Convention reveals something of that passion for unity which now fused together the French nation. Some peoples merge themselves slowly together under the shelter of kindred beliefs and institutions. Others again, after feeling their way towards closer union, finally achieve it in the explosion of war or revolution. The former case was the happy lot of the British nation; the latter, that of the French. Pitt, with his essentially English outlook, failed to perceive that the diverse peoples grouped together under the French monarchy had now attained to an indissoluble unity under the stress of the very blows which he and his Allies dealt in Flanders, Alsace, and Provence.

For by this time the counter-strokes dealt by the Republicans were telling with fatal effect on their adversaries. The failure of the Spanish campaign in Roussillon and the irruption of a French force into Catalonia dashed the spirits of that weak and wavering monarch, Charles IV; and already whispers were heard that peace with France was necessary. The disputes with England concerning Nootka Sound and affairs at Toulon predisposed the King and his people to think with less horror of the regicides of Paris. As for Sardinia, the childish obscurantism of the Court of Turin had nursed to quick life a mushroom growth of Jacobinism. The army defending the Alpine passes was honeycombed with discontent; and the suspicious conduct of Austria towards her little ally foreshadowed the divisions and disasters which quickly followed on the advent of Bonaparte at that theatre of the war.

It was clear that only from London could come the impulse which would invigorate this anaemic Coalition. Pitt sought to impart such an impulse in the King's Speech at the opening of the Session of 1794. It had throughout a defiant ring. The capture of three of the northern fortresses of France, the gains

[1] Thugut in the autumn of 1793 sketched a scheme for annexing the north of France from the Somme to Sedan.

in the East and West Indies (they amounted to Pondicherry, Chandernagore, and Tobago, together with Miquelon and St. Pierre), the blow dealt to her navy at Toulon, and the impossibility of her continuing the recent prodigious exertions, were in turn duly emphasized. And on 21st January 1794, when Fox moved an amendment in favour of peace, the Prime Minister spoke even more strongly of the madness of coming to terms with the present rulers of France. Could any statesman not gifted with second sight have spoken otherwise? At that time the Reign of Terror was approaching its climax. The Goddess of Reason had lately been enthroned in Notre Dame amidst ribald songs and dances. The schism between Robespierre and the atheistical party was beginning to appear ; and few persons believed that France would long bend the knee before the lords of the guillotine, whose resources were largely derived from the plunder of churches and banks, forced loans from the wealthy, and a graduated Income Tax resembling the Spartan proposals of Thomas Paine.

In such a case Pitt naturally repeated his statement of the previous session, that he altogether deprecated a peace with France, unless it possessed some elements of permanence, and secured due indemnity to Great Britain. Nay, he declared that he would rather persevere with war, even in the midst of disasters, than come to terms with the present rulers of France, who were alike enemies of order and rabid foes of England. They drove men into battle by fear of the guillotine; they formed rapine and destruction into a system, and perverted to their detestable purposes all the talents and ingenuity derived from the civilization around them. He was careful, however, to correct the mis-statement of Fox, that the Government was struggling for the restoration of the French monarchy. While believing that that nation would live most happily under a King, Pitt denied that a restoration was the object of the present war. We have already seen that he held this view in his correspondence with the Austrian Court. The House supported Ministers by 277 votes to 59.

These declarations, backed by so large a majority, caused great satisfaction at Vienna, and heartened that Government in the midst of its many uncertainties. There was every need of encouragement. In that age, when the great monarchs of the eighteenth century had passed, or were passing, away, Francis II stood somewhat low among the mediocrities on whom fell the strokes of destiny. He was a poor replica of Leopold II. Where the father was supple and adroit, the son was perversely obstinate or weakly pliable. In place of foresight and tenacity in the pursuit of essentials, Francis was remarkable for a more than Hapsburg narrowness of view, and he lacked the toughness which had not seldom repaired the blunders of that House. Those counsellors swayed him most who appealed to his family pride, or satisfied his other dominant feelings, attachment to the old order of things and a pedantic clinging to established usages. But the weakness of his character soon became so patent as to excite general distrust, especially as he was swayed by the wayward impulses of his consort, a daughter of Ferdinand IV and Maria Carolina of Naples. From her mother she inherited a hatred of French principles and the bent towards intrigue and extravagance which wrecked the careers of that Queen and of her sister, Marie Antoinette. Francis II and his consort longed to stamp out the French plague; but they lacked the strength of mind and of will that commands success. Our special envoy at Vienna, Thomas Grenville, questioned whether the Emperor "had steadiness enough to influence the Government."

According to the same competent judge, the Chancellor Thugut was the only efficient Minister, being very laborious in his work, and indeed "the only man of business about the Court." [1] Yet Thugut was rather a clever diplomat and ideal head-clerk than a statesman. In forethought he did not much excel his master. Indeed, his personality and his position alike condemned him to aim at cheap and easy gains. His features and figure were mean. Worse still, he was of low birth, a crime in the eyes of nobles and courtiers who for nearly half a century had seen the prestige of the Chancery enhanced by the lordly airs and whims of Kaunitz. Fear of courtly intrigues ever obsessed the mind of Thugut; and thus, whenever the horizon darkened, this coast-hugging pilot at once made for the nearest haven. In particular, as the recovery of Belgium in the year 1793 brought no financial gain, but unending vistas of war, he sought other means of indemnity, and discovered them in Alsace-Lorraine,

[1] "Dropmore P.," ii, 628. So, too, Morton Eden wrote to Grenville on 1st January 1793: "The steadfastness of the Emperor does not equal his moral rectitude" ("F. O.," Austria, 32).

South Poland, and Venice. The first was a concession to the pride of the House of Hapsburg-Lorraine; but Thugut saw in Venetia and in the land south of Warsaw the readiest means of indemnifying Austria for the loss of her Belgic Provinces, which after the defeat of Wattignies (October 1793) he probably expected and welcomed.

In this orientation of Hapsburg policy Thugut did but follow the impulse first imparted by Hertzberg at Berlin. As we have seen, Frederick William II entered on the French war in one of his chivalrous moods, which passed away amidst the smoke of Valmy. The miseries of the retreat Rhinewards, and the incursion of the French into the valley of the Main taught him prudence, while the ease of his conquest of Great Poland early in the year 1793 assured the victory of statecraft over chivalry. Morton Eden reported from Berlin that, had the preparations for the Valmy campaign equalled in thoroughness those for the invasion of Poland, events must have gone very differently in Champagne. The circumspection with which the Prussians conducted the siege of Mainz in the summer of 1793, and the long delays of the autumn, have already been noticed. The result of it was that at Christmastide of the year 1793 Pichegru and Hoche threw back Wurmser in disastrous rout, and compelled Brunswick hurriedly to retire to the Rhine.

As always happens between discordant allies after defeats, Berlin and Vienna indulged in a war of words, amidst which the Coalition would probably have broken up but for the efforts of British diplomacy. The Pitt Ministry had despatched to Berlin the ablest of British diplomatists, Lord Malmesbury, with a view to strengthening the accord between the three Powers; and the mingled charm and authority of his presence did much to thwart the petty prejudices and intrigues prevalent at that capital. He took Brussels and Frankfurt on his way to Berlin, and his diary shows the listlessness or discontent which had infected the officers of the British army. Many of them openly brought against the Duke of York the most outrageous and unfounded charges, and it seems that about fifty of them went on furlough to England, where they spread those slanders and played into the hands of the Opposition.[1] Malmesbury's converse with the Duke and others at Ath convinced him that the

---

[1] " Dropmore P.," ii, 491; " Malmesbury Diaries," iii, 17-19, 69.

commander-in-chief was striving manfully and generously against a situation full of difficulty.

At Frankfurt, and again at Berlin, Malmesbury found signs that Frederick William was ashamed at the ignominious issue of the campaign, and professed a desire to take up the duties which the Duke of Brunswick had so haltingly fulfilled. The King seemed rather pleased than otherwise at the Austrian reverses in the north of Alsace, but by no means indisposed to renew the attack upon France, always provided that England paid him a sufficient subsidy. He assured the envoy that his *chef-d'œuvre*, the Triple Alliance of 1788, was still a reality, but he declared, on the faith of an honest man, that the state of Prussia's finances would not enable him to face a third campaign. In point of fact, out of the reserve fund of 80,000,000 crowns which Frederick the Great had handed on, only 20,000,000 or perhaps only 14,000,000 remained in the early days of 1794.[1]

Other difficulties beset the Prussian monarch. Want of work had driven the weavers of Silesia to a state of frenzy and tumult almost resembling a *Jacquerie*; and there and elsewhere serfs and peasants talked openly of casting off the restraints and burdens of Feudalism. In such a case the veriest autocrat must pause before he commits his country to the risks of a loan (that of 1792 had exhausted Prussia's credit), or to a campaign where the losses were certain and the gains doubtful. On this last topic various schemes had been bandied to and fro between Berlin and Vienna. The debt of honour certainly bade Frederick William help to secure to his rival a counterpart to Prussia's acquisitions in Poland; but, apart from this consideration and the need of stamping out the French pest in the Rhineland, the politicians of Berlin found few reasons for prolonging the war. What wonder, then, that they set on foot intrigues with the regicides of Paris? Marshal Möllendorf, the commander whom Frederick William substituted for the weary and disgusted Duke of Brunswick, proved to be a partisan of peace.[2]

Royalist at heart, but beset by advisers and mistresses who fanned his jealousy of Austria and love of ease, Frederick William wavered under the whims of the hour or the counsels of the last comer. Malmesbury thus summed up the question now at issue in his letter to Pitt of 9th January 1794: "Can we

[1] "Dropmore P.," ii, 494; "Malmesbury Diaries," iii, 31, *et seq.*
[2] "Malmesbury Diaries," iii, 50; Sorel, iv, 17.

do without the King of Prussia or can we not? If we can, he is
not worth the giving of a guinea for. If we cannot, I am afraid
we cannot give too many." Malmesbury saw no means of keeping Frederick William steady up to the end of the war. Pitt and
Grenville, however, devised the following expedient. They offered
the sum of £2,000,000 for bringing 100,000 Prussians into the field.
Of this sum Great Britain would furnish two fifths (or £800,000),
and Austria and Holland each one fifth, the last fifth being
advanced by Prussia herself until she reimbursed herself from
France at the general peace. The device was suggestive of that
of the rustic who tempts his beast of burden onwards by dangling
a choice vegetable before his nose.

Frederick William alone might have been attracted by the
offer; but his advisers haggled long and obstinately over details.
Chief among the objectors was a Councillor of State, Haugwitz,
an oily, plausible creature, whose Gallophil leanings were
destined finally to place his country under the heel of Napoleon
and deal a death-blow to Pitt. For the present, he treated
Malmesbury with a moderation and courtesy that deftly veiled
a determined opposition. The British envoy was fully his match.
Finding that Haugwitz ascribed all difficulties and delays to the
Austrian embassy, he advised him to propose the transfer of the
negotiations to The Hague, where these annoyances would cease.
Vain and always prone to take the easiest course, Haugwitz
swallowed the bait and succeeded in carrying a point which was
all in Malmesbury's favour, especially as it saved time in com-
municating with Downing Street. After annoying delays they set
out on 23rd March; and with the aid of twenty-two horses at
each post traversed the 326 (English) miles to The Hague in 120
hours during the days, 23rd—30th March, when the campaign
ought to have opened.

The prospects at Vienna were equally gloomy. Morton Eden's
reports to Grenville form an unrelieved jeremiad. Even amidst
the alarms caused by the disasters at Toulon and in the
Palatinate, jealousy of Prussia was the dominant feeling. The
utmost efforts of our ambassador failed to convince Francis II
and Thugut of the need of humouring Prussia by meeting her
demand for an additional subsidy and by guaranteeing bread
and forage for the 20,000 men who formed her contingent in the
Austrian service. Into these wearisome quarrels we need not
enter, further than to note that they were envenomed by the

acerbity of the Prussian ambassador at Vienna. The Marquis
Lucchesini, born at Lucca in 1752, early entered the service of
Frederick the Great, to whom he acted as reader. He advanced
rapidly under his successor. His commanding demeanour and
vivacity of speech, added to great powers of work, and acuteness
in detecting the foibles of others, made him a formidable opponent. Further, his marriage with the sister of Bischoffswerder,
until lately the King's favourite adviser, added to his influence,
which, as was natural with a foreigner, inclined towards the
attractive and gainful course. Long afterwards the saviour of
Prussia, Baron vom Stein, classed him among the narrow,
selfish, insincere men who had been the ruin of nations.[1] Certainly he helped to ruin Poland; and now his conduct at Vienna
clogged the efforts of Morton Eden and Malmesbury to strengthen
the Coalition against France. Eden complained that he behaved
as an intriguing subaltern rather than as an ambassador; and
rumour credibly ascribed his tortuous and exasperating conduct
to French gold.

In the midst of his irritation against Prussia and her envoy,
Thugut heard with astonishment the British proposals, presented
at Berlin early in February, to bring 100,000 Prussians into the
field. Urgently he remonstrated with Eden, pointing out that
Prussia had played them false in two campaigns, and would do
so again, witness her late contention that France must not be
weakened. On no account, then, must Frederick William head a
compact mass of 100,000 men in the Palatinate. He would be
the arbiter of the situation. He would be between the Austrian
army in Brabant and the Hapsburg States. Nay, he might
march into Swabia, reach the Danube, take boats at Ulm, and,
sailing down that stream, have Vienna at his mercy![2] So pressing were these anxieties that, at the close of February, Thugut
sent a special request to Catharine II to guarantee the security
of Austria's possessions in case Frederick William withdrew
from the Coalition.

Despite the utmost efforts of the British Ministry and its envoys,
no plan of vigorous co-operation could be arranged between the
two German rivals; the sole link connecting them was the
clause of the treaty of 1792, whereby Austria, as having been
attacked by France, claimed the help of 20,000 Prussians.

[1] Seeley, "Stein," i, 65.
[2] "F. O.," Austria, 36. Eden to Grenville, 15th and 27th February.

Frederick William decided that this force must remain at Mainz, in order to guard the Empire from a French raid. He promised 80,000 more troops to Great Britain and Holland, provided that they were paid for. On one point alone the four Allies came near to agreement, namely, that the main Prussian army should operate in Flanders, so as effectively to defend the Dutch territory, secure conquests in the North of France, and, above all, preclude the quarrels which must ensue if it acted near the Austrians.[1] Thugut of course assented, his great aim being to remove the Prussians as far as possible from Swabia. Disputes on these subjects went on up to the end of March 1794, the time when an advance into French Flanders promised great results.

The reader will naturally ask—Can this be called a Coalition? A Coalition implies some power of coalescing. But among the four Powers there was far more of disunion than union. In fact, England was the sole link between these wrangling confederates, and that, too, solely by means of what Carlyle called the cash nexus. Grenville, using a more homely metaphor, averred that the German princes turned towards England as an inexhaustible milch-cow. The animal in this case could dictate her terms; and thus the relations of the three Powers resembled those of a rich but somewhat exigent employer to grumbling and distrustful employees. Holland also, in return for her sacrifices in men and money, demanded from Austria a better frontier on the side of Dutch Flanders and Maestricht, to which the Viennese Court opposed a quiet but firm resistance.

It speaks volumes for the confidence inspired by Pitt and Grenville, and for the tactful zeal of Malmesbury and Eden, that they induced the German rivals to make one more effort. The Duke of York also played an important part in the formation of the plan of campaign; for he it was who persuaded Colonel Mack to accompany him to London, and there discuss with Ministers the alternative schemes. The mention of Mack will excite surprise among those who know of him only by the futile Neapolitan campaign of 1799, and the frightful disaster of Ulm. In regard to strategy and the theory of war he displayed much ability; and his administrative talents and energy as Quarter-Master-General in 1793 should have screened him from the criticism that he discoursed brilliantly on war in *salons*, and in the council rhetorically developed specious and elegant plans.[2]

[1] "Malmesbury Diaries," iii, 81, 82.   [2] Sorel, iv, 13.

Mack's plan of operations was first submitted to the judgement of the Archduke Charles, the Prince of Coburg, Count Mercy, the Prince of Orange, and the Duke of York, at Brussels. Next, he proceeded, along with Counts Stahremberg and Merveldt to London, and on 13th February unfolded his plan to Pitt, Grenville, and Dundas. The Duke of York had preceded him by two days, but was absent from this conference. It became piquant when Pitt " playfully " remarked to Mack that a great general had recently arrived at London whose appointment to the command of the British force in Flanders would doubtless meet with his warm approval. After a little more fencing, Pitt gave the name of the Marquis Cornwallis, who had just returned from his Viceroyalty in India. Mack by no means welcomed the proposal, and made the irreverent remark that the best General, after fighting elephants in India, would be puzzled by the French. Pitt thereupon observed that the Duke of York had not the confidence of the army, to which Mack and Merveldt replied by praising his character, and decrying his critics as a set of influential but inexperienced youths.

The matter then dropped, and the Duke was present at the conference on the morrow. Finally, Austria and England bound themselves to make great efforts, the latter with at least 40,000 men, either British or German auxiliaries. The Prussian and Dutch forces were to be increased so as to bring the grand total to 340,000 men. Of this large number 170,000 were to operate in Flanders with a view to a march on Paris; 35,000 held the country along the right bank of the Meuse; 15,000 protected Luxemburg; 65,000 Prussians prolonged the line eastwards to the Rhine, which was guarded by 55,000 Austrians. Certainly the plan called for a third of a million of men, if all the frontier strongholds of Flanders were to be taken before the march to Paris began. In regard to details, Pitt, Grenville, and Dundas urged that Cornwallis should command the British and subsidiary forces defending West Flanders—a suggestion which George III warmly approved, on condition that the Duke of York, serving with the main body nearer the centre of the long line, had a number of troops proportionate to his rank and talents.

Thus the effort of Pitt and his colleagues to shelve the Duke of York was foiled. On another and weightier matter he had his way. Coburg's conduct had been so languid and unenterprising as to lead to urgent demands for his recall; and it was understood that the Emperor Francis would take the command, with Mack as Chief-of-Staff and virtual director of the campaign. Pitt expressed to Mack his marked preference of this arrangement to the alternative scheme, the appointment of the Archduke Charles; for the extreme youth of the Archduke might hinder a good understanding between him and his subordinate and senior, the Duke of York. Seeing, then, that Mack declined absolutely to serve under Coburg,[1] nothing but the presence of the Emperor could end the friction in Flanders.

But alas for the monarchical cause! At the very time when the Kaiser was to set out for Brussels, alarming news came from Cracow. The temper of the Poles, heated by the wrongs and insults of two years, burst forth in a rising against the Russian and Prussian authorities. Kosciusko, the last hope of Poland, issued an appeal which nerved his countrymen to dare the impossible. Rushing to arms, they astonished the world by exhibiting in the last throes of their long agony a strength which, if put forth in 1791, might have saved their land from spoliation. Even now their despairing struggles turned towards Warsaw much of the energy which should have trended towards Paris; and thus, once again, and not for the last time, did the foul crimes of 1772 and 1793 avenge themselves on their perpetrators. The last struggles of Poland helped on the French Republic to its mighty adolescence. Finally, on 2nd April, Francis II departed for Brussels. Thugut set out nine days later; and in the interval, on the plausible pretext that Prussia would seize more Polish land, he stopped the reinforcements destined for Flanders. He also urged the Czarina on no account to allow a partition of Poland.[2]

While the Continental States were thus pulling different ways, British diplomacy won two notable triumphs at The Hague. By dint of threatening Haugwitz with the rupture of the whole negotiation, Malmesbury induced that Minister to countermand the order for the retirement of the Prussian troops, which had already begun. He thereby saved the Allies in the Palatinate and Flanders from very serious risks in view of the

---

[1] Vivenot, iii, 89-96; "Dropmore P.," ii, 505-7.

[2] "F. O.," Austria, 36, Eden to Grenville, 31st March, 9th April. See, too, Vivenot, iii, 172, for proofs that Kosciusko sought to delay the rising, and looked to Vienna for help against Russia and Prussia.

gathering masses of the French.[1] Further, on 19th April, he induced Haugwitz to sign a treaty which promised to revivify the monarchical cause. Prussia agreed to furnish, by 24th May, 62,400 men, who were to act conjointly with the British and Dutch forces in Flanders. For this powerful succour the two Maritime States would pay a subsidy of £50,000 a month, besides the cost of bread and forage, reckoned at £1 12s. per man per month, and £300,000 for initial expenses. As Great Britain and Holland wholly supported this army, they prescribed the sphere of its operations, and retained any conquests that it might make. The treaty was for the year 1794; but its renewal was stipulated in a separate article. Prussia of course still supplied to Austria the 20,000 men due by the treaty of 1792.

If Malmesbury had not induced Haugwitz to sign the treaty then, it would never have been signed at all. Almost alone in the Court of Berlin, Frederick William desired to continue the struggle. His uncle, Prince Henry, had always opposed war with France, and long before Valmy, had prophesied that her untrained but enthusiastic levies would be a match for any professional army. His influence and that of the Duke of Brunswick, Lucchesini, and Möllendorf, were still cast against the western crusade, so that Grenville believed Prussia to be dragging on the negotiation solely in order to embarrass her Allies by throwing it up early in the campaign.[2] Moreover, Malmesbury's treaty contained its own death warrant. A Great Power can ill afford to hire out its troops to non-military States, unless they lessen the humiliation of such a proceeding by according the utmost possible freedom. But the Hague Convention specified that the subsidized Prussian army must operate where the paymasters directed; and they now decided on removing it from the Palatinate to the valley of the Meuse near Dinant, or even further west, provided that Austria could fill up the gap thus left in the Palatinate.[3] In passing, I may note that this important decision was due to George III, as appears in Grenville's final instruction to Malmesbury: "The King's determination is finally taken•not to agree to any plan by which the Prussians would be employed more to the left than the country of the Meuse."[4] No one who knows the rigour of the King's resolves can doubt

---

[1] "Malmesbury Diaries," iii, 85, 89.   [2] "Dropmore P.," ii, 516.
[3] "F. O.," Prussia, 33. Grenville to Malmesbury, 21st April.
[4] *Ibid.*, Same to same, 23rd May.

that he was responsible for a determination fraught with un-expected issues.

It is alien to my purpose to recount the ensuing disputes. I can glance only at the part played by Pitt. At one point his conduct was weak and dilatory. Early in May, when Malmes-bury proceeded to London for the purpose of securing the ratifica-tion of the treaty and the payment of the first subsidy to Prussia, he encountered most annoying delays. Pitt and Grenville left him severely alone, probably because they were then so occupied with the coercion of the English Jacobins as to have no time for the plans which promised the overthrow of the French Jacobins. Another topic engaging their attention was the hoped-for coali-tion with the Portland Whigs, which shrouded from their gaze the needs of the European Coalition. However we may explain the fact, it is certain that during sixteen days (6th to 22nd May) Malmesbury, despite his urgent entreaties to Grenville, could procure neither instructions as to his future conduct, nor a promise for the payment of the first Prussian subsidy. News of a British disaster in Flanders at last quickened the laggards of Whitehall. On the 23rd Malmesbury gained his heart's desire, and set out for the Prussian headquarters on the following day.[1] Meanwhile, owing to this long delay (one of the most discredit-able incidents in the careers of Pitt and Grenville), Prussia took no steps to carry out the terms of the compact. It so happened that on 24th May her army in the Palatinate, commanded by Möllendorff, gained a victory over the French at Kaiserslautern in the Palatinate; but that event set them the more against Malmesbury's treaty, which implied a march of some 120 miles through difficult country, and across an enemy's front.

Moreover, as has been hinted, reverses had by this time over-taken the right wing of the Allies, in West Flanders. At the centre, near the Sambre, the campaign opened with promise, the British cavalry gaining a brilliant success at Bethencourt. But Carnot, having drawn upon the French troops in Lorraine and the Palatinate, threw his heaviest columns at points on the extreme west of the French front, the result being that at Turcoing the Republicans shattered the isolated corps of the Duke of York and General Otto (18th May). The successes of the Prus-sians and of the Austrian army, on the Sambre, saved the situa-

---

[1] "Malmesbury Diaries," iii, 96.

tion for a time. But the prospects even in that quarter were overclouded by the resolve of the Emperor Francis to leave his army and return to Vienna. News of the critical state of affairs in Poland prompted this decision, the results of which soon appeared in quarrels at headquarters and discouragement in the rank and file. The Austrian soldiery saw in the withdrawal of the Kaiser the end of his rule in the Netherlands. They were right. The counsels of Thugut had now prevailed. South Poland was to be the prize of the Hapsburgs. The tiresome and distant Netherlands were to be given up, the pecuniary support of England, however, being assured as far as possible by a feint of defending them.

Here we have the explanation of the half-hearted effort made by the Austrians at Fleurus. There was every reason why Coburg, now again the commander of the main Austrian force, should strike vigorously at the French force besieging Charleroi. A decisive victory in front of Charleroi would not only save that place, but would give pause to the French forces further west, now advancing rapidly towards Ghent. Accordingly Coburg, advancing as far as Fleurus, hard by the village of Ligny, attacked the Republicans. He had on the whole the best of the fight, when the arrival of news of the surrender of Charleroi led him most tamely to call off his men and fall back. The retirement took place in discreditably good order, not a single gun being lost (25th June 1794). A bold leader would have beaten the enemy and probably would have saved Charleroi. With the same excess of prudence Coburg conducted his retreat, several positions and strongholds being abandoned in craven fashion.

Meanwhile Pitt and Dundas made great efforts to save West Flanders. In haste they despatched reinforcements to Ostend; and among the regiments which landed there on 25th and 26th June was the 33rd, commanded by Colonel Wellesley. The future Duke of Wellington found the small garrison of Ostend in a state of panic; and his chief, the Earl of Moira, deemed it best to meet the French in the open. By great good fortune Moira, with most of the regiments, reached Bruges, and beyond that town came into touch with Clerfait's force. Wellesley, taking ship, sailed round to Antwerp and reached that column by a safer route and earlier than his chief. His action is characteristic of a judgement that never erred, a will that never faltered. In this campaign, as he afterwards said, he learnt how not to

make war. But success not seldom crowns the efforts of him
who has the good sense to probe the causes of failure. Certainly
it rarely comes to British commanders save after very chastening experiences; and Wellesley now took part in what was, for
the Austrians, a fore-ordained retreat. Despite the manly appeals
of the Duke of York, Coburg declined to make a stand on the
fateful ridge of Mount St. Jean; and the name of Waterloo
appears in the tepid records of 1794 at the head of a plan for
arranging the stages of the retreat (5th July) which the nervousness of Coburg soon condemned to the limbo of unfulfilled
promises.[1] Is it surprising that, two days later, the Duke of York
declared to him that the British were "betrayed and sold to the
enemy"? Worse still, the garrisons of Valenciennes, Condé,
Quesnoy, and Landrecies, amounting to nearly 11,000 men, were
now left to their fate.

Indirectly Pitt and Dundas were responsible for these disasters. They weakened the British force in Flanders by sending
large drafts to the West Indies, as will in due course appear.
They also allowed Corsica to be occupied in the spring of 1794,
and yet they made little or no use of that island for expeditions
against the Riviera, which the royalist natives would readily
have undertaken under an inspiring leader. They also relied too
much on the Austrians and Prussians, though the former were
known to care little for their Netherlands, apart from the prospect of gaining the Barrier fortresses of French Flanders in
order to further the Belgic-Bavarian exchange. Above all, as
we have seen, Pitt's conduct towards Prussia was annoyingly
halting. Malmesbury's treaty could have no effect unless it led
the Prussians to move at once. The delay of sixteen days at
Whitehall must rank as one of the causes of the failures just
recounted; and though Grenville was technically guilty, Pitt
must be blamed for not ensuring the needful despatch in an all-
important decision. It is curious that he never realized his
responsibility. Speaking at a later date of the campaign of
Fleurus, he said that it turned upon as narrow a point as ever
occurred: that England was unfortunate, but the blame did not
rest with her.[2] This probably refers to the surrender of Charleroi

---

[1] "W. O.," I, 169. See an admirable article in the "United Service
Mag." (Aug. 1897), by Colonel E. M. Lloyd, founded on the papers of
General Sir James Craig, Adjutant-General of the Duke of York.

[2] "Parl. Hist.," xxxii, 1132.

and the retreat from Fleurus. But Pitt did not understand that the timely advent of part of the Prussian force on the Meuse, or even its advance into Lorraine, would have changed the situation; and for their inactivity he was in some measure responsible.

At times Pitt lived in dreamland. On 15th July, while the Austrians were quietly withdrawing from Central Belgium, he drew up a Memorandum as to the course of events. By the close of the year Austria was to bring 100,000 men into Flanders, a close alliance being framed on the basis of her acquisition of the French border districts (Valenciennes had not yet surrendered). England was to retain all conquests in the two Indies. The Prussians were to march towards Flanders, which they obstinately refused to do. Dutch and other troops were to be engaged by England, the presumption being that the year 1795 would see the losses of 1794 more than retrieved. The mistake of 10,000 in adding up the totals of the troops (78,000 instead of 88,000) enables one to conjecture at what time of the day this sketch was outlined.[1] One would not take it seriously had not the Foreign Office soon despatched Earl Spencer and Mr. Thomas Grenville as special envoys to Vienna to propose very similar plans, Austria being urged on by the prospect of acquiring the French Barrier fortresses from Lille to Sedan.[2]

They aroused in Thugut a spirit of greed, not of honourable emulation. In a private letter to Pitt, dated Vienna 16th August, Spencer warned him that that Government was "neither possessed of sufficient energy and vigour, nor sufficiently actuated by the true principles on which the cause in which we are engaged ought to be conducted" to justify the demands of Thugut. They included British subsidies for Austria, though she could well support the war, and the sacrifice of British maritime conquests at the general peace as a means of ensuring the recovery of her losses on land. As to Belgium, added Spencer, Thugut looked on it "as irrecoverably lost and not worth regaining, unless with the addition of a very strong and extended barrier, composed of fortresses which he to-day plainly told us he did not think there was the least chance of taking in the course of the war, but that they must be obtained as cessions from France at the peace.[3] Thus Thugut expected that, while

---

[1] "Dropmore P.," ii, 599. [2] "F. O.," Austria, 38. Despatch of 19th July.
[3] Pitt MSS., 180. See, too, "Dropmore P.," ii, 617-20, 626.

the Austrians were ignominiously evacuating the Netherlands, the British fleet should win French colonies valuable enough to induce France both to retire from Belgium, and to surrender to Austria her northern fortresses from Lille to Sedan or Thionville.

The capture of Valenciennes and the slaughter of the *émigrés* in the Austrian garrison was the retort of the French to these day-dreams (29th August). The fall of Robespierre a month earlier, and the enhanced authority now enjoyed by Carnot enabled the authorities at Paris to press on the conquest of Belgium with an energy which set at defiance the boyish miscalculations of Pitt and the wavering plans of the Hapsburgs.

Towards the close of July Pitt and Grenville saw the need of abating the rigour of their demands on Prussia. For of what use was it to move 60,000 Prussians more than 100 miles to defend West Flanders when that province was lost? Malmesbury therefore was empowered to pay the monthly subsidy of £50,000 on behalf of Great Britain and Holland, provided that Möllendorf's army attacked the French about Trèves, thus lessening the pressure on Coburg's left wing. On 27th July he framed such an agreement with Hardenberg. This statesman was destined to be one of the saviours of the Prussian State in its darkest days, 1810-12; but now, as always, his conduct was shifty; and it is questionable whether he, any more than Haugwitz, dealt honourably with England. It must suffice to say that Möllendorf made not even a demonstration towards Trèves. His inactivity was in part due to the withdrawal of several regiments towards Poland, though Great Britain and Holland still paid for the maintenance of the full quota on the Rhine.

So flagrant was the breach of faith as to elicit heated protests from Malmesbury; and Pitt, justly indignant at the use of British money for what was virtually a partition of Poland, decided to remonstrate with Jacobi, the Prussian ambassador at London. Summoning him to Downing Street, at the end of September, he upbraided him with this dishonourable conduct, declaring that, unless the Prussians moved forward at once, the British and Dutch subsidy for October would be withheld. Much as we may sympathize with this indignant outburst, we must pronounce it unwise. For firstly, Pitt was intruding upon the sphere of Grenville in making this declaration, which was far more acrid than the despatches of the Foreign Secretary.

Secondly, it was made in the presence of Dundas, with whom Grenville was already on bad terms. Is it surprising that the Foreign Secretary wrote sharply to Pitt protesting against his acting on a line different from that previously taken at Downing Street? In his despatch of 30th September to Berlin, Grenville was careful to make the withdrawal of the subsidy strictly conditional, and his protest was probably less sharp than that which Pitt addressed to Jacobi.

So annoyed was Grenville at Pitt's interference during his own temporary absence that he wrote to express his willingness to retire from the Foreign Office if this would solve the difficulties caused by the appointment of Earl Fitzwilliam to the Irish Viceroyalty. To that topic I shall recur in a later chapter on the Irish troubles which now became acute. Here it must suffice to say that Pitt declined to accept Grenville's offer, and affairs at Downing Street righted themselves.[1] But at Berlin the mischief was irremediable. Jacobi, a born intriguer, and ever hostile to England, represented the words of Pitt in the worst possible light. Accordingly Frederick William affected great indignation at the conduct of Pitt, accused him of ending the alliance, and discovered in his own ruffled feelings the pretext for giving rein to the dictates of self-interest. He gave orders to end the campaign on the Rhine; and though Grenville sought to patch matters up, compromise was clearly impossible between Allies who had lost that mutual confidence which is the only lasting guarantee of treaties.

At the autumnal equinox of 1794 Pitt was confronted by a far more serious crisis than at the beginning of the war in February 1793. The Republicans, after throwing back Clerfait beyond the River Roer, towards Aix-la-Chapelle, compelled the Duke of York to abandon the natural line of defence of Holland, the River Waal; and in the early days of October the British retired behind Bergen-op-zoom and other Dutch fortresses. These were found to be totally unprepared to sustain a siege. The sluggishness of the Orange party, dominant in Holland since 1787, stood in marked contrast to the eagerness of the Dutch Patriots to help the invaders. Consequently in a few weeks the friends of the Stadholder saw their hopes fade away.

[1] See "Pitt and Napoleon Miscellanies" for Grenville's letters. Pitt was the guest of Grenville at Dropmore at the end of November 1794 ("Buckingham P.," ii, 319).

There was but one chance of rescue. The Duke of Brunswick, who so skilfully led the Prussians to Amsterdam in 1787,
might be expected to impart some courage to the Dutch garrisons and some show of discipline to the disordered relics of
York's and Clerfait's forces now drifting slowly northwards. His
position as a Field-Marshal of the Prussian army also promised
to interest the Court of Berlin in recovering some part, at least,
of the supremacy of the Allies in the Dutch Netherlands. As
the crisis in Holland had served to unite the two great Protestant Powers, so now it might prevent the dissolution of that salutary compact. Further, George III, though greatly disliking the
substitution of Cornwallis for the Duke of York, favoured the
appointment of the veteran Brunswick to the supreme command. Family considerations, always very strong in the King,
here concurred with reasons of state. Not only had Brunswick
married the sister of George III; but their daughter, the Princess
Caroline, was now the reluctant choice of the Prince of Wales.
The parents, both at Windsor and at Brunswick welcomed the
avowal by the royal prodigal of the claims of lawful wedlock.
The Duchess of Brunswick fell into raptures at the brilliant
prospects thus opened out for her daughter; and it seemed that
both Hymen and Mars, for once working in unison, conspired to
bring from his inglorious retreat at Brunswick the man whom
that age still acclaimed as its war-lord.

Malmesbury therefore proceeded to Brunswick for the double
purpose of arranging the marriage and urging the Duke to take
the command of the allied forces on the Lower Rhine. Over-
joyed at leaving the atmosphere of intrigue at Möllendorf's
headquarters, the envoy journeyed into the northern plain in
hopes of assuring the safety of part of Holland. Early in
November Pitt and his colleagues received a refusal from the
Duke, but now they sent through Malmesbury an offer to sub-
sidize a corps of 20,000 or 30,000 Austrians in that quarter.
These, along with the British, Hanoverian, and Hessian troops,
when marshalled by Brunswick, might surely be trusted to stay
the French advance. The crisis was momentous. Brunswick
well understood that in reality the fate of North Germany was
at stake; for the French, if masters of the Rhine and Ems
valleys, could easily overrun the northern plain, including his
own duchy. Self-interest, pride in the German name, hatred of
French principles, and, finally, satisfaction at the marriage

alliance, bade the Duke draw his sword before it was too late. But here again the malign influence of Berlin thwarted the plans of Pitt. In vain did Malmesbury ply the Duke with arguments and the Duchess with compliments. On 25th November the Duke informed him that, as a Prussian Field-Marshal, he was bound to consult Frederick William: and " the answer he had received was not of a nature which allowed him to accept of an offer otherwise so highly honourable and flattering to him." He then handed to the envoy his formal refusal.[1]

Whether the elderly Duke of Brunswick could have withstood the impetuous onset of the ill-clad, half-starved, but unconquerable peasants now following the French tricolour in its progress through Holland, who shall say? The exploits of Pichegru and his levies border on the miraculous until we remember that half of the Dutch laboured on their behalf, while the troops of York and Clerfait distrusted or despised those leaders. This consideration it was that led Pitt to take a step which he deemed most necessary for the public service as well as for the reputation of the Duke of York. On Sunday, 25th November, he wrote at Holwood a very lengthy letter to the King, setting forth most deferentially the reasons which impelled him and his colleagues to request the withdrawal of the Duke from Holland.[2] He touched with equal skill and firmness on the unfortunate feeling prevalent in the army respecting the Duke of York; and, while eulogizing His Royal Highness, expressed the conviction of the Cabinet that, in his own interests as well as those of the country, he should be recalled from a sphere of action where the difficulties were wellnigh insuperable. Pitt also suggested to the King the advisability of transferring the British forces to a more promising sphere, Brittany or la Vendée. The King's answer evinced considerable irritation, a proof that he saw little but the personal aspects of the case. Pitt, however, held to his point, and the Duke was recalled in order to become a little later commander-in-chief, a position for which he was far better suited than for a command in the field. At the close of the year Pitt showed his regard for the public service by requesting from the King leave to displace his brother, the Earl of Chatham, from the Admiralty, where his lethargy had several times

---

[1] " F. O.," Prussia, 35. Malmesbury to Grenville, 25th November 1794.
[2] See " Pitt and Napoleon Miscellanies " for this letter.

hindered the naval operations. Lord Spencer became First Lord, the Earl of Chatham succeeding to Spencer's position as Lord Privy Seal.

Pitt's magnanimous resolve to brave the royal displeasure rather than keep a royal prince in a situation for which he was unfit met with general approval. The times were too serious to admit of pedantic trifling or unmanly shrinking. In quick succession there arrived news of the definite refusal of the Duke of Brunswick to come forward, of the incredible apathy of the Dutch, and of the demoralization of the Allies in their continued retreat. To add to their misfortunes, nature gripped that land of waters in a severe frost, so that the Dutch loyalists were unable, even if they had the hardihood, to let loose the floods against the invaders. In endless swarms these pressed on from the South, determined now to realize Dumouriez' dream of conquering Holland in order to appropriate its resources, pecuniary, naval, and colonial. Pichegru it was who won immortal fame by this conquest, which in truth needs not the legendary addition of his cavalry seizing a Dutch squadron in the Zuyder Zee. A singular incident attended the journey of Malmesbury with the future Princess of Wales towards Helvoetsluys, on their way to England. Unaware of the inroads of the French horse, they had to beat a speedy retirement, which, unfortunately for the Prince of Wales, placed them out of reach of the raiders. A little later the Duke and Duchess of Brunswick were fain to pack up their valuables and leave their capital in haste.

Such was the French conquest of Holland and part of Hanover in the winter of 1794-5. So speedy was it that Pitt and Dundas took no timely means to ensure the carrying off the Dutch fleet. As no small part of it was loyal to the Prince of Orange, who now fled to England, the oversight is to be censured. Surely Flushing or the Brill could have been secured. The Cabinet, however, as we shall see later, prepared to rescue from the general ruin the most valuable of the Dutch colonies, the Cape of Good Hope, the importance of which, for the safety of India, Pitt and Dundas rated most highly. Meanwhile, under the command of Abercromby, Harcourt, Cathcart, and Walmoden, the British and subsidized German forces fell back towards the River Ems, and thence to the Weser. Pitt, as we have seen, desired to recall the British regiments for service in the West of France. But various considerations told against this plan; and, as will appear later, the King obstinately opposed the withdrawal of the British cavalry from the confines of his beloved Electorate until the autumn of 1795. In April of that year the infantry, now reduced to some 6,000 effectives by the rigours of winter, embarked at Bremen.

Thus ended an expedition unprecedentedly fatal to the British arms. The causes of the disaster are not far to seek. The campaigns of 1793-4 were undertaken heedlessly, in reliance upon the strength of a Coalition which proved to have no strength, and upon the weakness of the French Republic which proved to be unconquerably strong. The Allies were powerful enough to goad France to fury, too weak to crush its transports. Their ill-concealed threats of partition bound France to the cause of the Jacobins, which otherwise she would have abjured in horror. Thus the would-be invaders drove France in upon herself, compelled her to organize her strength to the utmost; and that strength, when marshalled by Carnot, was destined to shatter the Coalition and overrun neighbouring lands. She then learnt the fatal secret that she could conquer Europe.

In a later chapter I propose to survey Pitt's conduct as War Minister. Here I need only point out that his mistakes resulted mainly from his unquenchable hopefulness. A singular proof of this admirable but dangerous quality is seen in his effort during the months of February and March 1795 to frame one more plan of co-operation with the Court of Berlin, which had so cynically deceived him. To this proposal Grenville offered unflinching opposition, coupled with a conditional threat to resign. Pitt persuaded him to defer action until the troubles in Ireland were less acute. But the King finally agreed with Pitt, and Grenville was on the point of retiring when news arrived of the defection of Prussia.[1] For some time she had been deep in negotiations with France, which had the approval of Möllendorf and the officers of her Rhenish army.[2] The upshot of it all was a treaty, which Hardenberg signed with the French envoy at Basle on 5th April 1795. By this discreditable bargain Frederick William of Prussia enabled France to work her will on the lands west of the Rhine, on condition of his acquiring a general ascendancy over North and Central Germany, which now became neutral in the strife. Austria and the South German States remained at

---

[1] "Dropmore P.," iii, 26-30, 50, 57.
[2] Ranke, "Hardenberg," i, 258; "Paget P.," i, 95, *et seq.*

war with France for two years longer, by which time the tottering Germanic System fell beneath the sword of Napoleon
Bonaparte.

Prussia's bargain with France marks a reversion to her traditional policy, which viewed that Power as the friend and Austria
as the enemy. It undid the life-work of Prince Kaunitz, now
nearing his end at Vienna, and left the Hapsburg States enfeebled. True, they had a profitable share in the third and last
Partition of Poland, which soon ensued; but this scarcely made
good the loss in prestige due to the undisputed hegemony of
Prussia in the greater part of Germany. The House of Hohenzollern, impelled by men like Lucchesini, Haugwitz, and Hardenberg, took the easy and profitable course and plumed itself on
over-reaching its secular rival at Vienna. In reality it sealed the
doom not only of the truly conservative policy of Pitt, but of
the European fabric. Prussia it was which enabled the Jacobins
to triumph and to extend their sway over neighbouring lands.
The example of Berlin tempted Spain three months later to sign
degrading terms of peace with France, and thus to rob England
of her gains in Hayti and Corsica. Thanks to Prussia and Spain,
France could enter upon that career of conquest in Italy which
assured the rise of Napoleon Bonaparte and the temporary ruin
of Austria. The mistakes of Pitt were great; but, after all, they
might have been retrieved were it not for the torpor of the
Viennese Court and the treachery of Prussia.

CHAPTER IX

THE WEST INDIES

Unfortunately, the war was carried on on the old principle of almost undivided attention to what was termed British interests—that is, looking to
and preferring the protection of trade and the capture of the enemy's
colonial establishments rather than to the objects which had involved Great
Britain in the contest with France.—COLONEL THOMAS GRAHAM'S *Diary*.

IF we try to picture the course of the war as mapped out by
Pitt, it would probably have appeared somewhat as follows.
Great Britain, after lending to the Dutch a few regiments as a
protection against the threatened raid of Dumouriez, withdraws
them, leaving the Dutch and the subsidized German corps to
guard the rear of the legions of Prussia and Austria during their
conquering march to Paris. England, in the meantime, harasses
the coasts of France, thereby compelling her to detain considerable forces at the important points, and further cripples her
by sweeping her fleets and merchantmen from the sea and seizing her colonies.

In short, Pitt's conception of the true function of Great Britain
in a continental war was based on that of his father, who accorded
comparatively little military aid to Frederick the Great even in his
direst need, but helped him indirectly by subsidies and by naval
expeditions that stalemated no small portion of the French army.
If Chatham's tactics succeeded when Prussia was striving against
France, Austria, and Russia, how much more might Pitt hope to
win a speedy triumph over anarchic France during her struggle
with Austria, Prussia, Spain, Naples, Sardinia, and Holland? He
expected, and he had a right to expect, that these States would
need British money, not British troops, while the Sea Power restricted its operations to a "minor offensive" along the sea-
boards of France and her colonies. Pitt's efforts in this direction
were constantly thwarted by the drain of men to Flanders; but

his letters to Murray, Chief of Staff to the Duke of York, evince his anxiety to strike at Toulon and the West Indies, and not merely to lighten the military duties of Austria and Prussia on the French borders.[1] It would be tedious to recount his various attempts to prepare an expedition for the West Indies.[2] Of more interest are the requests for protection which he received from the French colonists of Hayti, the western part of the great island of San Domingo.

As appeared in Chapter XX of the former volume, the decrees of the National Assembly of Paris fired the negroes of the French West Indies with the resolve to claim the liberty and equality now recklessly promised by the mother-land. The white settlers, on the contrary, having recently acquired autonomous rights, disputed the legality of that levelling legislation, and rejected all authority but that of Louis XVI. Amidst the ensuing strifes, the chief colonies, especially Hayti, were menaced by that most horrible of all commotions, a servile revolt, when, most opportunely, help arrived from Jamaica. The contrast between the timely succour of England and the reckless iconoclasm of Paris struck the imagination of the French settlers, and the Assembly of Hayti forthwith drew up a declaration, setting forth the illegality of the French decrees, the miseries resulting from them, and the resolve of the colonists to sever a connection absolutely fatal to their welfare. Citing the example of the United States fifteen years before, and recounting the misdeeds of the mother country, they proclaimed to the world the justice of the act of severance.

A copy of this declaration, signed by de Cadusey on 27th September 1791, was sent forthwith to Pitt, with a request for the protection of Great Britain. He received it at Burton Pynsent on 27th October.[3] One of the chief delegates from Hayti was de Charmilly, who on 14th November sought an interview with Pitt, and a fortnight later wrote to him, earnestly begging the help of the only nation which could avert ruin from those islands. France, he declared, had passed a decree of blood against her own colonies and was powerless to stop its effects. The National Assembly, having by its annexation of Avignon recognized the right of that papal district to belong to whom it would, Hayti of equal right now voted for union with England. He further advised that its ports should remain open to

[1] See "Eng. Hist. Rev.," October 1909.
[2] "Dropmore P.," ii, 395, 438, 443, 444, 464.   [3] Pitt MSS., 349.

all nations, a course of action which would herald the dawn of commercial and political freedom among the Spanish colonies of the New World.[1] These alluring prospects failed to entice Pitt from the strict neutrality to which he had pledged himself. So far was he from desiring to profit by the misfortunes of France, as the French princes first, and after them the Jacobins, maliciously asserted.

Once more the deputies of France flung the torch of discord across the Atlantic. By their decree of 4th April 1792 they declared absolute equality of rights between whites, half-castes, and blacks, and sent out commissioners to enforce this anarchic fiat. They forthwith took the side of the rebels, who in Toussaint l'Ouverture found a leader of terrible force of will. Martinique and Guadeloupe and the smaller islands were also a prey to civil war. In sheer desperation the planters and merchants of Guadeloupe sent over a delegate, Curt, to appeal to the British Government for protection. Lord Hawkesbury accorded to him an informal interview in the closing days of 1792. Curt pressed him for official help, without which his fellow colonists must lose their lives and property, and declared that he and many others abjured the name of Frenchmen.[2] Malouet, once prominent in the National Assembly and destined to become famous under Napoleon, also approached our Ministers, but with more caution. He knew that in some of the islands the Republic had many adherents; but after the outbreak of war in February 1793 he too advocated the sovereignty of Great Britain under certain conditions, and on behalf of the colonists of Hayti signed a compact with Dundas to that effect.

Fear of a revolt of the slaves had induced Ministers to send out reinforcements, so that, early in 1793, 19 battalions were in the British West Indies. In the month of April a small British force easily captured Tobago and restored that valuable little island to Great Britain. An attack on Martinique at midsummer was, however, a failure. These attempts, it may be noted, were made with forces already in the West Indies.[3] 'Pitt and Dundas have been severely blamed for sending further reinforcements to the West Indies.[4] But a letter which Pitt wrote to Grenville

[1] Pitt MSS., 121.   [2] "F. O.," France, 40.
[3] Malouet, "Méms.," ii, 209-11 ; Morse Stephens, "French Rev.," ii, 481-4 ; "Dropmore P.," ii, 388.
[4] Fortescue, iv, pt. i, 77, 78.

some time in June or July 1793 shows that the news of a French
expedition having set sail to the West Indies, escorted by six or
seven sail-of-the-line from Brest, led him to urge the despatch of
a force for the protection of that important group of colonies.[1]

Besides, was a forward policy in the West Indies unwise? In
these days it is hard to realize the value of those islands. The
mention of Hayti conjures up a vision as of a ship manned
by gorillas; for there and in Liberia is seen the proneness of
the negroes to aimless lounging varied by outbursts of passion.
But in the year 1789 Hayti far surpassed Jamaica in wealth and
activity. The French possessed only the western third of the
island; but the Spanish portion to the east was far less fertile,
and far worse cultivated. The French genius for colonization was
seen in the excellent system of irrigation carried on in the vast
and fertile plain, the *Cul-de-Sac*, east of the capital, Port-au-
Prince. But other portions, notably the long peninsula to the
south-west, were also highly prosperous. The chief towns
equalled in splendour and activity the provincial cities of France.
Port-au-Prince and Cap Français were the pride of the West
Indies; and the rocky fortress, Mole St. Nicholas, dominated
those waters as Gibraltar dominates the Eastern Mediterranean.
The population of Hayti was reckoned at 40,000 whites, 60,000
mulattoes or half-castes, and some 500,000 negro slaves. Its exports (chiefly sugar, coffee, and cotton) were assessed at upwards
of £7,500,000, or more by one third than that of all the British
West Indies. To some extent Jamaica flourished on its ruin.
For in May 1796 an official report stated that two coffee-
planters, refugees from Hayti, who had settled in the mountains
behind Port Royal, were introducing so many improvements as
to bring the exports of coffee up to 6,000,000 lb.; and they
would soon amount to 50,000,000 lb.[2]

The colonists of Hayti, who offered this valuable prize to
Great Britain, were far from being unprincipled adventurers.
Malouet, on whom fell the chief responsibility, was an upright
and able man; and both he and his comrades were deputed by
representative Assemblies which sought to save society from
sinking into a gulf of unutterable horrors. His letters to
Pitt[3] are instinct with the conviction that the men of Hayti

[1] "Dropmore P.," ii, 402, 403.   [2] Pitt MSS., 349.
[3] Pitt MSS., 155, 349. In the latter packet is Malouet's letter of 10th
March 1793 from Kingston, Jamaica, to M. Franklyn at London, dwelling

unanimously desired a British protectorate, and recognized that the colonists must pay for the support accorded to them. As we were framing an alliance with Spain, no difficulties were to be anticipated from the Spanish part of that island. When five or six valuable islands were to be had, to all appearance with little risk except from the slaves, Ministers would have been craven in the extreme not to push on an enterprise which promised to benefit British commerce and cripple that of France. Unfortunately, owing to the drain of the Flemish campaign, their action was tardy. The schisms between Royalists and Republicans at the city of Cap Francais enabled the negroes to burst in at midsummer of 1793 with fire and knife and glut their vengeance on some thousands of persons. Even after these atrocities the Jacobin commissioners continued to make use of the blacks in order to enforce their levelling decree; and the year ended amid long drawn out scenes of murder, rape, and pillage. By these infamous means did democracy win its triumph in the West Indies.

In their despair the French loyalists applied for further aid to Major-General Williamson, the governor of Jamaica. He sent a force which received a hearty welcome at the little fortress of Jérémie (19th September), and a few days later at that important stronghold, Mole St. Nicholas, then blockaded on land by the blacks. An attempt by the Republicans at the capital, Port-au-Prince, to send an expedition for the recapture of Mole St. Nicholas was thwarted; and late in the year 1793 five other towns accepted British protection. The rapid recovery of prosperity in the district forming the lower jaw of the griffin-like head of Hayti is seen in the official exports from the port of Grand Anse at its tip. During the quarter 20th September to 31st December 1793 it sent the following quantities to British ports, chiefly Kingston in Jamaica: Coffee, 644,751 lb.; Sugar, 91,593 lb.; Cotton, 56,339 lb.; Cocoa, 66,944 lb. Even larger quantities of coffee were exported to foreign ports.[1] In 1796 the produce of Hayti was valued at £1,500,000; the colony employed more than 400 ships.[2] Was not this a land for which some risks might be encountered?

on the woes of San Domingo and Martinique—all due to the folly and wickedness of one man, probably Brissot. He despairs of the French West Indies. See, too, "Dropmore P.," ii, 388.
[1] Pitt MSS., 349.   [2] "Parl. Hist.," xxxiii, 586.

Meanwhile the Spaniards from their part of the island had overrun certain districts, especially those to the north of Port-au-Prince. In particular, they for a time occupied the port of Gonaives, about midway between the capital and Mole St. Nicholas, a step almost as threatening to the British forces as to the French Republicans. It is hard to fathom the designs of the Spaniards at this time. Their pride, their hereditary claims to the whole of the Indies, and their nearness to this splendid prize, all urged them on to an effort from which lack of men, ships and money, and the hatred of the French and the blacks to their sway should have warned them off. Seeing also that the French colonists had officially handed over their possession to Great Britain, Spain should have come to some understanding with her Ally before invading what was now in effect British territory. She did not do so; and subsequent events proved that her King and statesmen harboured deep resentment against the transfer, and sought to thwart it by underhand means. For the present, however, their inroad into the north-central districts dealt one more blow to the power of the French Jacobins and their black friends. These last were formidable only when the quest was plunder. Even the iron will of their ablest leader, Toussaint l'Ouverture, could infuse no steadiness into the swarthy levies, which, roving almost at will in the mountainous interior, were wellnigh as dangerous to the Republicans as to the British.[1]

It is not surprising, then, that Pitt and Dundas, despite the drain of ships and men to Ostend and Toulon, did all in their power to secure this colony, which had always been deemed essential to the prosperity of French commerce. On 11th October 1793 Pitt reluctantly admitted the need of further postponing the West India expedition owing to the uncertainty of the fate of Ostend and the chance of a French raid on our shores. But when these dangers passed away the original plan held the first place; and it should be noted that, by the middle of November, when the expedition was finally decided on, the position of the Royalists at Toulon was thought to be satisfactory. Much, of course, can be urged against sending troops so far away, when the loyal Bretons needed succour; but Pitt, Gren-

[1] The facts stated above suffice to refute the strange statement of Mr. Morse Stephens ("Fr. Rev.," ii, 476) that the English invasion of San Domingo was "absurd." It was not an invasion, but an occupation of the coast towns after scarcely any resistance.

ville, and, still more, Dundas were bent on this colonial enterprise; and, viewing the situation as it then was, not as we with
our knowledge of later events see it, their decision seems
defensible.[1]

On 26th November, then, Sir John Jervis (afterwards Earl of
St. Vincent) set sail with some 7,000 troops commanded by Sir
Charles Grey. After touching at Barbados he made for Martinique and succeeded in reducing that island by 22nd March
1794. St. Lucia, Guadeloupe, Marie Galante, and the Saintes
surrendered in April, but after struggles which showed that the
Republicans, backed by mulattoes and blacks, were formidable
foes. This anarchic combination was already threatening the
small and scattered British garrisons in San Domingo. But,
when further reinforcements from England reached Mole St.
Nicholas, a force detached thence under Major-General Whyte
made a dash upon Port-au-Prince. Vigorously handled, and
under cover of a violent thunderstorm, the landing parties carried
an important outwork in handsome style, and thus assured the
surrender of the whole place. The spoils were 101 cannon and
32 ships, with cargoes worth about half a million sterling (4th
June 1794). This brilliant success cost the assailants very few
lives; but the heats of the summer and probably also the in-
temperance of the troops soon thinned their ranks. The French,
too, having received succours which slipped out from Rochefort,
recovered Guadeloupe in the month of September.[2] And from
this point of vantage they sought, often with success, to stir up
the slaves in the British islands.

Thus by the autumn of 1794 the position was somewhat as
follows. The British had secured all the French colonies in the
West Indies, excepting Guadeloupe. In Hayti they held nearly
all the coast towns, and maintained an intermittent blockade
over the others; but their position was precarious owing to the
thinness of their garrisons, the untrustworthiness of their mulatto
auxiliaries, and the ravages of disease. It seems probable that,
with ordinary precautions and some reinforcements, the garrisons
might have held out in the towns then occupied, provided that
the fleet intercepted French expeditions destined for the West
Indies; and this ought to have been possible after Howe's
victory of 1st June 1794. The fact that the Republic strenuously

[1] "Dropmore P.," ii, 443, 454, 464.
[2] Fortescue, iv, pt. i, chs. xiii, xiv; James, i, 250-2.

prepared to regain those islands at the very time when the Coalition in Europe and the revolt in Brittany threatened its existence, suffices to justify Pitt and his colleagues in attacking France in that quarter. A colony which is worth regaining must be worth gaining. To the capture of Louisburg, a weaker stronghold than Mole St. Nicholas, England devoted several expeditions a generation earlier. Had Pitt and Dundas declined to have as a gift this key to the Indies, what would not their critics have said of their incapacity and cowardice? For the West Indies were then far more highly prized than Canada.

Endless difficulties beset every expedition to the tropics, even when forethought and care minimize the risks from disease. The story of England's ventures in those seas is, in general, one of hasty action and long repentance. No one had made a special study of the needs of white men in that climate. In fact, the military martinets of those days made little allowance for the altered conditions of service under a broiling sun; and, until the advent of Abercromby, only slight changes took place either in the uniform or the time of drills. Dr. Pinckard, in his account of this enterprise, mentions cases of gross stupidity, slovenliness, and even of dishonesty on the part of army officials in those colonies;[1] and it is clear that to this cause the long death-roll was largely due. The following figures at the close of 1794 are instructive:[2]

	BRITISH.		COLONIAL.	
	Effective.	Sick.	Effective.	Sick.
Port-au-Prince . . .	366	462	496	48
Mole St. Nicholas . . .	209	166	209	38
Jérémie	95	59	—	—
St. Marc	48	33	813	321
Tiburon	34	18	—	—
Total .	1490		1925	

It will be observed that the French and coloured troops were far more immune from sickness. Indeed, the loyal French colonists felt much annoyance at the comparative uselessness of

[1] Pinckard, "Notes on the Expedition to the West Indies," ii, especially Letter 15.
[2] Bryan Edwards, "Hist. Survey of S. Domingo" (1801), 204. Fortescue (iv, 385) assesses the British losses in the West Indies in 1794 at 12,000 men, apart from deaths in battle.

the British force at this time. Charmilly, after a long visit to Hayti, returned to London in September 1794, and laid stress on this in several letters to Pitt. On 11th October he urges him to sanction a plan (already approved) for raising a force of French *émigrés* in service in Hayti. A month later he complains that nothing is being done, though the loyalists of Hayti are willing to pay their share of the expenses. As it is, they are growing disheartened; for the British troops remain in the strongholds, thus leaving the colonial troops in the country too weak to cope with the roving bands of brigands. As for himself, he is weary of soliciting help which is never vouchsafed; and he warns Pitt that opinion is gaining ground in Hayti as to the uselessness of maintaining a struggle in which the British people take no interest. The note of egotism rarely absent from Charmilly's letters appears in his assurance that, if something is not done soon, England will lose the splendid possession which he has placed in her hand.[1]

There were good reasons why Pitt and his colleagues should not commit themselves deeply to the Haytian embroglio. In that anxious time, the autumn of 1794, the most urgent needs were to save Holland from the Jacobins, to distract them by helping the Royalists of Brittany, and from our new base in Corsica to clog their attempts at an invasion of Italy. Owing to the slackness of our Allies, these enterprises proved unexpectedly difficult. In truth any two of them would have strained the scanty resources of the British army; and Pitt is open to censure for not ruling out all but the most essential of them. But here a word of caution is needful. For us, with our knowledge of the sequel, it is a comparatively easy task to assess the gains and losses of the war, and to blame perseverance in one course as wasteful folly or backwardness in another as stupid slothfulness. If later critics would seek to realize the amount of information possessed by fallible mortals at the time of their decisions, the world would be spared floods of censure. How was Pitt to know that the Dutch were about to hamper, rather than assist, the defence of their land by the Allies; that Prussia would play him false; that the schisms among the French Royalists would make Quiberon a word of horror; that Paoli would stir up strife in Corsica; or that Spain

[1] Pitt MSS., 121.

was preparing to ruin British rule in Hayti? With loyal co-operation on the part of the Allies, all these enterprises might have proceeded successfully side by side.

There were no solid reasons for distrusting Spain. The Court of Madrid had eagerly taken up arms against the regicides of Paris; and Pitt, as we shall see, early sought to avoid friction in the West Indies. Otherwise, he would be highly blameable; for England's easy acquisition of Hayti could not but ruffle the feelings of the Dons. No chord in the highly strung nature of the Spaniard vibrates so readily and so powerfully as that of pride in the retention or recovery of the conquests of his ancestors. The determination of the Court of Madrid to win back Louisiana and the Floridas, not to speak of Minorca, had potently influenced its policy in the recent past, and the prospect of seeing the Union Jack wave over Hayti and Corsica now envenomed the ever open wound of Gibraltar. True, the French colonists of Hayti, acting through their local Assemblies, had the right to will away their land to England. Spain, at least, could not say them nay; but none the less she longed to see her flag float once more over the western districts which had slipped from her grasp.

Pitt and Grenville had early foreseen trouble ahead with Spain on the subject of the West Indies. When affairs at Toulon were causing friction, Grenville instructed Lord St. Helens, British ambassador at Madrid, to urge that Court to secure the hoped-for indemnities in the French districts north of the Pyrenees. As for England, she had in view Hayti and certain of the French Leeward Islands. This plan, continued Grenville, could not offend Spain, seeing that the Haytian or western part of San Domingo fronted Jamaica and fell naturally to the Power holding that island. But, as the Court of Madrid was known to cherish desires for a part of Hayti, St. Helens must endeavour to ascertain their extent so as to come to a friendly compromise.[1] The Spanish Government, at that time incensed by the quarrels at Toulon, vouchsafed no reply to these courteous overtures. They were renewed during the year 1794, but with no better result.

Meanwhile, Don Garcia, the Spanish Governor of San

---

[1] "F. O.," Spain, 28. Grenville to St. Helens, 30th November 1793. On 1st October Pitt pressed Grenville to open this question to the Spanish Court ("Dropmore P.," ii, 433, 438).

Domingo sought to pour oil on the flames of civil strife. He
allowed the bands of negroes to retire into the Spanish districts,
and replenish their stores. In fact, his conduct was so openly
hostile to England, that on 11th November 1794 Grenville instructed Jackson, British *chargé d'affaires* at Madrid, to demand
the recall of that arrogant official.[1] Charmilly also averred that
the brigands often sallied forth from Spanish territory to ravage
the western districts.[2] Other facts point in the same direction.
Whence could the Republicans and their black allies have gained
supplies of arms and ammunition but from the Spaniards? The
survey of the British over the western coasts was close enough
to bar those supplies, at least in the quantities that the negroes
demanded. In truth, the enigmas of the Hayti affair can be solved
only by delving in the Spanish archives. The whole question is
closely connected with the extraordinary change that came over
Anglo-Spanish relations in the years 1795-6, a topic which will
be treated in the following chapter.

[1] "H. O." (Secretaries of State), 5.
[2] Pitt MSS., 349. He added that in 1788, 584 European and 699 American
ships set sail from Hayti: 37,447 negroes were imported.

CHAPTER X

SPAIN AND HAYTI

Are not Martinique, Mole St. Nicholas, and the Cape of Good Hope most important conquests?—PITT, *Speech of 9th December* 1795.

MORE than once it has happened that, after a time of national revival, Spain has fallen under the dominion of a ruler led by wrongheaded counsellors and intriguing favourites. Such was the case in the year 1788. Charles III, who then passed away, had restored the finances, the prosperity, the navy, and the prestige of that land. But his successor, Charles IV, proved to be one of the weakest and most indolent members of that dynasty. Fond of display, and devoted to the pleasures of the chase and the table, he squandered the resources of the State, and soon saw his finances fall into hopeless confusion. Worse still, his consort, a princess of the ducal House of Parma, and a woman of much energy, conceived a violent passion for Manuel Godoy, a young private in the royal guards, on whom she heaped favours and dignities, so that he forced his way into the highest circles with the title Duke of Alcudia. He was endowed with a dignified mien, handsome features, affable manners, and good abilities, so that the British ambassador, Lord St. Helens, happily characterized him as a Birmingham Villiers. The measure of his importance and of the degradation of the Sovereigns may be gauged from the fact that the paramour of the Queen became the chief Minister of the King. In truth, the Queen, her lover, and her two confessors governed Spain.

The habits of the favourite were as follows. He rose early, drove or rode for an hour, and after breakfast transacted business for a time. He then relieved the tedium of that time by witnessing exhibitions of skill and daring by his private matadors, after which he spent about three hours in the society of the Queen. He then devoted the same length of time to the conduct of public business with the King; and the day ended with dinner, fêtes, the opera, or the consideration of requests for patronage. This function of State generally occupied three evenings in the week; and on these occasions a crowd of some 250 suitors filled his meanly lit ante-room with jealous expectancy and long baffled hopes.[1]

Certainly the representatives of monarchy at this time of acute trial were unequal to the strain. Catharine of Russia was supremely able, but no less corrupt. Frederick William of Prussia equalled her in vice and in nothing else. Francis of Austria had the brain of a master of ceremonies; George III that of a model squire; Ferdinand of Naples was in his place in the kennel; Victor Amadeus of Sardinia, in the confessional. It is difficult to say to what place Charles IV of Spain and his consort can most fitly be assigned; for they could not live apart from Godoy; and with Godoy they would have been excluded from any residence but the royal palace of Spain. The policy of that Court wavered under his whims and devices. Hated by the grandees, loathed by honest people, and yet fawned on by all alike, he sought to strengthen his power by jobbery, with results fatal to the public services. Such a man evades difficulties instead of grappling with them. He lives for the day. "After me the deluge " is the motto of all Godoys.

The favourite soon perceived that the war with France pleased neither the Court, the merchants, nor the people. Charles IV had gone to war for the restoration of royalty; but, thanks to the perfidy of Prussia and the vacillations of Austria, that ideal had vanished; and in its place there appeared the spectres of want and bankruptcy. By the end of 1794 the Republicans had gained a firm foothold in Catalonia and Biscay; and the prospect of further campaigns was highly distasteful to a Court which kept up the traditional pomp of the Spanish monarchy. Even when the Spanish forces in Catalonia and Biscay were wellnigh starving, the Court borrowed £160,000 to defray the expenses of the usual migration to San Ildefonso ; and the British ambassador computed that the cost of a campaign could be saved by a sojourn in Madrid for the whole year. But parsimony such as this was out of the question. Accordingly the only possible alternatives were, peace with France, an issue of paper money,

[1] " F. O.," Spain, 36. Bute to Grenville, 26th June 1795.

or a bankruptcy. Godoy inclined strongly to peace, and discovered in Anglophobia a means of betraying the French
House of Bourbon. England, so he averred, had entered on the
war solely for her own aggrandisement, with the view of appro-
priating first Dunkirk, then Toulon, and, failing them, Corsica
and Hayti, to the manifest detriment of Spain. The argument
was specious; for Pitt's resolve to cripple France by colonial
conquests necessarily tended to re-awaken the old jealousies of
the Spaniards; and herein, as in other respects, the son had to
confront difficulties unknown in the days of his father. The task
of the elder Pitt was simple compared with that of humouring
and spurring on five inert and yet jealous Allies.

Among them Spain was not the least slothful and exacting.
After the quarrels between Langara and Hood at Toulon, the
despatches from Madrid to London were full of complaints.
Now it was the detention of Danish vessels carrying naval
stores, ostensibly for Cadiz, but in reality, as we asserted, for
Rochefort. Now it was the seizure and condemnation of a
Spanish merchantman, the " Sant' Iago," on a somewhat similar
charge. England had equal cause for annoyance. The embers
of the quarrel of 1790 were once more fanned to a flame by
Spanish officials. Captain Vancouver, of H.M.S. " Discovery,"
while on a voyage to survey the island which now bears his
name, had his ship and crew detained and ill-treated at Monterey
Bay by the Governor of California. The Court of St. James
warmly protested against this conduct as contrary to the
Nootka Sound Convention of 1790; and thereby inflamed that
still open wound. Valdez, Minister of Marine, the only rival of
Godoy, now openly avowed his hostility to England. Early in
February 1795, in a conference with the King, he hotly denounced
British designs in Corsica and Hayti. Thenceforth there was no
hope of securing the co-operation of the Spanish fleet for the
blockade of Toulon and other duties too exacting for Admiral
Hotham's squadron. On 11th February Godoy handed to Jackson, our *chargé d'affaires*, a state paper containing the assurance
that Spain desired to continue the struggle against France; but
" if His Christian Majesty finds another road less dangerous
than that which he follows, he will take it with the dignity becoming his rank; he will exhaust the means he may have till he
shall obtain the welfare of his people; but he will not look on
their annihilation with indifference, if those who have a similar

interest vary the mode of pursuing it." In plain language this meant that, as Prussia was then treating with France, Spain would follow her example when she thought fit.[1]

Thereafter the Spanish Ministers either manifested sullen reserve or indulged in petulant complaints respecting the "Sant' Iago," Corsica, and Hayti. The conduct of the Marquis del Campo at London was equally sinister; his despatches represented the policy and conduct of England in the darkest colours. In the hope of softening these asperities Pitt and Grenville decided to send the Earl of Bute to Madrid in place of Jackson, who desired to escape from the insolences of that capital. Thus by one of the subtle ironies of history, the son of Chatham despatched to the Court of Madrid the son of the man who thwarted Chatham's aims respecting that same Power. Bute's instructions (dated 5th April) bade him humour that Court, but none the less look out for any signs of a Franco-Spanish compact, and discover at what place in the Spanish colonies a blow might be dealt with most effect.

On 13th April, after receiving news of a Spanish success in Catalonia, Grenville urged Bute to re-awaken Castilian pride by holding out the prospect of gains beyond the Pyrenees, and expressed the hope that Spain might renew her treaty with England, promising also to consider her claims to parts of the north-west of Hayti. These hopes were futile. Early in that year France and Spain began to draw close together. The more moderate Republicans, Sieyès, Boissy d'Anglas, and Cambacérès, let it be known that France would offer moderate terms. Barthélemy, the able French envoy in Switzerland, furthered these plans, which came near to fulfilment when Prussia signed with France the Treaty of Basle (5th April 1795). Charles IV was only waiting for some excuse to follow suit. As a relative of Louis XVI, he scrupled to take the lead; but he was ready to follow the lead of Prussia. The sacrifices demanded of him in March 1795 were considerable, viz., the province of Guipuzcoa and San Domingo. But Bourgoing, the special envoy to Madrid, offered a prize which far counterbalanced these losses. He held out to Godoy the bait which in the more skilful hands of Napoleon was destined to catch both him and his credulous master. Portugal was to be theirs if they made

---

[1] "F. O.," Spain, 36. Jackson to Grenville, 2nd January and 11th February 1795.

common cause with France. Acting together, the two Latin nations would overwhelm this "province of England," and together they would chase the British from the Mediterranean. That Portugal had loyally supported Spain in the monarchist cause mattered little. In place of the costly war of principle, Godoy sought to substitute an effort with limited liability, effective partnership, and enormous profits. He knew not that in entering on this broad and easy path, he assured the ruin of Spain and the ultimate loss of her colonial empire.

In this secret chaffering Pitt and Grenville were worsted as inevitably as in the similar case of the Partition of Poland. The Power that cries "hands off" to abettors of robbery needs to have overwhelming force at its back; but both here and on the banks of the Vistula England was helpless. There was no Court of Appeal. Christendom had vanished amidst the schemes of the monarchs in the East, and under the stabs of regicides in the West. Thus, while the champions of monarchy were sharing the last spoils of Poland, France succeeded in detaching Spain from the royalist league by inciting her to the plunder of Portugal.

Few moves have been more mean and cowardly; though the conduct of the Court of Madrid in this matter touches far deeper depths of infamy. For its present position was far from hopeless. With the help of the British fleet the progress of the French troops towards Bilbao might have been stayed. Affairs in Catalonia wore a hopeful aspect. England offered to recognize the Spanish conquests in Hayti and to press for further indemnities from France at the general peace. But all representations were in vain. Godoy brushed them aside in order to compass the ruin of the House of Braganza. On this enterprise he concentrated all his faculties. He inveighed against the invasion of Hayti by British troops. "His Britannic Majesty," he said, "ought to have abstained from any interference with the island of San Domingo, upon the whole of which His Christian Majesty had a well-founded claim; or, if any enterprize was undertaken there by Great Britain, it should have been in the way of auxiliary to Spain in order to restore to her her ancient possessions in the West Indies." On other occasions he moaned over the heavy expenses of the war, the misery of the people, and the impossibility of resisting the superior power of France. But his chief theme was Hayti, and he finally suggested that the British acquisitions in that island should be held in trust for Louis XVII. He was not a little ruffled by the reply that they belonged of right to George III, who would keep them as compensation for the expenses of the war. Another significant fact was the removal of a fine corps of French *émigrés*, some 3,300 strong, from the northern provinces to Cadiz, on their way to the West Indies.

At the time of the arrival of Bute at that port (25th May), Fortune vouchsafed a few gleams of hope to the Allies. Spanish pride having kicked against the French demands, especially that of the province of Guipuzcoa, Bourgoing's mission proved fruitless. The diplomatic situation also improved. In February 1795, as we have seen, Catharine II of Russia signed a defensive treaty with Great Britain, to which Austria acceeded on 20th May. Thus did Pitt replace the outworn Triple Alliance with Prussia and Holland by a more powerful confederacy. With these bright prospects in view, and animated by the hope of rousing Western France from Quiberon, Pitt had a right to expect some measure of fortitude even in the Court of Madrid.[1] But Godoy remained obdurate. On 11th June, in his first interview with Bute, he said he had no faith in Russia; the vacillations of Austria were notorious; and Pitt was said to be about to send Eden to Paris to sue for peace. As for Spain, she was hard pressed; French and American emissaries had stirred up strife in her colonies; and affairs were most "ticklish" in San Domingo. His Government had therefore sought for a composition (not a definite peace) with France. In fact, the war as a whole had failed, for whereas the Allies had set themselves to crush French principles, they had succeeded merely in uniting the French people in one common cause. On 11th July he promised to recall the Anglophobe Governor of San Domingo; but he declared the island to be in so distracted a state that both Spaniards and British would probably be expelled. He then complained that somehow England always got the better of Spain; witness Nootka Sound, Hayti, and Corsica. In spite of Bute's assurance that he came to end these jealousies, Godoy continued to drift on the tide of events. "No plan is prepared," wrote Bute on 11th July, "no measures are taken. The accident of the day seems to determine everything, and happy do the

---

[1] "F. O.," Spain, 37. Grenville to Bute, 5th, 12th, and 19th June.

Ministers feel when the day is passed." He therefore advised that Godoy should be bribed.

The advice came too late. Already the favourite had instructed Don Domingo d'Yriarte, his envoy to the now extinct Polish Republic, to confer with Barthélemy, the French Ambassador at Basle. The actions of Yriarte, of course, depended on the secret behests of Godoy. On 2nd July Godoy informed him that peace was the only means of thwarting the efforts of the bad counsellors of the Crown; and four days later he wrote:

Every day makes peace more necessary. There is no hope of restoring affairs in Navarre. Cowardice has unnerved our army and the French will dictate their terms to us. . . . I fear that their claims will be excessive, and condescension is our only resource if we are to succeed in saving ourselves even in part. Your Lordship need not take alarm at the rigour of the terms of peace; listen to them, accept them, and forward them to me, saying to yourself that perhaps they will not be so fatal as the results of a delay in the negotiation might be.[1]

Yriarte, a nervous valetudinarian, eagerly accepted this despicable advice. Already one of his secretaries had allowed Barthélemy to see an almost equally base effusion from Godoy; so that the French ambassador on 21st July informed the Committee of Public Safety that the game was in their hands. This was the case. Yriarte, after receiving two packets from Madrid, hastily sought a nocturnal interview with Barthélemy by the help of a dark lantern. The French ambassador received him with some surprise, especially on hearing that he came to sign a treaty of peace on terms not yet known at Paris. When the Spaniard insisted on signing at once, Barthélemy examined the conditions, and finding them highly favourable to France, consulted his secretaries, with the result that he finally decided to conclude the affair.

Thus came about the Peace of Basle (22nd July 1795). Spain now waived her former demands, the restoration of religious worship in France, and French aid in the recovery of Gibraltar. The French, however, now agreed to restore all the districts held by their troops in the North of Spain, while the Court of Madrid ceded San Domingo. Spain also made peace with the Dutch or Batavian Republic, and offered to mediate between France and Portugal, Naples, Sardinia, and Parma.[2] Such were

[1] Del Cantillo, "Tratados," 660.
[2] "Papiers de Barthélemy," vi, Introd., xv, 71, 77-85.

the chief clauses of this astonishing compact. It dealt a deadly blow to Pitt. For at the very time when he was building up a formidable league and rousing Brittany against the Republic, Spain seceded from the monarchist cause, and by surrendering San Domingo to France, doomed to failure his costly efforts in Hayti. Further, as will appear in Chapter XI, by setting free large numbers of the French troops at the Pyrenees, she greatly enhanced the difficulties of the expedition of General Doyle to the coast of la Vendée. Worst of all, it soon appeared that Godoy was bent on reviving the policy of the Family Compact, making common cause even with the murderers of Louis XVI in order to thwart England's expansion oversea. Bute therefore warned our Government to prepare to strike a blow at once, before the Spanish fleet should be ready to help the French either in Corsica or Hayti. These precautions proved, for the present at least, to be unnecessary. The degradation of the Court and populace of Madrid may be measured by the joy with which the news of that inglorious peace was received. The Queen, fearful that the failures in the war would lead to the fall of her paramour, procured the speedy ratification of the Treaty of Basle and decorated him with the title Prince of the Peace.

On hearing of the defection of Spain, Pitt at once took steps to guard Hayti against a treacherous attack by detaching the greater part of the British force then preparing to help the French Royalists of la Vendée. The general opinion both in London and Madrid was that war must ensue. Godoy kept a close watch upon Bute, who took a mansion in Madrid on a long lease in order to lull that Court into security. It was of the highest importance to avert or delay a rupture with Spain; for the condition of the British West Indies was most critical. The French, having recovered Guadeloupe and St. Lucia, despatched thence emissaries to fire the slaves in the British islands with the hope of gaining liberty and equality. The peril became acute in Jamaica. There about 500 negroes had escaped to the mountains, especially in Trelawny and Charlestown Counties, and by night carried out murderous raids against the planters and their dependents. So fiendish were the atrocities of these Maroons, that the authorities in that island applied to the Spaniards in Cuba for one hundred bloodhounds and twenty huntsmen in order to track the Maroons to their fastnesses. This device proved successful; the murderers were by degrees hunted down, and were transported to British North America, £25,000 being voted by the Jamaica Assembly for settling them there.

Nevertheless the use of bloodhounds, which placed Britons on a level with the Spanish crusaders, aroused general disgust. Attempts were made in the House of Commons by General Macleod, Sheridan, and Courtenay to represent the Maroons as men worthily struggling for liberty. Dundas, while pruning these sprays of rhetoric, declared that Ministers would thereafter prohibit the use of bloodhounds. These troubles with the slaves prejudiced Parliament against any change in their condition. In vain did Francis, in one of the last speeches of an acrid but not discreditable career, press for the amelioration of their lot. At the outset he showed the bitterness of his enmity to Pitt by charging him with the betrayal of the cause which, in his oration of 2nd April 1792, he had irradiated with the beatific vision of a regenerated and blissful Africa. Why, he asked, did not the Minister resign office after his failure to realize his heart's desire? He then charged him with insincerity on the whole question, and urged the House to be content with alleviating the condition of the slaves by giving them the rudiments of education and some rights of property, above all by securing the sanctity of their marriages. Fox followed with a speech aimed more against Pitt than the slave-owners. The Prime Minister then replied. Ignoring the charges of his opponents, he pointed out that the proposed improvements were utterly inadequate to remedy the ills of the negroes so long as Parliament allowed shiploads of these unhappy creatures to be cast into the West Indies every year. What was needed, he said, was the abolition of that hateful traffic, indeed of the whole system of slavery. For himself, he still hoped that Parliament would adopt those measures, which alone could be effective. Wilberforce was absent through illness. Francis, having elicited in the main mere personalities, not declarations of principle, withdrew his motion.

The lapse of the question of Abolition in the years 1795-6 was a public misfortune; for the slaves, despairing of justice from England, turned to France. For the good of the cause they murdered men, women, or children, with equal indifference; and, when hunted down, died with the cry *Vive la République*. Here was our chief difficulty in the West Indies. Owing to the refusal of Parliament to limit the supply of slaves or to alleviate their condition, we had to deal with myriads of blacks, exasperated by their former hardships, hoping everything from France, and able to support climatic changes which dealt havoc to the raw English levies. In truth, the success of the West India expeditions depended on other factors besides military and medical skill. It turned on political and humanitarian motives that were scouted at Westminster. The French Jacobins stole many a march on the English governing classes; and in declaring the negro to be an equal of the white man they nearly wrecked Britain's possessions in the West Indies.

For a great negro leader had now appeared. Toussaint l'Ouverture, though probably not of pure negro blood, was born at Breda in the north of Hayti in 1746. His mental gifts were formidable; and when sharpened by education and by long contact with whites, they enabled him to play upon the elemental passions of his kindred, to organize them, to lead them to the fight, to cure their wounds, and to overawe their discontent. A barbarian in his outbursts of passion, and a European in organizing power, he became a zealot in the Republican cause. A quarrel with another masterful negro, Jean François, forced him for a time to retire into the Spanish part of San Domingo; but he soon returned, and proved to be our most formidable enemy.

The position in Hayti at the close of 1795 was somewhat as follows. The Republicans and their coloured allies, often helped by the Spaniards, held or ravaged the greater part of the territory which the French Royalists had invited us to possess. Their hopeful forecasts had led Pitt and Dundas to send far too few troops for what proved to be an increasingly difficult enterprise; and at this time British authority extended scarcely beyond the reach of the garrisons. The French Royalists had not given the help which Malouet and Charmilly had led our Ministers to expect.[1] And on the other hand, Victor Hugues, the Republican leader, managed to spread revolt in St. Vincent, Grenada, and Dominica. In this critical state of things, the Cabinet decided to accord to Major-General Williamson, Governor of Hayti, a long furlough, and to place in supreme command a man of great resourcefulness and power of character. Sir Ralph Abercromby was at this time sixty-one years of

[1] "W. O.," vi, 6, which contains other despatches of Dundas cited later.

age; but in zeal and ardour he excelled nearly all the junior officers. His toughness and energy had invested with dignity even the disastrous retreat from Holland early in the year. He was not a great commander; for he lacked both soundness and firmness of judgement, and he had no grasp of the principles of strategy; but he restored the discipline and prestige of the British army; and in him Moore and Wellesley hailed the dawn of a brighter era. "The best man and the best soldier who has appeared amongst us this war," was Moore's comment after Abercromby's glorious death near Alexandria.[1] Pitt has often been charged with lack of judgement in selecting commanders. Let it be remembered, then, that he sent Abercromby to the post of difficulty and danger.

Unfortunately, delays multiplied at Spithead. Though the Cabinet withdrew the marrow of the Vendean expedition, yet not enough troops were available to complete Abercromby's muster; and when the men were ready, the ordnance and transports were not at hand. What Department and what officials were answerable for this scandalous state of things it is hard to say. Buckingham, who had several correspondents at Portsmouth, suspected Abercromby of shiftlessness. However that may be, the autumn wore away amidst recriminations and growing discontent. When the fleet at last put to sea, it encountered a terrible storm off Portland; several transports were dashed to pieces on that point; while others in the van were flung back on to the Chesil Beach or the shore near Bridport (18th November). The horrors of the scene were heightened by the brutality of the coast population, which rushed on the spoil in utter disregard of the wretches struggling in the waves. The rest of the convoy put back to Spithead; and not till the spring of 1796 did Abercromby reach Jamaica. Dundas had instructed him first to recover St. Lucia and Guadeloupe, whence Victor Hugues had flung forth the brands of revolt. Ultimately the flames shrivelled up the colonies of France; but, for the present, they were more formidable than her fleets and armies. It was therefore sound policy to strike at those two islands. In a "secret" despatch of 4th November, Dundas also warned Major-General Forbes closely to watch the Spaniards in San Domingo, and, though not attacking their posts, yet to support the French Royalists with arms and money in case they desired to do so.

[1] "Diary of Sir John Moore," i, 208, 221, 233, 243; ii, 18, 19.

Among those who sailed from Portsmouth early in 1796 was Colonel (afterwards Sir John) Moore.[1] He found the West India service most unpopular. Yet the energy of Abercromby and Moore brought about the surrender of that almost impregnable fortress, Morne Fortunée, in St. Lucia. Moore was left as governor of the island, but with a garrison insufficient to complete the subjection of the fanatical blacks. General Whyte found the conquest of the Dutch settlement of Demerara a far easier task than its retention. Abercromby then relieved St. Vincent and strengthened the defences of Grenada, that island having been recaptured by General Nicols. Abercromby and his comrades thus saved those possessions from the most imminent danger. His services were almost as great in the quarters as on the field. He adapted the cumbrous uniform to the needs of the tropics, and, by abolishing parades and drills in the noontide heats, and improving the sanitary conditions of the camps, sought to stay the ravages of disease, of which the carelessness or stupidity of officials had been the most potent ally. On 21st April 1796 Sheridan moved for a return of the troops who had succumbed to disease in the West Indies. He asserted that several of them, on landing, were without shoes and stockings, that hospitals crowded with sick were without medicines or bandages, and that in one case a hundred patients had to spend the night on the bare beach. Dundas's reply was virtually an admission of the truth of these charges.

The declaration of war by Spain in the autumn of 1796 brought about a new situation. The Republicans and their black allies regularly took refuge and found their supplies in the central parts of San Domingo now ceded to France; but when the British sought to follow and attack them there, they were assured that it was neutral territory. The British Government warmly protested against this duplicity. Either the island was Spanish, or it was French. If the former, then Toussaint and his men had no right to retreat thither. If the latter, the British could attack them. In point of fact, plans for the transfer of San Domingo to France were at that time dragging slowly along at Madrid: and when the French General, Rom, failed to bend that Court to his terms, he departed for the island under the convoy of a Spanish squadron. This incident was typical of the recent policy of

---

[1] "Diary of Sir John Moore," 2 vols. Edited by General Maurice.

Madrid. In every possible way it favoured France. Early in 1796 seven French warships underwent extensive repairs in the royal dockyard at Cadiz. Merry, secretary of legation at Madrid, further reported numerous seizures of British merchantmen by French privateers which brought them into Spanish harbours. Twelve ships were thus brought into Alicante in the winter of 1795-6; and English merchants could get no redress for these seizures. French privateers also fitted out at Trinidad to act against Grenada and Tobago.[1]

Provocations were not all on one side. Early in 1796, three Spanish West Indiamen were overhauled by two English frigates and taken to Bermuda, in the belief that war had broken out. They were, however, at once released. Godoy protested angrily against this indignity, and early in March hinted that Spain's neutrality would cease on the establishment of a French Government. Two months later Bute found that Spain was seeking to form a Quadruple Alliance, namely, with France, Denmark, and Sweden, a scheme which Ehrenthal, the Swedish envoy, warmly furthered. The news of Bonaparte's victories in Italy and of the financial troubles in England evidently puffed up Godoy with the hope of playing the part of an Alberoni for the humiliation of England; and in 1796 Spain had better prospects of worsting the islanders than in 1718 when they had the alliance of France, Austria, and Holland. In truth, no period was more favourable for a revival of the Latin races than the years 1796-7, when England was in dire straits, when Austria succumbed under the blows of Bonaparte, and the Dutch, Danes, and Swedes opposed the British Power. With singleness of purpose and honesty in their administrations, France, Spain, and their Allies should have wrecked the life-work of the two Pitts.

The British Ministers felt the gravity of the situation. In view of the collapse of the Austrian Power in Lombardy, Pitt wrote to Grenville on 28th June in unusually despondent terms, that it was hopeless to expect Austria to prolong the war after the present campaign. We should be left alone to confront France and Holland, "probably joined by Spain, and perhaps favoured more or less openly by the Northern Powers."[2] Ac-

---

[1] "F. O.," Spain, 39, 40. Merry to Grenville, 20th and 25th December and 19th January, 10th February, 6th and 29th March.
[2] "Dropmore P.," iii, 214.

cordingly we must see to our home defences, and also consider the possibility of a general peace. Grenville therefore urged Bute to seek by all methods compatible with his dignity "to preserve the good understanding of the two countries." In fact, Pitt and his colleagues now decided to bring about a general pacification; and, as will appear later, they held to that resolve, in spite of the strong opposition of George III. But, on 5th August, while they were discussing details, Bonaparte won a crushing victory over Wurmser at Castiglione, and, eleven days later, Godoy definitely sided with France. Pitt feared that the hostile league would include Denmark and Sweden; and, but for his foresight in gaining over Catharine, this would have been the issue of events. Even so, Godoy hoped to form a Quadruple Alliance with France, Holland, and Prussia. He therefore took a high tone with Bute, declaring that England would not be allowed to attack San Domingo, as it was still Spanish, and there was a necessary connection between France and Spain; but he would not hear of Bute accepting that statement as a declaration of war.

Clearly, Spain was trying to gain time; for reports from Cadiz showed her fleet to be far from ready, several of the ships being leaky. The repairs to the French ships at that dockyard also went on in the most leisurely manner. But on 4th August all was ready. Admiral Mann with a small blockading force having been called by Jervis into the Mediterranean, the French ships set sail, escorted by twenty Spanish sail-of-the-line. The French squadron made for the Bank of Newfoundland and inflicted great damage. Why it did not proceed along with the Spaniards to the West Indies is hard to say. The impact of twenty-seven sail-of-the-line in that quarter would have been decisive; but probably Godoy did not yet feel warranted in throwing down the gauntlet. Pitt and Grenville decided to overlook the gross breach of neutrality at Cadiz, and even now hoped for a change in Godoy's mood. On 26th August Grenville informed Bute that, though England had good cause for declaring war, she would await the result of the recent proposals to Spain. On or about that date Las Casas, the Spanish ambassador, pettishly left London on a flimsy pretext; and two days later Dundas warned the commander-in-chief in Hayti of the imminence of war. Nevertheless, while taking every precaution, he was not to attack the Spaniards until definite news of a rupture arrived.

Further, on the 31st (as will appear in the following chapter) Portland despatched orders to Sir Gilbert Elliot, Viceroy of Corsica, to prepare for the immediate evacuation of that island.

It is therefore clear that Pitt and his colleagues used all possible means to avert war with Spain. Bute, acting on orders from London, carried complaisance to lengths derogatory, as he thought, to the honour of Great Britain, and Godoy humoured him to the top of his bent. Thus, on 10th September, in the course of a singular interview, Godoy assured him that, even if war broke forth, it would be brief. If (he continued) England had not annoyed Spain by her naval and colonial policy, the latter might have arranged to find some indemnity, either at the expense of Holland, or else "something on the coast of California. You English have a passion for California, and the trade is in the most flourishing state." Half amused by these dilatory tactics, Bute sought to find out the real state of the case; and he discovered that the Franco-Spanish compact aimed at the joint conquest of Portugal as well as of Naples, Sicily, and Gibraltar, while England was to be compelled to surrender Honduras and Hayti. On the 5th of October he received from Godoy the Spanish declaration of war. It laid stress on the disputes at Toulon, England's seizure of Corsica, Hayti, and Dutch Demerara, besides the founding of British mercantile posts on the River Missouri, which evidently aimed at securing the routes to the Pacific.[1] Of these schemes, the conquest of Portugal lay the nearest to the heart of Godoy.

The rupture with Spain is an event of prime importance. Because her fleet was disastrously beaten by Jervis off Cape St. Vincent in February 1797, it has too often been assumed that she counted for little in the war. An examination of the British Records reveals the error of that assumption. The evacuation of Corsica and of the Mediterranean by the British forces resulted solely from the Spanish offensive. Though weak in herself, Spain held so strong a position in Europe and the West Indies as to endanger British enterprises at many points, besides threatening the coasts of Ireland. In truth, but for Spanish support in the Mediterranean, Bonaparte could never have ventured upon his Eastern expedition. Thus the defection of the Court of Madrid changed the character of the war. Thenceforth

[1] "F. O.," Spain, 44. Bute to Grenville, 10th September and 21st October.

it revolved more and more around colonial questions, to the weakening of the royalist and republican motives which had worked so potently in its early stages. The oriental adventure of the young Corsican was to emphasize the contrast between the years 1793 and 1798; but the scene-shifting began with the intrigues of Godoy. In a sense Pitt himself helped on the transformation. He did not regard the struggle against France as one of political principle. He aimed solely at curbing the aggression of the Jacobins upon Holland; and the obvious device of weakening France by expeditions to the West Indies further helped to bring events back into the arena of eighteenth-century strife. Now that Spain, the protagonist of the French Bourbons, deserted their cause and attacked the Power in which they most trusted, all pretence of a war of principle vanished. The importance of the change was not perceived at the time, though signs of it were not wanting. Both in France and England democratic enthusiasm speedily died down, and the discontent, which now and again flared forth in both lands, was but a feeble sputter compared with the devouring flame of 1789.

In the West Indies the effects of the rupture with Spain were speedily felt. On 9th September 1796 Dundas instructed Forbes, commander-in-chief in Hayti, to help the Spanish settlers if they resisted the transfer of their part of the island to France. He also enjoined the utmost possible economy in public expenditure, and urged that the French settlers should have a large share in the conduct of local affairs. This zeal on behalf of local self-government was markedly opportunist. It arose from a suggestion of Colonel Wigglesworth, Commissary-General in Hayti, that the expenses of that colony would not lessen until there was a regular Government. In the midst of the financial strain at home Pitt and his colleagues desired that the French settlers should bear their share of the expense of maintaining bands of native auxiliaries. By one of the unaccountable impulses that sway the negro mind, a considerable force was now available; but it could not be utilized owing to the rigid economy enjoined by the Home Government. As the financial outlook darkened, Portland and Dundas sent urgent warnings to the new Governor of Hayti, Major-General Simcoe, bidding him concentrate the whole of the British force at Cape Nicholas Mole, the probable objective of the French and Spaniards. The military administration must be withdrawn to that fortress, the British cavalry being sent home. Further, as Great Britain could in no case bear a larger financial burden than £300,000 a year for Hayti, expenses were to be reduced on all sides, the residue falling to the share of the colonists. A larger naval force would, however, be sent; and Simcoe was advised to seize the island of Tortuga and to alarm the Spaniards by feints against Havannah.

This was the beginning of the end at Hayti. Ministers, in despair of pacifying that racial cauldron, now looked on the Spanish colonies as an easier prize. Dundas therefore ordered Abercromby to capture Porto Rico or Trinidad; and he even dallied with a fantastic scheme for shipping the Haytian colonists to Porto Rico. Abercromby, however, who again set sail from Portsmouth in November 1796, decided to make for Trinidad, and by a brilliant stroke captured its capital, Port of Spain. The attack on San Juan, in Porto Rico, met with unexpected difficulties, and ended in failure (February and April 1797). Matters now became desperate in Hayti. The rebels captured several posts near Port-au-Prince, largely owing to dissensions among the defenders. Simcoe, despite a serious illness on his way out, worked miracles with his skeleton regiments, but both he and his subordinates failed to cut down expenses as the Cabinet demanded. Accordingly, on 9th June 1797, Portland and Dundas reminded him that no further reinforcements could be sent out, and added this ominous sentence: " It is but too obvious that . . . the immense sacrifices this country has made for the protection of the French part of San Domingo have too frequently been diverted from purposes of public utility to answer the worst ends of private peculation and inordinate cupidity."

In a recent debate in the House of Commons St. John assessed the expenses of Hayti for January 1797 at £700,000; and stated that, for the discharge of judicial duties, a Frenchman was receiving £2,500 a year, which he was now squandering in London. Pitt remained silent. Dundas did not deny these allegations, but begged members to recollect the great difficulties of our officials in Hayti.[1] This was undeniable. It is the curse of a policy of retirement that waverers haste to leave betimes with all the spoils obtainable. The signs of abandonment of Hayti caused

---

[1] For the disgust of Pitt and Dundas, see " Dropmore P.," iii, 390.

a stampede, demoralizing to all concerned. On 1st January 1798, Portland and Dundas penned the order for the evacuation of Hayti, owing to the impossibility of making good the loss of troops or of recruiting in the island. After dwelling on the impossibility of reducing the expenditure to the requisite amount, Ministers explained that they had deferred the evacuation of Hayti " as long as the negotiation which His Majesty had opened with the enemy at Lille, and the disposition of a majority in the two Councils of Legislature in France, left a hope that some immediate arrangement might be made with that country, which in its consequences might operate to relieve England from the intolerable burdens by which the British part of St. Domingo is retained, and to a certain degree to ensure to its inhabitants a continuance of security and protection. . . . The rupture of the negotiation and the avowed system of the present Government of France appear on the one hand to render the attainment of this desirable end precarious, if not remote, whilst on the other they impose on H.M.'s confidential servants an additional obligation of reducing the heavy burdens of a war, the continuance of which is unavoidable, within the narrowest limits, in order to be able to persevere in it until adequate terms of peace can be obtained; and it is certainly their first and essential duty to appropriate the resources of the country with such management and economy as may ensure the preservation and defence of the essential possessions of the Crown. . . ."

The good faith of Pitt in the Lille negotiation appears clearly in this interesting statement, which further proves that he held on to Hayti in the hope of ceding it to France on terms satisfactory to Great Britain and the colonists. Doubtless it was the perception of this truth which led many of the settlers to decamp after spoiling the Egyptians. The thankless duty of evacuation devolved on Brigadier-General Maitland, who carried it out with skill and patience. Especially admirable is his secret bargain with Toussaint, whereby that able chief agreed not to molest the British either in Hayti or in Jamaica, while in return he was to receive provisions at certain ports under his control. Ministers had not advised any such proceeding, but they cordially approved of it, despite the clamour of the West India planters at a compact with a negro.[1] Thus was laid the basis of that good

---

[1] Malouet wrote to Pitt on 24th June 1798: "The wisdom of General Maitland's measures, the perfect order in which he has conducted the opera-

understanding which subsequently enabled Toussaint to defy Bonaparte.

The success attending this agreement shows what power England might have wielded had not her King, her Princes, and her Parliament insisted on maintaining intact the institution of slavery. They thereby aroused an enemy more terrible than yellow fever, the negro. France profited by the blunder; but she rushed blindly forward, using the black man with a recklessness which gave him the mastery. On the other hand, if Pitt and Wilberforce had succeeded in carrying out their programme in the years 1790-2, the incendiary devices of Brissot and Victor Hugues would have come to nought. In that case the transfer of Hayti to England would have placed at her disposal myriads of devoted blacks, ready and able to plant the Union Jack on every fortress in the West Indies, and to conquer the colonies of Spain if she changed sides. It was not to be. Far from gaining an accession of strength in that quarter, England lost heavily in men and treasure, and at the Peace of Amiens retained only Trinidad in return for all her sacrifices.

In no part does Pitt's war policy appear to more disadvantage than in the West Indies. He entered into those expeditions when the army at home was unable to meet the demands of the service in Flanders, and on the coasts of Brittany and Provence, not to speak of the needs of Ireland and the East Indies. He allowed Dundas to send out levies which were far too raw to withstand the strain of the tropics. This fact, together with the stupidity of the regulations and the inexperience, or worse, of the medical staff, accounts for the waste of life and the barrenness of these tedious campaigns. At no time had England in the West Indies a force sufficient to withstand the ravages of disease and to overcome the Republicans and their black allies. Nevertheless, while the conduct of the West Indian campaigns is open to censure, it is difficult to see what other course could have been adopted towards those important colonies, in view of the resolve of the French Jacobins to revolutionize them. The attempt was made and partly succeeded. Could Pitt and his colleagues stand merely on the defensive, while incendiaries sought to stir up

tions have lessened the disasters attending it, and by means of a truce and convention agreed on with the Republican chiefs, not an inconsiderable number of inhabitants has been induced to remain on their plantations" (Pitt MSS., 146).

a war of colour? Was it not the natural and inevitable step to en-deavour to extirpate those fire-brands? And when so attractive an offer as that of Hayti was made by the royalist settlers, could the British Government hold timidly aloof and allow that rich land to breed revolt? Surely a servile war could be averted only by intervention at the natural centre of influence. If from Guade-loupe, after its recapture by the French, the seeds of rebellion were sown broadcast, would not Hayti have become a volcano of insurrection? Finally, it is unquestionable that the change of front of the Court of Madrid in the years 1795-6 blighted the whole enterprise at the very time when success seemed attain-able. On Godoy, then, not on Pitt, must rest the responsibility for the lamentable waste of life in the West Indies and the ultimate lapse into barbarism of their most fertile island.

CHAPTER XI

THE CAPE OF GOOD HOPE: CORSICA: QUIBERON

THE French Jacobins early laid stress on the weakness of the British Empire. An official report issued in January 1793 at Paris advocated a close alliance with Tippoo Sahib, the Raja of Mysore, and recommended that the French force sent to assist him should threaten or secure the Dutch possessions at the Cape of Good Hope, and in Java and Ceylon. " There," it continued, " you would meet only with men enervated by luxury, soft beings that would tremble before the soldiers of liberty." The French conquest of Holland and the capture of the Dutch fleet in the winter of 1794-5 brought these schemes within measurable distance of fulfilment. Failing to save a single Dutch fortress or warship, Pitt and his colleagues became alarmed about the Dutch colonies; and when the lethargic Stadholder and his consort Wilhelmina landed in England, Ministers conferred with him on this topic.

On 7th February 1795, shortly after his arrival at Kew House, thenceforth the scene of his debauches, he drew up an order for the Governor of the Cape of Good Hope, bidding him welcome the arrival of a friendly British force, which would save Cape Town from the French. That important post belonged to the Dutch East India Company, then virtually bankrupt, and altogether unable to maintain its neutrality amidst the struggles for a world-empire now entering on a new phase. The officials of the Company at Amsterdam on 3rd February issued warnings to all Dutch ships in British ports to set sail forthwith, and further requested the French Government to secure Dutch vessels from attacks by its war vessels or privateers.[1] A few days later the invaders of Holland laid hands on British ships and detained even the packet-boats. In fact, though the Dutch did not frame an

---

[1] " F. O.," Holland, 57.

alliance with France until 16th May, it existed in effect from the month of February.[1] These facts explain the action of the Prince of Orange, which is otherwise unjustifiable. It was a natural retort to the conduct of the Dutch authorities. The British archives also show the alarm of our India Board and of its president, Dundas. On 5th February he urged the British East India Company to send in duplicate urgent messages to India. On 8th and 10th February he inquired whether the extra troops needed for India could sail on three of their ships now ready in the Thames; and he requested that some of the Company's troops stationed at St. Helena should proceed to India, their place being taken by drafts from home.[2]

Foremost among Dundas's plans for assuring British supremacy in India was the acquisition of the Cape. Not that he valued the Cape and Egypt on their own account. That generation regarded them merely as half-way-houses to India, witness the curious statement of Sir Francis Baring, Director of the East India Company, to Dundas, that the Cape was of no advantage whatever to us, and might be a dangerous drain upon our population; but in the hands of France it would most seriously menace our interests.[3] Of how many prosperous British colonies has not this been said? For similar reasons we took possession of large parts of India and Canada, not to speak of Malta, portions of Australia, New Zealand, and the Egyptian Soudan.

Early in March Commodore Blankett set sail from Spithead with four ships, having on board part of the 78th regiment, besides marines. The "Sphinx" was to join them at St. Helena. The land forces were commanded by Major-General Sir James Craig. Early in April Rear-Admiral Sir Keith Elphinstone sailed with a larger force, and a further expedition was in preparation under the command of Major-General Alured Clarke. The Cabinet expected little or no resistance, and even referred to a friendly reception as the probable issue. They had some grounds for hope. The Dutch force at the Cape consisted of about 800 German mercenaries, whose pay was far in arrears. It was suggested that we should take them into our pay, and quiet the people by the promise of abolishing the abuses of the Dutch Company. These hopes proved excessive. Craig, on making False Bay on 11th June, soon found Governor Sluysken totally unaffected by the

---

[1] " Cape Records," i, 98.   [2] " W. O.," vi, 67.

[3] " Cape Records," i, 17, 22.

Stadholder's letter. He was a man "of the most uncommon *sangfroid*," professing affection to England and dislike of France, but resolved to keep a firm hold of Cape Town. He offered to give the squadron all it wanted, and begged for time to consider the British demand.

Meanwhile mounted burghers poured in from the eastern settlements, and greatly strengthened the Dutch camp, situated in a pass half way between the town and False Bay. These sturdy farmers hoped to win entire independence; for indeed the Dutch East India Company cramped the life of the settlers at every turn. Despite the wealth of that land in corn, cotton, wine, and cattle, it made little progress. The fisheries might have been productive but for the regulations which forbade the colonists even a pleasure boat. The Company claimed one-tenth of the produce of all sales and had the right of pre-emption and of fixing the prices of goods. Settlers might not even kill their own cattle for food without the permission of officials. Cape Town was the only market for foreign commerce, and all products going in and out were subject to heavy dues.[1] Far from thriving on these exclusive rights, that corporation found its funds crippled by the very regulations which impoverished and irritated the burghers. In fact the first aim of the Boers was to trek beyond reach of the arm of the law. Thus came about the settlement of the remote townships, Swellendam and Graaf-Reinet, and thus was implanted in that virile race the resolve to secure complete independence of the enfeebled motherland.

The time seemed to have come when the British force menaced Cape Town. The Boers, no less than the Governor Sluysken, regarded the letter of the Prince as a forgery and the whole affair a mere trick. In vain did Elphinstone and Craig offer guarantees for good government. The officials and soldiery were impressed by the offer of enrolment in the British service, but the armed farmers proved intractable. Not having artillery or sufficient troops, Craig awaited the arrival of reinforcements from St. Helena; but on 14th July he landed about 1,600 men at Simon's Town, and somewhat later began the advance towards Cape Town. With little difficulty his men drove the Dutch from a strong position in the Pass of Muysenberg. On

---

[1] "Cape Records," i, 23-6, 138-40; Cory, "Rise of South Africa," i, ch. ii.

the next day the Dutch advanced from Cape Town with all their force and eight guns, but failed to dislodge Craig, despite his lack of artillery.

A period of much anxiety ensued, owing to the delay in the arrival of the reinforcements under Major-General Alured Clarke, without which an advance on Cape Town was perilous. The Dutch meanwhile received supplies from interlopers, concerning whom Elphinstone wrote with nautical emphasis: " The seas are infested with Americans, Danes, Genoese, Tuscans, etc., or in other terms smuggling ships, mostly belonging to Britain and Bengal, entrenched with oaths and infamy, who trade to the French islands [Bourbon, etc.] and all the ports in India, changing their flags as is most convenient to them."[1] He therefore forbade any of them to touch at the Cape. On the arrival of Clarke's force Craig took the offensive. About 4,000 strong, the British pushed on towards Cape Town, amidst a dropping fire from the mounted burghers, until they drew near to Wynberg. There the Dutch prepared to offer a stout resistance; but the diversion caused by three British ships entering Table Bay, and firing at Cape Town, unsteadied them; and, after little fighting, they retired towards the capital, crying out that Sluysken had betrayed them. Early on the morrow he offered to surrender; and the Union Jack was hoisted on 16th September.

The conquest was delusively easy. The mounted Boers, who were the heart of the defence, rode off with their arms, vowing vengeance against the invaders; and some hundred of the foreign mercenaries, who entered the British service, soon deserted. On 22nd September Craig wrote that, except the six principal merchants in Cape Town, all the population was hostile, and would certainly join the French, if they appeared, Jacobin ideas being rife alike in town and country. He hoped that the abolition of " the abominable monopolies " would have some effect. After Clarke and most of his troops sailed on to their destination, India, Craig viewed the future with concern, as Cape Town and the neighbouring bays needed a considerable force for adequate defence. The population of Cape Town and district then amounted to 4,957 settlers and their children, 6,068 servants, and 9,049 slaves. In the whole colony there were

---

[1] "W. O.," i, 323. In "F. O.," Holland, 57, is a memorial of Elphinstone and Craig to Grenville, stating why they had detained at the Cape the U. S. ship "Argonaut," whose owners now prosecuted them for £100,000.

14,929 free settlers, 11,555 servants, and 19,807 slaves. The oxen numbered 418,817.

The news of the capture of Cape Town caused great relief at Whitehall. Dundas on 16th January 1796 assured Craig that His Majesty would have preferred a peaceful acquisition. The remark does not evince much sagacity; for in that case the Boers would have represented the occupation as an act of trickery concocted with the Prince of Orange. As it was, the Cape was conquered after a fair fight. Undoubtedly in the month of August the burghers might have beaten Craig had they been either well led or enterprising. Dundas also instructed Clarke to leave a strong garrison at Cape Town, and forwarded news of the capture of Trincomalee, the Dutch stronghold in Ceylon. The Dutch soon sent a force of 2,000 troops convoyed by six warships, for the recapture of the Cape; but, while sheltering in Saldanha Bay, some fifty miles north of Cape Town, it was surprised by Elphinstone's squadron and capitulated (17th August 1796). The news of this disaster hastened the surrender of the burghers of Graaf Reinet who had defied British authority.

In order to mark the permanence of British rule, Pitt decided to send out as Governor Lord Macartney, who previously had undertaken a mission to "Louis XVIII" at Verona. His arrival in May 1797 helped to check the growth of discontent which was again becoming formidable. Macartney's difficulties were great. The Dutch held sullenly aloof, in the belief that England must give up her prize at the peace. Our military and naval officers disliked Cape Town, owing to the lack of amusements, the dearness of provisions, and the badness of the roadstead. Admiral Pringle declared to Lady Anne Barnard that, as a naval station, it was the worst that the devil could have contrived; that the people were objectionable, and the animals vile, even the hens being unable to lay fresh eggs. The soldiers grumbled at the high prices; for, though beef was only fourpence a pound, and good wine sixpence a bottle, yet an egg cost three-pence and a dish of cauliflowers eighteenpence. Readers of Lady Anne's sprightly letters will note in germ the problem that has beset the British in South Africa.[1] They formed a restless minority among a people curiously unreceptive and suspicious. They were bored by the surroundings, puzzled by

---

[1] "South Africa a Century ago." By Lady Anne Barnard.

Dutch elusiveness, and doubtful as to the future. The war was going far from well; and the alliance of Spain with France in the summer of 1796 facilitated attacks from the Canaries and Monte Video. These difficulties were enhanced by the cold and tactless behaviour of Macartney.

Nevertheless Pitt resolved at all costs to hold the Cape. Signs of disgust at the state of affairs in Corsica and the West Indies early figure in his letters; but as to the retention of Cape Town he never wavered. Bonaparte's capture of Egypt in 1798 showed that India was about to be assailed by way of the Red Sea. The greater, then, was the need to retain the stronghold which dominated the sea-route to the East Indies. The resolve of Pitt to assure the communication with India by one or other of the two routes will concern us later. But we may risk the assertion that he would certainly have avoided the blunder of the Addington Ministry in 1802 in giving up the Cape and neglecting to secure Malta against recapture by Napoleon. Early in the course of the Napoleonic War, Pitt resolved at all costs to retain Malta and to re-conquer the Cape. During the negotiations of 1805 with Russia he refused to allow the discussion of our title to Malta; and in the parleys with Prussia a little later he distinctly excepted the Cape from the list of the conquered colonies which Britain might be willing to restore at the general peace.[1] Six days before Pitt expressed this resolve, Nelson won his last and greatest triumph, thus enabling the Prime Minister to deal with full effect the blow which won Cape Colony for the British flag. It is clear, then, that Pitt discerned the enormous importance of that station as an outwork of India. In fact, after the expedition of Bonaparte to Egypt and the renewal of his oriental schemes in 1803, no statesman worthy of the name could fail to see that either Egypt and Malta, or the Cape of Good Hope, must belong to the mistress of the East Indies. In the last resort, then, it was the world-policy of Napoleon, which planted the Union Jack for ever both at Malta and the Cape of Good Hope.

Naval campaigns almost of necessity resolve themselves into a series of experiments; and after the failure of the attempt to hold Toulon, a blow at Corsica was the natural sequel. At a

[1] "F. O.," Prussia, 70. Pitt to Harrowby, 27th October 1805.

time when Great Britain had no post within the Mediterranean, that island was a most desirable prize. Its supplies of naval stores to the dockyard at Toulon were of the highest value to the French; and Nelson declared the occupation of Corsica to be imperatively necessary, as it furnished that dockyard with the decks, sides, and straight timbers for ships.[1] Accordingly, after the evacuation of Toulon by the Allies in December 1793, Admiral Hood decided to effect the reduction of the island for the royalist cause.

Already, while at Toulon, he had received an urgent invitation from Paoli, the leader of the Royalist, or British, party in Corsica, to help the islanders in driving out the French. Victor in the long feud against the Bonapartes, whom he expelled at midsummer, Paoli now resolved to root out the Jacobins, and his Anglophil leanings induced him to offer the crown of Corsica to George III. Both the King and his Ministers received the offer favourably, Pitt and Grenville regarding Corsica as one of the indemnities to be exacted from France. Sir Gilbert Elliot, the King's Commissioner in the Mediterranean, was therefore charged to administer Corsica. Disputes between Admiral Hood and General Dundas, the commander of the British troops, somewhat hampered the sieges of the three French garrisons still holding out; but by August 1794 Calvi, the last hope of the French, succumbed to the vigour of the attack of General Stuart, effectively helped by Nelson, who there lost the sight of his right eye.

Subsequent events in Corsica, although of great interest, are not closely connected with the life of Pitt; and I therefore propose to describe them and the details of the Quiberon expedition in the volume entitled "Pitt and Napoleon Miscellanies." In this chapter only the incidents which more particularly concern Pitt will be noticed.

The attempt to rule that most clannish and suspicious of Mediterranean peoples first called forth the administrative powers of Sir Gilbert Elliot, first Earl of Minto. Acting as Viceroy of Corsica, he sought to promote contentment by promulgating an excellent constitution and administrative reforms. But, being hampered from the outset by the factious behaviour of Paoli, he, with the consent of the Cabinet, deported him

---

[1] "Nelson Despatches," ii, 5.

to England in the autumn of 1795. An equally serious complication was the feud between the British army and navy. These disputes, originating at Toulon, grew apace in Corsica. Elliot sided with Hood, and was therefore detested by Dundas, his successor, Sir Charles Stuart, and their coadjutor, Colonel Moore. This brilliant young officer, by nature somewhat a *frondeur*, was finally guilty of expressions so disrespectful as to lead to his removal shortly before that of Paoli. He carried his complaints to Pitt, who bade him set forth his case dispassionately. Indeed, so impressed was he with Moore's abilities, that he decided to employ him in the West Indies, and afterwards advanced him to posts of high importance.

Pitt took little interest in Corsica, leaving it to the intermittent attentions of Portland. Consequently that interesting experiment had not a fair chance. The possession of the island was also nearly useless in a military sense; for the British garrison could spare no detachments, which, even with the help of the loyal Corsicans, could effectively harass the French forces campaigning in the Genoese Riviera. Elliot entered into relations with the Knights of Malta, and in other ways sought to develop a Mediterranean policy; but in this he met with scant support from London. In excuse of Pitt it must be said that he had his hands more than full elsewhere. Moreover the peace between France and Spain, framed in July 1795, caused him great concern, especially as the Court of Madrid manifested deep resentment at the British occupation of Corsica. In October 1795 Pitt inclined strongly towards peace, and thenceforth carried on the war mainly with a view to securing indemnities. Corsica apparently he now looked on as burdensome; for in his speech of 9th December 1795 he did not include it among the three valued acquisitions of the war—Martinique, Cape Nicholas Mole (in Hayti), and the Cape of Good Hope. Dundas always looked on the occupation of Corsica as prejudicial to the colonial efforts which held the first place in his thoughts. Accordingly it was not utilized in the spring of 1796, when expeditions ought to have set forth to hamper the march of Bonaparte's ill-equipped columns along the coast from Nice to Savona.

The opportunity then lost was never to return. Bonaparte's triumphs in Italy enabled him to prepare at Leghorn to deal a blow for the recovery of his native island. Checked for the time by the other claims of the war and the presence of Nelson, he kept this aim in view; and the conquest of North and Central Italy at the close of that campaign compromised the safety of the small British and *émigré* force in Corsica. The final reason, however, for the evacuation of the island was neither the menace from Italy nor the discontent of the islanders, but the alliance of Spain with France. As Nelson foresaw, that event endangered the communications with England. Ministers also knew that a plan was on foot for a French invasion of Ireland, which, as we shall see, was attempted at the end of the year. They therefore determined to concentrate their forces for home defence and the protection of the most important possessions, a decision which involved the abandonment of the Mediterranean. Accordingly, on 31st August 1796, Portland sent orders for the evacuation of Corsica and of Elba. For a few days in the latter half of October Ministers revoked these orders, and bade Elliot hold firm, their hope being to tempt the Empress Catharine to active co-operation against France by the cession of Corsica to her. Whether that wily potentate saw through this device is doubtful; for she died on 16th November. Her death put an end to the fleeting hope of opposing France with an equality of force; for the bent of her successor, Paul I, was at first towards peace.

Despite the comparative neglect of Mediterranean affairs by Pitt at this time, they exerted a profound influence upon his career. In view of the many claims upon the British navy, it was perhaps impossible to exert upon the coast of Nice and Genoa the pressure which Elliot desired; but the failure to do so in the spring of 1796 enabled Bonaparte to win the triumphs which changed the history of the world. Further, the British occupation of Corsica, scarcely less than that of Hayti, aroused keen jealousy at Madrid, and thus helped to set in motion forces which for the time checkmated England in the Mediterranean. Not until the Spaniards were beaten by Jervis and Nelson could she stretch forth her trident over that sea, first from Minorca and finally from Malta. The loss of Corsica was keenly felt. For, had England made full use of that island as a base of operations, Bonaparte could not have carried out his Egyptian expedition in 1798. Austria also ascribed her overthrow in Venetia and Styria to the withdrawal of the British fleet from the Mediterranean. That step seemed a confession of pitiable weakness, though in reality it enabled the Government to concentrate the fleet at points more important than Bastia and Ajaccio.

Amidst the disasters at the end of the Flemish campaign of 1794 Pitt sought to divert the energies of England to a more promising field. Thwarted on the Lower Rhine by the vacillations of the German Powers and the torpor of the Dutch, he hoped for success among the Royalists of Brittany and la Vendée. He framed this decision reluctantly; for it involved co-operation with the French princes, the Comte de Provence and the Comte d'Artois, and with the swarms of fanatical *émigrés* who had long pestered him with mad projects. Further, he had always been loath to declare for the restoration of the Bourbons. To do so would be to flaunt the *fleur-de-lis* in the face of a nation which hated all that pertained to the old régime. Besides, it implied a surrender to the clique headed by Burke and Windham, which scoffed at the compromise between monarchy and democracy embodied in the French constitution of 1791. Pitt, with his innate moderation and good sense, saw the folly of these reactionary views and the impossibility of forcing them upon the French people. Nevertheless, as an experiment in the course of that bewildering strife, he had recourse to the *émigrés*.

The accession of Windham to the Cabinet, in July 1794, had strengthened their influence at Westminster; and incidents which occurred in France during the winter of 1794-5 evinced a decline of Jacobinical enthusiasm. The sentiment of loyalty, damped by the chilling personality of Louis XVI and the follies of his brothers, revived now that the little Louis XVII was being slowly done to death by his gaolers in the Temple. The rapacity and vulgar ostentation of the Thermidorian party, then in power, provoked general disgust; and despair of any satisfactory settlement began to range friends of order on the side of the monarchy. The late American envoy at Paris, Gouverneur Morris, informed Bland Burges at our Foreign Office, on 28th June 1795, that the state of France was so desperate as to admit of cure only by the restoration of the old dynasty; that the recent death of Louis XVII was a benefit to the cause inasmuch as his mind had been completely brutalized; and finally the envoy heartily wished success to every effort to overthrow the despicable Government at Paris.

Though the Royalist leaders in the west of France early in the year 1795 made a truce with the Republic, yet the resumption of the civil war in that quarter was known to be only a question

of time. Windham, therefore, urged the despatch of an expedition to Brittany. His royalist zeal had now developed his
powers to their utmost. Early in the course of the French Revolution the chivalry of his nature detached him from the Foxites. The glow and beauty of his periods marked him out as the
successor of Burke in the House of Commons; yet in no respect
did he attain complete success. His speeches were too refined
and subtle for that audience; and, worse still, his diffidence or
torpor led him often to miss opportunities of effective intervention. The sensitiveness of his nature appeared in his falling in
love at first sight with a Highland girl whom Burke and he
casually met during a tour. His loss of her made a painful impression on him.[1] The butt of an unkind fate, he seemed
destined also to be the leader of lost causes; and the proud and
penniless *émigrés* found in him their most devoted friend.

Despite the opposition of Dundas, and the doubts of Pitt, his
views prevailed; and preparations began for an Anglo-French
expedition to the coast of Brittany. During the winter there had
arrived in London a Breton leader of gigantic stature and considerable mental powers, the Comte de Puisaye. He had fought
devotedly for the constitutional monarchy in that great province
and had the confidence of its inhabitants, whether nobles or
peasants (*Chouans*). But French princes and the cliques of
" pure " Royalists looked on him, as Marie Antoinette looked on
Mirabeau, merely as a rebel who had partly seen the error of his
ways. Secretly they resolved to make use of him, as he had
gained the confidence of Windham and Pitt, but to throw him
over at the first opportunity.

Meanwhile the Cabinet began to equip regiments of French
Royalists destined to form the spearhead of the " Royal and
Catholic Army." Various causes delayed the preparations, the
chief being the absence in North Germany of seasoned corps
of *émigrés* whose presence in Brittany was essential. Puisaye
therefore urged Ministers to allow him to enrol recruits from
among the French prisoners of war in England—a dangerous
device which, unfortunately, was adopted. Undoubtedly the
initiative in this matter rested with him; and it is noteworthy
that other royalist leaders had tried the plan, hitherto with
no untoward results.[2] Prisoners were not forced into the new

[1] " Corresp. of Sir John Sinclair," i, 141-3.
[2] Puisaye, " Mems.," ii, 594-603; Forneron, " Hist. des Emigrés," ii, 13, 14.

corps; but it is clear that some of them enlisted in order to get back to France. As for the finances of the enterprise, they were partly met by the manufacture of royalist *assignats*. Whether they were like the forged *assignats* manufactured, with the connivance of Government, near Hexham and Durham, is not clear. It is alleged by royalist writers that they bore a mark ensuring identification, so that, in case of a monarchist triumph, they would be duly honoured. The chief aim, however, certainly was to discredit the republican notes and to embarrass the Parisian Government. That Pitt should in any way have countenanced these underhand devices is discreditable.

Owing to the declaration of war by Holland (May 1795), the vacillations of Spain, and the determination of George III to keep troops in Hanover,[1] very few British were available for the enterprise. It is worth noting that the King disliked the *émigrés* and often shocked Windham by assertions at Court that they would prove false. His influence was used steadily against all attempts in their favour. There were, indeed, good grounds for suspicion even at this time. Seeing that Charette and other Breton leaders still observed the truce with the Republic, the risks of a landing were great; and this explains the reluctance of the Cabinet to allow the Comte d'Artois to proceed with the first contingent.[2] It was charged to occupy the Quiberon Peninsula as a base for further exertions, to supply arms to the Bretons, and thus prepare for a general rising, the effect of which would be clinched by the arrival of a larger force. The vanguard set sail from Spithead on 17th June 1795. It consisted of some 3,800 *émigrés*, under the general command of Puisaye, though by some mistake in drafting the orders, considerable power was given to Comte d'Hervilly, the senior officer of the subsidized regiments. At first all went well. The convoying fleet under Lord Bridport, after capturing three French sail-of-the-line off l'Orient, made Quiberon Bay and assisted in the capture of Fort Penthièvre, commanding the narrow isthmus (3rd July).

Disputes now began between Puisaye and Hervilly, the former desiring to push on boldly, while the latter insisted on remaining in the peninsula. Time was thus given for the republican general, Hoche, to collect his forces and make spirited attacks upon the invaders, who soon fell a prey to schism and dis-

---

[1] Cornwallis, "Corresp.," iii, 289.
[2] "F. O.," France, 44. Grenville to d'Harcourt, 19th June 1795.

couragement. The doom of the expedition was decided by the treacherous surrender of the fort to Hoche's men at the close of a night attack (21st July). As day dawned the Republicans drove their foes into the peninsula. Wild scenes of panic ensued. A storm having compelled the larger British warships to keep in the offing, Puisaye went off in a boat to beg succour from Admiral Warren. The defence speedily collapsed. De Sombreuil, who was left in command near the tip of the tongue of land, unaccountably surrendered, though a British corvette, the "Lark," and gunboats were effectively covering his flank. At the instigation of Tallien, the French Convention disavowed the promise of its officers at Quiberon to spare the lives of those who laid down their arms; and 712 Royalists were shot down in cold blood at Auray and neighbouring places.

The evidence proves that the Pitt Ministry had done its best for this expedition, which went to pieces owing to the quarrels of its leaders and the refusal of Charette to stir a finger on behalf of Puisaye, whom he detested. For the final massacre Tallien and the French Convention are wholly responsible. Yet it suited the tactics of the English Opposition to accuse Pitt of planning the death of the French Royalists. Fox, in one of his wildest outbreaks, charged Ministers with deliberately sending noble gentlemen to a massacre. Sheridan, too, declared that, though British blood had not flowed, yet "British honour had bled at every pore." These reckless mis-statements have been refuted by the testimony of La Jaille, Vauban, and Puisaye, royalist officers who escaped.

Before these horrible events were known in England, Ministers prepared to succour the vanguard at Quiberon. News that Spain had made peace with France in a highly suspicious manner weakened this second effort, it being necessary to safeguard the British West Indies from a probable attack by the Spaniards. As no more than four newly raised British regiments could be spared for the Biscay coast, the Earl of Moira threw up the command, which General Doyle then accepted. It seems probable that by 3rd August Pitt doubted the expendiency of sending a second expedition to Brittany or la Vendée. Nevertheless, the Comte d'Artois, who about that time arrived at Spithead from North Germany with a force of *émigrés*, desired to make the venture, relying on Charette, and other royalist chiefs who had once more aroused the men of the West. The Count also cherished the hope that the numerous bands of malcontents in Paris would overthrow that tottering Government.

Events turned out otherwise. The first plan, that of occupying Noirmoutier, an island close to the Vendéan coast, proving impracticable, Doyle sailed to a smaller island, Yeu, farther out at sea. There the 5,500 troops, miserably cramped and underfed, waited until the Comte d'Artois should make good his boast of throwing himself into a boat, if need be, in order to join his faithful Charette. It was soon apparent that he preferred to stay in Yeu with his mistress, Mme. Polastron. In vain did the Bretons under Puisaye and Vauban, and the Vendéans under Charette, beg him to join them. Meanwhile, amid the early autumn rains the troops deteriorated, and the royalist rising at Paris proved a miserable fiasco, some 30,000 National Guards being scattered by a small force well handled by Bonaparte and Barras (5th October). Finally, a deputation of Bretons proceeded to Yeu, and begged Artois to place himself at the head of the numerous bands of devoted gentlemen and peasants who still awaited his appearance. All was in vain. *Je ne veux pas aller Chouanner* (play the Chouan) was his reply (12th November). On the morrow he informed Vauban that he had received orders from England to return at once. This assertion was at the time generally believed to be false; the letters of Grenville to the Prince prove it to be grossly exaggerated. To the despair and disgust of his soldiers he departed, and finally sought refuge from his creditors in Holyrood Castle. The British and French royalist regiments were withdrawn with much difficulty during the storms of December 1795. Nearly all the horses had to be destroyed.

Undoubtedly Pitt and Grenville had become disgusted with the torpor of Artois and the follies of the French Royalists. In particular the absurd failure at Paris seems to have prompted the resolve of the Cabinet to withdraw the British troops from Yeu. Pitt's letters of the latter half of October also evince a desire to pave the way for some understanding with the French Directory. As that Government was firmly installed in power, an opportunity presented itself, for the first time since the opening of the war, of arranging a lasting peace. These hopes were to be blighted; but it is certain that Pitt cherished them; and, doubtless, among the motives operating in favour of peace the foremost was a feeling of disgust at the poltroonery of the French Princes and the incurable factiousness of their followers, in whom the faculties which command success were lost amidst vices and perversities sufficient to ruin the best of causes. Pitt continued to support the Chouans by money and arms; but, despite the frequent protests of Windham, not a British soldier was landed on that coast.[1]

---

[1] On 19th January 1798 Pitt, Windham, and Canning agreed to give £9,082 and £9,400 for the discharge of debts due for services of the Royalists in France, incurred in England and France respectively, leaving a balance of £8,000 for future payment. The following sums were paid to the Duc d'Harcourt for the support of "Monsieur": in 1796, £3,000; in 1797, £9,000; and after May 1798 at the rate of £500 per month (B.M. Add. MSS., 37844). I have not found the sums allowed to the Comte d'Artois.

CHAPTER XII

PITT AS WAR MINISTER (1793-8)

*Si vous affaiblissez vos moyens en partageant vos forces, si vous rompez en Italie l'unité de la pensée militaire, je vous le dis avec douleur, vous aurez perdu la plus belle occasion d'imposer des lois à l'Italie. . . . La guerre est comme le gouvernement, c'est une affaire de tact.—*NAPOLEON, *Letters of 14th May 1796.*

IN estimating the services of Pitt as War Minister during the first phases of the conflict we must remember that the ambition of his life was to be a Peace Minister. Amidst the exhaustion caused by the American War, he deemed it essential to ensure the continuous growth of savings and investments which, under favourable conditions, advance at the rate of Compound Interest. His success in the time of peace 1783-93, may be measured by the fact that, despite the waste of war, the rate of progress was not seriously checked in the years 1793-6. A Scotsman, MacRitchie, who travelled through England in 1795[1] was surprised to find the large towns in a most flourishing state; and it is well known that the exports of cottons largely increased in the last decade of the century. Seeing that the war became " a contention of purse," the final triumph of England may be ascribed to the reserve of strength which Pitt had helped to assure. He did not live on to witness the issue of the economic struggle brought about by the Continental System of Napoleon. But a study of the commercial war of the years 1806-13 shows that Pitt's forethought enabled Britain to foil the persistent efforts of her mightiest enemy.

Military critics will, however, reply that Pitt's economies in the earlier period so far weakened her army as to lead to the failures of the Revolutionary War. There is some force in this

[1] "Diary of a Tour through Great Britain in 1795," by W. MacRitchie (1897).

contention. A closer examination, however, will reveal facts that
necessarily weaken it. Firstly, England had never kept up a
large army in time of peace. Dislike of a standing army was
almost inconceivably strong; and it is certain that an attempt
by Pitt to maintain an army in excess of the ordinary peace
establishment would have aroused a powerful opposition. He
therefore concentrated his efforts on the navy; and the maritime triumphs of the war were due in the last resort to his
fostering care. As for the army, he kept it at its normal strength
until the spring of the year 1792, when he decided to effect some
reductions. In one sense this decision is creditable to him. It
proves that he neither desired nor expected a rupture with
France. In his view the risks of war were past. After his
surrender to the Empress Catharine in 1791 peace seemed
assured. Further, his decision to reduce the British Army was
formed before the declaration of war by France against Austria
(20th April 1792). After the rupture of France with Sardinia
and Prussia it appeared the height of madness for a single dis-
organized State to enlarge the circle of its enemies. Consequently, up to the second week of November 1792, Pitt and
Grenville were fully justified in expecting the duration of peace
for Great Britain. Here, as at many points in the ensuing
struggle, it was the impossible which happened.

Is Pitt to be blamed for effecting economies which led to a
reduction of taxes and an alleviation of the burdens of the
poor? The chief danger of the years 1791, 1792 came not from
the French Jacobins, but from their British sympathizers; and
experience warranted the belief that, with a lightening of the
financial load, the nation would manifest its former loyalty. On
23rd August 1791 Grenville wrote: "Our only danger is at home,
and for averting that danger, peace and economy are our best resources."[1] These considerations are political rather than military.
But it is impossible to separate the two spheres. The strength
of the army depends ultimately on the strength of the nation.

It is also well to remember that systematic preparation for
war was an outcome of that struggle. Conscription was a bequest
of the French Revolution. Planned first by Carnot, it was carried
out by Dubois Crancé and others in 1798. But in 1793 the days
of large armies had not dawned. It was usual to maintain
small forces of professional soldiers, together with a more or less

[1] " Dropmore P.," ii, 172.

inefficient militia. In England methods not unlike those of the age of Falstaff still held good. War was an adventure, not a science. In France first it became an intensely national effort. The Jacobins evoked the popular enthusiasm; the Committee of Public Safety embodied it in citizen armies; and the science of Carnot and Napoleon led them to victories which shattered the old-world systems and baffled the forecasts of Pitt.

Let us briefly survey the conduct of the war by Pitt in its chief stages up to the year 1798. The first period is from the declaration of war in February 1793, to the Battle of Fleurus, near the close of June 1794. At the outset he is alarmed by the irruption of Dumouriez into Holland, and hastily sends a small British force under the Duke of York, solely for the defence of Helvoetsluys and its neighbourhood. It answers its purpose; the French are held up at the Hollandsdiep, while the Austrians crush their main force at Neerwinden. Thereupon Coburg claims the Duke's assistance in driving the Republicans from the fortresses of French Flanders. Pitt and his colleagues give their assent, because the enterprise seems easy after the defection of Dumouriez, and Dunkirk is a tempting prize near to hand, but mainly owing to their urgent desire that Austria shall find her indemnity not in Bavaria, but in the French border fortresses. Thus, for reasons which are political, rather than military, the Cabinet embarks an insufficient force on what proves to be a lengthy and hazardous enterprise. Further, while the British push on, Prussia holds back; so that the Duke of York virtually takes the place of the Prussian contingent. Unaware of the duplicity of Berlin, and trusting that the Allies will soon master the border strongholds, Pitt and Dundas prepare to harry the coasts of France, and to secure her most valuable colony, Hayti. These are their chief aims in the war. But, while preparing maritime expeditions, they also drift into a continental campaign, from which they find it hard to withdraw.

The efforts put forth at Toulon and in Corsica were the out-come of the treaties with Austria, Sardinia, and Naples, which required the appearance of a British fleet off the coasts of France and Italy. While seeking to strengthen both the Coalition and the Royalists of Provence, Admiral Hood's force found an un-expected sphere of action at Toulon. In August 1793 that city admitted the British troops and a Spanish force a few days later. Thereupon Pitt claimed the help which he had a right to expect from his Allies. Naples and Sardinia sent contingents deficient in quality or numbers; and the Court of Vienna, after promising to send 5,000 troops from the Milanese, neglected to do so. Quarrels and suspicions hampered the defence; but the arrival of the Austrian contingent would probably have turned the scale. Owing to the length of time required for despatches from Toulon to reach London, Pitt and his colleagues did not hear of the remissness of Austria until 22nd December, that is, five days after the fall of that stronghold. Had they known it a month earlier, they could have sent thither the large force, then mustering in the Solent, which on 26th November set sail for the West Indies.

This seems an unpardonable diffusion of efforts. But Ministers must already have regretted their readiness to take up the duties incumbent on Prussia in Flanders; and doubtless they resolved not to play the part of the willing horse at Toulon. In the early days of every league there comes a time when an active Power must protest against the shifty ways which are the curse of Coalitions. Besides, Pitt had to keep in view the interests of Great Britain. These were, firstly, to guard the Low Countries against French aggression, and, secondly, to gain an indemnity for the expenses of the war either in the French West Indies, or in Corsica. The independence of the Low Countries was a European question. The maritime conquests concerned England alone. Were Britons to shelve their own interests for a question of international import? The statesman who does so will not long hold the reins at Westminster. Besides, no device for weakening France was deemed more effective than that of seizing her wealthiest group of colonies. On the other hand, there was pressing need of armed help for the Royalists of Brittany; and on this ground we must pronounce the West India enterprise ill timed. A still worse blunder was the continued inactivity of Moira's force in the Solent and the Channel Islands. The reports of an intended French invasion form a wholly inadequate excuse for his inaction. His troops could have rendered valuable service either in Brittany, Flanders, or at Toulon. The riddle of their inaction has never been solved. Ultimately the blame must rest with Pitt, Dundas, and Lord Chatham.[1]

---

[1] In "H. O.," Geo. III (Domestic), 27, are Dundas's instructions to Moira, dated 20th November 1793, appointing him Major-General in an expedition

In 1794 Pitt hoped to retrieve the failures of the first campaign and to wear down the French defence. For this purpose
he liberally subsidized Austria and concluded with Prussia a
treaty which, with better management, might have brought a
second highly efficient army into Flanders. The compacts of
that springtide warranted the hope that 340,000 allied troops
would advance on the north and north-east frontiers of France.
They were not forthcoming; but, even as it was, the Imperialists
and the Duke of York routed the French levies in Flanders and
seemed about to open the way to Paris. Earl Howe's victory,
named " the glorious first of June," ensured supremacy in the
Channel. Brittany and la Vendée were again aflame. The
Union Jack replaced the tricolour on the strongholds of Corsica
and in the most fertile parts of the West Indies. In April—
May 1794 the collapse of the Jacobins seemed imminent.

But these early triumphs of the Allies were almost as fatal as
their later disasters. Indeed they were largely the cause of them.
Believing that they had the game in their hands, Prussia and
Austria relaxed their efforts at the very time when France
girded herself for a mightier struggle. Moreover, the emergence
of the Polish Question in an acute phase served once again to
distract the German rivals and to weaken their efforts in the
West. Moreover, the Anglo-Prussian Treaty of May 1794 pre-
scribing the valley of the Meuse as the sphere of action of the
62,400 Prussians subsidized by England, and Holland was so
rigid as to furnish their generals with good excuses for refusing
to march from the Palatinate across the front of the French
columns now pressing forward. The upshot was that England
and the Dutch Republic got nothing in return for their subsidies,
while the Prussians on their side chafed at the insistent demands
from London and The Hague for the exact fulfilment of the
bargain. The situation was annoying for military men; and the
British Government erred in tying them down too stringently
to a flank march, which was fraught with danger after the long
delay of Pitt in ratifying the compact (6th-23rd May); while
the postponement in the payment of the first subsidies gave

to Guernsey, with Admiral MacBride, taking with him a Hessian corps as
soon as it arrives. He is to seize St. Malo or any place near it suitable for
helping the Royalists and harassing the enemy. If he deems success doubtful, he is to await reinforcements. The aim is to help the cause of Louis XVII
and lead to a general pacification.

the Prussians a good excuse for inaction.[1] His remonstrance to the Prussian envoy in London, at the close of September 1794, was also unwise. For it exceeded the more measured protests of Grenville, and furnished the Berlin Court with the desired excuse for recalling its troops from the Rhine. In short, the campaign of 1794 failed, not so much because the French were in superior force at the battles of Turcoing and Fleurus, as because the Allies at no point worked cordially together. The intrusion of political motives hampered their generals and turned what ought to have been an overwhelming triumph into a disgracefully tame retreat.

The disasters at Turcoing and Fleurus open up the second stage of the war. Realizing more and more the difficulty of defending Holland and Hanover, Pitt seeks to end that campaign and to concentrate on colonial enterprises and the war in Brittany and la Vendée. Experience of the utter weakness of his Administration for purposes of war also leads him to strengthen it at the time of the union with the Old Whigs. They demanded that their leader, the Duke of Portland, should take the Home Office. On Dundas demurring to this, Grenville generously assented to Pitt's suggestion that he should vacate the Foreign Office (6th July). Fortunately the Duke declined to take it; and Pitt resolved to make drastic changes, especially by curtailing the functions of the Secretary of State for Home Affairs, and creating a War Ministry of Cabinet rank. Some change was clearly requisite; for of late Dundas had supervised internal affairs, including those of Ireland, as well as the conduct of the war; as Treasurer of the Navy he managed its finances, and, as President of the India Board, he sought to control the affairs of that Empire. As for the War Office, it was a petty office, controlled by a nonentity, Sir Charles Yonge, who was soon to be transferred to the Mint.

In the haphazard allotment of military business to the Commander-in-Chief, Amherst, to the head clerk of the War Office, Yonge, and to the overworked pluralist, Dundas, we discern the causes of disaster. The war with France being unforeseen, Pitt had to put up with these quaint arrangements; but the reverses in Flanders and the incoming of the Portland Whigs now enabled him to reduce chaos to order. He insisted that the

[1] "Malmesbury Diaries," iii, 96-8.

Secretary of State for Home Affairs should cease to direct the course of the war, but consented that colonial business should fall to his lot. On the other hand he greatly enlarged the functions of the War Office. His will prevailed. On 7th July Portland agreed to become Home Secretary, while his supporter, Windham, came into the re-organized War Office as Secretary at War, Dundas becoming Secretary of State for War and the Colonies. Despite the obvious need of specializing and strengthening these Departments, the resistance of Dundas was not easily overcome. His letter to Pitt on this subject betrays a curious cloudiness of vision on a subject where clearness is essential:

Wimbledon, *July* 9, 1794.[1]

. . . The idea of a War Minister as a separate Department you must on recollection be sensible cannot exist in this country. The operations of war are canvassed and adjusted in the Cabinet, and become the joint act of His Majesty's servants; and the Sec^y of State who holds the pen does no more than transmit their sentiments. I do not mean to say that there is not at all times in H. M.'s Councils some particular person who has, and ought to have, a leading and even an overruling ascendency in the conduct of public affairs; and that ascendency extends to war as it does to every other subject. Such you are at present as the Minister of the King. Such your father was as Secretary of State. Such you would be if you was Secretary of State, and such Mr. Fox would be if he was Secretary of State and the Duke of Bedford First Lord of the Treasury. In short it depends, and must ever depend, on other circumstances than the particular name by which a person is called; and if you was to have a Secretary of State for the War Department tomorrow, not a person living would ever look upon him, or any other person but you, as the War Minister. All modern wars are a contention of purse, and unless some very peculiar circumstance occurs to direct the lead into another channel, the Minister of Finance must be the Minister of War. Your father for obvious reasons was an exception to the rule.

It is impossible for any person to controvert the position I now state; and therefore, when you talk of a War Minister, you must mean a person to superintend the detail of the execution of the operations which are determined upon. But do you think it possible to persuade the public that such a separate Department can be necessary? Yourself, so far as a general superintendence is necessary, must take that into your own hands. If it was in the hands of any other, it would lead to a constant wrangling between him and the various Executive Boards.

[1] Chevening MSS.

The illogicality of this letter would be amusing if it had not been so disastrous. Because war depends ultimately on money, therefore (said Dundas) the Chancellor of the Exchequer ought to control its operations and act virtually as Secretary of State for War. Then why not also as First Lord of the Admiralty? No sooner is the question formulated than we see that Dundas is confusing two very different things, namely, general financial control and the administration of military affairs. In fact, Dundas still clung to the old customs which allotted to the Secretaries of State wide and often overlapping duties. He did not see the need of a specialized and authoritative War Office, though the triumphs achieved by Carnot and the Committee of Public Safety during the past twelvemonth might have opened his eyes. Fortunately, Pitt discerned the necessity of strengthening that Department; and, as we have seen, he made Dundas and Windham War Ministers, with seats in the Cabinet. Thus from July 1794 military affairs had a chance of adequate treatment in that body; and Pitt deserves great credit for remodelling the Cabinet in a way suited to the exigencies of modern warfare.

Why did he not appoint that experienced soldier, the Marquis Cornwallis, Secretary of State for War? The answer is that he designed him as successor to the Duke of York in Flanders. As has already appeared, Pitt framed this resolve in February 1794, on the return of Cornwallis from India; and, though rebuffed then, he continued to revolve the matter until the beginning of the autumn, when the opposition of George III and of Francis II of Austria prevented the appointment of that experienced soldier to the supreme command of the Allies. As for the accession of Windham to the War Department, it seems to have been merely a device to satisfy the Old Whigs. Probably the question was not even discussed until 4th July, when the Duke of Portland first named it to Windham. As it finds no place in the Pitt-Grenville letters until 7th July, we may infer that Pitt and Dundas accepted Windham with some reluctance as an ardent partisan of Burke and the *émigrés*. Windham now persistently urged an expedition to Brittany; and the Quiberon and Yeu enterprises were largely due to him. Pitt and Dundas, after their experience of the *émigrés*, had no great hope in these efforts; and after the defection of Spain they discerned the increasing need of concentrating their efforts on home defence and operations which safeguarded British interests in the East and West Indies. To these causes may be ascribed their decision to withdraw the British force from the island of Yeu. The indignant letters of Windham to Pitt in 1796-8 show that, after the Yeu fiasco and the beginning of the peace negotiations with France, his advice was slighted. His moanings to Mrs. Crewe over the degeneracy of the age also tell their tale. In October 1796 he merely "drags on " at the War Office until he sees what turn things will take.

Pitt's determination to ensure efficiency in the services appears from two incidents of the closing weeks of 1794. He deposed Lord Chatham from the Admiralty in favour of the far more efficient Lord Spencer; and he removed the Duke of York from the command in Holland. Another change remains to be noted, namely, the retirement of the Master General of the Ordnance. The Duke of Richmond had for some time ceased to attend the meetings of the Cabinet. During six months Pitt put up with this peevishness; but on the receipt of alarming news from Holland, he exerted his authority. On 27th January 1795 he informed Richmond that his long absence from the Cabinet and his general aloofness would make his return unpleasant and " embarrassing to public business. This consideration," he added, " must decide my opinion . . . and at this critical time it seems indispensable to make some such arrangement as shall substitute some other efficient military aid in so important a Department."[1] This cutting note produced the desired result. Richmond resigned and Cornwallis took his place at the Ordnance and in the Cabinet. No change was more beneficial. During the next three years the Ministry had the advice of the ablest soldier of the generation preceding that of Wellington. Unfortunately the Cornwallis letters are so few that his share in the shaping of war policy is unknown; but it is clear that he helped Ministers finally to override the resolve of the King to keep the relic of the British force for the defence of Hanover.[2]

To conclude the survey of these changes, we may note that the Duke of York, after returning from Holland, became Commander-in-Chief of the British army, a situation in which he earned general approbation. Thus, when it is asserted that Pitt altogether lacked his father's power of discerning military talents, the reply must be that he rendered an incalculable service by

---

[1] Pretyman MSS.   [2] "Cornwallis Corresp.," ii, 289.

organizing a competent War Ministry, that he put the right men
in the right place, though at the cost of offending the King, the
Duke of York, a powerful nobleman, and his own brother; and
that he quickly noted the transcendent abilities of Moore even
when under censure for acts of disobedience in Corsica. The
results attained by the elder Pitt were far more brilliant; for he
came to the front at a time when the problems were far less
difficult and illusory than those of the Revolutionary Era; but,
if the very diverse conditions of their times be considered, the
services of Pitt will not suffer by comparison even with those of
his father.

The torpor of the Dutch in defending their country and the
refusal of the Duke of Brunswick to organize the defence of
North Germany virtually ended the war on that side. In one
respect the defection of Prussia in April 1795 proved beneficial;
for she undertook to keep the States of North and Central Germany entirely neutral. Had George III condescended at once
to place his Electorate under her covering wing, the whole British
and subsidized force might have been withdrawn in the spring
of that year. Pride, however, for some time held him back from
that politic but humiliating step. Consequently several battalions
remained in Hanover for so long a time as to weaken the blow
dealt at Paris through Quiberon. This was highly prejudicial to
the Breton movement, which would have found in the troops
detained in Germany the firm nucleus that was so much needed.
Even after the ghastly failure at Quiberon, had the French
émigré corps arrived at Spithead at the end of July instead of
August, the expedition to the Vendéan coast might have ended
differently. It is usual to blame Pitt or Dundas for the delay in
those preparations. But George must be held finally responsible. As to the Quiberon disaster, it has been proved to result
from the hot-headedness of Puisaye, the criminal carelessness
of Hervilly, and the ceaseless schisms of the Royalists.

With the alliance of the Dutch and French Republics in May
1795, and the almost open avowal of the French cause by the
Court of Madrid in July, the war entered upon a third phase.
Thenceforth the colonial motive was paramount at Westminster,
for Pitt and his colleagues questioned the wisdom of holding
Corsica. On the other hand they sought to safeguard India by
seizing the Cape of Good Hope, and to preserve Hayti from the

inroads of the French, to whom Spain handed over her posses-‹ sion, San Domingo. Unfortunately the greater the prominence accorded to colonial affairs, the wider grew the breach with Spain, until in October 1796 the Court of Madrid declared war. Is Pitt to be blamed for the rupture with Spain? From the standpoint of Burke and Windham he is open to grave censure. Surveying the course of events from their royalist minaret, these prophets ceased not to proclaim the restoration of the Bourbons to be the sole purpose of the war. Let there be no talk of indemnities. Be content with crushing Jacobinism and restoring order. Such was their contention; and much may be said for it.

On the other hand, we must remember that at first England was not a principal in the contest. It was thrust upon her by the aggressions of the Jacobins, and perforce she played a subordinate part in continental campaigns, the prizes of which Austria and Prussia had already marked out. The reproaches hurled by Burke and Windham were the outcome of ignorance as to the aims of the powerful Allies, whose co-operation, illusory though it came to be, was at that time deemed essential to success. Further, in striking at the French colonies, Pitt followed the course successfully adopted by England in several wars. But here again his difficulties were greater than those of Chatham. Indeed, they were enhanced by the triumphs of Chatham. Where now could he deal the most telling blow? Not against Canada; for his father had reft that prize. The French settlements in the East Indies were of small account. It was in Hayti, Martinique, and Guadeloupe that French commerce could be ruined. At them, therefore, he struck. But in so doing he reopened the old disputes with Spain. In vain did he seek to avert bickerings by suggesting a friendly understanding about Hayti. Godoy was determined to bicker. And, as the war changed its character, the old Latin affinities helped that adventurer to undermine the monarchical league and to draw back Spain to the traditional connection with France.

The Spanish declaration of war in October 1796 opens the fourth phase of the struggle. Thenceforth England stood on the defensive in Europe in order to guard and strengthen her Colonial Empire. She abandoned Corsica and Elba; she withdrew her fleet from the Mediterranean so that Ireland might be screened from attack. Pitt's views also underwent a change.

Foreseeing the collapse of Austria, he sought to assure peace with France and Spain by conquering enough territory oversea to counterbalance the triumphs of Bonaparte and Moreau in Italy and the Rhineland. If he could not restore the Balance of Power on the Continent, he strove to safeguard British interests at all essential points. Failing to save Holland from the Jacobins' grip, he conquered and held the Cape. This was the bent of his policy during the peace overtures of the year 1796. He struggled on reluctantly with the war, opposing as inopportune the motions of Fox, Grey, or Wilberforce for peace, but ever hoping that France would be compelled by the pressure of bankruptcy to come to terms and surrender some of her continental conquests on consideration of recovering her colonies. Wilberforce heard him declare that he could almost calculate the time when her resources would be exhausted. On the philanthropist repeating this at a dinner party, one of his guests, de Lageard, wittily remarked: " I should like to know who was Chancellor of the Exchequer to Attila." [1] This remark shore asunder Pitt's financial arguments and reveals the weak point of his policy. He conducted the war as if it were a Seven Years' War. It was a Revolutionary War; and at this very time a greater than Attila was at hand. Bonaparte was preparing to use the spoils of Italy for the extension of the arena of strife. Nelson, then seeking to intercept the supplies of Bonaparte's army in the Riviera, foresaw the danger and thus graphically summarized it: " Italy is the gold mine; and if once entered, is without means of resistance." As by a flash we see in this remark and in that of de Lageard the miscalculation which was to ruin the life work of Pitt and almost ruin his country.

Despite the opposition of the King and Grenville to the negotiations for peace, Pitt held firm; and early in 1796 advances were made through Wickham, our enterprising envoy in Switzerland. They were foredoomed to failure; on 26th March the Directory declared its resolve to listen to no proposals involving the surrender of any of the lands incorporated in France by the terms of the constitution of 1795. This implied that she would retain the Rhine boundary, along with Savoy, Nice, and Avignon. Grenville received the news with satisfaction, remarking to Wickham that the Directory had acted clumsily and " in fact played

---

[1] " Life of Wilberforce," ii, 92.

our game better than we could have hoped." [1] The effect on
public opinion was even better when it appeared that France
expected England to surrender her colonial conquests. That
France should gain enormously on land while the British acquisitions oversea were surrendered, was so monstrous a claim
as to arouse the temper of the nation. Even Fox admitted that
if France retained her conquests in Europe, England must keep
those gained at sea. As Pitt pointed out in his speech of 10th
May 1796, the French demands blighted all hope of peace; and
we must struggle on, "waiting for the return of reason in our
deluded enemy."

Pitt regarded the French conquest of Italy as counterbalanced
by the triumph of Jervis and Nelson at Cape St. Vincent in
February 1797; and he therefore refused to consider the cession
of Gibraltar to Spain. Wholeheartedly he sought for peace in
that year. But it was to be peace with honour. In fact, Great
Britain fared better after 1796 than before. As Allies fell away
or joined the enemy, her real strength began to appear. The
reasons for the paradox are not far to seek. Open enemies are
less dangerous than false friends. Further, the complexities of
the war, resulting from the conflicting aims of the Allies, vanished.
England therefore could act in the way in which Pitt would all
along have preferred her to act, namely, against the enemy's
colonies. In Europe her attitude was defensive; and for a time
in the summer and autumn of 1796 fears of invasion were rife.
Accordingly the Quarter-Master-General, Sir David Dundas,
drew up a scheme of coast defence, especially for the district
between Pegwell Bay and Pevensey Bay; he also devised
measures for "driving" the country in front of the enemy. In
November of that year he recommended the construction of
batteries or entrenchments at Shooter's Hill, Blackheath, on the
hills near Lee, Lewisham, Sydenham, Norwood, Streatham,
Merton, and Wandsworth. The failure of Hoche's attempt at
Bantry Bay and the victory off Cape St. Vincent somewhat

[1] Sorel, v, 41; "Wickham Corresp.," i, 269-74, 343. Some mis-statements
of Sorel may be noted here. On pp. 39, 40 of vol. v he states that Pitt was
intent on acquiring Malta and Egypt (though he was then in doubt whether
to retain Corsica): also that, after the insult to George III in London on
29th October 1795, Pitt proposed a loan of £18,000,000 and new taxes, which
Parliament refused. The facts are that Pitt asked for that loan on 7th December 1796, and it was subscribed in twenty-two hours. On the same day
Parliament voted the new taxes.

assuaged these fears; but, owing to the alarming state of Ireland, England remained on the defensive through the years 1797-8, until Bonaparte's Egyptian expedition enabled her to strike a crushing blow at the chief colonial enterprise of her antagonist. That adventure, together with the aggressions of France at Rome and in Switzerland, aroused the anger or fear of Russia, Austria, and Naples, and thereby led up to the war of the Second Coalition.

Amidst the conflict of aims which distracted the Allies in the First Coalition, Pitt's foresight was not seldom at fault. But only those who have weighed the importance of the diplomatic issues at stake, and have noted their warping influence on military affairs, have the right to accuse him of blindness and presumption. The problem before him was of unexampled complexity, and its solution could be effected only by a succession of experiments. That he put forth too many efforts at one time may be granted; and yet in each case, if the details are fully known, the reasons for making the attempt seem adequate. Did not Chatham fail in most of the expeditions which he sent against the coasts of France? Even those who censure Pitt for his blunders in the war will admit that the inspiring influence of his personality and patriotism nerved the nation and Parliament for the struggle. True, the Opposition indulged in petty nagging and in ingeniously unpatriotic tactics; but they only served to throw up in bold relief the consistent and courageous conduct of the Prime Minister. It was an easy task to refute the peevish efforts of Fox to justify the French Jacobins alike before the war, throughout its course, and in their rejection of the British overtures for peace. But in every encounter Pitt won more than a personal triumph. He proved that the war was forced upon us; that on our side it was a defensive effort; and that despite the perverse conduct of Prussia and Spain, England had won notable gains oversea and might expect an advantageous peace, provided only that the nation persevered.

One question remains. Why did not Pitt call the nation to arms? The reasons for his caution are doubtless to be found in the ingrained conservatism of the English character, and in the political ferment which marked the years 1794-5. The mere proposal to merge Line, Militia, and Volunteers in one national array would have seemed mere madness. For the populace had

recently been protesting against the facilities given to the loyal
to arm and drill themselves. It was rumoured that, by way of
retort, the men of Sheffield, Southwark, and Norwich secretly
mustered for practice with pikes. In such circumstances, conscription might well spell Revolution. Here was the weak place
in Pitt's armour. By parting company with the reformers, he
had embittered no small section of his countrymen. In 1794, as
we have seen, he was considered a reactionary and an oppressor.
He therefore could not appeal to the nation, as Carnot did in
France. Even his Bill of March 1794 for increasing the Militia
by an extension of the old custom of the ballot or the drawing
of lots produced some discontent. A similar proposal, passed a
year earlier by the Dublin Parliament for raising 16,000 additional
Militiamen in Ireland, led to widespread rioting, especially in
Ulster. Not until 1797 did the Scottish Militia Act ensure the
adoption of similar methods by Scotland, though regiments of
Fencibles were raised in the meantime.

The preparations for national defence continued to proceed in
these parochial ways. Pitt's authority at Westminster was at no
time more firmly founded than at the time of the meeting of the
new Parliament in the autumn of 1796. Yet the piecemeal
methods went on as before. He proposed to raise by means of
the ballot a levy of 15,000 men in order to recruit the navy and
the Line regiments; and he further asked for a levy of 60,000
men as a Supplementary Militia, one tenth being embodied by
turns so as not to withdraw from work too many hands at one
time. Nor was this all. For the purpose of strengthening the
irregular cavalry, he proposed that every person who kept ten
horses should be required to furnish one horseman and a horse
for such a corps, and those who owned more than ten horses
were to subscribe a proportionate sum towards its maintenance.
He also required gamekeepers and those who took out licenses
to shoot either to serve on horseback or to find a substitute.
In all he expected to raise 20,000 horsemen by these means.

The attitude of the House was on the whole highly favourable
to these proposals. Fox accused Ministers of raising an invasion
scare in order to compass their own nefarious designs; but Pitt's
first proposals passed without a division; that on the cavalry by
140 votes to 30. Nevertheless, Pitt did nothing towards securing cohesion in these diverse forces, except by a provision which
obliged Volunteers to enrol in the Supplementary Militia, to

take the oath as such, and to train by turns for twenty days at a time in any part of the country, instead of training once or twice a week in their own towns. This must have been beneficial where it was carried out; but, as the Militia was controlled by the Home Office, it is doubtful whether enough energy was thrown into the scheme to ensure success.

These arrangements are miserably inadequate in comparison with the *levée en masse* of Carnot, which baffled the calculations of foreign statesmen, flung back the armies of the Coalition, and opened up the path of glory for Bonaparte. Here the popular armament did not become in any sense national until after the renewal of war in 1803. The possibilities open to England, even in that trying year 1795, were set forth by Major Cartwright in a suggestive pamphlet—"The Commonwealth in Danger." After pointing out that, having been deserted by Prussia and Spain, we must now depend on ourselves alone, he depicted the contrast between England and France. The French Republic, relying on the populace, had more than a million of men under arms. Great Britain was "a disarmed, defenceless, unprepared people, scarcely more capable of resisting a torrent of French invaders than the herds and flocks of Smithfield." How, then, could the danger be averted? Solely (he replied) by trusting the people and by reviving the ancient laws which compelled house-holders to bear arms. But this implied the concession of the franchise. Be bold, he said. Make the Kingdom a Commonwealth and the nation will be saved. He continued in these noteworthy words: "The enemy is at the gates, and we must be friends or perish. Adversity is a school of the sublime virtues. Necessity is an eloquent reconciler of differences.... By saying to Britain— Be an armed nation, she secures her defence and seals her free-dom. A million of armed men, supporting the State with their purse, and defending it with their lives, will know that none have so great a stake as themselves in the Government. . . . Arming the people and reforming Parliament are inseparable."

At first sight this seems mere rhetoric, but on reflection it will appear the path of prudence. By the talisman of trust in the people France conjured up those armed hosts which overthrew old Europe. At the stamp of Napoleon's heel a new Europe arose, wherein the most potent defiance came from the peoples which drew upon their inmost reserves of strength. That these consist in men, not in money, is clear from the course of the struggle against the great Emperor. Spain, Russia, and Prussia adopted truly national systems of defence, and quickly forged to the front. Britain and Austria clung to their old systems, and, thanks to Wellington's genius and Metternich's diplomacy, they survived. But they did not play the decisive part which they might have done if George III and Pitt, Francis II and Thugut, had early determined to trust and arm their peoples. Unfortunately for England, she underwent no military disaster; and therefore Pitt was fain to plod along in the old paths and use the nation's wealth, not its manhood. He organized it piecemeal, on a class basis, instead of embattling it as a whole. In the main his failure to realize the possibilities of the situation arose from his abandonment of those invigorating principles which nerved him to the achievements of the earlier and better part of his career. It is conceivable that, had he retained the idealism of his youth and discovered a British Scharnhorst, Waterloo might have been fought in 1796 and won solely by British troops.

CHAPTER XIII

DEARTH AND DISCONTENT

The Waste Land Bill will turn the tide of our affairs and enable us to bear without difficulty the increased burdens of the war.—SINCLAIR TO PITT, 13th March 1796.

ON 29th October 1795 occurred an event unparalleled within the memory of Englishmen then living. An immense crowd, filling the Mall, broke into loud hissing and hooting when George III left Buckingham House in the state carriage to proceed to Westminster for the opening of Parliament. The tumult reached its climax as the procession approached the Ordnance Office, when a small pebble, or marble, or shot from an air-gun, pierced the carriage window. The King immediately said to Westmorland, who sat opposite, "That's a shot," and, with the courage of his family, coolly leaned forward to examine the round hole in the glass. Similar scenes occurred on his return to St. James's Palace. The mob pressed forward with an eagerness which the Guards could scarcely restrain, calling out "Peace, Peace; Bread, Bread; No Pitt; No Famine." With some difficulty the gates of the Horse Guards were shut against them. Opposite Spring Gardens a stone struck the woodwork of the carriage; and the intrepid monarch alighted at St. James's amidst a commotion so wild that one of the horses took fright and flung down a groom, breaking his thigh. Thereafter the rabble set upon the state carriage, greatly damaging it; and when George later on proceeded in his private carriage to Buckingham House, he again ploughed his way through a din of curses. Pitt kept discreetly in the background, or he would have been roughly handled.

A loyalist caricature of the period gives an imaginative version of the incident. In it Pitt figures as the coachman whipping on the horses of the royal carriage amidst a shower of stones, eggs, and cats. The King sits inside absolutely passive, with large protruding eyes; Lansdowne, Bedford, Whitbread, and others strive to stop the wheels; Fox and Sheridan, armed with bludgeons, seek to force open the door; while Norfolk fires a blunderbuss at the King. The sketch illustrates the fierce partisanship of the time, which stooped to incredibly coarse charges. But scarcely less strange was the insinuation of Lansdowne, immediately after the affair, that Ministers had themselves planned it in order to alarm the public and perpetuate their despotic rule. The same insinuation found favour with Francis Place, a rabid tailor of Holborn, and a prominent member of the London Corresponding Society, who charged Pitt with imperilling the life of George III in order to keep office. "It is a curious circumstance," he wrote, "that Pitt carried all his obnoxious measures, silenced or kept down his opponents and raised vast sums of money by means of the alarms which he and his coadjutors had created. The war was commenced after an alarm had been created, and it was kept up by the same means."[1] Fox and his followers often uttered similar taunts.

The insults to the King were but the climax of an agitation which had previously gone to strange lengths. On 27th October 1795 the London Corresponding Society convened a monster meeting in the fields near Copenhagen House, Islington, in order to protest against the war and to press for annual Parliaments and universal suffrage. A crowd said to number nearly 150,000 persons assembled under the chairmanship of John Binns, and passed an "Address to the Nation," which concluded as follows: "If ever the British nation should loudly demand strong and decisive measures, we boldly answer, 'We have lives and are ready to devote them either separately or collectively for the salvation of our country.'" Outwardly the meeting was orderly, if that epithet can be applied to a monster meeting which advocated civil war. But probably less than one tenth of the assemblage heard the resolution. Equally threatening was a hand-bill circulated in London on the practice of "King-killing." Place says nothing about this, and ridicules the "Address to the Nation" as a foolish production, which he had opposed no less strongly than the convocation of the meeting. This was the

[1] B.M. Add. MSS., 27808.

usual attitude of Place. He sought to figure as the apostle of reasonableness, deprecating all unwise acts and frothy talk on the part of his associates, but minimizing the follies of British democrats, which he usually ascribed to the insidious advice of the emissaries of Pitt.

Let us enlarge our survey. From the Home Office Records it is clear that dear food and uncertain work had aggravated the political discontent of the years 1792-4, until the autumn of 1795 witnessed almost an epidemic of sedition. To take one significant episode. An inflammatory placard, dated Norwich, 16th October 1795, was widely circulated. That city, as we have seen, was a hotbed of Radicalism. There it was that the democratic clubs sought to federate with the view of forming a National Convention. One of their members, named Besey, now posted up the following placard. After stating that the prevailing misery is due to the present unjust and unnecessary war, the number of abuses and sinecures, and "the monopoly of farms which disgraces this country," it continues thus: "The Minister would gladly instigate you to riot and plunder that he might send against you those *valiant* heroes who compose his devoted Volunteer corps. . . . This would accelerate his darling object of governing us by a military aristocracy. The countries which supplied us with quantities of corn now groan under the iron yoke of the Tigress of the North or lie desolate from this infernal war. We send immense stores to the emigrants and the *Chouans*. Those rebels, not satisfied with traitorously resisting the constituted authorities of their country, have desolated the face of it. These honourable Allies must be fed, as others of the kind are paid, by us." He then urges them to form popular Societies and demand redress of grievances. He concludes thus: "You may as well look for chastity and mercy in the Empress of Russia, honour and consistency from the King of Prussia, wisdom and plain dealing from the Emperor of Germany, as a single speck of virtue from our **Hell-born Minister**." [1]

In view of these facts, is it surprising that Ministers decided to issue a royal proclamation against seditious assemblies and the circulation of treasonable papers? Sheriffs, magistrates, and all law-abiding men were charged to apprehend those who distributed such papers and to help in the suppression of sedi-

[1] "H. O.," Geo. III (Domestic), 36.

tious meetings (4th November). Six days later Grenville introduced the Treasonable Practices Bill, while Pitt in the Commons moved the Seditious Meetings Bill. The Prime Minister
stated that, as soon as the Habeas Corpus Act came again into
operation, the political clubs renewed their propaganda and
brought about the present dangerous situation. In order to
suppress gatherings of a definitely seditious character, he proposed that, before a meeting of more than fifty persons which
was not convened by the local authorities, notice must be given
by seven householders and sent to the magistrates. The Bill
also required the presence of a magistrate, and invested him with
power to stop any speech, disperse the meeting, and order the
arrest of the speaker. But this was not all. The authorities had
been alarmed by the popularity of Thelwall's racy discourses,
resumed early in 1795, which represented Government as the
source of all the country's ills. Whether his sprightly sallies
were dangerous may be doubted; but Pitt, with characteristic
lack of humour, paid Thelwall the compliment of ordaining that
lecture-halls must be licensed by two magistrates; and a magistrate might enter at any time. The Bill was passed for three years.

Equally drastic was the Treasonable Practices Bill. Declaring
the planning or levying war within the kingdom to be an act of
substantive treason, it imposed dire penalties on those who devised evil against the King, who sought to coerce Parliament or
help the invaders. Even those who spoke or wrote against the
constitution came under the penalties for treason and might be
transported for seven years. As Fox indignantly exclaimed, if
he criticized a system which allotted two members to Old Sarum
and none to Manchester, he might be sent to Botany Bay. The
alarm of Pitt at the state of affairs appears in a request which he
and Portland sent to the Duke of York, on 14th November, for
reinforcements of cavalry. They asked him to despatch three
troops of the 1st Dragoon Guards from Romford to Hackney,
replacing the Pembroke Fencible Cavalry, which was utterly
useless; to order up two troops of the Cornish Fencible Cavalry
from Barnet to Hampstead and Highgate; to despatch the 11th
Light Dragoons from Guildford to Ewell or Kingston, and the
1st Fencibles from Reading to Uxbridge. These, along with
the Lancashire Militia at Lewisham and Greenwich, and the
Guards in London, would suffice for the crisis.[1]

[1] "H. O.," (Departmental), Secs. of State.

Such were the conditions under which the debates on the two Bills proceeded. They turned largely on the connection between the Islington meeting and the outrage on the King. Canning stoutly affirmed that connection, which Sheridan and Fox no less vehemently denied. Wilberforce on this occasion supported the Government. Pitt showed little zeal in defending his Bill, promising to safeguard the right of public meeting when lawfully exercised. The debate in the Lords elicited from the Bishop of Rochester the significant statement that he did not know what the great mass of the people had to do with the laws except to obey them. The Earl of Lauderdale pilloried this utterance, thereby consoling himself for being in a minority of 5. In the Commons Fox mustered 22, as against 167 for the Government (6th November—14th December 1795). Meanwhile monster meetings of protest were held on 12th November and 2nd and 7th December, the two last in Marylebone Fields, which now form the greater portion of Regent's Park. The orderliness of these vast throngs, comprising perhaps a quarter of a million of men, affords a strong argument against the two Acts. Lord Malmesbury much regretted that there was no rioting, now that all was ready for its repression. After the passing of those " barbarous bloodthirsty " measures (as Place called them) the country settled down into a sullen silence. Reformers limited their assemblies to forty-five members; but even so they did not escape the close meshes of the law. Binns and Jones, delegates of the London Corresponding Society who went to Birmingham, were arrested there; and the Society soon gave up its propaganda. All but the most resolute members fell away, and by the end of 1796 it was £185 in debt.[1]

Undoubtedly these measures mark the nadir of Pitt's political career. Nevertheless, the coincidence between the London Corresponding Society's meeting at Islington and the attempted outrage on George III was suspiciously close in point of time; and a dangerous feeling prevailed throughout the country. Pitt, as we shall see, took steps to alleviate the distress which was its chief cause; but after the insult to the King he could not but take precautionary measures against sedition. After such an incident, a Minister who did nothing at all would be held responsible if the monarch were assassinated. Some coercive measures were

---

[1] B.M. Add. MSS., 27808; "Hist. of the Two Acts," 330 et seq.

inevitable; and it is clear that they cowed the more restive spirits. Among other persons who wrote to Pitt on this topic, Wilson, formerly his tutor at Burton Pynsent and Cambridge, sent him a letter from Binfield, in which occur these sentences: "The Sedition Bills also have had so good an effect. Our farmers can now go to market without being exposed to the danger of having republican principles instilled into them while they are dining." Apparently, then, the loyal efforts of Berkshire magistrates extended to the interiors of inns. Whether the two Acts were not needlessly prolonged is open to grave question. Certainly, while driving the discontent underground, they increased its explosive force. General David Dundas, in his Report on National Defence of November 1796, states that at no time were there so many people disposed to help the invaders. Perhaps we may sum up by declaring the two Acts a disagreeable but necessary expedient during the time of alarm, and mischievous when it passed away.[1]

The insult to the King was but one symptom of a distemper widely prevalent. Its causes were manifold. Chief among them was a feeling of disgust at the many failures of the war. The defection of Prussia and Spain, the fruitless waste of British troops in the West Indies, the insane follies of the French *émigrés*, the ghastly scenes at Quiberon, and the tragi-comedy of Vendémiaire in the streets of Paris, sufficed to daunt the stoutest hearts. By the middle of the month of October 1795, Pitt decided to come to terms with France, if the Directory, newly installed in power, should found a stable Government and exhibit peaceful tendencies. His position in this autumn is pathetic. Reproached by the *émigrés* for recalling the Comte d'Artois from Yeu, taunted by Fox for not having sought peace from the Terrorists, and reviled by the populace as the cause of the dearth, he held firmly on his way, shelving the *émigrés*, maintaining that this was the first opportunity of gaining a lasting peace, and adjuring the people to behave manfully in order the more speedily to win it.

This advice seemed but cold comfort to men and women whose hardships were severe. Political discontent was greatly increased by dear food and uncertainty of employment. The symptoms had long been threatening. At midsummer of the year 1795 the men of Birmingham assembled in hundreds

---

[1] Pitt MSS., 190; "W. O.," 113.

opposite a mill and bakehouse on Snow Hill, crying out: " A
large loaf. Are we to be starved to death?" They were dispersed by armed force, but not without bloodshed. At that time
insubordination in the troops was met by summary executions
or repression at Horsham, Brighton, and Dumfries. In July a
drunken brawl at Charing Cross led to a riot, in the course of
which the mob smashed Pitt's windows in Downing Street, and
demolished a recruiting station in St. George's Fields, Lambeth.
The country districts were deeply agitated by the shortage of
corn resulting from the bad harvest of 1794. A report from Bea-
minster in Dorset stated that for six weeks before the harvest of
1795 no wheat remained; and the poor of that county would
have starved, had not a sum of money been raised sufficient to
buy cargoes of wheat which then reached Plymouth.

The suffering was increased by the extraordinary cold of that
midsummer which destroyed hundreds of newly-shorn sheep and
blighted the corn. Driving storms of rain in August laid the crops.
On heavy land they were utterly spoilt, so that even by October
the poor felt the pinch. From all parts there came the gloomiest
reports. In Oxfordshire there was no old wheat left, and the
insatiable demands from the large towns of the north sent up
prices alarmingly. In November Lord Bateman wrote from
Leominster that the wheat crop was but two thirds of the
average, and, if Government did not import wheat directly, not
through fraudulent contractors, riots must ensue. Reports from
Petworth, East Grinstead, and Battle told of the havoc wrought
by blight and rains. At Plymouth the price of wheat exceeded
all records. Lord Salisbury reported a shortage of one third in
the wheat crop of mid-Hertfordshire. Kensington sent a better
estimate for its corn lands. But the magistrates of Enfield and
Edmonton deemed the outlook so threatening that they urged
Pitt and his colleagues (1) to encourage the free importation of
wheat,(2) to facilitate the enclosure of all common fields and the
conversion of common and waste lands into tillage; (3) to pass
an Act legalizing relief of the poor in every parish by the weekly
distribution of bread and meat at reduced prices in proportion
to the size of the family and of its earnings.[1]

The protests against the Corn Laws are significant. In 1773
the bounty system of the reign of William III was revised, the

[1] " H. O.," Geo. III (Domestic), 36.

average price of wheat being reckoned at forty-four shillings the quarter. If it fell below that figure, a bounty of five shillings a quarter was granted on export, so as to encourage farmers to give a wide acreage to wheat, in the assurance that in bountiful seasons they could profitably dispose of their surplus. But when the price rose to forty-four shillings exportation was forbidden, and at forty-eight shillings foreign corn was admitted on easy terms so as to safeguard the consumer; for, as Burke said: " he who separates the interest of the consumer from the interest of the grower starves the country." Unfortunately, in 1791, Government raised the price at which importation was allowed to fifty-four shillings the quarter. The upward trend of prices may have called for some change; but it was too drastic. In view of the increase of the manufacturing townships, Pitt should have favoured the import of foreign corn, though not in such a way as unduly to discourage agriculturists. England, in fact, was then reaching the stage at which she needed foreign corn when nature withheld her bounties at home, and it is well to remember that 1792 was the last year in which England exported any appreciable amount of wheat. During the Great War she became an importing country, and at no time was the crisis worse than in the winter of 1795-6. Early in the year 1796 the best wheat sold at six guineas the quarter, or four times its present price; the inferior kinds were very dear, and many poor people perished from want if not from actual starvation. So grave was the crisis as to evoke a widespread demand for Free Trade in corn. This feeling pervaded even the rural districts, a report by John Shepherd of Faversham being specially significant. In the towns there was an outcry against corn merchants, who were guilty of forestalling and regrating. Possibly but for these tricks of trade the supply of home wheat might almost have sufficed.

Pitt seems to have thought so; for he wrote to the Marquis of Stafford, stating his desire to have powers for compelling exhaustive returns of the wheat supply to be sent in. On the whole, however, he deemed such an expedient high-handed and likely to cause alarm. He therefore decided to call for a special committee to inquire into the high price of corn, and explained his reasons to the House of Commons on 3rd November 1795. He urged the need of modifying the old and nearly obsolete law relating to the assize of bread, and he suggested the advisability of mixing wheat with barley, or other corn, which, while lessening the price of bread, would not render it unpalatable. As to prohibiting the distillation of whiskey, he proposed to discontinue that device after February 1796, so that the revenue might not unduly suffer. The committee was equally cautious. In presenting its report eight days later, Ryder moved that the members should pledge themselves to lessen the consumption of wheat in their households by one third. These proposals appeared wholly inadequate to Bankes and Sheridan, who urged that all classes should be compelled to eat the same kind of bread. Francis, however, asserted that the poor in his district now refused to eat any but the best wheaten bread. There was therefore every need for a law compelling bakers to make bread only two thirds of wheat. Nevertheless, the House agreed to the proposals of the committee. Members also bound themselves to forswear pastry, and by all possible means to endeavour to lessen the consumption of fine wheaten flour. History does not record how far these resolves held good, and with what hygienic results. An external sign of the patriotic mania for economy in wheat was the disuse of hair-powder, which resulted from the tax now imposed on that article. Thus Rousseau, Pitt, and Nature are largely responsible for a change which in its turn hastened the disappearance of wigs.

Pitt and his colleagues sought to check the practice of forestalling. But, as usually happens in a struggle with human selfishness, success was doubtful. More fruitful was the expedient of attracting foreign corn by granting large bounties on imports. As if this were not enough, British warships sometimes compelled neutral corn-vessels, bound for France, to put in at our harbours and sell their cargoes at the high prices then prevailing, a high-handed practice which prepared the way for the Armed Neutrality League of 1800. These exceptional expedients seem to have been due to what Sheffield called "a sure little junto,"— Pitt, Ryder, and Jenkinson. He further accused them of taking the corn trade out of the hands of the merchants and then dropping State management prematurely. Over against this captious comment may be placed the undoubted fact that, early in the year 1796, wheat sold at six guineas the quarter, and by the month of May was down nearly to normal prices. In that month Pitt deemed the crisis past; for the King's Speech of 19th May, at the end of the last session of that Parliament, congratulated members on the success of their efforts to afford relief to the people. The harvest of 1796 was more abundant; but confidence was not restored until late in the year. As Whitbread pointed out, the increase of large farms at the expense of the little men led to the holding back of the new corn. The small farmer perforce had to sell his corn at once. The wealthy farmer could bide his time.[1]

In these years of dearth, when the troubles in Poland restricted the supply of corn from that natural granary, the importance of the United States became increasingly obvious. Pitt had consistently sought to improve the relations with our kinsmen, and in 1791 sent out the first official envoy, George Hammond. The disputes resulting from the War of Independence and those arising out of the British Maritime Code during the Great War, brought about acute friction; but the good sense of Pitt, Washington, and John Jay, his special envoy to London, led to the conclusion of an Anglo-American Treaty (7th October 1794). Though hotly opposed by the Gallophil party at Washington, it was finally ratified in September 1796, and thus postponed for sixteen years the hostilities which had at times seemed imminent. For the present the United States sent us an increased quantity of cotton wool, but mere driblets of corn except in seasons of scarcity. Lancashire benefited from the enhanced trade, while the British farmer did not yet discern the approach of times of ruinous competition.[2]

Agriculture had long been an occupation equally fashionable and profitable. No part of the career of George III deserves more commendation than his patronage of high farming. That he felt keen interest in the subject appears from the letters which he sent to "The Annals of Agriculture" over the signature of "Ralph Robinson," one of his shepherds at Windsor. A present of a ram from the King's fine flock of merinos was a sign of high favour. Thanks to this encouragement and the efforts of that prince of agricultural reformers, Arthur Young, the staple industry of the land was in a highly flourishing condition. The rise in the price of wheat now stimulated the demand for the enclosure of waste lands and of the open or com-

[1] "Parl. Hist.," xxxii, 235-42, 687-700, 1156; Tooke, "Hist. of Prices," i, 185 et seq.; Porter, "Progress of the Nation," 147, 452.
[2] "Dropmore P.," iii, 87, 243, 526-30; "Report of the American Hist. Assoc." (1903), ii, 67-9, 354, 375, 440 et seq., 552-8; E. Channing, "United States," 148-50; Cunningham, 512, 694.

mon-fields which then adjoined the great majority of English villages. The reclamation of wastes and fens was an advantage to all but the very poor, who, as graziers, wood-cutters, or fishermen, dragged along a life of poverty but independence. Though they might suffer by the change to tillage, the parish and the nation at large reaped golden harvests.

The enclosure of common fields was a different matter. Though on them the traditional rotation of crops was stupid and the husbandry slipshod, yet the semi-communal tillage of the three open strips enabled Hodge to jog along in the easy ways dear to him. In such cases a change to more costly methods involves hardship to the poor, who cannot, or will not, adopt the requirements of a more scientific age. Recent research has also shown that villagers depended mainly on their grazing rights. Now, a small grazier does not readily become a corn-grower. Even if he can buy a plough and a team, he lacks the experience needful for success in corn-growing. Accordingly, the small yeomen could neither compete with the large farmers nor imitate their methods. While the few who succeeded became prosperous, the many sank into poverty. These results may also be ascribed to the expense and injustice too often attending the enclosures of this period. Far from striking off at one blow the fetters of the old system, as happened in France in 1789, English law required each parish to procure its own Enclosure Act. Thus, when the parishioners at the village meeting had decided to enclose the common fields and waste, there occurred a long and costly delay until the parochial charter was gained.

Then again, the difficult task of re-allotting the wastes and open fields in proportion to the rights of the lord of the manor the tithe-owner, and the parishioners, sometimes furnished an occasion for downright robbery of the poor. That staunch champion of high-farming and enclosures, Arthur Young, names many instances of shameful extortion on the part of landlord and attorneys. Where the village carried out its enclosure fairly and cheaply, the benefits were undoubtedly great. The wastes then became good pasture or tolerable tillage; and the common fields, previously cut up into small plots, and worked on a wasteful rotation, soon testified to the magic of individual ownership. A case in point was Snettisham, near Sandringham, where, as the result of the new wealth, the population increased by one fifth, while the poor-rate diminished by one half. Young also declared that large parts of Norfolk, owing to judicious enclosures, produced glorious crops of grain and healthy flocks fed on turnips and mangolds, where formerly there had been dreary wastes, miserable stock, and underfed shepherds.

The dearth of the year 1795 brought to the front the question of a General Enclosure Act, for enabling parishes to adopt this reform without the expense of separately applying to Parliament. To devise a measure suitable to the wide diversities of tenure prevalent in English villages was a difficult task; but it had been carried out successfully in Scotland by the Act of 1695; and now, a century later, a similar boon was proposed for England by one of the most enterprising of Scotsmen. Sir John Sinclair was born in 1754 at Thurso Castle. Inheriting large estates in the county of Caithness, he determined to enter political life, and became member for Lostwithiel, in Cornwall. Differing sharply from Pitt over the Warren Hastings affair, he adopted the independent line of conduct natural to his tastes, and during the Regency dispute joined the intermediate party known as the Armed Neutrality.

Above all he devoted himself to the development of Scottish agriculture, and began in 1790 a work entitled " A Statistical Account of Scotland." He also founded a society for improving the quality of British wool, and in May 1793 he urged the Prime Minister to incorporate a Board of Agriculture. Young bet that Pitt would refuse; for, while favouring commerce and manufactures, he had hitherto done nothing for the plough. He lost his bet. Pitt gave a conditional offer of support, provided that the House of Commons approved. The proposal won general assent, despite the insinuations of Fox and Sheridan that its purpose was merely to increase the patronage at the disposal of the Cabinet. Sinclair became president, with Young as secretary.[1] The Englishman complained that Sinclair's habit of playing with large schemes wasted the scanty funds at their disposal. But the Board did good work, for instance, in setting on foot experiments as to the admixture of barley, beans, and rice in the partly wheaten bread ordained by Parliament in 1795.

With the view of framing a General Enclosure Act, Sinclair sought to extract from parochial Enclosure Acts a medicine suitable to the myriad needs and ailments of English rural

[1] "Mems. of Sir John Sinclair," I, ch. iv; II, ch. i.

life. His survey of typical enactments is of high interest. He summarizes the treatment accorded to the lord of the manor, the rector or other tithe owner, and the parishioners. Thus, in the case of three parishes near Hull, namely, Hessle, Anlaby, and Tranley, the wastes and open fields, comprising 3,640 acres, were divided by an act of the year 1792 in a way which seems to have given satisfaction. Commissioners appointed by the local authorities divided the soil among the lords of the manors, the tithe-owners, and the parishioners, the landlords retaining half of their portions in trust for the poor. Other instances, however, reveal the difficulty of the question of tithes. Young and Sinclair felt bitterly on this subject, as their recent proposal to give a detailed description of the lands of every parish in England was successfully opposed by Dr. Moore, Archbishop of Canterbury.

Pointing out the need of a General Enclosure Act, Sinclair claimed that of the 22,107,000 acres of waste in England and Wales, a large portion could be afforested, while only one million acres were quite useless—a very hopeful estimate.[1] In order to investigate this question, a Select Committee was appointed, comprising among others Lord William Russell, Ryder, Carew, Coke of Norfolk, Plumer, and Whitbread. The outcome of its research was the General Enclosure Bill introduced early in the session of 1796, which elicited the sanguine prophecy of its author quoted at the head of this chapter.

The measure aroused keen interest. On 15th March the London Court of Aldermen urged its members to assist in passing some such measure with a view to increasing the food supply, and providing work for the poor, as well as for soldiers and sailors discharged at the peace. The proposals were as follows: The present method of enclosure would be extended so as to enable the parties concerned to frame an inexpensive and friendly agreement. In case of disagreement the Bill would enable the majority of the parishioners, voting, not by head, but according to the value of their rights, to decide on the question of enclosure. But, in order to safeguard the rights of the poor, the choice of commissioners charged with the duty of re-allotting

---

[1] "Mems. of Sir John Sinclair," ii, 60-4, 104; Sinclair, "Address . . . on the Cultivation of Waste Lands (1795)"; "Observations on . . . a Bill for facilitating the Division of Commons." He first urged this on Pitt on 10th January 1795 (Pitt MSS., 175).

the soil would rest with the majority, reckoned both according to heads and value. The lord of the manor could not veto enclosure; but his convenience was specially to be consulted in the re-apportionment of the land. Sinclair also pointed out to Pitt that, as tithe-owners were now " much run at," their interests must be carefully guarded. As for the cottagers, they would find compensation for the lapse of their fuel rights by the acquisition of small allotments near to their cottages. The poor also would not be charged with the expenses of enclosure, and might raise money on loan to fence the plots awarded to them in lieu of their share in the waste and the open fields. To insist, said Sinclair, on four acres being annexed to every cottage was really harmful. Finally he expressed the hope that, under his plan, the legal expenses of enclosure would on an average be £5 per parish as against the present burden of £500.[1]

Pitt's treatment of the General Enclosure Bill is somewhat obscure. Again and again Sinclair urged him to greater activity. In April 1796 he begged him to consult with the judges so as to meet the objections of tithe-owners. In May he warned him of the general disappointment that must ensue if no measure of that kind passed in that session. He asked him whether the Bill, as now amended by the committee, would not answer its purpose. Pitt gave no encouraging sign. On the contrary, he gratified the country gentlemen by opposing a Bill for the Reform of the Game Laws. The proposer, Curwen, sought merely to legalize the killing of game started on ground farmed by the occupier. But the squires took alarm, asserting that every small farmer could then pursue hares and rabbits from his ground into their preserves, and that country life, on those terms, would be intolerable. Pitt took their side, averring that sport was a relaxation well suited to the higher Orders of State, but likely to entice farmers away " from more serious and useful occupations." Much may be forgiven to a Prime Minister shortly before a General Election, which, in fact, gave to Pitt a new lease of power.

To Sinclair the election brought defeat and chagrin. He travelled northward to the Orkneys to seek a seat there, and, writing from Edinburgh on 6th July, tartly informed Pitt of his rejection after a journey of nearly a thousand miles. He must (he adds) either obtain a seat elsewhere, or take no further

[1] Pitt MSS., 178.

interest in the Board of Agriculture. If Pitt approves of his labour at the Board, will he show it in some way? " If, on the other hand," he continues, " you feel the least hesitation about giving it support, your candour, I am persuaded, will induce you to inform me at once, that I may no longer be tempted to waste so much time and labour in such pursuits. . . . I still flatter myself, however, that you will see the object in such a light that you will give the President of the Board of Agriculture a seat either in the Upper or the Lower House, that he may be encouraged to carry on the concerns of that useful institution with redoubled energy." Pitt's comment on the back of the letter is suggestive: " That he has lost his election, but flatters himself that a seat will be given him either in the *Lower* or Upper House, or he must decline taking further concern in the proceedings of the Board of Agriculture." A little later Sinclair renewed his appeal for a seat either at Midhurst, or in Scotland. Failing that, he hinted that the President of the Board of Agriculture ought to be a Peer. Is it surprising that Pitt fulfilled the suggestion by giving his influence in favour of Lord Somerville, who displaced Sinclair at the Board in 1798? Loughborough it was who suggested the change;[1] but Pitt must have approved it; and thereafter the Board deteriorated.

In truth the thane of Thurso had become a bore. His letters to Pitt teem with advice on foreign politics and the distillation of whisky, on new taxes and high farming, on increasing the silver coinage and checking smuggling, on manning the navy and raising corps of Fencibles. Wisdom flashing forth in these diverse forms begets distrust. Sinclair the omniscient correspondent injured Sinclair the agrarian reformer. Young treated the Prime Minister with more tact. His letters were fewer, and his help was practical. A pleasing instance of this was his presence at Holwood in April 1798, when Pitt was draining the hillside near his house, so as to preserve it from damp and provide water for the farm and garden below. Young drew up the scheme, went down more than once to superintend the boring and trenching, and then added these words: " I beg you will permit me to give such attention merely and solely as a mark of gratitude for the goodness I have already experienced at your hands."[2]

[1] " Corresp. of Sir John Sinclair," i, 124.
[2] Pitt MSS., 193. Sinclair raised two corps of Fencibles. The list of his works, pamphlets, etc., fills thirty-two pages at the end of his Memoirs.

Sinclair, now member for Petersfield, brought his General Enclosure Bill before Parliament in 1797. In order to meet the objections of tithe-owners and lawyers, he divided it into two parts, the former applying to parishes where all the persons concerned were unanimous, the latter where this was not the case. Even so the measure met with opposition from the legal profession; and on 13th May he wrote to Pitt expressing deep concern at the opposition of the Solicitor-General. In July he besought Pitt to make the Bill a Cabinet measure in order to " prevent either legal or ecclesiastical prejudices operating against it." Nevertheless Pitt remained neutral, and the Bill was lost in the Lords, mainly owing to the opposition of the Lord Chancellor.[1] In December Sinclair announced his intention of bringing in a Bill for the improvement of waste land; but, he added significantly, " I should be glad previously to know whether it is your intention to support that measure or not." Pitt gave no sign, and the proposal did not come forward.

Pitt's treatment of one of the most important questions of that time deserves censure. We may grant that the fussiness of Sinclair told against his proposals. It is also true that the drafting of a Bill applicable to every English parish was beset with difficulties, and that enclosures, while adding greatly to the food supply of the nation, had for the most part told against the independence of the poorer villagers. But this was largely due to the expense and chicanery consequent on the passing of parochial Acts of Parliament; and what objections were there to facilitating the enclosure of wastes and open fields by parishes where everyone desired it? In such a case it was the bounden duty of Parliament to end the law's delays and cheapen the procedure.

That Pitt did little or nothing to avert the hostility of bishops and lawyers in the Upper House convicts him either of apathy or of covert opposition. He is largely responsible for the continuance of the old customs, under which a parish faced the expense of procuring a separate Act of Parliament only under stress of severe dearth; and, as a rule, the crisis ended long before the cumbrous machinery of the law enabled the new lands to come under the plough. It is, however, possible that he hoped to inaugurate a system of enclosures of waste lands by a clause which appeared in his abortive proposals of the year 1797 for the relief

[1] " Mems. of Sir John Sinclair," ii, 106-9.

of the poor. His Bill on that subject comprised not only very generous plans of relief, but also the grant of cows to the deserving poor, the erection of Schools of Industry in every parish or group of parishes, and facilities for reclaiming waste land. His treatment of the question of poor relief is too extensive a subject to admit of adequate description here; but I propose to return to it and to notice somewhat fully the criticisms of Bentham and others.[1] It must suffice to say that the draft of that measure bespeaks a keen interest in the welfare of the poor, and indeed errs on the side of generosity. Abbot, afterwards Lord Colchester, was asked by Pitt to help in drafting the Poor Bill; and he pronounced it " as bad in the mode as the principles were good in substance."[2]

After the withdrawal of Pitt's Poor Bill, nothing was done to facilitate enclosures until the accession of Addington to power. His General Enclosure Act of the year 1801 afforded timely relief in the matter of food-supply, a fact which shows that the difficulties in the way of such a measure were far from serious. The passing of that Bill, it is true, was helped on by the terrible dearth of that year, when the average price of wheat was close on 116 shillings the quarter. But Pitt was content to meet the almost equally acute crisis of 1795-6 by temporary shifts, one of which exasperated the neutral States of the North and prepared the way for the renewal of the hostile League of the Baltic.

[1] " Pitt and Napoleon Miscellanies."
[2] " Lord Colchester's Diary," i, 82.

CHAPTER XIV

THE YEARS OF STRAIN (1796-7)

Torn as we are by faction, without an army, without money, trusting entirely to a navy whom we may not be able to pay, and on whose loyalty, even if we can, no firm reliance is to be placed, how are we to get out of this cursed war without a Revolution?—CORNWALLIS TO ROSS, 15th December 1797.

THE year 1797, which opened with events portending the overthrow of Austria and the financial collapse of England, brought a passing gleam of sunshine into the gray life of Pitt. For some time he had been a frequent visitor at Eden Farm, Beckenham, the seat of Lord Auckland. It was on the way to Holwood, and the cheerful society of that large family afforded a relief from cares of state not to be found in his bachelor household. His circle of friends, never large, had somewhat diminished with the wear and tear of politics. His affection for Wilberforce, perhaps, had not quite regained its former fervour. As for the vinous society of Dundas, a valuable colleague but a far from ideal companion, Pitt must in his better moments have held it cheap. He rarely saw his mother, far away in Somerset; and probably his relations to his brother had cooled since he removed him from the Admiralty. In truth, despite his loving disposition, Pitt was a lonely man.

The voice of rumour, in his case always unfair, charged him with utter indifference to feminine charms. His niece, Lady Hester Stanhope, who later on had opportunities of observing him closely, vehemently denied the charge, declaring that he was much impressed by beauty in women, and noted the least defect, whether of feature, demeanour, or dress. She declared that, on one occasion, while commending her preparations for the ball-room, he suggested the looping up of one particular fold. At once she recognized the voice of the expert and hailed the experiment as an artistic triumph. Hester's recollections, it is true, belong to the lonely years spent in the Lebanon, when she indulged in ecstatic or spiteful outbursts; and we therefore question her statement that Pitt was once so enamoured of a certain Miss W——, who became Mrs. B——s of Devonshire, as to drink wine out of her shoe. But Hester's remarks are detailed enough to refute the reports of his unnatural insensibility, which elicited coarse jests from opponents; and we may fully trust that severe critic of all Pitt's friends, when, recalling a special visit to Beckenham Church, she pronounced the Honourable Eleanor Eden gloriously beautiful.[1]

To this bright vivacious girl of twenty years Pitt's affections went forth in the winter of 1796-7;[2] and she reciprocated them. Every one agrees that Eleanor combined beauty with good sense, sprightliness with tact. Having had varied experiences during Auckland's missions to Paris, Madrid, and The Hague, she had matured far beyond her years. In mental endowments she would have been a fit companion even to Pitt; and she possessed a rich store of the social graces in which he was somewhat deficient. In fact, here was his weak point as a political leader. He and his colleagues had no *salon* which could vie with those of the Whig grandees. The accession of Portland had been a social boon; but Pitt and his intimate followers exerted little influence on London Society. He and Grenville were too stiff. Neither Dundas nor Wilberforce moved in the highest circles. Portland, Spencer, and Windham held somewhat aloof, and Leeds, Sydney, and others had been alienated. Accordingly, the news that Pitt was paying marked attentions to Auckland's eldest daughter caused a flutter of excitement. Her charm and tact warranted the belief that in the near future the Prime Minister would dominate the social sphere hardly less than the political.

Among his friends who knew how warm a heart beat under that cold exterior, the news inspired the hope that here was the talisman which would reveal the hidden treasures of his nature. The stiff form would now unbend; the political leader would

---

[1] "Mems. of Lady Hester Stanhope," i, 177-81. Tomline asserted that a lady of the highest rank desired to marry Pitt. Various conjectures have been made on this topic. Lord Rosebery suggests that the Duchess of Gordon was hinted at.

[2] "Auckland Journals," iii, 356, 363, 369, 373-4.

The Hon. Eleanor Eden

(From a miniature)

figure as a genial host; the martinet would become a man. Assuredly their estimate was correct. Pitt's nature needed more glow, wider sympathies, a freer expression. A happy marriage would in any case have widened his outlook and matured his character. But a union with Eleanor Eden would have supplied to him the amenities of life. We picture her exerting upon him an influence not unlike that which Wordsworth believed that his sister had exerted upon his being:

> thou didst plant its crevices with flowers,
> Hang it with shrubs that twinkle in the breeze,
> And teach the little birds to build their nests
> And warble in its chambers.[1]

It was not to be. After toying with this day-dream, Pitt suddenly broke away to Downing Street. His letter to Auckland, written there on 20th January 1797, announced the decision of the Minister in chillingly correct terms. In pathetically halting and laboured phraseology he implied that he had throughout observed a correct aloofness. After five long sentences of apology to the father he proceeded thus:

Whoever may have the good fortune ever to be united to her is destined to more than his share of human happiness. Whether, at any rate, I could have had any ground to hope that such would have been my lot, I am in no degree entitled to guess. I have to reproach myself for ever having indulged the idea on my own part as far as I have done, without asking myself carefully and early enough what were the difficulties in the way of its being realised. I have suffered myself to overlook them too long, but having now at length reflected as fully and as calmly as I am able on every circumstance that ought to come under my consideration (at least as much for her sake as for my own) I am compelled to say that I find the obstacles to it decisive and insurmountable.[2]

Auckland had a right to feel the deepest pain at this official missive. The matter had been discussed in newspapers. Indeed, a caricaturist ventured to publish a sketch showing Pitt as Adam conducting Eve to the nuptial bower in the garden of Eden, while behind it squatted Satan as a toad, leering hatred through the features of Fox. It is to be hoped that Auckland did not

---

[1] Wordsworth, " Prelude," bk. xiv.

[2] Pretyman MSS. Quoted in full, with Pitt's second letter and one of Auckland, by Lord Ashbourne ("Pitt," 241-4).

know of this indelicate cartoon when he replied to Pitt. That letter has very properly been destroyed. But we have Pitt's second letter to Auckland, in which he again assures him how deeply he is affected by hearing of " the sentiments of another person, unhappily too nearly interested in the subject in question." He adds these moving words: " Believe me, I have not lightly or easily sacrificed my best hopes and earnest wishes to my conviction and judgment." Auckland's reply of 23rd January reveals the grief of his wife and daughter. For two or three days they remained in absolute solitude, and that, too, in a household remarkable for domestic affection. To Pitt also the decision was a matter of deep pain and life-long regret. Thenceforth he trod the path of duty alone. On 7th February the Archbishop of Canterbury wrote to Auckland (his brother-in-law) that Pitt lived in seclusion and seemed dreamy. At a recent Council meeting his face was swollen and unhealthy looking. Probably this was the time at which Pitt informed Addington that he must take the helm of State.[1]

We can only conjecture as to the insuperable obstacles to the union; but it seems highly probable that they were of a financial kind. In the Pitt MSS. (No. 196) there is a brief Memorandum in Pitt's writing, of the year 1797, which must refer to his yearly expenses, either at Downing Street or at Holwood. It gives the liquor account of the steward's room as " £300 and upwards," and states that the other expenses of that room might be reduced from £600 to £300, those of his own wardrobe from £600 to £400, and those of the stable from £400 to £300. These figures do not tally with those of the Downing Street or Holwood accounts for the latter half of 1797, which will be stated later; and the loose way in which Pitt estimates his expenses is highly suggestive. We now know that he was heading straight for bankruptcy throughout this period; and probably on looking into his affairs he discovered the fact. It is also certain that he lent money to his mother. She seems to have lost on farming experiments at Burton Pynsent; for she charged her sons to defray her just debts incurred in this manner, and the Bishop of Lincoln in July 1801 stated that she owed to Pitt the sum of £5,800 on which she ought to pay interest but did not. Chatham also borrowed £1,000 from Pitt in August

Pellew, i, 183.

1791, and the fact that he paid not a penny to help to discharge the debts of his brother in the year 1801 seems to show that he himself was still in low water.[1]

Piecing together these fragments of evidence, we may infer that Pitt's near relations were a source of considerable expense, and that his own heedlessness had by this time further served to embarrass him. Therefore, his conduct towards Miss Eden, which at first sight seems heartless, was probably dictated by sheer financial need. We may also reject the spiteful statement in which Lady Hester Stanhope represented Pitt as saying: "Oh, there was her mother [Lady Auckland],—such a chatterer! and then the family intrigues! I can't keep them out of my house; and for my King's and my country's sake I must remain a single man." This is mere romancing. Pitt went to the Aucklands' house, not they to his. As for the remark about Auckland's intrigues, it clearly refers to the painful days after 1801, when Pitt broke with the household at Beckenham.

There was only one method whereby Pitt could have assured his marriage with Eleanor Eden, namely, by condescending to political jobbery. It was beyond the power of Auckland, a comparatively poor man, burdened with a large family, to grant a dowry with her unless Pitt awarded to him a lucrative post and sinecures. Of course any such step was wholly out of the question for either of them. In fact, Pitt opposed Auckland's promotion, opened up by the death of Lord Mansfield, President of the Council, though the public voice acclaimed Auckland as the successor.[2] Equally noteworthy is the fact that, early in the year 1798, Pitt appointed Auckland Postmaster-General, with an annual stipend of £2,500, but required him to give up his pension of £2,000 for diplomatic services.[3] It is pleasing to record that their friendship was not overclouded, except for a brief period.

There, then, we must leave this painful incident, but with heightened admiration for Pitt. Outwardly his conduct appears frigid in the extreme. Those, however, who probe the secrets of that reserved soul see that his renunciation of conjugal bliss resulted from a scrupulous sense of honour. As to

[1] Ashbourne, 162, 179; G. Rose, "Diaries," i, 410, 429.
[2] "Auckland Journals," iii, 359. George III, who disliked Auckland, ordered the appointment of Chatham.
[3] Ibid., iii, 387.

the tenderness of his feelings at this time, Addington, who knew him well, gives striking testimony, averring that in his disposition there was " very much of the softness and milkiness of human nature." That was the real Pitt.

Finance was the all-absorbing question in that gloomy winter of 1796-7. The triumphs of Bonaparte in Italy and Hoche's attempt to invade Ireland sank into insignificance in comparison with the oncoming shadow of bankruptcy. The causes of this phenomenon are too technical to receive adequate treatment here. Certainly the Bank Crisis of February of 1797 was not due to the exhaustion of the nation; for the revenue testified to its abounding vitality. The Permanent Taxes maintained nearly the high level reached in the prosperous year of peace, 1792, and the figures for British Imports and Exports told the same tale, but the sums of money borrowed in the years 1796, 1797 undoubtedly strained the national credit.[1] Austria also applied to England for loans to enable her to continue the war; and Pitt helped her to borrow in London the sum of £4,600,000 in 1795, and £4,620,000 in 1796.

In one particular Pitt's action was unprecedented. In July 1796, during the interval between the seventeenth and eighteenth Parliaments of Great Britain, Austria sent urgent requests for pecuniary help so as to stay the triumphs of the French in Italy and Swabia. Pitt yielded and secretly remitted the sum of £1,200,000 as a loan. Undoubtedly this opportune help enabled Austria to make the surprising efforts which flung back the French to the Rhine, and checked the triumphal progress of Bonaparte. Nevertheless, Fox threatened his rival with impeachment for this unconstitutional action. Pitt replied with irresistible cogency that the crisis called for bold handling, and that England helped her ally to save the Empire and to maintain the contest in Italy. The House condoned his action by 285 votes to 81, a proof that he dominated the new Parliament as completely as its predecessor. He has been accused of lavishing money on the Allies; but, except in this instance, he did not by any means satisfy their claims. Moreover, they were justified in expecting England to provide money in lieu of the troops which her War Office failed to raise. Austria also solemnly covenanted to repay the loans; and her neglect to do so

[1] See Appendix for the sums borrowed, expended on the army and navy, and raised by the Permanent Taxes in 1792-1801.

occasioned a bitter dispute which long held the two Powers apart. Pitt also refused her request for a loan in the year 1797. As far as possible, he discouraged the raising of war loans in London. Early in 1796 he did so in the case of Portugal from a fear that the export of bullion would impair credit.[1]

At that time a novel expedient was shaping itself in his mind. On New Year's Day he drove Sir John Sinclair from Dundas's house at Wimbledon up to town; and on the way the baronet suggested the raising a great loan on easy terms by an appeal to the loyalty of Britons.[2] The need of some such device became increasingly apparent; for sinister symptoms began to appear amidst the alarms of the autumn of 1796. The threats of invasion led the Ministry to propose a special levy of 15,000 men to reinforce the army, of 20,000 irregular cavalry, and of 60,000 supplemental Militia (18th October). These expenses, in addition to the ever growing demands for the public services, involved a deficit of £18,000,000. It was most important to raise this sum promptly in order to uphold the credit and display the loyalty of the nation; for, as we shall see, Pitt had recently opened negotiations for peace at Paris in the hope that the late successes of the Austrians both in Italy and the Rhineland (which proved to be only temporary), would induce the Directory to accord fair terms to enemies who thus evinced their energy and vitality. After consultation with the officials of the Bank of England, he decided to raise the required sums, not by means of "contractors," but by appealing direct to the public. Accordingly, on 1st December, he adopted the unusual course of appealing to the Lord Mayor and the Directors of the Bank of England to encourage in every possible way the raising of an extraordinary loan of £18,000,000. The rate of interest, $5\frac{5}{8}$ per cent., seems somewhat high in the case of a "Loyalty Loan," especially as Consols rose from $53\frac{3}{4}$ in September to 57 in November; but competent authorities agree that it was not too high.[3]

The response was most gratifying. The Bank subscribed £1,000,000, the Directors in their private capacity further contributing £400,000. Similar feelings were displayed in the City

---

[1] "Parl. Hist.," xxxii, 1297-1347; Pitt MSS., 102. Pitt to Boyd, 4th January 1796.

[2] "Mems. of Sir John Sinclair," ii, 276.

[3] W. Newmarch, "Loans raised by Pitt (1793-1801)," pp. 16, 25-33.

and in the provinces. Before the hour of 10 a.m. on 5th December, when the subscription list was opened at the Bank, the
lobby of the hall and even the approaches were crowded with
eager patriots, who fought their way towards the books. Those
in the rear called to more fortunate friends in the front to in-
scribe their names. Within an hour and twenty minutes the
amount which could then be allotted was made good, and hundreds retired disappointed. Similar scenes ensued on the two
following days, the whole sum of £18,000,000 being subscribed
in less than fifteen and a half hours.[1]

It was under these encouraging conditions that on 7th December 1796 Pitt made his Budget Statement, which included
the proposal of further advances of £3,000,000 to our Allies.
As a set-off to this, he pointed to the yield of the taxes and the
Imports and Exports for the quarter as affording gratifying
proof of the strength of the country. But, he added, "this
flourishing state of our affairs ought not to lessen our moderation or abate our desire for peace." Those who blame him
for continuing to pay £200,000 into the Sinking Fund, while
he had to borrow large sums at a ruinous rate of interest, should
remember that he believed this costly device to be only temporary in view of his efforts for peace.

The usually dull details of finance are at this point enlivened
by the ingenious suggestions poured in upon Pitt for opening up
new sources of revenue. The aim of financiers then being to
press on the taxpayer at all points with the imperceptible im-
partiality of air, the hints as to the taxation of neighbours and
rivals are of refreshing variety. Among the less obvious are
duties on barges, pawnbrokers' takings, toys, theatre and concert
tickets, buttons, corks, glass bottles, umbrellas, sheriffs and
under-sheriffs, county commissioners and attorneys who keep
clerks. On behalf of the last suggestion an anonymous writer
points out that it would enhance the dignity of the legal pro-

---

[1] On 2nd December 1796, Thomas Coutts, Pitt's banker, wrote to him:
"Mr. Dent, Mr. Hoare, Mr. Snow, Mr. Gosling, Mr. Drummond, and myself met today, and have each subscribed £50,000. . . . I shall leave town
tomorrow, having staid solely to do any service in my power in forwarding
this business, which I sincerely wish and hope may be the means of procuring peace on fair and honourable terms. P.S.—We have subscribed £10,000
in your name, and shall take care to make the payments" (Pitt MSS., 126).
Mr. Abbot ("Lord Colchester's Diary," 76) states that fear of a compulsory
contribution helped on the Loyalty Loan.

fession. Another correspondent suggests a similar impost on physicians, surgeons, and chemists, ranging from ten guineas in London to three guineas in the provinces, in order to discourage the entry of illiterates. He also urges the need of stopping the increase of luxury and amusements by taxing hot-houses, horses and carriages let out on Sundays, organs, pianos, and all musical instruments, as well as the owners thereof, on the ground that this step will lessen the alarming growth of bankruptcies and divorces. A tax on armorial bearings is suggested as one which will not be resented by the rich. A fourth correspondent advocates a graduated Income Tax, ranging from 6d. in the pound on incomes under £400, up to 5s. in the pound on incomes of more than £30,000 a year, and estimates the total yield at £62,625,000. The same writer urges the need of a tax on sinecures and pensions, and finally begs Pitt for a place for life, devolving on his son.[1]

The Chancellor of the Exchequer therefore had the choice of the direct attack on the purse or the increase of atmospheric pressure. For the present he chose the latter method, enhancing the duties on tea, wines, sugar, spirits, game licences, glass, tobacco, and snuff, besides raising the "Assessed Taxes" by ten per cent. The produce of some of these imposts is curious. Hair-powder yielded £197,000; the extra tea and wine duties £186,000 and £923,000, severally; those on tobacco and snuff only £40,000. Pitt's procedure in December 1796 was very cautious. He carefully watched the yield of the new taxes, in order to see whether the increase of price checked consumption. Finding that this did not happen in the case of tea and spirits, he further raised the duties on those commodities; but, on behalf of the poor, he exempted the cheaper kinds of tea. On the other hand he proposed to check the consumption of spirits by imposing an extra duty of five pence a gallon along with a surcharge on distillery licences. Further, as the duties on bricks, auction sales, sugar, bar iron, oil, wines, and coal had not lessened consumption, he again increased them. A questionable experiment was an increase in the postage of letters and parcels, and in the duties on newspapers, stage coaches, and canal tolls. A new House Duty, levied in proportion to the number of servants, is open to less objection. On the whole he expected

---

[1] Pitt MSS., 272.

the new taxes to yield £2,138,000. The total supply asked for was £27,640,000.

The financial outlook grew darker in the year 1797. At the close of January came the news of Hoche's expedition to Bantry Bay, which revealed the possibility of revolutionizing Ireland. On 4th February Pitt heard of the triumph of Bonaparte at Rivoli. The tidings told disastrously on markets already in a nervous state. A correspondent of Pitt attributed the decline to the action of the Bank of England at the close of 1795, in reducing their discounts. Fox and his friends ascribed it to the export of specie to Vienna; while Ministers and their friends gave out that it resulted from the fears of invasion, and the desire of depositors everywhere to withdraw their money and place it in hiding. Privately, however, Pitt confessed to Auckland that the export of gold brought matters to a climax.

The amount of specie in the Bank of England, which was nearly £8,000,000 in 1795, fell to £1,272,000 in February 1797. In reality the Bank was solvent, but it could not have realized its securities; and on several occasions the Directors warned Pitt that any further withdrawals of specie would bring on a crisis.[1] The final cause of alarm was a loan of £1,500,000 to the Irish Government, the first occasion on which any large sum was raised for that Administration.[2] On 25th and 26th February, then, crowds rushed to withdraw money from the Bank into which eleven weeks before they thronged in order to procure shares in the Loyalty Loan. So serious was the crisis that Ministers decided to intervene. On Sunday the 26th a meeting was held of the Privy Council, which issued an Order in Council empowering the Directors to refuse payments in cash until Parliament gave further orders on the subject.[3]

---

[1] Ann. Reg. (1797), 130-42.
[2] Sir J. Sinclair, " Hist. of the Public Revenue," ii, 143.
[3] Pitt MSS., 272; "Parl. Hist.," xxxii, 1517; Gilbart, "History . . . of Banking" (ed. by E. Sykes), i, 46. On 25th February 1797 Pitt wrote a memorandum (Pitt MSS., 102), stating that the crisis was due to the too great circulation of paper notes by banks having limited resources. Their stoppage affected larger Houses and paralysed trade. He had wanted to meet the City men, who met on the 22nd to discuss the situation, but failed to agree on any remedy. Finally they agreed to meet at the Mansion House to discuss the issue of Exchequer Bills. Coutts, on 19th March 1797, informed Pitt that gambling in the Prince of Wales' Debentures, which exceeded £432,000, ruined the market for ordinary securities (Pitt MSS., 126). Sinclair had

For a few hours there was the prospect of a general collapse; and as the Bank issued no notes for less than £5, though Sinclair and others had advised the issue of £3 and £2 notes, small traders were threatened with a recurrence to barter. Fortunately on 27th February the Directors published a reassuring statement, and the Lord Mayor presided at an influential meeting on the same day, which decided to accept banknotes as legal tender for any amount. Thus a crash was averted. But Fox, Sheridan, and the Opposition ably accused Pitt of leading his own country to the brink of bankruptcy, even while he proclaimed the imminent insolvency of France. They thundered against the export of gold to the Emperor, and demanded a searching inquiry into the high-handed dealings of the Minister with the Bank and with national finance. "We have too long had a confiding House of Commons," exclaimed Fox; "I want now an inquiring House of Commons." Despite Pitt's poor defence of his loans to the Emperor, the Government carried the day by 244 votes to 86 (28th February); but the unwonted size of the minority was a sharp warning to curtail loans and subsidies. Apart from a small loan to Portugal in 1798, nothing of note was done to help Continental States until Russia demanded pecuniary aid for the War of the Second Coalition. In order to provide a circulating medium, the Bank was empowered to issue notes for £2 and £1, and to refuse cash payments for sums exceeding £1 (March to May 1797).

Meanwhile, shortly after the Bank crisis, came news of the failure of an American, Colonel Tate, with some 1,400 French gaol-birds, to make a raid at Fishguard in Pembrokeshire. A later legend sought to embellish this very tame affair by ascribing his failure to the apparition on the hills of Welsh women in high hats and scarlet cloaks, whom the invaders took for regulars. Unfortunately for lovers of the picturesque, the apparition occurs only in much later accounts.[1] Far more important were the tidings from Cape St. Vincent. There Jervis, with only fifteen ships, boldly attacked twenty-seven Spaniards while still in confusion after a foggy night. As is well known, the boldness of Nelson, in wearing out of the line so as to prevent the reunion

vainly urged Pitt to compel bankers to find and exhibit securities for the paper notes which they issued ("Corresp. of Sir J. Sinclair," i, 87).
[1] H. F. B. Wheeler and A. M. Broadley, "Napoleon and the Invasion of England," ch. ii, have proved this.

of the enemy's ships, crowned the day with glory (14th February). The weakness of the Spanish navy stood glaringly revealed, and the fear of invasion, which turned mainly on a junction of their fleet to that of France, thenceforth subsided.

Jervis remarked before the fight that England never stood in more need of a victory. The news reached London most opportunely on 3rd March; for, along with the Bank crisis, came rumours of serious discontent among our seamen. Even Jervis could scarcely stamp out disaffection in the fleet that rode triumphantly before Cadiz; and in home waters mutiny soon ran riot. Is it surprising that sailors mutinied? In large part they were pressed men. Violence swept the crews together, and terror alone kept them together. The rules of the service prescribed flogging for minor offences, hanging for refusal to work. How men existed in the over-crowded decks is a mystery. On paper the rations seem adequate, a pound of meat per day, a proportionate amount of biscuit, and half a pint of rum. But these provisions were issued by pursers who often eked out their scanty pay by defrauding the crew. Weevilly biscuits and meat of briny antiquity were therefore the rule, excess of salt and close packing being deemed adequate safeguards against decay. Finally the indurated mass became so susceptible of polish as in the last resort to provide the purser with a supply of snuff-boxes. One little comfort was allowed, namely, cocoa for breakfast. But the chief solace was rum, cheap, new, and fiery, from the West Indies. This and the rope-end formed the *nexus* of the crew. As for the pay, from which alone the sailor could make his lot bearable, it had not been increased since the reign of Charles II. Thanks to the Duke of York, that of the army had been raised from $8\frac{1}{4}d$. to 1s. a day, though not in proportion to the cost of living, the net gain being only 2d. a day. The sailor alone was forgotten, and, lest he should come into touch with Radical clubs, leave of absence was rarely if ever accorded.

The men of the Channel Fleet were the first to resolve to end their chief grievances, namely, insufficient pay, withdrawal of leave of absence, and the unfair distribution of prize money. On putting back to Spithead in March 1797, they sent to Admiral Howe several round-robins demanding an increase of pay. He was then ill at Bath, and, deeming them the outcome of a single knot of malcontents, ignored them. This angered the men. His successor in command, Lord Bridport (formerly Lord Hood), was less popular; and when it transpired that the fleet would soon set sail, the men resolved to show their power. Accordingly, on 15th April, on the hoisting of the signal to weigh anchor, the crew of the flag-ship, the "Queen Charlotte," manned her shrouds and gave three cheers. The others followed her example, and not an anchor was weighed. On the next day (Easter Sunday) the men formed a central committee, sent ashore some hated officers, and formulated the demands outlined above, promising to fight the French if they put to sea, and afterwards to renew the same demands.

That Easter was a time of dismay in London. Ministers at once met in Cabinet Council and agreed to despatch to Portsmouth Spencer, first Lord of the Admiralty, along with Admiral Young, and others. Spencer's reputation for sincerity, love of justice, and regard for the seamen inspired general confidence; and when the Commissioners were joined by Bridport, Parker, Colpoys, and Gardner, there was hope of a compromise. The men allowed Bridport to retain his command, provided that he did not issue orders for sea; they enforced respect to officers; they flogged one man who became drunk, and ducked more venial offenders three times from a rope tied at the main-yard. Their committee of thirty-two (two from each ship), met every day on the "Queen Charlotte"; it demanded an increase of pay from 9¾d. to 1s. a day. But when Spencer promised to lay this request before the King, on condition of immediate restoration of discipline, the men demurred. Conscious of their power, they now claimed that rations must be served out, not 12 ounces, but 16 ounces to the pound; that the power of awarding heavy punishments for petty offences should be curtailed, extended opportunities being also granted for going ashore. In vain did Spencer and his colleagues protest against this dictation of terms. A personal appeal to the crew of the "Royal George" had no effect; and when Gardner vehemently reproached the men for skulking from the French, they ran at him; and he would have fared badly had he not placed his neck in a noose of a yard-rope and called on the men to hang him provided they returned to duty. The men thereupon cheered him and retired.

On 18th April the men's committee formulated their demands in two manifestoes. Further conferences took place, in one of which Gardner shook a delegate by the collar and was himself nearly murdered. The whole fleet then defiantly flew the red flag. Spencer and his colleagues returned to London for an interview with Pitt; and along with him and the Lord Chancellor they posted to Windsor to urge the need of compliance with the men's demands. Grenville, journeying from Dropmore, joined them, and a Privy Council was held. Pitt's and Spencer's views prevailed, and a Royal Proclamation was drawn up on 22nd April, pardoning the crews if they would return to duty. A horseman riding at full speed bore the document to Portsmouth in seven hours, and the fleet, with the exception of the "Marlborough," re-hoisted the white ensign and prepared for sea. The discontent rife at Plymouth also subsided. On 26th April, during a Budget debate, Pitt promised to provide for the extra pay to seamen and marines.

But on 3rd May an indiscreet opening of the whole question in the House of Lords by the Duke of Bedford led to a revival of discontent at Spithead. He upbraided Pitt with delay in introducing a Bill to give effect to the Royal Proclamation. Howe thereupon proceeded to justify his former conduct; and Spencer remarked that he did not expect to receive the King's commands to bring down any communication on the affair to the House of Lords. By an unscrupulous use of these remarks agitators inflamed the crews with the suspicion of ministerial trickery; and on 7th May, every ship refused to obey Bridport's orders to weigh anchor. The men arrested Colpoys and sent fifteen officers on shore. Pitt thereupon, on 8th May, moved a resolution in the terms of the decision framed at Windsor on 22nd April. He begged the House for a silent vote on this question; but Fox and Sheridan could not resist the temptation to accuse him of being the cause of this second mutiny. Clearly it resulted from the remarks in the House of Lords on 3rd May, which led the seamen to believe that Pitt was about to play them false.

The Commons passed the resolution; but Whitbread, on the morrow, moved a vote of censure on Pitt for delay in dealing with this important question. Again Pitt pointed out that the promise given during the Budget debate sufficed for the time, but he admitted that preliminary forms and inquiries had absorbed an undue amount of time. Fox and Sheridan pounced down on this admission, the latter inveighing against the "criminal and murderous delay" of Ministers, whose incapacity earned the contempt of the House. Spying a party advantage in protracting these debates, Whitbread renewed his attack on the next day (10th May). Pitt replied with admirable temper, and showed that the delay in presenting a Bill arose partly from the action of the Opposition itself. Will it be believed that Parliament wasted two days, while the navy was in mutiny, in discussing whether Pitt had or had not been guilty of delay? The results were deplorable. An anonymous chronicler, hostile to Pitt, confessed that the men at Spithead were " better pleased with reading Fox and Sheridan's speeches than with the long-expected settlement of their claims." [1]

In this state of things Pitt despatched Howe (" Black Dick "), the most popular of the admirals, in order to convince the seamen of the sincerity of Government. The following is the letter in which he apprised Bridport of Howe's mission:

Downing Street, *May* 10, 1797.[2]

The account we have received this morning led to a great degree of hope that the distressful embarrassments which you have experienced may already in a great degree have subsided. You will, however, have learnt that in the suspense in which we remained yesterday, it had been determined to send Lord Howe with such instructions under the sign manual as seemed to us best adapted to the very difficult emergency. His presenting this commission seems still [more] likely to confirm the good disposition which had begun to show itself, and his not coming after the intention had once been announced might lead to unpleasant consequence [*sic*]. It was thought best to make this a civil commission in order not to interfere with the military command of the fleet, and at the same time to give the commission to a distinguished naval character, though not with any naval authority or functions. It was also thought that making a communication of this nature after all that had passed through some other channel than the commander of the fleet was for other reasons preferable and likely to be thought so by you.

I earnestly hope this measure will produce good effects and will both in itself and in its consequences be satisfactory to you. At all events I am sure you will continue to contribute your exertions with the same zeal and public spirit which you have shewn under such trying diffi-culties to bring this arduous work, if possible, to a happy termination.

[1] " Parl. Hist.," xxxiii, 473-516; " Hist. of the Mutiny at Spithead and the Nore" (Lond. 1842), 61-2 ; " Dropmore P.," iii, 323.

[2] Pitt MSS., 102. Lord Mornington deemed the surrender to the seamen destructive of all discipline in the future (" Buckingham P.," i, 373).

I hope I need not say how sincerely and deeply, in addition to the public difficulties, I have felt for the situation in which you have been placed. If the favourable turn which has been given to affairs should be happily confirmed, I look forward to the hope that your command may still be attended with circumstances which may repay you for the labour and anxiety with which you have had to struggle.

Howe found it no easy task to vindicate the good faith of Ministers; but by visiting each ship in turn, he prevailed on the men to submit to discipline. The 14th of May was a day of great rejoicing at Spithead; the men's delegates landed and carried the venerable admiral in triumph to Government House, where he and his lady entertained them at dinner. Three days later the whole fleet put to sea.

But already there had fallen on Pitt a still severer blow. On 10th May appeared the first signs of discontent in the ships anchored off Sheerness. In all probability they may be ascribed to the factious wrangling at Westminster and the revival of the mutiny at Spithead on 7th May. Seeing that the demands of the sailors had been conceded before this outbreak occurred at the Nore, nothing can be said on behalf of the ringleaders, except that amidst their worst excesses they professed unswerving loyalty, firing salutes on 29th May in honour of the restoration of Charles II and on 4th June for King George's birthday. Apart from this their conduct was grossly unpatriotic. On 12th May the crew of H.M.S. "Sandwich," headed by a supernumerary named Parker, captured the ship, persuaded eleven other crews to mutiny, and sent delegates to Portsmouth to concert action with Bridport's fleet.

In this they failed; and, had Vice-Admiral Buckner, in command at the Nore, acted with vigour, he might have profited by the discouragement which this news produced. He acted weakly; and the men paid no heed to the Royal Proclamation issued on 23rd May, offering the same terms as those granted at Portsmouth and pardon to all who at once returned to duty. Spencer and his colleagues came from London in the hope of persuading the men, but in vain. The men sought to tempt the one loyal ship, the "Clyde," from its duty. Fortunately this Abdiel of a false company was able to slip off by night and guard the entrance to Sheerness harbour. Government then hurried up troops and had new batteries constructed to overawe the fleet. Unfortunately, at the end of May, thirteen more ships, deserters from the fleets of Duncan and Onslow, joined the mutineers at the Nore. This event might have led to a double disaster. Stout old Duncan with only two ships sailed on undaunted to the Texel, where lay a Dutch fleet of fifteen sail preparing for sea. In order to impose on them he kept flying signals as if to consorts in the offing, a stratagem which entirely succeeded. The danger was, however, acute until, acting on Spencer's suggestion, Vorontzoff ordered a Russian squadron, then in British waters, to sail to Duncan's help.

Equally serious was the situation at the Nore. The mutineers, strong in numbers but lacking beef and beer, stopped the navigation of the Thames and captured provisions from merchantmen, thus causing a panic in London. On 5th June, after firing the royal salute, the crews seized some unpopular officers and boatswains, tarred and feathered them, and landed them at Gravesend, a spectacle for gods and men. In these and other reckless acts the fever expended its force. Food and water ran short; for the banks were strictly guarded, and ships ceased to arrive. The desperate suggestion of handing the ships over to the Dutch was frustrated, if it were ever seriously considered, by the removal of the outer buoys. One by one ships fell away and replaced the red flag by the white ensign. Enough force was now at hand to quell the desperate minority; and on 15th June the "Sandwich," renouncing the authority of Parker, sailed under the guns of Sheerness. A fortnight later Parker swung from the yardarm of that ship. His had been a strange career. The son of a tradesman of Exeter, he is said to have entered the navy as a midshipman, but to have been thrice dismissed from his ship for bad conduct. Settling down at Perth, he was imprisoned for debt, but gained his freedom and also a bounty for enrolling in the navy as a volunteer. His daring spirit and sturdy frame brought him to the front in the way that we have seen, the moral perversity of his nature largely determining the course of the mutiny at the Nore. After him twenty-two other mutineers were hanged.

Few men have done more harm to England than Parker. So heavy a blow did the Nore mutiny deal to credit that 3 per cent. Consols, which did not fall below 50 at the Bank crisis, sank to 48 in June, the lowest level ever touched in our history. After the collapse of the mutiny they rose to 55½. The serenity of Pitt never failed during this terrible time. A remarkable proof of his self-possession was given by Spencer. Having to consult him hastily one night, he repaired to Downing Street and found that he was asleep. When awakened, he sat up in bed, heard the case, and gave his instructions, whereupon Spencer withdrew. Remembering, however, one topic which he had omitted, he returned, and found him buried in slumber as profound as if he had not been disturbed. Fox and his friends were far from showing the same equanimity. Because the House by 256 votes to 91 opposed a motion for Reform which Grey most inopportunely brought forward in the midst of the mutiny, they decided to leave Parliament. But the effect of this "secession" was marred by the occasional reappearance of Sheridan, Tierney, and others who had loudly advocated it.[1] Unpatriotic in conception, it speedily became ludicrous from its half-hearted execution.

The question has often been raised whether the mutineers were egged on by malcontent clubs. There are some suspicious signs. A mutineer on board H.M.S. "Champion" told his captain that they had received money from a man in a black coat. This alone is not very convincing. But the malcontents at the Nore certainly received money, though from what source is uncertain. The evidence brought before the Committee of Secrecy as to the connection of the United Irishmen with the mutineers, seems rather thin. As to French bribery, the loyal sailors at Spithead in their address to the Nore mutineers bade them not to be any longer misled by "French principles and their agents, under whatsoever mask." It was also reported in August 1798 that the French Government paid an Irishman, Duckett, to go and *renew* the mutiny. The officials of the Home Office believed the London Corresponding Society to be guilty; and on 16th June one of them, J. K[ing], issued a secret order to two of his agents at Sheerness to discover whether two members of that society, named Beck and Galloway, had had dealings with the rebel crews. The agents, A. Graham and D. Williams, on 24th June sent to the Duke of Portland the following report, which merits quotation almost in full:[2]

. . . Mr. Graham and Mr. Williams beg leave to assure his Grace that they have unremittingly endeavoured to trace if there was any connexion or correspondence carried on between the mutineers and any private person or any society on shore, and they think they may with

[1] Holland, i, 84-91.   [2] "H. O.," Geo. III (Domestic), 137.

the greatest safety pronounce that no such connexion or correspondence ever did exist. They do not however mean to say that wicked and designing men have not been among the mutineers; on the contrary they have proof sufficient to found a belief upon that several whose mischievous dispositions would lead them to the farthest corner of the kingdom in hopes of continuing a disturbance once begun have been in company with the delegates on shore, and have also (some of them) visited the ships at the Nore, and by using inflammatory language endeavoured to spirit on the sailors to a continuance of the mutiny, without however daring to offer anything like a plan for the disposal of the fleet or to do more than insinuate that they were belonging to clubs or societies whose members wished well to the cause, but from which societies Mr. Graham and Mr. Williams are persuaded no such persons were ever regularly deputed. Neither do they believe that any club or society in the kingdom or any of those persons who may have found means of introducing themselves to the delegates have in the smallest degree been able to influence the proceedings of the mutineers, whose conduct from the beginning seems to have been of a wild and extravagant nature not reducible to any sort of form or order and therefore capable of no other mischief than was to be apprehended from a want of the fleet to serve against the enemy. In this state however they were unfortunately suffered to go on without interruption until they began to think themselves justifiable in what they were doing, and by stopping up the mouth of the Thames they were suspected of designs for which Mr. Graham and Mr. Williams can by no means give them credit. The want of beer and fresh beef prompted them to revenge, and that and nothing else induced them to interrupt the trade of the river. It was done on the spur of the occasion, and with a view of obtaining a supply of fresh provisions. Another thing, namely the systematic appearance with which the delegates and the sub-committees on board the different ships conducted the business of the mutiny may be supposed a good ground of suspecting that better informed men than sailors in general are must have been employed in regulating it for them. This Mr. Graham and Mr. Williams at first were inclined to believe too; but in the course of their examinations of people belonging to the fleet they were perfectly convinced that without such a combination and with the assistance of the newspapers only (independent of the many cheap publications to be had upon subjects relating to clubs and societies of all descriptions) and the advantage of so many good writers as must have been found among the quota-men, they were capable of conducting it themselves.

Graham and Williams arrested at Sheerness three strangers, Hulm, McLaurin, and McCan, who were making mischief. Nothing seems to have come of these arrests; and, despite the opinion of Pitt, expressed in his speech of 2nd June, we may dismiss the charge against the London Corresponding Society. It is clear, however, that busybodies circulated newspapers and pamphlets at Sheerness, Chatham, and Maidstone. The reports of the parliamentary debates of 3rd, 8th, 9th, and 10th May would alone have encouraged the mutineers; and the chiefs of the Opposition must bear no small share of responsibility for the disastrous events at Spithead and the Nore. They were warned that their nagging tactics would cause trouble in the navy. They persisted, in the hope of discrediting the Ministry. They succeeded in paralysing the navy; and the only excuse for their conduct is that their hatred of Pitt blinded them to the obvious consequences. From this censure I must except Sheridan, whose speech of 2nd June was patriotic; and he further is said to have suggested the plan of removing the buoys beyond the mutinous fleet.

For a brief space disquieting symptoms appeared in the army. An inflammatory appeal to the troops was distributed at Maidstone by Henry Fellows; and the same man addressed a letter to some person unnamed, asking him to send on 100 copies of the Ulster Address, 50 of "Boniparte's [sic] Address," 50 of " the Duke of Richmond's Letter," and 50 of Payne's " Agrarian Justice." The last named was found among the papers of John Bone, a member of the London Corresponding Society.[1] It is not unlikely that this propaganda was connected with that at Chatham barracks, where a seditious handbill was left on 21st May 1797, urging the men to cast off the tyranny misnamed discipline, to demand better food, better clothing, and freedom from restraint in barracks. "The power is all our own," it concludes. "The regiments which send you this are willing to do their part. They will show their countrymen they can be soldiers without being slaves . . . Be sober, be ready."[2] The paper was probably connected with the mutiny at the Nore. There were also some suspicious doings in London barracks. One of the incendiaries there was, " wicked Williams," who certainly had run through the whole gamut of evil. First as a clergyman, he ruined himself by his excesses; then as a penitent he applied to Wilberforce for relief, and, after disgusting even that saintly man, he in revenge carried round to certain barracks

---

[1] " Report of the Comm. of Secrecy " (1799), 23; App., v, vi.
[2] From Mr. Broadley's MSS.

the signature of his would-be benefactor appended to a seditious appeal. Busybodies lacking all sense of humour therefore
buzzed it about that the abolitionist leader sought to stir up a
mutiny. On 13th May Pitt sent to him to sift any grains of
truth that there might be in this peck of lies. The following
unpublished letter from Wilberforce to Pitt shows that he advised
him to use Williams so as to get at the grains:

2.20 Sat.^y mng. [May 1797?][1]

Williams has been with Windham and is to wait on him again. The
latter has been with me, and I have been guarding him about W^{ms's}
character, telling him that we wish to enable some proper person to
watch W^{ms's} motions by becoming acquainted with his person. Now, if
this watch should be at or near Windham's, this point could be obtained.
My other means of making the discovery have failed, and I can devise
no other. Williams avowed to Windham that he had been employed in
endeavouring to inflame the soldiery, but that his mind was not prepared to go the lengths he found it would be required to go. I am
pretty sure the best way would be to give Williams money, a little, to
infuse a principle of hope. I dare say he is hungry. You must place no
dependence whatever on him, but if he would act for you, he would be
a useful agent, and I think a little money in his case indispensable. I
intreat you not to neglect this. I suppose there will now be no use in
my seeing Ford.

In a second letter, written an hour later, Wilberforce urges
Pitt not to neglect this note. Williams some years ago sought to
make a mutiny; he was skilled in intrigue, had "held Jacobinical
language, and was going on in the most profligate and abandoned
way." This is all the information that the Pitt MSS. yield upon
this question. But in the private diary of Wilberforce there
is the significant entry: "Pitt awaked by Woolwich artillery
riot and went out to Cabinet." The cool bearing of Lord
Harrington, commander of the forces in London, helped to
restore confidence. On 3rd June Government introduced and
speedily passed a Bill for preventing seduction of the soldiery.
There were rumours of an intended mutiny in the Guards; but
fortunately the troops remained true to duty, and some of
them helped to quell the mutiny at the Nore.

A survey of Pitt's conduct during these critical months

---

[1] Pitt MSS., 189. See, too, "Life of Wilberforce," ii, 217; Windham
("Diary," 363) saw Williams on and after 13th May.

reveals the limitations of his nature. He was wanting in fore-sight. He seems to have been taken unawares both by the Bank crisis and the mutinies. He met the financial crisis promptly when it became acute, though by means which caused incalculable inconvenience at a later time. The mutinies also ought to have been averted by timely concessions to the sailors, who needed increase of pay fully as much as the soldiery. For this neglect, however, the Admiralty Board, not Pitt, is chiefly to blame. When the storm burst, Ministers did not display the necessary initiative and resourcefulness; and the officials of the Admiralty must be censured for the delay in bringing forward the proposals on which Parliament could act. The Opposition, as usual, blamed Pitt alone; and it must be confessed that he did not exert on officials the almost terrifying influence whereby Chatham is said to have expedited the preparation of a fleet of transports. The story to that effect is of doubtful authenticity.[1] But there is no doubt that Chatham's personality and behaviour surpassed those of his son in face of a national crisis. The eagle eye of the father would have discerned the growth of discontent in the navy, and his forceful will would have found means to allay or crush it. Before the thunder of his eloquence the mewlings of faction must have died away. The younger Pitt was too hopeful, too soft, for the emergency. But it is only fair to re-member the heartache and ill health besetting him since the month of January, which doubtless dulled his powers during the ensuing period of ceaseless strain and anxiety.

[1] J. Corbett, "England in the Seven Years' War," i, 191.

CHAPTER XV

NATIONAL REVIVAL

A common feeling of danger has produced a common spirit of exertion, and we have cheerfully come forward with a surrender of part of our property, not merely for recovering ourselves, but for the general recovery of mankind.—PITT, *Speech of 3rd December* 1798.

THE desire of Pitt for peace with France led him in the autumn of 1796 to renew more formally the overtures which he had instituted early in that year. His first offer was repelled in so insolent a way that the King expressed annoyance at its renewal being deemed necessary to call forth the spirit of the British lion. Pitt, however, despatched Lord Malmesbury on a special mission to Paris; and the slowness of his journey, due to the bad roads, led Burke to remark: "No wonder it was slow; for he went all the way on his knees." Pitt's terms were by no means undignified. He offered that France should keep San Domingo and her conquests in Europe except those made from Austria. The French reverses in Swabia and the check to Bonaparte at Caldiero made the French Directory complaisant for a time; but his victory at Arcola (17th November), the death of the Czarina Catharine, and the hope of revolutionizing Ireland, led it to adopt an imperious tone. Its irrevocable resolve to keep Belgium and the Rhine boundary appeared in a curt demand to Malmesbury, either to concede that point or to quit Paris within forty-eight hours (19th December).[1]

It argued singular hopefulness in Pitt that, despite the opposition of the King, he should make a third effort for peace in the summer of the year 1797, when the loyalty of the fleet was open to grave doubt, when rebellion raised its head in Ireland, and Bonaparte had beaten down the last defences of Austria;

[1] "Malmesbury Diaries," iii, 259-368; "Dropmore P.," iii, 239-42, 256, 287, 290.

but so early as 9th April he urged on George the need of making pacific overtures to Paris, seeing that Austria was at the end of her resources and seemed on the point of accepting the French terms. The untoward events of the next weeks deepened his convictions; and to a letter of the Earl of Carlisle, pressing on him the urgent need of peace, he replied as follows:

[*Draft.*]   *Private.*

Downing St., 4 *June* 1797.[1]

I can also venture to assure you that I feel not less strongly than yourself the expediency of taking every step towards peace that can be likely to effect the object, consistent with the safety and honour of the country; and I have no difficulty in adding (for your *private* satisfaction) that steps are taken of the most direct sort, and of which we must soon know the result, to ascertain whether the disposition of the enemy will admit of negotiation. On this point the last accounts from Paris seem to promise favourably. You will have the goodness to consider the fact of a step having been actually taken, as confidentially communicated to yourself.

Three days previously Pitt had sent to Paris suggestions for peace. Delacroix, the Minister of Foreign Affairs, whose asperities were so unbearable in 1796, now replied with courtesy. Pitt therefore persevered, declaring it to be his duty as a Christian and a patriot to end so terrible a war. On the other hand Grenville pronounced the negotiation mischievous at the present crisis, when the French Government would certainly proffer intolerable demands. Much, it was true, could be said in favour of concluding peace before Austria definitely came to terms with France; and if Russia and Prussia had shown signs of mediating in our favour, the negotiation might have had a favourable issue. But neither of those Courts evinced good-will, and that of Berlin angered Grenville. He therefore strongly opposed the overture to France, and herein had the support of the three Whig Ministers, Portland, Spencer, and Windham. The others sided with Pitt, Lord Liverpool after some hesitation. On 15th June there were two long and stormy meetings of the Cabinet, the latter lasting until midnight; but on the morrow, the day after the collapse of the Nore Mutiny, the Cabinet endorsed the views of Pitt.

---

[1] Pitt MSS., 102. See Stanhope, iii, App., for the letters of the King and Pitt; "Dropmore P.," iii, 310 *et seq.*; also C. Ballot, "Les Négociations de Lille," for an excellent account of these overtures and the European situation.

Thereupon Grenville entered a written protest, and wrote to the King, stating that he would offer his resignation if the times were not so critical. George thanked him, and in a highly significant phrase urged him to remain at his post so as "to stave off many farther humiliations."[1] Malmesbury proceeded to Lille and entered into negotiations with the French plenipotentiaries, Letourneur, Pléville, and Maret. The last was he who came on a fruitless errand to London in January 1793, and finally became Duc de Bassano, and Foreign Minister under Napoleon. It soon appeared that the only hope of peace lay in the triumph of the Moderates over the Jacobins at Paris. The former, who desired peace, and had an immense majority in the country, at first had the upper hand in the Chambers. They were willing to give up some of the French conquests on the Rhine and in the Belgic Provinces, if their distracted and nearly bankrupt country gained the boon of peace. Their opponents, weak in numbers, relied on the armies, and on the fierce fanaticism which clung alike to the principles and the conquests of the Jacobins. Pitt was willing to meet France half-way. He consented to leave her in possession of her "constitutional" frontiers, i.e., Belgium, Luxemburg, Avignon, Savoy, and Nice, besides restoring to her and her allies all naval conquests, except the Cape of Good Hope and Trinidad. Ceylon, a recent conquest, was to be reserved for exchange. So far, but no farther, Pitt consented to go in his desire for peace. Later on he assured Malmesbury that he would have given way either on Ceylon or the Cape of Good Hope. But this latter concession would have galled him deeply; for, as we shall see, he deemed the possession of the Cape essential to British interests in the East. Spain's demand for Gibraltar he waived aside as wholly inadmissible, thus resuming on this question the attitude which he had taken up in the years 1782-3.[2] Far though Pitt went on the path of conciliation, he did not

[1] See Pitt's letter of 16th June to the King and new letters of Grenville in "Pitt and Napoleon Miscellanies"; "Windham's Diary," 368; C. Ballot, *op. cit.*, ch. v and App.; Luckwaldt (*vice* Hüffer) "Quellen," pt. ii, 153, 161, 176, 183.

[2] On 1st August 1797 Wilberforce wrote to Pitt a letter (the last part of which is quoted in Chapter XX of my former volume) urging him, even if the negotiation failed, to declare on what terms he would resume it. In Mr. Broadley's library is a letter of Lord Shelburne to Vergennes, dated 13th November 1782, which makes it clear that Pitt in 1782-3 was wholly against the surrender or the exchange of Gibraltar.

satisfy the haughty spirits dominant at Paris. It was soon
evident that the only means of satisfying them were subter-
ranean; and a go-between now offered himself. An American,
Melvill, who claimed to be on intimate terms with the most
influential persons at Paris, assured Malmesbury that he could
guarantee the concession of the desired terms, on consideration of the payment of £450,000 to the leading men at Paris.
Malmesbury at first believed in Melvill's sincerity and sent
him over to see Pitt. They had some interviews at Holwood
at the close of August, apparently to the satisfaction of the
Prime Minister; for, after referring the proposal to Grenville, he
laid it before the King. His reply, dated Weymouth, 9th September, advised a wary acceptance of the terms, provided that
France also gave up her claim of indemnity for the ships taken
or burnt at Toulon in 1793.

The King did not then know of the *coup d'état* of Fructidor 18
(4th September), whereby Augereau, the right hand of Bonaparte,
coerced the Moderates and installed the Jacobins in power. The
work was done with brutal thoroughness, prominent opponents
being seized and forthwith deported, while the triumphant
minority annulled the elections in forty-nine Departments, and
by unscrupulous pressure compelled voters to endorse the *fiat* of
the army. Thus did France plunge once more into a Reign of
Terror, and without the golden hopes which had made the
former experiment bearable. Such was virtually the end of
parliamentary government in France. It is indeed curious that
critics of Pitt, who label his repressive measures a " Reign of
Terror," bestow few words of regret on the despicable acts of
the " Fructidorians," whose policy of leaden repression at home
and filibustering raids abroad made the name of Liberty odious
to her former devotees.

The new tyrants at Paris withheld all news of the *coup d'état*
until they could override the policy of the French plenipotentiaries at Lille. There it seemed probable that peace might
ensue, when, on 9th September, the first authentic news of
Augereau's violence arrived. Even so, Pitt hoped that the
triumphant faction would be inclined to enjoy their success in
peace. It was not to be. A member of the French embassy at
Lille discerned far more clearly the motives now operating at
Paris, that the new Directory, while making peace with Austria,
would continue the war with England in order to have a pretext

for keeping up its armies and acquiring compensations. In any case the successors of the pacific trio with whom Malmesbury had almost come to terms, demanded that England should restore every possession conquered from the French or their allies. This implied the surrender of the Cape, Ceylon, and Trinidad, besides minor places on which Pitt and his colleagues held firm. Brief discussions took place, Malmesbury continuing to show tact and good temper; but on Sunday, 17th September, the French plenipotentiaries requested him, if he could not grant their demands, to leave Lille within twenty-four hours. He departed early on Monday, reached London by noon of Wednesday, and saw Grenville and Canning immediately. Pitt, owing to news of the death of his brother in-law, Eliot, was too prostrate with grief to see him until the morrow. It then appeared that the Directory on 11th September issued a secret order to its plenipotentiaries to send off Malmesbury within twenty-four hours if he had not full powers to surrender all Britain's conquests.[1]

Even now there was a glimmer of hope. By some secret channel, Melvill, O'Drusse, or else Boyd the banker, Pitt received the startling offer, that Talleyrand, if he remained in favour at Paris, could assure to England the Dutch settlements in question if a large enough sum were paid over to Barras, Rewbell, and their clique. Pitt clutched at this straw, and on 22nd September wrote to the King, stating that for £1,200,000 we could retain Ceylon, and for £800,000 the Cape of Good Hope. While withholding the name of the intermediaries, known only to himself and Dundas, he strongly urged that £2,000,000 be paid down when a treaty in this sense was signed with France, provided that that sum could be presented to Parliament under the head of secret service. George, now at Windsor, cannot have been pleased that Pitt and Dundas had a state secret which was withheld for him; but he replied on the morrow in terms, part of which Earl Stanhope did not publish. "I am so thoroughly convinced of the venality of that nation [France] and the strange methods used by its Directors in carrying on negotiations that I agree with him [Pitt] in thinking, strange as the proposal appears, that it may be not without foundation."

[1] Ballot, *op. cit.*, 302, who corrects Thiers, Sorel, and Sciout on several points.

George, then, was more sceptical than Pitt; and Grenville and Malmesbury soon had cause to believe the offer to be merely an effort of certain Frenchmen to speculate in the English funds. Nothing came of the matter. Melvill, O'Drusse, and Talleyrand on the French side, and Boyd in London, seem to have been the wire-pullers in this affair, which was renewed early in October; it may have been only a "bull" operation. The secret is hard to fathom; but Pitt and Dundas were clearly too credulous. Such was the conclusion of Malmesbury. It tallied with the pronouncement of Windham, who in one of his captious moods remarked to Malmesbury that Pitt had no knowledge of the world, and kept in office by making concessions, and by "tiding it over." Grenville (he said) thought more of the nation's dignity, but was almost a recluse. In fact, the Cabinet was ruled by Dundas, whom Grenville hated. Dundas it was who had sacrificed Corsica, which involved the loss of Italy.[1] Windham of course detested the author of the colonial expeditions, which had diverted help from the Bretons. In the Chouans alone he saw hope; for how could England struggle on alone against France if she could use all the advantages offered by Brest and Cherbourg?

Much can be said in support of these contentions; for now that the Directory threw away the scabbard, England felt the need of the stout Bretons, whose armies had become mere predatory bands. The last predictions of Burke were therefore justified. That once mighty intellect expended its last flickering powers in undignified gibes at the expense of Pitt and his regicide peace. Fate denied to him the privilege of seeing Malmesbury again expelled from France and whipped back "like a cur to his kennel." The great Irishman passed away, amidst inconceivable gloom, in his 68th year, at Beaconsfield (8th July 1797). In the view of Windham and other extreme Royalists, Burke was wholly right, and Pitt's weakness was the cause of all his country's ills.

We may grant that the summer of the year 1797 was one of the worst possible times in which to open a negotiation with triumphant France; for she was certain to exact hard terms from a power whose credit and whose prestige at sea had grievously suffered. Nevertheless, the mistake, if mistake it was,

[1] "Dropmore P.," iii, 377, 380-2; "Malmesbury Diaries," iii, 590.

is venial when compared with the unstatesmanlike arrogance of the French Directors, who, when an advantageous and brilliant peace was within their reach, chose to open up a new cycle of war. Of late France had made use of the pretext that she must gain her " natural frontiers "—the Rhine, the Alps, the Pyrenees, and the Ocean—for the sake of security against the old dynasties. By rejecting Pitt's overtures, her leaders now proclaimed their resolve to dominate Italy and Germany and to secure supremacy at sea. Their intrigues with British malcontents and the United Irishmen also showed their determination to revolutionize our institutions. Thus England was to be abased and insulted, while France lorded it over all her neighbours and prepared to become mistress of the seas. The war therefore ceased to be in any sense a war of principle, and became for France a struggle for world-wide supremacy, for England a struggle for national existence; and while democratic enthusiasm waned at Paris, the old patriotic spirit revived everywhere in Great Britain. The newspapers were full of appeals for unanimity; and on 20th November appeared the first number of that bright and patriotic paper, the " Anti-Jacobin," under the editorship of Canning and Hookham Frere, which played no small part in arousing national ardour. On the next day the French Directory issued an appeal to France to bestir herself to overthrow the British power, and to dictate peace at London.

There was need of unanimity; for while France was stamping out revolt, and Great Britain felt increasingly the drag of Ireland, Pitt encountered an antagonist of unsuspected strength. Over against his diffuse and tentative policy stood that of Bonaparte, clear-cut, and for the present everywhere victorious. While Pitt pursued that will o' the wisp, a money-bought peace, the Corsican was bullying the Austrian negotiators at Udine and Campo Formio. Finally his gasconnades carried the day; and on 17th October Austria signed away her Netherlands to France and her Milanese and Mantuan territories to the newly created Cisalpine Republic. Bonaparte and the Emperor, however, agreed to partition the unoffending Venetian State, the western half of which went to the Cisalpines, the eastern half, along with Venice, Istria, and Dalmatia, to the Hapsburgs. The Court of Vienna struggled hard to gain the Ionian Islands; but on these, and on Malta, the young general had set his heart as the natural stepping-stones to Egypt. At the close of the year he returned

to Paris in triumph, and was invited by the Director, Barras, to
go and conquer England.

   Some such effort, either directly against London, or by a deadly
ricochet through Ireland, would have been made, had not Duncan,
on 11th October, crushed the Dutch off Camperdown, taking
nine ships out of fifteen. The consequences were far reaching.
The Dutch navy was paralysed; and without it the squadrons
at Cherbourg and Brest were not yet strong enough to attack
our coasts, until the Toulon and Cadiz fleets sailed northwards.
Bonaparte, who was sent to survey the ports in Flanders and the
north of France, reported to the Directory on 23rd February
1798 that there were fitting out at Brest only ten sail-of-the-
line, which moreover had no crews, and that the preparations
were everywhere so backward as to compel Government to
postpone the invasion until 1799. The wish was father to that
thought. Already he had laid his plans to seize Egypt, and
now strongly advised the orientation of French policy. A third
possible course was the closing of all continental ports against
England, an adumbration of the Continental System of 1806-13
for assuring the ruin of British commerce.

   The news of Camperdown and Campo Formio added vigour
to Pitt's appeal for national union in his great speech of
10th November, in which he gave proofs of the domineering
spirit of the party now triumphant at Paris. Very telling,
also, was his taunt at the Whig press, "which knows no other
use of English liberty but servilely to retail and transcribe
French opinions." Sinclair, who had moved a hostile amendment, was so impressed as to withdraw it; and thus at last the
violence of the French Jacobins conduced to harmony at
Westminster.

   Already there were signs that the struggle was one of financial
endurance. At the close of November 1797 Pitt appealed to the
patriotism of Britons to raise £25,500,000 for the estimated expenses of the next year, in order to display the wealth and
strength of the kingdom. He therefore proposed to ask the
Bank of England to advance £3,000,000 on Exchequer bills;
and he urged the propertied classes to submit to the trebling of
the Assessed Taxes on inhabited houses, windows, male servants,
horses, carriages, etc. The trebling of these imposts took the
House by surprise, and drew from Tierney, now, in the absence
of Fox, the leader of Opposition, the taunt that Pitt had to

cringe to the Bank for help. A few days later Pitt explained that the triple duty would fall only upon those who already paid £3 or more on that score. If the sum paid were less than £1 it would be halved. Those who paid £3 or more would be charged at an increasing rate, until, when the sum paid exceeded £50, the amount would be quadrupled. Nor was this all. By a third Resolution he outlined the scheme of what was in part a progressive Income Tax. Incomes under £60 were exempt; those between £60 and £65 paid at the rate of 2d. in the pound; and the proportion rose until it reached 2s. in the pound for incomes of £200 or more.

Though Pitt pointed out the need of a patriotic rejoinder to the threats of the French Government, the new Assessed Taxes aroused a furious opposition. "The chief and almost only topic of conversation is the new taxes," wrote Theresa Parker to Lady Stanley of Alderley. "How people are to live if the Bill is passed I know not. I understand the Opposition are much elated with the hope of the Bill's being passed, as they consider Mr. Pitt infallibly ruined if it does, and that he must go out."[1] The patriotism of London equalled that of the Foxites. City men, forgetting that the present proposals were due to the shameless evasions of the Assessed Taxes, raised a threatening din, some of them declaring that Pitt would be assaulted if he came into the City. Several supporters of Pitt, among them the Duke of Leeds, Sir William Pulteney and Henry Thornton, opposed the new imposts, and the Opposition was jubilantly furious. Sheridan, who returned to the fray, declared that though the poor escaped these taxes they would starve; for the wealth which employed them would be dried up. Hobhouse dubbed the Finance Bill inquisitorial, degrading, and fatal to the virtues of truthfulness and charity. Squires bemoaned the loss of horses and carriages and the hard lot of their footmen. Arthur Young warned Pitt that if the taxes could not be evaded, gentlemen must sell their estates and live in town. Bath, he was assured, welcomed the new imposts because they would drive very many families thither. He begged Pitt to reconsider his proposals, and, instead of them, to tax "all places of public diversion, public dinners, clubs, etc., not forgetting debating societies and Jacobin meetings"; for this would restrain

[1] "Parl. Hist.," xxxiii, 1076; "The Early Married Life of Lady Stanley 149.

"that violent emigration to towns, which the measure dreadfully threatens."[1]

A sign of the hopes of the Opposition was the re-appearance of Fox. Resuming his long vacant seat, he declared Pitt to be the author of the country's ruin. For himself, he upheld the funding system, that is, the plan of shelving the debt upon the future. The palm for abusiveness was, however, carried off by Nicholls and Jekyll. The former taunted Pitt with losing all his Allies and raising France to undreamt-of heights of power, with failing to gain peace, with exhausting the credit and the resources of England until now he had to requisition men's incomes. As for Jekyll, he called the present proposals "a detestable measure of extortion and rapacity." The debates dragged on, until, after a powerful reply by Pitt in the small hours of 5th January 1798 the Finance Bill passed the Commons by 196 to 71. The Lords showed a far better spirit. Carrington declared that Pitt's proposals did not go far enough. Lord Holland in a maiden speech pronounced them worse than the progressive taxes of Robespierre. But Liverpool, Auckland, and Grenville supported the measure, which passed on 9th January 1798 by 75 to 6.

For a time the Finance Bill injured Pitt's popularity in the City. During the State procession on 19th December 1797, when the King, Queen, and Ministers went to St. Paul's to render thanks for the naval triumphs of that year, he was hooted by the mob; and on the return his carriage had to be guarded by a squadron of horse. Nevertheless, it is now clear that Pitt's proposals were both necessary and salutary. The predictions of commercial ruin were soon refuted by the trade returns. Imports in 1798 showed an increase of £6,844,000 over those of 1797; exports, an increase of £3,974,000. In part, doubtless, these gratifying results may be ascribed to renewed security at sea, the bountiful harvest of 1798, and the recent opening up of trade to Turkey and the Levant. But, under a vicious fiscal system, trade would not have recovered from the severe depression of 1797. Amidst all the troubles of the Irish Rebellion of 1798, Pitt derived comfort from the signs of returning prosperity.

The confidence which he inspired was proved by the success of a remarkable experiment, the Patriotic Contribution. In the

[1] Pitt MSS., 193. Mr. Abbott, afterwards Lord Colchester, differed from his patron, the Duke of Leeds, on this question. See "Lord Colchester's Diaries," i, 124-31.

midst of the acrid debates on the Finance Bill, the Speaker, Addington, tactfully suggested the insertion of a clause enabling the Bank of England to receive voluntary gifts, amounting to one-fifth of the income. Pitt gratefully adopted the proposal, and early in the year 1798 patriots began to send in large sums. Pitt, Addington, Dundas, the Lord Chancellor, and Lords Kenyon and Romney at once gave £2,000 each; the King graciously allotted from the Privy Purse £20,000 a year during the war. The generous impulse speedily prevailed, and the City once more showed its patriotism by subscribing £10,000; the Bank gave £200,000. A platform was erected near the Royal Exchange for the receipt of contributions. Among others, a wealthy calico printer, Robert Peel, father of the statesman, felt the call of duty to give £10,000. He went back to Bury (Lancashire) in some anxiety to inform his partner, Yates, of this unbusinesslike conduct, whereupon the latter remarked, "You might as well have made it £20,000 while you were about it." If all Britons had acted in this spirit, the new taxes would have met the needs of the war. But, as will subsequently appear, they failed to balance the ever growing expenditure, and Pitt in 1799-1800 had to raise loans on the security of the Income Tax to make up its deficiencies.

A pleasing proof of the restoration of friendship between Auckland and Pitt appears in a letter in which the former asked advice as to the amount which he should give to this fund. He was now Postmaster-General, and stated that his total gross income was £3,600, out of which the new taxes took £320. Should he give £1,000? And what should he give for his brother, Morton Eden, ambassador at Vienna? Pitt answered that £700 should be the utmost for him; the sum of £500 for Morton would also be generous.[1] On the whole, £2,300,000 was subscribed—a sum which contrasts remarkably with the driblets that came in as a response to Necker's appeal in the autumn of 1789 for a patriotic contribution of one fourth of the incomes of Frenchmen.

Even so, Pitt had to impose new taxes in his Budget of 1798, and to raise a loan of £3,000,000. Further, on 2nd April, he proposed a commutation of the Land Tax. Of late it had been voted annually at the rate of 4s. in the pound, and produced about

---

[1] B.M. Add. MSS., 34454.

£2,000,000. Pitt now proposed to make it a perpetual charge upon parishes, but to enable owners to redeem their land from the tax at the existing valuation. The sums accruing from these sales were to go to the reduction of the National Debt. His aim, that of enhancing credit, was as praiseworthy as his procedure was defective. For there had been no valuation of the land for many years, and the assessments varied in the most surprising manner even in neighbouring districts. Doubtless it was impossible during the Great War to carry out the expensive and lengthy process of a national valuation; but, as manufactures and mining were creating a new Industrial England, the time was most unsuited to the imposition of a fixed quota of Land Tax.

Nevertheless, Pitt took as basis the assessment of 1797, and made it a perpetual charge upon each parish. The results have in many cases been most incongruous. Agricultural land, which was generally rated high, continued to pay at that level long after depreciation set in. On the other hand, large tracts in the manufacturing districts, rapidly increasing in value, paid far less than their due share. In some cases where a barren moor has become a hive of industry, the parish now raises its quota by a rate of .001 in the pound. In a few cases, where the fall in value has been severe, the rate is very heavy, in spite of remedial legislation. Pitt could not have foreseen differences such as these; but, in view of the rapid growth of manufactures in the Midlands and North, he should have ensured either a re-valuation of the parochial quotas or a complete and methodical redemption from the Land Tax. He took neither course, and that, too, in spite of the warnings of Lord Sheffield and Sinclair as to the injustice and impolicy of his proposals. They passed both Houses by large majorities, perhaps because he offered to landlords the option of redeeming their land at twenty years' purchase. Less than one fourth of the tax was redeemed before the year 1800, a fact which seems to show that the landed interest was too hard pressed to profit by the opportunity. As Sir Francis Burdett said, country gentlemen had to bear a heavy burden of taxation, besides poor-rates, tithes, and the expense of the mounted yeomanry. Thurlow compared the country magnates to sheep who let themselves be shorn and re-shorn, whereas merchants and traders were like hogs, grunting and bolting as soon as one bristle was touched. In defence of Pitt's action, it may be said that he hoped to secure a considerable gain by the investment of the purchase money in Consols and to enhance their value; but it appears that not more than £80,000 a year was thus realized.[1]

The prevalence of discontent early in 1798 and the threatened coalition of Irish and British malcontents will be noticed in the following chapter. Pitt was so impressed by the danger as to press for the suspension of the Habeas Corpus Act and the renewal of the Aliens Act (April 1798). As happened in 1794, the revival of coercion produced vehement protests. Already the Duke of Norfolk had flung defiance at Ministers. Presiding at a great banquet held at the Crown and Anchor, on the occasion of Fox's birthday, 24th January, he not only compared the great orator to Washington, but hinted that the 2,000 men present might do as much as Washington's handful had done in America. Finally he proposed the distinctly Jacobinical toast, " Our Sovereign, the Majesty of the People." For this he was dismissed from the command of a militia regiment and from the Lord Lieutenancy of the West Riding of Yorkshire.

Fox chose to repeat the toast early in May 1798, when large parts of Ireland were on the brink of revolt. In so dire a crisis it behoved a leading man to weigh his words. But the wilful strain in his nature set all prudence at defiance. Thereupon several of Pitt's friends recommended a public prosecution for sedition, or at least a reprimand at the bar of the House of Commons. To the former course Pitt objected as giving Fox too much consequence, besides running the risk of an acquittal; but he saw some advantage in the latter course; for (as he wrote to Dundas) Fox, when irritated by the reprimand, would probably offer a new insult and could then be sent to the Tower for the rest of the Session. The suggestion is perhaps the pettiest in the whole of Pitt's correspondence; but probably it was due to the extremely grave situation in Ireland and the fear of a French invasion. Further, Fox had ceased to attend the House of Commons; and a member who shirks his duty is doubly guilty when he proposes a seditious toast. Pitt, however, did not push matters to extremes, and the course actually adopted was the removal of the name of Fox from the Privy Council by the hand of George III on 9th May.

[1] " Parl. Hist.," xxxiii, 1434-54, 1481; " Mems. of Sir John Sinclair," i, 310, 311.

Sixteen days later, Pitt and Tierney had a passage of arms in the House. That pugnacious Irishman had thrust himself to the fore during the secession of Fox and other prominent Whigs from the House, and had to bear many reproaches for his officiousness. He also nagged at Pitt at every opportunity, until, on his opposing a motion of urgency for a Bill for better manning the Navy, Pitt's patience gave way. He accused the self-constituted leader of seeking to obstruct the defence of the country. The charge was in the main correct; for Tierney's opposition to a pressing measure of national defence was highly unpatriotic. Nevertheless, Tierney had right on his side when he called Pitt to order and appealed to the Speaker for protection. Rarely has that personage been placed in a more difficult position. Pitt was right in his facts; but etiquette required that he should withdraw or at least attenuate his charge. Addington politely hinted that the words were unparliamentary, but suggested that the Minister should give an explanation. Pitt stiffly refused either to withdraw his words, or to explain their meaning. There the incident closed. On the next day, Saturday, 26th May, Tierney sent Pitt a challenge, which was at once accepted.

We find it difficult now to take seriously a duel between a slim man of near forty who had rarely fired a shot in sport, never in anger, and a stoutly built irascible Irishman, for whom a good shot meant lynching or lasting opprobrium. Visions of Bob Acres and Sir Lucius O'Trigger flit before us. We picture Tierney quoting " fighting Bob Acres " as to the advantage of a sideways posture; and we wonder whether the seconds, if only in regard for their own safety, did not omit to insert bullets. The ludicrous side of the affair soon dawned on contemporaries, witness the suggestion that in all fairness Pitt's figure ought to be chalked out on Tierney's, and that no shot taking effect outside ought to count. But, on the whole, people took the incident seriously. Certainly the principals did. Pitt made his will beforehand, and requested Addington as a friend to come and see him, thereby preventing his interposition as Speaker. He asked Steele to be his second; but, he being away from town, Dudley Ryder took his place. Leaving Downing Street about noon on Whitsunday, 27th May, the pair walked along Birdcage Walk, mounted the steps leading into Queen Street, and entered a chaise engaged for their excursion. After passing the villages of Chelsea and Putney, and, topping the rise beyond, they proceeded along the old Portsmouth Road, which crosses the northern part of Putney Heath. At the top of the steep hill leading down into Kingston Vale they alighted, made their way past the gibbet where swung the corpse of a well-known highwayman, Jerry Abershaw, long the terror of travellers on that road. Did Pitt know that libellers likened him to the highwayman; for " Jerry took purses with his pistols, and Pitt with his Parliaments "? Lower down Pitt and Ryder found Tierney and his second, General Walpole, in a charming dell radiant with golden gorse and silver birches.[1]

But they were not alone. That fine Whitsuntide had brought many chaises along the road; and not a few curious persons skirted the rising ground towards Putney and Wimbledon. To these inquisitive groups rode up a tall bland-looking man, now more than usually sedate. It was Addington. Probably he was the most anxious man alive. He knew that his weakness as Speaker had freed Pitt from the necessity of apologizing to Tierney as the occasion demanded. Now, too, as Speaker, he ought to intervene. As a friend, pledged by Pitt to secrecy, he could do nothing but look on. Below, in the dell, the seconds saw to the pistols and measured the distance—twelve paces. Pitt and Tierney coolly took aim, and, at the signal, fired. Addington's heart must have leaped with joy to see Pitt's figure still erect. Again the seconds produced pistols, and again the pair fired: but this time Pitt discharged his weapon into the air. Was it a sign of his contrition for his insult to Tierney, or of his chivalrous sense of Tierney's disadvantage in the matter of target-space? Certain it is that Walpole leaped over the furze bushes for joy on seeing the duellists still erect.

Thus ended the duel, to the satisfaction of all present. Pitt had behaved with spirit, and Tierney had achieved immortal fame. But that the duel was fought at all caused deep concern. Hannah More was inexpressibly shocked at the desecration of Whitsunday; Wilberforce also was deeply pained. Indeed, he deemed the matter so serious as to propose to give notice of a

---

[1] Addington's description (Pellew, " Sidmouth," i, 206) fixes the spot. Mr. A. Hawkes, in an article in the "Wimbledon Annual" for 1904, places it in front of the house called "Scio," but it must be the deeper hollow towards Kingston Vale. Caricatures of the time wrongly place the duel on the high ground near the windmill. A wag chalked on Abershaw's gibbet a figure of the two duellers, Tierney saying: " As well fire at the devil's darning-needle."

motion for preventing duelling; but he dropped it on Pitt frankly assuring him that, if carried, it would involve his resignation. George III signified to Chatham his decided disapproval, and expressed to Pitt a desire that such an incident should never occur again. " Public characters," he added, " have no right to weigh alone what they owe to themselves; they must consider what they owe to their country." Thomas Pitt strongly repro- bated the conduct of Tierney in challenging Pitt; for we find the latter replying to him on 30th May: " I shall feel great concern if the feelings of my friends betray them into any observations on Mr. Tierney's conduct reproachful or in the smallest degree unfavourable to him, being convinced that he does not merit them." This is the letter of a spirited gentleman. Buckingham evidently sympathized with Thomas Pitt; for he expressed his surprise that the Prime Minister should risk his life against such a man as Tierney. A more jocular tone was taken by the Earl of Mornington, soon to become the Marquis Wellesley. Writing to Pitt from Fort St. George on 8th August 1799 (three months after the capture of Seringapatam), he expressed strong approval of his Irish policy and concluded as follows: " I send you by Henry a pair of pistols found in the palace at Seringapatam. They are mounted in gold and were given by the late King of France to the ' citizen Sultan ' (Tippoo). They will, I hope, ans- wer better for your next Jacobin duel than those you used under Abershaw's gibbet." [1]—What became of those pistols?

The general opinion was adverse to Pitt's conduct. For at that time the outlook in Ireland could scarcely have been gloomier, and Bonaparte's armada at Toulon was believed to be destined for those shores. In such a case, despite the nice punctilio of honour, neither ought Tierney to have sent a chal- lenge nor Pitt to have accepted it. The recklessness of Pitt in this affair is, however, typical of the mood of the British people in the spring and summer of that year. The victories of Jervis and Duncan, the rejection of Pitt's offers of peace by the French Directory, and its threats to invade these shores, aroused the fighting spirit of the race. As the war became a struggle for existence, all thoughts of surrender vanished. The prevalent feeling was one of defiance. It was nurtured by Canning in the Anti-Jacobin," in which he lampooned the French democrats

[1] Pretyman MSS.; "Dropmore P.," iv, 222.

and their British well-wishers. Under the thin disguise of "the Friend of Humanity" he satirized Tierney in the poem, "The Knife-Grinder," a parody, in form, of Southey's "Widow," and, in meaning, of Tierney's philanthropic appeals. In a play, "The Rovers," he sportfully satirized the romantic drama of Schiller, "The Robbers." In one of the incidental poems he represented the hero, while in prison, recalling the bright days

> at the U-
> -niversity of Göttingen,
> -niversity of Göttingen.

Pitt was so charmed with this *jeu d'esprit* that he is said to have added the following verse in the same mock-heroic style:[1]

> Sun, moon, and thou, vain world, adieu,
> That Kings and priests are plotting in;
> Here doomed to starve on water gru-
> -el, never shall I see the U-
> -niversity of Göttingen,
> -niversity of Göttingen.

A Prime Minister who can throw off squibs, and a nation that can enjoy them, will not succumb even in the worst crisis.

In truth, all patriots were now straining their utmost to repel an aggressive and insolent enemy. The Volunteer Movement more than ever called forth the manly exertions of the people; and one of the most popular caricatures of the time (May 1798) shows Pitt as a Volunteer standing rigidly at attention. Sermons, caricatures, pamphlets, and songs, especially those of Dibdin, served to stimulate martial ardour. Singular to relate, Hannah More (now in her fifty-third year) figured among the patriotic pamphleteers, her "Cheap Repository" of political tracts being an effective antidote to the Jacobinical leaflets which once had a hold on the poorer classes. Space will not admit of an account of all the agencies which heralded the

---

[1] The hero is probably Robert Adair, the Whig "envoy" to St. Petersburg in 1791,

> "the youth whose daring soul
> With *half a mission* sought the frozen pole."

Pitt's authorship of the lines quoted above is denied by Mr. Lloyd Sanders in his Introduction to the "Anti-Jacobin" (Methuen, 1904); but his arguments are not conclusive. Lines 370-80 of "New Morality" are also said to be by Pitt.

dawn of a more resolute patriotism. Though the methods were varied, the soul of them all was Pitt.[1]

The tone of public opinion astonished that experienced writer, Mallet du Pan, who, on coming from the Continent to England, described the change of spirit as astounding. There the monarchical States, utterly devoid of dignity and patriotism, were squabbling over the details of a shameful peace. "Here," he writes in May 1798, "we are in the full tide of war, crushed by taxation, and exposed to the fury of the most desperate of enemies, but nevertheless security, abundance, and energy reign supreme, alike in cottage and palace. I have not met with a single instance of nervousness or apprehension. The spectacle presented by public opinion has far surpassed my expectation. The nation had not yet learnt to know its own strength or its resources. The Government has taught it the secret, and inspired it with an unbounded confidence almost amounting to presumption." No more striking tribute has been paid by a foreigner to the dauntless spirit of Britons. Rarely have they begun a war well; for the careless ways of the race tell against the methodical preparation to which continental States must perforce submit. England, therefore, always loses in the first rounds of a fight. But, if she finds a good leader, she slowly and wastefully repairs the early losses. In September 1797 the French Directory made the unpardonable mistake of compelling her to prepare for a war to the knife. Thenceforth the hesitations of Pitt, which had weakened his war policy in 1795-6, vanished; and he now stood forth as the inspirer of his countrymen in a contest on behalf of their national existence and the future independence of Europe.

[1] In "Pitt and Napoleon Miscellanies" I shall describe Pitt's work in the national defence. See an excellent account of the popular literature of the time in "Napoleon and the Invasion of England," by H. F. B. Wheeler and A. M. Broadley, i, ch. vii.

CHAPTER XVI

THE IRISH REBELLION

The dark destiny of Ireland, as usual, triumphed.—T. MOORE, *Mems. of Lord Edward Fitzgerald.*

VARIOUS orders of minds ascribe the Irish Rebellion of 1798 to widely different causes. The ethnologist sees in it the incompatibility of Celt and Saxon. To the geographer it may yield proofs of Nature's design to make Ireland a nation. If approached from the religious standpoint, it will be set down either to Jesuits or to the great schism of Luther. The historian or jurist may trace its origins back to the long series of wrongs inflicted by a dominant on a subject race. Fanatical Irishmen see in it a natural result of the rule of "the base and bloody Saxon"; and Whig historians ascribe it to Pitt's unworthy treatment of that most enlightened of Lords-Lieutenant, Earl Fitzwilliam. Passing by the remoter causes, I must very briefly notice the last topic.

The appointment of the Whig magnate, Fitzwilliam, to the Irish Viceroyalty in 1794 resulted from the recent accession of the "Old Whigs," led by the Duke of Portland, to the ministerial ranks. That union, as we have seen, was a fertile cause of friction. Fitzwilliam was at first President of the Council; but that post did not satisfy the nephew and heir of the Marquis of Rockingham. He aspired to the Viceroyalty at Dublin; and Portland, who, as Home Secretary, supervised Irish affairs, claimed it for him. Pitt consented, provided that a suitable appointment could be arranged for the present Viceroy, the Earl of Westmorland. This was far from easy. Ultimately the position of Master of the Horse was found for him; but, long before this decision was formed, Fitzwilliam wrote to the Irish patriot, Grattan, asking him and his friends, the Ponsonbys, for their support during his Viceroyalty. This move implied a complete change of system at Dublin, Grattan and the Ponsonbys having declared for the admission of Roman Catholics to the then exclusively Protestant Parliament. True, this reform seemed a natural sequel to Pitt's action in according to British Catholics the right of public worship and of the construction of schools (1791). Further, in 1792, he urged Westmorland to favour the repeal of the remaining penal laws against Irish Catholics; but the Dublin Parliament decisively rejected the proposal. Nevertheless, in 1793 he induced Westmorland to support the extension of the franchise to Romanists, a measure which seemed to foreshadow their admission to Parliament itself. There is little doubt that Pitt, who then expected the war to be short, intended to set the crown to this emancipating policy; for even in the dark times that followed he uttered not a word which implied permanent hostility to the claims of Catholics. His attitude was that of one who awaited a fit opportunity for satisfying them.

Unfortunately, the overtures of Fitzwilliam to Grattan and the Ponsonbys became known at Dublin, with results most humiliating for Westmorland. The exultation of the Ponsonbys and the Opposition aroused the hopes of Catholics and the resentment of the more extreme Protestants. Chief among the champions of the existing order was the Irish Lord Chancellor, Baron Fitzgibbon, afterwards Earl of Clare. A man of keen intellect and indomitable will, he swayed the House of Lords, the Irish Bar, and the Viceregal councils. It was he who had urged severe measures against the new and powerful organization, the United Irishmen, started in Ulster by Wolfe Tone, which aimed at banding together men of both religions in a solid national phalanx. Scarcely less influential than Fitzgibbon was Beresford, the chief of the Revenue Department, whose family connections and control of patronage were so extensive as to earn him the name of the King of Ireland. Like Fitzgibbon he bitterly opposed any further concession to Catholics; and it was therefore believed that the dismissal of these two men was a needful preliminary to the passing of that important measure. Rumours of sweeping changes began to fly about, especially when Grattan came to London, and had interviews with the Lord Chancellor. The frequent shifts whereby the Scottish Presbyterian, Wedderburn, became the reactionary Lord Loughborough were notorious; and it is one of the suspicious features of the Fitzwilliam affair that he, now Lord

Chancellor of Great Britain, should urge Pitt to treat Fitzwilliam with the confidence due to his prospective dignity. The Attorney-General, Sir Richard Pepper Arden, sent to Pitt the following caution:

September 1794.[1]

. . . My wife says she dined the other day with Grattan at the Chancellor's. I am sadly afraid that preferment in Ireland will run too much in favour of those who have not been the most staunch friends of Government; but, pray, for God's sake, take care that the new Lord Lieutenant does not throw the Government back into the hands of Lord Shannon and the Ponsonbys, nor turn out those who behaved well during the King's illness to make way for those who behaved directly the reverse. Excuse my anxiety on this head but I fear there is good reason for it.

Arden was correctly informed. Now or a little later, Fitzwilliam formed the resolve to dismiss Fitzgibbon and Beresford. On the other hand, the lowering outlook in Holland in the autumn of 1794 induced in Pitt the conviction that the time had not yet come for sweeping changes at Dublin. Accordingly, late in October, or early in November, he and Grenville thoroughly discussed this subject with the newly appointed Ministers, Portland, Fitzwilliam, Spencer, and Windham. Grenville's account of this conference, which has but recently seen the light, refutes the oft repeated statement,[2] that Pitt accorded to Fitzwilliam a free hand at Dublin. On the contrary, it was agreed, apparently with the full consent of the Viceroy-elect, that he should make no change of system.[3] Fully consonant with this decision was the reply of Pitt to Sir John Parnell, Grattan, and the two Ponsonbys, who in the third week of November 1794 begged him to lower the duties on inter-insular imports. While expressing his complete sympathy with their request, he declared the present critical time to be inopportune for a change which must arouse clamour and prejudice.[4] The conduct of Fitzwilliam was far different. Landing near Dublin on 4th January 1795, he on the 7th sent Daly to request Beresford to retire from office. Beresford refused, and sent off an appeal

---

[1] Pitt MSS., 108. See "Pitt and Napoleon Miscellanies," for a fuller investigation of the Fitzwilliam affair in the light of new evidence.
[2] Lecky, vii, 41-4.   [3] "Dropmore P.," iii, 35-8.
[4] Pitt MSS., 331.

to his old friend, Auckland, with the result that the Cabinet soon met to consider the questions aroused by this and other curt dismissals. It being clear that Fitzwilliam was working with the Ponsonbys for a complete change of system, he was asked to modify his conduct. He refused to do so.

The King now intervened in an unusually incisive manner. He informed Pitt that it would be better to recall Fitzwilliam than to allow further concessions to Catholics, a subject which was "beyond the decision of any Cabinet of Ministers." Accordingly, Fitzwilliam was recalled, his departure from Dublin arousing a storm of indignation which bade fair to overwhelm the Administration of his successor, Earl Camden.

Such is a brief outline of the Fitzwilliam affair. No event could have been more unfortunate. It led Irish patriots and the Whigs at Westminster to inveigh against the perfidy and tyranny of Pitt. He was unable to publish documents in his own defence, while Fitzwilliam crowned his indiscretions by writing two lengthy letters charging the Cabinet with breach of faith and Beresford with peculation. Nominally private, they were published at Dublin, with the result that Pitt and Camden were held up to execration and contempt. On reviewing this question, we may conclude that Pitt erred in not procuring from Fitzwilliam a written statement that he would make no sweeping changes at Dublin, either in regard to men or measures, without the consent of the Cabinet. It is, however, clear that Ministers regarded the verbal understanding with Fitzwilliam as binding; for Grenville, Portland, Spencer, and Windham sided with Pitt in this painful dispute, Portland's chilling behaviour to the Earl on his return marking his disapproval of his conduct.

Never did a Lord-Lieutenant enter on his duties under auspices more threatening than those besetting the arrival of Camden on 31st March 1795. After the swearing-in ceremony the passions of the Dublin mob broke loose. Stones were flung at the carriages of the Primate and Fitzgibbon. The rabble then attacked the Speaker's residence and the Custom House, and not till two of their number fell dead under a volley of the soldiery did the rioters disperse. The rebellion which Fitzwilliam predicted on his departure seemed to be at hand.

Camden, on whom this storm was to burst three years later, was not a strong man. He entered on his duties doubtfully and before long sent requests for his recall on account of his family concerns. He might well quail at the magnitude of his task. His instructions bade him by all available means discourage the claims of the Catholics, and rally the discouraged Protestants. Thereafter he might conciliate the Catholics by promising relief for their parochial clergy, the foundation of a seminary for the training of their priests, and some measure of education for the peasantry. The instructions ended thus: " Moderate, soothe, conciliate these jarring spirits. We have great confidence in your judgment, firmness, discretion." [1] The despatch refutes the oft-repeated assertion that the Ministry sought to inflame the animosities of Protestants and Catholics in order to force on the Union. That was the outcome of the whole situation; but in the spring of 1795 Ministers hoped to calm the ferment, which they rightly ascribed to the imprudence of Fitzwilliam. Their forecast for a time came true. In the first debates at Dublin the lead given by Camden's able Secretary, Pelham, served to close the schism in the Protestant ranks. Despite the vehement efforts of Grattan, his Bill for the admission of Catholics was thrown out by a majority of more than one hundred; and Ireland entered once more on the dreary path of reaction.

In the hope of softening the asperities of Irish life, Pitt favoured the plan of founding a seminary for the training of Catholic priests in Ireland. The proposal was alike one of justice and expediency; of justice, because the expense of training Irish priests in foreign seminaries had been a sore burden to their co-religionists; and of expediency, because the change promised to assuage the anti-British prejudices of the priests. Moreover, amidst the sweeping triumph of secularism in France and Belgium, most of the seminaries frequented by Irish youths had disappeared. The chief objections urged against the scheme were the narrowness of view certain to result from the curriculum of a semi-monastic institution, and the desirability of educating priests at Trinity College along with Protestants. On these grounds we must regret Pitt's decision to found a separate training college, albeit at first intended for the education of lay youths as well. The considerations above set forth, however, prevailed; and the chief legislative result of the year 1795 at Dublin was the charter establishing Maynooth College. Undoubtedly it was the outcome of Pitt's

[1] Quoted by Froude, " The English in Ireland," iii, 158-61.

desire to pacify Catholic Ireland; but the unhappy conditions of the ensuing period told heavily against success. Indeed, as Wolfe Tone predicted, that institution fostered insular patriotism of a somewhat narrow type.

The trend of things in the years 1795-7 set steadily towards rebellion. The discontent was most threatening among the sturdy Presbyterians of Ulster, chafed as they were by the exaction of tithes by the Protestant Established Church. The founders and the ablest leaders of the League of United Irishmen were Protestants. For a time they aimed merely at a drastic measure of Parliamentary Reform similar to that advocated by English Radicals. But the disappointment of the hopes of Grattan and Irish Whigs in the spring of 1795 exasperated all sections of reformers and impelled the League towards revolutionary courses. Sops like Maynooth they rejected with scorn; and at the close of that year, after the passing of certain repressive measures, their organization became secret; they imposed an oath on members and gradually devised means for organizing the whole of Ireland in brotherhoods, which by means of district and county delegations, carried out the behests of the central committee at Dublin.

Yet their system was far from absorbing the whole of the nation. The vivacity of the Celt and the hardness of the Saxon tell against close union; and where the two races dwell side by side, solidarity is a dream. Now, as always, in times of excitement the old animosities burst forth. The Catholic peasantry banded together in clubs, known as Defenders, to glut their hatred upon Protestant landlords and tithe-reaping clergy. Their motives seem in the main to have been agrarian rather than religious; but, as in Leinster, Munster, and Connaught the dividing lines between landlords and peasants were almost identical with those between Protestants and Catholics, the land feud became a war of creed. The ensuing horrors, midnight attacks, cattle-maiming, and retaliation by armed yeomanry, exerted a sinister influence upon Ulster, where the masses were fiercely Protestant. Certain of the Catholic villages were ravaged by Protestant Peep o' Day Boys, until the Irishry fled in terror to the South or West, there wreaking their vengeance upon squires and parsons. By degrees the Peep o' Day Boys became known as Orangemen, whose defiant loyalty sometimes caused concern to Camden and Pitt; while the Defenders joined the better drilled ranks of United Ireland, which therefore became a preponderatingly Catholic body.

Thus affairs revolved in the old vicious circle. Feuds, racial, religious, and agrarian, rent Ireland asunder. Disputes about land have ever sunk deep into the brooding imagination of the Celt; and the memories of holdings absorbed, or of tithes pitilessly exacted in lean years, now flashed forth in many a deed of incendiarism or outrage. To Camden there appeared to be only one means of cure, coercion. An Indemnity Act was therefore passed to safeguard squires and yeomen who took the law into their own hands. Then followed the Insurrection Act, for disarming the disaffected, and the suspension of the Habeas Corpus Act for strengthening the arm of the law.

The outcome was that the United Irishmen turned towards France. Even in the year 1793 the Republic sent agents into Ireland to stir up revolt. Nothing definite came of those efforts, except that a section of Irish patriots thenceforth began to strive for separation from Great Britain. Early in 1796 Wolfe Tone proceeded to Paris to arrange for the despatch of a French auxiliary corps. On 20th April General Clarke, head of the Topographical Bureau at the War Office, agreed to send 10,000 men and 20,000 stand of arms. The mercurial Irishman encountered endless delays, and was often a prey to melancholy; but the news of Bonaparte's victories in Italy led him to picture the triumph of the French Grenadiers in Ireland.[1]

Another interesting figure is that of Lord Edward Fitzgerald. Sprung from the ancient line of the Geraldines, and son of the Duke of Leinster, he plunged into life with the gaiety and bravery of a Celt. After serving with distinction in the British army in America he returned, became a member of the Irish Parliament, and in 1790 during the acute friction with Spain, received from his uncle, the Duke of Richmond, an introduction to Pitt, who offered him the command of an expedition against Cadiz. Nothing came of the proposal; but the incident reveals the esteem in which the chivalrous young officer was held. He soon married Pamela, the reputed daughter of the Duke of Orleans and Mme. de Genlis, whence he himself was often dubbed " Egalité." The repressive policy of Camden made him a rebel; and in May 1796 he made his way to Hamburg, hoping to con-

---

[1] "Autobiography of Wolfe Tone," ii, chs. iv-vi ; Guillon, "La France et l'Irlande."

cert plans for a French invasion. There he was joined by Arthur O'Connor, who impressed Reinhard with a sense of ability and power. Together the two Irishmen travelled to Basle, where they induced Barthélemy to favour their scheme. Meanwhile the French Directory entered into the plan of Wolfe Tone; the mission of Fitzgerald had no direct result, apart from the revelation of his plan to a travelling companion, who had been the mistress of a British Minister, and now forwarded a description of it to London.[1]

Meanwhile Wolfe Tone had sketched the outline of the enterprise to Clarke and General Hoche, predicting to the latter, the commander-elect, that he would "amputate the right hand of England for ever."[2] As is well known, Hoche's expedition to Bantry Bay at the close of the year 1796 was an utter failure; and the sterner spirits in Ulster believed that the French had designed that it should end so. The malcontents therefore relaxed their efforts for a time, until, in the spring following, the mutinies in the British fleet aroused new hopes. It seems probable that their intrigues had some effect on events at the Nore. In quick succession United Ireland despatched to Paris two delegates, named Lewins and McNevin, to concert plans for another landing. The Directory sent an agent to treat with the League. Fitzgerald met him in London, and declared that the Irish Militia and Yeomanry would join the French on their landing. The United Irishmen also sought help from Spain.[3]

In Ireland the organisation went on apace until Camden struck sharp blows through the military. In the middle of May 1797, when the malcontents were excited by news of the second mutiny at Portsmouth, they rose in the North, but in three or four engagements the loyal Militia and Yeomanry broke up their bands. The South remained quiet, and the efforts to seduce the army and Militia were fruitless; but Lord Clifden, writing to Abbot on 15th May, predicted a general rising when the French attempted a second invasion, as they certainly would.[4] On 19th June Beresford wrote from Dublin to Auckland, stating that, but for the repressive measures and wholesale seizures of arms, not a

---

[1] "Mems. of Ld. E. Fitzgerald," ch. xx.   [2] Tone, "Autob.," ii, 99.
[3] "Report of the Comm. of Secrecy" (1799), 22, 25; W. J. Fitzpatrick, "Secret Service under Pitt," ch. x; C. L. Falkiner, "Studies in Irish History," ch. iv; "Castlereagh Corresp.," i, 270-88.
[4] "Lord Colchester's Diary," i, 103.

loyalist's head would have been safe.[1] The spring of 1797 was
indeed a time of great risk. But for the weakness of the Dutch
and French navies, a landing in Ireland could have taken place
with every chance of success. As it was, Camden's vigorous
measures so far cowed the malcontents that the rebellion was
deferred for a year. This respite probably saved the British
Empire. Amidst the financial and naval difficulties of the first
half of the year 1797, a telling blow struck at Ireland could
scarcely have failed of success. Rarely were the enemies of
England so formidable; never were her means of defence so
weak. Fortunately, no blow was aimed at her until the month
of October; and then, when the Dutch fleet set out to convoy
an expedition to Ireland, it was utterly crushed by Duncan at
Camperdown. There was therefore little risk of an invasion in
force after October 1797, the very month which saw Napoleon
Bonaparte set free from his lengthy negotiations with Austria.
Verily, if Fortune pressed hard on Pitt at Toulon and in Flanders and Hayti, she more than redressed the balance by her
boons at sea in the year 1797.

Camden's letters to Pitt reveal the imminence of bankruptcy
in Ireland throughout that year; and it is noteworthy that the
loan raised for the Irish Government in January and February was
the final cause of the Bank crisis in London. Even so, the Irish
Exchequer was in dire need. On 25th April Camden informed
Pitt that only £8,000 remained in the Exchequer, and he had
no means for equipping the troops if the French should land.
The sum of £200,000 must be sent at once. Such a demand at
that time was impossible; and not until the end of May could
Pitt forward the half of that sum, Camden meanwhile borrowing
money in Dublin at 8¾ per cent. On 1st June he wrote to Pitt
a confidential letter, laying bare his real aims. He urged him
to do all in his power to procure peace from France. He had
recommended this step in April; but now his language was most
insistent. Assuming that it would be sheer madness to tempt
fortune in another campaign, he suggested that, if the French
terms were too onerous, Pitt should leave it to another Prime
Minister to frame a peace. But whatever happened, Pitt must
not lower his dignity by conceding Reform and Catholic Emancipation in Great Britain and Ireland. If those measures were

[1] B.M. Add. MSS., 34454.

inevitable, others must carry them. The latter would only satisfy
the Irish Catholics for a time, their aim being to rule the country.
The only way of escaping these difficulties was a Union of the
Parliaments; but he (Camden) could not undertake to carry it,
still less Catholic Emancipation. Finally he declared the Presbyterians of Ulster to be Republicans who would rise *en masse*
if the French landed; but if Cornwallis were sent over to lead
the troops, even that crisis might be overcome.[1]

Pitt received this letter at the height of the mutiny at the
Nore. He seems to have sent no answer to it: indeed, silence
is the best reply to such an effusion. Camden's letters to Pitt
show that he longed for his recall. In that of 16th November
1796 he concluded with the significant remark that he looked
forward to the time when they would once more live as country
gentlemen in Kent. Pitt had the same longing; but he never
wrote a line expressing a desire to leave the tiller at the height
of the storm. Obviously Camden was weary of his work. Fear
seems to have been the motive which prompted his proclamation
of martial law in several counties and the offer of an amnesty to
all who would surrender their arms before Midsummer 1797.
Those enactments, together with the brutal methods of General
Lake and the soldiery in Ulster and Leinster, crushed revolt for
the present but kindled a flame of resentment which burst forth
a year later. As the danger increased, so did the severities of
the Protestant Yeomanry and Militia. Thus, fear begot rage,
and rage intensified fear and its offspring, violence. The United
Irishmen had their revenge. In the summer of 1797 their two
delegates, Lewins and McNevin, did their utmost to defeat the
efforts of Pitt to bring about peace with France; and the former
had the promise of the Director, Barras, that France would never
sheathe the sword until Ireland was free.[2]

Again Camden begged Pitt to seek the first opportunity of
freeing him from his duties in order to disentangle his private
affairs which were in much confusion, the excess of expenditure
over income at Dublin being a further cause of embarrassment.
In fact nothing but a sense of public duty, in view of a hostile
invasion, kept him at his post. So far from the truth are those
who, without knowledge of the inner motives of statesmen,

[1] Pitt MSS., 326. Quoted with other extracts from Camden's letters, in
"Pitt and Napoleon Miscellanies."
[2] Tone, "Autob.," ii, 272.

accuse them of delight in cruelty and of intriguing to provoke ,
a revolt.

Early in the year 1798 the hopes of malcontents centred in
the naval preparations progressing at Brest and Toulon.[1] Bonaparte also seemed about to deal a blow at London. In February
he surveyed the flotilla at Dunkirk and neighbouring ports;
and the hearts of English Jacobins beat high at the thought of
his landing in Kent or Sussex. The London Corresponding
Society, after a time of suspended animation, had now become
a revolutionary body. On 30th January its new secretaries,
Crossfield and Thomas Evans, issued an encouraging address to
the United Irishmen. Somewhat later Evans and Binns formed
a society, the United Englishmen, which imposed on its members an oath to learn the use of arms, its constitution in local,
or baronial, committees being modelled on that of the United
Irishmen. A society of United Scotsmen was founded about
the same time; a society of United Britons also came to being,
and issued a fraternal address to the United Irishmen on 5th
January.

Most significant of these effusions is one, dated 6 Pluviôse
An VI [25th January 1798], by "the Secret Committee of England" to the French Directory, containing the assurance that
Pitt had come to the end of his borrowing powers and that the
people were ready to throw off his yoke. "United as we are," it
concluded, "we now only await with impatience to see the Hero
of Italy and the brave veterans of the great Nation. Myriads
will hail their arrival with shouts of joy: they will soon finish
the glorious campaign." This address was drawn up fourteen
days before Bonaparte set out for Dunkirk. It is clear, then,
that its compilers were not so ignorant as that consequential
tailor, Francis Place, represented them. Their chief mistake lay
in concluding that Bonaparte intended to "leap the ditch." As
we now know, his tour on the northern coast was intended merely
to satisfy the Directors and encourage the English and Irish malcontents to risk their necks, while he made ready his armada at
Toulon for the Levant.[2] Meanwhile the United Britons and
United Irishmen sought to undermine Pitt's Government so that
it might fall with a crash at the advent of the hero of Italy.

---

[1] "Castlereagh Corresp.," i, 165-8.

[2] B.M. Add. MSS., 27808; "Report of the Comm. of Secrecy" (1799),
App. x; "Nap. Corresp.," iii, 486-92. For Place see *ante*, ch. vii.

They knew not that the chief efforts of the "soldiers of liberty" were then being directed to the pillage of Rome and of the cantonal treasuries of Switzerland in order to provide funds for Bonaparte's oriental adventure.

Already Irish, English, and French democrats had been fraternizing. In January 1798 the United Englishmen sent over two delegates to Dublin to concert action, and about the same time a priest of Dundalk, named O'Coigly (*Anglicé* Quigley), came over from Ireland as a delegate from the United Irishmen to Evans's Society. Place asserts that his plan of proceeding to France was not known. But, as Place habitually toned down or ridiculed the doings of that Society, this is doubtful. Owing to secret information (probably from Turner, a British spy at Hamburg) the Government arrested Quigley, Arthur O'Connor, and Binns, a leading member of the London Corresponding Society, at Margate as they were about to board a hoy for France (28th February). A little later Colonel Despard, Bonham, and Evans were arrested. The evidence against all but Quigley was not conclusive, and they were released. The case against Quigley depended on a paper found by a police officer in his pocket, urging a French invasion of England. He was therefore condemned for high treason and was hanged on 7th June 1798. Probably Quigley had that paper from a London Society; but if so, why were not its officials seized? In some respects the Quigley affair still remains a mystery. Certainly it added fuel to the hatred felt for Pitt by British and Irish Jacobins.[1]

The evidence against O'Connor was weighty. It was proved that he was the leader of the party and that he knew Quigley well. He had a cipher in his possession, which was surely superfluous if, as he stated, he was travelling on private business. Probably his acquittal was due to his relationship to Lord Longueville, an influential Irish peer. Fox, Sheridan, and the Duke of Norfolk also proceeded to Maidstone to answer for the virtuous and patriotic character of O'Connor, a fact which probably led the judge to give a strangely favourable summing-up. The conduct of the Opposition leaders in this matter led their former comrade, the Earl of Carlisle, to declare that they had now sunk to a lower political hell than any yet reached.

[1] W. J. Fitzpatrick, "Secret Service under Pitt," ch. iii; "Report of the Comm. of Secrecy" (1799), App. xxvi. For Despard, the plotter of 1802, see "Castlereagh Corresp.," i, 306, 326; ii, 4.

The Government, however, had not done with O'Connor. He was at once arrested at Maidstone on another charge (22nd May), and was in prison in Dublin during the rebellion. He then confessed that he had done more than any one to organize Leinster for revolt, also that he had had conferences with French generals with a view to invasion so far back as 1793; and he stated that he knew the member of the United Irishmen who in the winter of 1796 advised the French not to come until the spring of 1797.[1] There certainly was some misunderstanding between the Irish rebels and their would-be helpers; but the full details are not known. Finally O'Connor was allowed to retire to France; he became a French general, and helped Napoleon to concert plans for the invasion of Ireland, assuring him that, after the work of liberation was done, 200,000 Irishmen would help him to conquer England.

Meanwhile further news respecting the Franco-Irish plans reached Pitt through a man named Parish at Hamburg. An American friend of his at Brussels, while waiting at the municipal office for passports, saw those of two young Irishmen, named O'Finn, delegates of the United Irishmen of Cork. They had a large packet for the Directory at Paris, which contained the plans of the United Irishmen, the numbers and positions of the British troops and of the British warships between Dungeness and the North Foreland. The O'Finns stated this to the commissary of the Brussels bureau, who heard it with joy. The American secretly forwarded the news to Parish. The fact that the O'Finns had a list of the forces on the Kentish coast implied information from the English malcontents. Accordingly, on 19th April, Government seized the papers of the London Corresponding Society. They contained nothing of importance except the constitution of the Society, the oath to learn the use of arms, and the address to the United Irishmen. The Parliamentary Committee of Secrecy also believed that a plan was afoot for bringing to London a band of Irish fanatics to strike a blow which would paralyse Government while the French landed and Ireland revolted. This inference seems far-fetched; but the evidence at hand warranted the suspension of the Habeas Corpus Act, which Pitt procured from Parliament on the following day.

[1] "Auckland Journals," iv, 52. I have published the statements of O'Connor, etc., and the news sent by a British agent at Hamburg, in the "Eng. Hist. Rev." for October 1910.

Place, with his usual perverse ingenuity, argued that Pitt nursed the conspiracy in order to be able to create alarm and govern despotically.[1]

Events were now moving fast in Ireland. Chief among the exciting causes were the repressive measures of Camden and the licence of the Militia and Yeomanry. So able and active a commander as General Abercromby failed to keep discipline and prevent military outrages. Not long after his return from the West Indies he reluctantly accepted these thankless duties (November 1797). His dislike of the work appears in the following letter, addressed probably to one of Pitt's colleagues:

> Bantry, *Jan.* 28, 1798.[2]
>
> DEAR SIR,
>
> . . . I have found the country everywhere quiet, but there exists among the gentlemen the greatest despondency: they believe, or affect to believe, that there is a plot in every family, and a conspiracy in every parish, and they would abandon the country unless the troops were dispersed over the face of it for their protection. I believe the lower ranks heartily hate the gentlemen because they oppress them, and the gentle-

---

[1] Pitt MSS., 324; B.M. Add. MSS., 27808; "Dropmore P.," iv, 167.

On 24th May 1798 Thelwall wrote to Thos. Hardy from Llyswen, near Brecknock, describing his rustic retreat, and requesting a new pair of farmer's boots for "Stella." He hopes that O'Connor has returned in triumph to his friends. Tierney's vote in favour of suspending the Habeas Corpus Act does not surprise him, for he is vulgar and a sycophant. Hardy is too angry with Sheridan, whose chief offence is in going at all to the House of Commons. Sheridan surely does well in encouraging the people to resist an invasion. "I remain steady to my point—'no nation can be free but by its own efforts.' As for the French Directory and its faction, nothing appears to me to be further from their design than to leave one atom of liberty either to their own or to any nation. If, however, Mr. Sheridan supposes that all his talents can produce even a temporary unanimity while the present crew are in power, even for repelling the most inveterate enemy, he will find himself miserably mistaken. No such unanimity ever can exist: I am convinced, nay, the Ministers themselves seem determined, that it *shall* not. The only way to produce the unanimity desired is to stand aloof, and let these ruffians go blundering on till our most blessed and gracious sovereign shall see that either Pitt and Co. must bow down to the will of the people or his British crown bow down to five French shillings. . . . But what have we to do with Directories or politics? Peaceful shades of Llyswen! shelter me beneath your luxuriant foliage: lull me to forgetfulness, ye murmuring waters of the Wye. Let me be part farmer and fisherman. But no more politics—no more politics in this bad world!" (From Mr. A. M. Broadley's MSS.)

[2] Pretyman MSS. See, too, "Diary of Sir J. Moore," i, ch. xi.

men hate the peasants because they know they deserve to be hated. Hitherto rents have been paid, tithes have not been refused or taxes withheld. No arms or ammunition have anywhere been introduced, and there are no tumultuous assemblings of the people. I have often heard of disaffection among the militia; it may perhaps exist among a few individuals; but it cannot exist to any considerable amount. My inquiries have been unremitted in this particular. Were, however, a landing of the enemy to take place, I cannot say what might happen to a people dissatisfied with their situation and naturally of great levity; the new doctrines would give activity. We are preparing for whatever may happen and no labour or exertion shall be wanting.

Abercromby soon proclaimed his disgust at the excesses of his troops in unmeasured terms. True, he had much provocation. The militia officers under him were a loose swaggering set, whose cruelties to the peasantry during the prolonged search for arms were unpardonable. Further, their powers had been enlarged by Camden's order of May 1797, allowing them to use armed force without the requisition of magistrates, a step deemed necessary to screen the civil authorities from outrage or murder. Seeing that officers often put these powers to a brutal and arbitrary use, exasperating to the peasants and demoralizing to the soldiery, Abercromby determined publicly to rescind the viceregal mandate. The language in which he announced his decision was no less remarkable than the decision itself. On 26th February 1798 he stated in a general order: " That the frequency of courts-martial, and the many complaints of irregularities in the conduct of the troops in this kingdom having too unfortunately proved the army to be in a state of licentiousness which must render it formidable to everyone but the enemy, the commander-in-chief" forbids officers ever to use military force except at the requisition of magistrates.

That the army and militia did not assault their commander after this outrageous insult shows that their discipline had not wholly vanished. In face of the vehement outcries of the Irish loyalists against Abercromby, Camden showed much forbearance. He issued a guarded statement that Abercromby had been accustomed to command troops abroad, and did not realize the impression which would be caused in Ireland by his censure of the soldiery. Portland, however, openly blamed the commander-in-chief. Pitt's letter of 13th March to Camden shows that, had he seen Portland's censure before it went off, he would have

toned down some of its expressions; but on the whole he
heartily disapproved of Abercromby's indiscriminate rebuke to
the army as not only unjust, but calculated to depress its spirits
and encourage those of the French and the Irish malcontents.
Portland's reprimand brought about Abercromby's resignation,
which Camden sought to avert. Thus again events took the worst
possible course. Abercromby was an able and energetic man; and
his resignation, at the time when the arrival of the French was
expected, undoubtedly helped to raise the hopes of malcontents.
Well might Camden write to Pitt on 25th April that Abercromby
had done much harm. With that commander's desire to repress
the outrages of the soldiery everyone must sympathize. The
manner in which he sought to effect it was incredibly foolish.

Meanwhile, the work of the conspirators had been undermined by treachery. One of the conspirators, named Reynolds,
took fright and revealed the secret of the plot to an official at
Dublin Castle (26th February), adding the information that the
Dublin committee would hold a secret meeting on 12th March.
The police, bursting in, seized eighteen members, including
McNevin, along with their papers, amongst which were some in-
criminating O'Coigly. Lord Edward Fitzgerald escaped for a
time; but an informer gained knowledge of his movements, and
those of two brothers named Sheares. On his warning the Castle
that they were about to arouse Dublin to revolt, Camden resolved to anticipate the blow. Two police officers, Swan and
Ryan, tracked Fitzgerald to his lair on the 19th of May. They
found him in bed. At once the fierce spirit of his race surged up.
He sprang at them with the small dagger ready by his side and
struck at Swan. The blow went home, while the pistols aimed
by the officers missed fire. Turning on Ryan, he dealt thrust
upon thrust. The two wounded men clung to him while he
struggled and struck like a wild beast. He was dragging them
towards the door when Major Sirr rushed in and shot him in
the shoulder. Even then his convulsions were so violent that two
or three soldiers, who ran upstairs, scarcely overpowered him.
Swan soon died. The wounds of Ryan were not mortal. That
of Fitzgerald was not deemed serious, but it mortified, and he
passed away on 4th June, mourned by all who knew his chivalrous daring spirit.[1]

[1] "Castlereagh Coresp.," i, 458-67; "Life and Letters of Lady Sarah
Lennox," ii, 299-302; "Mems. of Lord E. Fitzgerald," chs. 27-30.

The fury of Fitzgerald is intelligible. He was the one necessary man in the plot then coming to a head for the capture of Dublin on 23rd May. Among his effects were found a green uniform, the seal of the Irish Union, the line of route for the Kildare rebels in their advance, together with a plan for the seizure of the chief officials. The triumph of the Castle was completed by the capture of Neilson and the Sheares. Their papers showed that no quarter was to be given. Irish historians (among them Plowden) maintained that Pitt and Camden all along knew of the plot and allowed the conspirators to drive on their mine in order at the right moment to blow them up. There is no evidence to this effect, except during the few days preceding the blow. Camden's efforts were uniformly directed towards disarmament and coercion, so much so that he is reproached for his cruelty by the very men who accuse him of playing with the conspiracy. It is clear that he sought to prevent a rising, which was expected to coincide with a French invasion. In fact the only prudent course was to repress and disarm at all possible points.

The severity of the crisis appears in the letters which Beresford, Cooke, and Lees, officials at Dublin Castle, wrote to Auckland. In answer to Lord Moira's reckless charge in the Irish Parliament, that they were pushing on the country to rebel, Beresford on 10th April asks Auckland how can they, who are daily exposed to murder, push on a nation to deeds of violence which must fall on them? On 1st May he writes: "We think the Toulon squadron will join the expedition against Ireland. . . . Pikes are making in numbers, and the idea of a rising prevails. Kildare and Wicklow are armed, organized, and rebellious. Dublin and the county are very bad. The rebels expect the French within a month. Such is their last Gazette." On 7th May Lees writes to Auckland: "Lord Camden must steel his heart. Otherwise we are in great jeopardy." On 9th May Beresford states that it would be a good plan to seize a number of malcontents, threaten them with flogging and induce them to turn informers. He adds: "At present the quiet which prevails in some parts is deceptive. Where the country is organized, quiet appears. Where the organization is going on there is disturbance. In Kildare there are complete regiments, with large quantities of arms in their possession." On 10th May Lees writes that Galway is arming for revolt, and, nine days later, after the arrest of Fitzgerald, he states that they expect a rising in Dublin on the morrow. On 21st May after the arrest of the Sheares, Cooke writes: " A rising is not given up; but I think it will not take place. Parts of Kildare will not give up arms. . . . A search for arms will commence. We are in good spirits." On 20th May Beresford informs Auckland of the receipt of news at the Castle from three different quarters that there would be a rising on the 21st, owing to the vigorous measures now taken by the Government.[1]

This is not the language of men who are nursing a plot. It evinces a resolve to stamp out disaffection before the Brest and Toulon fleets arrive. As for Pitt, his letters show a conviction of the need of continuing the repressive measures whereby Camden had " saved the country." He approved the plan of allowing officers to act without the orders of magistrates, seeing that the latter were often murdered for doing their duty. The thinness of his correspondence with Camden is somewhat surprising until we remember that his energies mainly went towards strengthening the army and navy. His letter to Grenville early in June shows that he expected news of the arrival of the French off the Irish coast, since they had got out from Toulon on 19th May.

It is not surprising that Ireland was thought to be their goal. Bonaparte and the Directory had kept the secret of their Eastern Expedition with far more care than Pitt displayed in worming it out. Certainly Pitt's spy system was far less efficient than has been imagined.[2] With ordinary activity the oriental scheme could have been found out from one of Barras' mistresses or from some official at Toulon. The fact that Bonaparte had some time previously engaged Arab interpreters might surely have enlightened an agent of average intelligence. So far back as 20th April French engineers in uniform, accompanied by interpreters, had arrived at Alexandria and Aleppo in order to prepare for the reception of large forces. The interpreters, it is said, " collect all possible information respecting Suez and the navigation of the Red Sea, as also particularly whether the English have any ships in the Persian Gulf. It is supposed that General Buonaparte will divide his army, one corps to be embarked from the Red Sea and pass round to the Gulf of Persia, the other part to proceed from Syria overland to the Euphrates,

---

[1] B.M. Add. MSS., 34454.   [2] " Dropmore P.," iv, 230, 239.

by which river they are to advance and join the remainder near the mouth of this river; from thence to make, *united*, the grand descent on the coast of Malabar or Deccan." [1] In these days it is difficult to imagine that this news did not reach Pitt until about 5th July.

The Irish malcontents were as ill informed as Pitt. Basing their hopes on the arrival of the French fleet, they prepared to rise about the end of May. But the arrests in Dublin hurried on their plans. The men of Kildare and Westmeath received orders from the secret Directory in Dublin to take arms on 23rd May, on the understanding that the whole of Ireland would revolt. They were to seize the towns and villages on the roads to Dublin, while the rebels in the city murdered the authorities and captured the chief positions. But on the 22nd the Government seized quantities of arms, and the presence of General Lake's garrison of 4,000 Yeomen daunted the United Irishmen; on the night of the 23rd-24th only the more daring of them stole about the environs, waiting for a signal which never came; and by dawn their bands melted away. In Meath also the rising failed miserably. A large concourse assembled on the historic slopes of Tara Hill, whence 400 Fencibles and Yeomen drove them with ease (25th May).

In Kildare and the north of Wicklow, where the influence of the Fitzgeralds made for revolt, large throngs of men assembled on the night of 23rd-24th May, and made desperate attacks on Naas and Clane, important posts on the roads leading to the capital. Their headlong rushes broke in vain against the stubborn stand of the small garrisons. But at a village hard by, named Prosperous, the rebel leaders fooled the chief of a small detachment by a story of their intention to deliver up arms. Gaining access to the village, they surprised the soldiers in the barracks, girdled them with fire, and spitted them on their pikes as they jumped forth. That night of horror ended with the murder of the Protestant manufacturer, whose enterprise had made their village what it was. A few days later General Ralph Dundas somewhat indiscreetly granted an armistice to a large body of Kildare rebels at Kilcullen on the promise that they would give up their arms and go home. Nevertheless a large body of them were found on the Curragh and barred the way to General Duff,

---

[1] B.M. Add. MSS., 34454. News received through Sir F. d'Ivernois.

who courageously marched with 600 men to the aid of Dundas. Duff was informed that these rebels would be willing to lay down their arms. His men were advancing towards them when a shot or shots were fired by the rebels, whether in bravado or in earnest is doubtful. The troops, taking it as another act of treachery, charged with fury and drove the mass from the plain with the loss of more than 200 killed. Thus, here again, events made for animosity and bloodshed. Protestants remembered the foul play at Prosperous; the rebels swore to avenge the treachery at the Curragh.

News of the first of these events sped across the Irish Sea on 25th and 26th May. They reached Pitt just before or after his Whitsunday duel on Putney Heath. Thick and fast came the tales of slaughter. On 29th May Camden wrote in almost despairing terms—The rebellion was most formidable and extensive. It would certainly be followed by a French invasion. It must be suppressed at once. The Protestants and the military were mad with fury, and called aloud for a war of extermination. The strife would be marked by unheard-of atrocities. For the sake of human nature, Pitt must at once send 5,000 regular troops. Camden added that cavalry were useless against lines of pikemen, a phrase which tells of the dogged fury of the peasantry. Nevertheless, his assertion that the rebellion was extensive proves his lack of balance. The saving facts of the situation were that the Ulstermen had not yet moved; that Connaught and Munster were quiet; and of Leinster, only Kildare, Wexford, and parts of Carlow and Wicklow were in arms. In Dublin murder was rife, but the pikemen did not muster.

Pitt's reply of 2nd June to Camden is singularly cool. In brief and businesslike terms he stated that, despite the difficulties of the situation, he had already prepared to despatch 5,000 men; but Camden must send them back at the earliest possible moment in order not to disarrange the plans for the war. Still more frigid was the letter of George III to Pitt. The King lamented the need of sending troops to Ireland, as they would thereby be cut off from "active service." Camden (he wrote) must really not press for them unnecessarily. However, as the sword was drawn in Ireland, it must not be sheathed until the rebels submitted unconditionally. Eleven days later the King wrote to Pitt that the new Lord Lieutenant "must not lose the present moment of terror for frightening the supporters of the Castle into an Union with this country; and no further indulgences must be granted to Roman Catholics, as no country can be governed where there is more than one established religion."[1] The thinness of the King's thought is in part redeemed by its tenacity. His mind resembled an elemental two-stringed instrument, which twanged forth two notes—Church and State.

In strange contrast to the calculations of the King and Pitt were the effusions of Camden. On 7th June he referred plaintively to Portland's despatch, stating that only 3,000 men could be sent. He warned Pitt that it was a religious war; priests marched at the head of the rebels, who swept together and drove at their head the reluctant. For the sake of humanity Pitt must send larger reinforcements. He added that Lake was unequal to the emergency. Fortunately, on that day Pitt received the consent of the Marquis Cornwallis to act as Lord Lieutenant and Commander-in-Chief in Ireland. As Camden had more than once pointed out the urgent need of that appointment, it is surprising to find him on 16th June upbraiding Pitt with the suddenness of the change. Surely it was no time for punctiliousness. Already the Ulstermen were rising, and 30,000 rebels were afoot in Wexford. But, as it happened, the worst of the trouble was over before Cornwallis could take the field. Landing on 20th June near Dublin, he heard news portending a speedy decision in Wexford.

It is not easy to account for the savagery of the revolt in that county. The gentry resided among their tenants on friendly terms; and the search for arms had been carried out less harshly than elsewhere. Gordon, the most impartial historian of the rebellion, admits that the floggings and half-hangings had been few in number, yet he adds that the people were determined to revolt, probably from fear that their turn would come. Neither is the religious bigotry of the rebels intelligible. The Protestants were numerous in Wexford town, Enniscorthy, and New Ross; but there seems to have been little religious animosity, except where tales were circulated as to intended massacres of Catholics by Orangemen. The Celt is highly susceptible to personal in-

[1] Pretyman MSS. The King also stated that Pitt had "saved Ireland" by persuading Pelham to return and act as Chief Secretary. Pelham was a clever man, but often disabled by ill health.

fluence; and, just as that of the Fitzgeralds largely accounts for the rising in Kildare, so does the personality of Father John Murphy explain the riddle of Wexford. The son of a peasant of that county, he was trained for the priesthood at Bordeaux, and ardently embraced the principles of the French Revolution and the aims of United Ireland. His huge frame, ready wit, and natural shrewdness brought him to the front in Wexford; and he concerted the plan of establishing an Irish Republic on a strictly Romanist basis, a programme incompatible with that of Wolfe Tone and the United Irishmen.

Murphy, marching with his flock to the house of a neighbouring Protestant clergyman, bade him and his terrified friends surrender. Meeting with a refusal, they fired the outbuildings; and when the flames gained the house, they granted the prayers of the occupants for mercy if they came out. On coming out the adult males were forthwith butchered. Meeting with large reinforcements from the hills, Father John's pikemen beat off a hasty attack by 110 men of the North Cork Militia, only seven of whom escaped to Wexford. Such were the doings on that Whitsunday in Wexford (27th May). Next, the rebels swept down upon Enniscorthy; and though beaten back from the very heart of the town by the steady valour of the defenders, these last were yet fain to fall back on Wexford. But for the plundering habits of the peasantry, not a man could have reached that town. The priest and his followers now took post on Vinegar Hill, a height east of the River Slaney, which overlooks Enniscorthy and the central plain of the county. There on successive days he and his council dealt out pike-law to some four or five hundred Protestants and landlords. Meanwhile, as no help drew nigh, Maxwell, the commander at Wexford, deeming that town untenable, beat a timely retreat westwards to Duncannon Fort on Waterford Harbour (30th May).

Master of Wexford county, Murphy and his colleague, Father Michael, proposed to raise Wicklow and Waterford. If these efforts succeeded, it was probable that Dublin and Munster would rise. Ulster might then revolt; and the advent of the French would clinch the triumph. In full confidence, then, the masses of pikemen moved against the loyalists at New Ross, an important position on the River Barrow. Parish by parish, the priests at their head, they marched, some 30,000 strong. At dawn of 5th June, when near the town, they knelt during the celebration of Mass. Then they goaded on herds of cattle to serve as an irresistible vanguard, and rushed at the old walls. General Johnstone and the 1,400 defenders were at first over-borne and had to retreat over the bridge; but the plundering habits of the victors were their ruin. The soldiery re-formed, regained their cannon, and planting them skilfully, dealt such havoc among the disorderly mass, that finally it surged out into the plain.[1] After their defeat the rebels deposed Harvey, a Pro-testant, from his nominal command.

This success of the loyalists saved Waterford and Kilkenny from anything more than local riots; and Moore, moving up from Fermoy and Clonmel, soon threatened the rebel county from the west. The beaten peasants glutted their revenge on Protestant prisoners near New Ross; and a general massacre of prisoners at Wexford was averted only by the rapid advance of Moore. Meanwhile, Father John, moving into County Wick-low with a force some 30,000 strong, sought to break down the defence at Arklow. But that important post on the River Avoca was stoutly held by General Needham with some 1,500 men, mostly militia and yeomen. There, too, the priests led on the peasants with a zeal that scorned death. One of the peasant leaders rushed up to a gun, thrust his cap into it, and shouted, " Come along, boys; her mouth is stopped." The next moment he and his men were blown to pieces. Disciplined valour gained the day (9th June), and John and his crusaders retired to Vinegar Hill. His colleague, Father Michael Murphy, who had claimed to be able to catch Protestant bullets, was killed by a cannon-shot; and this may have decided the rebels to retreat.

The British Guards had now arrived, to the inexpressible relief of Camden and his advisers. Beset by reports of a general rising in Ulster and by the furious protests of loyalists against the inaction of Pitt, the Lord Lieutenant had held on his way, acting with energy but curbing the policy of vengeance, so that, as he informed Pitt, he was now the most unpopular man in Ireland. Nevertheless, before he left her shores, he had the satisfaction to see his measures crowned with success. The converging moves of Lake, Needham, Dundas, and Johnstone upon Vinegar Hill cooped up the rebels on that height; and on 21st June the royal troops stormed the slopes with little loss. The dupes of Father

---

[1] J. Alexander, ". . . Rebellion in Wexford " (Dublin, 1800).

John no longer believed in his miraculous powers. The survivors broke away southwards, but then doubled back into the mountains of Wicklow. The war now became a hunt, varied by savage reprisals. Father John was hanged on 26th June. By his barbarities he had ended the dream of United Ireland. Few of the malcontents of Antrim and Down obeyed the call to arms of the United Irishmen early in June; and the risings in those counties soon flickered out. Religious bigotry enabled Dublin Castle once more to triumph.

Pitt was vehemently blamed by Irish loyalists for his apathy at the crisis. The accusation, quite natural among men whose families were in hourly danger, was unjust. As we have seen, even before the arrival of Camden's request, he took steps to send off 5,000 men. As the Duke of York and Dundas cut down that number to 3,000, and endeavoured to prevent any more being sent, they were responsible for the despatch of an inadequate force. If the French detachments intended for Ireland had arrived early in June, they must have carried all before them. But it was not until 22nd August that General Humbert, with 1,100 men, landed at Killala. Even so his little force was believed to be the vanguard of a large army, a fact which explains the revival of rebellion at the end of the summer.

Not until 1st September did Pitt hear this alarming news. At once he ordered all possible reinforcements to proceed to Ireland. There was need of them. The Irish militiamen under Lake and Hutchinson who opposed the French at Castlebar rushed away in wild panic from one-fourth of their numbers (27th August). Such were "the Castlebar Races." Probably the Irishmen were disaffected; for many of them joined the enemy. Cornwallis proceeded to the front, and with 11,000 men made head against the rebels and the French. The latter were now but 800 strong, and after a most creditable stand finally surrendered with the honours of war (8th September). Cornwallis issued a tactful bulletin,[1] commending his troops for their merit-

---

[1] "Cornwallis Corresp.," ii, 395-404. For the panic in Dublin see " Dropmore P.," iv, 289 et seq. Cooke wrote to Castlereagh on 28th September that the Bishop of Killala and his family were saved from slaughter by a few French officers, " who execrate our savages more than they whom they have plundered." He adds that though the United Irishmen began the plot the Catholics are turning it solely to their own interests (Pitt MSS., 327). See, too, H. F. B. Wheeler and A. M. Broadley, "The War in Wexford" (1910).

orious exertions and trusting to their honour not to commit acts of cruelty against their deluded fellow subjects. In point of fact 11,000 men with difficulty brought 800 to surrender and then gave themselves up to retaliation on the rebels. Fortunately the French Directory sent only small parties of raiders. A month later, Wolfe Tone, with a squadron, appeared off Lough Swilly; but the French ships being overpowered by Sir John Warren, Tone was captured, taken to Dublin, and cut his throat in order to escape the ignominy of a public hanging. Another small French squadron entered Killala Bay late in October, but had to make for the open. Thus flickered out a flame which threatened to shrivel up British rule in Ireland.

What causes contributed to this result? Certainly not the activity and resourcefulness of Pitt and his colleagues; for their conduct at the crisis was weak and tardy. The Duke of York and Dundas must primarily be blamed for the despatch of inadequate reinforcements; but Pitt ought to have overruled their decision. Perhaps the Cabinet believed England to be the objective of Bonaparte and the fleet at Brest; but, thanks to the rapid growth of the Volunteer Movement, England was well prepared to meet an invading force and to quell the efforts of the malcontent Societies. In Ireland the outlook was far more gloomy. After the resignation of Abercromby, Camden and the officials of Dublin Castle were in a state of panic. Pitt did well finally to send over Cornwallis; but that step came too late to influence the struggle in Leinster. In truth the saving facts of the situation were the treachery of informers at Dublin and the diversion of the efforts of Bonaparte towards the East. The former event enabled Camden to crush the rising in Dublin; the latter left thousands of brave Irishmen a prey to the false hopes which the French leaders had designedly fostered, Barras having led Wolfe Tone to believe that France would fight on for the freedom of Ireland. The influence of Bonaparte told more and more against an expedition to her shores; but the Irish patriots were left in the dark, for their rising would serve to distract the energies of England, while Bonaparte won glory in the East. To save appearances, the French Government sent three small expeditions in August to October; but they merely prolonged the agony of a dying cause, and led that deeply wronged people to ask what might not have happened if the promises showered on Wolfe Tone had been made good.

It is recorded of William of Orange, shortly before his intended landing in England, that, on hearing of the march of Louis XIV's formidable army into the Palatinate, he serenely smiled at his rival's miscalculation. Louis sated his troops with plunder and lost a crown for James II. Similarly we may imagine the mental exultation of Pitt on hearing that Bonaparte had gone the way of Alexander the Great and Mark Antony. Camden and he knew full well that Ireland was the danger spot of the British Empire, and that the half of the Toulon force could overthrow the Protestant ascendancy. Some sense of the magnitude of the blunder haunted Napoleon at St. Helena; for he confessed to Las Casas: "If, instead of the expedition to Egypt, I had undertaken that against Ireland, what could England have done now?" In a career, illumined by flashes of genius, but wrecked by strange errors, the miscalculation of the spring of 1798 was not the least fatal. For of all parts of the British Empire Ireland was that in which the Sea Power was most helpless when once a French *corps d'armée* had landed.

CHAPTER XVII

THE SECOND COALITION

To reduce France within her ancient limits is an object of evident and pressing interest to the future tranquillity and independence of Europe.—
Foreign Office Despatch of 16th November 1798.

IT is difficult to realize that the independence of Europe was endangered by the French Republic. We associate the ascendancy of France in Spain, Italy, Germany, Switzerland, and Holland with the personality of Napoleon; and by contrasting him with the pygmies who strutted on the stage after the death of Pitt we find the collapse of Europe intelligible. But a backward glance of one decade more shows France dominating the Continent. True, it was Bonaparte's genius which brought Austria to the humiliating Peace of Campo Formio (October 1797); but his triumphs in Italy merely crowned the efforts of France in 1793-5. After the close of his Italian campaigns a touch of her little finger unseated the Pope. At the Congress of Rastadt her envoys disposed of German duchies and bishoprics in the lordliest way. Switzerland she overran, plundered, and unified. Ferdinand IV of Naples and his consort, Maria Carolina, quaked and fumed at her threats. Prussia was her henchman. And in the first months of his reign Paul I of Russia courted her favour. French policy controlled Europe from the Niemen to the Tagus, from the Zuyder Zee to the Campagna.

Yet this supremacy was in reality unsound. So fitful a ruler as the Czar Paul was certain to weary of his peaceful mood. He had good ground for intervention. By the Treaty of Teschen (1779) Russia became one of the guarantors of the Germanic System which the French now set at naught. Moreover his chivalrous instincts, inherited from his mother, Catharine, were chafed by the news of French depredations in Rome and

Switzerland. The growth of indignation at St. Petersburg begot new hopes at Vienna. In truth Francis II, despite his timidity, could not acquiesce in French ascendancy. How could his motley States cohere, if from Swabia, Switzerland, and Italy there dropped on them the corrosive acid of democracy? The appeals from his father-in-law, Ferdinand of Naples, also had some weight. In fine the Court of Vienna decided to make overtures to London. On 17th March 1798 the Chancellor, Thugut, urged his ambassador, Stahremberg, to find out whether England would help Austria against "a fierce nation irrevocably determined on the total subversion of Europe, and rapidly marching to that end"; also whether Pitt would send a fleet to the Mediterranean, and, if necessary, prolong the struggle into the year 1799.[1] The entreaties from Naples were still more urgent.

Pitt resolved to stretch out a helping hand. Early in April he sought to induce Earl Spencer, First Lord of the Admiralty, to send to that sea a strong squadron detached from Earl St. Vincent's force blockading Cadiz. His letter asking for information on several topics is missing; but Spencer's letter to Grenville throws so much light on the situation that I quote parts of it, summarizing the remainder:[2]

Admiralty, *April* 6, 1798.

" I send you by Mr. Pitt's desire a sketch I have made out of answers to the queries he put down upon paper yesterday in Downing Street. The result is to my mind a decision which I fear will not tally very well with our wishes and the views you have formed as the groundwork of the communication at present proposed with Vienna." He then states that, even if a Russian squadron appears in the North Sea, yet we cannot keep a permanent squadron in the Mediterranean. " For that purpose we should at least have 70 sail, as the Channel cannot be trusted with safety with less than 35, including the coast of Ireland, and the remaining 35 would be but barely enough to watch Cadiz and command the Mediterranean. Our best plan appears to me to be to maintain as long as we can a position between Lisbon and Cadiz, and when we are excluded (which I conclude we soon shall be) from the Tagus, to send Lord St. Vincent with the fleet he now has to take a sweep round the Mediterranean and do all the mischief he can to the French navy." If,

---

[1] " F. O.," Austria, 51; " Dropmore P.," iv, 170. The French took nearly 33,000,000 francs from the Swiss cantonal treasuries.

[2] Pitt MSS., 108.

he adds, the Spaniards come northward, our home fleet can deal with them: if they go to the Mediterranean and join the French there will not be much danger from so ill-combined a force when opposed to St. Vincent's fleet, "which I consider as being the best formed to act together that perhaps ever existed." If Austria would be satisfied with our sweeping round the Mediterranean, Spencer advocates that plan, but not that of keeping a fleet there, "because, exclusive of the great expense, it would leave the Spaniards too much at liberty."

In answer to Pitt's questions Spencer states the force disposable for the Channel and the coast of Ireland as 34, for the Mediterranean 24; 3 more were fitting for sea, and 8 others were nearing completion; but the chief deficiency was in men, 8,000 more being needed. He adds that the Neapolitans have 4 sail-of-the-line and 7 frigates: the French have 6 sail at Corfu; but he thinks not more than 10 sail can be equipped at Toulon. He regards the Venetian fleet as valueless.

Clearly Spencer underrated the force at Toulon and in the ports of North Italy. But, even so, the position was critical. To send an undermanned fleet into the Mediterranean, while France was preparing a blow at Ireland, seemed almost foolhardy. Nevertheless, Pitt resolved to do so. For, as he stated to Grenville on 7th April, they must encourage Austria to play a decisive part in resisting French aggression; and, in view of the revival of the old English spirit, he was prepared to brave the risks of invasion, deeming even that event preferable to a lingering and indecisive war. As usual, Pitt's view prevailed; and a few days later orders went forth to St. Vincent to despatch a squadron under Nelson to the Mediterranean, Austria being also apprised of this decision, in terms which implied the formation of a league against France. While Russia and, if possible, Prussia defended Germany, Austria was to expel the French from Italy.[1] Here again Pitt's hopeful nature led him to antedate the course of events. The new Coalition came about very slowly. England and Austria were held apart by disputes respecting the repayment of the last loan, on which Pitt and Grenville insisted, perhaps with undue rigour. Distrust of Prussia paralysed the Court of Vienna, and some time elapsed before it came to terms with Russia. But in the midst of the haggling came news which brought new vigour to the old monarchies. On 1st August 1798 Nelson destroyed the French fleet in

[1] "Dropmore P.," iv, 166, 172; "F. O.," Austria, 51. Grenville to Eden, 20th April.

Aboukir Bay; and thus, at one blow, naval supremacy in the Mediterranean passed from the tricolour to the Union Jack. This momentous change resulted primarily from the bold resolve of Pitt to encounter even a French descent on our coasts, provided that he could strike at France in the Mediterranean. Thus he exchanged the defensive for the offensive in a way no less bewildering to the French than reassuring to friendly Powers; and it is noteworthy that he adopted the same course in 1805, in sending Craig's expedition into that sea, thereby replacing Addington's tame acceptance of events by a vigorous policy which heartened Austria and Naples for the struggle against Napoleon. On both occasions he ran great risks, but his audacity proved to be the highest prudence. The results of the Battle of the Nile were immeasurably great. Bonaparte and his 30,000 veterans were cooped up in Egypt. The Maltese rose against the French garrison of Valetta two days after the arrival of the glad tidings from the Nile. At Naples the news aroused a delirium of joy, and filled Queen Maria Carolina with a resolve to drive the French force from the Roman States.

To Pitt also the news of Nelson's triumph brought intense relief. The disappearance of Bonaparte's armada after the capture of Malta had caused much concern. True, Naples, which was thought to be his objective, was safe; but Ireland and Portugal were deemed in jeopardy. No one at Whitehall anticipated the seizure of Malta and Egypt, still less the emergence of plans for a French conquest of India. A tone of anxiety pervades Pitt's letter of 22nd August to his mother: " The account of Bonaparte's arrival at Alexandria is, I am afraid, true; but it gives us no particulars, and leaves us in entire suspense as to Nelson." [1] All the greater, then, was the relief on 2nd October, when tidings of Aboukir at last arrived.

Further, there were signs of a Russo-French war. The romantic nature of the Czar was fired by the hope of acquiring Malta. At Ancona, early in 1797, Bonaparte had intercepted a Russian envoy bearing offers of alliance to the Knights of the Order of St. John; and their expulsion by the French at Midsummer 1798 seemed to Paul a personal affront. Some of the Knights proceeded to St. Petersburg and claimed his protection. The affairs of the Order became his most cherished concern; and on 24th July Sir

---

[1] The Earl of Crawford's MSS.

Charles Whitworth, British ambassador at that Court, reported that Russia would now become a principal in the war against France, her aim being the re-establishment of peace on safe and honourable terms, but not the restoration of the French monarchy, on which Catharine had insisted. With this declaration the British and Austrian Cabinets were in full accord; and thus at last there was a hope of framing a compact Coalition. Fortunate was it that Bonaparte's seizure of Malta incensed Paul against France; for, early in August, the Swiss thinker, Laharpe, tutor of the future Czar Alexander I, brought tempting offers from Paris, with a view to the partition of the Turkish Empire.[1] That glittering prize was finally to captivate the fancy of Paul; but for the present he spurned the offer as degrading.

Nevertheless, the news of Aboukir did not wholly please him. For, while rejoicing at the discomfiture of the French atheists. he saw in Nelson's victory a sign of England's appropriation of Malta. In truth, that island now became the central knot of far-reaching complications. Formerly the bulwark of Christendom against the infidels, it now sundered European States.[2] So doubtful was the attitude of Paul and Francis that Pitt, in October 1798, twice wrote despondingly as to any definite decision on their part. All that was clear was their inordinate appetite for subsidies. These he of course withheld, knowing full well that neither would Paul tolerate for long the presence of the French at Malta, nor Francis their occupation of Switzerland. In any case he resolved not to give more than £2,000,000 to the two Empires for the year 1799.[3] For the time his hope lay only in the exertions of England, Europe being meantime "left to its fate." In order to humour the Czar, who was about to become Grand Master of the Knights of St. John, Grenville, on 23rd November, wrote to assure his Government that England renounced all aims of conquest in the Adriatic, or of the possession of Malta.

At the close of the year Pitt proudly displayed the inexhaustible resources of Great Britain. His Budget speech of 3rd December 1798 marks an epoch in economic history, alike for the boldness of the underlying conception and the statesmanlike

---

[1] "F. O.," Russia, 40. Whitworth to Grenville, 6th August 1798.

[2] See my Introduction to "The History of Malta, 1798-1815," by the late W. Hardman.

[3] "Dropmore P.," iv, 344, 355.

assessment of the national resources. Well might Mallet du Pan declare that the speech surpassed all previous efforts in its illuminating exposition of a nation's finance. As appeared in our survey of the Budget of 1797, Pitt then sought to meet the year's expenses within the year. To a generation accustomed to shift present burdens on to its successors the proposal seemed Quixotic; and Fox blamed him for not adopting this device. Pitt held to his plan, and outlined a ten per cent. tax upon income. Having failed to gain the requisite tenth by means of the Assessed Taxes, he proposed to raise it by methods which even the shirkers could with difficulty circumvent.

In order to lay a first rough actuarial basis for his Income Tax, he made a careful study of the nation's resources in the autumn of 1798. The results he summarized in an interesting statement. There were available at that time only rough estimates, even as to the area of cultivated land and its average rental. Relying upon Davenant, King, Adam Smith, Arthur Young, and Middleton, he estimated the area at 40,000,000 acres, and the average rental at 15s. an acre. He prudently fixed the taxable value at 12s. 6d. an acre. The yearly produce of mines, timber, and canal shares he assessed at £3,000,000. He reckoned house rent at double that sum, and the earnings of the legal profession at one half of it. Half a million he deemed well within the total of doctors' fees. He assessed the incomes derived from the British West Indies at £4,000,000, and those from the rest of the world at £1,000,000, a highly suggestive estimate. Tithes were reckoned at £4,000,000; annuities from the public funds at £12,000,000; the same sum for profits derived from foreign commerce; and £28,000,000 for the profits of internal trade, whether wholesale or retail. Fixing the rental of land at £6,000,000, he computed the total national income as £102,000,000, which should therefore yield not less than £10,000,000 a year. He proposed to safeguard the collection by imposing an oath at the declaration of income, and enjoining absolute secrecy on the Crown commissioners. The new tax, beginning from April 1799, would take the place of the Assessed Taxes. As will appear in a later chapter, the new impost did not yield the amount which Pitt expected; but the failure was probably due to defects in the methods of collection. Pitt further proposed to set aside £1,200,000 for the Sinking Fund.

His purpose in making this prodigious effort was to inspirit other nations to similar patriotic exertions. He pointed out with pride that after nearly six years of war British exports and imports exceeded those of any year of peace. Thus, far from declining in strength and prowess, as croakers averred, England had never shone so transcendently in the arts of peace and the exploits of war, a prodigality of power which presaged the vindication of her own rights and of the liberties of Europe.

What was the new Europe which Pitt sought to call to being? The question is of deep interest, not only as a psychological study, but as revealing glimpses of British policy in the years 1814-15. The old order having been rudely shaken in Germany, the Netherlands, Switzerland, and Italy, Pitt sought to effect a compromise between the claims of tradition and those of expediency. It being of paramount importance to safeguard Europe against France, Pitt and Grenville insisted on the limitation of that Power within its old boundaries, and the complete independence of Switzerland and Holland. That of the Kingdom of Sardinia afterwards figured in their stipulations. But one significant change now appears. The restoration of Austrian rule at Brussels being impracticable, it was suggested that the Belgic Provinces should go to the Prince of Orange when restored to his rights at The Hague. In the desperate crisis of 1805, as we shall see, Pitt sought to allure Prussia by offering Belgium to her; but that was a passing thought soon given up. The other solution of the Netherlands Question finally prevailed, thanks to the efforts of Pitt's pupil, Castlereagh, in 1814. The Foreign Office did not as yet aim at the retention of the Cape of Good Hope and Ceylon as a set off to British efforts for the Dutch and their acquisition of Belgium; but this thought was already taking shape. The barrier against French aggressions in the south-east was to be found in the reconstituted Kingdom of Sardinia, the House of Savoy rendering in that quarter services similar to the House of Orange in Flanders and Brabant. In other respects the British Cabinet favoured Austria's plans of aggrandisement in Italy as enhancing her power in a sphere which could not arouse the jealousy of Prussia. The aims of Berlin not being known, except that the restoration of the House of Orange was desired, Pitt and Grenville remained silent on that topic.[1]

[1] See Rose, "Napoleonic Studies," 54-8, for this despatch of 16th November 1798.

The question whether the peoples concerned would submit to this under-girding of the European fabric did not trouble them. They saw only the statics of territories; they had no conception of the dynamics of nations. A future in which Nationality, triumphant in Italy and Germany, would bring about a Balance of Power far more solid than any which their flying buttresses could assure, was of course entirely hidden from them. But they failed to read the signs of the times. The last despairing efforts of the Poles, and the *levée en masse* of the French people, now systematized in the Conscription Law of 5th September 1798, did not open their eyes to the future. For they were essentially men of the Eighteenth Century; and herein lay the chief cause of their failure against Revolutionary France. They dealt with lands as with blocks. She infused new energy into peoples.

Meanwhile the return of Nelson to the Neapolitan coast intoxicated that Court with joy. Queen Maria Carolina, ever the moving spirit at Naples, now laid her plans for the expulsion of the French from Italy. Trusting to her influence over her son-in-law, Francis II, and to a defensive compact which the Courts of Vienna and Naples had framed on 20th May 1798, she sought to incite him to take the offensive. Her close friendship with Lady Hamilton, wife of the British ambassador at Naples, also enabled her to gain complete ascendancy over Nelson, who, with his usual hatred of "the French villains," counselled open and immediate war. For abetting this design, Sir William Hamilton received a sharp rebuke from Downing Street. Francis II and Thugut were even more annoyed. They repulsed the Neapolitan emissary who begged for help, and roundly accused the Pitt Ministry of inciting Naples to war in order to drag in Austria. Their anger was not appeased by the successes of the Neapolitans near Rome, which the French evacuated on 29th November. The counter-stroke soon fell. The French, rallying in force, pushed the Bourbon columns southwards; and the early days of 1799 witnessed in swift succession the surrender of Naples, the flight of its Court and the Hamiltons to Palermo on Nelson's fleet, the foundation of the Parthenopean Republic, and the liquefaction of the blood of St. Januarius in sign of divine benediction on the new *régime*.[1]

[1] For a fuller account see "Camb. Mod. Hist." viii, ch. xxi, by the present writer.

Nevertheless, Nelson and the royal fugitives had set in motion forces which elsewhere made for triumph. Paul, re-assured as to England's desire to re-establish the Order of St. John at Malta, entered into an alliance with her on 29th December 1798, whereby the two Powers agreed to reduce France within her old boundaries, Russia furnishing to England an army of 45,000 men, mainly with a view to the support of Prussia, on condition of receiving £75,000 per month and three months' subsidies in advance. She also promised to send 3,000 men to help in the siege of the French garrison at Malta and others to assist England in the defence of the Neapolitan lands. Austria, resentful towards Pitt and fearful of Prussia's designs, still held back, though the events in Italy, especially the dethronement of Charles Emmanuel IV of the House of Savoy by the French should have spurred her to action. Probably she waited until the needs of England and Russia should enable her to dictate her terms. The cupidity of Thugut had been whetted by Pitt's speech as to the wealth of England; and the efforts of Cobenzl at St. Petersburg led Whitworth to sign a compact on terms so onerous to the British Treasury as to draw on him a sharp disclaimer and reprimand from London.[1] So matters dragged on far into the year 1799, when plans for the ensuing campaign ought to have been matured.

Still more luckless were the dealings of the British Cabinet with Prussia. In the hope of winning over Frederick William III, Grenville in November 1798 despatched his brother Thomas on a mission to Berlin. His journey thither was one of the longest and most eventful on record. At Yarmouth he was detained by easterly gales; and when at last the packet boat made the mouth of the Elbe it was wrecked. The passengers and crew succeeded in making their way to shore over the pack-ice, Grenville saving his papers, except the "full-power" needful for signing a treaty. He reached Cuxhaven in great exhaustion; and arrived at Berlin on 17th March, only to find that the French by daring and intrigue had cowed the North German States into subservience. The terrible winter of 1798-9 largely accounts for the delays which ruined the subsequent campaign. Whitworth remained long without news from Downing Street; and at last, on 12th February, announced that he had received nine

[1] "F. O.," Russia, 42. Despatches of 2nd, 8th and 25th January 1799.

posts at once. Meanwhile France, controlling all the coasts from
Bremen to Genoa, not only excluded British messengers, but
carried on her diplomatic bargaining in Germany without let or
hindrance. For all his trouble, Thomas Grenville could get no
firm footing amidst the shifting sands of Prussian diplomacy.
So nervous were the Austrian Ministers as to Prussia's future
conduct that they seemed about to come to terms with France
and join in the plunder of the smaller German States. This
might have been the upshot had not French armies crossed the
Rhine (1st March 1799), and shortly afterwards invaded the
Grisons Canton.[1] Goaded to action, Francis II declared war
eleven days later. On 28th April Austrian hussars seized the
French envoys withdrawing from Rastatt, murdering two of the
four and seizing the papers of all.

Thus began the war of the Second Coalition. Bonaparte's
seizure of Malta and Egypt without a declaration of war, and
the unbearable aggressions of the French in Switzerland, Italy,
and on the Rhine, stirred to action States which the diplomatic
efforts of Pitt and Grenville had left unmoved. For none of the
wars of that period was France so largely responsible. Even
now, when the inroad of the French into Germany threatened
the ascendancy of Prussia, Frederick William declined to join
the Allies; and his unstatesmanlike refusal thwarted the plans
of Pitt for the march of the subsidized Muscovite force through
Prussia for the recovery of Holland.

Another essential point was Switzerland. Like a bastion
frowning over converging valleys, that Alpine tract dominates
the basins of the Po, the Inn, the Upper Rhine, and the Upper
Rhone. He who holds it, if strong and resolute, can determine
the fortunes of North Italy, Eastern France, South Germany, and
the West of the Hapsburg domains. Further, by closing the
passes over the Alps he can derange the commerce of Europe;
and the sturdy mountaineers will either overbear the plain-
dwellers, or will serve as mercenaries in their forces. Accordingly Switzerland, like her Asiatic counterpart, Afghanistan, has
either controlled her neighbours, or has been fought for by
them. As commerce-controller, provider of troops, and warden
of the passes, she holds a most important position. Fortunate
it is that the Swiss have loved freedom, or money, more than

[1] Hüffer, " Quellen," i, 23-9.

dominion. For so soon as a great State possesses their land, the Balance of Power becomes a fiction.

Pitt evinced sure insight in his resolve to free the Switzers from the Jacobin yoke. To it the men of the Forest Cantons succumbed only after desperate struggles, which inspired Words-worth with one of the noblest of his sonnets. There is no sign that Pitt set much store on winning over the public opinion of Europe by siding with the oppressed against the oppressor, as his disciple, Canning, did during the Spanish National Rising; but help from the Swiss was certainly hoped for. So early as August 1798 Pitt proposed to allot £500,000 for assistance to them, and, but for the delays at St. Petersburg and Vienna, the Allies might have rescued that brave people before it fell beneath the weight of numbers. Even in March 1799, when the rising against the French had scarcely begun, he set apart £31,000 per month for the purpose of equipping a corps of 20,000 Swiss. On 15th March, after hearing of the outbreak of war on the Rhine, Grenville urged that the Russian force subsidized by England should march towards Switzerland, now that Prussia's doubtful behaviour prevented a conquest of Holland by land. He also insisted that this addition to the allied forces destined for Switzerland must not be allowed to lessen the number of Austrians operating there.[1]

The Court of Vienna at once saw in the subsidized Russian army a tool useful for its own plans, and requested that it should serve with the Austrians in Swabia. The answer to this singular request can be imagined. For a day or two Whitworth was also disturbed by a belated effort of the French Directory to restore peace. It offered Poland to the Elector of Saxony, and Saxony to Prussia for her friendly services, Austria being led to expect Bavaria, if she would keep Russia "within her ancient limits." Whitworth mentioned this overture to Cobenzl, and saw him blush for the first time on record.[2] Probably, then, the scheme had some powerful backing; but now Austria had crossed the Rubicon.

At first all went well. The French had played a game of bluff which they could not sustain. On all sides they were worsted in a way which suggests how decisive the campaign might have been had the Allies heartily seconded the salutary

---

[1] "Dropmore P.," iv, 297, 338, 505; "F. O.," Russia, 42.
[2] "F. O.," Russia, 42. Whitworth to Grenville, 29th March.

plans of Pitt. Unfortunately, despite his efforts, no compact came about between Great Britain and Austria. Russia and the Hapsburg State were but loosely connected; and, owing to a long delay in the arrival of the ratification of the Anglo-Russian Treaty, Paul did not until the beginning of May send forward the subsidized army under the command of Korsakoff.

On the other hand, the auxiliary Russian force sent forward to the help of Austria had by that time helped the white-coats to win notable triumphs in North Italy. In the months of April and May, Melas and the Imperialists, powerfully backed by Suvóroff's Muscovites, carried all before them, and drove the enemy from Milan. Soon afterwards the Allies entered Turin; and only by hard fighting and heavy losses did Moreau with the chief French army cut his way through to the Genoese coast. Meanwhile General Macdonald, retiring with a French corps from Naples, left that city to the vengeance of Nelson and Maria Carolina with results that are notorious. The French general made a brave stand in North Italy, only to fall before the onsets of the Allies at the Trebbia (17th-19th June). He, too, barely escaped to Genoa, where the relics of the two French armies faced about. These successes aroused the highest hopes at Westminster. Canning, who resigned his Under-Secretaryship of Foreign Affairs in March 1799, wrote that he cared not whether the Austrians were beaten; for their failure would serve as a good example to Europe. But in June, after their brilliant successes, he expressed a confident hope of the collapse of "the monstrous fabrick of crimes and cruelties and abominations" known as French policy; he added that Prussia could not be so stupid as to hold aloof from the Coalition; and that Pitt, again vigorous in mind and body, would carry through the war to the end.

But now in the train of victory there appeared its parasite, discord. The re-conquest of Italy was so brilliant and easy as to arouse disputes about the spoils; and when the Imperialists began to treat Suvóroff and his heroes cavalierly, the feud became acute. His complaints to his Sovereign that the Austrians thwarted him at every turn threw the irascible Czar into a rage, and he inveighed against the insolence of the Court of Vienna and its minions. Finally, in order to end these disputes, the British Ministry proposed the departure of Suvóroff to Switzerland in order to take command of Korsakoff's subsidized force.

In the third week of June Grenville urged this plan on the Russian Court as securing concentration of force and unity of command, the result in all probability being the liberation of Switzerland, whereupon the Allies could prepare for an invasion of France on her undefended flank, Franche Comté. England (added Grenville) disapproved of the presence of " Louis XVIII " at the Russian headquarters; and if Monsieur, his brother, issued a declaration, it must be drafted with care. The need of caution appears in Monsieur's offer of pardon and clemency to the misguided French, provided that they joined his standard.[1]

The Allies, it will be seen, built their hopes on a revolt of the royalists of the East of France. In fact, widespread risings were expected. Bordeaux had been the centre of a conspiracy for leaguing together the malcontents of la Vendée with those of the South, these again being in touch with the royalists of the Lyonnais and Franche Comté. Wickham, who was sent as British agent to Switzerland in June 1799, opened up an extensive correspondence which promised to lead to a formidable revolt whenever the Allies invaded Franche Comté and Nice. The malcontents had as leaders Generals Précy, Pichegru, and Willot. In due course the Comte d'Artois (" Monsieur ") was to appear and put himself at their head. Accordingly, in August 1799, he left Holyrood, came to London, and dined at Grenville's house with him and Pitt. The Prime Minister afterwards paid him a private visit: but the details of their conference are not known. It is certain, however, that the Cabinet accorded large sums of money to Wickham for use in the East of France. Even after the failure in Switzerland, he pressed for the payment of £365,000 in order to maintain the royalist movement.[2]

Pitt, then, was bent on using all possible means for humbling France; and, in view of her disasters in the field, the discontent at home, and the absence of Bonaparte's army in Egypt, the triumph of the Allies seemed to depend solely on their unanimity. Much can be said in favour of the British plan of uniting the two Russian armies in Switzerland to act with that of the Archduke Charles, in order to strike at Franche Comté in overwhelming force, while the Austrians in Italy invaded Nice. If all the moves had taken place betimes, formidable forces

[1] " F. O.," Russia, 43. Grenville to Whitworth, 23rd June.
[2] G. Caudrillier, " L'Association royaliste . . . et la Conspiration anglaise en France " (Paris, 1908); Wickham, " Corresp.," ii, *passim*.

would have been massed for an attack upon the weakest parts of the French frontier. The Czar agreed to the plan on 9th July; but the Emperor Francis withheld his sanction for a suspiciously long time. Here again, as in 1794-6, the men of the pen interfered with the men of the sword. Immersed in plans for a vast extension of Austria's domains in Italy, Thugut turned a deaf ear to the demands of Russia and England for the restoration of the House of Savoy to the throne of Turin. He declared that, as Austria had recovered the continental domains of that dynasty, she could therefore dispose of them. It soon appeared that she sought to appropriate Piedmont, as well as Venetia, Lombardy, Parma, Modena, and the northern part of the Papal States in place of her troublesome Belgic domains, thus liberally fulfilling Pitt's suggestion that her chief gains should be on the side of Italy.

On this question Pitt and Grenville differed. The latter, sympathizing with Russia, strongly objected to Austria annexing Piedmont. Pitt, however, maintained that such an acquisition would not resemble the partition of Poland or of Venetia; for Charles Emmanuel had lost his lands through his own weakness, and now did nothing towards recovering them. Further, it was to the advantage of Europe that the rescuing Power, Austria, should hold them as a barrier against France. If the Czar Paul could not be induced to take this view we might leave the two Empires to settle the matter; but, at present this solution offered the best chance of arriving at a compact with Austria so much to be desired. Thus, in order to strengthen the Barrier System against France, Pitt was prepared to sacrifice legal rights to expediency, while Grenville upheld the claims of justice.

Limits of space preclude an investigation of the causes of the humiliating failure of the campaign in Switzerland. Suffice it to say that, when Korsakoff's army finally entered the north-east of Switzerland, the Archduke Charles was compelled by imperious mandates from Vienna to withdraw into Swabia. He foresaw disaster; and it soon came. While Suvóroff's army was toiling down the northern defiles of the St. Gotthard, Masséna, after receiving strong reinforcements, overwhelmed Korsakoff at Zurich (25th-26th September). That Pitt expected defeat after the withdrawal of the Archduke Charles appears from his letter to Windham:

Downing Street, 30*th August* 1799.[1]

I should gladly accept your proposal to join the water-party today, but I came to town to meet Lord Grenville; and, having seen him, I am preparing to return part of the way to Walmer in the course of the evening. I was brought to town by the vexatious accounts from Vienna, which give too great a chance of our being disappointed in our best hopes by the blind and perverse selfishness of Austria's counsels.

Grenville was equally indignant and accused Austria of treachery.[2] Much can be said in support of that charge. Whatever may have been her motive, her conduct ruined the campaign. South-east of Zurich, Soult routed Hotze's Austrian corps, which might have linked the movements of Suvóroff with those of Korsakoff, and Suvóroff on arriving at Altorff found no other course practicable than to strike away eastwards over the Panixer Pass to Coire in the Grisons. There he arrived after severe hardships on 8th October, and swore never again to act with the Austrians. Paul, on hearing these dire tidings, registered the same vow, and informed the Viennese Court that thenceforth he separated his interests entirely from hers. Thus was it that Pitt's plans miscarried. Thus was it that British subsidies were flung away into the limbo strewn with tokens of Hapsburg fatuity.

The Anglo-Russian effort against the Batavian Republic is often referred to as if it were the principal event of the year 1799. On the contrary, it was little more than a diversion intended to help the chief enterprise in Switzerland and Franche Comté. The Czar Paul and Pitt probably did not intend to hold the Dutch Provinces unless the Allies pressed France hard on the Swiss frontier and the Orange party rose in force. If these contingencies held good, then Holland might be held as far as the River Waal. If not, then the effort must be temporary. Even so, its advantages were great. The seizure of the Dutch fleet at the Texel and Helder would end all chance of invasion from that quarter. Fears of such an attempt had prompted a counter-stroke dealt by General Coote's force in the spring of 1798 at the sluice-gates near Ostend. Its surrender under un-

---

B.M. Add. MSS., 37844.

[2] " Dropmore P.," v, 400. I propose to examine this campaign in " Pitt and Napoleon Miscellanies."

toward circumstances was, perhaps, nearly counterbalanced by the destruction of canal works necessary for the assembly of the flat-bottomed boats at Ostend.

For a brief space the doubtful attitude of Prussia led Pitt and Grenville to concert a larger scheme. They hoped to form a great array of Prussians, Russians, Britons, and Hanoverians which would sweep the French out of Holland; but obviously such a plan depended on the support of the Berlin Cabinet. If it were hostile, or even unfriendly, no force could advance through Hanover for the delivery of Holland; for it would be at the mercy of Prussia. In order to bring her into the league, Pitt and Grenville held out the promise of gains near the Dutch frontier; but she held coyly aloof, doubtless from a conviction that Austria would oppose her aggrandisement. So at least Thugut declared to Eden on his departure from Vienna. Well might his successor, Lord Minto, remark that the Allies spent as much time in watching each other's moves as those of the enemy.

Prussia being immovable, England and Russia laid their plans for a naval expedition to Holland. By a Convention signed at midsummer 1799 at St. Petersburg, Russia agreed to send a squadron of 11 ships, convoying an expeditionary force of 17,500 men to the Dutch coast, England paying £44,000 per month for their services after embarkation. The Czar hoped that England would send some 6,000 men. The help of 8,000 Swedes was also expected; but the King of Sweden, annoyed at England's seizure of Swedish merchantmen, refused all assistance. For a time Pitt desired both to attack the Island of Voorn below Rotterdam, and to effect a landing in the estuary of the Ems, provided that 25,000 British, 18,000 Russians, and 8,000 Swedes were available. Here, as so often, Pitt's hopes outran the actuality. Windham believed that he wished to conquer Flanders. But Windham's moods were so various and perverse that he can scarcely be trusted. In his view every effort not directed towards Brittany was wasted ; and certainly feints against the coasts of Brittany and Spain promised to further the Dutch expedition.[1]

---

[1] "F. O.," Russia, 43. Whitworth to Grenville, 23rd June 1799; "Dropmore P.," v, 133, 259; Windham, "Diary," 411. On 22nd July Windham urged Pitt to send a force to help the Bretons rather than to Holland. "If we succeed in France, Holland falls of course, but not *vice versa*" (Pitt MSS., 190).

Early in August Pitt and his colleagues finally resolved to send the expedition to the Dutch coast; but they had not decided as to the length or extent of the occupation. So, at least, it appears from a letter of Pitt to Sir Charles Grey:

Downing Street, *Aug.* 23, 1799.[1]

You will not wonder that the circumstances of the present moment have strongly recalled to Mr. Dundas's mind and mine the conversations which we have at different times had with you respecting the possibility of a successful stroke against Brest. The assemblage of the combined fleets[2] in that port renders such an object more tempting than ever. We have a prospect, if the expedition in Holland should terminate speedily, of having a large army of 30,000 men at least, and a large body of marines, with any number of sail-of-the-line that may be thought necessary, applicable to such a service by the month of October; and if the Allies continue to push their operations on the other side of France, the bulk of the French force will find sufficient occupation at a distance from their coast. In all these respects the time seems as favourable as it can ever be expected to be to such an enterprise; and if it is to be undertaken, we shall derive the greatest confidence of success from seeing the execution of it placed in your hands. Many circumstances may undoubtedly arise in the course of the next six weeks which may oblige us to abandon the idea. . . .

This letter proves that Pitt did not expect a prolonged occupation of Holland, at least by British troops; but the notions of Ministers on this topic were singularly hazy. All things considered, the expedition at first fared well. Sir Ralph Abercromby, the leader of the first detachment of some 12,000 British troops, effected a landing near the forts at the Helder, and on 27th August speedily captured them. Three days later Admiral Mitchell captured a squadron of 10 sail-of-the-line and several frigates anchored behind the Texel. Pitt was elated by these successes, and wrote from Walmer Castle on 5th September: " We are impatiently waiting till this east wind brings our transports in sight to carry the remainder of our troops, in order to compleat speedily what has been so gloriously begun." He adds that in a short autumn session he hopes speedily to pass by acclamation a Bill ensuring the doubling of the regular army by

---

[1] Pretyman MSS.

[2] That of Bruix, which after entering the Mediterranean, returned to Brest on 13th August along with the Spanish fleet.

another levy from the militia.[1] Other letters bespeak his anxiety as to the safety of his brother, the Earl of Chatham, who served on the Council of War directing the operations of the Duke of York.

Abercromby's first successes were for a time maintained. At dawn of 10th September the British force beat off a sharp attack by Vandamme at the Zuype Canal on the way southwards to Alkmaar. Three days later the Duke of York arrived and took the command, including that of a Russian corps under General Hermann. Moving forwards with some 30,000 men, the Duke attacked a Franco-Dutch force somewhat inferior in numbers but very strongly posted at and around the village of Bergen. The onset failed, mainly owing to the fierce but premature and disorderly onset of the Russians on the right wing, which ended in a rout. Abercromby's flanking movement came too late to restore the fight, which cost the British 1,000 men and the Russians more than double as many (19th September). Hermann was taken prisoner.[2]

On 2nd October the Allies compelled the enemy to retreat from Bergen; but the success was of little service. The defenders, now strongly reinforced, held several good positions between Alkmaar and Amsterdam. Meanwhile the Orange party did not stir. Torrents of rain day after day impaired the health of the troops and filled the dykes. An advance being impossible in these circumstances, the Duke of York retreated to the line of the Zuype (8th to 9th October). There he could have held his own; but, in view of the disasters in Switzerland, Ministers decided to evacuate Holland (15th October). Accordingly, by the Convention of Alkmaar, on the 18th, the Duke of York agreed to evacuate the Dutch Netherlands by the end of November, 8,000 of the prisoners of war then in England being restored. Most questionable was the decision of Ministers to evacuate the Helder and the Texel. Grenville desired to hold those posts as bases for a second attempt in 1800; but this was not done. The only result, then, was the capture of the Dutch fleet, a prize gained without loss by the end of September.

---

[1] The Earl of Crawford's MSS.

[2] Fortescue, iv, 662, 673-6; Bunbury, "Narrative of the War (1799-1810)," 50. Hermann wrote to the Emperor blaming the British for not supporting his advance ("Dropmore P.," v, 425); but on 10th October Paul dismissed him from the Russian service ("F. O.," Russia, 44).

The censures bestowed on this undertaking are very natural. Success was scarcely possible in the narrow, marshy strip of land north of Amsterdam. In such a district victory must be costly, while defeat spelt disaster. The whole enterprise was unwarrantable, unless the Orange party was about to rise; but on this subject Ministers were deceived. The Prince of Orange and his son assured them that it was necessary even to hold back the loyalists until armed help appeared, so eager were they to expel the French.[1] Not a sign of this eagerness appeared.

Undaunted by this failure, which Sheridan wittily called nibbling at the French rind, Pitt sought to utilize the Russian force withdrawn from Holland for the projected blow at Brest. It was therefore taken to the Channel Islands, greatly to the hurt of the inhabitants. Pitt and Grenville also concerted plans with the Austrian Court, which, chastened by the disasters in Switzerland, now displayed less truculence. It agreed to repay the loan of May 1797, to restore Piedmont to the House of Savoy, and to give back to France any provinces conquered in the war, on condition of the re-establishment of monarchy. Thus, a friendly understanding was at last arrived at; and on 24th December 1799 Grenville empowered Minto to prepare a treaty, adding that on the first opportunity the French Government should be informed of this engagement.

The occasion occurred at once. Bonaparte, having become master of France by the *coup d'état* of Brumaire (10th November), wrote on Christmas Day to Francis II and George III proposing terms of peace. The statesmanlike tone of that offer has been deservedly admired; but his motives in making it do not concern us here.[2] Suffice it to say that Pitt and Thugut saw in it a clever device for sundering the Anglo-Austrian compact. As appears from a letter of Canning, Pitt looked on the new Consular Government as a make-shift. Writing early in December to Canning, Pitt stated that the new French constitution might prove to be of a moderate American kind. To this Canning answered on the 7th that it might perhaps last long enough to admit of Bonaparte sending off a courier to London and receiving the reply if he were kicked back. Or more probably, France would fall under a military despotism, "of the actual and manifest instability of which you seem to entertain

---

[1] "Dropmore P.," v, 446.   [2] See Rose, "Napoleon I," 240-2.

no doubt." In answer to Pitt's statement "that we ought not to commit ourselves by any declaration that the restoration of royalty is the *sine qua non* condition of peace," Canning advised him to issue a declaration "that you would treat with a monarchy; that to the monarchy restored to its rightful owner you would give not only peace, but peace on the most liberal terms."

Clearly, then, Pitt was less royalist than Canning; but he decided to repel all overtures from Paris (so he wrote to Dundas on 31st December), because the condition of France did not provide a solid security for a peace. He added that he desired "to express strongly the eagerness with which we should embrace any opening for general peace whenever such solid security should be attainable. This may, I think, be so expressed as to convey to the people of France that the shortest road to peace is by effecting the restoration of Royalty, and thereby to increase the chance of that most desirable of all issues to the war." As Grenville and Dundas concurred in this view, the Foreign Office sent off a reply stating that the usual diplomatic forms would be observed; that His Majesty sought only to maintain the rights of his subjects against a war of aggression; and that the present time was unsuitable for negotiations with persons recently placed in power by a Revolution, until they should disclaim the restless and subversive schemes which threatened the framework of society. His Majesty, however, would welcome peace when it could be attained with security, the best pledge of which would be the restoration of Royalty.

This reply ranks among the greatest mistakes of the time. It made the name of the Bourbons odious and that of Bonaparte popular throughout France; and the scornful references to the First Consul's insecurity must have re-doubled the zeal of Frenchmen for the erection of a truly national and monarchical system under his auspices. In truth, it is difficult to see why Pitt, who held out the olive-branch to the newly-established Directory in the autumn of 1795, should have repelled the proffered hand of Bonaparte. The probable explanation is that he thought more of the effect of the reply at Vienna than at Paris. On 6th January Grenville forwarded a copy to Minto, expressing also the hope that it would be regarded as a sign of the fidelity of England to the Emperor. Further, Pitt's oration on 3rd February 1800 on this topic was marked by extreme acerbity against Bonaparte. He descanted on his perfidy and rapacity at the expense of Venice and the Sultan's dominions, and deprecated a compact with "this last adventurer in the lottery of Revolutions. . . . As a sincere lover of peace," he added, "I will not sacrifice it by grasping at the shadow, when the reality is not substantially within my reach. *Cur igitur pacem nolo? Quia infida est, quia periculosa, quia esse non potest.*"[1] In reply to a verbal challenge from Tierney a fortnight later, he fired off an harangue which ranks among the ablest and most fervid of improvisations. The Whig leader having defied him to state in one sentence without *ifs* and *buts* the object of the war, Pitt flung back the retort:

... I know not whether I can do it in one sentence, but in one word I can tell him that it is security; security against a danger the greatest that ever threatened the world; . . . against a danger which has been resisted by all the nations of Europe, and resisted by none with so much success as by this nation, because by none has it been resisted so uniformly and with so much energy. . . . How or where did the honourable gentleman discover that the Jacobinism of Robespierre, of Barère, of the Triumvirate, of the Five Directors, which he acknowledged to be real, has vanished and disappeared because it has all been centred and condensed into one man, who was reared and nursed in its bosom, whose celebrity was gained under its auspices, who was at once the child and champion of all its atrocities and horrors? Our security in negotiation is to be this Buonaparte, who is now the sole organ of all that was formerly dangerous and pestiferous in the Revolution. . . . *If* peace afford no prospect of security; *if* it threaten all the evils which we have been struggling to avert; *if* the prosecution of the war afford the prospect of attaining complete security; and *if* it may be prosecuted with increasing commerce, with increasing means, and with increasing prosperity, except what may result from the visitations of the seasons; then I say it is prudent in us not to negotiate at the present moment. These are my *buts* and my *ifs*. This is my plea, and on no other do I wish to be tried by God and my country.

One who heard that spirited retort left on record the profound impression which it produced on the House.[2]

Seeing that Bonaparte was then known merely as an able *condottiere*, not as the re-organizer of French society, Pitt's haughty attitude, though deplorable, is intelligible. The pro-

[1] Cicero, Seventh Philippic, ch. iii.

The father of the present Master of Trinity College, Cambridge. See his work, "Ten Great and Good Men," 49.

spects of the war were not unfavourable. He hoped that Austria, now about to invade Nice and Savoy, would be able by her own efforts to reduce France within her old limits, England's duty being to offer help on the Riviera, to make a dash at Brest, and to seize Belleisle as a base of supplies for the Breton royalists, now once more in revolt. It is significant that Dundas wrote to Pitt on 4th January expressing his belief that Bonaparte must be serious in his desire for peace because he had no other game to play.[1]

Many influences conspired to mar these hopes. The enterprises against Brest and Belleisle proved to be impracticable, and a landing at Quiberon failed because the Breton rising occurred too soon. The royalists of Provence did not rise at all. An attempt by Sir James Pulteney and a small force upon Ferrol was an utter failure. All the operations were paralysed by uncertainty as to the future conduct of Russia. The indignation of the Czar against Austria extended to England after the failure of the joint expedition to Holland; and his testiness increased owing to maritime disputes and the friction caused by the outrages of his troops in the Channel Islands. In the Riviera the Austrians continued their successes, and finally shut up Masséna in Genoa, where the British fleet rendered valuable service. But it is not surprising to find Grenville writing on 10th April to Dundas: "For God's sake, for your own honour, and for the cause in which we are engaged, do not let us, after having by immense exertions collected a fine army, leave it unemployed, gaping after messengers from Genoa, Augsburg, and Vienna till the moment for acting is irrecoverably passed by."

This, however, was the outcome of events. The French, acting on interior lines, and propelled by the will of Bonaparte, utterly crushed these sporadic efforts. The Royalists were quelled or pacified, the coasts were well guarded, while the First Consul, crossing the Great St. Bernard, overthrew the Austrians at Marengo (14th June). Before long Naples made peace with the conqueror. Meanwhile the Sea Power, operating on diverse coasts, delayed, but did not reverse, the progress of the French arms. British forces for a time defended Portugal and held Minorca and the citadel of Messina, but without any appreciable effect on Spain or Italy. The fleet played an important part in starving out the

---

[1] Pretyman MSS.

French garrisons of Genoa and Valetta. But elsewhere the action, or inaction, of the British forces was discreditable. True, the conditions were adverse, but an army numbering more than 80,000 men, and costing nearly £10,000,000 sterling, should have accomplished something in Europe.

Only at one point did the British arms win a decisive success, The French occupation of Egypt had aroused the apprehensions of Dundas for India; and throughout the year 1800 he continued to urge an expedition to Egypt, though other Ministers inclined to put it off. Finally, when Bonaparte's triumph at Marengo shattered all hopes of an Austrian invasion of Provence, and the surrender of Valetta, early in September, set free the British squadron long blockading that port, Dundas pressed the Egyptian project in a letter to Pitt, dated Wimbledon, 19th September 1800. The gist of it is as follows: [1]

On reconsidering the discussion on Egypt at the Cabinet meeting of yesterday, I am impressed by the danger of delaying action. The importance of expelling the French from Egypt is obvious; for it is clear that Bonaparte will subordinate every object to the retention of that colony. The danger to India may not be immediate, but it must be faced. Besides, our sacrifice of Turkish interests to those of Austria [that is, by refusing to ratify the Franco-Turkish Convention of El Arish] may induce the Sultan to bargain with France on terms very unfavourable to us. Or, again, France and Russia may plan a partition of the Ottoman Empire. The objections, that we are pledged to do what we can for Portugal and Austria, are not vital. For Portugal is safe while the Viennese Court opposes France; and by our subsidies and naval help we have borne our fair share in the Coalition. Further efforts in that direction will be fruitless. We must now see to our own interests. By occupying all the posts of Egypt, we can coop up the French and force them to capitulate. Action must not be postponed for any consideration whatever.

The opinion of Dundas soon prevailed; for, on 6th October, Grenville wrote that the Egyptian Expedition was decided on. As is well known, the joint efforts of forces from England, India, and the Cape of Good Hope brought about the surrender of the French garrisons, and the acquisition for the British Museum of the treasures designed for the Louvre. This brilliant result was in the last instance due to Abercromby, Hutchinson, Popham, and

[1] Pretyman MSS.

their coadjutors. But the enterprise resulted from the untiring championship of the interests of India by Dundas. Long afterwards at Perthshire dinner-tables he used to tell with pride how George III once proposed a toast to the Minister who planned the expedition to Egypt and in doing so had the courage to oppose not only his colleagues but his King.

As the year 1800 drew to its close, the opposition of the Baltic Powers to the British maritime code became most threatening. The questions at issue are too technical to be discussed here. Pitt and his colleagues believed the maintenance of the rights of search and of the seizure of an enemy's goods on neutral ships to be essential to the existence of England. For this view of the case much was to be said. In every war France used neutral ships in order to get supplies; and the neutrals themselves sought to filch trade from British merchants. Now, to hinder or destroy the commerce of the enemy, and to prevent neutrals from bringing naval stores to his ports, were the only means of bringing pressure from the sea upon the dominant Land Power. In a strife for life or death Pitt and his colleagues perforce made use of every weapon, even to the detriment of non-combatants. This stiff attitude, however, contrasted with that of Bonaparte, who, in July 1800 flattered the Czar by sending back Russian prisoners and by offering to cede Malta to him. Paul, not knowing that the fall of Valetta was imminent, was duped by this device; and, a few weeks later, occurred the rupture between Russia and England.

Thus, within a year, the Second Coalition against France went to pieces, and was succeeded by a league against England. Thanks to the victory of Nelson at Copenhagen and the murder of the Czar Paul in the spring of 1801, that unnatural alliance speedily collapsed. These events, however, belong to a time subsequent to Pitt's resignation of office, after the completion of the union with Ireland, to which we must now return. Enough has been said to show the statesmanlike nature of his plans for the vindication of European independence. The intrigues of Thugut, the selfish isolation of Prussia, and the mad oscillations of Paul marred those plans and left the Continent a prey to the unbridled ambition of Bonaparte, from which it was to be saved only after a decade of exhausting wars.

CHAPTER XVIII

THE UNION

I am determined not to submit to the insertion of any clause that shall make the exclusion of the Catholics a fundamental part of the Union, as I am fully convinced that, until the Catholics are admitted into a general participation of rights (which, when incorporated with the British Government, they cannot abuse) there will be no peace or safety in Ireland.—CORNWALLIS TO ROSS, 30*th September* 1798.

THE fairest method of dealing with the Act of Union of the British and Irish Parliaments seems to be, firstly, to trace the development of Pitt's thoughts on that subject; secondly, to survey the state of affairs in Ireland after the Rebellion of 1798; and thirdly, to trace the course of the negotiations whereby the new Lord Lieutenant, Cornwallis, succeeded in carrying through the measure itself.

Firstly, it is clear that Pitt had long felt the need of closer commercial ties between the two islands. As was shown in Chapter XI of the former part of this work, he sought to prepare the way for such a measure in the session of 1785. The importance which he attached to the freeing of inter-insular trade appears in a phrase of his letter of 6th January 1785 to the Duke of Rutland as to Great Britain and Ireland becoming "one country in effect, though for local concerns under distinct legislatures." This represents his first thoughts on the subject. Obviously they were then limited to a commercial union. If the two Parliaments and the two nations could have shaken off their commercial jealousies, Pitt would probably have been satisfied with fostering the prosperity of both islands, while leaving their legislative machinery intact. But, being thwarted by the stupidity of British traders and the nagging tactics adopted at Dublin, he wrote to Rutland that his plan was not discredited by failure and they must " await times and seasons for carrying it into effect."

Times and seasons brought, not peace and quiet, but the

French Revolution. With it there came an increase of racial and religious feuds, which, however, did but strengthen his conviction of the need of a closer connection between the two islands; witness his letter of 18th November 1792 to the Lord Lieutenant, the Earl of Westmorland:

> The idea of the present fermentation gradually bringing both parties to think of an Union with this country has long been in my mind. I hardly dare flatter myself with the hope of its taking place; but I believe it, tho' itself not easy to be accomplished, to be the only solution for other and greater difficulties. The admission of Catholics to a share of suffrage could not then be dangerous. The Protestant interest, in point of power, property and Church Establishment, would be secure because the decided majority of the supreme Legislature would necessarily be Protestant; and the great ground of argument on the part of the Catholics would be done away, as, compared with the rest of the Empire, they would become a minority. You will judge when and to whom this idea can be confided. It must certainly require great delicacy and management; but I am heartily glad that it is at least in your thoughts.[1]

These words show why Pitt allowed proposals so imperfect as the Franchise Bill of 1793 to become law. It enfranchised most of the Irish peasantry, the great majority of whom were Catholics, though men of their creed were excluded from Parliament. But he hoped in the future to supplement it by a far greater measure which would render the admission of Catholics to Parliament innocuous, namely, by the formation of a united Parliament in which they would command only a small minority of votes. Pitt's words open up a vista which receded far away amidst the smoke of war and the mirage of bigotry, and did not come into sight until the second decade of the period of peace, when Canning, Pitt's disciple, was the chief champion of the measure here first clearly outlined. Pitt, then, desired a Union as the sole means of ending commercial disputes, otherwise as insoluble as those between England and Scotland previous to the year 1707; but also for an even weightier reason, because only so could the religious discords of Irishmen be ended; only so could the chafing of the majority against the rule of a cramping caste cease. By the formation of an Imperial Parliament, the Irish Protestants would have solid guarantees against the subversion of all that they held most dear.

---

[1] Salomon, "Pitt," 599. See, too, the similar letter of Richmond to his sister, Lady Conolly, in June 1795 (Lecky, vii, 134).

The full realization of these aims was impossible. Early in 1793 came war with France, with its sequel, the heating of nationalist and religious feeling in Ireland; and while the officials of Dublin Castle embarked on a policy of repression, the United Irishmen looked for help to Paris. The results appeared in the Rebellion of 1798. The oft-repeated assertion that Pitt and Camden brought about the revolt in order to force on the Union is at variance with all the available evidence. They sought by all possible means to prevent a rising, which, with a reasonable amount of help from France, must have shaken the British Empire to its base. When the rebellion came and developed into a bloody religious feud, they saw that the time for a Union had come.

The best means of checking hasty generalizations is to peruse letters written at the time, before ingenious theories could be spun. Now, the definite proposal of a Union very rarely occurs before the month of June 1798. One of the first references is in a letter of the Lord Chancellor, Loughborough, to Pitt, dated 13th June 1798. After approving the appointment of Cornwallis as the best means of quelling the revolt in Ireland, he adds: " Every reasonable man in that country must feel that their preservation depends on their connection with England, and it ought [to] be their first wish to make it more entire. It would be very rash to make any such suggestion from hence: but we should be prepared to receive it and to impose the idea whenever it begins to appear in Ireland." [1]

More important, as showing the impossibility of continuing the present chaotic administration at Dublin, is the following letter from the Earl of Carlisle, formerly Lord Lieutenant, to Pitt. It is undated, but probably belongs to 2nd June 1798: [2]

. . . It may perhaps be but a weak apology for this interruption to own I cannot help looking at that country [Ireland] with a sort of affection, like an old house which one has once inhabited, not disliking the antient arrangement of its interior, and perhaps unreasonably prejudiced against many of its modern innovations. The innovation that has long given me uneasiness, and which now seems most seriously to perplex the Irish Government, was the fatal institution of an Irish Cabinet, which has worked itself into being, considered almost as a component part of that deputed authority. A Government composed of Lords Justices,

[1] Pitt MSS., 328.   [2] Ibid., 169.

natives of that country, as a permanent establishment, absurd as such an expedient might be, would not have at least that radical defect of authority disjoined from responsibility. We now feel all the bad effects of a power which should never have been confer'd, and which is strengthen'd from hence by many acting with you, so as to make it impossible for the Lord Lieutenant to manage with it or without it.

You have, in my poor judgment, an opportunity offer'd to crush at one blow this defective system. Ireland, I scruple not to say, cannot be saved if you permit an hour longer almost the military defence of that country to depend upon the tactical dictates of Chancellors, Speaker of the House of Commons, etc. I mean to speak with no disrespect of Lord Camden; I never heard anything but to his honour; but I maintain under the present circumstances the best soldier would make the best Lord-Lieutenant; one on whom no Junto there would presume to fling their shackles, and one who would cut them short if they presumed to talk of what they did not understand. With this idea, I confess, Ld Cornwallis naturally occurs to me. Next to this, but not so efficacious, would be sending some one equal to the military duties, freed from all control, saving that, for form's sake, good sense would acquiesce under to [sic] the King's Deputy. But I cannot doubt but a deeper change would be most advisable. The disaffected to our Government (and I fear it is too general) may perhaps have their degrees and divisions of animosity against it, and some possibly may be changed by a change of men more than by a professed change of measures, which perhaps they think little about. I know they are taught to believe a particular set of men are their enemies; in truth I question if, in tyrannising over and thwarting the Castle, and talking so injudiciously, they ought to be considered as our friends. . . .

Thus the man to whom in 1795 Earl Fitzwilliam poured forth his grievances against Pitt, now advised him to end the mischievous dualism at Dublin, which enabled Lords Justices and the Speaker of the Irish House of Commons to paralyse the Executive. There, as at Berlin, advisers who had great influence but no official responsibility, often intervened with disastrous results; and not until Stein took the tiller after Tilsit did the Prussian ship of State pursue a straight course. At Dublin the crisis of 1798 revealed the weakness of the Irish Executive, and naturally led to a complete break with the past.[1]

Amidst the mass of Pitt's papers relating to Ireland there is no sign of his intention to press on an Act of Union before the

[1] Porritt, ii, ch. lii; Seeley, "Stein," i, 267-82.

middle of the month of June 1798, that is, in the midst of the Rebellion. The first reference to it occurs in a memorandum endorsed by Pitt "received June 19, 1798," and obviously drawn up by Camden a few days before he resigned the Viceroyalty in favour of Cornwallis. Pitt's letter of inquiry is missing. Camden's reply is too long for quotation, but may be thus summarized:

The plan of a Union should be detailed as far as possible before it is attempted. The King's Cabinet should be at once consulted, also leading persons in both islands. If their opinion is favourable, the measure should then be brought forward. If the Catholic claims are to be met, the advice of their leading men, as for instance Lords Fingal and Kenmare, should be sought. The legal attainments of the Irish Chancellor, the Earl of Clare, and the parliamentary and commercial connections of the Speaker, Foster, entitle their opinions to great weight. Foster may perhaps be won over by the offer of an English peerage. The Irish Bar, as also Lords Shannon and Ely, will probably oppose a Union. Some persons will object to the admission of Catholics even to the United Parliament, though that measure cannot do harm. The Scottish Catholics should have the same privileges accorded to them, and a provision should be made for the Dissenting clergy. Parliamentary Reform must be considered, but it will not be dangerous now. The French will never make peace until Great Britain is weakened. The religious difficulty of a Union will not be great, for the Protestants will always form the majority in the United Parliament. Legal expenses in the case of Irish suits will be little more than in Scottish suits. As Dublin will suffer from the removal of the Parliament, the Lord Lieutenant's Court must be kept up in great splendour, the residence of influential persons in Ireland being encouraged in every possible way. The communications between the two islands must be improved, free packet-boats being provided. In a postscript Camden adds that he hopes Cornwallis will continue the present repressive policy, which otherwise must appear unduly harsh by contrast.[1]

The most significant passages are those in which Camden refers to the plan of a Union as so unformed as to require preliminary inquiries, and in which he presumes that after the Union Dissenters and Catholics will have "the same advantages as are bestowed upon the rest of the inhabitants of the three kingdoms." Clearly, then, Pitt and Camden had come to no decision on the Union; but Camden, from what he knew of Pitt's views,

---

[1] Pitt MSS., 326. For the text in full see " Pitt and Napoleon Miscellanies."

believed that he favoured a broad and inclusive policy, not a Union framed on a narrowly Protestant basis. Neither of them seems to have anticipated serious resistance on the religious question, even though the King, at the time of the Fitzwilliam crisis of 1795, had declared the admission of Catholics to the Irish Parliament to be a matter which concerned his conscience, not his Cabinet.

It is also obvious that the question of the Union was forced to the front by the cumbrous dualism of the Irish Executive, which proved to be utterly unable to cope with the crisis of the Rebellion. The King, as we have seen, shrewdly suggested that Cornwallis ought to make use of the fears of Irish loyalists in order to frighten the Dublin Parliament into acquiescence in an Act of Union. The same opinion was gaining ground; but several of Pitt's supporters doubted the advisability of so far-reaching a measure. Thus, on 4th July 1798, Hatsell, Clerk of the House of Commons, wrote to Auckland that of all possible plans a Union was the worst, " full of difficulties, to be brought about by errant jobs; and, when done, not answering the purpose. You must take out the teeth, or give the Catholics sops to eat. One or other; but the half-measure won't do." Better balanced was the judgement of the Earl of Carlisle, as stated to Auckland some time in September. After asking whether the recurrence of local risings in Ireland did not prove the unwisdom of the policy of lenience pursued by Cornwallis, he added these significant words: " In this distress it is not strange that we should turn to the expedient of Union; but this is running in a dark night for a port we are little acquainted with. . . . If you did not satisfy Ireland by the measure and take off some part of those ill-disposed to England, you would only make matters worse. But in truth something must be done, or we must fight for Ireland once a week." [1]

That the activity of the rebels varied according to the prospects of aid from France was manifest. Thus, on 25th July Beresford wrote to Auckland that the people seemed tired of rebellion, which would die out unless the French landed. But on 22nd August, after the arrival of Humbert's little force in Killala Bay, he described the whole country as in revolt. The State prisoners, O'Connor, McNevin, and Addis Emmett, sent

[1] B.M. Add. MSS., 34454.

to the papers a denial of their former pacific assurances;[1] and even after the surrender of Humbert's force, Beresford wrote to Auckland on 15th September: ". . . Should the French or the Dutch get out an armament and land, there will be a very general rising. I have it from a man on whose veracity I can depend, and who was on the spot in Mayo, during the French invasion, that the Catholics of the country ran to join them with eagerness, and that they had more than they could arm; that, as they moved on, they were constantly joined; but he says the Irish behaved so ill that the French made use of discipline, which thinned their ranks; however, they had 4,000 of them when they were attacked by Colonel Vereker, and about 200 of the Limerick militia. By our late accounts there are said to be in Mayo and Roscommon 10,000 rebels up: they are destroying the country."[2] Beresford then blames the Viceroy's proclamation, offering pardon to rebels who come in within a month, and he says their leaders tell them that 20,000 French will soon land. Equally significant is the statement of George Rose in a letter of 23rd September. Referring to the fact that two French warships had got away from Brest towards the Irish coast, he writes: "If they land, the struggle may be more serious. The truth is that it will be nearly impossible to keep Ireland as a conquered country. Union is become more urgent than ever." This was also the opinion of Lord Sheffield. Writing on 29th September from Rottingdean to Auckland, he remarks on the disquieting ease with which the French squadrons reach Ireland. He has had a long argument with the Irish Judge, Sir William Downes, and proved to him the necessity of a Union with Ireland. But (he proceeds) it will never take place, if it is set about publicly.

Irish loyalists united in decrying the comparatively lenient methods of Cornwallis; but, despite the urgent advice of Camden to Pitt, the change of system met with approval at Downing Street. This is the more remarkable as letters from Dublin were full of invectives against Cornwallis. Buckingham wrote almost daily to his brother, Grenville, foretelling ruin from the weakness and vacillation of the Lord Lieutenant. Still more furious were Beresford, Cooke, and Lees. Their correspondence with Auckland, Postmaster-General at London, was so systematic as to imply design. Probably they sought to procure the dismissal of

[1] See my article in the "Eng. Hist. Rev." for October 1910.
[2] B.M. Add. MSS., 34454.

Cornwallis and the nomination of Auckland in his place. There can be little doubt that Auckland lent himself to the scheme with a view to maintaining the Protestant ascendancy unimpaired; for he wrote to Beresford that public opinion in England favoured the maintenance of the existing order of things in Church and State in both kingdoms. The following extracts from the letters which he received from Cooke and Lees are typical. On 4th October Lees writes: "I am afraid Lord Cornwallis is not devil enough to deal with the devils he has to contend with in this country. . . . The profligacy of the murderous malignant disposition of Paddy soars too high for his humane and merciful principles at this crisis." Cooke was less flowery but equally emphatic: "If," he wrote on 22nd October, "your Union is to be Protestant, we have 100,000 Protestants who are connected by Orange Lodges, and they might be made a great nstrument. . . . Our robberies and murders continue; and the depredations of the mountain rebels increase."[1]

Nevertheless Cornwallis held on his way. In the period 22nd August 1798 to the end of February 1799, he reprieved as many as 41 rebels out of 131 on whom sentence of death had been passed, and he commuted to banishment heavy sentences passed on 78 others. It is clear, then, that, despite the efforts of Buckingham and the officials of Dublin Castle, Pitt continued to uphold a policy of clemency. But it is equally clear that the reliance of Irish malcontents on French aid, the persistent efforts of the Brest squadron to send that aid, and the savage reprisals demanded, and when possible enforced, by the loyal minority of Irishmen, brought about a situation in which Ireland could not stand alone.[2]

Preliminary inquiries respecting the Act of Union were set on foot, and the results were summarized in Memoranda of the summer and autumn of 1798. One of them, comprised among the Pelham manuscripts, is annotated by Pitt. The compiler thus referred to the question of Catholic Emancipation: "Catholics to be eligible to all offices, civil and military, taking the present oath. Such as shall take the Oath of Supremacy in the Bill of Rights may sit in Parliament without subscribing the Abjuration. Corporation offices to be Protestant." On this Pitt wrote the following note: "The first part seems unexceptionable, and

---

[1] B.M. Add. MSS., 34455.
[2] *Ibid.*; "Cornwallis Corresp.," iii, 13.

is exactly what I wish . . . but if this oath is sufficient for office, why require a different one for Parliament? And why are Corporation offices to be exclusively Protestant, when those of the State may be Catholic?"[1] Well might Pitt ask these questions, for the whole system of exclusion by religious tests was condemned so soon as admission to Parliament ceased to depend on them. Other Memoranda dealt mainly with the difficult question of compensation to the borough-holders and placemen who would suffer by the proposed change. But for the present it will be well to deal with the question of the abolition of religious tests.

The procedure of Pitt in regard to this difficult subject was eminently cautious. As was the case before dealing with the fiscal problem in 1785, so now he invited over certain leading Irishmen in order to discuss details. About the middle of October he had two interviews with the Earl of Clare, Lord Chancellor of Ireland. These important conferences took place at Holwood, where he was then occupied in marking out a new road; for his pastime every autumn was to indulge his favourite pursuit of planting trees and otherwise improving his grounds. The two ablest men in the sister kingdoms must have regarded one another with interest. They were not unlike in figure except that Clare was short. His frame was as slight as Pitt's; his features were thin and finely chiselled. Neither frame nor features bespoke the haughty spirit and dauntless will that enabled him at times to turn the current of events and overbear the decisions of Lords Lieutenant. In forcefulness and narrowness, in bravery and bigotry, he was a fit spokesman of the British garrison, which was resolved to hold every outwork of the citadel.

The particulars of their converse are unknown. Probably Clare had the advantage which a man of narrow views but expert knowledge enjoys over an antagonist who trusts in lofty principles and cherishes generous hopes. Clare, knowing his ground thoroughly, must have triumphed. Pitt did not confess his defeat. Indeed, on 16th October, he wrote reassuringly to Grenville: "I have had two very full conversations with Lord Clare. What he says is very encouraging to the great question of the Union, in which I do not think we shall have much difficulty; I mean, in proportion to the magnitude of the subject.

<hr />

[1] Lecky, viii, 328 note.

At his desire I have written to press the Speaker [Foster] to come over, which he seems to think may be of great importance." Here is Clare's version of the interviews in a letter of the same day to his fellow countryman, Castlereagh: "I have seen Mr. Pitt, the Chancellor, and the Duke of Portland, who seem to feel very sensibly the critical situation of our damnable country, and that the Union alone can save it. I should have hoped that what has passed would have opened the eyes of every man in England to the insanity of their past conduct with respect to the Papists of Ireland; but I can very plainly perceive that they were as full of their popish projects as ever. I trust, and I hope I am not deceived, that they are fairly inclined to give them up, and to bring the measure forward unencumbered with the doctrine of Emancipation. Lord Cornwallis has intimated his acquiescence in this point; Mr. Pitt is decided upon it, and I think he will keep his colleagues steady."[1]

The mention of Castlereagh seems to call for a short account of one who, after assisting in carrying the Act of Union, was destined to win a European reputation as a disciple of Pitt. Robert Stewart, Viscount Castlereagh, and second Marquis of Londonderry (1769-1822), was the son of Robert Stewart of Ballylawn in County Londonderry by his first marriage, that with the daughter of the Earl of Hertford. Educated at Armagh and at St. John's College, Cambridge, he soon returned to contest the seat of County Down with Lord Downshire, and succeeded by dint of hard work and the expenditure of £60,000. He entered the Irish Parliament as a representative of the freeholders as against the aristocracy; but the second marriage of his father (now Marquis of Londonderry) with the eldest daughter of the late Earl Camden brought the family into close connection with the second Earl, who, on becoming Lord Lieutenant in 1795, soon succeeded in detaching young Stewart from the popular party, already, from its many indiscretions, distasteful to his cool and cautious nature. Stewart had recently married Lady Emily Hobart, the daughter of the late Earl of Buckinghamshire, and became Viscount Castlereagh in October 1795. Though continuing to support the claims of the Catholics, he upheld Camden's policy of coercion; and his firm and resolute character made his support valuable in Parliament.

---

[1] "Dropmore P.," iv, 344; "Castlereagh Corresp.," i, 393.

The sagacity of his advice in committee, and the straightforward boldness of his action as an administrator, are in marked contrast to his rambling and laboured speeches, in whose incongruous phrases alone there lurked signs of Hibernian humour. "The features of the clause"; "sets of circumstances coming up and circumstances going down"; "men turning their backs upon themselves"; "the constitutional principle wound up in the bowels of the monarchy"; "the Herculean labour of the honourable member, who will find himself quite disappointed when he has at last brought forth his Hercules"—such are a few of the rhetorical gems which occasionally sparkled in the dull quartz of his plentiful output. Nevertheless, so manly was his bearing, so dogged his defence, that he always gained a respectful hearing; and supporters of the Government plucked up heart when, after a display of dazzling rhetoric by Grattan or Plunket, the young aristocrat drew up his tall figure, squared his chest, flung open his coat, and plunged into the unequal contest. Courage and tenacity win their reward; and in these qualities Castlereagh had no superior. It is said that on one occasion he determined to end a fight between two mastiffs, and, though badly bitten, he effected his purpose. These virile powers marked him out for promotion; and during the illness of Pelham, Chief Secretary at Dublin, Castlereagh discharged his duties. Cornwallis urged that he should have the appointment; and to the King's initial objection that a Briton ought to hold it, Cornwallis successfully replied that Castlereagh was "so very unlike an Irishman" that the office would be safe in his hands. Castlereagh received the appointment early in November 1798. He, the first Irishman to hold it, was destined to overthrow the Irish Parliament.[1]

We must now revert to the negotiations between Pitt and Clare. It is surprising to find Clare convinced that the Prime Minister would keep faithful to the Protestant cause its unfaithful champion, Loughborough, also that Cornwallis had acquiesced in the shelving of Catholic Emancipation. Probably Clare had the faculty, not uncommon in strong-willed men, of reading his thoughts into the words of others. For Cornwallis, writing to Pitt on 8th October, just after saying

---

[1] "Castlereagh Corresp.," i, 424 *et seq.*; "Cornwallis Corresp.," ii, 439-441; Brougham, "Statesmen of George III"; Lecky, viii, 311; Wilberforce ("Life," iii, 178) calls Castlereagh "a cold-blooded creature."

arewell to Clare at Dublin, describes him as a well-intentioned man, but blind to the absolute dependence of Irish Protestants on British support and resolutely opposed to the admission of Romanists to the united Parliament. As to himself, Cornwallis pens these noble words: "I certainly wish that England could now make a Union with the Irish nation, instead of making it with a party in Ireland"; and he expresses the hope that with fair treatment the Roman Catholics will soon become loyal subjects. Writing to the Duke of Portland in the same sense, Cornwallis shows a slight diffidence in his ability to judge of the chief question at issue.

Probably the solution of the riddle is here to be found. It seems that the Lord Lieutenant was politely deferential to Clare; that at Holwood Clare represented him as a convert to the ultra-Protestant tenets; and that Pitt accepted the statements of the Irish Chancellor. William Elliot, Under-Secretary at War at Dublin, who saw Pitt a week later, found him disinclined to further the Catholic claims at the present juncture, though equally resolved not to bar the way for the future. Possibly the King now intervened. It is a significant fact that Clare expected to have an interview with him before returning to Ireland. If so, he must have strengthened his earlier resolve. Pitt, then, gave way on the question of the admission of Dissenters and Catholics to the Irish Parliament. But he kept open the more important question of the admission of Catholics to the United Parliament. Obviously, the latter comprised the former; and it was likely to arouse the fears of the Irish Protestants far less. On tactical grounds alone the change of procedure was desirable. It is therefore difficult to see why Elliot so deeply deplored his surrender to the ultra-Protestants. Pitt had the approval of Grenville, who, owing to the religious feuds embittered by the Rebellion, deprecated the imposition of the Catholic claims on the fiercely Protestant Assembly at Dublin.[1] Yet he warmly supported them in the United Parliament, both in 1801 and 1807.

The next of the Protestant champions whom Pitt saw was Foster, Speaker of the Irish House of Commons, whose forceful will, narrow but resolute religious beliefs, and mercantile connections gave him an influence second only to that of Clare. In the course of a long conversation with him about 15th Novem-

[1] "Castlereagh Corresp.," ii, 29; "Buckingham P.," ii, 411, 412.

ber, Pitt found him frank in his opinions, decidedly opposed to
the Union, but not so fixedly as to preclude all hope of arrangement. On this topic Pitt dilated in a "private" letter of 17th
November, to Cornwallis:

· . . . I think I may venture to say that he [Foster] will not obstruct
the measure; and I rather hope if it can be made palatable to him personally (which I believe it may) that he will give it fair support. It
would, as it seems to me, be worth while for this purpose, to hold out
to him the prospect of a British peerage, with (if possible) some ostensible
situation, and a provision for life to which he would be naturally entitled on quitting the Chair. Beresford and Parnell do not say much on
the general measure, but I think both, or at least the former against
trying it, but both disposed to concur when they understand it is finally
resolved on. They all seem clearly (and I believe sincerely) of opinion
that it will not be wise to announce it as a decided measure from
authority, till time has been given for communication to all leading individuals and for disposing the public mind. On this account we have
omitted all reference to the subject in the King's Speech; and the communication may in all respects be more conveniently made by a separate
message when the Irish Parliament is sitting, and it can be announced
to them at the same time. In the interval previous to your Session there
will, I trust, be full opportunity for communication and arrangement
with individuals, on which I am inclined to believe the success of the
measure will wholly depend. You will observe that in what relates to
the oaths to be taken by members of the United Parliament, the plan
which we have sent copies the precedent I mentioned in a former
letter of the Scotch Union; and on the grounds I before mentioned, I
own I think this leaves the Catholic Question on the only footing on
which it can safely be placed. Mr. Elliott when he brought me your
letter, stated very strongly all the arguments which he thought ought to
induce us to admit the Catholics to Parliament, and office; but I confess he did not satisfy me of the practicability of such a measure at this
time, or of the propriety of attempting it. With respect to a provision
for the Catholic clergy, and some arrangement respecting tithes, I am
happy to find an uniform opinion in favor of the proposal, among all
the Irish I have seen; and I am more and more convinced that those
measures, with some effectual mode to enforce the residence of *all* ranks
of the Protestant clergy, offer the best chance of gradually putting an
end to the evils most felt in Ireland.[1]

The suggestion that Foster's opposition might be obviated

[1] Pitt MSS., 325; "Cornwallis Corresp.," ii, 441-3.

by the promise of a peerage emanated first from Camden. Its adoption by Pitt marks the first step in the by-paths of bribery on which he now entered. In this case his action is not indefensible; for the abolition of the Speakership at Dublin naturally involved some indemnity. Besides, in that Parliament no important measure passed without bribery. That eager democrat, Hamilton Rowan, foresaw in the Union "the downfall of one of the most corrupt assemblies I believe ever existed." The proprietors of the pocket-boroughs were needy and grasping, some of them living by the sale of presentation of seats. Government generally managed to control them, but only on condition of dispensing favours proportionate to the importance of the suitor and the corruptness of the occasion. As Beresford remarked with unconscious humour, the borough-mongers "cannot be expected to give up their interest for nothing; and those who bought their seats cannot be expected to give up their term for nothing." Here he expressed the general conviction of that age, which Pitt recognized in his Reform Bill of 1785 by seeking to indemnify the borough-holders of Great Britain.

A typical specimen of the borough-owner was that "ill-tempered, violent fellow," Lord Downshire, who controlled the Crown patronage in the North by virtue of his seven borough seats. Lord Ely had six seats; and the Duke of Devonshire, and Lords Abercorn, Belmore, Clifden, Granard, and Shannon, four apiece. In the counties, Downshire, the Ponsonbys, and the Beresfords controlled about twenty seats. Camden, writing to Pitt on 11th August 1799, thus described Downshire: "He is not personally corrupt; but the larger the compensation for the boroughs is to be, the more readily will he listen to you or Lord Castlereagh."[1] Lord Longueville, a borough-owner of great influence in County Cork, wrote as follows to Pitt on 3rd December, 1798:

. . . Long attached to you, and confirmed in that attachment for life by the direction and advice of Lord Westmorland, I have now no object to look up to, to prevent my falling a sacrifice to my political enemies, but to you. When Lord Shannon opposed your measures, I spent £30,000 of my own money to frustrate his intentions and support your measures. I shall now act by your advice and opinion on this great business of a Union with Great Britain. My friends are numerous and

[1] Pretyman MSS.

firm; they look up to you for decision on every occasion. My interest in Ireland is extensive. I wish to be a British peer before the measure of a Union takes place, or after. I wish the city of Cork to have two members, Bantry one and Mallow one.

Longueville gained his desire and the patronage of the Revenue offices in Cork City.[1] From Pitt's letter to Cornwallis it is clear that he believed that the promise of Government stipends for the Catholic clergy, and a reform in tithes would induce them to support the Union. But it seems impossible to reconcile his statement as to Beresford's opposition to the Union with the assertion of the latter, that, in an interview of 12th November, he pressed Pitt to take immediate steps to ensure the success of the measure, which otherwise would have to struggle against unfair odds at Dublin. The curious tendency of Hibernian affairs towards confusion also appears in Cornwallis's statement, on 15th November, that he had urged Pitt not to close the door to the Catholics in the United Parliament. Whereas Pitt was resolved to admit them at an early opportunity.[2]

On the various interests at stake there is in the Pretyman archives a long but undated Memorandum, with notes at the side by Pitt, or perhaps by Grenville; for their writing, when cramped, was similar. It recommends that the precedent of the Union with the Scottish Parliament shall be followed where possible; that few changes shall be made in the Irish legal system, appeals being allowed to the Irish Lord Chancellor and three chief judges, who may also deal with evidence for parliamentary and private Bills affecting Ireland. The general aim should be to lessen the expense of resort to the United Parliament for private business. Pitt here added at the side—"Particularly in divorces and exchange of lands in settlement," also in certain "private" Bills. The compiler then refers to the difficulty of assessing or equalizing the Revenues, National Debts, and the fiscal systems of the two islands, but suggests that on the last topic Pitt's Irish proposals of 1785 shall be followed. To this Pitt assents, suggesting also that the proportions of Revenue and Debt may soon be arranged provisionally, Commissioners being appointed to

---

[1] Pretyman MSS. "Cornwallis Corresp.," iii, 3; Macdonagh, "The Viceroy's Post Bag," 19.

[2] "Beresford Corresp.," ii, 189; "Cornwallis Corresp.," ii, 436; "Castlereagh Corresp.," i, 404.

discuss the future and definitive quotas. Further, Pitt expresses
the desire to model the election of Irish peers on that of
Scottish peers. The compiler of the plan advises a delegation
of 40 Irish peers, and not less than 120 Commoners to Westminster; but, as electoral changes are highly dangerous to both
countries, he drafts a scheme by which either 125 or 138 Irish
Commoners will sit in the United Parliament.[1]

Here Pitt and his colleagues differed from their adviser. Probably they heard rumours of the fears aroused by the advent of
Irish members. The repose of Lord Sheffield was troubled by
thoughts of the irruption of " 100 wild Irishmen "; and he deemed
the arrival of 75 quite sufficient, if staid country gentlemen were
not to be scared away from St. Stephen's. By way of compromise the Cabinet fixed the number at 100 on or before 25th
November 1798.[2] At that date Portland also informed Cornwallis that the number of Irish Peers at Westminster must not
exceed 32.

Meanwhile, the tangle at Dublin was becoming hopeless.
There, as Beresford warned Pitt, the report of the proposed
Union was the letting out of water. Captain Saurin, an eminent
counsel who was commander of a corps of lawyers nick-named
the Devil's Own, insisted on parading his battalion in order to
harangue them on the insult to Ireland and the injury to their
profession. His example was widely followed. On 9th December the Dublin Bar, by 168 votes to 32, protested strongly
against the proposal to extinguish the Irish Parliament. Eloquent
speakers like Plunket warned that body that suicide was the
supreme act of cowardice, besides being *ultra vires*. The neighbouring towns and counties joined in the clamour. The somnolence of Cornwallis, his neglect to win over opponents by tact
or material inducements, and the absence of any Ministerial declaration on the subject, left all initiative to the Opposition. On
24th December Cooke wrote to Auckland in these doleful terms:[3]

. . . Our Union politics are not at present very thriving. Pamphlets
are in shoals, in general against a Union; a few for it; but I do not yet
see anything of superior talent and effect. The tide in Dublin is difficult

[1] For the plan and notes, see "Pitt and Napoleon Miscellanies."
[2] "Cornwallis Corresp.," ii, 456, 457.
[3] B.M. Add. MSS., 34455. William C. Plunket (1764-1854), born in co.
Fermanagh, was called to the Irish Bar in 1787, and entered Parliament in

to stem. In the country hitherto, indifference. We have no account from the North, and that is the quarter I apprehend. The South will not be very hostile. The Bar is most impetuous and active, and I cannot be surprized at it. The Corporation have not sense to see that by an Union alone the Corporation can be preserved. Most of the best merchants are, I know, not averse. The proprietors of Dublin and the county are violent, and shopkeepers, etc. The Catholics hold back. They are on the watch to make the most of the game, and will intrigue with both parties. . . . In the North they expect the Dutch fleet. If we had a more able active conciliating Chief, we might do; but the *vis inertiae* is incredible. There is an amazing disgust among the friends of Government. The tone of loyalty is declining, for want of being cherished. Do not be surprized at a dreadful parliamentary opposition and a personal opposition.

Cooke's reference to the mediocrity of the pamphlets for the Union is a curious piece of *finesse*; for he was known to be the author of an able pamphlet, " Arguments for and against an Union between Great Britain and Ireland." In it he dilated on the benefits gained by Wales and Scotland from a Union with England. He dwelt on the recent increase of strength in France consequent on the concentration of political power at Paris, and demonstrated the unreality of the boasted independence of the Dublin Parliament, seeing that Irish enactments must be sealed by the Seal of Great Britain. After touching on the dangerous divergence of policy at Westminster and Dublin during the Regency crisis of 1789, he showed that peace and prosperity must increase under a more comprehensive system, which would both guarantee the existence of the Established Church, and accord civic recognition to Catholics. At present, said he, it would be dangerous to admit Catholics to the Irish Parliament; but in the United Parliament such a step would be practicable. This semi-official pronouncement caused a sensation, and before the end of the year twenty-four replies appeared. In one of the counterblasts the anonymous author offers " the reflections of a plain and humble mind," by stating forthwith that the policy of the British Government had been to foment discontent, to excite

1798. He speedily made his mark, and in 1803 was State Prosecutor of Emmett. In Pitt's second Administration (1804) he was Solicitor-General: he was created Baron Plunket in 1827 and was Lord Chancellor of Ireland in 1830-41. William Saurin sat in the Irish Parliament as a nominee of Lord Downshire (" Cornwallis Corresp.," iii, 212).

jealousies, to connive at insurrections, and finally to "amnestize" those rebellions, for the purpose of promoting its favourite and now avowed object of a Union.[1]

Far abler is the "Reply" to Cooke by Richard Jebb, who afterwards became a Justice of the King's Bench in Ireland. He showed that only in regard to the Regency had any serious difference arisen between the two Parliaments; he scoffed at the notion of Ireland's needs finding satisfaction at Westminster. Would Pitt, he asked, who whirled out of the Cabinet the gigantic Thurlow, ever attend to Irish affairs? Jebb then quoted with effect Clare's assertion that the Irish Parliament alone was competent to deal with the business of the island. He admitted the directing power of the British Cabinet over Ireland's concerns; but he averred that under the new system the Lord Lieutenant would be little more than a Great Contractor. As to the satisfaction to be granted to Catholics, the Under-Secretary had done well not to be too explicit, lest he should offend jealous Protestants. But, asked Jebb, would the Catholics have much influence in the United Kingdom, where they would be, not three to one as in Ireland, but three to fourteen? Nature herself had intended England and Scotland to be one country; she had proclaimed the need of some degree of independence in Ireland. Finally, he deprecated in the mouth of an official a reference to the success attending the policy of annexation pursued by France, which Pitt had always reprobated. The effect produced by these replies appears in a letter of Lees to Auckland on 29th December. Dublin, he writes, is in a frenzy against the Union. As for Cornwallis, he was as apathetic as usual: "We are asleep, while the disaffected are working amain."[2]

Not until 21st December did Pitt and his colleagues come to a final decision to press on the Act of Union at all costs. On that day he held a Cabinet meeting in Downing Street, all being present, as well as the Earl of Liverpool and Earl Camden. The following Minute of their resolution was taken by Lord Grenville.

That the Lord Lieutenant of Ireland should be instructed to state without delay to all persons with whom he may have communication

---

[1] "Strictures on a Pamphlet, etc.," 5 (Dublin, 1798).

[2] B.M. Add. MSS., 34455. The term "Contractor" used above is equivalent to "Undertaker," *i.e.*, one who undertook to get business through the Irish Parliament for certain rewards (Lecky, iv, 353).

on this subject, that His Majesty's Government is decided to press the measure of an Union as essential to the well-being of both countries and particularly to the security and peace of Ireland as dependent on its connection with Great Britain: that this object will now be urged to the utmost, and will even in the case (if it should happen) of any present failure, be renewed on every occasion till it succeed; and that the conduct of individuals on this subject will be considered as the test of their disposition to support the King's Government.[1]

Portland forthwith informed the Lord-Lieutenant, Cornwallis, of the purport of this resolution. Drastic proceedings were now inevitable; for mischievous rumours were rife at Dublin that nobody would suffer for his vote against the Union.

A brief Declaration as to the essentials of the Government plan was issued at Dublin on 5th January 1799. It stated that twenty-eight temporal peers elected for life would be delegated to Westminster, and four Protestant bishops, taken in rotation. Irish peers not elected might sit for British counties and boroughs, as before. The Crown retained the right of creating Irish peers. As to the delegation of the Commons of Ireland, each county or large town now returning two members could send only one to Westminster, except Dublin and Cork, each of which would return two members. Of the 108 small boroughs, one half would return members for one Parliament, the other half for the next Parliament. In the sphere of commerce Ireland would enjoy the same advantages as Great Britain, the duties between the two islands being equalized, the linen manufacturers retaining their special privileges. The Exchequer and National Debt of each island were to continue separate, the quota paid by Ireland into the Imperial Exchequer being reserved for future consideration, it being understood that when the Irish Revenue exceeded its expenses, the excess must be applied to local purposes, the taxes producing the excess being duly modified.

Apart from the inevitable vagueness as to the proportion of Ireland's quota, the Declaration was calculated to reassure Irishmen. The borough-mongers lost only one half of their lucrative patronage. True, the change bore hard upon the 180 Irish peers, of whom only one in six would enter the House of Lords at Westminster. But commerce was certain to thrive now that

[1] Pretyman MSS.

the British Empire unreservedly threw open its markets to Irish products; and in the political sphere the Act of Union, by shattering the Irish pocket-borough system, assigned an influence to the larger towns such as those of Great Britain did not enjoy until the time of the Reform Bill. Nothing, it is true, was said to encourage the Catholics; but in Cooke's semi-official pamphlet they had been led to hope for justice in the United Parliament.

The following letter of Cooke to Castlereagh (6th January) is interesting:

We shall have difficult work; but there is no need to despair. I do not hear of anything formidable from the country. Armagh is stirred by Lord Charlemont; Louth, I suppose, by the Speaker; Lord Enniskillen will move Fermanagh; Queen's County will be against [us]. I hear Waterford, Cork, Kerry, Limerick is [sic] with us. Sir Edward O'Brien in Clare is against and is stirring. Derry will be quiet, if not favourable. The North is so in general at present. The sketch of terms thrown out is much relished. I cannot tell you how our numbers will stand on the 22nd. The Catholics will wait upon the question, and will not declare till they think they can act with effect. Many persons are anxious to make them part of the measure. Grattan is come. I know not yet what he is doing. I hope all friends in London will be sent over. The first burst is everything. It would be decisive if the Prince of Wales would declare publicly in favour and hoist his banner for the Union.[1]

Apart from this enigmatical reference, there were few grounds for hope. The landlords and traders of Dublin naturally opposed a measure certain to lessen the importance of that city. Trinity College, the Corporation of Dublin, and the gentry and freeholders of County Dublin all protested against Union. Equally hostile were most Irish Protestants. In their pride as a dominant Order, they scorned the thought of subordination to Great Britain. Sixteen years of almost complete legislative independence had quickened their national feelings; and many of them undoubtedly set love of country before the promptings of caste. How was it possible, they asked, that the claims of Ireland should receive due attention amidst the clash of worldwide interests at Westminster?

Doubts like these should have been set at rest. Surely Pitt missed a great opportunity in not promising the appointment of a perpetual committee at Westminster, elected by the Irish

[1] Pretyman MSS.; also in Pitt MSS., 327.

members for the consideration of their local affairs. A similar committee for Scottish business would also have been a statesmanlike proposal, in view of the increase of work certain to result from the Union. Doubtless those committees would have interfered with the functions of the Lord Lieutenant at Dublin, and the Scottish patronage controlled by Henry Dundas. But some such measure would have appeased the discontent rife in both kingdoms, and, while easing the strain on the Imperial Parliament, would have nurtured the growth of that wider patriotism which has its roots in local affections.

A survey of the facts passed under review must, I think, lead to the conclusion that the conduct of Pitt in preparing for the Act of Union was halting and ineffective. It is true that Camden had advised him to make careful preliminary inquiries; but they were not instituted until October 1798, and they dragged on to the end of the year, by which time the fear of a French invasion had subsided. There were but two satisfactory ways of carrying the Act of Union through the hostile Parliament at Dublin. In June—October, during the panic caused by the Rebellion and the French raids, Pitt might have intimated secretly though officially to the leading loyalists that Great Britain could not again pour forth her blood and treasure for an unworkable system, and that the acceptance of that help must imply acquiescence in a Union. Such a compact would of course be termed unchivalrous by the rhetoricians at St. Stephen's Green; but it would have prevented the unchivalrous conduct of many so-called loyalists, who, after triumphing by England's aid, then, relying upon that aid for the future, thwarted Pitt's remedial policy. Prudence should have enjoined the adoption of some such precaution in the case of men whose behaviour was exacting towards England and exasperating towards the majority of Irishmen. In neglecting to take it, Pitt evinced a strange lack of foresight. At this point George III showed himself the shrewder tactician; for he urged that Cornwallis must take steps to frighten the loyal minority into accepting an Act of Union.

But there was an alternative course of action. Failing to come to an understanding with the ultra-Protestant zealots of Dublin, Pitt might have elicited a strong declaration from the many Irishmen who were in favour of Union. He seems to have taken no such step. Though aware that Cornwallis was in civil affairs a figure-head, he neglected to send over a spokesman capable of giving a decided lead. In the ensuing debates at Dublin, Castlereagh showed the toughness, energy, and resourcefulness which, despite his halting cumbrous style, made him a power in Parliament; but his youth and his stiff un-Hibernian ways told against him. Beresford was detained by illness in London; and Clare, after his return to Dublin, did strangely little for the cause. Thus, at this critical time the Unionists were without a lead and without a leader. The autumn of 1798 was frittered away in interviews in London, the purport of which ought to have clearly appeared two or three months earlier. The passive attitude and tardy action of Pitt and Portland in these critical weeks offer a strange contrast to the habits of clear thinking and forceful action characteristic of Napoleon. It is painful to compare their procedure with the action of the First Consul in speedily bringing ecclesiastical bigots and fanatical atheists to the working compromise summed up in the Concordat. In the case of the Union, the initiative, energy, and zeal, which count for much among a Celtic people, passed to the side of Pitt's opponents. Thenceforth that measure could be carried through the Irish Parliament only by coercion or bribery.

CHAPTER XIX

THE UNION (CONTINUED)

"We must consider it as a measure of great national policy, the object of which is effectually to counteract the restless machinations of an inveterate enemy, who has uniformly and anxiously endeavoured to effect a separation between the two countries."—PITT, Speech on the Union, 21*st April*, 1800.

ON 22nd January 1799 the long talked-of Act of Union was pointedly referred to in the King's Speech read out to the Irish Parliament. The Speech was adopted by the House of Lords, amendments hostile to the proposed measure being rejected by large majorities. But in the House of Commons nationalist zeal raged with ever-increasing fury from dusk until the dawn of the following day. In vain had Castlereagh made liberal use of the sum of £5,000 which he begged Pitt to send over to serve as a *primum mobile* at Dublin. In vain had he "worked like a horse." The feeling against the measure was too strong to be allayed by bribery of a retail kind.

Owing to ill health Grattan was not present. Sir John Parnell, Chancellor of the Exchequer, was among the less violent opponents; but the most telling appeal was that of Plunket, an Ulsterman. With an eloquence which even won votes he denied either the right of the Government to propose such a measure or the competence of that Assembly to commit political suicide. If the Act of Union were passed, he said, no one in Ireland would obey it. Then, turning to the Speaker, he exclaimed: "You are appointed to make laws and not Legislatures. You are appointed to exercise the functions of legislators, and not to transfer them; and if you do so, your act is a dissolution of the Government." On behalf of Government Castlereagh made a well-reasoned reply; but his speech was too laboured to commend a cause which offended both the sentiments and interests of members; and the Opposition was beaten by only one vote—106 to 105. The debate was marked by curious incidents. Sir Jonah Barrington, a chronicler of these events, declared that Cooke, perturbed by the threatened defection of a member named French, whispered to Castlereagh, and then, sidling up to the erring placeman, spoke long and earnestly until smiles spread over the features of both. A little later French rose to state his regret at the opinions which he had previously expressed. The story is not convincing in the case of a building provided with committee-rooms; but there can be no doubt that bribery went on before the debate. The final voting showed that there were limits to that form of influence. Even the canvassing of Castlereagh failed to persuade members to pass sentence of political death on half of their number and of transportation on the remainder. The joy of the men of Dublin found expression in a spontaneous illumination, and the mob broke all windows which were not lit up.

On all sides the procedure of the Government met with severe censure. As usual, blame was lavished upon Cornwallis, Lord Carysfort warning Grenville that the defeat was due to the disgust of " Orangemen and exterminators " at his clemency. Buckingham, writing to Pitt on 29th January, reported that on the estimate of Archbishop Troy, nine-tenths of the Irish Catholics were for the Union: " Remember, however," he added, " that this can only be done by the removal of Lord Cornwallis and Lord Castlereagh. . . . I protest I see no salvation but in the immediate change. Send us Lord Winchilsea, or rather Lord Euston, or in short send us any one. But send us Steele as his Secretary, and with firmness the Question (and with it Ireland) will be saved. Excuse this earnestness."[1] Pitt took no notice of this advice, but continued to support Cornwallis. As for the Irish Executive, it proceeded now to the policy of official coercion recommended from Downing Street. Parnell was dismissed from the Exchequer; the Prime Serjeant was deposed, and four opponents of Union were removed from subordinate posts, among them being Foster, son of the Speaker.

So confident was Pitt of victory at Dublin that he introduced the Bill of Union at Westminster on 23rd January. The King's Speech referred to the designs of enemies and traitors to separate Ireland from Great Britain, and counselled the adoption of means for perpetuating the connection. Forthwith Sheridan

[1] Pretyman MSS.

moved a hostile amendment. With his wonted zeal and eloquence, he urged the inopportuneness of such a measure when
40,000 British troops were holding down Ireland, and he denied
the competence either of the British or Irish Parliament to decide
on it. Pitt promptly refuted Sheridan's plea by referring to the
action of the English and Scottish Parliaments at the time of
their Union, and he twitted him with seeking to perpetuate at
Dublin a system whose injustice and cruelty he had always reprobated. Allowing that British rule in Ireland had been narrow and intolerant, Pitt foretold the advent of a far different
state of things after the Union. Then, pointing to the divergence of British and Irish policy at the time of the Regency crisis
he pronounced it a dangerous omen, and declared the Union to
be necessary to the peace and stability of the Empire. The
House agreed with him and negatived the amendment without a
division.

It is worth noting that of Sheridan's hypothetical colleagues
in office under the Prince Regent in the Cabinet outlined in
February 1789, not one now supported him. Fox was not present, being engrossed in Lucretius and the "Poetics" of Aris-
totle. He, however, informed Lord Holland that he detested the
Union and all centralized Governments, his predilection being
for Federalism.[1] The remark merits notice in view of the concentration of power in France, and in her vassal Republics at
Rome, Milan, Genoa, and Amsterdam. That eager student of
the Classics wished to dissolve the British Isles into their component parts at a time when the highly organized energy of the
French race was threatening every neighbouring State. While the
tricolour waved at Amsterdam, Mainz, Berne, Rome, Valetta, and
Cairo, Fox thought it opportune to federalize British institutions.
The means whereby Pitt sought to solidify them are open to
question. But which of the two statesmen had the sounder sense?

On 31st January, after the receipt of the disappointing news
from Dublin, Pitt returned to the charge. Expressing deep
regret that the Irish House of Commons should have rejected
the plan of a Union before it knew the details, he proceeded to
describe the proposals of the Government. Firstly, he insisted
that it was the concerted action of invaders from without and
traitors within that made the measure necessary. He then

---

[1] "Mems. of Fox," iii, 150; "Grattan Mems.," iv, 435.

argued that the settlement of 1782, according legislative independence to the Irish Parliament, was far from final, as appeared
in the ministerial declarations of that time. Moreover, Irish
Bills did not become law unless sanctioned by the King and
sealed by the Great Seal of Great Britain on the advice of British
Ministers, facts which implied the dependence of the Irish Parliament. Turning to the commercial issues at stake, he effectively
quoted the statement of Foster to the Irish House of Commons
in 1785, that they would be mad to reject the commercial proposals then offered, which, if thrown out, would not be renewed.
But now, said Pitt, they are renewed in the projected Union;
and Foster has used his influence to reject a measure which
breaks down the fiscal barriers between the two kingdoms. After
referring to the Regency Question, he pointed out the danger of
France attacking the British race at its weakest point. Never
would she cease to assail it until the Union was indissoluble.
Commerce, he said, was the source of wealth; and the wealth
needed to withstand the predatory designs of France would be
enhanced by a free interchange of British and Irish products.
The Union would encourage the flow into the poorer island of
British capital which it so much needed. Next, adverting to the
religious feuds in Ireland, he remarked on the danger of granting
concessions to the Irish Catholics while Ireland remained a distinct kingdom. He then uttered these momentous words:

On the other hand, without anticipating the discussion, or the propriety of agitating the question, or saying how soon or how late it may
be fit to discuss it, two propositions are indisputable; first, when the
conduct of the Catholics shall be such as to make it safe for the
Government to admit them to the participation of the privileges granted
to those of the established religion, and when the temper of the times
shall be favourable to such a measure—when these events take place, it
is obvious that such a question may be agitated in an United Imperial
Parliament with much greater safety, than it could be in a separate
Legislature. In the second place, I think it certain that, even for whatever period it may be thought necessary after the Union to withhold
from the Catholics the enjoyment of those advantages, many of the
objections which at present arise out of their situation would be removed, if the Protestant Legislature were no longer separate and local,
but general and Imperial: and the Catholics themselves would at once
feel a mitigation of the most goading and irritating of their present
causes of complaint.

Pitt then deprecated the effort to inflame the insular pride of Irishmen. Could Irishmen really object to unite with Britons? For it was no subordinate place that they were asked to take, but one of equality and honour. Most happily then did he quote the vow of Aeneas for an equal and lasting compact between his Trojans and the Italians:

> Non ego nec Teucris Italos parere jubebo,
> Nec nova regna peto: paribus se legibus ambae
> Invictae gentes aeterna in foedera mittant.[1]

He ended his speech by moving eight Resolutions on the question; and the House approved their introduction by 140 votes to 15. This statesmanlike survey lacked the fire and imaginative elevation of his speech on the Slave Trade in 1792. But there was little need of rhetoric and invective. Pitt's aim was to convince Ireland of the justice of his proposals. And his plea, though weak at one point, must rank among the ablest expositions of a great and complex question. How different the course of events might have been if the Commons of Ireland had first heard Pitt's proposals of Union, clearly and authoritatively set forth, not in the distorted form which rumour or malice depicted. In this respect Gladstone proved himself an abler tactician than Pitt. His Home Rule Bill of 1886 remained a secret until it was described in that masterly statement which formed a worthy retort to Pitt's oration of 31st January 1799. Pitt prepared it with great care, so Auckland avers; and, as he and Long had secured the presence of the best reporters, the text of the speech is among the most accurate that we possess for that period. He now resolved to bring forward specific Resolutions, instead of, as before, proposing merely to appoint Commissioners to consider the details of the Bill of Union. It is unfortunate that he did not take this step at first. The mistake probably resulted from his besetting sin—excess of confidence. On 26th January he expressed to Cornwallis his deep disappointment and grief at the action of the Dublin Parliament, which he ascribed to prejudice and cabal. Clearly he had underrated the force of the nationalist opposition.

---

[1] Virgil, "Aen.," xii, 189-91. "As for me, I will neither bid the Italians obey the Trojans, nor do I seek a new sovereignty. Let both peoples, unsubdued, submit to an eternal compact with equal laws." The correct reading is "Nec mihi regna peto," which Pitt altered to "nova."

Meanwhile Castlereagh endeavoured to reckon the value of the pecuniary interests in Ireland opposed to the Union. In a characteristically narrow spirit he assessed the losses to borough-holders at £756,000; to controllers of counties at £224,000; to barristers at £200,000; to purchasers of parliamentary seats at £75,000; and he estimated the probable depreciation of property in Dublin at £200,000. Thus, moneyed interests worth £1,433,000 were arrayed against the Union. He proposed to whittle down these claims by raising the number of Irish members in the United Parliament either to 127 or 141. Both at Dublin and Westminster Ministers were intent on appeasing hostile interests on the easiest terms. Among Pitt's papers is a curious estimate of the opinion of the propertied classes in the counties and chief towns of Ireland. "Property" is declared to favour the Union in Antrim, Clare, Cork, Donegal, Galway, Kerry, Leitrim, Londonderry, Mayo, Waterford, and Wexford. It was hostile in Carlow, Cavan, Dublin, Fermanagh, Kildare, and Louth. In the other counties it was divided on the subject. Among the towns, Cork, Galway, Lisburne, Londonderry, Waterford, and Wexford supported Union. Clonmell, Drogheda, and Dublin opposed it; while Belfast, Kilkenny, and Limerick were doubtful. Most of the Grand Juries petitioned for Union, only those of Dublin, Louth, Queen's County, and Wicklow pronouncing against it.[1] In view of the expected attempt of the Brest fleet, the Grand Jury of Cork burst into a patriotic rhapsody which must be placed on record:

March 26, 1799.[2]

. . . At the present awful moment whilst we await the threatened attempt of the enemies of religion and of man to crush us in their sacrilegious embrace; whilst their diabolical influence cherishes rebellion and promotes assassination in the land, we look back with gratitude to the timely interposition of Great Britain, which has more than once rescued us from that infidel yoke under which so great a portion of distracted Europe at this moment groans. We have still to acknowledge how necessary that interposition is to protect us from the further attempts of an unprincipled foe, . . . and to her assistance we are . . . indebted for keeping down an unnatural but wide extended rebellion

---

[1] Pitt MSS., 196, 320.
[2] Pretyman MSS. See "Cornwallis Corresp.," iii, 125, 210, for Unionist sentiment in Cork.

within the bosom of this country. To become a constituent part of that Empire to whose protection we owe our political existence and whose constitution is the admiration of the civilized world; to participate in those resources which are inexhaustible; to become joint proprietors of that navy which is irresistible; and to share in that commerce which knows no bounds, are objects beyond which our most sanguine wishes for the wealth and prosperity of Ireland cannot possibly extend, whilst the prospect which they hold forth of terminating the jarring interests of party and reconciling the jealous distinctions of religion, promises a restoration of that tranquillity to which the country has too long been a stranger.

This exuberant loyalty may have been heightened by the hope that Cork would reap from the Union a commercial harvest equal to that which raised Glasgow from a city of 12,700 souls before the Anglo-Scottish Union, to one of nearly 70,000 in the year 1800. But the men of Cork forgot that that marvellous increase was due to the coal, iron, and manufactures of Lanarkshire, no less than to free participation in the trade of the Empire.

The fact that Cork was then far more Unionist than Belfast is apt to perplex the reader until he realizes that Roman Catholics for the most part favoured Union, not so much from loyalty to George III, as from the conviction that only in the Imperial Parliament could they gain full religious equality. On the other hand the Presbyterians of Ulster had fewer grievances to be redressed, and were not without hope of gaining satisfaction from the Protestant Legislature at Dublin. It is certain that the Catholic Archbishops of Dublin and Tuam, besides Bishop Moylan of Cork and other prelates, used their influence on behalf of the Union. Cornwallis was known to favour the Catholic claims; and Wilberforce, writing to Pitt, says: " I have long wished to converse with you a little concerning the part proper for you to take when the Catholic Question should come before the House. I feel it due to the long friendship which has subsisted between us to state to you unreservedly my sentiments on this very important occasion, especially as I fear they are different from your own." [1] Pitt does not seem to have welcomed the suggestion couched in these magisterial terms, and, as the sequel will show, he had good grounds for concealing his

[1] Pitt MSS., 189.

hand. Only at one point did the Cabinet declare its intentions.
There being some fear that the Opposition at Dublin would
seek to win over the Catholics by the offer of Emancipation, the
Government declared its resolve to oppose any step in this
direction so long as that Parliament existed.[1]

It is well also to remember that the concession of the franchise
to the bulk of the Irish peasantry in 1793, with the full approval
of Pitt, enabled the Catholics to control the elections in the
counties and "open" boroughs except in Ulster. Therefore,
though they could not send to Parliament men of their creed,
they could in many instances keep out Protestants who were
inimical to their interests. In the present case, then, Catholic
influence was certain to tell powerfully, though indirectly, in
favour of Union. These facts explain the progress of the
cause early in the year 1799. Opponents of the measure began
to tremble for their seats owing to the action either of Government or of the Catholic vote. Accordingly, despite the frantic
efforts of Lord Downshire and Foster, Government carried the
day by 123 to 103 (15th February). Fear worked on behalf of
Union. A great fleet was fitting out at Brest, the Dutch ports
were alive with work, and again Ireland was believed to be the
aim of the Republicans. As was the case in 1798, they encouraged numbers of Irishmen to make pikes, to muster on the
hills of Cork and Wicklow, dealing murder and havoc in the
plains by night. Cornwallis therefore proclaimed martial law,
armed the yeomen, and sought to crush the malcontents, a
proceeding which led critics to charge Government with inciting
the people to outrage in order to coerce them. Those who
flung out the sneer should also have proved that the naval preparations at Brest and the Texel were instigated from Downing
Street in order to carry the Union.

The real feelings of Dublin officials appear in the letters of
Beresford, Cooke, and Lees to Auckland. On 15th March
1799 Beresford writes: "Our business is going on smoothly in
Parliament; from the day that Government took the courage
[*sic*] of dividing with the Opposition, they have grown weaker
and weaker every day as I foretold to you they would. The
Speaker [Foster], as I hear, appears to be much softened. I am
sure he sees that he has pledged himself too far, and that he

[1] "Cornwallis Corresp.," iii, 52, 54; Hunt, "Pol. Hist. of England," x,
447.

cannot depend upon those who heretofore supported him! and both he and Ponsonby are conscious that the point will be carried and they, of course, left in the lurch. . . . The country is in a wretched way, organization going on everywhere ; and if the French should land, I much fear that there will be very universal risings." On the subject of inter-insular trade Beresford informs Auckland on 29th March that Ireland depends almost entirely upon Great Britain and her colonies, having a balance in her favour in that trade but an adverse balance in her dealings with foreign lands. She exports 41,670,000 yards of linen to Great Britain and only 4,762,000 yards to other lands. Besides, the British trade is increasing fast, as England uses less and less foreign linen. On the morrow, Cooke declares that, if the French do not land, the Irish malcontents will settle down. Commending the policy of going slowly with the Union, he says: " By letting the subject cool, by opening its nature, tendencies, and advantages, and seeming not to press it, and by insinuating that no other course of safety to property remains, the mind begins to think seriously and faints. I think during the Vacation pains may be taken with the House of Commons so as to give us a fair majority, and if the Catholics act steadily we should be able to carry the point. I could wish that Mr. Pitt would suffer some person of ability to prepare all the necessary Bills, and to fill up every detail; so that the measure might be seen in its complete stage. I despair of this being done, tho' obviously right; for Ministers never will act till they are forced, and I do not wonder at it."[1]

Again, all the energy was on the side of the Opposition. On 11th April Foster passed the whole subject in review in a speech of four hours' duration. In order to weaken one of the strongest of Pitt's arguments, he proposed that in case of a Regency, the Regent, who was chosen at Westminster, should necessarily be Regent at Dublin. This proposal of couse implied the dependence of the Irish Parliament on that of Great Britain; but, as invalidating one of the chief pleas for Union, Foster pressed it home. He also charged Pitt with endeavouring to wring a large sum of money every year from Ireland. The speech made a deep impression. The only way of deadening its influence and stopping the Regency Bill was to postpone it until August and

[1] B.M. Add. MSS., 35455.

summarily to close the session on 1st June. The meanness of
this device is a tribute to the power of Foster and the mediocrity
of the officials of Dublin Castle.

Meanwhile the naval situation had cleared up, so far as concerns
Ireland. On 25th April Admiral Bruix, with a powerful fleet,
slipped out from Brest by night past Lord Bridport's blockading
force. For some days panic reigned in London, and it is significant that Bridport took especial measures to guard the coasts of
Ireland, thus enabling the French to get clear away to the Mediterranean. With bolder tactics they should have been able to
reduce the new British possession, Minorca, or annihilate the
small force blockading Malta. The relief felt at Dublin Castle,
on hearing of Bruix' southward voyage, appears in Beresford's
letter of 15th May, in which he refers to the revival of loyalty
and the terrible number of hangings by courts martial: "We
consider ourselves as safe from the French for this year; but I
am in great anxiety for my friend St. Vincent. What steps will
be taken against those damned dogs in the Mediterranean? . . .
I expect that the French going to the Mediterranean, instead of
coming to the assistance of their friends here, will have a very
great effect upon the people of this country, who, as soon as
they find that they have been made fools of will endeavour to
get out of the scrape they are in." On 1st June Cooke writes
"secretly" to Auckland, expressing regret that Pitt ever attacked
Foster, whose opposition is most weighty. The Cabinet lost the
measure by want of good management in 1798: and the same is
now the case. Nothing has been done to win over Lord Downshire with his eight votes, or Lords Donegal and De Clifford,
who had half as many. He even asks whether Pitt will think it
worth while to spend three months' work on the Union now that
the French had gone to the Mediterranean.[1] The question reveals
the prevalence of the belief that Pitt paid little attention to
Irish affairs. Probably it arose from his stiffness of manner and
his execrable habit of leaving letters unanswered. This defect
had become incurable, witness the complaint of Wilberforce to
Addington—"You know how difficult, I may say next to
impossible, it is to extort a line from Pitt."[2]

In July the return of Bruix with the Cadiz fleet into the Atlantic renewed the fears of Irish loyalists and the hopes of the

[1] B.M. Add. MSS., 35455.   [2] "Life of Wilberforce," ii, 227.

malcontents. The combined fleet managed to enter Brest on
13th August 1799; and its presence there was a continual source
of unsettlement to Ireland, preparations for revolt being kept up
in several parts. A large British force was therefore kept in
Ireland, not for the purpose of forcing through the Union, as
Pitt's enemies averred, but in order to guard against invasion
and rebellion. Though reinforcements arrived, Cornwallis complained that he had not enough troops. On 24th July 1799 he
informed the Duke of Portland that he had only 45,000 regular
infantry, a number sufficient to preserve order but totally inadequate to repel an invasion in force. Thus the facts of the case
are, that French threats to tear Ireland from Great Britain kept
up the threatening ferment and necessitated the presence of a
considerable military force; but they also led Pitt to insist on
the Union as a means of thwarting all separatist efforts whether
from without or from within. It is clear, however, that Pitt and
Earl Spencer trusted to Bridport's powerful squadron to intercept any large expedition of the enemy. The blow then preparing against the Dutch was in part intended to ensure the safety
of the British Isles.

Meanwhile at Westminster the cause of the Union met with
almost universal approval. The debate in the Lords on 11th
April elicited admirable speeches, from Dr. Watson, the learned
Bishop of Llandaff, and from Lords Auckland and Minto. Only
Lords Holland, King, and Thanet protested against the measure.
In the Commons, Lord Sheffield, while supporting the Union,
reproved Ministers for allowing their aim to become known in
Ireland several weeks before the details of their proposals were
made public. The measure received warm support from Canning,
who a month earlier had resigned the Under-Secretaryship for
Foreign Affairs, and was now for the time merely on the India
Board of Control, with a sinecure superadded. The sensitive
young Irishman had found it impossible to work with the cold
and austere Grenville; and his place was taken for a time by his
coadjutor on the " Anti-Jacobin," Hookham Frere, to whom the
Grenville yoke proved scarcely less irksome.

Canning flung himself with ardour into the struggle for the
Union, and proved a match for his brilliant fellow countryman,
Sheridan. He combated the notion that the Irish Parliament
was unalterably opposed to the measure, and, arguing from the
contemptuous manner in which the French had met our over-

tures for peace, he inferred their resolve to sever Ireland from the Empire. In animated style he declared that Ireland would not lose but gain in dignity by the Union, which would confer on her what she most needed, stronger and steadier government. On this occasion Sheridan did not speak, and Fox was absent. After a protest by Lord William Russell against infringing the final settlement of 1782, Pitt arose merely in order to challenge this statement and to read the letters of the Duke of Portland to Lord Shelburne of May—June 1782; they refuted Russell's contention only in so far as to show that Ministers then designed to legislate further on the subject. The Irish Parliament certainly regarded the legislative independence then granted as complete and final. The House of Commons supported Pitt by a unanimous vote.

During the summer the outlook at Dublin became somewhat brighter, as appears from the following " secret " letter of Cooke to Lord Camden. After congratulating him on receiving the Garter, he continues:

Dublin, 14 *Aug.*, 1799.

. . . I think Union gains ground. Lord Cornwallis is in earnest on the subject and feels himself committed. The Catholics have been chiefly courted by him, and he has always been of opinion that, if they would act heartily in support, the Protestants would not resist the efforts of the British Government, assisted by the population of the kingdom. I believe this position to be true. It cannot, however, be fully acted upon, in my mind, unless there be a determination to make futher concessions to that body. To such concessions I confess I do not see insuperable, tho' I do strong, objections. I think they vanish in the superior importance of the question of Union. From the present state of the country I conceive the question may be brought forward with safety. If the Catholics were steady, Dublin might be preserved quiet, tho' the Opposition would be clamorous. Our difficulties will be in Parliament. I think the Speaker will not relax. Lord Downshire, I am sorry to say, seems very hostile. Lord de Clifford is also unfriendly. Lord Donegal I hear is coming round. Could Lord Downshire and Lord de Clifford be made cordial, the Parliament would be secure. I see not any great difficulty in settling the terms except as to the representation of the Commons and compensation to the boroughs. Allowing two members for each county—which makes 64—there is no principle which can be exactly applied for classing the boroughs and selecting the great towns, and tho' it would be easy to compensate the close boroughs, it is almost

impossible to compensate pot-walloping boroughs.[1] The difficulties here
are enhanced by the consideration that in this case private not public
interests are concerned. When I thus represent the probability of success, I am aware of the strange volatility of the Irish mind; and I should
not be surprised at any sudden turn of the present appearances. . . .

Very interesting is the statement as to the courting of the
Catholics by Cornwallis. Pitt certainly knew of these advances;
for on New Year's Day 1801 Castlereagh reminded him by
letter that Cornwallis did not venture to make them until the
Cabinet had discussed the matter sometime in the autumn of
1799, and had come to a conclusion entirely favourable to the
Catholic claims, finally assuring him that he " need not hesitate in
calling forth the Catholic support in whatever degree he found it
practicable to obtain it." This and other passages in Castlereagh's
letter prove conclusively that not only Pitt, but the Cabinet as
a whole was responsible for the procedure of Cornwallis, which
ensured the more or less declared support of the Irish Catholics.[2]
The chief difficulty was with the Protestant clique which largely
controlled State patronage. In the autumn Pitt had another interview with Downshire, but found him full of complaints, demanding among other things that Ireland should send at least 300
Commoners to Westminster. He departed for Dublin declaring
that he would do his duty. In October the Government's cause was
furthered by a state progress of Cornwallis through the North of
Ireland, during which he received numerous addresses in favour
of Union. At Belfast 150 of the chief citizens attended a banquet
in his honour; Londonderry was enthusiastic in the cause; and
it was clear that the opposition of the Protestants of the North
was slackening. But, as often happened in Ireland, many
Catholics now began to doubt the utility of a measure commended by their opponents. The interest which Pitt felt in this
complex problem and in Cornwallis's tour appears in the following Memorandum which he wrote probably at the end of October 1799:

The number of placemen in Ireland is 71. Of these such as hold
office for life or during good behaviour, 11, and 2 holding places for
pleasure, vote against. It is said 63 seats have been vacated by Govern-

---

[1] These were boroughs in which all holders of tenements where a pot could
be boiled had votes. See Porritt, ii, 186, 350.
[2] " Castlereagh Corresp.," iv, 8-10.

ment by a misuse of the Place Bill. This number is exaggerated; but at least 10 were vacated to serve Opposition. A charge is made against Lord Cornwallis for canvassing for declarations in favour of Union. The fact is that Lord Cornwallis, being commander-in-chief, thought it his duty to make a progress of inspection thro' the kingdom in order to examine the state of the army and to be a judge of the means of defence he could rely on. In this progress he received numerous addresses in favour of Union. A charge is made against Government of intimidation and the exertion of martial law. There was only one attempt to substantiate such a charge which was by Sir L. Parsons, which, instead of terminating in censure, produced a vote of unanimous approbation in favour of Government. There have been general charges of corruption adduced, but no proof attempted. The charge retorted by Government on Opposition for forming the most extensive subscriptions for the purpose of corruption has not been denied by them.

The last sentence refers to a curious incident. Downshire, the most influential opponent of the Union, had opened a fund for influencing members of Parliament. It reached a large amount, probably £100,000. Beresford in a letter to Auckland states that £4,000 was paid to win over a supporter of Government. Pitt, as we have seen, believed that Downshire's fund necessitated the extensive use of bribery by Government. But it is on the whole more likely that Dublin Castle opened the game by its request early in 1799, for £5,000 immediately from London. Further sums were forwarded, for on 5th April, Cooke, after interviews with Pitt and Portland, assured Castlereagh that Portland would send " the needful " to Dublin. He adds: " Pitt will contrive to let you have from £8,000 to £10,000 for five years," though this was less than Castlereagh required. After this, it is absurd to deny that Pitt used corrupt means to carry the Union. He used them because only so could he carry through that corrupt Parliament a measure entailing pecuniary loss on most of its members. Probably he disliked the work as much as Cornwallis, who longed to kick the men whom he had to conciliate.—" I despise and hate myself every hour," so Cornwallis wrote to Ross, " for engaging in such dirty work, and am supported only by the reflection that without an Union, the British Empire must be dissolved." [1]

---

[1] "Cornwallis Corresp.," iii, 101, 102, 226; "Castlereagh Corresp.," iii, 260; Plowden (ii, 550), without proof, denies the existence of Downshire's fund.

The winter of 1799-1800 was marked by fierce discontent; and again, after the rise of Bonaparte to power, there were rumours of invasion which excited the peasants of South Ireland. The men of Dublin on some occasions assaulted Unionist Members of Parliament. Cornwallis, however, believed that the country as a whole favoured the cause; and Castlereagh received favourable assurances as to the attitude of the great majority of Catholics except in County Dublin.[1] Some leading Episcopalians were appeased by the insertion of a clause uniting the Protestant Churches of England and Ireland in one body. This concession did not satisfy the Orangemen, who, despite the prohibition of their Grand Lodge, clamoured against the Union, and threatened to oppose it by force.

So doubtful were the omens when Cornwallis opened the Irish Parliament on 5th February 1800, in a speech commending the present plan of unification. Castlereagh then defended the proposals and declared them to have the support of three fourths of the property there represented. After showing the need of keeping the debts of the two islands distinct, he explained that an examination of the Customs and Excise duties warranted the inference that the contribution of Ireland towards Imperial expenses should be two fifteenths of that of Great Britain. He claimed that this plan would press less heavily on Ireland than the present duty of contributing £1,000,000 to the British armaments in time of war and half that amount in peace. Further, the Union would tend to assuage religious jealousies and to consolidate the strength of the Empire. Early on the next morning the House divided—158 for and 115 against Government. This result did not wholly please Dublin Castle. Cooke wrote on the morrow to Auckland: "The activity and intimidation of Opposition, together with their subscription purse, does sad mischief. They scruple not to give from 3,000 to 4,000 guineas for a vote." Government therefore had to mourn over seven deserters.[2] Nevertheless, this division was decisive. Castlereagh rounded up his flock, and by the display of fat pasture called in some of the wanderers. Is it possible that the Opposition purse was merely

---

[1] "Castlereagh Corresp.," iii, 135, 226. On the proposed changes in the Catechism there is a long *précis* in the Pretyman MSS., being a summary of the correspondence of Lords Castlereagh and Hobart with Archbishop Troy and Bishop Moylan.

[2] B.M. Add. MSS., 35455; "Dropmore P.," vi, 121.

the device of a skilful auctioneer, who sends in a friend to raise the bids?

The triumph of Government at Dublin had its effects at Westminster. On 21st April 1800 Pitt explained the Resolutions as recently accepted by the Irish Parliament. He spoke very briefly, probably owing to ill health, which beset him through many weeks of that year.[1] He soon met a challenger. Thomas Jones dared him to combat by accusing Ministers of seeking to disfranchise Ireland by corrupt means. Foiled in argument, they now acted on the principle

Flectere si nequeo superos, Acheronta movebo.

After a further display of classical knowledge, Jones declared that the introduction of 100 Irish members into that House must destroy the British constitution, which, like Damocles, would for ever be threatened with the sword of Dionysius suspended over it by a single hair.

Disregarding rhetoric and classical allusions, Pitt plunged into business. In none of his speeches is there a simpler statement of a case. He declared the Union to be absolutely necessary as a means of thwarting the machinations of an enemy ever intent on separating the two kingdoms. It would further allay the religious animosities rife in Ireland, and would conduce to her freedom and happiness. He then uttered these words: " It may be proper to leave to Parliament an opportunity of considering what may be fit to be done for His Majesty's Catholic subjects, without seeking at present any rule to govern the Protestant Establishment or to make any provision upon that subject." This statement is not wholly clear; but it and its context undoubtedly opened up a prospect of Catholic Emancipation such as Cornwallis had far more clearly outlined. The significance of Pitt's declaration will appear in the sequel.

On the subject of commerce Pitt laid down the guiding principle that after the Union all Customs barriers between the two islands ought to be swept away as completely as between England and Scotland. If at present they swerved from this grand object, it was for the sake of reaching it the more surely. In compliance with the demand of Ireland, they would allow her to maintain a protective duty of 10 per cent. on cottons and

[1] " Castlereagh Corresp.," iii, 263, 278.

woollens, in the latter case for not more than twenty years. He
then added these words: "The manufacturers of this country
do not, I believe, wish for any protecting duties; all they desire
is a free intercourse with all the world; and, though the want of
protecting duties may occasion partial loss, they think that
amply compensated by general advantage." No more statesmanlike utterance had been heard in the House of Commons.
Only by degrees had Pitt worked his way to this conviction. In
his early Budgets, as we saw, he clung to the system of numerous
duties; but, despite the cramping influence of war, he now relied
on the effects of a two-shilling Income Tax and aimed at the
abolition of protective Customs dues. He was fated never to
reach this ideal; but there can be no doubt that he cherished it
as one of the hopes of his life.

Turning next to the question of Ireland's contribution to the
Imperial Exchequer, Pitt set forth his reasons for fixing it at
two fifteenths of the revenue of Great Britain; but, as this decision might in the future unduly burden the smaller island, it
would not be final; and he suggested that at the end of twenty
years the resources of each would so far have developed as to
admit of a more authoritative assessment. If, however, in the
meantime the amount paid by Ireland should be in excess of
what ought to be paid, the surplus should be applied either
to the extinction of her Debt or to local improvements. He
further expressed the hope that in course of time the Debts and
the produce of taxation would be so far assimilated in the two
kingdoms as to admit of the formation of one National Debt
and one system of taxation. Despite the favourable nature of
these proposals, Pitt encountered a spirited opposition. Grey
declared the measure to be a gross violation of the rights of the
Irish people. Sheridan, Dr. Laurence (the friend of Burke), and
Tierney continued in the same strain; and Grey finally dared
the Minister to dissolve the Irish Parliament and appeal to the
people. Throwing off all signs of bodily weakness, Pitt took up
the challenge. Last year, he said, when the Commons of Ireland rejected the Union, certain members applauded them.
Now, when they passed it, the same members said "appeal to
the people." He refused to do so, knowing well the scenes of
violence and intimidation that would result from consulting
primary assemblies of Irishmen. The reference to those bodies,
so notorious during the French Revolution, clinched his reply;

and the House expressed approval of the Union by 236 votes
to 30 (21st April 1800).

The further debates on the Bill are of little interest. In the
absence of Fox, Grey was the protagonist of Opposition. Bankes,
once a firm supporter of Pitt, opposed the measure. Wilberforce
confessed to tremulous uncertainty about it, ostensibly because
the addition of 100 Irish members to the House would add to
the influence of the Crown, but more probably because he foresaw Catholic Emancipation. Peel, already known as one of the
most successful and patriotic of Lancashire manufacturers, spoke
up manfully for the Union, though he deeply regretted that
Ireland would retain certain protective duties against Great
Britain. Very noteworthy, in view of the son's championship of
Free Trade in 1845, was the contention of the father that a weak
country (Ireland) had no need of "protection" against a stronger
one. In reality it would be as if a poor family shut its doors
against assistance from a wealthy one. On the trading proposals
Pitt's following was thinned down to 133; but the main question
went through in May by overwhelming majorities in both Houses.
In the following month it passed through the Irish Parliament.

Castlereagh thereupon introduced a Bill to indemnify the
holders of pocket boroughs who would lose patronage by the
proposed changes. The Government, having now revised its
previous resolve, proposed to disfranchise as many as 84 small
Irish boroughs, and allotted £15,000 for each, or £1,260,000 in
all. In explanation of this payment it must be remembered that
the owning of such boroughs was a recognized form of property,
as appeared in Pitt's proposal of 1785 to compensate British
owners whom he sought to dispossess. Nothing but the near
approach of revolution in 1832 availed to shatter the system of
pocket boroughs in Great Britain; and then their owners were
sent empty away. The difference in treatment marks the infiltra-
tion of new ideas. In England and Ireland a vote and a seat had
been a form of property. According to the Rights of Man the
franchise was an inalienable right of citizenship.

The list of Union honours and preferments having been published, we need not dwell on that unsavoury topic, except to
remark that the promotions in the peerage conferred for services
in connection with the Union numbered forty-six; that the
opposition of the Protestant Archbishop of Cashel was bought
off by the promise of the Archbishopric of Dublin; and that the

number of ecclesiastical jobs consequent on the Union was nearly twenty. The promotions in the legal profession numbered twelve. Twelve pensions and four titular honours were also granted. Five aspirants refused the posts offered to them because they expected "snug sinecures" which "require no attendance at all." In March 1805 Lord Hardwicke, successor to Cornwallis, complained that his funds were so embarrassed by the various claims that the Irish Civil List had only £150 in hand.[1] These sordid bargainings cannot be said to amount to wholesale corruption, and did not much exceed those which usually were needed to carry an important Bill through that Parliament. On the whole Pitt and his colleagues might reflect with satisfaction that the use of bribes served to cleanse the political life of Ireland in the future.

The Union of the British and Irish Parliaments is generally considered from the insular point of view. This is quite natural; for primarily it concerned the British Isles. Nevertheless the influences which brought it about were more than insular. The formation of the United Kingdom, by the Act which came into effect on 1st January 1801, was but one among many processes of consolidation then proceeding. France was the first State which succeeded in concentrating political power at the capital; and the new polity endued her with a strength sufficient to break in pieces the chaotic systems of her neighbours. The mania of the French for centralization was seen in their dealings with the Batavian Republic, and with the Swiss Confederation, which they crushed into the mould of an indivisible Republic. Everywhere the new unifying impulse undermined or swept away local Parliaments or provincial Estates. Liberty, Equality, and Fraternity in practice meant a single, democratic, and centralized Government. In self defence the Powers threatened by France borrowed her political weapons. In succession Great Britain, Prussia, and for a time even Austria, pulled themselves together for the struggle. As the binding powers of commerce also tended towards union, the Nineteenth Century witnessed the absorption of little States, except where they represented a distinct nationality.

Confronted by the new and threatening forces in France, Pitt

[1] M. Mac Donagh, "The Viceroy's Post-Bag," 43-53; "Cornwallis Corresp.," iii, 245, 251-6, 267, 318-21.

was virtually compelled to abrogate a system under which the Speaker of the Irish House of Commons, and Ministers who had no definite responsibility, could meddle in military affairs. Under the sway of Mars dualism cannot exist. In the crises of a great war Cabals and Juntos go by the board. The Irish Ministry was little more than a Junto; and Ireland need not mourn its loss.

The loss of her Parliament was far more serious; and if that body had represented the Irish people, Pitt's action would be indefensible. But Grattan's Parliament represented only a small minority of the Irish people; and that minority was resolved not to admit Catholics to full civic rights. It would have fought to maintain Protestant Episcopalian ascendancy; and under the conditions then existing England must have drawn the sword on behalf of her exacting "garrison."

Even in ordinary times such a state of things was unbearable; and the French saw it. Their aim was to strike at England through Ireland; and, but for Bonaparte's dreams of conquest in the East, this blow would have been dealt. Fortunately for Great Britain, his oriental ambitions served to divert to the sands of Egypt a thunderbolt which would have been fatal at Dublin. Even as it was, the mere presence of Bruix' great fleet at Brest prolonged the ferment in Ireland, thus emphasizing the force of the arguments in favour of Union. As we have seen, Pitt placed them in the forefront of his speeches; and those who charge him with hypocrisy, because France did not strike vigorously at Ireland during or after the Rebellion of 1798, only expose their ignorance of the facts and sentiments of that time. Throughout the years 1799 and 1800 the thought of invasion filled the minds of loyalists with dread, of malcontents with eager hope.

Nevertheless Pitt saw in the Union, not merely an expedient necessitated by war, but a permanent uplift for the whole nation. From the not dissimilar case of the Union with Scotland he augured hopefully for Ireland, believing that her commerce would thrive not less than that of North Britain. Still more did he found his hopes upon the religious settlement whereby he sought to crown his work. Ever since the days of Queen Elizabeth the strife between the Protestants and Catholics had marred the fortunes of that land. Pitt believed that it could be stilled in the larger political unity for which he now prepared.

CHAPTER XX

RESIGNATION

It is well known that no quiet could subsist in a country where there is not a Church Establishment.—GEORGE III TO ADDINGTON, 29th January 1801.

ON 25th September 1800 Pitt wrote to the Lord Chancellor, Loughborough, then in attendance on the King at Weymouth, requesting his presence at a Cabinet meeting in order to discuss the Catholic Question and proposals respecting tithes and a provision for the Catholic and Dissenting clergy. Five days later he explained to his colleagues the main proposal. In place of the Oaths of Supremacy and Abjuration he desired to impose on members of Parliament and officials merely the Oath of Allegiance, which would be no bar to Romanists. The change won the approval of all the Ministers present except Loughborough. He strongly objected to the proposal, upheld the present exclusive system, and demurred to any change affecting Roman Catholics except a commutation of tithes, a measure which he had in preparation. His colleagues, astonished at this firm opposition from the erstwhile Presbyterian of East Lothian, begged him to elaborate his Tithe Bill, and indulged the hope that further inquiry would weaken his resistance to the larger Reform. They did not know Loughborough.

There is a curious reference in one of Pitt's letters, of October 1798, to Loughborough as the Keeper of the King's conscience.[1] The phrase has an ironical ring well suited to the character of him who called it forth. Now, in his sixty-seventh year, he had run through the gamut of political professions. An adept in the art of changing sides, he, as Alexander Wedderburn, had earned the contempt or envy of all rivals. Yet such was the grace of

---

[1] "Dropmore P.," iv, 337.

431

his curves and the skill of his explanations that a new turn caused less surprise than admiration. Unlike his rival, Thurlow, who stormed ahead, Wedderburn trimmed his sails for every breeze and showed up best in light airs. Making few friends, he had few inveterate enemies; but one of them, Churchill, limned him as

> Adopting arts by which gay villains rise
> And reach the heights which honest men despise;
> Mute at the Bar and in the Senate loud,
> Dull 'mong the dullest, proudest of the proud,
> A pert prim prater of the northern race,
> Guilt in his heart, and famine in his face.

This was before Wedderburn had wormed himself into favour with Lord North and won the office of Solicitor-General (1778). Two years later he became Lord Loughborough, a title which Fox ascribed to his rancorous abuse of the American colonists. Figuring next as a member of the Fox-North Administration, he did not long share the misfortunes of his colleagues, for he alone of his colleagues contrived not to offend either the King or Pitt. This sleekness had its reward. The perversities of Thurlow having led to his fall in 1792, Loughborough became Lord Chancellor. His sage counsels heightened his reputation; and in October 1794 Pitt assigned to him the delicate task of seeing Earl Fitzwilliam and Grattan in order to smooth over the difficulties attending the union with the Old Whigs. At his house in Bedford Square, Bloomsbury, occurred some of the conferences which ensured Fitzwilliam's acceptance of the Irish Viceroyalty. Loughborough urged Pitt to do all in his power to prevent a rupture with the Portland Whigs or the Irish people. Counsels of conciliation then flowed from his lips and were treasured up. In fact, Pitt seems to have felt no suspicion of him despite his courtier-like ways and his constant attendance on the King. For Loughborough, like Dundas, had outlived the evil reputation of an earlier time. The Marquis of Buckingham, writing to Grenville on an awkward episode affecting Lord Berkeley, advised him to consult Loughborough as a man of discretion and undoubted private honour.[1]

Neither Pitt nor Grenville knew that Loughborough had

---

[1] "Dropmore P.," v, 82; "Malmesbury Diaries," ii, 507. Sir John Macpherson called Loughborough by far the cleverest man in the country ("Glenbervie Journals," 54).

played them false in 1795. The man who urged them to send Fitzwilliam to Dublin with the olive-branch soon tendered to George III official advice of an exactly opposite tenour, namely, that assent to Catholic Emancipation would involve a violation of the Coronation Oath. A day or two later he stated to Rose that he had given to the King wholly different counsels, to the effect that the Coronation Oath did not apply to the question at issue, which referred to a legislative enactment, not to an act of the King in his executive capacity.[1] Two other legal authorities unequivocally declared for this view of the case.

Whether in the autumn and winter of 1800 Loughborough's secret counsels had much effect on the King may be doubted; for George, in his letter of 6th February 1795 to Pitt, declared Catholic Emancipation to be "beyond the decision of any Cabinet of Ministers." As for the Church Establishment, it was essential to every State, and must be maintained intact. When George had once framed a resolve, it was hopeless to try to change it. Moreover, during the debates on the Union, early in 1799, he remarked to Dundas at Court that he hoped the Cabinet was not pledged to anything in favour of the Romanists. "No," was the wary reply, "that will be a matter for future consideration." Thereupon he set forth his scruples respecting the Coronation Oath. Dundas sought to allay them by observing that the Oath referred, not to his executive actions, but only to his assent to an act of the Legislature, a matter even then taken for granted. The remark, far from soothing the King, elicited the shrewd retort, "None of your Scotch metaphysics, Mr. Dundas! None of your Scotch metaphysics!"

The action of Loughborough, then, can only have put an edge on the King's resolve; and all speculation as to the exact nature of his "intrigues" at Weymouth or at Windsor is futile. In truth a collision between the King and Pitt on this topic was inevitable. The marvel is that there had been no serious friction during the past eighteen years. Probably the knowledge that a Fox Cabinet, dominated by the Prince of Wales, was the only alternative to Pitt had exerted a chastening influence on the once headstrong monarch; but now even that spectre faded away before the more potent wraith of mangled Protestantism. The King was a sincerely religious man in his own narrow way;

---

[1] Campbell, viii, 172; G. Rose, "Diaries," i, 300.

and arguments about the Coronation Oath were as useless with him as discussions on Modernism are with Pius X.

Pitt therefore kept his plans secret. But we must here digress to notice an assertion to the contrary. Malmesbury avers that Loughborough, while at Weymouth in the autumn of 1800, informed his cousin, Auckland, and the Archbishop of Canterbury of the danger to the Established Church; that the latter wrote to the King, who thereupon upbraided Pitt. Now, it is highly probable that Auckland knew nothing of the matter until the end of January 1801,[1] and the secret almost certainly did not come to light until then, when the Archbishop, Auckland's brother-in-law, was a prey to nervous anxieties resulting from recent and agitating news. Further, no such letter from the King to Pitt is extant either at the Public Record Office, Orwell Park, or Chevening; and if the proposals were known to George why did he fume at Pitt and Castlereagh on 28th January for springing the mine upon him? Finally, if the King, while at Weymouth, blamed Pitt for bringing the matter forward, why did Malmesbury censure him for keeping it secret? It is well to probe these absurdities, for they reveal the untrustworthiness of the Earl on this question.

To revert to Pitt's procedure; there were two arguments on which he must have relied for convincing the King of the need of granting Catholic Emancipation. Firstly, the Irish Catholics had, on the whole, behaved with marked loyalty and moderation during the wearisome debates on the Union at Dublin, a course of conduct markedly different from the acrid and factious tactics of the privileged Protestant Episcopalians. Secondly, as the summer of 1800 waned to autumn, the position of Great Britain became almost desperate. Her ally, Austria, had lost Lombardy and was fighting a losing game in Swabia. Russia had not only left the Second Coalition, but was threatening England with a renewal of the Armed Neutrality League. At home a bad harvest was sending up corn to famine prices; and sedition again raised its head. In such a case would not a patriotic ruler waive his objections to a measure essential not only to peace and quiet in Ireland, but to the stability of the United Kingdom? The latter consideration derived added force from the fact that Bonaparte, fresh from his triumphs in Italy, was inaugurating a policy of

---

[1] "Malmesbury Diaries," iv, 21; "Auckland Journals," iv, 114-25.

conciliation which promised to end the long ferment in the west of France and to make of her a really united nation. While he was allaying Jacobinical zeal and royalist bigotry, could Britons afford to keep up internal causes of friction, and, disunited among themselves, face a hostile world in arms? In such an emergency would not the King waive even his conscientious scruples, and at the cost of some qualms pacify and consolidate his nominally united realms?

For it was certain that the Irish Catholics would not rest now that the boon of Emancipation was well within reach. Pitt and Cornwallis had aroused their hopes. While not openly promising that the portals at Westminster should be thrown open to Roman Catholics, Ministers had allowed hints to go forth definite enough to influence opinion, especially in Cork, Tipperary, and Galway. In fact, Castlereagh assured Pitt that the help of Catholics had turned the wavering scales in favour of Union.[1] The claims of honour therefore required that Pitt should do all in his power to requite the services of a great body of men, long depressed and maligned, who, when tempted by the foreigner to revolt, had on the whole shown remarkable patience and fidelity. The pressure of this problem was too much for the scanty strength of Pitt. Worried by private financial needs, and distressed at the bewildering change in European affairs, he broke down in health in September—October; and a period of rest and change at Addington's seat at Woodley, near Reading, was all too short for a complete recovery (18th October to 5th November). Addington, describing this visit, remarked that Pitt had become one of his family. Neither of them knew that a time of feud was at hand.

At the close of the year Castlereagh came from Dublin to London to confer with Ministers on legal and other details connected with the proposal of Catholic Emancipation. By that time Loughborough's sharp opposition to the measure was known at Dublin Castle, where Cornwallis declared all resistance to the measure to be mere madness. The Catholics, he reported, were quiet merely because they were confident of success. Cooke, though once opposed to Catholic Emancipation, now accepted it as a necessity.[2] Nevertheless in the King's view Catholic Emancipation was wholly incompatible with his Corona-

---

[1] "Castlereagh Corresp.," iv 8-12.   [2] *Ibid.*, iii, 418; iv, 13, 17-20.

tion Oath and with the Church Establishment in England. In the middle of December the Chancellor drew up an able and very detailed Memorandum on the legal aspects of the case. He even discoursed on the proselytizing zeal of Romanists and the material causes of discontent in Ireland which the Union would probably dispel. As Cooke remarked, the paper seemed designed to close the question for ever.[1]

Pitt was equally determined to set the question at rest. He and Castlereagh had confidence in the issue; and Cornwallis declared that if Pitt were firm he would meet with no difficulty. Accordingly Pitt inserted in the King's Speech for the ensuing session a passage expressing confidence that Parliament would seek to improve the benefits already secured by the Act of Union. The phrase was smooth enough to leave the King's conscience unruffled, and on 23rd January he assented to the Speech, requesting that no change be made.[2] But while Pitt sapped the approaches to the citadel, Loughborough countermined him. On what day and in what manner he informed the King of the proposed measure of Catholic Emancipation is not clear. Possibly George scented mischief in a short conversation with Spencer and Grenville about the middle of January. But his brain was set on fire by something which he heard on 27th or 28th January. On the latter day (Wednesday), during the *levée* at St. James's Palace, his behaviour betrayed unusual excitement, and he said warmly to Windham, a friend of the measure, that he regarded all supporters of it as " personally indisposed " to him. Waxing hotter in the course of the function, he declared in a loud voice to Dundas: " What is this that the young Lord [Castlereagh] has brought over, which they are going to throw at my head? Lord C. came over with the plan in September. . . . I shall reckon any man my personal enemy who proposes any such measure. The most Jacobinical thing I ever heard of."

This extraordinary outburst naturally led Ministers to confer together on the morrow; and they requested Grenville to prepare

---

[1] Pellew, i, *ad fin.* The original is in " H. O.," Ireland (Corresp.), 99, together with nine others for or against Catholic Emancipation, some with notes by Castlereagh.

[2] The first Imperial Parliament met on 22nd January; but time was taken up in swearing in members and choosing a Speaker. Addington was chosen. The King's Speech was fixed for 2nd February.

a paper explaining the proposed changes in the form of oath for members of Parliament and officials. Grenville declined this task, which Pitt himself then undertook. This question, I may note, was far more difficult than outsiders could understand. Castlereagh's interviews with Pitt in September, and now again in January, had only recently brought Ministers near to an agreement, a fact which fully accounts for the delay in drafting the proposals in a form suitable for the King's inspection.[1] On that day George took another step betokening irrevocable opposition. He begged Addington to see Pitt and convince him of the danger of the measure. The King confessed that he could scarcely keep his temper in speaking about it; for it portended the destruction of the Established Church and the end of all order in civil life. Addington therefore paid a visit to Pitt, who cannot have been well pleased to see him acting as a tool of the King. The interview, however, seems to have been friendly, and it inspired Addington with the complacent hope that he had dissuaded Pitt. Possibly he or Auckland alarmed Dr. Moore, Archbishop of Canterbury, and set the bishops in motion. Other persons working to this end were the Earl of Clare and the Irish Primate. The latter took a prominent part in arousing the fears of the King. Cooke wrote: " The Primate was a great card, was much consulted by the King, for ever with him, or in correspondence with him. . . . The Archbishop of Canterbury was at first so nervous that for ten or twelve nights he could not sleep, and our Primate was daily with him, encouraging him."[2]

It is uncertain how far Pitt was aware of the many adverse influences playing upon the King; for his papers on this topic are unusually scanty. On the 30th he sent a draft of his proposals to Loughborough, a sign that he would persevere with them. On the morrow George again summoned Addington to the palace, and adjured him to form a Ministry. This offer preceded the arrival of any intimation from Pitt of his desire to resign if his advice were rejected. Addington for his part begged to be excused; whereupon the King exclaimed: " Lay your hand upon your heart and ask yourself where I am to turn for support if *you* do not stand by me." [3] Meanwhile Pitt was inditing his

[1] "Castlereagh Corresp.," iv, 17-20; G. Rose, "Diaries," i, 303.

[2] *Ibid.*, iv, 81.

[3] G. Rose, "Diaries," i, 309; Pellew, i, 287. Addington afterwards de-

famous letter of 31st January, to the King, of which this summary must suffice:

Pitt has heard with deep regret of the opposition displayed by His
Majesty to the proposals of Catholic Emancipation, which are approved
by the majority of the Cabinet and regarded as a natural sequel to the
Act of Union. The admission of Catholics and Dissenters to certain
offices, and of Catholics to Parliament, now involves little or no danger
to the Established Church or to the Protestant interest, as the Catholics
disclaim the obnoxious tenets once held by them. A form of oath can
be devised to exclude those Dissenters who may have designs against
the constitution either in Church or State. The Irish Catholic clergy
may be attached to the Government by making their maintenance partly
dependent on the State. These changes would adapt the constitution to
present needs. Pitt therefore earnestly commends the measure to the
consideration of His Majesty. Meanwhile no steps will be taken in the
matter; but, if on examination the measure should not be approved,
Pitt will beg to be allowed to resign, though in such a way as to occasion the least possible difficulty. Finally he takes the liberty " of most
respectfully, but explicitly, submitting to Your Majesty the indispensable
necessity of effectually discountenancing, in the whole of the interval,
all attempts to make use of Your Majesty's name, or to influence the
opinion of any individual on any part of the subject."

In the last sentence Pitt administered a telling and dignified
rebuke for the outrageous behaviour of the King at the *levée*. A
reply came on the morrow, couched in pompously ungrammat-
ical terms, which sufficiently refute the rumour that it was composed by that polished talker, Loughborough. George declared
that his Oath bound him to support the Established Church;
that State officials must be in active communion with that
Church. He therefore refused to discuss the present proposals,
which tended to destroy the groundwork of the Constitution.
Respecting the suggested truce of silence he wrote as follows:
" Mr. Pitt once acquainted with my sentiments, his assuring
me that he will stave off the only question whereon I fear from
his letter we can never agree—for the advantage and comfort of
continuing to have his advice and exertions in public affairs I
will certainly abstain from talking on this subject which is the
one nearest my heart." The meaning of these words is not easy
to fix; but apparently the King meant to say that his silence

stroyed those letters of the King to him which he considered unsuitable
for publication.

on the subject was conditional on Pitt promising never to bring it forward again. Now, Pitt had made no such promise. He required that, while the King was examining the proposals of his Cabinet, he would abstain from setting his counsellors against it. George III evaded this request, thereby leaving himself free to talk at large against Catholic Emancipation while he was supposed to be examining its details. We may be sure that this sentence clinched Pitt's resolve to resign at the earliest possible moment.[1]

He said so in his reply of 3rd February to the King. He expressed both regret at the King's resolve on this question, and a desire to consult his convenience, though continuance in office even for a short time became very difficult in view of the King's refusal to undertake to discountenance the use of his name during the interval. In every respect the accession of another Minister was to be desired. Pitt closed this painful correspondence with a letter, also of 3rd February, requesting a pension of £1,500 a year for Long, one of the secretaries of the Treasury, whose private means were so slender as to leave him in discomfort if he should resign. The King briefly assented to Pitt's retirement and to Long's pension. To Long's services the King accorded a few words of thanks: to those of Pitt not a word. This is the more remarkable as Pitt was then suffering from an attack of gout which depressed him greatly; but, as we shall see, the King in private expressed his deep obligations, and requested him to keep in office until all the new appointments were settled.[2] This involved a delay of nearly six weeks, which were among the most trying of his career.

On 5th February the King succeeded in persuading Addington to form a Ministry. Accordingly on the 10th he resigned the office of Speaker, being succeeded by Sir John Mitford, afterwards Lord Redesdale. There is no ground for the insinuation that Addington snatched at office. He took it without eagerness but from conscientious conviction; and Pitt, with the usual generosity of his nature, assured him of his support as a

---

[1] Grenville agreed with Pitt's letter to the King, but doubted the possibility of precluding discussion on the question, as it was already in the papers. He assured Pitt that he would act closely with him (Grenville to Pitt, 1st February 1801; Pretyman MSS.). Pitt afterwards declared that his resignation was largely due to the manner in which the King opposed him.

[2] "Lord Colchester's Diaries," i, 224.

private member. Of Pitt's colleagues Grenville, Dundas, Spencer, and Windham offered their resignations; so also did Cornwallis and Castlereagh at Dublin. Portland retained the Home Secretaryship. Of late he had wavered on the subject of Catholic Emancipation, perhaps owing to the arguments of Loughborough. Westmorland and Chatham also kept their positions of Lord Privy Seal and Lord President. The retention of office by the latter aroused some comment; but as the earnest desire of Pitt was to disarrange the Ministry as little as possible, he probably approved conduct which outsiders condemned as unbrotherly.

The following letter from Chatham, dated Winchester, 6th February, is of interest. After expressing his regret at Pitt's resignation, he continues: " Upon the measure itself of granting further indulgence to the Catholics I have neither time, nor indeed would it be of any use, to say anything at present. I will only observe that if, by being on the spot, I could in any degree have contributed even to put off the extremity to which the agitation of it has led, I should think I had done much, and I should be most unhappy in having been absent ; otherwise I consider myself as fortunate in having avoided a discussion which could only have been painful to me in many respects. As things stand, I shall certainly think it my duty to come to town in a few days, and I will defer, till we meet, any further remarks; I will only add that if your part is irrevocably taken, the King could not have acted more wisely than in having recourse to the Speaker. . . . I see all the difficulty and delicacy of your situation." [1]

Far less charitable were the sentiments of Dundas in the following letter:

Wimbledon, 7 *Feb.*, 1801.[2]

I know not to what stage the Speaker's endeavours to form an Arrangement have proceeded; but it is impossible for me not to whisper into your ear my conviction that no Arrangement can be formed under him as its head that will not crumble to pieces almost as soon as formed. Our friends who, as an act of friendship and attachment to you agree to remain in office, do it with the utmost chagrin and unwillingness; and among the other considerations which operate upon them the feeling that they are embarking in an Administration under a head totally incapable to carry it on and which must of course soon be an object of

<hr>

[1] Pitt MSS., 122.   [2] Pretyman MSS.

ridicule is uppermost in their minds. Add to this that, though they will
not certainly enter into faction and opposition, all the aristocracy of the
country at present cordially connected with Government, and part of it
under you, feel a degradation in the first Minister of the Country being
selected from [*sic*] a Person of the description of Mr. Addington without the slightest pretensions to justify it, and destitute of abilities to
carry it on. Depend upon it I am not exaggerating the state of the case;
and a very short experience will prove that I am right; and the Speaker
will ere long feel that he has fallen from a most exalted situation and
character into one of a very opposite description. Save him from it if
not too late. Yourself excluded from it, I am afraid nothing permanent
can be formed; but if the Speaker was to advise the King to call upon
the Duke of Portland to form an Administration, I am persuaded His
Grace at the head of it, with either Steele, Ryder, Lord Hawkesbury, or
even Mr. Abbott as his Chancellor of the Exchequer, would fill the
public eye infinitely more than anything that can be found upon the
plan now in agitation. By the answer I have received from the King to
my resignation I must entreat you without delay to send for my correspondence with Lord Westmorland in order that I may be sure of what
my recollection suggests, that I refused to give the promise of the
Government at home that what was then proposed was the ultimatum
of concession.

The last sentence of Chatham's letter refers to the difficulties
of Pitt's position. These have nearly always been overlooked.
Yet his decision turned finally on a question of honour. It is
true that neither Pitt nor Cornwallis gave a distinct pledge to
the Irish Catholics that the Cabinet would press their claims
if they would support the Union. But no such pledge could
have been given without exasperating the King and the privileged phalanx at St. Stephen's Green. Therefore, when the
critics of Pitt demand to see the proof that he made a promise,
they ask for what, in the nature of the case, could not be forthcoming. Cornwallis and Castlereagh were aware of the need of
extreme caution in making overtures to the leading Catholics;
and they afterwards denied that they gave a distinct pledge.
Nevertheless, some of their agents induced the Catholics of the
south and west of Ireland, to act in a "highly useful" manner,
which averted an otherwise dangerous opposition. Castlereagh
explained this to Pitt early in January;[1] and the scrupulous

---

[1] "Castlereagh Corresp.," iv, 8-12. Both Grenville and Windham declared
in Parliament in May 1805 that hopes were held out to the Irish Catholics,
and that their support of the Union was the result (Hansard, iv, 659, 1022).

Minister must have considered these promises as a debt of honour. That some of the leading Irish Catholics viewed them in the same light appears in an account of a representative meeting held at Ryan's house in Marlborough Street, Dublin, on 27th October 1804. Ryan then set forth the condition of his co-religionists at the time of the Union, and referred to the stipulations made to them by Government. Others, including Lord Fingall and a barrister, Scully, followed; and after two more meetings, they resolved to petition Pitt, who had by that time returned to office, it being known that he was at heart favourable to their claims.[1] But in his speech of 14th May 1805 on this topic, he said, " I did not make a distinct pledge. On the contrary, I believe the line of argument I took was, that if it should be thought right to give what the Catholics required, it might be given with more safety to the Empire.[2]

What the stipulations were is not clear; for with this exception the Irish Records are disappointingly silent. But it is clear that Canning finally came to consider them binding on an honourable man. In his great speech on Catholic Emancipation in March 1827, while admitting that Pitt in 1800 made no definite promise to the Catholics, he added these notable words: " The Catholics were made to believe, and that belief was a powerful inducement to them to lend their aid towards the accomplishment of the measure [the Union] that in the Imperial Parliament the question which so nearly concerned them would be more favourably entertained. . . . There is no tribunal, however solemn, before which I am not prepared to depose to my firm belief in the sincerity of Mr. Pitt's wishes and intentions to carry it." This passage once for all refutes the charges of insincerity which certain of Canning's biographers have brought against Pitt.

Light is thrown on this topic by notes of Bishop Tomline. Pitt consulted his former tutor at this crisis; for on 6th February he wrote warning him of his approaching resignation on grounds which he desired to explain. He added : " I am in the firm persuasion that an Arrangement can be formed to which I can give a cordial general support, and which may keep everything safe."[3] The bishop thereupon came to town and saw much of Pitt, whose conduct he thus describes: " I never saw Mr. Pitt in more uniformly cheerful spirits, although everyone about him was de-

---

[1] " H. O.," Ireland (Corresp.), 99.   [2] Hansard, iv, 1015.
[3] Pretyman MSS.

jected and melancholy. He talked of his quitting office with the utmost composure, gave the King the highest credit for the notions on which he acted, and also fully acquitted those who were supposed to have influenced his sentiments and conduct. He felt some dissatisfaction at the conduct of one who was *not* a Cabinet Minister, and was under great obligations to Mr. Pitt, who had by intrigues and misrepresentations and every unfair means in his power endeavoured to influence people's opinion on the question and to excite alarm and prejudice against him." The reference here is to Lord Auckland, but nothing definite is known as to his conduct. The bishop then states that Pitt's equanimity was surprising, inasmuch as his resignation would reduce his income to less than that of a country gentleman and necessitate the sale of Holwood. Nevertheless, no hasty word fell from him even in the most confidential conversation; but he talked cheerfully of living in privacy for the rest of his life, and expressed satisfaction that men who were attached to the constitution would carry on affairs of State. The safety of the country seemed to be his only concern. Tomline then describes the cause and the circumstances of Pitt's resignation:[1]

While the business of the Union was going on, Lord Cornwallis had informed the Ministers in England that the support of the Catholics to the measure would in a great degree depend upon the intention of Ministers to remove those disabilities under which they at present laboured. This produced in the Cabinet a discussion of the question of Catholic Emancipation, as it is called, and Lord Cornwallis was authorized to declare that it was intended by Government, after the Union should have taken place, to grant to the Catholics some further indulgences; but he was not authorized to pledge the Government to any particular measure, nor was any plan of this kind settled by the Cabinet. When the King's Speech was to be drawn up for the opening of the Imperial Parliament, the Catholic Question naturally occurred and gave rise to a good deal of discussion in the Cabinet. Mr. Pitt, Lord Grenville, Lord Spencer, Mr. Dundas, and Mr. Wyndham declared themselves in favour of Catholic Emancipation; and the Lord Chancellor, the Duke of Portland and Lord Westmorland against it. Lord Chatham and Lord Liverpool did not attend the Council, the former being at Winchester as military commander of that district and the latter was confined to his house by illness.

The King was of course informed of this division in the Cabinet and

[1] Pretyman MSS.

took a decided part by talking against the question freely and openly to everyone he saw. On Wednesday, the 28th of January, the King said to Mr. D[undas] at the *levée* in such a voice that those who were near might hear him—"So here is an Irish Secretary come over to propose in Parliament the Emancipation of the Irish Catholics, as they call it"—and then he declared himself in the strongest degree hostile to the question. This was of course reported to Mr. Pitt. On the Friday (the 30th) the King sent for the Speaker to the Queen's House and conversed with him a long time. Upon my mentioning this circumstance to Mr. Pitt, he said he knew what happened at that interview and seemed perfectly satisfied with it. He had before told me (namely, the first night he saw me, Saturday, Feb. 7th) that he knew nine days before that he should be under the necessity of resigning. On the 31st Mr. Pitt wrote his first letter to the King. Two letters only passed on each side, which see. Mr. Pitt did not see the King till at the *levée* on Wednesday the 11th [February]. The King spoke to him in the most gracious manner— "You have behaved like yourself throughout this business. Nothing could possibly be more honourable. I have a great deal more to say to you."—"Your Majesty has already said much more than the occasion calls for."—"Oh no, I have not; and I do not care who hears me: it was impossible for anyone to behave more honourably." After more conversation of the same kind the King desired to see Mr. Pitt in the closet. The *levée* continued, and, some little time after, Mr. Pitt said to the King: "Your Majesty will pardon me if I take the liberty of saying that I fear I shall not be able to attend Your Majesty in the closet." "Oh yes: you must; I have just done." The King went to the closet and Mr. Pitt attended him. Nothing could exceed the kindness of the King towards Mr. Pitt: he was affected very much and more than once. The conversation lasted more than half an hour; and in the course of it the King said that, tho' he could no longer retain Mr. Pitt in his service, he hoped to have him as his friend. Mr. Pitt, with strong expressions both of duty and attachment and love to His Majesty, submitted that any intercourse of that kind might be injurious to His Majesty's Government; for that it was very important that his new Ministers should appear to act by themselves and for themselves, and that if he was frequently with His Majesty, unfavourable conclusions might be drawn concerning his interference or influence. This seemed to satisfy the King, and they parted. At the *levée* the King spoke in the highest terms of Mr. Pitt's conduct throughout the business of his resignation, and said that it was very different from that of his predecessors.

This narrative needs little comment, except on the phrase that the Cabinet had promised to grant the Catholics "some further indulgences." Probably the schism occurred on the extent of those concessions, Pitt and the majority desiring the admission of Catholics to Parliament and to offices of trust, while Loughborough and the minority refused to do more than grant some measure of support to the Irish priests.[1] The King probably opposed both concessions; and Pitt seems to have ascribed his strenuous opposition more to the intrigues of Auckland than to those of Loughborough. In this he was probably mistaken. The best judge on this question, the monarch himself, certainly looked on the Chancellor as a traitor. But in truth the crisis could not be avoided. The King acknowledged as much in his effusive comments on the extremely honourable conduct of Pitt, but he also most firmly declared that he could no longer retain him in his service. This was in effect a dismissal. On 18th February, George wrote a brief letter expressing his sorrow at the close of Pitt's political career and his satisfaction that Parliament had passed the Ways and Means without debate. Thus did he close his correspondence with a Minister who had devotedly served him for more than seventeen years.

There is little need to notice the hasty and spiteful comments of Lord Malmesbury, that Pitt was playing a selfishly criminal game by resigning, with the evident aim of showing his own strength and being called back to office on his own terms.[2] The Malmesbury Diaries at this point consist chiefly of hearsays, which can readily be refuted. But this calumny spread widely, and Fox finally barbed it with the hint that the substitution of Addington for Pitt was " a notorious juggle," the former being obviously a dummy to be knocked down when it suited Pitt to come back fancy-free about the Catholics. Fortunately, the correspondence of statesmen often supplies antidotes to the venomous gibes of bystanders; and a case in point is a phrase in Grenville's letter of 13th February to Minto: " There was no

[1] In " H. O.," Ireland (Corresp.), 99, are long reports of the Irish Catholic bishops, dated November 1800, on the state of their dioceses. The bishops' incomes did not average more than £300 a year. The Archbishops of Dublin and Tuam reckoned the total number of parish priests and curates at 1,800, of whom 1,400 were seculars and 400 regulars. The benefices numbered 1,200; each required the services of two priests. The destruction of the seminaries in France and the poverty of the Irish made it impossible to supply or support 2,400 clergy. Other papers follow for and against Catholic Emancipation. See also " Castlereagh Corresp.," iii, *ad fin.*

[2] " Malmesbury Diaries," iv, 3, 8, 9, 14.

alternative except that of taking this step [resignation] or of agreeing to the disguise or dereliction of one's opinion on one of the most important questions in the whole range of our domestic policy."[1]

Pitt has been sharply censured for his excessive scrupulousness in resigning at so serious a crisis. But the verdict must depend on three main issues, the importance of the question at stake, that of the services rendered by the Irish Catholics, and the nature of the promises made to them. Now, no one will deny that in the days when France was striving to effect the independence of Ireland—for Bonaparte was thought to be pressing on the war with that aim in view[2]—the question of the Union stood paramount. It was the most important problem confronting Parliament since the Union with Scotland in 1707; and the difficulties encountered were greater than those raised by the Scots. The services of the Irish Catholics to the cause of the Union are not easy to assess; but Castlereagh, a cool judge, rated them high. In such a case a man of sensitive conscience will deem himself bound to those who, in reliance on his sense of honour, acted in a way that ensured the success of his measure. Above all, in so tangled a situation the final decision will depend on the character of the statesman. Walpole would have waived aside the debt of honour. Pitt resolved to discharge it.

It is scarcely necessary to notice another slander, that Pitt resigned because, in his inability to procure peace from France, he intended to put Addington in office merely for that purpose, to be ousted when it was fulfilled. No evidence is forthcoming in support of this version, which found no small favour with Continental historians of a former generation; but it is now clear that the split occurred solely on Catholic Emancipation. Those Ministers who approved it resigned; while its opponents remained in office, namely, Portland, Chatham, and Westmorland. The same is true of the subordinate offices. The new Cabinet decided to grant only occasional relief and a "compassionate allowance" to the Irish priests.[3] In several other matters its

[1] "Dropmore P.," vi, 445. Mulgrave, who knew Pitt well, was convinced of his sincerity in resigning. His letter of 9th February 1801 (quoted by R. Plumer Ward, "Memoirs," i, 44) refutes the insinuations of Sorel (vi, 101) that Pitt resigned because he could not make peace with France.
[2] "Castlereagh Corresp.," iii, 285.
[3] "Lord Colchester's Diaries," i, 286.

policy differed from that of Pitt; and Addington soon made it apparent that he was no stop-gap.

But now this clear issue was to be blurred in the blinding glare of the King's lunacy. The causes of the malady of February 1801 were partly physical, partly mental. While still agitated by the dismissal of his trusted Minister, the King, two days later, went to church on the day appointed for the National Fast. That day of supplication for delivery from the perils of the time was shrouded in gloom and snow. He remained a long time in church and took a chill. Nevertheless, with his wonted energy he persisted in transacting business with Addington, until the stress told on the brain. On the 16th slight feverish symptoms began to develop. Yet Addington saw him often about new appointments, until on Sunday the 22nd the symptoms caused some concern. Willis, son of the man who had so much control over him during the illness of 1788-9, now came to the Queen's House, and resumed the old regimen. Dr. Gisborne was also in attendance. From the notes of Tomline we glean curious details about the illness. The bilious symptoms were very pronounced, and after the 23rd the King became worse. His manner became nervous and "hurried." He went up to Willis and shook him eagerly by the hand. When the Queen and princesses rose to leave, he jocosely extended his arms so as to stop them; whereupon Willis stepped forward, and, looking at him earnestly, told him he was very ill. The King at once said with a deep sigh: "I see, I cannot deceive you. I have deceived all the rest. They think me well; but I cannot deceive you." He then burst into an agony of weeping, threw himself into Willis's arms, and said: "You are right. I am ill indeed. But oh! for God's sake, keep your father from me, and keep off a Regency."

After weeping for a quarter of an hour, he walked about the room with Willis for an hour and a half. In the evening he grew worse. At 2.30 a.m. he went to bed, while the Duke of Kent and Willis watched by the door. As in the previous seizure, intervals of calm and reasonableness alternated strangely with fits of delirium or even of violence. Now and again he spoke collectedly, and at such times those about him rejoiced to hear the familiar "What, what," wherewith he prefaced his remarks.[1]

[1] Pretyman MSS.

Frequently he declared that he would uphold the Church of England ; or again his thoughts started away from the loathed spectre of a Regency. On 2nd March the illness took so violent a turn that his life seemed in danger; but, as was the case twelve years before, long spells of sleep supervened and brought his pulse down from 136 to 84. His powers of recovery surprised every one about him. By 6th March he was so far well as to be allowed to see the Dukes of York, Kent, and Cumberland. Not until 9th March did he undergo the more trying ordeal of seeing the Prince of Wales. On that same day he requested to see Pitt, who very properly declined, suggesting, with all deference, that Addington was the proper person for an interview.[1]

Meanwhile, at or just after the crisis of the illness, Pitt gave a very important pledge. If we may trust the far from convincing statements of Lord Malmesbury, who had the story from Pelham, the King on 7th March charged Willis to inform Pitt of the improvement in his health, and to add the biting words: " But what has not *he* to answer for who is the cause of my having been ill at all? " Pelham further asserted that Pitt, in a " most dutiful, humble and contrite answer," wrote down his resolve to give up Catholic Emancipation.[2] Now it is almost certain that Pitt sent no such letter, for none exists either at the Public Record Office, Orwell Park, or Chevening. Tomline asserts that Pitt sent by Willis a verbal assurance that he would not agitate Catholic Emancipation again during the King's reign ; whereupon George III exclaimed: " Now my mind will be at ease." The bishop, however, believed that Pitt's assurance was reported in a more emphatic form than was warranted; and the statesman does not seem to have considered himself absolutely bound by it. Yet the written assurance sent by Rose to the King on behalf of Pitt seems binding during that reign.[3]

Thus had the King conquered—by madness. No incident in the life of Pitt is more unfortunate than this surrender. The King had made an ungenerous use of the privileges of an invalid, and the pressure which he put on Pitt passes the bounds even of the immorality of a sick-room. The illness began with a chill due to his own imprudence; but he used its later developments to extort a promise which otherwise would never have been

---

[1] G. Rose, " Diaries," i, 313, 330; " Lord Colchester's Diaries," i, 244.

[2] " Malmesbury Diaries," iv, 31, 32.

[3] G. Rose, " Diaries," i, 360; Stanhope, iii, 304, 305.

forthcoming. Nothing but the crisis in the King's illness led Pitt to waver. For at the end of February he authorized Castlereagh to send to Cornwallis at Dublin a declaration intended to reassure the Irish Catholics. It pointed out that the majority of the Cabinet had resigned owing to the impossibility of carrying Catholic Emancipation at the present juncture. He (Pitt) still resolved to do his utmost for the success of that cause; and therefore begged them to refrain from any conduct which would prejudice it in the future. Cornwallis delivered this and another paper to the titular Archbishop of Dublin and Lord Fingall for circulation among their friends and found that it produced good results.[1] Far different, of course, was the effect produced on those few who knew of Pitt's private promise to the King. They contrasted it with the contrary promise to the Irish Catholics and drew the most unfavourable inferences, forgetting that between 27th February and 2nd March the King's illness had taken so dangerous a turn as perhaps to justify the use of that political sedative.

While blaming Pitt for weakness in giving this pledge to the King, we must remember that the prolongation of the reign of George III was the first desire of all responsible statesmen. The intrigues of the Prince of Wales and Fox for a Regency were again beginning; and thus there loomed ahead an appalling vista of waste and demoralization. In these circumstances Dundas and Cornwallis came to the conclusion that the King's conscience must not again be troubled. Grenville seems to have held firm on the Catholic Question.[2] But his colleagues now took an opportunist view. Pitt had two or three interviews with the Prince of Wales, late in February and early in March, and made it clear that the Prince would be well advised to accept the Regency Bill drafted in 1789. On the Prince asking whether this was the opinion of certain of Pitt's colleagues, who then opposed that Bill as derogatory to his interests, Pitt at once replied in the affirmative; and when the Prince further objected to certain restrictions on the power of the Regent, Pitt declared that no change would be acceptable. They parted courteously but coolly; and we may be sure that the Prince

[1] "Cornwallis Corresp.," iii, 343-9.
[2] Ibid., iii, 346; "Lord Colchester's Diaries," i, 243. The writer in the "Edinburgh Review" for 1858, who censured Pitt, failed to notice the entire change in the political situation brought about by the King's acute malady.

never forgave Pitt for his uncompromising assertion of the rights of Parliament.

So dark was the outlook at home and abroad that Pitt was persuaded, probably by Dundas, Tomline, Rose, and Canning, to re-consider the whole question with a view to continuance in office, provided that some suitable position were found for Addington. The bishop penned some notes of sharp criticism on the conduct of Addington, affirming that, if he had been patriotic and sincere, he would have pressed Pitt to remain in office. The following words are remarkable: " Mr. Pitt, Mr. Dundas and myself had a long conversation upon this point at Wimbledon; and I am satisfied that, if Mr. Addington had entered into the idea cordially, Mr. Pitt's resignation might have been prevented." He adds that they drew up a tentative scheme of a Cabinet, Pitt remaining as chief, while Addington was to be a Secretary of State; but the latter rejected this indignantly.[1] Pitt also finally deemed the plan " utterly improper," and threatened to hold aloof from those who would not support the new Administration or croaked about its instability. The action of Dundas and the bishop was unfortunate; for it gave rise to the report that Pitt was intriguing with them for a shuffling of offices in which he would again come out at the top; and, as usually happens, the meanest version overshadowed the truth.

Fortune willed that the new Ministry, by far the weakest Ministry of recent times, should win two brilliant successes and secure a not inglorious peace. So bewildering a change seemed impossible in the dark days of February—March 1801, when it was the bounden duty of every strong man to remain at his post, and of under-studies to stand aside. The fates and Addington willed otherwise. Pitt resigned on 14th March, nineteen days before Nelson triumphed at Copenhagen.

Meanwhile Pitt had endeavoured to place the nation's finance on a sound footing. His Budget speech of 18th February has a ring of confidence and pride. True, the expenses were unprecedentedly heavy. Great Britain had to provide £12,117,000, and Ireland £3,785,000, for the army alone. The navy cost £15,800,000; the Ordnance £1,938,000. The bad seasons or other causes having lessened the yield of the Income Tax and the Malt Tax, he proposed further imposts upon sugar, raisins,

---

[1] Pretyman MSS.

tea, paper, timber, lead, and all exports without exception. He increased the Excise duty on horses, even those used for agriculture, on stamp duties, and on the postage of letters. He also urged that not less than £200,000 (the normal amount) should be set apart for the reduction of the British National Debt. Over against these depressing proposals he set the notable fact that British commerce prospered more than ever, and that the revenue showed remarkable buoyancy. From these extraordinary symptons he augured that the strength and spirit of the people were equal to all the demands of the crisis; and he declared that the attachment of the nation to its revered monarch and beloved constitution furnished a moving spectacle to Europe. The House accepted these crushing imposts without demur.

He found it more difficult to reconcile his followers to the sway of Addington. As we have seen, Dundas had already expressed to Pitt his scorn of him and his desire for a Portland Ministry. Rose also refused to serve under a man whom he accused (unjustly, as we now know) of worming his way to office; and the high-spirited Canning declined to give to Pitt any pledge except that he would not laugh at the new Prime Minister. It is clear that Canning, like his chief, disliked resignation. As the gifted young Irishman wrote, it was not at all good fun to move out of the best house in London (Downing Street) and hunt about for a little dwelling.[1] Ryder and Steele kept their posts.

Singular to relate, the Mr. Pliable of so many Ministries was soon to be turned out. Loughborough, on whose back Addington climbed to power, forthwith received a direct intimation to withdraw. The Lord Chancellor therefore closed his career, the King bestowing on him for his services to religion the title Earl of Rosslyn. To finish with him, we may note that his settlement near Windsor and his assiduous courting of the royal favour finally secured an epitaph quite as piquant as any which George bestowed. On hearing of Rosslyn's sudden death early in 1805, the King earnestly asked the messenger whether the news was trustworthy; and, on receiving a reassuring reply, he said: " Then, he has not left a greater knave behind him in my dominions." The comment of Thurlow on this gracious remark

---

[1] Bagot, " Canning and his Friends," i, 180.

is equally notable: "Then I presume that His Majesty is quite sane at present."

One of Pitt's friendships was severed by the crisis. As we have seen, he deeply resented the part played by Auckland. To his letter of remonstrance he replied very briefly that, widely as they differed on the topic at issue, they differed quite as much as to the question on which side there had been a failure of friendship, confidence, or attention. The rupture became complete on 20th March, when Auckland declared in the Lords that Pitt's resignation was involved in mystery which the eye could not penetrate. The insinuation wounded Pitt deeply; and his intercourse with Auckland entirely ceased. Pitt was not exacting in his social intercourse; but no man of high feeling can endure secret opposition, followed by a veiled insinuation that what he has done from high principle resulted from motives that cannot bear the light. This is an unpardonable sin that ends friendship.

With all his outward composure, Pitt must have felt deep distress at his failure to complete the Union by the act of grace which he had in contemplation. The time was ripe, indeed over-ripe, for a generous experiment, whereby seven tenths of the Irish people would have gained religious equality. If the populace of Dublin hailed with joy the St. Patrick's cross on the new Union Jack,[1] we may be sure that Irishmen, irrespective of creed, would have joined heart and soul in the larger national unity which it typified. It is probable that Pitt, when granting the franchise to Irish Catholics in 1793, resolved to make the other concessions at an early date. But the cause of Catholic Emancipation having been prejudiced by the unwise haste of Fitzwilliam in 1795, and by raids and revolts soon after, the time of the Union was the first which he could seize with any chance of success; and he hoped to vitalize that Union by an act which would then have been hailed as a boon. Such acts of grace are all too rare in the frigid annals of British Parliaments. The Anglo-Saxon race builds its political fabric too exclusively on material interests; and the whole structure is the uglier and weaker for this calculating hardness. At the time of the Union with Scotland, the counsellors of Queen Anne utterly failed to

---

[1] "Castlereagh Corresp.," iv, 14.

touch the hearts of the Scots; and it was left to commerce sluggishly and partially to mingle the two peoples. In contrast with this dullness, how inspiring are the annals of France in the early and best days of the Revolution. Then the separatist Provincial System vanished as a miasma; and amidst the eager hopes and class renunciations of that golden day the French people found a unity such as legislators alone can neither make nor unmake. With the insight of a statesman Pitt now sought to clinch legislation by sentiment. He desired to vivify the Union with Ireland by a concession which would come with all the more graciousness because he had not introduced it into the legal contract of marriage. But the outcome of it all was, for himself resignation, for the two peoples the continuance of their age-long feud.

CHAPTER XXI

PITT AND HIS FRIENDS (1794-1805)

Nothing could be more playful, and at the same time more instructive, than Pitt's conversation on a variety of topics while sitting in the library at Cirencester. You never would have guessed that the man before you was Prime Minister of the country, and one of the greatest that ever filled that situation. His style and manner were quite those of an accomplished idler. —"Malmesbury Diaries," iv, 34.

THE conflict of parties and interests is apt to thin the circle of a statesman's friends; and in that age of relentless strife the denuding forces worked havoc. Only he who possesses truly lovable qualities can pass through such a time with comparatively little loss; and such was the lot of Pitt. True, his circle was somewhat diminished. The opposition of Bankes had been at times so sharp as to lessen their intimacy; and the reputation of Steele had suffered seriously from financial irregularities.[1] Pitt's affection for Dundas and Grenville had also cooled; but on the whole his friendships stood the test of time better, perhaps, than those of any statesman of the eighteenth century. Certainly in this respect he compares favourably with his awe-inspiring father. Not that Pitt possessed the charm of affability. On most persons his austere self-concentration produced a repellent effect; and it must be confessed that the Grenville strain in his nature dowered him with a fund of more than ordinary English coldness. Such was the opinion not only of the French *émigrés*, whom he designedly kept at arm's length, but even of his followers, to whom his aloofness seemed a violation of the rules of the parliamentary game. But it was not in his nature to expand except in the heat of debate or in congenial society. In general his stiffness was insular, his pre-occupation profound. Lady Hester Stanhope, who saw much of him in the closing

---

[1] Wraxall, iii, 458. For Pitt's earlier friendships see my former volume.

454

years, pictures his thin, tall, rather ungainly figure, stalking
through Hyde Park, oblivious of all surroundings, with head
uptilted, "as if his ideas were *en air*, so that you would have
taken him for a poet."[1]

The comparison is as flighty as Lady Hester's remarks usually
were, though the passage may depict with truth the air that Pitt
assumed when walking with her. No one else accused him of
having affinities to poets. In truth, so angular was his nature,
so restricted his sympathies, that he never came in touch with
literary men, artists, or original thinkers. His life was the poorer
for it. A statesman should know more than a part of human
life; and Pitt never realized the full extent of his powers
because he spent his time almost entirely amongst politicians of
the same school. His mind, though by no means closed against
new ideas, lacked the eager inquisitiveness of that of Napoleon,
who, before the process of imperial fossilization set in, welcomed
discussions with men of all shades of opinion, and encouraged
in them that frankness of utterance which at once widens and
clarifies the views of the disputants. It is true that Pitt's private
conversations are almost unknown. They appear to have ranged
within political grooves, with frequent excursions into the loved
domains of classical and English literature; but he seems
never to have explored the new realms of speculation and
poetry then opened up by Bentham and the Lake Poets. A
letter of the poet Hayley to him will serve to suggest the extent
of his loss in limiting his intercourse to a comparatively small
coterie:

Felpham, near Chichester, *Sept.* 9 [?].[2]

DEAR PITT,

Why are you slow in doing the little good in your power? Yes:
great as you are, the real good you can do must be little; but that little
I once believed you would ever haste to do with a generous eagerness
and enthusiasm, and therefore I used to contemplate your character
with an enthusiastic affection. That character, high as it was, sunk in

---

[1] "Mems. of Lady Hester Stanhope," iii, 187.
[2] From Mr. Broadley's MSS. Hayley's efforts on behalf of Cowper have
been described by Professor E. Dowden, "Essays: Modern and Eliza-
bethan" (1910). Ultimately a pension of £300 a year was assigned to Cowper: the authorization, signed by the King and Pitt, and dated 23rd April
1794, is now in the Cowper Museum, Olney, Bucks, so the secretary, Mr.
Thomas Wright (editor of Cowper's Letters), kindly informs me.

my estimation from the calamitous delay concerning the promised pension of Cowper, a delay which allowed that dear and now released sufferer to sink into utter and useless distraction before the neglected promise was fulfilled. Will you make me some amends for the affectionate concern I suffered for the diminution of your glory in that business by expediting now a pension eagerly but ineffectively solicited by many *great people*, as I am told, for a most deserving woman, the widow of Mr. Green, the consul at Nice? . . . Deserve and receive a kind and constant remembrance in the benedictions of a recluse who has still the ambition to live in your regard by the good which he would excite you to perform. At all events forgive this very unexpected intrusion and importunity from the old and long sequestered admirer of your youth,

W. Hayley.

Hayley's letter is a trifle too presumptuous in tone even for an old friend; but it affords one more proof of Pitt's neglect of literary men, though it is but fair to remember that in 1793-4 he was hard pressed by the outbreak of war with France and the struggle to keep the Allies together. Still, the greatest of statesmen is he who, in the midst of world politics, neither neglects old friends, nor forgets the claims of literature and art. In this connection it is painful to add that he allowed the yearly stipend of the King's Painter, Sir Joshua Reynolds, to be reduced from £200 to £50. On Reynolds soliciting the secretaryship to the Order of the Bath, he was told that it had been promised to an official of the Treasury. Another request, proffered through his patron, the Duke of Rutland, also proved fruitless, and he had reason to write with some bitterness—" Mr. Pitt, I fear, has not much attention to the arts."[1] His neglect of literature and the arts was the more unfortunate because George III and his sons did not raise the tone of the Court in this respect, witness the remark of the King to Gibbon at a State function. "Well, Mr. Gibbon, it's always scribble, scribble, I suppose."[2]

Apart from these obvious limitations in Pitt's nature, there was a wealth of noble qualities, which ensured life-long devotion from those who penetrated the protective crust and came to

---

[1] "Rutland Papers," iii, 229, 241 (Hist. MSS. Comm.). Soo, too, Tomline said that Pitt had no ear for music, and little taste for drawing or painting, though he was fond of architecture, and once drew from memory the plan of a mansion in Norfolk, with a view to improving it (Lord Rosebery, "Tomline's Estimate of Pitt," 34).

[2] "Glenbervie Journals," 195.

know, not the statesman, but the man. In him the qualities that command respect and excite affection were happily balanced. To a manly courage which never quailed in the hour of disaster, and a good sense that provided sage counsels alike in private and public affairs, he added the tenderer gifts. His affection once given was not lightly withdrawn. He looked always on the best side of men, and to that noble failing, if failing it be, most of his blunders may be ascribed. Even when his confidence was abused, he was loth to take revenge, so that Canning expressed regret at his reluctance to punish those who betrayed him.[1] Such a man will often make mistakes, but he will also inspire the devotion that serves to repair them. Moreover, even his opponents were forced to admit the conscientiousness of his conduct. On this topic the testimony of his friend Wilberforce is of value; for they had differed sharply as to the rupture with France in 1793; and, somewhat later, Wilberforce lamented the relaxation of Pitt's efforts against the Slave Trade. Yet their differences did not end their friendship; on 30th November 1797 the philanthropist wrote as follows to Sir Richard Aclom on the subject of the reformation of morals:

. . . There is one point only on which I will now declare we perfectly coincide, I mean, that of a general moral reform being the only real restorative of the health of our body politic. But I hesitate not to say that, tho' the Government is in its system and principle too much (indeed ever so little is, as I think, too much) tainted with corruption, yet it is more sound than the people at large. You appear to feel the disposition of the public to yield an implicit assent to Ministers without stopping to investigate the causes of that disposition (which are chiefly to be found in the violence of the Opposition and the established predominance of party). I will frankly avow no man has lamented this more than myself; I may indeed say more than this. I have endeavoured both in public and in private to fight against it. But selfishness has diffused itself thro' the whole mass of our people, and *hinc illae lacrymae*. You mistakenly conceive, as do many others, that I am biassed by personal affection for Mr. Pitt. When we meet, I will rectify your error on that head. . . .[2]

Again, on 20th February 1798, Wilberforce wrote to William Smith, an active Abolitionist and now prominent in the Oppo-

---

[1] "Malmesbury Diaries," iv, 26; G. Rose, "Diaries," i, 4.
[2] Pitt MSS., 189.

sition, deploring the dilatoriness of Pitt, but maintaining that
his patriotism was purer and more disinterested than that of
anyone not under the direct influence of Christian principles.
He adds these words:

> I speak not this from the partiality of personal affection. In fact for
> several years past there has been so little of the *eadem velle et eadem
> nolle* that our friendship has starved for want of nutriment. I really love
> him for his public qualities and his private ones, though there too he
> is much misunderstood. But how can I expect that he should love me
> much, who have been so long rendering myself in various ways vexatious
> to him, and, above all, when, poor fellow, he never schools his mind by
> a cessation from political ruminations, the most blinding, hardening,
> and souring of all others?[1]

These passages explain why the personality of Pitt attracted
all that was purest and most patriotic in the public life of
England. Men might disagree with particular actions, but they
saw in him the saving genius of the State; and this was the
dominant feeling until the year 1801 when events scattered his
following and reduced public life almost to a state of chaos.

His character, then, was strong in the virtues of steadfastness
and loyalty, on which the social gifts can root deeply and bear
perennial fruit. Of these he had rich store. His conversations
possessed singular charm; for his melodious voice, facile fancy,
and retentive memory enabled him to adorn all topics. His
favourite themes were the Greek and Latin Classics. The rooms
at Holwood or Walmer were strewn with volumes of his favourite
authors, on whom he delighted to converse at length. Grenville
declared to Wellesley that Pitt was the best classical scholar he
had ever met. Yet, with the delicate tact which bade him enliven, not dominate, the social circle, he refrained from obtruding
those subjects on occasions when they would be neither known
nor appreciated. Equally good was his knowledge of English
literature; so that in the company of kindred spirits, the flow of
wit and learning, imagination and experience, must have rivalled
that of the Literary Club over which Dr. Johnson held sway.

Unfortunately, only the merest scraps survive; but the testimony of Pitt's friends suffices to refute the Whig legend as to
his cold and calculating selfishness, which filled even the hours
of leisure with schemes for making himself necessary to the King

[1] "Life of Wilberforce," ii, 270.

and country.[1] On the contrary, he was fond of society, throwing himself so heartily into the conversation that the *savant* was merged in the wit, the Prime Minister in the genial companion. His jests were of that Attic flavour which seasons without stinging; and this was the outcome, not of calculation, but of a kindly disposition, which delighted to throw off political cares amidst the tide of mirth which he helped to carry to the full. He also felt increasingly the charms of country life, and at Holwood was never more happy than when labouring along with his gardeners in the effort to enhance the beauty of his grounds. This strenuous work, together with horse exercise and occasional bursts with the West Kent or Dover hunt, provided the recreation which enabled his naturally weak and gout-ridden frame to withstand the wear and tear of official life up to his forty-seventh year.

In town he delighted to visit friends in an informal manner, and was never more pleased than when he could have games with children. His romp with young Napier and the two Stanhopes when they succeeded in corking his face, has been already described; but it appears that even in 1805, when beset by manifold cares, he often dropped in at Broom House, Parson's Green, the residence of Sir Evan Nepean, and would "take a chair in a corner, and, laying aside state and gravity, would gambol and play with the boys."[2] At times his repartees were piquant. When his friend and admirer, the Duchess of Gordon, who had not seen him for some time, met him at the *levée* and asked whether he talked as much nonsense as of yore, he laughingly replied: " I do not know whether I talk so much nonsense: certainly I do not *hear* so much."[3]

Is it surprising that a character so benevolent, and social gifts of so much charm, should attract men about him? Of those who came forward to fill the gaps of the circle, only two, Wellesley and Canning, were men of powers so exceptional as to claim more than passing notice. Though descended from families domiciled in Ireland, they differed widely, except in versatility

[1] The estimate of Pitt by Wellesley, summarized above, refutes the ungenerous remark of Lecky (v, 72) that he took little delight in books and "was a politician, and nothing more." Lecky was perhaps misled by the ignorant libel on Pitt in Wraxall, iii, 223.

[2] "Diary of D. Scully," quoted by Dr. Hunt, "Transactions of Royal Hist. Soc." (1908), p. 12.

[3] Lord Rosebery, "Tomline's Estimate of Pitt," 33.

and devotion to Pitt. Wellesley's nature was Saxon in its inner hardness. Like his younger brother, the future Duke of Wellington, he rarely displayed signs of emotion; but his temperament, though cold at the heart, thrilled at the approach of great and perilous enterprises, amidst which he rivalled his brother in activity and resourcefulness. Accordingly, his Viceroyalty of India moved Bonaparte to envy, patriotic Britons to rapturous applause, and the parsimonious Directors of the Company to carping criticisms. Those who deny to Pitt the gift of choosing able and inspiring men, forget that he made Wellesley Governor-General of India, and supported him in his quarrels with the India House. As Earl of Mornington, Wellesley had helped the Irish Administration in various ways, and became closely acquainted with the Grenvilles. His first letter to Pitt, dated Dublin, January 1785, expresses thanks for assistance and for the offer of support in case the annoyances of his situation drove him to England. Thus, Mornington was first attracted to Pitt by his loyalty to subordinates; and, later, after his return to England, respect for the Minister ripened into admiration and love of the man.

They had much in common. Manly in bearing, persistent of purpose, and prompt in decision, they were also richly dowered with social gifts. Like Pitt, Mornington had classical attainments and literary gifts of no mean order; and his high spirits and powers of repartee must have brought new energy to the jaded statesman. Entering Parliament as member for Windsor, he found his duties far from congenial. On some occasions nervousness marred the effect of his speeches; and his constituents involved him in so much expense and worry as to prompt a request, in the autumn of 1794, for the intervention of Pitt, seeing that his rival, Isherwood, had " the means of supplying the rapacity even of the electors of Windsor." On 4th October he thanked Pitt for relieving him from further obligations to " the worthy electors of that loyal borough "; but he continued for a time to sit in Parliament. Meanwhile his fine presence and lively converse brought him into favour with the Prince of Wales. On 4th August 1793, writing at Brighthelmstone, he heartily congratulated Pitt on the surrender of Valenciennes, which sanguine persons hoped might hasten the end of the war. But, he added, " I own my most sanguine expectations cannot reach the notion of our being able to bring down the power of

France in one campaign to the level to which I think it must be
reduced for our safety and for that of the rest of the world.
H.R.H. the Prince of Wales has been pleased to be most gracious
to me. . . . I suppose you have heard of his dinner on the capture of Valenciennes. We sat from five till half-past ten, and
many were very drunk, particularly H.R.H. He really did the
honours most admirably. . . ." In the next letter, of the early part
of August 1796, Mornington sends a quatrain of Latin Elegiacs
which he had composed at Dundas's house, on the exploits of
Wurmser in relieving Mantua, of Davidovitch at Roveredo, and
Quosdanovitch at Brescia (not Verona), which seemed to presage
the ruin of Bonaparte.

> Mantua Vurmisero gaudet, Rovereda Davido,
> Et Verona tibi, Quosdanovice, patet.
> Vae mihi (raptor ait Gallus) ne forte per Alpes
> Heu! Bona pars in rem cogar abire malam.[1]

For some time Mornington had felt the charm of Indian history;
and the blend of energy with romance in his being may have
prompted Pitt's selection of him as Viceroy in 1797. After a
most tedious voyage he reached the Hooghly in time to foil the
blow which Tippoo Sahib, Bonaparte's prospective ally, aimed
at Madras. In his letter to Pitt, written there on 20th April
1799, he expressed a hope of the capture of Seringapatam, and
continues thus: " I assure you that my nerves are much strengthened by all the exertions which I have been obliged to make,
and in this land of indolence I pass for rather an active, stout,
hardy fellow and can now fast till four o'clock (save only a bit
of biscuit and a glass of port). I am happy to hear that you are
better than you have ever been in your life. There is no comfort in mine but the distant hope of seeing you all again safe,
well, and quizzing in England. I have only one request to make
to you if you do not mean to abridge either my doleful days or
the period of my Government—do not suffer that *cantancerous*
[*sic*] fellow, Sir J[ames] Craig, to be made commander-in-chief
in Bengal. Send me a sober discreet decent man, but do not
allow the etiquette of throwing inkstands to be revived at the
Council Board."[2]

[1] *I.e.*, Mantua rejoices in Wurmser, Rovereda in Davidovitch, Verona is
open to Quosdanovitch. "Woe is me," says the greedy Gaul, Bonaparte,
" I shall have to be off through the Alps and go to the dogs."

[2] Pitt MSS., 188.

On 12th May, after announcing to Pitt the capture of Seringapatam, Mornington adds: "If Buonaparte should now chuse
to visit Malabar, I think he will find supper prepared for him
before he has reached Calcutta." Reviewing the events of his
Viceroyalty he writes on 8th August: "I suppose you will
either hang me or magnificently honour me for my deeds (mine
they are, be they good or bad). In either case I shall be gratified;
for an English gallows is better than an Indian throne; but
these words must be buried in your own breast; for here I pre-
tend to be very happy and humble; although I am as proud as
the D. and as wretched as his dam. I think you will enjoy 'Le
Citoïen Tipou' and 'Citoïen Sultan' in the papers found at
Seringapatam. I admire your conduct with respect to the
Union [with Ireland]. I hope you will persevere, but I *trust* you
will not *trust* Ireland to my old friend Hobart. He used to be
a good humoured fellow; but from what I have heard of his
reign here, he is utterly unfit to govern anywhere."[1]

Pitt did not receive this letter by 6th November, when he
informed Wellesley that the King, as a mark of high approbation, conferred on him the title the Marquis Wellesley, suitable
arrangements being also in contemplation for his family. An
Irish marquisate was far from the magnificent reward which the
Viceroy desired; and on 28th April 1800 he expressed his
anguish of mind at receiving only an Irish and pinchbeck
reward for exploits neither Irish nor pinchbeck. Nevertheless,
while requesting a speedy recall so that he might hide his
chagrin in retirement, he uttered no vindictive word against
Pitt. Despite its morbid expressions, the letter is that of a
friend to a friend. On 27th September Pitt wrote in reply one
of the longest of his private letters. With equal tact and frankness he reviewed the whole question, proving that Wellesley's
services were not undervalued, that the bestowal of an English
marquisate would have been an advance of four steps in the
peerage for what was after all a short Viceroyalty; and that the
present honour equalled that conferred on Cornwallis at the end
of his term. The question was whether Wellesley should receive
an English earldom or an Irish marquisate; and the latter was
deemed preferable. Further, if the notion prevailed at Calcutta

[1] Pitt MSS., 188. Hobart married Pitt's early love, Eleanor Eden, and
became Minister at War under Addington. For Mornington's comments on
his factious conduct at Madras, see "Dropmore P.," iv, 384, 476; v, 268; vi, 338.

that Wellesley had been slighted, it might be due to a suspicion that he himself harboured it. Pitt then begged Wellesley to regard this frankness as the best proof of real friendship.[1]

Wellesley showed his good sense by acquiescing, and their letters though rare, became thoroughly cordial. Writing at Patna on 6th October 1801, he gently reproached Pitt for his long silence, especially for not explaining the reason of his resignation; he also expressed the hope that he approved his remaining at Calcutta until a successor was appointed. He added that his state progress up the Ganges to Patna had been favoured by an easterly gale of unusual strength which the natives ascribed either to his happy star or to an Order in Council. As for his health, it was better than in " the reeking House of Commons." Again at the beginning of 1804 he expressed regret that Pitt had neither written nor vouchsafed any sign of approbation at recent events, including the victory of Assaye, which assured British ascendancy in the East.

At last, on 30th August 1804, three months after resuming office, Pitt apologized for his neglect on the ground of excess of work in preparing to meet a French invasion, in which he had so far succeeded as to hope that the attempt might be made. At that time he expected Wellesley to come home in order to escape the petty cabals of the Company's Directors; but he left the decision entirely to him. Pitt's next letter, at Christmastide, breathes a profound hope for Wellesley's speedy arrival as a means of lightening the then heavy burden of political life. Wellesley, however, on 25th March 1805, announced his chivalrous resolve to remain in India another season owing to financial troubles and disputes with the Company. To Dundas, in May 1805, he wrote: " I imagined myself to be one of the best friends of the Company, but I hear that I am a traitor, and a conspirator, and an interloper. Time discovers truth, and I must leave the Honourable Courts' opinions to that test." [2] In August, after transferring his duties to Cornwallis, he set sail for England, and landed in time to have a few last words with Pitt. The interview must have been deeply affecting. At its conclusion Pitt fainted away. Of all the estimates of Pitt none breathes deeper devotion than that of Wellesley. Was it not because he at last saw the pettiness of his own pride and petulance when con-

---

[1] Stanhope, iii, 232; Rosebery, "Pitt," 213-7.   [2] Pitt MSS., 188.

trasted with the self-abnegation of him who was truly the Great Commoner? And did not even his meteoric career in the East pale before the full-orbed splendour of the quarter of a century of achievement which made up the public life of Pitt?

The other enthusiastic friend was typically Irish in temperament. Celtic in vivacity and charm, feminine in sensitiveness, Canning was dowered with virile persistence and pugnacity. In histrionic and versifying power he rivalled his countryman, Sheridan, who never forgave him for deserting the Whigs and going over to Pitt. The loss was indeed serious; for the young orator was far more than a *frondeur*. As editor of the "Anti-Jacobin," conjointly with Hookham Frere, he covered with ridicule the detractors of their country, and helped on the revival of national spirit which began in 1798. But he also possessed great administrative talents, displaying as Under-Secretary for Foreign Affairs an insight into character in which his chief, Grenville, was signally lacking. Canning's letters to Pitt on the negotiation at Lille in 1797 show signs of those inductive powers which appear at their zenith in his brilliantly correct inference ten years later that the Danish fleet must be snatched from the clutch of Napoleon.

The statuesque calm of Pitt's personality charmed and overawed this impressionable Irishman from the time of their first interview in the summer of 1792. Always versatile and sometimes shifty, he seems instinctively to have felt in him the needed counterpart. As the Czar Alexander leaned on the rocklike Stein in the crisis of 1812, so Canning gained strength and confidence from reliance on Pitt. He on his side took a keen interest in his disciple, discerning in him the propagator of the Pitt doctrine and tradition. At times the fostering care became fatherly. A case in point was Canning's marriage with a wealthy Scottish heiress (July 1800). Pitt regarded this event as essential to his success as the future leader of the party. Indeed, so absorbed was he in his own thoughts during the ride to the church as not to notice a pert remark of Canning's friend, Hookham Frere. The clergyman, Frere, and he were in a coach driving along Swallow Street towards Brook Street when a carter who saw them called out: "What! Billy Pitt! and with a parson too!" Thereupon Frere burst out with the daring jest, "He thinks you are going to Tyburn to be hanged privately!" But Pitt was too pre-occupied to notice the gibe. Again, after the ceremony, in the vestry Pitt was so nervous as to be unable to sign as a witness, and Canning had to whisper to Frere to sign without waiting for him.[1] They ascribed his strange inaction to extreme regard for Canning. But surely another explanation is more natural. How could a man of keenly affectionate nature share in that ceremony without feeling deeply his own lonely lot? Three and a half years ago poverty and debt had stepped in to part him and Eleanor Eden. Was it not the wraith of his buried love which now hovered before him, blotting out the sight of the carter, deafening his ears to the jest, and palsying his hand?

Pitt's resignation of office sorely tried his friends; for, without informing them of the inmost reasons that prompted that step, he pressed them to remain in office under his successor, Addington. As we have seen, some of them refused. Of those not holding Cabinet appointments, Rose and Long, joint Secretaries of the Treasury, Lord Granville Leveson-Gower, a Lord of the Treasury, and Canning, joint Paymaster of the Forces, decided to resign. Pitt's silence and his urgent requests to his friends to remain in office were of course open to misconstruction ; and several of his supporters echoed the malicious assertion of Frere, that his aim was for Addington to take office as a *locum tenens*, and sign a discreditable peace, whereupon he (Pitt) would come back to power and find his former supporters in their old places. Malmesbury gave colour to the story by stating that Addington described himself as *locum tenens*, a remark utterly inconsistent with all that is known of his complacent pride. Nevertheless the slander gained general currency, and, even now, despite convincing refutation, dies hard. That Canning and others resented Pitt's silence and his pressure to remain in office is undeniable; but, while saying nothing as to the cause of his own conduct, he explained clearly to Canning that, as a friend, he was gratified by his conduct in resigning, however much he deplored his action on public grounds. Of course the *tu quoque* retort was inevitable ; but Canning's curiosity was not gratified.[2]

For a time he talked of breaking with Pitt, and sent him a copy of a letter to Frere couched in those terms. Pitt replied

[1] Gabrielle Festing, "J. H. Frere and his Friends," 31.
[2] "Malmesbury Diaries," iv, 8; Pellew, i, ch. xi; G. Festing, "Hookham Frere," 42-4; R. Bell, "Canning," 176; H. W. V. Temperley, "Canning," 62-3.

calmly on 26th April 1801 that on reviewing his conduct he
found it neither unkind nor unfair. While lamenting that Canning should thus have misunderstood his conduct, he expressed
a resolve to forget the incident and a hope that their friendship
might endure. Serenity such as this is the best cure to Celtic
susceptibility. But other grievances were discovered, and on
12th July Canning dashed off to Frere a furious missive full
of dashes and underlinings, charging Pitt with showing to him
" confidence just enough to mislead and not enough to guide ";
on which promising theme he fired off clause upon clause of an
incoherent sentence which fills thirty-five lines of print and then
expires in a dash. What it was all about is far from clear, except that Canning believed Pitt to have done " scrupulously
and magnanimously *right* by everybody but *me*." [1] Before long
the sensitive youth was moving heaven and earth to bring back
Pitt to power. But, even in December 1803, when his whole
soul was bound up in him, he reproached him with lover-like
vehemence for having inspired a derogatory article in the
" Accurate Observer." Apparently the wounded friend had no
proof whatever that Pitt had sped or barbed the shaft.

Among those who won Pitt's confidence in his closing years
was Spencer Perceval, an able young barrister, who entered
Parliament in 1796 as member for Northampton, and showed
considerable skill in finance and debating powers of no mean
order. " He spoke (says Sinclair) without the disagreeable cant
of the Bar, was never tedious, was peculiarly distinct in matters
of business, and explained his financial measures with clearness
and ability. His style was singularly acute, bold, sarcastic, and
personal." The same authority avers that Pitt, on being asked—
" If we lose you, where could we find a successor?"—answered
at once, " Perceval." The reply is remarkable; for Perceval,
besides opposing Catholic Emancipation, displayed little tact in
dealing with men and a strangely narrow outlook. Probably it
was his power of hard work, his grasp of finance, and his resolute disposition which led Pitt to prefer him to Canning, who in
other respects was far better qualified to act as leader.

I must here notice charges which have been brought against
Pitt, that his creations of peers, or promotions in the peerage,
which by the year 1801 exceeded 140, were fraught with evil to

[1] Stanhope, iii, 315; Festing, 47-51.

the Upper House, lowering the intellectual level of its debates, and impairing the balance of parties, with results damaging to the constitution.[1] It has even been suggested that the friction between the two Houses in the years 1830-1911 resulted in no small degree from the reckless conduct of Pitt in this respect. Vague and sweeping assertions like these can neither be substantiated nor refuted. But the only definite part of them, namely, that Pitt's creations degraded the House of Lords, is obviously overstrained. At no period was the tone of its debates higher than in that of Pitt's supremacy, witness those on Warren Hastings, the disputes with Spain and Russia, and the Great War. They have not the brilliance of those of the Commons in the days of Burke, Fox, Pitt and Sheridan; but they often excel them in statesmanlike qualities; and a perusal of them reveals the fact that the ablest of the Lords were, not those of the old governing families, which at that period showed signs of decadence, but those for whose creation Pitt was mainly responsible. Malmesbury, Buckingham, Grenville, Auckland, Carrington, Minto, and at a later period, Sidmouth and Castlereagh, excelled in ability and weight the representatives of the older nobility. Far from degrading and weakening the peerage, Pitt strengthened it by an infusion of new blood which was sorely needed at that time of strain and stress. Further, it must be remembered that Burke's Economy Bill had abolished many of the sinecures which were considered due for steady support in Parliament; and, while at Bath in the year 1797, he admitted that his reform was accountable for the large increase of peerages, thenceforth the chief hope of the faithful.[2] Pitt's correspondence also shows that he frequently repulsed the insistent claims of his supporters for titles, a theme on which piquant letters might be adduced.

Surely, too, it is unjust to say that Pitt entirely altered the political complexion of the Upper House. During the greater part of his career the so-called political differences were based mainly on personal considerations; and throughout the struggle against France, Whigs and Tories, with the exception of a small coterie, were merged in the national party which recognized in Pitt the saviour of British institutions. The charge that he was largely responsible for the friction between the two Houses after 1830 needs little notice; for that friction was clearly due to the

---

[1] May, "Constit. Hist.," i, 232-8; Lecky, v, 27.   [2] Wraxall, ii, 286.

progress of democratic principles and the growth of an enormous industrial community in these islands. Both of those developments told strongly against the parity of political influence of the two Houses of Parliament. Amidst the torpor of the previous age the prerogatives of the Peers had gone unchallenged. After the French Revolution and the Industrial Revolution a challenge was certain to come; and in this, as in many other respects, the conduct of Pitt was such as to strengthen our institutions. By adding to the House of Lords a considerable number of commoners he enabled it to withstand the storms of the Revolutionary age and the inevitable conflicts of the future.

To revert to the year 1801, there occurred early in the autumn an event of high import. The struggle of eight years between Great Britain and France ended in stalemate. The collapse of the Armed Neutrality League together with the capture of Malta and the surrender of the French garrisons in Egypt left the Union Jack triumphant at sea and the tricolour on the Continent. Each State had need of rest to restore its finances and consolidate its conquests. Therefore, though Bonaparte had at the end of March 1801 sharply repelled the pacific overtures of the Addington Cabinet, yet negotiations were resumed at the close of summer, a fact which proves that the First Consul was influenced, not by spite to Pitt and goodwill to his successor, but by the constricting grip of the Sea Power. Hawkesbury, Grenville's successor at the Foreign Office, asserted that shortly before the end of the negotiation Pitt sat up with him through part of a night discussing finance, and finally advising the cessation of hostilities.

Not that Pitt directed the negotiations; for both Addington and Hawkesbury were proud and sensitive men, and Pitt at some points criticized the conditions of the Preliminaries of London (1st October 1801). They were as follows: Great Britain agreed to restore to France, Spain, and the Batavian, or Dutch, Republic all their possessions recently conquered by her, with the exception of Trinidad and Ceylon, ceded to her by Spain and the Dutch respectively. She also retired from Elba and restored Malta to the Knights of St. John, under conditions to be further specified. The French restored Egypt to the Sultan, and evacuated Naples and the Papal States. Portugal was also saved from danger of partition. Nothing was said respecting the resumption of trade between England and France; and no assurance was forthcoming as to the independence of the Republics bordering on France. By his recent compact with Austria the First Consul agreed to respect their independence; but England had no definite ground for complaint if it were violated.

While the London rabble shouted itself hoarse with joy at the advent of peace, Grenville, Windham, and Canning saw disgrace and disaster ahead. Pitt thought otherwise. At the small house in Park Place which he had leased for his visits to London, he wrote to Long on 1st October, describing the terms as not all that could be wished but "highly creditable, and on the whole very advantageous." Finding that Grenville considered them disastrous, he on the 5th expressed concern at their disagreement. Though regretting the surrender of the Cape, and the uncertainty of the fate of Malta, he considered the acquisition of Ceylon and Trinidad most beneficial; and he hailed with satisfaction a peace which saved Turkey and Portugal from spoliation. He therefore suggested an interview for the sake of reconciling their differences. To this Grenville somewhat coolly assented, remarking that the differences were fundamental and could not be concealed, and that his confidence in the Addington Cabinet was irretrievably destroyed by a treaty which ceded to France Martinique, Malta, Minorca, the Cape, Cochin China, and all the Dutch settlements. Clearly, then, Grenville looked on the Dutch Republic and Spain as dominated by Bonaparte, who would seize Minorca, Malta, and the Cape whenever it suited him. He also wrote to the King expressing regret that he could no longer support Addington, whose conduct towards France and Russia was "marked throughout by a tone of unnecessary and degrading concession."[1]

Here, then, the two cousins began sharply to differ. On 3rd November, during the debates on the Peace, Pitt rose to rebut the censures of Thomas Grenville on a policy which implied the surrender of the Mediterranean to France. He deprecated these sweeping criticisms; for he had ever been ready to frame a treaty which, though falling short of our just pretensions, was not inconsistent with honour and security. The present terms did not fulfil all his wishes; but the difference between them and the best possible

[1] Stanhope, iii, 352; "Dropmore P.," vii, 49-51. For new letters of Canning and Grenville, see "Pitt and Napoleon Miscellanies."

terms was not worth the continuance of war. If both Trinidad and Malta could not be retained, he commended Ministers for choosing Trinidad; for the sight of the Union Jack at Malta would have hurt the pride of France. With regard to the Cape of Good Hope he deemed it a far more important possession than Hawkesbury had represented, though inferior to Ceylon. He deplored our failure to restore the House of Savoy to its capital, Turin; but the chief object of the war, the security of Great Britain, had been attained. True, the restoration of the French monarchy would have furnished a better safeguard for peace; but we had never insisted on it as essential, though it might have been assured if the Allies had fulfilled their duties. As to the future, if the First Consul aimed at founding a military despotism, he probably would not select England as the first object of his attack; and we had every prospect of enjoying a long peace. Remembering, perhaps, that he made the same prophecy early in 1792, he uttered this warning: " I am inclined to hope every-thing that is good; but I am bound to act as if I feared other-wise." In none of his speeches did Pitt display less foresight. The preference of Trinidad to Malta and of Ceylon to the Cape is curious enough; but the prophecy as to a long period of peace and the probable immunity of England from Bonaparte's attack argues singular blindness to the colonial trend of French policy since the year 1798. Despite acrid comments by Fox and Windham, the speech carried the day and firmly established Addington in power.

The sequel is well known. In the interval of six months, during which the aged and gouty Cornwallis sought to reduce the Preliminaries of London to the Treaty of Amiens (27th March 1802), Bonaparte remodelled the Batavian, Ligurian, and Cisalpine Republics in a way wholly at variance with the Treaty of Lunéville. Against these breaches of faith the Addington Cabinet made no protest; and the treaty in its final form pro-vided a complex and unsatisfactory compromise on the Maltese question.[1] Canning and Windham strove to elicit from Pitt a public expression of his disapproval of the treaty; but their efforts were in vain. On 20th April 1802 Canning, while at his country seat, South Hill, Bracknell (Berks), wrote thus to Windham:[2]

[1] See Rose, " Life of Napoleon," i, ch. xiv, for details.
[2] B.M. Add. MSS., 37844.

. . . Do not suppose that this is because I have the slightest doubt as to the impression which may be made by pointing out the gross faults and omissions, the weakness, and baseness, and shuffling, and stupidity, that mark this Treaty even beyond the Preliminaries that led to it. But I think people do not want to be convinced of this; that they will not take it kindly, but rather otherwise, to have it forced upon their observation; that, if parted to a division, they will vote for the Treaty with all its imperfections upon its head. . . . Now as to Pitt himself. He cannot and does not think of this as he did of the Preliminary Treaty. But debate it; and he will, he must, debate as warmly for it. He can take no distinction without seeming to abandon Addington; and that he will not do. He cannot object to any part of the Peace in public, without weakening the grounds upon which he contends peace upon the whole to be preferable to war, and *that* he will not do. . . . Leave it possible for Pitt to say six or eight months hence that the Preliminaries promised well, but that the Treaty did not come up to them. I do not promise you that he ever will say this. But I am fairly persuaded that, if you force from him a public approbation of the Treaty, you defer for at least as many months as have passed since the debates of October, the chance of his coming to see things almost as you and I see them. . . .

April 27 1802.

Since I wrote to you, I have seen Lord Grenville, and I think the plan of action, which he tells me had been concerted between you and him, so perfect, that I retract everything in what I wrote to you (if anything there were) which could be construed as making against it. To debate "about it and about it," as much as you will, to move for papers, to move for taking the Treaty into consideration—all this may be done with great and good effect, but a condemnation of the Treaty, such as would force P[itt] into a defence of it, and identify him with the makers of it, is what of all things is to be avoided. I hope you think so.—Whether P[itt] *will* save us I do not know. But surely he is the only man that *can*.

All was in vain. Pitt, having promised to support Addington, deemed himself in honour bound to fulfil that pledge. But, as the events of the year 1802 showed more and more the imbecility of the Addington Cabinet, torturing doubts preyed upon his mind. His friends, especially Canning, now began to discern the pathos of his position, but sought to draw him from his seclusion at Walmer. An opportunity occurred in the month of May. Pitt's birthday was on the 28th. Would not all who foresaw ruin for England in the supremacy of "the Doctor" welcome a demonstration on behalf of his predecessor? For more than a year Pitt's friends had been puzzled and abashed by his unexplained retirement, witness the uncharitable surmise of the usually benevolent Dr. Burgh—"Can I see Addington climb upon the stooping neck of Mr. Pitt, and not believe that it is done in hostility or in a masked confederacy? If the former, how am I to estimate the man who comes in? If the latter, what judgement can I form of the man who goes out?"[1] Slander also was busy in the guise of that gadfly, Nicholls, who proposed to thank the King for dismissing him. By way of retort Pitt's friends triumphantly carried a motion of thanks to Pitt for his great services, against a carping minority of fifty-two; but members were heard to mutter their preference for Addington over all "the d—d men of genius."

Was it not time to arouse the country from sloth? The England of 1802 seemed to Wordsworth

> a fen of stagnant waters.

While he invoked the memory of Milton, Canning resolved to appeal to Pitt. In a day or two he threw off a poem which, though slighted by him, gained a wider vogue than any of his effusions, "The Pilot that weathered the Storm." The last and best stanza is as follows:

> And O! if again the rude whirlwind should rise,
>   The dawning of peace should fresh darkness deform,
> The regrets of the good and the fears of the wise
>   Shall turn to the pilot that weathered the storm.

The song was enthusiastically received by the company assembled at the Merchant Taylors' Hall; and the reference to the recall of Pitt roused the company to a high pitch of excitement. The song, as a whole, is laboured and strained. The only stanza which happily weds phrase and thought is the last. The others form a lumbering prelude to this almost Sibylline cadence.

Despite these efforts to sow discord between Pitt and Addington, they remained on excellent terms;[2] and the support given by the former to the Peace of Amiens ensured to the Minister an overwhelming victory at the polls in the General Election of the

[1] "Private Papers of Wilberforce," 110.
[2] For the passing misunderstanding of February 1802, see Pellew, ii, 489-92, with Pitt's letters.

summer of 1802. Pitt was of course returned by the University of Cambridge, " with every mark of zeal and cordiality "—so he wrote to Rose on 10th July. The rest of the summer he passed either near London or at Walmer. It is unfortunate that he did not visit France, as Fox, Romilly, and many others now did. Probably his sharp rebuff to Bonaparte's overture at the end of 1799, and his subsequent diatribes against him precluded such a step. But he also needed rest and quiet. On 8th June he wrote to Windham: " The sea air and the contrast of the scene to that which I left behind me in London have, as usual, done me a great deal of good." [1] He set to work to improve the grounds adjoining the castle, and invited Addington, who was then spending some weeks at Eastbourne, to come over and see the changes. Further, he leased a large farm near Walmer, and expressed a hope that he might spend the rest of the year in farming. The splendour of that summer and the bounteous crops of corn evidently captivated Pitt. The supreme need of England was more corn. A man who could not serve her at Westminster could serve her by high farming. This was Pitt's forecast, unless " the *pacificator* of Europe takes it into his head to send an army from the opposite coast to revenge himself for some newspaper paragraph." [2]

At this time, too, he finally succeeded in disposing of Holwood. The sale was inevitable; for Pitt's finance had long been a source of deep anxiety. So far back as 18th October 1800 Rose informed the Bishop of Lincoln that bailiffs threatened the seizure of Pitt's furniture in Downing Street for debts of £600 and £400. Then, referring to Pitt's ill health, he wrote: " I conceived till this morning [it] was owing to the state of public matters; but I am now strongly inclined to think he is agitated by the state of his own affairs. Bullock came to me this morning and forced upon me such a history of debts and distresses as actually sickened me. . . . Something must be done before Pitt returns to town. His expenses in the last years were nearly £26,000. I am quite certain Holwood must be parted with." [3]

Pitt's private finance is involved in mystery. His official stipend was £6,000 a year; and as Lord Warden of the Cinque Ports he drew £3,000 more. Yet he was now insolvent. Among

---

[1] B.M. Add. MSS., 37844.   [2] Pellew, ii, 75, 76.
[3] Pretyman MSS. Bullock paid the servants and supervised the accounts at Downing Street. Pitt was then staying with Addington near Reading.

his papers systematic accounts are extant only for the latter
half of the years 1794 and 1799. Even these are not complete, especially for the household at Walmer Castle. Those
for the house in Downing Street are the fullest; but, for the last
six months of 1799, they amount to £3,789 at Downing Street,
and £2,382 at Holwood, the latter sum including a charge of
£1,163 for farm expenses which cannot much have exceeded the
income.[1] The Walmer accounts vary according to the duration
of Pitt's residence. Those for the summer and autumn of 1794
amount only to £458. Evidently, then, Pitt benefited by the
King's gift of the Wardenship of the Cinque Ports. But he gave
£1,000 in 1793 to start the Dover Volunteer corps and doubtless
other sums towards the Fencibles of the other Cinque Ports.

At all times the servants at Downing Street and the farm at
Holwood were a heavy drain. The amount of the servants' private
bills charged to Pitt at Downing Street is disgraceful. Pitt kept
a good table and a good cellar, as the customs of the age required; but neither these expenses nor his heavy outlay on his
tailor would have brought about a crisis, had not his town servants and tradesmen plundered him. Morse, the tailor, charged at
the rate of £130 to £140 a quarter for Pitt's clothes. Now Pitt
was neat and punctilious in his attire, but he was no dandy. As
for the farm at Holwood, accounts for straw and manure were
charged twice over, as some friendly accountant pointed out.
Probably, too, his experiments in landscape-gardening were as
costly as they had been to Chatham; for lavishness was in the
nature both of father and son. Pitt once confessed to his niece,
Hester Stanhope, that he never saw a house and grounds without at once planning improvements. In this phrase as in the
suggestive item on farm expenses we can see why the sale of
Holwood was necessary; but for various reasons it did not take
place until the autumn of 1802.

Meanwhile his friends bestirred themselves to prevent the
scandal of an execution. They succeeded in staving off a crisis

---

[1] Omitting shillings, the details for Downing Street and Holwood for
July—December 1799 are respectively: Table, £344, £231; Cellar, £169,
£126; Housekeeping, £531, £156; Private Account, £357, £—; Servants'
Wages, £251, £69; Servants' Board Wages, £329, £80; Servants' Bills,
£353, £15; Liveries, £41, £—; Taxes, etc., £747, £77; Farm, £—, £784;
Farm Labourers, £—, £379; Garden, £—, £125; Stable, £155, £—; Job
Horses, £165, £—; Incidentals, £347, £340. (Pitt MSS., 201.)

until schemes of relief were concerted, but here again there was much difficulty; for, on hearing of the proposed private subscription on his behalf, he declared that he would rather return to practice at the Bar than submit to such a humiliation. Fox might allow friends to pay his gambling debts; but the pride of Pitt scorned to accept help on behalf of liabilities even if due to pre-occupation in public affairs. Rose deemed a sum of £25,000 necessary to his peace and quietness, seeing that the total liabilities were £45,064. The letters which passed between Camden, the Bishop of Lincoln, and Rose, evince deep affection for the shy, proud man. The following is a *précis* of a letter of Rose to Tomline which is among the Pretyman MSS.:

Christchurch, *July* 21, 1801.

I am in great perplexity about Pitt's affairs. Joe Smith has been strangely misled respecting them.[1] The unforeseen demands have been very large. If Holwood fetches a good price, the sum of £24,000 will set the matter at rest. Pitt's diamonds have been sold for £680 to pay pressing claims. The unpaid bills now amount to £9,618. Old debts come to £9,600 more. Mr. Soane and Mr. Coutts might be asked to wait, as neither would suffer from it. The debt due to Banker (£5,800) cannot surely be a separate one of Pitt's; for I think he could give no security on it. Probably it is a debt contracted jointly with Lord Chatham, the whole of which Pitt may have to pay. Of the last sum which in his own deep distress he borrowed on the security of Holwood, he gave (I know) £1,000 to Lord Chatham. These are trifling considerations compared with that of getting him to accept the means of relief. They are as follows: (1) a vote from Parliament; (2) a free gift from the King; (3) a private subscription; (4) an additional office for life. The first and second of these Pitt has peremptorily declined. The third he refused in 1787 when the London merchants offered £100,000. The fourth course would not be wholly creditable, but Pitt thinks it the least objectionable. He dislikes the second and third alternatives because the second (as he thinks) would give the King a hold over him and the third would entitle the subscribers to his favour. The notion of an execution by bailiffs in his house is too painful to contemplate. I consider the first or second alternatives the best.

The reference here to a gift, or loan, from Pitt to his brother prompts the inquiry whether similar acts of benevolence may

---

[1] Joseph Smith (no relative of "Bob Smith," Lord Carrington) became Pitt's private secretary in 1787. His letters, published along with "The Beaufort Papers" in 1897, throw no light on Pitt's debts.

not explain his difficulties. We find the second Earl of Chatham in August 1797 acknowledging a loan of £1,000 from Pitt. The bishop, replying to Rose on 24th July 1801, states that the debt of £5,800 was to the best of his knowledge a sum advanced through Thomas Coutts, the banker, to Lady Chatham upon the Burton Pynsent estate. He adds that she ought to pay interest to Pitt upon it, but did not. It seems that Pitt advanced £11,750 in all on behalf of the Burton Pynsent estate. Here, then, was a grievous family burden. Probably the debt was left by his father, and may have been increased by his mother. So far back as November 1793 he wrote to her stating his desire to help her at any time of need; and in August of the following year, when she believed her end to be near, she begged her sons to pay her "just debts," which were due, not to vain expenses, but to outlays upon the farm which she at the time believed to be for the best.[1] The eldest son could not help her, for he required succour from Pitt. If, then, the farming experiments at Burton Pynsent failed, the loss fell upon Pitt. We may infer, then, that his debts were occasioned partly by rapacious servants and tradesmen in London, partly by farming and gardening at Holwood, but also by the needs of his mother and brother. The fact that Chatham paid not a shilling towards the discharge of Pitt's liabilities proves that he was in low water; and as no one, not even Tomline, knew of the source of Pitt's embarrassments, they must have been of a peculiarly delicate character.

Tomline's decision, that Pitt could never accept a sinecure from Addington, is indisputable. The words in which Pitt declared that he could not accept the sum of £30,000 graciously offered by the King breathe more independence than those in which he first expressed his gratitude for the offer. There remained, then, the plan of a private subscription. The Bishop of Lincoln mentioned it to him with admirable delicacy on 6th August 1801, and gained his consent. The following were the subscribers: Lords Bathurst, Camden, and Carrington, together with Tomline, Rose, and Steele, £1,000 each. From Scotland came £4,000, probably in equal parts from the Dukes of Buccleugh and Gordon, Dundas, and the Chief Baron. Wilberforce, Long, and Joseph Smith each gave £500, and another (Lord Alvanley?) £200. Bishop Tomline and Rose showed equal

[1] Ashbourne, 162. See, too, ch. xv of this work.

activity and tact in raising this sum of £11,700, so that the details remained unknown to Pitt.[1] Later on he felt pecuniary embarrassments, partly owing to his share in maintaining the Cinque Ports Volunteers, and at his death his debts amounted to £40,000.

His relations to his bankers, Messrs. Coutts, continued cordial, though on 24th April 1805 Thomas Coutts ventured to state that there was an overdraft against him of £1,511, which, however, was redressed by the arrival of his quarterly official stipends.[2] Pitt's loyalty to his friends appears in his effort during his second Ministry to procure the royal assent to his nomination of Bishop Tomline to the Archbishopric of Canterbury shortly after the death of Dr. Moore early in 1805. The King, however, who did not admire Tomline, and believed the Bishop of Norwich to have prior claims, refused his reiterated requests. Pitt's second letter to the King on this subject is couched in terms almost of remonstrance.[3]

Reverting to Pitt's life at Walmer, we find that in the summer of 1802 he fell a prey to nausea and lassitude; so that Lady Hester Stanhope, who visited him in September, found him very weak. Probably his indisposition was due less to the exceptional heat of that season than to suppressed gout aggravated by anxiety. As we saw, he invited Addington to come over from Eastbourne and discuss public affairs. The conference seems to have caused him much concern; for Tomline in July 1802 jotted down notes of a conversation with Pitt, in which Addington is described as "without exception the vainest man he (Pitt) had ever met with." Pitt's advice had often been asked before the Preliminaries of Peace were signed, but afterwards he was neglected. Cornwallis, too, had evidently believed that by the Treaty of Amiens all former treaties with France were revived without being named; and probably Ministers were under the same delusion. The last King's Speech was also annoying to Pitt, who characterized Addington as "a man of little mind, of consummate vanity and of very slender abilities." As to resumption of office Pitt thought it impossible during the life of the King, except in case of some great emergency.[4]

---

[1] G. Rose, "Diaries," i, 429; ii, 215.

[2] Pitt MSS., 126. Coutts and five other bankers each subscribed £50,000 to the "Loyalty Loan" in 1797 and invested £10,000 on behalf of Pitt.

[3] Stanhope, iv, 233, 252; Ashbourne, 351-4. [4] Pretyman MSS.

Equally frank were Pitt's confessions to Canning, who stayed at Walmer in September—October 1802. He admitted that his resignation was due partly to the manner in which the King opposed him on Catholic Emancipation. But he quitted office with a clear conscience, leaving full means for attacking Egypt and the Armed Neutrals, so that the reproaches of desertion of duty were unjust. He pledged himself to support Addington; and from this only Addington could release him. He admitted that this was a mistake, now that current events showed Bonaparte's ambition to be insatiable; but none the less he waved aside Canning's reiterated appeals that he would apply to Addington for release from the pledge, on the ground that such a step would seem an intrigue for a return to power. "My ambition (he proudly said) is character, not office."

Was a statesman ever placed in a more embarrassing situation? Pitt had resigned office on a point of honour, and yet felt constrained to humour the royal invalid by abandoning the very measure which caused his resignation. Incautiously he pledged himself to support Addington, thereby alienating some of his own supporters. He defended his pacific policy until it led to a bad treaty followed by a series of humiliations. By October 1802 Bonaparte was master of four Republics bordering on France, and had annexed Piedmont and Elba, besides securing Parma and Louisiana by profitable exchanges. Such a peace was worse than a disastrous war. Yet Addington made no protest except against the virtual subjugation of Switzerland. True, the Cabinet now clung to the Cape and Malta as for dear life; but elsewhere the eye could see French influence creeping resistlessly over Europe, while the German Powers were intent only on securing the spoils of the Ecclesiastical States. Well might Pitt write to Wilberforce on 31st October: "You know how much under all the circumstances I wished for peace, and my wishes remain the same, if Bonaparte can be made to feel that he is not to trample in succession on every nation in Europe. But of this I fear there is little chance, and without it I see no prospect but war." Worst of all, there were sure signs that France and the other Powers distrusted and despised Addington. Vorontzoff, the Russian ambassador, declared that he would work hard to form an alliance with Pitt, but despaired of effecting anything with his successor.[1] In truth, Pitt's excessive scrupulousness at

---

[1] "Private Papers of Wilberforce," 34; G. Rose, "Diaries," i, 508.

the time of his resignation had enclosed himself and his country in a vicious circle from which the only means of escape was war.

A prey to these harassing thoughts, Pitt left Walmer near the close of October 1802 to take the waters at Bath. On the way he visited Sir Charles Middleton at Teston in Kent, and sought distraction by inquiries on farming. Middleton wrote to Wilberforce on 26th October: " His inquiries were very minute and judicious; and it is incredible how quickly he comprehended things, and how much further he reasons on them than I can follow him. ... I believe Mr. Pitt has it in his power to become the first farmer in England if he thinks the pursuit worth his time and attention."[1] The treatment at Bath suited Pitt so well that he prolonged his stay. Rose, whom he invited to Bath in the second week of November, thus describes to Bishop Tomline his manner of life:

Bath, *Nov.* 21, 1802.[2]

Mr. Pitt's health mends every day: it is really better than it has been ever since I knew him. I am quite sure this place agrees with him *entirely*, he eats a small [*illegible*] and a half for breakfast, and more at dinner than I ever saw him at $\frac{1}{2}$ past 4: no luncheon: two very small glasses of Madeira at dinner and *less* than a pint of port after dinner: at night, nothing but a bason of arrowroot: he is positively in the best possible train of management for his health. . . . He is positively decided to have no responsibility whatever respecting what has been done or is doing on the subject of foreign politics; he not only adheres to his resolution of not going up for the opening [of Parliament]; but will not attend even on the estimates unless a necessity should arise: he writes to day both to Mr. Addington and Lord Hawkesbury in a style that will not only manifest the above, *but will prevent all further attempts to draw him into confidential communication.* He has also made up his mind to take office again whenever the occasion shall arise, when he can come in properly, and has now no reluctance on the subject. I dare not say more by the Post. If my letter is opened, the Ministers will know the first part is true, and I don't care about their learning the latter. Lord Grenville will positively not take a line to render it difficult for Mr. Pitt and him to act together; he will move no amendment to the Address. . . .

Rose, as we have seen, disliked Lord Auckland, who was joint Postmaster-General; and if Pitt's letters were opened at the

[1] " Letters of Wilberforce," i, 256.   [2] Pretyman MSS.

Post Office, we can understand the thinness of his correspondence.[1] Recently he had advised Addington not to retain Alexandria, Malta, Goree, and Cape Town, but to trust rather to
defensive preparations, which might include a friendly understanding with other aggrieved Powers. This surely was the
dignified course. Even Malta was not worth the risk of immediate war unless we were ready both with armaments and
alliances. The foregoing letter, however, shows that Pitt believed
his advice to be useless. Possibly he heard that the Cabinet had
decided to retain those posts; and finally, as we shall see, Pitt
approved their action in the case of Malta. Meanwhile matters
went from bad to worse. Ministers complained of Pitt's aloofness; but his friends agreed that he must do nothing to avert
from Addington the consequences of his own incompetence.
Even the cold Grenville declared Pitt to be the only man who
could save England. But could even he, when under an incompetent chief, achieve that feat?

For by this time Addington had hopelessly deranged the
nation's finance. While giving up Pitt's drastic Income Tax,
which had not brought in the expected £10,000,000 but a net
sum of £6,000,000, he raised the Assessed Taxes by one third,
increased Import and Export duties with impartial rigour, and
yet proposed to raise £5,000,000 by Exchequer Bills, which were
to be funded at the end of the Session or paid off by a loan. This
signal failure to meet the year's expenses within the year exasperated Pitt. At Christmas, which he spent with Rose at his
seat in the New Forest, he often conversed on this topic; and
his host thus summed up his own conclusions in a letter to
Bishop Tomline:

Cuffnells, *December* 24, 1802.[2]

. . . There is hardly a part of the Budget that is not too stupidly
wrong even for the doctor's dullness and ignorance. I am sure Mr. Pitt
must concur with me; and I have all the materials for him.—Wrong
about the increase of the revenue; wrong as to the produce of the

[1] Auckland, while ambassador at The Hague, was suspected of too great
inquisitiveness as to the British despatches which passed through that
place. On 20th July 1790, Aust, of the Foreign Office, wrote to Sir R. M.
Keith at Vienna that Keith's new cipher puzzles " our friends at the Hague,"
and that Auckland's curiosity is "insatiable" (B.M. Add. MSS., 35543).
See, too, a note by Miss Rose in G. Rose " Diaries," ii, 75.
[2] Pretyman MSS.

Consolidated Fund; scandalously wrong as to what is to be expected from it in future by at least £2,800,000 a year; wrong as to the money he will want this year by millions. . . .

During his stay at Cuffnells Pitt received a letter from Addington urging the need of an interview. Viewing the request as a sign of distress with which he must in honour comply, Pitt agreed to stay a few days early in January 1803 at the White Lodge in Richmond Park, which the King had for the time assigned to his favoured Minister. Addington described him as looking far from well, though his strength had improved and his spirits and appetite were good.[1] Apparently Pitt found the instruction of his host in finance a subject as dreary as the winter landscape. He afterwards told Rose that Addington mooted his entrance to the Cabinet awkwardly during their farewell drive to town. But this does not tally with another account, which is that Pitt, on the plea of winding up the transfer of Holwood, suddenly left the White Lodge on 6th January. On the 11th he wrote from Camden's seat, The Wilderness, in Kent, that his views on foreign affairs were nearly in accord with those of the Cabinet, but that he failed to convince Addington of his financial error.

This, then, was still the rock of offence. Nevertheless, Pitt begged Rose not to attack the Cabinet on that topic, as it would embarrass him. If it were necessary on public grounds to set right the error, he (Pitt) would do so himself on some fit occasion. Malmesbury and Canning did their utmost to spur him on to a more decided opposition; and the latter wrote him a letter of eight pages "too admonitory and too fault-finding for even Pitt's very good humoured mind to bear."[2] Pitt replied by silence. In vain did friends tell him that Ministers had assured the King of his intention to bring forward Catholic Emancipation if he returned to office. In vain did Malmesbury declare that Pitt must take the helm of State, otherwise Fox would do

---

[1] Pellew, ii, 113. Lord Holland, writing early in 1803 to his uncle, General Fox, then at Malta, says that there are three parties in Parliament, besides many subdivisions, "Grenville and Windham against peace and nearly avowed enemies of the present Government; the old Opposition; and Addington [sic]. Pitt, as you know, supports Addington, but the degree of intimacy and the nature of his connection with Ministers are riddles to every one." (From Mr. Broadley's MSS.)

[2] "Malmesbury Diaries," iv, 168; G. Rose, "Diaries," ii, 6-9; Pellew, ii, 113.

so. In vain did Rose predict the country's ruin from Addington's appalling ignorance of finance. Pitt still considered himself in honour bound to support Addington. At the close of January he held friendly converse with him, before setting out for Walmer for a time of rest and seclusion. Canning's only consolation was that Bonaparte would come to their help, and by some new act of violence end Pitt's scrupulous balancing between the claims of national duty and of private obligations. The First Consul dealt blow upon blow. Yet even so, Canning's hopes were long to remain unfulfilled. As we saw in the former volume, the relations of Pitt to Addington had for many years been of an intimate nature; but occasions arise when a statesman ought promptly to act upon the maxim of Mirabeau—" *La petite morale est ennemie de la grande.*" In subordinating the interests of England to the dictates of a deep-rooted but too exacting friendship, Pitt was guilty of one of the most fatal blunders of that time.

CHAPTER XXII

ADDINGTON OR PITT?

Once more doth Pitt deem the land crying loud to him—
Frail though and spent, and an hungered for restfulness
Once more responds he, dead fervours to energize
Aims to concentre, slack efforts to bind.

THOMAS HARDY, *The Dynasts*, Act i, sc. 3.

ON 30th January 1803 there appeared in the " Moniteur "
the official Report of Colonel Sebastiani, Napoleon's envoy
to the Levant. So threatening were its terms respecting the
situation in Egypt and Corfu, that the Addington Ministry at
once adopted a stiffer tone, and applied to Parliament for
10,000 additional seamen and the embodying of the militia.
But the House, while readily acceding on 9th March, evidently wanted not only more men but a man. The return of Pitt
to power was anxiously discussed in the lobbies. The Duke
of Portland and Lord Pelham strongly expressed their desire
for it. Yet Pitt remained at Walmer, feeling that he could not
support financial plans fraught with danger to the State. Addington therefore resolved to sound him again with a view to
his entering the Cabinet as a coadjutor. The envoy whom he
chose for this delicate mission was Henry Dundas, now Lord
Melville. He could count on his devotion; for, besides nominat-
ing him for the peerage, he is said to have opened to his gaze
a life of official activity and patronage as First Lord of the
Admiralty in place of the parsimonious and unmannerly St.
Vincent.[1] Pitt received his old friend at Walmer with a shade
of coolness in view of his declaration, on quitting office, that he
could accept no boon whatever from Addington. To come now
as his Cabinet-maker argued either overwhelming patriotism
or phenomenal restlessness.

---

[1] Addington desired the retirement of St. Vincent. See " Dropmore P.,"
vii, 121; Stanhope, iv, 21.

Nevertheless, the two friends resumed at Walmer the festive intercourse of the Wimbledon days; and in due course, after dinner and wine, Melville broached the subject of his visit. It was that Addington, who was First Lord of the Treasury and Chancellor of the Exchequer, should resign the latter office to Pitt, and take Lord Pelham's place as Secretary of State for Home Affairs. We can picture the astonishment and wrath of Pitt as this singular proposal came to light. At once he cut short the conversation, probably not without expletives. But Melville was pertinacious where patriotism and office were at stake; and their converse spread over the two days, 21st-22nd March, Melville thereupon sending a summary of it to Addington, couched in terms which Pitt deemed too favourable. The upshot was that on personal grounds Pitt desired not to return to office; and, if affairs were efficiently conducted, would prefer to continue his present independent support. If, however, the misleading statements of the Treasury were persisted in, he must criticize them. Above all, if he returned to office it must be as First Lord of the Treasury and Chancellor of the Exchequer.

But Addington, foreseeing that Pitt would claim his two former offices, had concocted a sovereign remedy for all these personal sores. Pitt was to take office as Chancellor of the Exchequer, serving under his brother, the Earl of Chatham, as Prime Minister. Is it surprising that he negatived this singular proposal "without reserve or affectation"? By way of retort to this family prescription he charged Melville to point out the absolute need of the Cabinet being under the control of "the First Minister," who must not only have the confidence of the King and administer the finances, but also in the last resort impose his will on his colleagues. For himself he declared he would never come forward unless bound by public duty and with the enjoyment of the fullest confidence of the King.[1] There is a discrepancy between Melville's letter to Addington and a short account given by Pitt to Wilberforce two years later, to the effect that Melville, on cautiously opening his proposals at Walmer, saw that it would not do and stopped abruptly. "Really," said Pitt with a sly severity, "I had not the curiosity to ask what I was to be." Such was the bomb-shell exploded on Addington's bureau on

[1] Pellew, ii, 114-6.

Henry Dundas, First Viscount Melville

(From a painting by Sir T Lawrence)

23rd March. It must have cost him no less concern than Bonaparte's outrageous behaviour to our ambassador, Lord Whitworth, ten days before. That scene before the diplomatic circle at the Tuileries portended war. How would Addington and his colleagues behave in this crisis? Would they sink all personal feelings, and, admitting that they could not weather the storm, accept the help and guidance of long tried navigators? Or would they stand on their dignity and order the pilot-boat to sheer off? Clearly it was a case where half measures were useless. The old captain and his chosen subalterns must command the ship. Pitt made this clear during conversations with Addington at Long's house at Bromley Hill (10th April). While declaring that he would not urge any point inconsistent with His Majesty's intentions, he demanded that Grenville, Melville, Spencer, and Windham should enter the Cabinet with him on the clearly expressed desire of the King, and at the request of the present Ministry. The last conditions seem severe. But Pitt's pledge to Addington made it essential that the Prime Minister should take the first step. To these terms two days later Addington made demur, but promised to communicate them to his colleagues; whereupon Pitt declared that he had said the last word on the matter; and when Ministers objected to Grenville and Windham, he was inexorable.[1] That their anger waxed hot against him appears from the following letter sent to Pitt by Lord Redesdale, formerly Sir John Mitford, and now Lord Chancellor of Ireland, who had been with Pitt and Addington at their conferences at Bromley:

Albemarle St., *April* 16, 1803.[2]

What passed yesterday and the day before at Bromley Hill, has made so strong an impression on my mind that I have been unable to relieve myself from the anxiety which it has occasioned. However you may flatter yourself to the contrary, it seems to me most clear that your return into office, with the impression under which you have appeared to act, must have the effect of driving from their situations every man now in office, and making a greater change than has ever been made on any similar occasion. I think myself as one of those persons individually intitled to call upon your honour not to pursue the line of conduct which you seem determined to adopt. The present Administration, so

---

[1] " Lord Colchester's Diaries," i, 415. Pellew, ii, 121-4.
[2] Pretyman MSS.

far from having been formed in hostility to you, was avowedly formed
of your friends. When you quitted office, you repeatedly declared that
you should consider yourself as obliged to those friends who would
continue in office or would accept office under Mr. Addington. You
must recollect that I expressed to you my disapprobation of the change
and my wish to retire to my situation at the Bar, quitting the office of
Attorney-General; and that you used to me these words—" That you
must not do, for my sake." The words were too strongly impressed
upon my mind at the moment to have escaped my memory. You encouraged me to take the office of Speaker much against my will. If I
had not taken that office, nothing should have induced me to take that
in which I am now placed, and by which I have been brought into a
position of much anxiety, separated from all my old friends. Many
many others are in similar situations, and all are to be sacrificed to
those men who were said by yourself at the time to be acting in contradiction to your wishes in quitting their offices or those who dragged
you out of office with them. You will probably tell me that you have
no such intentions, particularly with respect to myself. But, whatever
may be your intentions, such must be the unavoidable consequence of
the changes which you have determined upon. I thought, when I took
a situation under the Administration at the head of which you placed
Mr. Addington, that I was doing you service. It was of no small importance to you, whether you looked to a return to office, or to retirement from public life, that the Government should not fall into the
hands of those who had been engaged in violent opposition to you;
and you yourself stated to me that you apprehended that must be the
consequence if Mr. Addington should not be able to form an Administration. . . . Some of your last words to me induce me to think that
you have not yourself abandoned the plan formed for giving to the
Roman Catholic Church full establishment in Ireland—for such I consider the plan suggested by Lord Castlereagh, with any modification of
which it is capable. Indeed, if all those who went out of office because
that measure was not approved then (such being the ostensible cause of
their quitting their stations) are to come into office again, there can be
no doubt in the mind of the public that it is determined to carry that
measure. . . .

That at so critical a juncture a supporter of Addington, not
of Cabinet rank, should rake up personal reasons why Pitt
should let things drift to ruin is inconceivable. And did Redesdale really believe Protestantism to be endangered by Pitt's
return to office, after his assurance at Bromley that he would
not press any point at variance with the royal resolves? The

King, who knew Pitt far better than Redesdale did, had no fear that he would belie his word by bringing forward Catholic Emancipation. But the phrases in the letter quoted above show that some of the Ministers were preparing to beat the drum ecclesiastic, and, in the teeth of the evidence, to charge Pitt with ingratitude and duplicity if he became Prime Minister. Ignoring the national crisis, they concentrated attention solely on the personal questions at issue; and it is humiliating to have to add that their petty scheming won the day. A compromise between Pitt and Addington was exceedingly difficult, but their reproaches and innuendoes made it impossible.[1]

The outcome was disastrous. The failure to form a strong and truly national Administration ended all hope of peace. Over against Addington set Bonaparte; with Hawkesbury compare Talleyrand; with Hobart, Berthier.[2] The weighing need go no further. The British Ministry kicks the beam; and in that signal inequality is one of the chief causes of the war of 1803. The first Consul, like the Czar Alexander I, despised the Addington Cabinet. He could not believe that men who were laughed at by their own supporters would dare to face him in arms. Twice he made the mistake of judging a nation by its Ministers—England by Addington in 1803, Spain by Godoy in 1808. Both blunders were natural, and both were irreparable; but those peoples had to pour forth their life blood to recover the position from which weakness and folly allowed them to slide. Politics, like meteorology, teaches that any sharp difference of pressure, whether mental or atmospheric, draws in a strong current to redress the balance. Never were the conditions more cyclonic than in 1803. A decade of strife scarcely made good the inequality between the organized might of France and the administrative chaos of her neighbours; between the Titanic Corsican and the mediocrities or knaves who held the reins at London, Vienna, Berlin, and Madrid.

War having been declared on 18th May 1803, Pitt sought the first opportunity of inspiriting Parliament and the nation. On

---

[1] G. Rose, "Diaries," ii, 156; "Lord Colchester's Diaries," i, 416, 417; Pellew, ii, 119-28.

[2] Hawkesbury's remissness (so Vorontzoff told Rose) then lost an opportunity of gaining the friendly mediation of the Czar (G. Rose, "Diaries," ii, 43, 157). Romilly ("Mems.," i, 427) calls the Ministry a thing of no account in comparison with Pitt, and says it was universally despised.

the 23rd a great concourse crowded the House in the hope of hearing him speak; and cries of "Pitt, Pitt" arose as he strode to his seat on the third row behind Ministers, beside one of the pillars. The position gave point to a remark of Canning to Lord Malmesbury, that Pitt would fire over the heads of Ministers, neither praising nor blaming them, but merely supporting the policy of the war. Such was the case. Replying to a few criticisms of Erskine, he defended the Cabinet and powerfully described the unbearable aggressions of the First Consul.

The speech aroused a patriotic fervour which cannot be fully realized from the meagre and dreary summary of it which survives. Romilly pronounced it among the finest, if not the very finest, which he had ever made;[1] and Sheridan, in a vinous effusion to Lady Bessborough, called it "one of the most magnificent pieces of declamation that ever fell from that rascal Pitt's lips. Detesting the dog, as I do, I cannot withhold this just tribute to the scoundrel's talents." There follows a lament over Pitt's want of honesty, which betokens the maudlin mood preceding complete intoxication.[2] On the morrow Fox vehemently blamed the Cabinet in a speech which, for width of survey, acuteness of dialectic, wealth of illustration and abhorrence of war, stands unrivalled. Addington's reply exhibited his hopeless mediocrity; but, thanks to Pitt, Ministers triumphed by 398 votes to 67. As they resented the absence of definite praise in his speech, he withdrew to Walmer, there to serve his country and embarrass his finances by raising the Cinque Ports Volunteers.

Before recounting Pitt's services in East Kent, I must mention a bereavement which he had sustained. His mother died, after a very short seizure, at Burton Pynsent on 3rd April 1803. Thus was snapped a link connecting England with a mighty past. A quarter of a century had elapsed since her consort was laid to rest in the family vault in Westminster Abbey; she followed him while the storm-fiends were shrouding in strife the two

---

[1] Romilly Memoirs, i, 427.

[2] Sichel, "Sheridan," i, 440. Spencer Stanhope declared Pitt's speech the finest he ever heard. His wife wrote to their son: "He (Pitt) spoke for two hours, but unless he can be prevailed upon to give it himself, as the shorthand-writers were excluded, the speech will be lost for ever. Your father thinks it will be made out by some of his friends and submitted to his inspection; therefore, tho' we may lose much, we shall not lose the whole" (A. M. W. Stirling, "Annals of a Yorkshire House," ii, 282).

hereditary foes; and the Napoleonic War was destined to bring her gifted son thither in less than three years. The father had linked the name of Pitt with military triumphs; the son, with futile efforts for peace and goodwill; but the lives both of the war-lord and of the would-be peacemaker were to be ended by tidings of national disaster.

> No parleying now. In Britain is one breath;
> We all are with you now from shore to shore;
> Ye men of Kent, 'tis victory or death!

We all know these lines of Wordsworth. Do we know equally well that on Pitt, as Lord Warden, fell the chief burden of organization on the most easily accessible coast, that which stretches from Ramsgate to Rye?[1] It was defenceless but for the antiquated works at Sandown, Deal, Walmer, Dover, and a few small redoubts further west. Evidently men must be the ramparts, and Pitt sought to stimulate the Volunteer Movement, which now again made headway. He strove to make it a National Movement. At the close of July he sent an official offer to raise 3,000 Volunteers in Walmer and its neighbourhood; and he urged Ministers to have recourse to a *levée en masse*, whereupon Yorke, Under Secretary at War, proposed a scheme somewhat on those lines. Probably the encouragement offered to Volunteers was too great; for, while they were required to do less than was necessary to ensure efficiency, they were freed from all risk of compulsory enrolment in the Militia. This force and the Army consequently suffered, while the Volunteer Associations grew apace. On 27th October 1803 the King reviewed in Hyde Park as many as 27,000 of the London Volunteers and showed his caustic wit by giving the nickname of " the Devil's Own " to the Inns of Court Volunteers.

Pitt was not present on this occasion, he and his neighbour, Lord Carrington, on whom in 1802 he bestowed the command of Deal Castle, being busy in organizing the local Volunteers. As Constable of Dover Castle, Pitt summoned the delegates of the Cinque Ports to meet him there to discuss the raising of local corps; and he gave the sum of £1,000 towards their expenses. Dover contributed £885; Sandwich, £887; Margate,

---

[1] " Dumouriez and the Defence of England against Napoleon," by J. H. Rose and A. M. Broadley.

£538, and so on. As Lord Warden, he also took steps to secure
a large number of recruits for the new Army of Reserve, and he
further instructed local authorities to send in returns of all men
of military age, besides carts, horses, and stock, with a view to
the " driving " of the district in case of a landing.[1] At Walmer
he kept open house for officers and guests who visited that coast.
By the end of the year 1803 more than 10,000 Kentishmen had
enrolled as Volunteers, and 1,040 in the Army of Reserve,
exclusive of Sea Fencibles serving on gunboats. For the whole
of Great Britain the totals were 379,000 and 31,000 respectively.[2]
Pitt's joke at the expense of a battalion which laid more stress
on privileges than drills, has become historic. Its organizers
sent up a plan containing several stipulations as to their duties,
with exceptions " in case of actual invasion." Pitt lost patience
at this Falstaff-like conduct, and opposite the clause that they
were on no account to be sent out of the country he wrote the
stinging comment—" except in case of invasion."

The pen of Lady Hester Stanhope gives life-like glimpses of
him during the endless drills between Deal and Dover. She had
fled from the levelling vagaries of Earl Stanhope at Chevening
to Lady Chatham at Burton Pynsent; but that home being now
broken up, Pitt offered to install her at Walmer Castle. He did
so with some misgiving; for her queenly airs and sprightly
sallies, however pleasing as a tonic, promised little for comfort
and repose. But the experiment succeeded beyond all hope.
She soon learnt to admire his serenity, while his home was the
livelier for the coming of this meteoric being. Her complexion
was dazzlingly bright. Her eyes, usually blue, would flash black,
as did those of Chatham in moments of excitement. Her
features, too, had a magical play of expression, lighting up at a
pleasing fancy, or again darting forth scorn, with the April-like
alternations that irradiated and overclouded the brow of her
grandsire. Kinglake, who saw her half a century later in her
Syrian fastness, was struck by the likeness to the Chatham of
Copley's famous picture.

Certainly she had more in common with him than with the
younger Pitt. During the time when she brought storm and
sunshine to Walmer, Park Place, and Bowling Green House,
she often rallied her uncle on showing undue complaisance to

[1] Lyon, " Hist. of Dover," p. xxxiii.   [2] Hansard, i, 1899-1902.

the King or to stupid colleagues whom the Great Commoner
would have overawed. Pitt laughingly took the second place,
and at times vowed that when her voice rang with excitement,
he caught an echo of the tones of his father.[1] Perhaps it was
this which reconciled him to her vagaries. For her whims and
moods even then showed the extravagance which made her the
dreaded Sultana of that lonely Syrian castle where she ended
her days amidst thirty quarrelsome but awe-struck servants,
and an equal number of cats, over whom an apprehensive doctor
held doubtful sway.

But that bitter, repining, spirit-haunted exile was far different
from the joyous creature who shed light on Pitt. Her spasmodic
nature needed his strength; her waywardness, his affectionate
control. As for her tart retorts, terrifying to bores and toadies,
they only amused him. In truth she brought into his life a beam
of the sunshine which might have flooded it had he married
Eleanor Eden. Hester soon found that, far from being indifferent
to the charms of women, he was an exacting judge of beauty,
even of dress. In fact, she pronounced him to be perfect in
household life. His abilities in gardening astonished her; and
we may doubt the correctness of the local legend which as-
cribes to her the landscape-gardening undertaken in the grounds
of Walmer Castle in 1803. The dell at the top of the grounds
was Hester's favourite haunt.

The varied excitements of the time are mirrored in her
sprightly letters. Thus, on 15th November 1803, she wrote at
Walmer:

We took one of their gunboats the other day: and, as soon as she
came in, Mr. Pitt, Charles,[2] Lord Camden and myself took a Deal boat
and rowed alongside of her. She had two large guns on board, 30
soldiers and 4 sailors. She is about 30 feet long, and only draws about
4 feet of water; an ill-contrived thing, and so little above the water
that, had she as many men on board as she could really carry, a
moderate storm would wash them overboard. . . . Mr. Pitt's 1st battalion of his newly-raised regiment was reviewed the other day by
General Dundas, who expressed himself equally surprised and pleased
by the state of discipline he found them in. . . . I like all this sort of
thing, and I admire my uncle most particularly when surrounded with a

---

[1] " Mems. of Lady Hester Stanhope," i, 174.
[2] Lady Hester's second brother.

tribe of military attendants. But what is all this pageantry compared with the unaffected simplicity of real greatness!

Walmer Castle, *Nov.* 19, 1803.

To F. R. Jackson, Esq.

To express the kindness with which Mr. Pitt welcomed my return and proposed my living with him would be impossible; one would really suppose that all obligation was on his side. Here then am I, happy to a degree; exactly in the sort of society I most like. There are generally three or four men staying in the house, and we dine eight or ten almost every other day. Military and naval characters are constantly welcome here; women are not, I suppose, because they do not form any part of our society. You may guess, then, what a pretty fuss they make with me. Pitt absolutely goes through the fatigue of a drill sergeant. It is parade after parade at 15 or 20 minutes' distance from each other. I often attend him; and it is quite as much as I am equal to, although I am remarkably well just now. The hard riding I do not mind, but to remain almost *still* so many hours on horseback is an incomprehensible bore, and requires more patience than you can easily imagine. However, I suppose few regiments for the time were ever so forward; therefore the trouble is nothing. If Mr. Pitt does not overdo and injure his health every other consideration becomes trifling. [She then states her anxiety on this score. She rarely speaks to him on it, as he particularly dislikes it. She adds:] I am happy to tell you, sincerely, I see nothing at all alarming about him. He had a cough when I first came to England, but it has nearly or quite left him. He is thin, but certainly strong, and his spirits are excellent. . . . Mr. Pitt is determined to remain acting colonel when his regiment is called into the field.

On this topic Pitt met with a rebuff from General (afterwards Sir John) Moore, commander of the newly formed camp at Shorncliffe, near Folkestone. Pitt rode over from Walmer to ask his advice, and his question as to the position he and his Volunteers should take brought the following reply: "Do you see that hill? You and yours shall be drawn up on it, where you will make a most formidable appearance to the enemy, while I with the soldiers will be fighting on the beach." Pitt was highly amused at this professional retort; but at the close of 1804 his regiment was pronounced by General David Dundas fit to take the field with regulars. Life in the open and regular exercise on horseback served to strengthen Pitt's frame; for Hester, writing in the middle of January 1804, when her uncle was away in London for a few days, says: "His most intimate

friends say they do not remember him so well since the year
'97. . . . Oh! such miserable things as these French gunboats.
We took a vessel the other day, laden with gin—to keep their
spirits up, I suppose." Bonaparte was believed to be at Boulogne;
and there was much alarm about a landing; but she was resolved
"not to be driven up country like a sheep."

This phrase refers to the arrangements for "driving" the
country, that is, sweeping it bare of everything in front of the
invaders. The plans for "driving" were thorough, but were finally
pronounced unworkable. His efforts to meet the Boulogne flotilla
were also most vigorous. On 18th October 1803 he informs Rose
that he had 170 gunboats ready between Hastings and Margate
to give the enemy a good reception whenever they appeared.
He adds: "Our Volunteers are, I think, likely to be called upon
to undertake permanent duty, which, I hope, they will readily
consent to. I suppose the same measure will be recommended
in your part of the coast [West Hants]. I wish the arrangements for defence were as forward everywhere else as they are
in Hythe Bay under General Moore. We begin now to have no
other fear in that quarter than that the enemy will not give us
an opportunity of putting our preparations to the proof, and will
select some other point which we should not be in reach of in
the first instance." On 10th November he expresses a hope of
repelling any force that attempted to land in East Kent, but
fears that elsewhere the French cannot be stopped until they
arrive disagreeably near to London.[1]

It is clear, then, that Pitt was not dismayed by the startling
disparity of forces. On the coast of Flanders and Picardy were
ranged regular troops amounting to 114,554 men seemingly
ready for embarkation on an immense flotilla of small craft, part
of which was heavily armed. It is now known that these imposing forces were rarely, if ever, up to their nominal strength;
that part of the flotilla was unseaworthy; that the difficulties of
getting under way were never overcome; and that the unwieldy
mass would probably have been routed, if not destroyed, by the
cruisers and gunboats stationed on the Kentish coast. Still, even
if part of it made land, the crisis would be serious in view of the

---

[1] G. Rose, "Diaries," ii, 70-2; Desbrière, "Projets de Débarquement,"
iii, 98-105; Wheeler and Broadley, "Napoleon and the Invasion of England," ii, ch. 14; Cornwallis ("Corresp.," iii, 500) thought ill of our chances
if the French landed, but he doubted if they could. (*Ibid.*, iii, 503.)

paucity and want of organization of the British forces. As bearing on this subject, a letter of Lord Melville to a relative deserves quotation:

"Dunira, 16 *Dec.*, 1803.[1]

"DEAR ALEXANDER,

"I received your letter from Walmer and was extreamly happy to learn from it that Mr. Pitt was in such excellent health. Long, I pray, may it continue. He has been very usefully and creditably employed, but not exactly in the way his country could have wished; but that is a subject on which I never now allow myself to think. . . . If Mr. Pitt, from what he feels within himself or from the enthusiasm he may have inspired in those he commands, conceives that the defence of the country could at any time be safely entrusted with the Volunteers alone, as the newspapers seem to convey as his sentiments, he is by much too sanguine. On the other hand it is talking wildly, or like old women, to contend, as Mr. Windham and Mr. Fox do, that great bodies of Britains [*sic*], with arms in their hands and trained to the use of them, are not a most important bulwark of security to the Empire. My opinion, however, lays perhaps in the middle, and I would have greatly preferred a much smaller number to have secured more effectually their uniform efficiency. I would much rather have had 200,000 on the footing of Lord Hobart's first letter in June than double that number selected and formed in the loose and desultory manner they have more recently been under the variety of contradictory orders they have since received and by which Government have annoyed every corner of the country." Melville adds that they would be useful if thoroughly trained and not allowed to leave their corps; but exemptions from the Militia and Army of Reserve ballots granted to the recent Volunteer Corps are mischievous, and interfere with the recruiting. The Militia is unnecessarily large and interferes with recruiting for the regular army. He would have enough trained troops at home to be able to send abroad "50,000 infantry for offensive operations either by ourselves or in co-operation with such European Powers as may recover their senses, as sooner or later they must and will do."

Pitt did not leave his post for long, except when high winds made an invasion impossible. At such times he would make a trip to London. A short sojourn in town in the early spring elicits from Lady Hester the words: "I cannot but be happy anywhere in Mr. Pitt's society"; and she hoped that she helped to amuse and entertain him. Certainly Pitt did his utmost to

[1] Pitt MSS., 157.

enliven her stay at the little residence at Park Place. In the Memoirs of the Comtesse de Boigne, who claims to have known her well, we catch a glimpse of Pitt acting as *chaperon* at balls which obviously bored him. Yet he would patiently wait there until, perhaps, four a.m., when Lady Hester returned to end his *ennui*. Is it surprising that after his death she called him that adored angel?

Early in the year 1804 a ministerial crisis seemed at hand. The personal insignificance of Ministers, the hatred felt for St. Vincent at the Admiralty, the distrust of Hobart at the War Office, and the deep depression caused by the laboured infelicities of Addington's speeches presaged a breakdown. So threatening was the outlook that Grenville urged Pitt to combine with him for the overthrow of an Administration which palsied national energy. For reasons which are far from clear, Pitt refused to take decisive action. During his stay in London in mid-January he saw Grenville, but declined to pledge himself to a definite opposition. Grenville and his coadjutors, among them Lord Carysfort, were puzzled by this wavering conduct, which they ascribed to *finesse*, pettiness, or even to insincerity.[1] But it is clear that Pitt objected only to their proposed methods, which he termed a teasing, harassing opposition. In vain did the Bishop of Lincoln, who came to town at Pitt's request, seek to reconcile their differences. The most to be hoped for was that Pitt would be compelled by force of circumstances to concert a plan with the Grenvilles for Addington's overthrow. The following letter of Carysfort to the bishop is of interest:

Jany. 18, 1804.[2]

Lord Grenville and Mr. Pitt being agreed upon so material a point as the necessity of removing Mr. A[ddington] from his present situation, it must be a matter not only of regret but of surprise, that they should not be able to reconcile any difference of opinion between them as to the sort of opposition to be carried on in Parliament; and I cannot help thinking that Mr. Pitt's avowal that he intends opposition would in itself be sufficient to incline (not merely Lord Grenville and his friends, who have made it a principal object to be united with Mr. Pitt and place him again at the head of affairs) but all the parties who may mean

---

[1] " Dropmore P.," vii, 193, 196.
[2] Pretyman MSS. It is in answer to the one referred to in " Dropmore P.," vii, 209.

to oppose, to leave the mode pretty much at his option! . . . [Your letter] leads me to think that Mr. Pitt and he may not have understood each other. Lord Grenville's attachment to Mr. Pitt has been so conspicuous, and I am persuaded his communications have been so frank and so explicit, that I cannot account for Mr. Pitt using any reserve with him, and must be of opinion that greater openness, where there is such solid ground of confidence, would lead to more satisfactory results. [Lord Carysfort then says that Pitt should not keep public opinion so long in suspense; for] the public danger from a Ministry confessedly incapable is already great and urgent and will be continually increasing.

Failing to get help from Pitt, Grenville, at the end of January, sought the help of Fox! Through his brother, Thomas Grenville, as go-between he offered the Whig leader his alliance for the overthrow of Addington and the formation of a Ministry of the talented men of all parties. Here, then, is the origin of the broad-bottomed or All the Talents Administrations which produced so singular a muddle after the death of Pitt. The Fox-Grenville bargain cannot be styled immoral like that of Fox and North in 1782; for it expressly excluded all compromise on matters of conviction. Nevertheless it was a tactical mistake, for which Pitt's exasperating aloofness was largely responsible. Few occurrences in this time of folly and blundering were more untoward. Pitt's letter of 4th February to Grenville shows that he discerned the magnitude of the error, little though he saw his own share in it. The result of the union of Fox and Grenville was likely to be the fall of Addington, an appeal ot the King to him (Pitt) to form a Cabinet, which would be narrowed and weakened by the present effort of Grenville to form a strong and comprehensive Administration.[1]

Presumably the national crisis was not yet acute enough to satisfy Pitt that he might conscientiously oppose Addington. But that he was drifting to this convicton appears in the following letter from Rose to the Bishop of Lincoln.

Feb. 11, 1804.[2]

I showed Mr. Pitt your letter because it expressed so entirely my own view of the interesting subject: he appeared at first against anything like hostility, but I think is now disposed to point out pretty strongly the neglect of proper measures of defence in the naval and military de-

[1] " Dropmore P.," vii, 211-14.   [2] Pretyman MSS.

partments and to suggest the necessary ones; so [as] to throw on the Government the just responsibility and odium of rejecting them if they shall determine to do so.

Rose then states that the Bishop of St. Asaph calls the new Volunteer Bill "the most wishy-washy thing that ever was produced." He also adds that the King is ill, probably of dropsy. The fact was even worse. A chill caught in drenching rain developed into the former mental malady. Thus the nation was for a time kingless, leaderless, and open to a deadly thrust from Boulogne. For a short time his life was in danger, and all the troubles of a Regency loomed ahead. The Prince of Wales having ventured on the compromising prophecy that the illness "*must* last several months," Pitt quoted to his informant, Malmesbury, the damning line

Thy wish was father, Harry, to that thought.

In truth, there now began a series of intrigues, in which the Prince, Fox, and the Duke and Duchess of Devonshire played the leading parts, for assuring a Regency and the formation of a Fox Administration. While England needed to keep her gaze on Boulogne, the intriguers thought only of the death or lunacy of the King, the accession of the Prince and the apportionment of the spoils of office. Sheridan on this occasion played his own game and for this was heartily cursed by the expectant Creevey.[1]

In view of these last complications and the prospect of an invasion, Pitt revised his former judgement, and informed Malmesbury that, while declining the offers of the Grenvilles to help to overthrow Addington, he would not refuse to take office if for any reason Ministers resigned. On that day (19th February) Melville wrote to him from Melville Castle that the outlook was full of horror, and everything depended on the formation of a steady and permanent Government with which foreign nations could treat. For this reason he (Melville) urged that the King should be relieved of his executive duties, which it was sheer cruelty to exact from him.[2] Pitt's answer to this daring proposal is not known; but later, on 29th March, in answer to further overtures from Melville, he stated that the King's illness was less serious than was reported by the Earl of Moira, the *confidante* of the Prince of Wales; and that while it lasted he doubted the pro-

[1] "Creevey Papers," i, 25-7.   [2] Pretyman MSS.

priety of taking any steps to overturn the Ministry.[1] To this scrupulousness Melville was a stranger, and on 4th April again urged him to form a compact opposition for the overthrow of Addington, and promised him the votes of at least twenty-six Scottish members (out of forty-five) for any such effort.[2]

Meanwhile the King recovered but slowly. The nervous, excited, irritable symptoms showed little abatement; and in the third week in March he fell into a fit of anger of such violence that he had to be strapped to his bed. Even more threatening was the military situation. Yorke, early in March, proposed a Volunteer Consolidation Bill, which met with general derision. As the state of the Navy was also unsatisfactory, Pitt freely criticized Ministers, especially St. Vincent; and, on one occasion, when Addington showed boyish petulance, he met with a serene and courteous answer. Tierney, Treasurer of the Navy, attacked Pitt coarsely; Sheridan, with his usual wit and brilliance; but neither coarseness nor eloquence could rehabilitate that Ministry. The urgency of the crisis appears in the following letter written by Pitt at Walmer Castle to some person unknown:

April 11, 1804.

. . . The experience of the last summer and the discussions of this session confirm me in the opinion that while the Government remains in its present shape and under its present leader, nothing efficient can be expected either to originate with them or to be fairly adopted and effectually executed. With this persuasion, and thinking that a system of more energy and decision is indispensable with a view to the immediate crisis and the many difficulties he may have to encounter in the course of the present contest, I mean to take an early opportunity of avowing and acting on these sentiments more explicitly and decidedly than I have hitherto done; and I shall endeavour to give effect to my opinion by the support of all the friends whom I can collect. My object will be to press to the utmost those points which I think essential to the public defence, and at the same time in doing so to make it, if I can, impossible for the present Government to maintain itself. In this object I have every reason to believe that I shall have the fullest concurrence of all those with whom I have the most differed on former occasions and with whom possibly I may as little agree in future. With their number added to my own more immediate friends, and to the few who have acted with L[d] Grenville and Windham, I am persuaded that our

---

[1] Stanhope, iv, 139-44.   [2] Pretyman MSS.

division on any favourable question will probably be such as would be sufficient to shake a much stronger Government than the present. . . .[1]

On the same day he promised Melville to return to town in the middle of April, and to make the " principal push " against Addington on 23rd April, on the subject of Yorke's Bill for suspending the completion of the Army Reserve. If they failed, he would return to Walmer for another kind of contest. The joint assault by Fox and Pitt against the Ministry on 23rd April produced a great sensation, the speech of Pitt being remarkable for its suppressed sarcasm and thinly veiled charges of inefficiency. As a call to arms, it stands without a rival. Ministers were utterly beaten in argument, and escaped defeat only by thirty-seven votes. Addington became alarmed, and advised the King, who was now convalescent, to instruct the Lord Chancellor, Eldon, to confer with Pitt, a fact which refutes the charges of Brougham and Dean Pellew against Eldon.

Finally the King allowed Pitt to make proposals concerning a new Ministry. Pitt did so fully and courteously in a paper which George III forthwith described to Eldon as containing " many empty words and little information." To Pitt himself the King, on 5th May, expressed his deep regret that he had taken such a dislike to Mr. Addington, after the praiseworthy services of the latter to our glorious Constitution in Church and State. He could never forget the wound which Pitt proposed to deal it, and " the indelicacy (not to call it worse) of wanting His Majesty to forego his solemn Coronation Oath." He therefore required Pitt to give a solemn pledge not to propose the least alteration in the Test Act. As to a proposal to admit Fox to the Cabinet, the King expressed " his astonishment that Mr. Pitt should one moment harbour the thought of bringing such a man before his Royal notice." References to the " wild ideas " of Burke, and to Grenville being guided by obstinacy, " his usual director," filled up the interstices of this strange composition.[2] Evidently the enfeebled brain of George could form no notion of the national danger. While Pitt thought only of the safety of England, the King's thoughts continued to gyrate angrily around the Test Act, the Coronation Oath, and the iniquities of Fox.

It was therefore with grave apprehension that on 7th May

---

[1] From Mr. A. M. Broadley's MSS.   [2] Stanhope, iv, App. viii-ix.

Pitt went to Buckingham House for attendance upon the King, the first for nearly three and a quarter years. He expected an outburst of rage when he mentioned the chief subject at issue, namely the inclusion of Fox and the Grenvilles in the future Administration. The King, however, kept surprising control over his feelings, behaved graciously to Pitt, tactfully waived aside smaller questions that he disliked, even consented to admit the Grenvilles, but for ever barred the way to the return of Fox. The utmost that he would hear was the employment of Fox as an ambassador. Once again, then, the royal convalescent outwitted Pitt. " Never," said Pitt to Eldon, " in any conversation I have had with him in my life has he so baffled me." Fox being excluded by the King, there was scant hope of bringing in his new allies, the Grenvilles and Windham. Pitt broached the matter to Lord Grenville on 7th May, and received on the morrow a friendly but firm refusal. The following sentences are noteworthy: " We rest our determination solely on our strong sense of the impropriety of our becoming parties to a system of Government which is to be formed at such a moment as the present on a principle of exclusion. . . . We see no hope of any effectual remedy for those mischiefs but by uniting in the public service as large a proportion as possible of the weight, talents, and character to be found in public men of all descriptions and without any exception."

The refusal of Grenville to join Pitt has often been ascribed to jealousy of Pitt, and the latter is reported to have said that he would teach that proud man that he could do without him. The sentiment is alien to the tolerant nature of Pitt,[1] who must have respected his cousin's decision, based as it was on a determination to break down the bigoted resolve of the King. But Grenville's conduct punished Pitt far more severely than the King. For while George in his feeble, irritable condition thought only about the Test Act and Fox, Pitt was intent on forming a truly national Administration, including Fox, Fitzwilliam, and Melville as Secretaries of State, with Spencer at the Admiralty, Grenville as Lord President, and Windham as Chancellor of the Duchy of Lancaster.[2]

The actual result was far inferior. Fox, Fitzwilliam, Spencer, Grenville, and Windham being ruled out by the King's action

[1] G. Rose, " Diaries," i, 4.   [2] Stanhope, iv, 177.

and Grenville's resolve, the Cabinet was formed as follows: Pitt, First Lord of the Treasury and Chancellor of the Exchequer; Harrowby, Foreign Secretary; Hawkesbury, Home Secretary; Camden, Secretary at War and for the Colonies; Portland, Lord President; Eldon, Lord Chancellor; Westmorland, Privy Seal; Melville, Admiralty; Chatham, Master of Ordnance; Mulgrave, Duchy of Lancaster; Castlereagh, President of the India Board; the Duke of Montrose, President of the Board of Trade. Of these twelve Ministers, six had been with Addington, namely, Hawkesbury (though at the Foreign Office, which he unwillingly vacated), Portland, Eldon, Westmorland, Chatham, and Castlereagh.[1] Pitt dispensed with the services of Addington, St. Vincent, and Pelham. Of non-Cabinet appointments, the chief were those of the Earl of Hardwicke as Lord Lieutenant of Ireland; Sir Evan Nepean, Irish Secretary; William Dundas, War Office; Canning, Treasury of the Navy, in place of Tierney, who declined to serve with Pitt; Lord Charles Somerset and George Rose, Joint Paymasters of the Forces; and Perceval, Attorney-General. Canning and Rose were dissatisfied with their appointments, the latter writing to Bishop Tomline in deep chagrin at Pitt's neglect of his faithful services.

The new Cabinet, besides being too large, was half Addingtonian and half Pittite, a source of weakness which soon led to further changes. It was also weighted with inefficient members—Chatham, Hawkesbury, and Portland. The King disliked Hawkesbury, and said he had no head for business, no method, and no punctuality. Harrowby, though a man of brilliant parts in private life, and an excellent speaker, was oppressed by a delicate frame, precarious health, and a peevish temper. During no small part of his tenure of office he had to take the waters at Bath, and was therefore a poor substitute for the experienced and hard-working Grenville. Pitt, for some unexplained reason, disliked placing Melville at the Admiralty, a strangely prophetic instinct. Camden and Mulgrave were also misfits. Hawkesbury did better work at the Home Office than the Foreign Office; but on the whole, the new arrangement aroused widespread grumbling and distrust. The result of it all was the dissolution of the great national party formed in the year 1794 and the

[1] Pitt thoroughly approved of Castlereagh taking the India Board under Addington in July 1802; in October he entered the Cabinet ("Private Papers of Wilberforce," 131).

formation of three groups, following Pitt, Addington, and Grenville, the Addingtonians showing much bitterness at the treatment of their chief, while the Grenvilles and Windham inveighed
against the new Ministry, as formed on the principle of exclud-
ing Fox.[1] The charge was unfair; for at that crisis Pitt could
not stand by and see the national resources frittered away by
Addington. The King's Government had to be carried on; and,
like Wellington a generation later, Pitt consented to do so in the
only way which was practicable.

The limitations of his power were soon obvious. The two unfriendly groups eagerly criticized him at all times and accorded
grudging and doubtful support even on measures which they
approved. This was especially the case with regard to the
Abolition of the Slave Trade. Thanks to the untiring exertions
of Wilberforce, Clarkson, and others, that movement had made
considerable progress during the interval of peace. The outbreak of war in May 1803 darkened the outlook; for once again
the cry was raised that England must not cut off a trade which
was essential to the welfare of the West Indies, highly lucrative
to British shipowners, and a necessary adjunct to the mercantile
marine. Nevertheless, the accession of Pitt to power and the
goodwill of the majority of the Irish members inspired Wilberforce with hope. True, Addington always strenuously opposed
him; and among the younger members of the Cabinet Castlereagh had declared his hostility; but at first all went well. At
the close of May 1804 Pitt and Fox united in expressing
approval of Wilberforce's proposals. Addington, in remarks
which lasted exactly forty seconds, scouted the measure, but
carried with him only 49 members as against 124. The majorities were nearly as great at the second and third readings.

In the Lords the omens were inauspicious. Some bishops
were away in their dioceses: the supporters of the West India and
shipping interests were at hand, using their utmost endeavours to
delay, if not to defeat, the measure. Pitt despaired of thwarting
these dilatory tactics, backed by wealth and influence from all
quarters. Wilberforce wrote indignantly to Lord Muncaster:
" It was truly humiliating to see four of the Royal Family come
down to vote against the poor, helpless, friendless slaves." A
wild speech by Stanhope told against the cause which he

---

[1] Wraxall (iii, 281) with his usual bias says that Pitt " affected " to desire
the inclusion of Fox.

meant to further, and the motion was adjourned to avoid defeat.

Pitt's subsequent conduct in 1805 disappointed Wilberforce. Certainly it was half-hearted and procrastinating. But, seeing that he had to rely more on Addington and finally to bring him into the Cabinet, his difficulties were great. The Irish members also showed signs of defection; and it was certain that the Bill would fail in the Lords. Accordingly, Pitt begged Wilberforce to wait for a more propitious time. A sense of religious duty impelled him to persevere, with the inevitable result, a crushing defeat (19th February 1805).[1] On a smaller question, connected with the prohibition of the supply of slaves to Guiana, then recently conquered from the Dutch, he finally brought Pitt to acquiesce. But here again the conduct of the Minister was tardy. Wilberforce urged Pitt to abolish the Guiana Slave Trade by an Order in Council, and early in May wrote: " One very power-ful and important reason for your abolishing the Guiana Slave Trade by an act of Government, not by, or in consequence of a vote of Parliament, is that it would tend to confirm the dis-position so strongly manifested by the Dutch to abolish the Slave Trade, and give them the sort of compensation they demand." The British Order in Council did not appear until 13th September 1805.[2]

Nevertheless, their friendship remained firm to the end. " Had much talk with him [Pitt] on political topics, finding him very open and kind." Such is Wilberforce's account of his last inter-views with Pitt; and he certainly could not have remained on friendly terms with one who was deliberately untrue to the cause. He knew better than recent critics the difficulties resulting from the compromise with Addington and from the ceaseless friction with the followers of Fox and Grenville.

The case of the Slave Trade serves to illustrate the peculiar difficulties of Pitt's position, which were to appear on even more important questions. The King, Addington, Grenville, and Pitt had all contributed to the tangle. Limiting our survey to the conduct of Addington and Pitt, we must pronounce both of them culpable. Addington should have seen that Pitt's promise of support, given at the time of the King's lunacy in February—March 1801, was not morally binding three years later when

[1] " Life of Wilberforce," iii, 168, 182, 184, 211, 212.
[2] *Ibid.*, iii, 230-4; Pitt MSS., 189.

the existence of the nation was at stake in the Napoleonic War. At such a time an enlightened patriot does not stand upon punctilio, but gladly takes a second place if he can thereby place in authority an abler man. Addington alone could release Pitt from the debt of honour incurred in February 1801, and faithfully discharged for three weary years, at the cost of the alienation of friends and the derision of opponents. He never spoke or wrote that word of release, but held Pitt to the bargain with an insistence which would be contemptible were it not in large measure the outcome of a narrow complacent nature blind to its own shortcomings.

Pitt, also, behaved weakly. The original promise, to support an untried man, was a piece of astounding trustfulness; and when the weakness of Addington's Administration involved the nation in war and brought it to the brink of disaster, he should openly have claimed release from a pledge too hastily given, leaving the world to judge between them. As it was, for nearly a year he wavered to and fro between the claims of national duty and private honour, thereby exasperating his friends and finally driving the Grenvilles, Windham, and Spencer to a union with Fox which in its turn blighted the hope of forming a national Administration. Finally, he made only one effort to induce the King to accept Fox. True, the situation was a delicate one; for pressure brought to bear on George on that topic would have brought back the mental malady. But the Grenvilles, viewing the situation with pedantic narrowness, considered the attempt so half-hearted as to warrant their opposition to the new Cabinet. On the whole, then, Pitt's punctiliousness must be pronounced a secondary but vital cause of the lamentable *dénouement*, which left him exposed at forty-five years of age, enfeebled by worry and gout, to a contest with Napoleon at the climax of his powers.

CHAPTER XXIII

PITT AND NAPOLEON

I made a mistake about England, in trying to conquer it. The English are a brave nation. I have always said that there are only two nations, the English and the French; and I made the French.—NAPOLEON TO MACNAMARA (1814), *Lord Broughton's Recollections*, i, 180.

THE two protagonists now stood face to face—Napoleon, Emperor of the French, President of the Italian Republic, Mediator of the Swiss Republic, controller of Holland, absolute ruler of a great military Empire; Pitt, the Prime Minister of an obstinate and at times half-crazy King, dependent on a weak Cabinet, a disordered Exchequer, a Navy weakened by ill-timed economies, and land forces whose martial ardour ill made up for lack of organization, equipment, and training. Before the outbreak of war in May 1803, Napoleon had summed up the situation in the words—"Forty-five millions of people must prevail over sixteen millions." And now after a year of hostilities his position was far stronger. In Hanover the French troops were profitably installed on the Elector's domains. Soult's corps occupied the Neapolitan realm, thus threatening Malta, the Ionian Isles, the Morea, and Egypt. The recent restitution of several colonial conquests by England not only damaged her trade, but enabled her enemy to stir up trouble in India. There, thanks to Wellesley's dramatic victory at Assaye, the Union Jack waved in triumph; but at other points Napoleon might hope to gain the long contested race for Empire.

So convinced was Pitt of the need of fighting out the quarrel thrust upon us by Napoleon's aggressions, that he waved aside an offer of Livingston, American envoy at Paris, to effect a reconciliation. During a brief visit to London, Livingston sent proposals to this effect through Whitworth, who declined to meet a man hitherto remarkable for a strong anti-British bias; and

Pitt approved this repulse.[1] Nevertheless, on 5th June Livingston, accompanied by Fox and Grey, called on Pitt at Downing
Street; but his proposals proved to be merely the outcome of
informal conversations with Joseph Bonaparte, who was known
to be far more peacefully inclined than his brother. Joseph's
notions were that Malta should perhaps be garrisoned by Russians, and must in any case be relinquished by England; that
France should withdraw her troops from the Dutch and Swiss
Republics, the status of which was not defined.[2] Pitt set little
store by these shadowy proposals, doubtless seeing in them a
way of discovering whether England was concerting a league
against France.

Already, in spite of many obstacles, he was taking the first
steps in that direction. An initial difficulty lay in the mental
aberrations of the King, whose conduct still caused intense
anxiety or annoyance.[3] Scarcely a day passed without a lapse
into incoherence or violence. Moreover, his conversation often
showed a lack of discrimination, being the same to the Queen,
the physicians, or the servants. He made the most capricious
changes, turning off the Queen's favourite coachman, and making
grooms footmen, and footmen grooms, to the distraction of the
household. On assuming office, Pitt consulted the royal physicians and received a reply, dated Queen's Palace, 16th May
1804, stating that the King was equal to the discharge of important business, but must avoid long conferences or any deviation from his usual habits, quiet being essential. Thereupon Pitt
and Lord Eldon wrote to the King urging this prudent course.
They frequently visited Buckingham House, where five physicians were in almost constant attendance, a state of things
viewed with alarm by patriots and with eager hope by the
Foxites and their hangers on.[4]

Unfortunately George could not compose himself to rest.
Such is the tenor of hasty notes sent to Pitt by Villiers, now
high in favour at Kew and Windsor. They describe the King's
fussy intervention in household affairs, his orders for sudden and
expensive changes in the palaces, his substitution of German for
English servants, his frequent visits to the stables unaccompanied

---

[1] Pitt MSS., 102. Pitt to Whitworth, 28th May 1804; G. Rose, "Diaries,"
ii, 136. See, too, Rose, "Despatches relating to the ... Third Coalition," 27.
[2] Stanhope, iv, 199-201.   [3] Czartoryski, "Memoirs," ii, 35.
[4] "Creevey Papers," i, 28.

by the equerry, his irritability on the most trifling occasions, and, alternating with this undignified bustle, fits of somnolence which at times overtook him even on horseback. Then, too, there were quarrels with the Queen, whose conduct, said Villiers, was such as to aggravate these troubles and check the course of recovery. Indeed, the King's violent headaches seemed to Dr. Milman to presage an attack of apoplexy. At all times he showed a marked preference for the company of servants and workmen, declaring the higher officials to be "Court nuisances." Villiers therefore begged Pitt to request an interview with the King, now at Kew, for he took no notice of letters. On Midsummer day Villiers suggested means for assuring the veto of the physicians on the projected visit to Weymouth, in view of the extravagance and inconvenience of the plans to which it gave rise.

Among them was the collection of a large military force in Dorset, George being convinced that the French would land there rather than in Kent or Essex. Fortunately, the Duke of York dissuaded him from a step so eminently favourable to Napoleon; for about this time the King wrote to the Duke: "As I am no friend to obstinacy, I will agree to lessen the demand from other districts" (i.e., for an "Army of Reserve" in Dorset). The visit to Weymouth was also postponed; and Camden, Secretary at War, countermanded the construction of huge barracks at that town, which the King had ordered without consulting the Cabinet or the Duke of York. On 1st August Villiers reported the refusal of the King to see the Prince of Wales, with whom no complete reconciliation was possible. George wished Villiers to come and reside near Windsor and manage all his private affairs, and would take no refusal. But how, asked Villiers, was he to do this on £330 a year? He therefore requested the advice and help of Pitt.[1]

At Weymouth, late in the summer, the quarrels between the King and Queen again became acute, as appears from confidential letters which Lord Hawkesbury wrote to Pitt. The latter sided with the Queen and Princes on some points; and indeed through these months the conduct of George seems to have been so exasperating that the Princesses almost sank under the ceaseless strain, for Queen Charlotte, too, was "ill and cross." In vain did Pitt seek to effect a reconciliation between

[1] Pretyman MSS.

the King and the Prince of Wales. The only result of his efforts was a formal and fruitless interview. Last but not least of Pitt's Court worries was the conduct of the Princess of Wales. Her wayward and extravagant habits increased the aversion of the Prince, and produced scandals so serious that Pitt urgently but ineffectually remonstrated with her at her residence in Black-heath. Such were the diversions of a Minister on whom almost singly rested the burden of defending his country at this crisis.

The eccentricities of the King seriously hampered British diplomacy. For how could Russia and Austria bind themselves to an Administration which might at any time be succeeded by one which was under the domination of the Prince of Wales, Fox, and Sheridan? True, offers of a defensive alliance were mooted at St. Petersburg to our ambassador, Admiral Warren. But it was obvious even to that misplaced sailor, whom Pitt soon recalled, that Russia merely aimed at securing English subsidies and help for her garrison at Corfu, now threatened by Soult. The timid conduct of Francis II, who, as if in imita-tion of Napoleon, assumed the title of Hereditary Emperor of the Austrian Empire, further prescribed caution; and only by slow degrees did the Czar Alexander feel his way towards an understanding with England. His jealousy respecting Malta, and the uncertainties at London and Windsor, held these natural allies apart for many months. Pitt did not hurry matters, doubtless from a conviction that the conduct of Napoleon must before long bring both Russia and Austria into the field. Meanwhile, he withheld subsidies which would have helped them to arm for an almost inevitable struggle.[1] We need not therefore trace the course of these coy advances until they led to definite overtures. Here as always Pitt showed a dignified reserve and a cautious regard for British finances, which refute the stories officially circulated at Paris as to his lavishly bribing the Continental States to attack France. As usually happens, the prosaic truth long remained hidden in British despatches, while the piquant slander gained all but universal acceptance.

Pitt's first thought was to enhance the value of England's friendship by strengthening her navy and enabling her to take the offensive if an occasion offered. The French royalist refugee,

[1] Rose, "Despatches relating to the . . . Third Coalition" (Royal Hist. Soc., 1904), 14-19; also Rose, "Napoleonic Studies," 364-6, for the tentative Russian overture of November 1803.

General Dumouriez, in a long Memoir which he drew up for the Cabinet, pointed out that nothing was more perilous than a perpetual defensive, as it allowed the enemy quietly to perfect his plans for attack at any point over the whole field.[1] Pitt was well aware of this danger. In fact, his policy of military pin-pricks, while apparently wasteful and inconclusive, had prevented that concentration of the enemy's force which alone could ensure the capture of London. Once more, then, he aimed at strength-ening the regular army, reducing the Militia to its usual quota, and raising a large force of Volunteers. On 5th June 1804 he brought forward his proposal for repairing the defects of Yorke's Army of Reserve Act. They arose from the following provisions. A man, when drawn to serve in that force, must either come forward, find a substitute, or pay a fine of £20 for each year of default. A penalty also fell on every parish failing to supply its quota. The consequence was that parishes and individuals offered high bounties in order to escape the fine—sometimes as much as £40 or £60 per man.[2] These bounties naturally drew the best recruits to the Army of Reserve, to the detriment both of the army and navy. Another source of loss to the line regi-ments was the addition to the strength of the Militia, the net result being that 9,000 more recruits were required annually for the regular forces. These therefore suffered from the competi-tion of the second and third lines of defence; and in this com-petition (then unusually severe) has always lain the crux of the British military problem.

Pitt sought to solve the problem by reducing the Militia (now 74,000 strong) to the old standard of 52,000 men, transferring the surplus to the Army of Reserve. He also suggested various inducements to men in the latter force to enter the line regi-ments. Further, he proposed to lessen the penalties levied on defaulters. While maintaining the principle of compulsory serv-ice, at least for a considerable part of the population, he lessened the inducements which told in favour of the Army of Reserve and against the Line. Further, in place of the irritating plan of recruiting by the compulsion of the ballot, Pitt made the parish authorities responsible for the supply of their quota. If, even so,

---

[1] Rose and Broadley, "Dumouriez and the Defence of England against Napoleon," 260.

[2] Fortescue, v, 204-13. Half of the fine went to the overseers of the parish, who were bound under penalties to provide a parochial substitute.

the parishes could not find the men, the commander of the district was empowered to raise them by the ordinary means of recruiting. He further proposed to associate in each district the battalions of the Army of Reserve with those of the Line, in the well-grounded hope of increasing *esprit de corps* and stimulating the flow of men into the first line of defence.

The chief critic of these proposals was Sheridan who, on 18th June brilliantly declaimed against the formation of a great Regular Army, as alien to the spirit of our people, and by all the arts of rhetorical necromancy sought to raise the spectre of a Standing Army. When others bemoaned the threatened increase of taxation and Windham and Craufurd ("Craufurd of the Light Division") criticized the measure severely, the Opposition cherished the hope of defeating the Ministry. The debate dragged on till 4 a.m. when 265 members supported Pitt against 223 Noes. The Bill became law on 29th June. Undoubtedly it failed to answer his hopes. Recruits did not come in, probably because most parishes were thenceforth content to pay the smaller fines now imposed. Grenville even ventured to assert that the Regular Army was smaller at the beginning of 1805 than a year earlier. Certainly the numbers were deficient; and Pitt accordingly on 31st March 1805 brought in a Bill to attract men from the Supplementary Militia into the Regular Army by a bounty of ten guineas per man. This brought forward 11,000 men, but at the expense of the Militia.[1] Thus Pitt did not solve the military problem. Who indeed has solved it?

Most fortunately for England, the Emperor had made serious miscalculations respecting the flotilla now preparing at the ports between Ostend and Etaples. First he armed his gun-boats heavily so that they might fight their way across against a fleet. On finding this to be impossible, he had to face the delay and expense of reconstruction. Next the harbours at and near Boulogne proved to be too shallow and too small for the enlarged flotilla. The strengthening of the French fleet was also a work of time. England therefore gained a year's respite. Indeed not a few experienced naval officers scouted an invasion by the flotilla as impossible. General Moore also believed that Napoleon would never be so mad as to make the attempt, which must end in our glory and his disgrace. Only by continuing to

---

[1] Fortescue, v, 239, 240.

threaten us could he do harm.[1]   Another sceptic was Lord
Melville, First Lord of the Admiralty, who, in a letter of 14th
October, urged Pitt during his stay at Weymouth to represent
to the King the importance of attacking the flotilla at Boulogne,
if only in order to show the impracticability of Napoleon's
scheme. Experienced officers, said Melville, reported that the
flotilla must embark the troops in the outer road; yet the
work of getting that vast concourse of boats out of the inner
harbour could not be accomplished in less than four, five, or
perhaps even six tides. We must therefore attack them during
this tedious operation. " Our officers and seamen," he continues,
" have a perfect confidence that they can attack them under
their own batteries, and put them into immediate confusion. . . .
Their confidence is founded on the experiment they have already
made of entering in the night the Bay of Boulogne and sustain-
ing for many hours the whole fire of the enemy's batteries without a single man being hurt." Moreover, the British fire-ships,
being like ordinary ships, will take the enemy by surprise and
cause irremediable confusion.[2]   Apparently the King and Pitt
thought an attack not only too risky, in view of the failures at
Boulogne in 1801 and on 3rd October 1804, but also needless, if
the flotilla were no more formidable than Melville pronounced.
While inspecting the " Royal Sovereign " at Portsmouth on 6th
October the King wrote to Pitt enjoining great caution, as a
failure would be very discreditable.[3]

I do not propose to discuss here the much debated question
whether Napoleon intended to invade England, or to wear us
out by threats of invasion.[4]   Suffice it to say that no responsible
Minister could ignore those formidable preparations. Pitt therefore strove might and main to raise martial enthusiasm by
attending drills and reviews of Volunteers. A cynical phrase in
Grenville's letter of 25th August 1804 dwells on the ridiculous
figure which he cut, riding from Downing Street to Wimbledon
Common and thence to Cox Heath in Kent "to inspect military
carriages, impregnable batteries, and Lord Chatham's reviews.
Can he possibly be serious in expecting Bonaparte now?" The

---

[1] "Creevey Papers," i, 29.   [2] Pitt MSS., 157.
[3] Pretyman MSS. See "Ann. Reg." (1805) for the failure at Boulogne on
3rd October 1804.
[4] See Desbrière, "Projets . . . de Débarquement, etc.," vol. v; J. Corbett,
"The Campaign of Trafalgar," chs. ii, iii, ix.

sneer is a sign of the strained relations between the cousins. Assuredly, if Bonaparte had come, Grenville and his Foxite allies would have impeached a Minister who left his country defenceless. Pitt showed a good example to country gentlemen by drilling his corps of Volunteers at Walmer, so that it became a model of efficiency. There was the greatest need at that point, for the coast between Ramsgate and Dungeness presented exceptional facilities for a landing except under the guns of Sandown, Deal, Walmer, and Dover. Pitt's attention was specially directed to the open shelving beach between Folkestone and Dungeness.

In truth, the district of Romney Marsh, which is not normally marshy, offered the maximum of attractions to an invader, who, after beaching his boats and entrenching himself behind a fosse, would find few, if any, physical obstacles to his advance into the level tract between Ashford and Tonbridge. As this route was undefended, Pitt and Camden, by the month of October 1804, decided on the construction of the Hythe Military Canal. On 24th October Pitt attended a meeting of the "surveyors, lords, bailiffs and jurats" of Romney Marsh held at Dymchurch, Generals Sir David Dundas and Moore, and Colonel Brown being also present. It was agreed that the proposed canal from Sandgate to Rye would be beneficial to Romney Marsh, and landlords were urged forthwith to put their property at the disposal of Government, trusting to receive compensation assessed by a duly qualified local jury. On Pitt's recommendation the matter was passed at once, and he returned to Walmer Castle.[1] By the end of 1804 the work was well in hand, the expense of cutting the fosse of ten feet deep being estimated at £150,000. Batteries and martello towers were designed for its protection especially around Hythe and Dymchurch. At the latter place were sluices for flooding the marsh. Criticisms have fallen freely upon Pitt's canal, the report gaining currency that it was intended for the conveyance of military stores. Its true purpose was to isolate the most vulnerable part of the coast and to form a barrier which would at least delay an

---

[1] "Kentish Gazette," 26th October 1804. Apparently Moore agreed to the scheme, despite his opinion quoted above. For information on this topic I am indebted to Lieutenant-Colonel Fynmore of Sandgate. In the manœuvres of 1910 regiments were told off to extemporize means of crossing the canal in the quickest and most effective way.

invader until reinforcements arrived. In its original condition it was an excellent first line of defence of South Kent; and, unless the French flotilla brought over pontoons, it formed a barrier not easily penetrable, which fully justified its comparatively small cost.

The same remarks apply to the martello towers. The responsibility for them rests mainly with Colonel Twiss and Captain Ford, who in the summer of 1803 recommended their construction at exposed points of the shore, at a cost of about £3,000 apiece. The experience of our troops in Corsica showed that such towers, even when held by small garrisons, could hold at bay a greatly superior force.[1] The towers were begun soon afterwards; but those in Pevensey Bay were not undertaken till 1805-6. The first points to be defended were those nearest to France.

In the winter of 1804-5 there was need to strengthen the coast defences; for the declaration of war by Spain placed the whole of the coast line from the Texel to Toulon at Napoleon's disposal for shipbuilding. There seemed therefore every prospect of our being finally overwhelmed at sea, a consummation which the French Emperor might have ensured had he refrained from irritating the monarchs of Russia and Austria. Fortunately for England, his nature was too restless and domineering to admit of the necessary concentration of effort on the naval problem; and that besetting sin, megalomania, marred prospects which then seemed easily realizable. Playing with coolness and patience, he had the game in his hands in 1804, when as yet there was little prospect of an Anglo-Russian alliance.

An offensive alliance of Spain with France was the natural result of the treaty of 1796 between the two Powers. In vain did the luxurious Charles IV and his pampered minion, Godoy, Prince of the Peace, seek to evade their obligations. Under threat of a French invasion they gave way and agreed to pay 72,000,000 francs a year into the French exchequer, and to force the hand of Portugal. That little Power purchased immunity for a time by paying an annual subsidy of 12,000,000 francs to France. Spain also repaired French warships which took refuge at Ferrol in July 1804, and allowed reinforcements

[1] "W. O.," 76; "Diary of Sir J. Moore," ii, 71-4.

to their crews to travel thither overland. When Pitt and Harrowby remonstrated on this conduct, Spain armed as if for war;
and in answer to inquiries from London, Godoy alleged certain
disputes with the United States as the cause of his alarm. The
arrival in London of Frere, our ambassador at Madrid, on 17th
September 1804 revealed the unreality of this excuse; for he
reported that Spain had previously decided to yield on that
question. As the Spanish fleet was evidently preparing to co-
operate with that of Napoleon, Pitt resolved to deal the blow
which Chatham was not allowed to deliver in 1761. The weak
point of Spain was her treasure fleet; there was an inner fit-
ness in wrenching from her the gold which was soon to go into
Napoleon's coffers.

On Tuesday, 18th September, the Cabinet assembled, Eldon,
Camden, Hawkesbury, Melville, Mulgrave, and Pitt being
present. In view of the news brought by Frere, and other tidings
from Rear-Admiral Cochrane off Ferrol, Ministers decided to
order Cochrane closely to blockade that port, preventing both
French and Spanish ships from sailing out. Admiral Cornwallis,
then blockading Brest, was to reinforce Cochrane, thereby assuring
the capture of the Spanish treasure ships bound from South
America to Cadiz.[1] Pitt at once reported this decision to Harrowby, then in attendance on the King at Weymouth, and urged
a speedy ratification of it.[2] Hence without delay the order went
forth which enlarged the area of strife. The four frigates despatched for the seizure of the treasure-ships were not so
superior in force to the convoying corvettes as to avert a conflict. One of the Spanish ships blew up: the others surrendered
(5th October 1804). Resenting this outrage, Spain declared war
on 12th December.[3] Pitt did not consider the capture of the
treasure-ships as necessarily involving war, but rather as a sharp
warning, called for by the hostile conduct of Spain; for on 23rd
September he wrote to Harrowby stating that they must wait
for the Spanish answer to our ultimatum, and in the meantime
Spanish merchantmen might leave British ports unmolested.[4]

The seizure of the Spanish treasure-ships caused resentment

[1] Pretyman MSS.   [2] Harrowby MSS.
[3] Mahan, ii, ch. xv, *ad fin.*; "Ann. Reg." (1804), 555; "Mems. of R. P.
Ward," i, ch. vii. For the subsequent plan of Ministers to attack Ferrol,
from which Moore dissuaded them, see "Diary of Sir J. Moore," ii, ch. xxi.
[4] Harrowby MSS.

at St. Petersburg until the causes of Britain's action were more fully known. But the event did not long delay a góod understanding. The prospect of Sicily falling a prey to the French army of occupation in South Italy alarmed both the Czar Alexander and Pitt. The former was bound by a Convention signed in 1798 to befriend the Neapolitan Court; and it was also to his interest to prevent France dominating the Mediterranean and expelling the Russians from Corfu. He therefore demanded from Napoleon the evacuation of Italy and North Germany, a suitable compensation for the King of Sardinia for the loss of his mainland possessions, and the recognition of the complete neutrality of the Germanic Empire. Far from complying with these demands, Napoleon kept his troops in South Italy and Hanover, and early in November seized Sir Horace Rumbold, British ambassador at Hamburg. At once Pitt and Harrowby made effective use of this incident to prove the impossibility of peace with Napoleon. The Russian and Prussian Courts sent sharp remonstrances to Paris; and, to humour Frederick William, Napoleon ordered the release of the envoy, though in the most grudging way possible. This violation of international law served to counterbalance our irregular action against Spain.

In short, Napoleon's evident resolve everywhere to carry matters with a high hand convinced the Czar that war was inevitable; and he prepared to espouse the cause of Britain, not so much from sympathy with her as from detestation of her restless adversary.[1] On 20th November Pitt wrote from Downing Street to Harrowby, who was then taking the waters at Bath, expressing joy that the views of Russia coincided entirely with ours, especially as to the reduction of the French Power within its ancient limits. He added these noteworthy words: "The restoration of the [French] monarchy may become in the course of events an object to be distinctly aimed at, but it certainly cannot be made a substantive object in the first instance; and it is very satisfactory to see that in this important point there is no apparent difference in our sentiments."[2] The hope of ending Prussia's subservience to Napoleon, and of inspiring Francis of Austria with a manly resolve, proved futile. Frederick William and Haugwitz hoped to creep into Hanover, under the French

[1] Rose, "Third Coalition," 32, 53, 61, 65, 67, 71, 75.
[2] Harrowby MSS.

Emperor's cloak, and Austria had not yet suffered enough humiliation to lead her to fling down the gauntlet. True, she signed a compact with Russia on 6th November 1804; but it was timidly defensive in tone. Alexander therefore held back in the hope that events would compel her to take sides against Napoleon.

Far less calculating was Gustavus IV of Sweden. With the chivalrous zeal of his race he stood forth the first among the European monarchs as the declared ally of England. After the execution of the Duc d'Enghien by the French Emperor, he informed " Monsieur " Napoleon Bonaparte of the rupture of all relations between them; and now, on 3rd December 1804, an Anglo-Swedish Convention was signed, placing at our disposal the Isle of Rügen and the fortress of Stralsund in Swedish Pomerania, in return for a subsidy of £80,000. This sum served but to whet his appetite for subsidies, his demands almost equalling in extravagance his Quixotic summons to a royalist crusade.

Pitt therefore based his hopes on the statesmanlike policy of the Czar, who in that month despatched to London one of his confidants, a clever but viewy young man, of frank and engaging manners, Count Novossiltzoff. Ostensibly the mission was for scientific purposes; but French agents discovered that he took with him a plan of a Coalition against Napoleon.[1] This seems to have led the Emperor to take a step similar to that of Christmastide 1799. On 2nd January 1805 he wrote a letter direct to George III, proposing terms of peace. The King at once expressed to Pitt his astonishment that "the French usurper " had addressed him in this objectionable manner, and highly approved the draft of an answer which Pitt had thoughtfully forwarded to Windsor. In it Pitt declared that His Majesty could not enter upon the proposed overtures for peace until he had communicated them to the Powers with which he had confidential ties, especially to the Emperor of Russia. At the King's command, he sent a copy of this answer to St. Petersburg. At London, then, as also at Paris, Napoleon's offer was deemed a diplomatic device for getting news, though it also enabled him to represent himself as the friend of peace and Pitt as its worst enemy.

[1] Lefebvre, " Cabinets de l'Europe," ii, 33.

While the French Emperor played his game with the advantages conferred by a daring initiative, superior force, and unquestioned authority at home, Pitt had to employ all possible means to conciliate allies abroad and half-hearted friends at Westminster. His position was far from secure. True, the King had now recovered almost his usual health; but in Parliament the Ministry with difficulty repelled the bitter attacks of Fox, Sheridan, Grenville, and Windham. The speech of Grenville on the seizure of the Spanish treasure ships was of singular bitterness. Though aware of the provocations of the Spanish Court, he chose to represent that affair as a cowardly, and almost piratical attack on an unprepared Power. Pitt had expected some such misrepresentations. He knew that the Opposition would strain every nerve to overthrow him; and in the Christmas Vacation he made timely overtures through Hawkesbury for the support of Addington. The two old friends met on 23rd December 1804, at Hawkesbury's residence, Coombe Wood, near Richmond Park. The host contrived to be absent when Pitt entered the room, and he advanced with the cordial greeting: " I rejoice to take you by the hand again."

Converse of three hours ensued between them alone. Addington demurred to Pitt's request that he should retire to the Upper House. Finally, however, he agreed to do so, accepting the title of Viscount Sidmouth, taking also the Presidency of the Council, which the Duke of Portland, for reasons of health, wished to relinquish, though he finally agreed to remain in the Cabinet without office. Lord Hobart, now Earl of Buckinghamshire, also entered the Cabinet as Chancellor of the Duchy of Lancaster in place of Lord Mulgrave, who now succeeded Lord Harrowby at the Foreign Office. Pitt further promised to promote some of Addington's supporters, including his brother-in-law, Bragge Bathurst.

These changes were resented by several of Pitt's supporters, especially by Rose. We have already noticed his contempt for Addington's financial shifts; and he now, on 8th January 1805, wrote to Bishop Tomline deploring Pitt's junction with " a man whose imbecility and falsehood, under Mr. Pitt's own sanction," had weakened the country. Pitt would now gain a few votes, no additional talents, and an increase of rancour in the Opposition. " We shall," adds Rose, " drag on a wretched existence and expire not creditably. What next will happen God only

knows." [1] Canning was equally annoyed at the new Coalition. [2]
His sharp tongue and still sharper pen had deeply annoyed
Addington. Who, indeed, would not have resented this reference
in the " Apothecary's Hall (First of April)":

> When his speeches hobble vilely
> How " Hear him " bursts from brother Hiley !
> When his faltering periods lag
> Hark to the cheers of brother Bragge !

Sarcasms on Hawkesbury had also annoyed that susceptible
Minister; so that in June 1804 Canning offered to resign his
Treasurership of the Navy. The matter was patched up, only
to be opened once more in the winter. Pitt sought to mediate
between the bard and his victim, but failed to elicit from
Canning an apology as complete as Hawkesbury demanded.
Finally, on 18th January, Canning informed Pitt that, as Hawkes-
bury had left his letter unanswered for three days, he declined
to take the further steps which Pitt recommended. [3] Is it sur-
prising that the health of the Prime Minister began to suffer?
Friends noted with concern his thinness and a hacking cough.
Nevertheless, he rode out successfully the squalls of the session
of 1805, beating off the onset of Sheridan against his Defence
Bill, and defeating an inopportune motion of Fox for Catholic
Emancipation.

On this subject Pitt secretly sympathized with Fox, but his
hands were tied both by his promise of March 1801 to the King
not to bring up the subject during his reign, and recently by his
union with Addington. The Irish Catholics knew of these difficulties; and at meetings held by their leading men at the house
of James Ryan, a wealthy Dublin merchant, in the autumn of
1804, both Lord Fingall and Counsellor Scully deprecated a
petition to Parliament as alike useless and embarrassing. Scully
urged that they must conciliate one whose " opinions had literally
proved of great weight in the Catholic cause. . . . The Catholics
owe him [Pitt] respect for his enlarged and manly conceptions
of the necessity of relieving them, and the dignified energy with
which he publicly expressed those conceptions." A Committee
was chosen to consider the matter and communicate with Pitt.
It included Fingall, Sir Thomas French, Scully, and others. At

---

[1] Pretyman MSS.   [2] Stanhope, iv, 244-8.
[3] See the letter in " Pitt and Napoleon Miscellanies."

the third meeting at Ryan's house, on 17th November, Keogh sharply blamed Fingall for opposing the petition, and commented adversely on the silence of Pitt. Scully inferred from it "that he is favourably disposed, but in some way, to them unknown, not in a situation in which he can freely act," or even explain his reticence; but no Catholic wished to embarrass him.[1] Nevertheless, the petition was resolved on; and it is clear that Fox encouraged the petitioners rather from the hope of embarrassing Pitt than of carrying Catholic Emancipation.[2]

In March 1805 Scully came to London, and saw Fox, Nepean, and Grey. Pitt received him and others of the Irish deputation at Downing Street on the 12th. Scully noted in his diary: "He [Pitt] wore dirty boots and odd-fashioned, lank leather breeches, but otherwise well dressed and cleanly, his hair powdered, etc. He was very courteous and cordial in words and looks, but his carriage was stiff and strait, perhaps naturally so. His face cold and harsh, rather selfish, but acute and sensible. We took our seats after much reciprocal ceremony." Pitt declined Fingall's request that he should present the Catholic petition, though he admitted that the measure would be most salutary whenever the proper time would arrive; but he added with a smile that he could not tell when that would be. The deputation failed to move him from this position, and thereafter committed its cause to the Opposition.[3] Despite excellent speeches by Fox and Grey, and by Grenville and Holland in the Lords, the motions for Catholic Emancipation were rejected by large majorities. The speech of Pitt on 14th May, to which reference has already been made, naturally lacked energy and fire; he opposed Fox's motion solely on the ground of present expediency.[4]

The worst trial of the session was the impeachment of his old friend, Lord Melville. As Treasurer of the Navy in Pitt's former Administration, he had been guilty of a serious irregularity in not preventing Deputy Treasurer Trotter from using the sum of £10,000 for private speculation. Suspicions having been aroused on this and other grounds, a Commission was appointed to sift the matter to the bottom. The tenth Report dealing with these

[1] "H. O." Ireland (Corresp.), 99.
[2] "Mems. of Fox," iv, 45, 68, 72, 75.
[3] See an interesting account by Dr. Hunt, "Transactions of the Royal Hist. Soc." (1908), pp. 7-16.
[4] Hansard, iv, 1013-22, 1060.

charges came out on 17th or 18th March; and Wilberforce, who then chanced to be with Pitt, noted how eagerly, without waiting to cut open the pages, he sought to tear out the secret. It proved to be highly unfavourable to Melville. In vain did Wilberforce and Bankes seek to persuade Pitt to adopt a judicial attitude on this question. Though his friendship with Melville had cooled, yet it was still strong, and he finally agreed with Lord Sidmouth to press for a committee of inquiry. Only so could he count on the support of the Addingtonians. On 8th April, then, he resolutely defended Melville against the aspersions of Whitbread, maintaining that the evidence before the Commission was far from conclusive, and moving that a select Committee of the House should make further investigations.

The debate was long and stormy. Petty, Tierney, George Ponsonby, and Fox censured Melville severely. Canning with his wonted brilliance, Castlereagh with the usual laboured infelicity, sought to strengthen the defence; but it had almost collapsed when, about 4 a.m. of 9th April, Wilberforce arose. At once Pitt bent forward and sent an eager glance down the Treasury bench at his old friend; for the verdict of a conscientious and independent member at such a time is decisive. Speaking with the calm of deep conviction, the member for Yorkshire declared against Melville, whereupon Pitt sank back with signs of deep pain. The division showed 216 for and 216 against the motion of censure. The Speaker, Abbott, turned deathly white, and after a long and trying pause gave the casting vote against the Government. Then the pent up feelings burst forth. The groups of the Opposition united in yells of triumph; one member gave the "view holloa," and others shouted to Pitt to resign. He meanwhile pressed forward his hat to hide the tears which stole down his cheeks. Fitzharris, son of Lord Malmesbury, and a few devoted friends formed a phalanx to screen him from the insolent stare of Colonel Wardle and others who were crowding round the exit to see "how Billy Pitt looked after it"; and he was helped out of the House in a half unconscious state. The blow told severely on a frame already enfeebled by overwork and worry.[1]

Whitbread's further motion for impeachment was rejected (11th June), but a similar motion succeeded a fortnight later.

[1] Hansard, iv, 255-325; "Life of Wilberforce," iii, 219-23; "Malmesbury Diaries," iv, 338, 347; "Lord Colchester's Diaries," i, 544-9.

Public opinion, however, soon began to veer round and pronounce the conduct of the Opposition rancorous. Melville's relative, Sir Charles Middleton, in a letter to Wilberforce, denounced it as sheer persecution, seeing that the nation had suffered no loss, and Melville had served it many years with indefatigable zeal. As for Melville, he retired to his Highland seat, " Dunira," and in the last letter which he wrote to Pitt, dated 11th November 1805, expressed gratitude for Pitt's recent message that his energy at the Admiralty had largely contributed to the triumph at Trafalgar. Melville's feelings further appeared in the postscript, that Nelson's death was "enviable beyond expression," as placing "his fair fame beyond the reach of caprice, envy, or malevolence." [1] Pitt did not live on to see the vindication of his old friend. On 12th June 1806, after a trial of twelve days in Westminster Hall, the Peers acquitted Melville on all the ten counts, the prosecution failing to prove that he had benefited by Trotter's irregular use of the sum of £10,000. It is worth noting that Whitbread in his final attack declared his belief that Pitt in similar circumstances would have died rather than connive at such an irregularity. [2] This statement may be set against the Bacchic outburst of Creevey, after the hostile vote in Parliament, that Pitt had betrayed Melville in order to save himself from ruin. [3]

Pitt, seconded in this by Grenville, urged the appointment of Middleton, whose sagacity and long experience at the Admiralty had of late furnished the First Lord with invaluable counsel. True, he was eighty years of age, but neither had his frame lost vigour nor his mind alertness. Seeing that his reputation as a naval expert was unequalled, Pitt little expected to encounter the stiff opposition of Lords Sidmouth and Buckinghamshire to the appointment, which they designed for Buckinghamshire, Hawkesbury, or Charles Yorke. The King, too, probably influenced by Sidmouth, expressed his disapproval of Middleton, preferring those just named, or Castlereagh, or even Chatham. In a matter which concerned the safety of the nation Pitt was inexorable, facing for several days the threats of resignation of his two colleagues and the disapproval of the King. Finally he carried his point, the two lords being pacified by the assurance that Middleton's appointment would be temporary. The King

[1] Chevening MSS.   [2] "Trial of Lord Melville" (1806), 256-9, 370, 378.
[3] "Creevey Papers," i, 34.

also consented to raise him to the peerage as Lord Barham, adding, however, the proviso that he should attend the Cabinet only during the discussion of naval affairs. In this grudging way did the Monarch and Sidmouth permit Middleton to reap the reward of life-long service and the nation to benefit by his unique experience. Only of late has the work done by Barham during the Trafalgar campaign been duly set forth; and it is therefore possible now to estimate the service rendered by Pitt in insisting on his appointment even at the risk of the secession of the Addingtonian group.[1]

Before referring to naval affairs, we must glance at the efforts of Pitt to frame a Coalition of the Powers against France. In the middle of January 1805 he had important interviews with Novossiltzoff, the envoy whom the Czar Alexander had despatched to London on an important mission. For this ardent young reformer Alexander had drawn up secret instructions which the curious may read in the Memoirs of his Minister, Czartoryski.[2] They illustrate the mingling of sentimentality and statecraft, of viewiness and ambition, which accounts for the strange oscillations of Muscovite policy between altruistic philosophy and brutal self-seeking. At present the Russian Janus turned his modern face westwards. Alexander insisted on the need of tearing from France the mask of liberty which she had so long and so profitably worn. Against the naturalism of Rousseau, which supplied Napoleon with excellent reasons for every annexation, Alexander resolved to appeal to historical rights and the Balance of Power. Yet he also resolved to uphold the rights of all the peoples concerned. They must be reconciled to their rulers so as to harmonize the claims of legitimacy and liberty. Thus, the King of Sardinia, when restored to his throne at Turin, was to be induced to grant a Constitution. The Germanic System was to be rescued from chaos by the grant of free federal institutions. The independence of the Italian, Helvetic, and Dutch Republics was a matter of urgency, those States being also strengthened against French aggressions. Finally, Russia and England were, if possible, to secure the friendship of Turkey.

With these aims Pitt declared his entire concurrence, a just

[1] "Barham Papers" (Navy Records Society), iii; Corbett, "Trafalgar Campaign," 70-2; Stanhope, iv, 287; Pellew, ii 356-64.
[2] Czartoryski, "Mems.," ii, ch. vii.

and lasting peace being the first of British interests. He developed these notions in a remarkable document of date 19th
January 1805. We may be sure that it is his; for, an accident
having befallen the Earl of Harrowby at the close of 1804, Lord
Mulgrave took his place at the Foreign Office, and a new comer
would not have ventured to impose his own views as to the
future of Europe. Pitt now recurred to his plans of the year
1798 for assuring the repose of the Continent. In brief, they
were the aggrandisement of Austria in Northern Italy and of
Prussia in the Low Countries so as to form barriers against
France. The Italian Republic must therefore be divided between
the Hapsburgs and the King of Sardinia, the latter also absorbing
the Genoese Republic, which had forfeited all claim to consideration. Pitt did not enter into details respecting Belgium;
but probably he intended to offer it to Prussia, in order to still
her cravings for Hanover. Such was his proposal to the Court
of Berlin in October 1805.[1] Conscious, perhaps, that the present
plans were not consonant with the benevolent idealism of Russian policy, which, however, stole sidelong glances at Constant-
inople, Pitt declared that only by these arrangements could the
peace of Europe be secured. They were therefore "not repugnant to the most sacred principles of justice and public
morality." In order further to curb the aggressions of Napoleon,
the Great Powers were mutually to guarantee their possessions,
thus laying the foundation of a system of public right.[2]

This scheme clearly foreshadows the system of alliances and
compromises carried out by Castlereagh in the Treaty of Chaumont nine years later. Pitt also assented to the Czar's proposal
that the final settlement should be guaranteed by international
agreements forming a basis for the new European polity, a suggestion in which lies the germ of the Holy Alliance. It would
be absurd to hold Pitt responsible for the strange and unforeseen developments of the years 1815-25. But it is to be regretted
that fear of Napoleon should have obliterated his earlier aim of
forming a defensive league of the weaker States. His cure for
the evils of French domination was scarcely better than the evils
themselves. The installation of the Hapsburgs at Venice and
Milan, of Victor Emmanuel I at Genoa, of Frederick William of

---

[1] "F. O.," Prussia, 70; Rose, "Napoleonic Studies," 54-8; Rose, "Napoleon," ii, 54.

[2] Garden, "Traités," viii, 317-23; Alison, App. to ch. xxxix.

Prussia at Brussels, could not permanently improve the lot of the Italian and Belgian peoples. So soon as we formulate the question we see that, as in 1798, Pitt left their welfare out of count. He aimed merely at piling up barriers against France, and trusted to some vague arrangement with the Czar for safeguarding the political rights of the bartered peoples.

Pitt's reliance on the statics of statecraft rather than on the dynamics of nationality tells against the credibility of the oft-repeated story that he prophesied the liberation of Europe by the enthusiasm and efforts of the Spaniards. Wellington afterwards told the Spanish general, Alava, that Pitt, on hearing of the disaster of Ulm, made this prophecy at a dinner party at which he (then Sir Arthur Wellesley) was present. Difficulties of time and place militate against the anecdote, which, moreover, is out of harmony with the sentiments expressed in Pitt's speeches, letters, and despatches.[1] Further, his experience of Spain was such as to inspire him with deep distrust; and, finally, the cast of his mind was so far objective as to forbid the indulgence of speculations on the little-known topic of nationality. Distrusting novel theories, he sought to utilize forces of tried potency. He worked by diplomatic methods through Governments, not through the tumultuary efforts of peoples. Dependence on a nation so backward as the Spaniards would have seemed to him madness. Even if he could have seen the surprising events of May—June 1808, he would probably have distrusted the spirit which prompted them. In truth, he lacked the sympathetic instinct which led Canning at that crisis to side with the Spanish patriots and thus open a new chapter in the history of Europe.

Yet it is but just to remember that Pitt the diplomatic bargainer of 1805 differed from Pitt the upholder of weak States in 1790, only because the times had completely changed. Against the destructive schemes of Joseph II, Catharine II, and Hertzberg he worked on the whole successfully. But now Poland was gone; Sweden and Turkey were safe; the German tangle had been cut by the Secularizations of Church domains in 1803.

[1] Toreno ("War of Independence in Spain, vol. i, *ad fin.*) had the story from Alava, who connected it with the arrival of the news of Ulm, on 2nd November. Pitt said: "All is not lost if I can succeed in raising up a national war in Europe, and this must have its commencement in Spain." But Malmesbury ("Diaries," iv, 340), who was present, does not name the incident, and states that Pitt disbelieved the news (see ch. xxiv).

Now the danger was from the West. France had swallowed up her weaker neighbours. Napoleon dominated Spain, Italy, Switzerland, the Rhenish States, and the Netherlands. Russian policy, subversive under Catharine, was in a European sense conservative under Alexander. Then the most damaging thrusts to the European fabric came from Vienna and St. Petersburg. Now they came from Paris. Pitt therefore sought to construct a rampart out of the weak States bordering on France. As the Barrier Treaties of a century earlier were directed against Louis XIV, so now Pitt sought to inaugurate an enlarged Barrier policy as a safeguard against Napoleon. The efforts of at least half a million of trained troops being available, the time had apparently come for a final effort to preserve the Balance of Power before it was irretrievably impaired.

For a time the Russian and British Governments seemed in complete accord. Novossiltzoff, on his return to St. Petersburg, wrote to Pitt on 20th March 1805 (N.S.), describing the entire concurrence of his master with the principles on which they had agreed at London. In about eight days he would leave for Berlin to put forth his utmost endeavours to gain the alliance of that Court. He would then proceed to Paris to present the Czar's ultimatum. A refusal was expected; but his master believed it more dignified to take all reasonable means of ensuring peace. The orders for mobilizing the Russian troops would go forth at the time of his departure for Berlin. Before his arrival at Paris, he hoped to receive from London full powers authorizing him to speak for Great Britain as well as for Russia.[1]

All this implied the closest union and sympathy. But now Alexander showed the other side of his nature. He sought to drive a hard bargain with Pitt. Firstly, he strove to obtain the promise of a larger British force to form an integral part of a Russian expedition for the deliverance of the Kingdom of Naples. In view of the paucity of our disposable forces, Pitt had sought to limit the sphere of action to Sicily and the neighbouring parts of Calabria, the defence of Sicily, the key of the Mediterranean and the outwork of Egypt, being now and throughout the war one of the cardinal aims of British policy. An expedition under General Sir James Craig was about to set sail for Malta and Messina; and the Czar required that, when strengthened, it

[1] Pretyman MSS.

should act in any part of South Italy, under a Russian general. After wearisome correspondence, a compromise was arrived at; and on 19th April 1805 Craig set sail from Portsmouth on his perilous voyage over seas now and again swept by French and Spanish warships. By good fortune he escaped these many dangers, and reached Malta, there setting free seasoned troops for operations in South Italy. The hardihood of Pitt in sending forth this expedition has often provoked criticism. But it was worth while to run serious risks to save Sicily from the grip of Napoleon, and to wrest from him the initiative which he had hitherto enjoyed unchallenged. Besides, the Czar insisted on that effort, and made it almost a *sine quâ non* of his alliance. In a military sense the results were contemptible; in the diplomatic sphere they were very great.[1]

Twelve days before Craig set sail, Czartoryski worried or coaxed the British ambassador at St. Petersburg, Lord Granville Leveson-Gower, into signing a provisional treaty of alliance. The Czar now promised to set in motion half a million of men (half of them being Austrians, and only 115,000 Russians) so as to drive the French from Italy, Switzerland, Germany, and the Low Countries, England subsidizing the allied forces at the rate of £1,250,000 a year for every 100,000 men actually employed. The liberated lands were to have the right of building their own fortresses and choosing their own constitutions. But firstly, Alexander would seek to restore peace to Europe; and to this end he would consent to Napoleon placing his brother Joseph on the throne of North Italy, either in Piedmont or in the Italian Republic, shadowy realms being outlined in the Peninsula for the consolation of the dispossessed King of Sardinia. But the sting of the proposal was in its tail. Alexander suggested that, to secure the boon of peace, England should restore her maritime conquests in the war, and also Malta if Napoleon insisted on this last, the island being then garrisoned by Russians. In 'its blend of hazy theorizings on general topics with astute egotism in Russian affairs, the scheme is highly characteristic, peace being assured by means which would substitute Muscovite for British rule at Malta; while in the event of war, Great Britain was to pay at the rate of £6,250,000 a

---

[1] Rose, "Third Coalition," 25, 32, 44, 61, 66, 73, 76, 87, 97, etc.; Mr. Julian Corbett, "The Trafalgar Campaign," chs. i, ii. For a critique on Pitt's Mediterranean plans, see Bunbury's "Great War with France," 183-95.

year for campaigns that would aggrandise the continental States at the expense of France.[1]

What must have been the feelings of Pitt when he perused this Byzantine offer? While prepared to give way on some parts of the January proposals, he was determined to hold fast to Malta. The island had not been named by him and Novoss-iltzoff, its present destiny being assumed as irrevocably fixed. But now Alexander swung back to the aims of his father, the domination of the Central Mediterranean from the impregnable fortress of Valetta. Probably some of the Knights of the Order of St. John who had sought refuge in Russia gained the ear of Alexander in the spring of 1805, and produced the startling change in his policy just described. Whatever the cause, Pitt's answer could be none other than a firm refusal. In Count Simon Vorontzoff, Russian ambassador at London, he found a secret sympathizer, who entered heartily into his plans for the salvation of Europe, foreseeing that only by the retention of Malta for the Union Jack could the Mediterranean be saved from becoming a French lake; and that if either Gower or Pitt wavered on this question, the country would disown them.[2] Official etiquette, of course, compelled him to proffer Alexander's demand, and to declare that, unless Pitt gave way about Malta, there was an end of all hope of the alliance. Here Pitt intervened with the statesmanlike remark: " It will not save Europe. The Mediterranean, the Levant and Egypt, will be in the power of France the moment a British squadron ceases to have for base a good port protected by formidable fortifications. . . . So, whatever pain it causes us (and it is indeed great) we must give up the hope of seeing the alliance ratified, since its express condition is our renunciation of Malta. We will continue the war alone. It will be maritime."

Thus Malta, the final cause of the Great War, now promised to limit that war. Vorontzoff prevailed on Pitt to defer reporting his refusal to St. Petersburg. But on 27th May he stated that the last ray of hope had disappeared, as neither Court would give way. On 5th June, then, Mulgrave penned for Gower a despatch summarizing Pitt's reasons why England must retain Malta. She was ready to restore her valuable conquests in the East and West Indies, but the key of the Mediterranean she

[1] Rose, "Third Coalition," 127-30.   [2] Czartoryski, "Mems.," ii, 74-6.

must not and would not surrender. Neither would she relax her maritime code as the Emperor of Russia now insisted; for experience had shown it to be necessary for the equipment of the British fleets and the crippling of the enemy's naval construction. In the maintenance of these fleets lay the only hope of assuring the salvation of Europe. A more convincing exposition of the importance of Sea Power has never gone forth from a Government office.[1]

The deadlock was therefore complete. But now, as happened more than once in the development of the Coalitions, Napoleon himself came to the rescue. Whether he was aware of the breakdown of the Anglo-Russian negotiation is uncertain; but his remark to Fouché—" I shall be able to strike the blow before the old Coalition machines are ready "—and his conduct in Italy in the months of May and June 1805 bear the imprint of a boundless confidence, which, on any other supposition, savours of madness. He well knew that no continental ruler but Gustavus of Sweden desired war with him. Austria maintained her timid reserve. Alexander was ready to negotiate with him through the medium of Novossiltzoff, who was now at Berlin awaiting permission to proceed to Paris. The predilections of Frederick William of Prussia for France were notorious; for Hanover was his goal; and he and his counsellers saw far more hope of securing it from Napoleon than from King George.[2]

Prudence and patience were therefore peculiarly necessary for Napoleon at this juncture. He had the game in his hands if he would but concentrate all his energies against England and leave severely alone the land which then most interested Russia and Austria, namely, Italy. But, either from the ingrained restlessness of his nature, which chafed at the stalemate at Boulogne, or from contempt of "the old Coalition machines," or from an innate conviction that Italy was his own political preserve, he now took two steps which aroused the anger of the Russian and Austrian Emperors. On 26th May 1805 he crowned himself King of Italy in the cathedral of Milan, thereby welding that populous realm indissolubly to his Empire. On 4th June he annexed outright the Genoese or Ligurian Republic. Both acts were flagrant infractions of his

---

[1] Czartoryski, " Mems.," ii, 78; Rose, "Third Coalition," 155-64.

[2] *Ibid.*, 232; Ulmann, "Russisch-preussische Politik"; Hansing, "Hardenberg und die dritte Coalition."

Treaty of Lunéville with Austria of four years before; and they contemptuously overturned the Balance of Power which Alexander was striving to re-establish. The results were soon apparent. "This man is insatiable," exclaimed Alexander; "his ambition knows no bounds; he is a scourge of the world: he wants war; well, he shall have it, and the sooner the better."

Novossiltzoff left Berlin for St. Petersburg; and his despatches of 10th July to Vorontzoff and to Hardenberg, Foreign Minister at Berlin, prove conclusively that it was Napoleon's annexation of Genoa which ended all hope of peace on the Continent.[1] The French Emperor himself admitted as much a few years later when he visited Genoa. Looking down on that beautiful city, he exclaimed: "Ah! It was worth a war." In order to work French patriotism up to the necessary pitch he on 30th May 1805 ordered Fouché to have caricatures made at Paris depicting John Bull, purse in hand, entreating the Powers to take his money and fight France. Insults to Russia and England make up the rest of that angry and almost illegible scrawl.[2] In his heart he knew that the war sprang from his resolve to make the Mediterranean a French lake and Italy an annexe of his imperial fabric.

The sequel may be told very briefly. On 28th July the Court of St. Petersburg agreed to Pitt's version of the Anglo-Russian compact; and on 9th August the British ambassador at St. Petersburg pledged his country to join the two Empires if Napoleon rejected the conditions of peace still left open to him. In that case Gower promised to assure the advance of five months' subsidy at the rate mentioned above.[3] It is needless to say that Napoleon rejected all thought of compromise; and Austria began to hurry her troops up the banks of the Danube for the Bavarian campaign.[4] Thus Pitt won the diplomatic game. Or rather, his opponent gave it to him by the last reckless move at Genoa. The wrath of Alexander at this affront obliterated his annoyance at the retention of Malta by Great Britain;

---

[1] "Paget Papers," ii, 186; Sir G. Jackson, "Diaries," i, 304, 458-60; Rose, "Third Coalition," 180.   [2] "Lettres inédites de Napoléon," i, 50.

[3] Rose, "Third Coalition," 279-82. On 9th August Austria allied herself to Russia.

[4] For a time her action was unknown at London; and Pitt and Mulgrave outlined a plan of campaign turning largely on the liberation of South and Central Italy. See Mr. Corbett, "Trafalgar Campaign," App. B.

and both he and the Emperor Francis now prepared to enter the lists against Napoleon.

Meanwhile, Pitt sought to strengthen his Ministry in view of the desertion of the Addingtonians. Two of them, Hiley Addington and Bond, spoke bitterly against Melville during the debates of June, which led Gillray to represent them as jackasses about to kick a wounded lion. So annoyed was Pitt as to refuse them promotions which they expected, whereupon Sidmouth and Buckinghamshire tendered their resignations. The old friends parted sorrowfully after a final interview at Pitt's house on Putney Heath (7th July). Camden now became President of the Council, and Castlereagh Minister at War, Harrowby re-entering the Cabinet as Chancellor of the Duchy of Lancaster.

As the prospect of further taxation was calculated to depress Pitt's supporters and inspirit the Opposition, he proceeded to Weymouth in the middle of September to lay before the King an important proposal. The formation of a truly national Administration being more than ever essential, he besought George to admit certain members of the parties of Fox and Grenville, especially in order to facilitate the passing of the next Budget. The Monarch, however, was obdurate, asserting that Pitt had done well in the past session and would probably fare better still in the next. On 22nd September he repeated these statements to Rose, whom he called to him on the esplanade, and was quite unconvinced by his arguments that in the present state of parties the Budget could scarcely be passed, and that, if Pitt chanced to be laid up with a fit of gout for two or three weeks, there would be an end of the Administration. The King would not hear of any change, and proved more intractable on this topic than in the year before, during his stay at Cuffnells.[1] In fact, in Rose's manuscript is a statement, prudently omitted from the published Diaries, that George, on returning to his residence at Weymouth, declared his resolve rather to risk a civil war than to admit Fox into his councils.[2] Thus ended Pitt's last effort to form a national Administration fitted to cope with the gigantic power of Napoleon.

It is difficult to realize the multiplicity of the cares which pressed upon Pitt. Rose feared that he would soon succumb to the burden; for, apart from the defence of a weak Government against a strong Opposition, Pitt transacted very much of the

---

[1] G. Rose, "Diaries," ii, 198-200.   [2] Pretyman MSS.

business of the War Office and Foreign Office, besides assisting the Admiralty and the Commander-in-Chief. No one in Europe, with the exception of Napoleon, worked so hard; and Pitt, besides being ten years older than the Emperor, had far less physical strength. We may judge, then, of the effect produced by a life such as Lady Hester Stanhope described in a passage of more than usual credibility: "Ah doctor," she said in her Lebanon days, "what a life was his! Roused from sleep (for he was a good sleeper) with a despatch from Lord Melville; then down to Windsor; then, if he had half an hour to spare, trying to swallow something; Mr. Adams with a paper, Mr. Long with another; then Mr. Rose: then, with a little bottle of cordial confection in his pocket, off to the House until three or four in the morning; then home to a hot supper for two or three hours more, to talk over what was to be done next day:—and wine, and wine. Scarcely up next morning, when 'tat-tat-tat,' twenty or thirty people one after another, and the horses walking before the door from two till sunset, waiting for him. It was enough to kill a man—it was murder."[1]

One who knew Pitt well gave wise advice to his secretary, William Dacre Adams. "Attend to your meals regularly even if you sit up or rise the earlier for it to get through the business. I have often been told that half Mr. Pitt's complaints were originally brought on by fasting too long and indeed only eating when he found it convenient, which ruined the tone of his stomach."[2] These statements explain the reason for the collapse of Pitt's strength late in the year. Hester's concluding remark is somewhat hysterical, but it is nearer the truth than the charge that Pitt was greedy of power. He killed himself by persistent overwork on behalf of a nation which did not understand him, and in the service of a Monarch who refused to allow him to strengthen his Administration.

It is impossible now to feel one's way along all the threads which Pitt held in his hands. But occasionally a chance reference reveals his connection with designs of vast moment. The following is a case in point. Castlereagh wrote to him, probably on 20th August 1805, in terms which show that Pitt took a leading part in one of the decisions bearing on the fate of the naval campaign which culminated at Trafalgar. The daring

[1] "Lady Hester Stanhope's Mems.," ii, 63.
[2] Chevening MSS. See, too, G. Rose, "Diaries," ii, 235, as to Pitt's reliance on "cordial medicines."

and wisdom of his naval policy in 1805 has lately been fully
vindicated.[1] But the following letter throws new light on the
complex problem which arose after the indecisive success gained
by Admiral Calder over Villeneuve's French and Spanish fleets
off Cape Finisterre on 22nd July, and while the subsequent movements of those fleets were not yet definitely known. Baird's
expedition at Cork was destined for the reduction of the Cape
(ever Pitt's pre-occupation) so soon as the way was fairly safe.

Downing St Tuesday 3 P.M.[2]

My dear Sir,

I have just seen Lord Hawkesbury and Lord Barham, Adm^l
Cornwallis having anticipated your intentions by detaching 20 sail of
the line off Ferrol, and the wind being now favourable, it appears to us
that no time should be lost in ordering Sir D. Baird to sail. As L^d H.
and Ld B. seem to entertain no doubt of your approving of this step, I
shall send the orders without delay. I shall remain in town tonight and
be at your disposal as best suits your engagements.

Ever yours,

CASTLEREAGH.

The most interesting words in this letter are " your intentions."
They seem to imply that the plan of detaching part of Admiral
Cornwallis's fleet off Brest to the assistance of Calder off the
North West of Spain was originally Pitt's own, not Lord Barham's,
as has been hitherto supposed. They must not be pressed too
much; for the advice of Barham, First Lord of the Admiralty,
must have been paramount. Nevertheless the proposal was
evidently Pitt's as well as Barham's. The fact that Cornwallis

[1] By Mr. Julian Corbett, "The Campaign of Trafalgar." Mr. Corbett has
kindly helped me to fix the probable date of Castlereagh's letter.

[2] Pitt MSS., 121. In Pitt MSS., 111, is a hasty and undated note of Pitt
to Middleton (probably of February 1805) asking him to consider "whether
it might not be expedient to direct Sir John Warren to proceed to Cape de
Verde, and if he there found that Sir James Duckworth was gone to the
West Indies, but not upon certain information of the enemy having preceded
him, that Sir J. Warren should be ordered on to the Cape, unless he
received intelligence that the enemy had taken another course." He adds
that this suggestion arises out of the news received from the Cape, where
French troops were expected. In that case the operations would be pro-
tracted. Pitt hoped that Warren would be back in five months, that is by
1st June, before which time the French preparations for the invasion of
England would not be far advanced. Evidently, then, Pitt sought Middleton's advice direct on the complex problem of defending England and
guarding the overland and the sea routes to India at the same time. On
this see Corbett, "Trafalgar Campaign," 236-8.

anticipated it bespeaks the resolve alike of Ministers and the admiral at all costs to stop Villeneuve off Finisterre and prevent the naval concentration in French waters on which Napoleon laid so much stress. The success of the British counter-stroke is well known. Villeneuve, having been roughly handled by Calder, put into Ferrol, and finally, a prey to discouragement, made off for Cadiz, thus upsetting Napoleon's scheme for the invasion of England. In due course Nelson returned to England for a brief time of rest at "dear, dear Merton," and then set off on his last cruise. Before his departure he had an interview with Pitt at Downing Street—the only occasion, I believe, on which they met—and found in the ante-room Sir Arthur Wellesley, just returned from India. At the end of the interview Pitt flattered the great seaman by an act of attention which he thus described: "Mr. Pitt paid me a compliment, which, I believe, he would not have paid to a Prince of the Blood. When I rose to go, he left the room with me and attended me to the carriage." By attentions such as these Chatham was wont to stimulate the patriotism of our warriors; and on this occasion his son played an equally inspiriting part. Imagination strives to picture the scene, especially when England's greatest statesman and greatest seaman passed through the ante-room where stood the future victor of Waterloo.[1]

Never again were those three heroes to meet. Nelson departed for Trafalgar. Pitt resumed the work which was wearing him to death, nerved, however, by the consciousness that the despatch of Nelson to the Mediterranean would foil Napoleon's project of making that sea a French lake, "the principal aim of my policy" as he declared it to be. In that quarter, then, Pitt won a decisive victory which was destined to save not only that sea, but the Continent from the domination of France. Whether a glimpse of the future course of events opened out to the wearied gaze of the statesman we know not. All we know is that in mid-December, when the "Victory" lay jury-masted and wind-bound for three days off Walmer Castle, the Lord Warden was at Bath, in hope of gaining health and strength for a struggle which concerned him even more nearly than that in the Mediterranean, namely, the liberation of North Germany and the Dutch Netherlands from the Napoleonic yoke.

[1] Wellington in 1834 told Croker that they met in the anteroom of the Secretary of State, Castlereagh (Croker, "Diaries," ii, 234).

CHAPTER XXIV

THE LAST STRUGGLE

Heavens! What has Prussia to answer for! For nothing less, in my mind, than every calamity which has befallen Europe for more than ten years.—GENERAL PAGET TO SIR ARTHUR PAGET, 24*th January* 1806.

THE opening moves in the great game between Pitt and Napoleon were divided with a curious evenness. As we have seen, the French Emperor's defiant annexation of Genoa obliterated the anger of the Czar at Pitt's insistence on the retention of Malta; and if Pitt's high-handed conduct forced Spain to declare against England, yet, on the other hand, Napoleon wantonly challenged Austria and Russia to a conflict. The first events of the war showed a similar balance. On 20th October the French Emperor compelled the Austrian commander, General Mack, to surrender at or near Ulm in Swabia with almost the whole of an army of some 70,000 men. On the next day Nelson destroyed the French and Spanish fleets at Trafalgar. So quickly did the forcefulness or ineptitude of four commanders determine the course of events. By the end of October the tricolour waved triumphant over Central Europe; but the Union Jack was thenceforth scarcely challenged by sea; and Britain began to exert that unseen but resistless pressure upon her enemy which gradually edged him to his ruin. Consequently the appalling failures of the Third Coalition on land only delayed the final triumph on which the serene genius of Pitt surely counted.

At first everything seemed to favour his designs. Part of Napoleon's army in its hurried march from North Germany towards Ulm violated the neutrality of the Prussian principality of Anspach, apparently by command of the Emperor. This short cut to success nearly entailed disaster; for it earned the sharp resentment of Prussia at a time when he especially valued her friendship. Indeed, so soon as he resolved to turn the "Army of England" against Austria, he despatched his most trusted aide-de-camp, Duroc, to Berlin, to tempt that Court with that alluring bait, Hanover. Russia and England were, however, making equal efforts in the hope of gaining the help of the magnificent army of Frederick William III. For a time Pitt also hoped to add the South German States, and in all to set in motion a mass of 650,000 men against France, Austria contributing 250,000, Russia 180,000, Prussia 100,000 (later on he bargained for 180,000), Sardinia 25,000, Naples 20,000, Sweden 16,000, and the small German States the remainder. Napoleon, on the other hand, strove to paralyse the efforts of the Coalition by securing the alliance or the friendly neutrality of Prussia. With 200,000 hostile or doubtful troops on her frontier, Austria could do little, and Russia still less. Further, as he still had French troops in one or two fortresses of Hanover, he could utter the words so often on the lips of Bismarck—*Beati possidentes*. Hanover belonged of right to George III; but Napoleon could will it away to Prussia.

Thus the fortunes of Europe depended largely on Frederick William. Unfortunately he was incapable of rising to the height of the situation; for he utterly lacked the virile qualities which raised the House of Hohenzollern above petty compeers in Swabia to fame and prosperity. Essentially mediocre, and conscious of his slender endowments, he, like Louis XVI, nearly always hesitated, and therefore generally lost. His character was a dull compound of negations. Prone neither to vice nor to passion, he was equally devoid of charm and graciousness. Freezing men by his coldness, he failed to overawe them by superiority; and, with a weak man's dislike of genius and strength, he avoided great men, preferring trimmers like Haugwitz and Lombard, who played upon his foibles, and saved him from disagreeable decisions. The commanding personality of Stein inspired in him nervous dislike which deepened into peevish dread. Only in the depths of disaster, into which his own weakness was to plunge him, did he have recourse to that saviour of Prussia.

By the side of Frederick William was that radiant figure, Queen Louisa, who recalls the contrast between Marie Antoinette and her uninteresting, hapless spouse. For Louisa, too, had ambition and the power of inspiring devotion, though etiquette and jealousy forbade her intervention in affairs of State;[1] otherwise the Prussian Government would have shaken off that paralysing indecision which left its people friendless and spiritless on the bursting of the storm a year later. For the present, the King's chief adviser, Hardenberg, sought to impart to Prussian policy a trend more favourable to England and Russia. Conscious of the need of a better frontier on the west and of the longing of his master for the greater part of Hanover, he sought to attain this end by means not wholly opposed to the feelings of George III and the policy of Pitt. Above all, he strove to end the humiliating subservience of his Court to France, which galled the spirit of all patriotic Prussians. Their great desire was to join the new Coalition even though such a step entailed war with Napoleon. They rejoiced at the news of Admiral Calder's victory off Finisterre, and hailed every sign of war at St. Petersburg and Vienna.[2] On the other hand, the French party was strong at Court. Haugwitz, its head, was still nominally Minister for Foreign Affairs, and, though often absent for long periods on his Silesian domain, resumed the control of them when he returned to Berlin. This singular arrangement enabled the King to keep up the game of political see-saw which brought relief to him, disgust to his would-be allies, and ruin to his country.

To tilt the balance in favour of the Coalition was now the chief aim of Pitt. And who shall say that, if Prussia, with strength still unimpaired, had played the part which her enfeebled people insisted on taking up in 1813, the doom of Napoleon might not have been assured in the autumn and winter which we associate with the names of Ulm and Austerlitz? All this was possible, nay, probable, had Frederick William surveyed the situation with the sound judgement of Pitt. But the British statesman laboured under one great disadvantage. He could not offer to Prussia what she most wanted. He could do no more than promise to extend her western confines to Antwerp and Ostend; and she far preferred Hanover, as solidifying her straggling western lands, without bringing her near to France. Here was an almost insuperable obstacle; and we can imagine that, like his father, he cursed Britain's connection with Hanover. His chief hope was, that Prussia would discern her true interest

---

[1] G. Jackson ("Diaries," i, 270) gives a supposed instance of her interference in favour of Haugwitz.

[2] *Ibid.*, i, 301, 305, 314-9.

in acquiring less by honourable means than very much from Napoleon, whose gifts were often perilous. Russia, too, at that time seemed to adopt the British view of the Hanoverian question; and in the early autumn that Power mustered her second army on the borders of Prussia in a highly threatening manner. Finally, the Czar declared that if his troops were refused a passage through Silesia, he would make his way by force, the Pitt Cabinet informing him that, in that case, the liberal subsidies intended for Prussia, would be added to those already on their way to St. Petersburg. But even threats failed to bring Frederick William to a decision; and Hardenberg announced that a forcible entry of the Russians would involve war with Prussia.[1]

While Frederick William fumed at the Muscovite threats, came news of the violation of his Anspach domain on 3rd October. At once he declared his intention to avenge the insult and to expel Duroc from Prussian territory. He also raised high the hopes of the Allies by allowing the Russians to enter Silesia, and by favouring Pitt's plan of a joint expedition of the Allies to Hanover with a view to the liberation of Holland; and when he ordered the mobilization of the whole Prussian army, there appeared good grounds for expecting the speedy accession of at least 150,000 troops trained in the school of Frederick the Great. Even Haugwitz now suggested that if war came England must give Prussia a subsidy.[2] The Anglophil party at Berlin raised its head in triumph at the approach of the Russian Emperor; and when on 28th October he entered Berlin with enthusiastic greetings from the populace, Europe seemed about to be leagued against Napoleon. Chivalry and prudence alike counselled such a union, for on the morrow arrived news of the annihilation of Mack's army. Nothing but prompt action could save Germany from the Napoleonic deluge.

The first rumours of the disaster at Ulm did not reach London until 2nd November. Lord Malmesbury was dining with Pitt and mentioned the report to him, whereupon the Prime Minister exclaimed in loud and angry tones, " Don't believe a word of it: it is all a fiction." [3]   But on the morrow a Dutch newspaper was brought, and Malmesbury translated the account, which was so clear and detailed as to leave little room for doubt. Pitt's coun-

---

[1] Metternich, " Mems.," i, 57 (Eng. ed.); Hardenberg, " Mems.," ii, 220-4.
[2] Hardenberg, " Mems.," ii, 292-300.
[3] " Malmesbury Diaries," iv, 340.

tenance changed. There came over him that look which his
friends saw imprinted more deeply with every week of deepen-
ing gloom. For a brief space it passed away. On 6th November London heard the joyful yet painful news of Trafalgar. It
reached Downing Street at 3 a.m. Pitt was so moved by conflicting emotions that he, the soundest of sleepers, could not find
repose, but roused himself for work. The Stock Exchange registered the swift oscillations from confidence to doubt, for
though all fear of the French and Spanish fleet was at an end,
yet, as Nelson perished, national security seemed imperilled, and
Consols sank.

The contrast between the victorious constancy of Britain and
the wavering and hapless counsels of the Germanic States inspired Pitt with one of the most magnanimous utterances of that
age. At the Lord Mayor's banquet on 9th November, that
dignitary proposed his health as the Saviour of Europe. Pitt
concentrated his reply into these two memorable sentences:
" I return you many thanks for the honour you have done me;
but Europe is not to be saved by any single man. England has
saved herself by her exertions, and will, as I trust, save Europe
by her example." In its terseness and strength, its truth and
modesty, its patriotism and hopefulness, this utterance stands
unrivalled. The effect must have been all the greater because
Pitt then bore on his countenance signs of that anxious forethought in which now lay the chief hope of European independence.

Six days before the arrival of news of the Austrian disaster,
Pitt had sought to expedite a union with Prussia. In view of the
urgency of the case, he decided to send his trusted friend, the
Earl of Harrowby, the Dudley Ryder of former days. Harrowby's great abilities have never met with due recognition,
probably owing to the persistent ill health which impaired alike
his equanimity and his power of work; but Wilberforce had
good cause for commending Pitt's choice; and he added in a
letter of 25th October that the capacity of Harrowby was rated
far higher by foreigners than by Englishmen.[1] The instructions
to the Earl, drafted by Lord Mulgrave on 27th October, reveal
Pitt's resolve to go very far in order to buy the support of
Prussia. They empowered Harrowby to offer her the Belgic

[1] Pretyman MSS.; "Life of Wilberforce," iii, 412.

provinces and such German lands as would connect them with the Westphalian domains of Prussia. The need of money for the immediate equipment of her army being also urgent, Harrowby was to offer a yearly subsidy of £12 10s. for each Prussian soldier actually serving against France, the hope being expressed that from 150,000 to 200,000 men would be forthcoming. At the same time Pitt explained that at the general peace Great Britain would restore all her acquisitions oversea, Malta and the Cape of Good Hope alone excepted. Harrowby was also charged to do all in his power to effect the liberation of North Germany and Holland by the Russo-Swedish force then mustering at Stralsund. Such were the plans of Pitt. Even in this brief outline, their magnanimity is apparent. In order to assure the freedom of the Continent, he was ready to pour forth the wealth of Britain, and to sacrifice all her conquests, except those two bulwarks of Empire, Malta and the Cape.[1] Already even before Nelson gained the mastery of the seas at Trafalgar, Baird's force had set sail for the reduction of the Cape. It achieved its purpose in the month in which Pitt died. It is not generally known that the foundation of our South African Empire was due primarily to his foresight. The war having originated in Napoleon's aggressions and his threats respecting Egypt and the Orient generally, Pitt resolved that England should thenceforth dominate both the sea route and the overland route to the East Indies.

Unfortunately, owing to the fogs on the River Elbe and other delays at Hamburg, Harrowby did not reach Berlin until the middle of November;[2] and a fortnight earlier (3rd November) the sovereigns of Russia and Prussia had framed the Treaty of Potsdam. Ostensibly, it bound Prussia to side with the Allies unless within four weeks Napoleon accepted her armed mediation, which she proposed to offer forthwith. She required from the French Emperor a full recognition of the independence of Germany, Holland, Switzerland, and Naples, which of course implied the withdrawal of French troops from those lands. Napoleon was also to grant to the dispossessed King of Sardinia

---

[1] Rose, "Third Coalition," 208-20.

In "F. O.," Russia, 59, is a ciphered despatch of 25th October 1805 that, if circumstances favoured, a second British expedition (i.e., besides that destined for Hanover) would be made ready to seize Walcheren.

[2] Pitt MSS., 142.

the following indemnities—Genoa, Parma, and Piacenza; while
Austria was to recover Central Venetia as far as the River
Mincio. The Allies flattered themselves that Napoleon would
at once reject these terms and throw Prussia into their arms.
Such, too, was the conviction of Pitt. While regretting that France
should keep Piedmont and find no barrier opposed to her in
Holland,[1] he felt so convinced of Napoleon's refusal and of
Prussia's good faith that he prepared to satisfy her demand for
a British subsidy. Prussian troops were marching into Hanover,
as if with the aim of ousting the French and restoring the
authority of George III; and Hardenberg assured Harrowby in
their first interview, on 16th November, that that force would protect the flank of the Anglo-Russian expedition then about to
enter the Electorate.

On the surface, then, everything seemed to augur a brilliant
success for Pitt's policy. As had happened before, the recklessness of Napoleon favoured the British cause; and it is probable
that, if Frederick William had sent to the French headquarters
any one but Count Haugwitz, Prussia would have drawn the
sword. Napoleon was in great danger. True, he met with little
opposition in his advance to Vienna and thence into Moravia.
But the deeper he plunged into that province, the worse would
be his position if 180,000 Prussians were launched at his
flank and rear. The Court of Berlin was well aware that the
destinies of Europe lay in its hands; and for once a fatal confidence possessed Frederick William. He and his advisers used
the crisis, not in the magnanimous spirit which impelled Pitt to
sacrifice nearly the whole of Britain's naval conquests, but in
order to assure Prussia's gain even at the expense of the solidarity of the European League. The Coalition's extremity was
Prussia's opportunity. Hanover was her price for joining it.
Such was the purport of a secret article of the Treaty of
Potsdam, to which the Czar had most reluctantly given his
consent.

In order to bring the utmost possible pressure to bear upon
the British Government, a special Russian envoy, Count d'Oubril,
set out from Berlin to London, crossing Harrowby on the way.
Oubril arrived in London on or about 16th November; and

[1] See Hansing, "Hardenberg und die dritte Coalition" (Appendix), for a
comparison of these terms with those of the Anglo-Russian treaty of 11th
April 1805.

after a short delay Vorontzoff and he communicated to Pitt the document containing the ominous demand. The Russian ambassador noted that Pitt, despite long training in the concealment of his feelings, displayed some emotion on reading the fateful words. In truth, they dealt the second of the strokes which struck him to the heart. But, collecting himself with an effort, he informed Vorontzoff that, so great was the King's attachment to Hanover, the patrimony of his family for upwards of a thousand years, that no Minister would venture ever to name the proposal, as it might either kill him or drive him mad. All the arguments of Vorontzoff and Oubril on behalf of the Prusso-Russian demand utterly failed. Pitt expressed a desire to meet Prussia's wishes for a better western frontier, but never at the expense of Hanover.[1] Thus he deliberately faced a terrible diplomatic reverse rather than expose the King to a recurrence of his mental malady. A little later he recovered his equanimity; for on 19th November he informed Harrowby that, though Hanover was out of the question, yet he hoped to find an equivalent which would satisfy Prussia. The two Emperors could not in their present plight object to her gaining a large accession of territory. Moreover it would be an infinite disgrace to them now to make a separate peace with Napoleon.

Still [he added] even if this should happen, we have a strong interest that a separate peace should provide all the security that can be obtained for the Continent. If decent terms are obtained, particularly if France is obliged *really* to evacuate Holland and leave it in a state of independence, and if the three great Continental Powers after extorting concessions from France in the moment of victory, unite cordially in an obligation to resist all future encroachments, not only Europe will have gained much, but we shall have gained for the separate objects of this country more than enough to compensate for all the expense of subsidies in this year; and we may return to a state of separate war with little to guard against but the single point of Boulogne and with increased means of concentrating both our naval and land defence. The first object therefore of my wishes is, the immediate rejection of the mediation [2] and the *embarking Prussia at any rate in active and decisive*

---

[1] Czartoryski, "Mems.," ii, ch. ix. The editor wrongly gives the date of Vorontzoff's letter as $\frac{17}{29}$ September 1805, though it contains references to Ulm and Trafalgar. It is of 18th-21st November. " F. O.," Prussia, 70. Mulgrave to Harrowby, 23rd November.

[2] *I.e.*, the Prussian mediation by Napoleon.

operations towards Germany and Holland, leaving it to be considered afterwards what territorial arrangements can be agreed upon to secure her permanent co-operation. The next would be, in the event of negotiation, our being included in it, on the terms of restoring all our conquests except Malta and the Cape—and the third (and tho' the worst not a bad one) as good a separate peace as possible for our perfidious Allies, leaving us to fight our battle for ourselves. . . .[1]

Pitt's indignation against Prussia did not lead him to fling a refusal at her. On the contrary, he sought to postpone that announcement until the expiration of the four weeks, within which she must make her decision to side with or against Napoleon. Such was the purport of his letter of 23rd November to Harrowby. He also announced an increase in the numbers of the British force destined to serve in Hanover. This expedition under General Don was now being pushed on with great zeal. It met with disapproval from Canning, who with much sagacity pointed out, on 29th November, that if the war were continued the gain of a month or two was a trifling object; whereas, if the Allies ended the war, France would certainly offer Hanover to Prussia.[2] The dash of pessimism in Canning's nature enabled him to discern difficulties and dangers which were hidden from Pitt's ever hopeful vision. Mulgrave seems to have shared Pitt's view; for he signed all the despatches relating to the Hanoverian expedition. On 23rd November he informed Harrowby that, early in the year 1806, as many as 70,000 British and Hanoverian troops would be ready for service, either in Hanover or wherever they could be employed to most effect. He therefore expected that by that time the Allies would have nearly 300,000 men in North Germany; and, as the resources of Austria were not depleted by the disaster at Ulm, she and Russia ought then to have nearly half a million of men on foot.[3]

Pitt's eagerness to receive news from Harrowby appears in the closing phrases of his letter of 29th November to that envoy: "We are counting moments till we hear in what state you found things on your arrival [at Berlin], and what has been Haugwitz's reception at the French headquarters." Again, on 5th December, he sent off to him a letter, which as being the

---

[1] Harrowby MSS.
[2] See "Pitt and Napoleon Miscellanies" for the letter in full.
[3] Rose, "Third Coalition," 230-5.

last of any importance written by him at Downing Street, must be given in full:

Downing St. *Dec. 5th,* 1805.

DEAR HARROWBY,

I am grieved to hear by your letter of the 24th that you had been so much persecuted by headaches, and that you had allowed the secret article of Potsdam [*sic*] to give you so much uneasiness. You must I am sure be satisfied that the way in which you have treated it is *the best possible,* because it gives no hopes of the thing being consented to, and at the same time avoids the necessity of any formal and official negative. The great object I think is that Prussia should if possible, decide on the result of C^t Haugwitz's mission, without giving to the evil councillors of the King of Prussia the advantage of stating to him that this object is precluded for ever. At the same time we cannot in good faith give the least assurance that it is likely to be ever attainable. Woronzow [Vorontzoff] who has been in town for ten days but is gone again, writes to Alopeus that he has received from him the *mémoire raisonné* on the exchange of Hanover, but cannot present it to us till he has orders to do so from his own Court. We are therefore supposed to know nothing more of the matter.

On the whole state of things, you will perhaps be angry with me for saying that my hopes are still sanguine. I think I see great chance of Prussia agreeing to co-operate either for a definite object or a limited time, in return for subsidies and for our assurance (which you know to be a very sincere one) of wishing to procure for them important acquisitions. The question of Hanover may I think be left aloof. As to plans of operations, it is almost idle to say anything. But you will have seen that we think the first and *essential* point is to act (as Prussia seems to intend) with a force sure of success in the rear of the French Army in Germany. Still I cannot conceive what can be the military reasons why an attack on Holland should not take place at the same time, or at least should not be prepared so as to be put into execution whenever the effect of any great success of the Allies, or a frost, or an appearance of good disposition in the country, should afford a favourable opening for such an enterprise, the advantages of which in its impression and consequences I need not state to you. We have finally decided with a view to this chance and for the sake of shewing at any rate our readiness to co-operate, to send the 12,000 men which have been prepared, to Embden [*sic*], and if this wind continues, I hope they will sail within three days. Endeavour to make Prussia send under General Kalkreuth (or whoever may be the general they destine for that quarter) not merely 10,000 men, but enough to make such an army as can scarce be resisted. Our force with the Russians (exclusive of the Swedes and after allowing for something to watch Hameln [1]) will be near 40,000 men. It surely cannot be difficult for Prussia to add 30,000 to that number within a very few weeks on increased subsidies beyond the number they now propose, and that without at all impairing the effort against Bonaparte's army. As to your stay at Berlin I can only say that if your health will permit, *everything that we value most* may depend on your remaining till you have seen the leading points of the negociation fairly through. As to details with Saxony and Hesse, they cannot be worth your waiting for, if they require any time, which, however, supposing you once to settle with Prussia, they cannot. The important moment seems to be that when the issue of Haugwitz's negociation shall have been known in Berlin and time given to communicate with Austria and Russia on the result. Under these circumstances it will I am afraid hardly be as pleasant to you as it is to me to know that Parliament will not meet till the 21st of Jany [1806] and that you have not on that account any reason for your immediate return. If, however, (as I most earnestly hope will not be the case) you should really find the fatigue and anxiety too much for you, it is certainly among *the things that we value most*, that you should return, having suffered as little as possible. A frigate will be sent to wait your orders at the Elbe, but I hope you will have no occasion to use it, till after you have signed a provisional treaty, and seen the Prussians on their march against the enemy.

Ever most sincerely yours
W. P.

Three days before Pitt poured forth this sanguine forecast, Napoleon struck the Coalition to the heart. As "the sun of Austerlitz" set, the two Emperors were in flight eastwards, while their armies streamed after them in hopeless rout, or struggled through the funnel of death between the two lakes (2nd December). Marbot's story of thousands of Russians sinking majestically under the ice is a piece of melodrama. But the reality was such as to stun the survivors. In his dazed condition the Emperor Francis forthwith sent proposals for a truce. It proved to be the precursor of the armistice of 6th December, which involved the departure of the Russian army and the exclusion of that of Prussia from Austrian territories. In the calculating balance maintained at Berlin, this diplomatic surrender proved to be a greater calamity than the military disaster. True, the news of the battle caused consternation; but for the present Frederick William held firm and on 8th Dec-

---

[1] The French held the fortress of Hameln.

ember ordered part of the Prussian army (now 192,000 strong) to enter Bohemia for the succour of the Allies.[1] Not until after the 13th, after the arrival of news of the armistice, did he seek to evade his obligations to Russia; and, obviously, a new situation arose when Alexander gave up the campaign, and Francis promised to bar out the Prussians. Hardenberg sought to hide from Harrowby this change of front, hinting, however, that Prussia might have to consult her own interests. In the light of the events of 1795, that phrase was clear enough; and Harrowby forthwith sent orders to General Don to countermand the advance of his troops towards Hanover.[2]

To complete this chapter of misfortunes, Harrowby's health broke down. On discovering the truth about Prussia's secret demand for Hanover, he fell into the depths of despair and nervous prostration, as appears from the postscript of his letter of 24th November to Pitt:

This horrible secret article has finished me. It stood with its mouth open, and from mere cowardice I have run into it, and it will devour me. I am persuaded, however, that it would equally have caught me if I had run away. There is something, however, in every view of it which agonises me. I am anxious beyond imagination to know what passes in England upon it and conclude I shall by the next newspaper. Would it be impossible to prevail upon the King to listen to the idea of a sort of Barrier-treaty for Hanover, which would give Prussia a military frontier but not the territorial possession?[3]

On 8th December, after hearing the first news of Austerlitz, he writes in equally dolorous strains, concluding with a request that Pitt would send a frigate to the mouth of the Elbe to bring away his coffin. Again he writes in these pathetic terms:

Most secret.

Berlin, 12 *Dec.* 1805.[4]
DEAR PITT,
   The current of events has been so rapid, and the embarrassments they produce from every quarter is [*sic*] so intolerable, that, weakened as my brain has been by nervous spasms of giddiness, I hardly keep my senses. Cool judgment is required; and I can only take steps in a state of agitation—repent; and there is something more to be

---

[1] Rose, "Third Coalition," 259. [2] *Ibid.*, 260, 261.
[3] Pitt MSS., 142. [4] Pretyman MSS.

repented of. I shall not long stand it; but, in the meantime, what mischief may not have happened! The sacrifice of myself is nothing. All is over with me even if I survive. I am tolerably at intervals, but every fresh occurrence brings with it distraction. I tremble at the consequences. You can conceive no state of mind, or rather of mind and body operating upon each other; you cannot even pity it; you can only despise it. Good God. If it be possible, do not betray me. I may recover. I try to disguise my feelings. I write to my wife with affected cheerfulness. She would not survive. For heaven's sake, keep this to yourself.

> Yours ever,
>
> HARROWBY.

To what mistake Harrowby here alludes is a mystery. But George Jackson states that he had three fits at Berlin, besides spasms every day. Indeed his state was so pitiable that his selection for this difficult post was matter of general comment. The physicians strongly urged him to return to England at once.[1] Pitt cannot have received Harrowby's pathetic confession when he replied as follows, probably to the letter of the 8th:

> Bath, *Dec.* 21st, 1805.[2]

DEAR HARROWBY,

I was prevented from writing a few lines as I intended by the messenger we sent from hence yesterday. We are sending orders for another today to pass through Berlin on his way to the Emperor's head-quarters, to remind them of sending the ratification which we have never yet received. We have nothing very authentic from the armies later than your despatch of the 9th by estafette, but there are accounts thro' Hamburg from Berlin of the 10th, corroborated by reports from various quarters, which lead us to hope that the sequel of the battle at length terminated in great success on the part of Russia. If this proves true, I flatter myself your subsidiary treaty will have been soon brought to a prosperous issue, and you will be delivered from all your fatigue and anxiety. I am quite grieved to think how much you have suffered, tho' I trust your complaint is only temporary, and that a good battle and a good treaty will send you back to us in better health than you went. I see no danger of your exceeding our limit in the amount of subsidy, as we looked if necessary to an actual annual payment of £3,000,000, and the number proposed in the treaty, of 180,000

---

[1] G. Jackson, "Diaries," i, 377, 381, 384. Harrowby left Berlin on 7th or 8th January 1806 (*ibid.*, 390).

[2] Harrowby MSS.

Prussians and 40,000 Allies, will not require more than £2,750,000, which still leaves room for 25,000 men more if they are wanted and can be had. I have been here for ten days and have already felt the effect of the waters in a pretty smart fit of the gout from which I am just recovering, and of which I expect soon to perceive the benefit.

Ever yours,
W. PITT.

I need hardly tell you that every step you have taken has been exactly what we should have desired.

He who wrote these cheering words was in worse health than Harrowby. The latter lived on till the year 1847; Pitt had now taken his last journey but one. Sharp attacks of gout had reduced him to so weak and tremulous a state that he could scarcely lift a glass to his lips. So wrote Mrs. Jackson on 9th December, long before the news of Austerlitz reached these shores.[1] So far back as 27th November, Canning, in prophetic strains, begged him not to defer a projected visit to Bath until it was too late for the waters to do him good. But "the pilot that weathered the storm" refused to leave the tiller in case decisive news came from Harrowby. He also prepared to strengthen his Cabinet against the attacks certain to be made in the ensuing session, by including in it two excellent speakers, Canning and Charles Yorke, the latter taking the Board of Control. Why he did not complete these changes, as Canning begged him to do, is far from clear. Possibly the sharp though friendly criticism which Canning levelled against the Anglo-Russian expedition to Hanover made him apprehensive of divisions in the Cabinet on a question which was very near his heart. Certainly much could be said in favour of an expedition to Walcheren, which Canning urged should be entrusted to General M[oore?]. Pitt preferred the Hanoverian enterprise, doubtless because it would lay Russia and Prussia under a debt of honour to co-operate to the utmost of their power.

At last the strain became too great, and on 7th December Pitt set out for Bath, arriving there on the 11th. He resided at Harrowby's house, 11, Laura Place. His stay in Bath aroused interest so intense that he found it necessary to vary the time of his visits to the Pump Room in order to escape the crowd

---

[1] G. Jackson, "Diaries," i, 381.

which would otherwise have incommoded him.[1] As has just
appeared, he expected a speedy recovery; for, as was the case
with his father, if the attack of gout ran a normal course, the
system felt relief. Freedom from worry was the first condition
of amendment. After his retirement from office in 1768 Chatham recovered so quickly that his opponents gibed at the illness
as a political device.[2] Ten years later he succumbed to excitement and strain.

During the first part of his stay at Bath, Pitt was in good
spirits and wrote cheerfully about his health. The following
letter to his London physician, Sir Walter Farquhar, is not that
of a man who feels death approaching:

Bath, Dec. 15. 1805.[3]

The gout continues pretty smartly in my foot; and I find from
Mr. Crooks that it is attended with a feverish pulse and some other
symptoms of the same nature. I have communicated to Mr. Crooks
your directions, and he is to send me the saline draughts with some
little addition, which he will explain to you. I thought he would detail
symptoms more precisely than I could, and have therefore desired him
to write to you. On the whole, I have no doubt the plan you have laid
down will answer, and I do not at present see the smallest occasion to
accept your kind and friendly offer of coming here.

P.S. 4.30 P.M. I enclose Mr. Crooks' letter to you. His account to
me of the pulse was that it was not strong, but quick and beating near
an hundred. One of the saline draughts which I have taken since I
wrote the foregoing letter, seems, as far as I can judge from feeling,
already to have had a very good effect.

Not until ten days later do we find signs of alarm in the letters
of his friends; for it is characteristic of his buoyant nature that
he never wrote despondingly about himself. There is a well-
known story to the effect that, on hearing the news of Austerlitz, he called for a map of Europe, to see where the place was,
and then said with a sigh: " Roll up that map: it will not be

[1] Peach, "Historic Houses of Bath." The "Bath Herald" of 11th January
1806 has an ode containing the lines:

Oh prepare, prepare
The renovating draught! He comes by stealth
(For so unconscious worth is ever seen)
With thoughts uplifted but retiring mien.

[2] Ruville, "Chatham," iii, 246.   [3] Chevening MSS.

wanted these ten years." One version assigns the incident to
Shockerwick House, near Bath. Pitt is looking over the picture
gallery, and is gazing at Gainsborough's portrait of the actor
Quin. His retentive memory calls up the lines in Churchill's
" Characters":

> Nature, in spite of all his skill, crept in—
> Horatio, Dorax, Falstaff—still 'twas Quin.

At that moment he hears the beat of a horse's hoofs. A courier
dashes up. He comes in, splashed with mud, hands the despatches. Pitt tears them open and hurriedly reads them. His
countenance changes, he calls for brandy, then for a map, and
is finally helped to his carriage, uttering the historic phrase.[1]
In another version he mournfully rolls out the words to
Lady Hester Stanhope, as she welcomes him in the hall of
Bowling Green House, after his last journey to his home on
Putney Heath.[2] The words probably fell from him on some
occasion. But at the risk of incurring the charge of pedantry, I
must point out that the news of Austerlitz did not come on him
as one overwhelming shock: it filtered through by degrees. As
we have seen, he wrote to Harrowby on 21st December, stating
that reports from Berlin and other quarters represented the
sequel to the battle as a great success for the Russians. It
appears that Thornton, our envoy at Hamburg, wrote as follows
on 13th December to Mulgrave: "From everything I can learn
(for the details are even yet far from being circumstantial
and decisive) the tide of success had completely turned in
favour of the Russian and Austrian armies, tho', as the conflict still continued to the 4th and perhaps to the 5th, it could
not be positively said on which side the victory had been declared. The certain intelligence cannot now be long delayed."[3]
Castlereagh also, writing to Pitt on 19th December, assured
him that he had heard similar news through various channels,
and therefore cherished high hopes that something good had
happened.[4] Mulgrave, who was then also at Bath along with
Bathurst, Hawkesbury, and Canning, shared these hopes. Despite the first reports of Austerlitz, which were promptly contra-

---

[1] Thomas Hardy ("The Dynasts," i, Act vi, sc. 7) places the incident in
the week after Austerlitz. The date is impossible.
[2] Stanhope, iv, 369.   [3] Pitt MSS., 337.
[4] *Ibid.*, 121. See, too, in his letter of 23rd December ("Castlereagh Corresp.," vi, 92).

dicted, the Ministerial circle at Bath had no want of diversion.
On 12th December Mulgrave sent to Pitt a short poem on
Trafalgar for his correction, and Pitt touched up a few lines.
On 21st December Mulgrave wrote to him: " I send you
Woronzow [Vorontzoff] and Ward, *faute de mieux*. I was rejoiced to find you were gone out in your carriage when I called
at your home after church. As Bathurst, Canning, and the
gout have left you, I hope you will be able to return to the mess
to-morrow." This does not imply that Pitt was living the life of
an invalid, or was kept to so strict a diet as during his sojourn
at Bath three years before.

Equally hopeful was the estimate of Canning. He spent a
week with Pitt at Bath, and, after leaving him shortly before
Christmas, informed a friend that Pitt was " recovering from a
fit of the gout, which has done him abundance of good, and puts
off the time of his driving after old Frere—I trust to an incalculable distance. . . . There wants only an official confirmation of
all the good news (that has reached us through every possible
channel except those of Office) to complete it."[1]

Canning, we may note here, had discussed with Pitt his projected poem—" Ulm and Trafalgar" (which bore the motto
" Look here, upon this picture, and on that "). It began:

> While Austria's yielded armies, vainly brave,
> Moved, in sad pomp, by Danube's blood-stained wave

and ended with a noble acclaim to Nelson:

> Thou, bravest, gentlest Spirit, fare thee well.

On the first line Canning plumed himself until he remembered
the warning of an old tutor at Magdalen, that when anything in
your verses pleased you very much, it was best to strike it out.
Canning referred the phrase " yielded armies " to Pitt, who
probably found relief from his cares in touching up the poem.[2]
That Christmastide, then, was a time of anxiety, but not of
settled gloom. There is no sign that Pitt or his colleagues felt
the position to be desperate until the end of the year. On

[1] J. Bagot, "Canning and his Friends," i, 227. The statement about the
gout corrects Malmesbury ("Diaries," iv, 343) that the attack of gout left
Pitt far weaker and with digestion impaired. Malmesbury was not at Bath.
Frere's father had lately died.
[2] Bagot, "Canning, etc.," 415-9; H. Newbolt, "Year of Trafalgar," 190-3.

Christmas Day Castlereagh wrote from Downing Street to Pitt: "I am sorry to add to your materials for criticism and speculation. I send you Cooke's 'Courant.' There is intelligence in the City from Amsterdam of the 21st. Nothing official known here of an *armistice*. You have received from Lord B[arham?] every information from that quarter."[1]

Indeed, the hopefulness of Ministers now involved them in greater difficulties. Building on Prussia's promises, they decided early in December to order the despatch of strong reinforcements to the British corps then on the point of entering Hanover.[2] In all, as many as 65,000 British and King's Germans were to be sent—the largest force that had ever set sail from these shores, a fact which testifies to the ardour of Pitt's desires for the liberation of Hanover and Holland. Even the immediate results of this decision were disastrous. Sixty-seven transports, forthwith setting sail, encountered a terrible storm, which flung three of them on the enemy's coast, while one sank with all hands on the Goodwins. Such was the purport of the news sent by Castlereagh to Pitt at Bath on 19th December. He added that, in spite of these losses, "the little Cabinet of five" (with Lord Barham in attendance) decided to order all the remaining transports to sail, so that Prussia might be encouraged to "throw her strength to the southward. We have acted for the best, and I hope you and your companions will approve."[3] Pitt, of course, did approve, not knowing that while England was encountering heavy risks in order to effect the liberation of North Germany, her Allies had come to terms with Napoleon.

At last, on 29th December, definite news concerning the armistice of 6th December reached London. It must have chilled the hearts of the boldest. For, trusting in the continued exertions of the Allies, England had sent to North Germany as many as 257 transports, and of these 8 were now known to be lost, involving the death of 664 men, and the capture of about 1,000 on the enemies' coasts. All this effort and loss of life now appeared to be useless, in view of the vacillating conduct of Prussia. Only with her good will could the British troops, with the Russian and Swedish contingents, hope to conquer Holland. If she declared against us, the whole force would be in jeopardy. Such were the tidings which Castlereagh bore with

[1] Pitt MSS., 121.   [2] "Castlereagh Corresp.," vi, 70-85.
[3] Pitt MSS., 121.

him to Pitt at the end of the year.[1] Not a line survives respecting that mournful interview; but we can picture the deathly look coming over Pitt's emaciated features as he now for the first time faced the prospect of the dissolution of the mighty league which he had toiled to construct. Probably it was this shock to the system which brought on a second attack of the gout, accompanied with great weakness and distaste for food.[2]

Nevertheless he clung to the hope that Prussia would stand firm. On 3rd January 1806 further news reached him from the Austrian and Prussian Governments. The Austrian despatches represented Austerlitz as a repulse, but not a disaster, and the armistice as a device for enabling Prussia to prepare her blow at Napoleon's flank or rear. On 5th January Mulgrave found in the despatches from Berlin grounds for believing that that Court might under certain conditions assist the two Emperors in Moravia and the British force in Hanover. On the morrow he wrote to Pitt in emphatic terms, urging him to offer to Prussia the Dutch Republic. That little State (he urged) could not again be independent, save in circumstances now scarcely imaginable, much less realizable. Further, the Stadholder having very tamely accepted the domain of Fulda as an indemnity, we need feel no qualms for the House of Nassau; and, as Prussia was influenced solely by territorial greed, and Hanover was out of the question, she might well acquire the Dutch Netherlands, which would link her to British interests.[3] Again we have to admit ignorance of Pitt's opinion on this degrading proposal. Certainly it never took definite shape.[4] Though willing to assign to Prussia the Belgic Netherlands, he laid great stress on the independence of the Dutch Netherlands, which indeed was the corner-stone of his foreign policy. Moreover, to barter away an unoffending little State was to repeat the international crimes of the partitions of Poland and Venetia. We may be sure that that proud and just spirit would rather have perished than stoop to such ignominy.

[1] "Castlereagh Corresp.," vi, 100; "Malmesbury Diaries," iv, 344.

[2] Gifford, "Life of Pitt," vi, 802; Lord Rosebery, "Tomline's Estimate of Pitt" (1903), p. 16.

[3] Pitt MSS., 142.

[4] In the "Hardenberg Memoirs" (ii, 353) it is stated that Harrowby offered Holland to Prussia. Every despatch that I have read runs counter to this assertion. If Harrowby made the offer, it was in sheer desperation and on his own authority; but he nowhere mentions it.

In effect, he fell a victim to his resolve never to barter away the patrimony of George III. We now know that Prussia's policy at this crisis turned mainly on the acquisition of Hanover. Her envoy, Haugwitz, whom she sent to Napoleon's headquarters charged with the offer of Prussia's armed mediation on behalf of Europe, had on 15th December signed with him the humiliating Convention of Schönbrunn, whereby Prussia agreed to make certain cessions of territory on condition of acquiring Hanover. About Christmastide Frederick William decided to close with this offer, which involved the expulsion of the Anglo-Russian force from the Electorate. Premonitory signs of this change of front were soon visible at Berlin. Indeed, the trend of Prussian policy during the last decade prepared the British Ministry for the ruin of their hopes. Pitt must have been racked with anxiety lest Prussia should doff the lion's skin and don that of the jackal; for he alone knew of the nervous breakdown of Harrowby.

Perhaps it was the hope of helping on that negotiation from Downing Street, added to the verdict of Sir Walter Farquhar that the Bath waters were now of no avail, which induced him on 9th January to set out on his homeward journey. He was believed to be in better health than at the time of his arrival; such at least was the announcement of the " Bath Herald " on the 11th; and his hopeful outlook appears in a curious detail which afterwards came to light. In order to beguile the tedium of the journey he had taken out from a circulating library in Bath the following works, each in two volumes, " The Secret History of the Court of Petersburg," and Schiller's " History of the Thirty Years' War." [1] A man who believes death to be near does not undertake a study of the manifold intrigues of Catharine II, or of the Thirty Years' War. He also had the prospect of seeing the liveliest and most devoted of friends, Canning, at his country home, South Hill, Bracknell, in Windsor Forest. Canning sent the invitation on the 5th, and it was accepted on the 8th in terms which implied a sojourn of some days. He offered to accompany him from Bath, if he felt strong enough to converse on the way; but Pitt declined this offer, and it is doubtful whether he stayed at South Hill; for Malmesbury declares that he had to remain a

[1] Chevening MSS.; "Notes and Queries," 12th November 1864. Mr. John Upham of Bath on 10th March 1806 sent these particulars to Lord Chatham. Gifford (" Life of Pitt," vi, 803) wrongly states that the journey took four days.

long time in bed at Reading. On the other hand the Bishop of Lincoln declared that the journey took only two days, and that at its close Pitt showed no very marked signs of fatigue. Lady Hester Stanhope, however, was shocked by his wasted appearance on reaching his home, Bowling Green House, on Putney Heath.

Some eighteen months earlier he had leased that residence. It stands on the (old) Portsmouth Road, and had earlier been an inn frequented by lovers of that game and patrons of cock-fighting. After enlargement it had been converted into a gentleman's abode which well suited the modest requirements of Pitt and of his niece, Lady Hester Stanhope.[1] There, not far from the scenes of his youthful frolics with Wilberforce, and only a quarter of a mile from the dell where he fought the duel with Tierney, he found solace from the ever-increasing cares of state. In those last months Hester felt for him feelings akin to adoration.

On the morrow, Sunday, their circle was enlarged by the arrival of his old friend and counsellor, Bishop Tomline, who was shocked at the change which had taken place in him since he left for Bath. The physicians, Farquhar, Reynolds, and Baillie, however, saw no cause for alarm, the only disquieting symptoms being intense weakness and dislike of animal food. There is a forcibly significant phrase in a recent letter of George Rose to Tomline, that he dreaded the effect on the invalid of an excessive use of medicines.[2] Evidently Rose believed the digestive organs to be impaired by this habit. Pitt's daily potations of port wine for many years past must further have told against recovery. Whether Farquhar and his colleagues cut off medicine and sought to build up that emaciated frame is uncertain. All that we know is that they prescribed complete quiet, and therefore requested the bishop to open all Pitt's letters so as to preclude all chance of excitement.

On 12th January, Pitt wrote an affectionate letter to the Marquis Wellesley, welcoming him on his return from his memorable Vice-royalty in India. He begged him to come to Bowling

---

[1] The house has been very little altered since 1806, and not at all on the side shown in the accompanying sketch, which, by kind permission of Mr. and Mrs. Doulton, was done by my daughter. The room over the veranda is that in which Pitt died.

[2] Pretyman MSS.

BOWLING GREEN HOUSE, PUTNEY HEATH

(FROM A PENCIL SKETCH BY ELSIE H. ROSE)

Green House at the earliest opportunity. The letter closes with these remarkable words: " I am recovering rather slowly from a series of stomach complaints, followed by severe attacks of gout, but I believe I am now in the way of real amendment."[1] The Bishop also describes him as gaining ground until Monday the 13th. On that day he went out in his coach in the morning, but in the evening Lords Castlereagh and Hawkesbury, having obtained permission from the physicians to interview their chief, communicated news which had a most agitating effect. Pitt afterwards assured the Bishop "that he felt during that conversation some sensation in his stomach which he feared it might be difficult to remove."[2] It is surprising that the physicians allowed an interview of an agitating nature; but the ministerial pressure brought to bear on them may have overborne their better judgement. In matters of Cabinet discipline Pitt was an autocrat, insisting that no important action should be taken without his cognizance. Probably, then, it was his own sense of responsibility which exposed him to the death blow.

Certainly the question at issue was of the gravest kind. Should Ministers order the return of the British reinforcements last sent to Hanover? That expedition was the work of Pitt. He it was who had reared the fabric of a European Coalition; and, even after the withdrawal of Austria, he clung to the hope that Prussia would take her place, and, with the help of British, Prussian, Russian, and Swedish troops, drive the French from North Germany and the Dutch Republic. How could his colleagues order back a large part of the British force, thereby justifying the vacillations of Prussia and ensuring a parliamentary triumph to Fox and Grenville? And yet Ministers knew, better than Pitt could know, the danger of relying on the Court of Berlin. Though not yet fully aware of its resolve to take Napoleon's side, they had strong reasons for expecting this course of action; and in that case the British expedition would be in grave danger between the Prussians on the east, the Franco-Dutch forces on the south-west and the ice-floes which were forming on the River Weser. Prudence counselled the timely return of our troops who were yet on board ship at or near Bremen.[3] Patriotic pride prompted a bold offensive. But the King and Pitt alone could utter the decisive words. The King approved the return

---

[1] Stanhope, iv, 374.			[2] Pretyman MSS.
[3] " Castlereagh Corresp.," vi, 103-112, 119.

of the last reinforcements, and Pitt, it seems, must have conceded the point. But the concession struck him to the heart. It was the last of the deadly stabs which fate dealt him thick and fast in his time of weakness.

Nevertheless, on the morrow he drove out in his carriage, but was visibly weaker than before the interview. For a few minutes he saw his brother and then Lord Wellesley. The latter found his mind as clear as ever; and he uttered these remarkable words about Sir Arthur Wellesley: " He states every difficulty before he undertakes any service, but none after he has undertaken it." What a prophecy of Vittoria and Waterloo there is in these words—the swan-song of Pitt. It was too much for him. He fainted before Wellesley left the room. On the 18th he rallied for a time, and the doctors saw a gleam of hope.[1]

In reality there was only one faint chance of recovery, that good news might arrive. The chief cause of physical collapse was the torture of the brain; and it was possible that the whole system might even now rally under the vitalizing thrills of hope. But as day by day passed by and brought nearer that dreaded occasion, the opening of Parliament on 22nd January, this last chance vanished. The news which reached the Foreign Office became more and more gloomy. On 10th January Mulgrave decided, when recalling Harrowby, to entrust his mission at Berlin to the Earl of Harrington, in the hope that that Court would keep troth.[2] But all negotiation was useless. By the 19th the conduct of Prussia respecting Hanover appeared so threatening that Ministers ordered the immediate recall of the whole British force.[3] Thus, England had sent forth some 60,000 troops in order to bring them back again. She had paid a million sterling to Austria, and the results were Ulm and Austerlitz. Nearly as much had gone to Russia, and the outcome was the armistice. A British subsidy had been claimed by Prussia, and in return she was about to take Hanover as a gift from Napoleon. It is to be hoped that Ministers kept the last bitter truth from Pitt; but from their silence he must have augured the worst. Surely death itself was better than to be driven from power by

---

[1] Stanhope, iv, 375; " Malmesbury Diaries," iv, 346; " Dropmore P.," vii, 327.

[2] " F. O.," Austria, 77. Mulgrave to Harrington, 10th January 1806.

[3] " Castlereagh Corresp.," vi, 126.

the combined attacks of Fox, Grenville, and Windham, the success of which was now assured.

A touching instance of Pitt's thoughtfulness during these days of waning strength is recorded by Robert Plumer Ward. He had accepted office as Under Secretary for Foreign Affairs; but, in the event of the overthrow of the Ministry, he would be in a far worse position than before. Pitt remembered this fact, and whispered to Farquhar the words "Robert Ward." He also made signs for paper and ink and sought to pen a request for a pension; but he succeeded only in tracing strokes which could not be deciphered.[1] His thoughts were also with his nieces, especially Lady Hester Stanhope. Farquhar sought to prevent a parting interview with her; but during his temporary absence she slipped into the bedroom, there to receive the blessing of her uncle and an affectionate farewell. To her brother James, who then came in, he said; "Dear soul, I know she loves me. Where is Hester? Is Hester gone?" Early on the 22nd he dictated these words to the bishop: "I wish £1,000 or £1,500 a year to be given to my nieces if the public should think my long services deserving it; but I do not presume to think I have earned it."[2] He then named those to whom since 1801 he owed sums of money: Long, Steele, Lords Camden and Carrington, the Bishop of Lincoln and Joseph Smith; he also entrusted his papers to the bishop and to Lord Chatham.

Already Bishop Tomline had warned him of his approaching change and besought him to prepare his mind for the Sacrament. This he declined, alleging his unworthiness to receive it. Thereupon the bishop prayed with him. He calmly murmured the responses and humbly confessed that he had too much neglected prayer. Nevertheless, he affirmed the steadiness of his religious faith and principles, and declared that he had ever sought to fulfil his duty to God and to mankind, though with many errors and failures. While the bishop was overcome with emotion, the dying man thanked him earnestly for all his kindness throughout life. Once his thoughts recurred to his own conduct; he expressed heartfelt satisfaction at the innocency of his life, and declared that he died in perfect charity with all mankind.[3]

[1] R. P. Ward, "Memoirs," i, 176.   [2] Pretyman MSS.
[3] Lord Rosebery, "Tomline's Estimate of Pitt," 18; "Dropmore P.," vii, 330.

He lingered on to the early hours of 23rd January, the twenty-fifth anniversary of his entry into Parliament. During that night the cares of state once more pressed upon him. He spoke often about a private letter from Lord Harrowby, probably the pathetic effusion quoted above. At times he asked his nephew the direction of the wind, and on hearing it was in the east he murmured: "East—ah that will do: that will bring him quick."[1] Then he fell into conversation with a messenger, or, again, he murmured "Hear, hear," until sleep enfolded him. The last thoughts of Napoleon are said to have centred in his early love and his army—"Joséphine:—Tête d'armée" he gasped as he neared his end. In Pitt's being there was but one master passion; and to it his wandering fancies returned during a last brief spell of consciousness. As James Stanhope listened to the breathing, there fell on his ears with a strange clearness the words: "My country! How I leave my country!" Then the sufferer fell once more into a deep sleep; and so he lay, until, some three hours before the dawn, his spirit passed away in a long-drawn sigh.

[1] Stanhope, iv, 381.

EPILOGUE

Now is the stately column broke
The beacon-light is quench'd in smoke,
The trumpet's silver sound is still
The warder silent on the hill.
SCOTT, *Marmion*.

THIS noble epitaph to the memory of Pitt conveys an impression alike of heroic endeavour and of irretrievable failure. It is the Funeral March of Chopin, not of Handel, and it echoes the feeling of the time. An impenetrable darkness hung over England. Ulm, Austerlitz, the armistice, and the desertion of the Allies by Prussia were successive waves of calamity, which obliterated all landmarks and all means of safety. The dying words of Pitt found response in every breast, with this difference, that, while he was proudly conscious of the correctness of his aims, the many, who judge solely by tangible results, imputed to him the disasters of the war and the collapse of the Coalition. Even Auckland exclaimed that the continental alliances had been wretchedly mismanaged, a remark which Malmesbury treated with quiet contempt. Grenville, who was about to move a vote of censure on the Ministry, burst into an agony of tears on hearing that Pitt was at death's door. His distress of mind probably arose from a belated perception of the factiousness of his own conduct and from grief at the unrelieved gloom of the end of a career whose meridian splendour had shed lustre upon him.

The House of Commons did not whole-heartedly accord to the deceased statesman a burial in Westminster Abbey in the tomb of Chatham. A motion to that effect, moved by Lascelles and seconded by the Marquis of Titchfield, was strongly opposed by Fox, George Ponsonby, Windham, and three other speakers. It passed by 258 votes to 59. Still more painful was the discussion in the Common Council of the City of London, where a proposal to erect a monument to Pitt was carried only by 77 votes to 71. It is safe to say that, if the fortune of war had gone against France at Ulm and Austerlitz, Pitt would have been ecstatically hailed as the saviour of Europe, as indeed he was at the Guildhall after Trafalgar. How long was it before it dawned on Auckland, Windham, and the seventy-one councillors of the City of London, that the censures cast on the memory of Pitt ought to have been levelled at the defender of Ulm, the Czar Alexander and his equally presumptuous advisers at Austerlitz, and most of all at the cringing politicians of Berlin?

It is now abundantly clear that Pitt fell a victim to his confidence in the rulers of three great monarchies, whose means were vast, whose promises were lofty, and whose surrender after the first reverses baffled all forecasts. The descendants of Maria Theresa and Catharine tamely retired from the fray after a single adverse blow; and the successor of the great Frederick sheathed his sword after the unpardonable insult at Anspach.

In truth, the career of Pitt came to a climax at a time of unexampled decadence of the ancient dynasties. The destinies of the allied Houses of Bourbon rested upon Louis XVI of France and Charles IV of Spain. To the ineptitude of the former the French Revolution was in large measure due. To the weakness and falsity of the latter we may ascribe the desertion of the royalist cause by Spain in 1795-6, with the train of disastrous results in the Mediterranean and the West Indies. In Central Europe Francis of Austria was scarcely more than a tool in the hands of those subtle schemers, Thugut and Cobenzl. The boundless resources of Russia were at the disposal of Paul and Alexander, who, with all their generous impulses, were incapable of steadily applying them to one definite end. Only after weary years of subservience to Napoleon did Alexander develop that firmness of character which finally brought salvation to the Continent. From Frederick William even deeper humiliations failed to evoke any heroic resolve. Among the statesmen of those three monarchies at the time of Pitt there is but one who was a fit compeer to him; and the fates willed that Stein should not control affairs until the year 1807. The age of Pitt was the age of Godoy, Thugut, and Haugwitz — weavers of old-world schemes of partition or barter, and blind to the storm gathering in the West.

The importance of his achievements in curbing their ambitions and saving the smaller States has not received due recognition. He did much to rescue the Dutch Netherlands from anarchy, and Sweden and Turkey from the clutches of powerful neighbours. He failed, indeed, in his diplomatic contest with Catharine; but the duplicity of the Court of Berlin, and the factious opposition of the Whigs, made success impossible; and he had thereafter to look on helplessly at the final Partitions of Poland. Only those who have probed the policy of Russia, Austria, and Prussia in the years 1787-92 can fully realize the difficulties which attended his efforts to frame a solid league against Revolutionary France. As well might one attempt out of rubble to build a cannon-proof rampart.

At home Pitt had to deal with George III. Now, even under a limited monarchy the fortunes of a statesman depend largely on the character of his Sovereign. While possessing the initiative which proffers timely advice, it should be under the control of unfailing tact. Dowered with insight into character and foresight as to the trend of events, the Monarch must, for the most part, subordinate energy to self-repression and the prophetic instinct to the warnings of courtly sagacity. Yet the ideal British ruler must at times assert his will, albeit indirectly, and with the personal charm which ensures the smooth working of this delicately poised machine. He should therefore be the embodiment of all the political virtues. Will even the admirers of George claim that he realized that ideal? However excellent as Elector of Hanover, he was a doubtful blessing as King of Great Britain and Ireland.

In truth, the Hanoverian strain in his nature had not been toned to the degree of fineness needful for the kingly office in these islands. In a time of peculiar difficulty he sought to govern almost absolutely by means which ensured the temporary subservience of Parliament, and in a spirit which brought disruption upon the Empire. The former half of Pitt's career was largely occupied in repairing the financial waste consequent on the American War, or in making good long arrears of legislation. Here, indeed, is his most abiding contribution to the national welfare. But his indebtedness to the King on questions of foreign and domestic policy is rarely apparent. Reform, whether Economical or Parliamentary, encountered the more or less declared opposition of the Sovereign. On the other hand, George showed marked ability in the support of corporate interests and the management of men; so that his relations to Pitt were not unlike those of the Duke of Newcastle to Chatham. The Pitts supplied the brain power while the Monarch or the Duke by the award of favours ensured the needful degree of subservience at the polls or in the lobbies of St. Stephens.

After the " surrender " at the close of the American War, the attitude of George towards his British subjects was one of scarcely concealed scorn. Now and again his feelings burst forth uncontrollably. Shortly before his second attack of lunacy, which occurred near the end of the fortieth year of his reign, he astonished the congregation in church by repeating in loud and emphatic tones the response: " Forty years long was I grieved with this generation and said: ' It is a people that do err in their hearts, for they have not known My ways.' " The tones of the voice betokened the approach of lunacy, but the conviction of the mind was always the same. For the most part, however, scorn was tempered by calculation. His letters to Pitt are full of commendation of the House of Commons when it unquestioningly passed Government Bills or the Supplies; whereas he looked on Fox and Burke as baneful and wearisome talkers, consumers of time, and foes to healthful slumber. Similarly, in his political catechism, the whole duty of Parliament was to help Ministers to govern; while their proper function was to raise the maximum of revenue with the minimum of fuss and change. In short, to maintain the existing social order; to allow no change in a constitution which aroused the wonder or envy of other nations; to use peerages and bishoprics, pocket boroughs and sinecures, as a means of buttressing that fabric, such were the aims of the third George.

Failing materially to weaken the force of this mighty engine of patronage, Pitt was fain to make the best of things as they were. The defeat of his Reform Bill in 1785 was the chief crisis in his early career; for it involved the failure of the Abolition Bill, perhaps also of the schemes for the relief of the poor which he outlined in 1797. In fact, after the year 1785, and still more so after 1790, he had to govern mainly as King's Minister, not as the people's Minister. Worst of all, the centre of political gravity remained dangerously high throughout the storms of the Revolutionary Era. How much of the nation's energy then went forth in justifiable discontent and futile efforts at repression has already appeared. Up to the year 1798 the struggle against France was largely one of the governing class against a nation; and for this the King and the British oligarchy, not Pitt, were responsible. Personal charm and the magnetic gift of evoking enthusiasm have in some monarchs counterbalanced defects of narrowness and intolerance. George was not deficient in courtly grace and tact—witness his remark to Pitt at their first interview after the long separation of the years 1801-1804. When Pitt ventured to compliment the King on his looking better than after the illness of 1801, the latter at once replied: "That is not to be wondered at: I was then on the point of parting with an old friend. Now I am about to regain one." But these gracious remarks came rarely in his closing years, which were marked by increasing harshness to his family, petulance on the most trivial affairs, and an outlook more narrowly personal than ever.

Such a nature chafes its surroundings. It arouses no enthusiasm; it merely begets heat by friction. Pitt has been blamed for spending too much time and energy in speeches about the war. But there was no other way of kindling the nation's zeal. The Princes very rarely spoke in the House of Lords, except under an overmastering fear of the abolition of the Slave Trade. None of the Ministers, except Windham, had the gift of oratory. On Pitt alone devolved the task of arousing a national spirit; and a cruel destiny cut short his life at the very time when his inspiring presence was most needed. How much England then lost can never be known. Vorontzoff, Russian ambassador at London, who had earlier been a bitter enemy of Pitt, now expressed the fervent desire that death had carried off his weary old frame, rather than that of the potential Saviour of Europe. The words are instinct with prescience. The personality and the actions of Pitt were alike a summons to a life of dignity and manly independence. His successors had perforce to take a course not unlike that which they were about to censure in him; and the distrust which the Czar Alexander felt for them in part accounts for the collapse at Tilsit and the ensuing years of bondage to Napoleon.

The disintegrating effects of the party system, or rather of its factious use by the Whig leaders, have been explained in these pages. Its first result was seen in the divergence of the careers of Pitt and Fox. The cause of Reform ought to have received their undivided support; but little by little they were edged apart, and their hostility was perhaps the most lasting of the many evils wrought by the unnatural Coalition of Fox and North. For a time Pitt gathered around him a national party, which became avowedly so on the junction of the Old Whigs in 1794. But in the last years of his life the denuding influences of partisan and personal feuds disastrously thinned his following. From the refusal of George to grant Catholic Emancipation, and the consequent resignation of Pitt in the spring of 1801, we may trace three sinister results. The Union with Ireland was bereft of its natural sequel, Catholic Emancipation; the Ministerial ranks were cleft in twain; and the crisis brought to the front Addington, a man utterly incapable of confronting Napoleon. Had Pitt remained in power, the Peace of Amiens would have been less one-sided, its maintenance more dignified; and the First Consul, who respected the strong but bullied the weak, would probably have acquiesced in a settlement consonant with the reviving prestige of England. But though the Union Jack won notable triumphs in the spring of 1801, yet at London everything went awry. Moved by consideration for the King, then recovering from lunacy, Pitt weakly promised not to bring forward Catholic Emancipation during his life, an act which annoyed the Grenville-Windham group. His rash promise to support Addington tied his hands in the following years; and even after the renewal of war he too scrupulously refrained from overthrowing a Ministry whose weakness had invited foreign aggressions and was powerless to avenge them. Finally, the Grenvilles joined Fox; and thus the King's perversity nullified the efforts of Pitt to form an Administration worthy to cope with Napoleon.

Nevertheless, the challenge flung down to England by the French regicides in 1793 was such as to enhance the person of the Monarch in these islands; and the Revolutionary War, which was fatal to several dynasties on the Continent, served to consolidate the power of the House of Brunswick. For, though Pitt sought to keep the war from becoming a royalist crusade, it almost inevitably assumed that character. During hostilities there can be but two sharply defined parties. Accordingly, Pitt, who opened his career with a bold attack upon the prerogatives of George III, ended it as his champion, even consenting to surrender a cherished conviction in order that the Monarch's peace of mind might not be troubled. Was ever a Minister beset by more baffling problems, by more hampering restrictions? Peace might have solved and shattered them.

But peace he could not secure in the years 1796, 1797; and when finally it came it proved to be no peace, merely a pause before a still greater cycle of war.

The grandeur of Pitt's efforts for ensuring the independence of Europe has somewhat obscured his services as Empire builder. Yet, with the possible exception of Chatham, no statesman has exercised a greater influence on the destinies of the British race. On two occasions he sternly set his face against the cession of Gibraltar; he took keen interest in the settlement of New South Wales; his arrangements for the government of Canada deserve far higher praise than they have usually secured; and his firmness in repelling the archaic claims of Spain to the shores of the Northern Pacific gained for his people the future colony of British Columbia. Cherishing a belief in the pacific nature of Bonaparte's policy at the time of the Treaty of Amiens, he condoned the retrocession of the Cape of Good Hope and of Malta, on condition of the gain of Ceylon and Trinidad; but after the revival of French schemes of aggression in the East he saw the imperative need of planting or maintaining the Union Jack at those commanding points. He, who has been accused of excessive trust in allies, prepared to forego the alliance of Russia rather than give up Malta; and, even before Nelson gained the mastery at sea, Pitt sent forth an expedition to conquer the Cape. In his magnanimous desire of securing to Europe the blessings of a lasting peace he was ready to surrender maritime conquests of greater pecuniary value so long as England held the keys of the overland and sea routes to India. To that empire his just and statesmanlike policy brought a new sense of confidence and therefore a time of comparative rest, until the threatening orientation of Bonaparte's plans once more placed everything at hazard. Thanks to the exertions of Dundas and the Wellesleys, the crisis was averted; but the policy which assured British supremacy in the East was essentially that of Pitt.

It is far easier to assess the importance of the life work of Pitt than to set forth his character in living traits. Those who knew him well agree as the charm of his personality; but they supply few illuminating details, perhaps out of respect for the reserve which was his usual panoply. Like Chatham he rarely revealed his inmost self. The beauties of his conversation, informed with learning, sparkling with wit, always vivacious yet never spiteful, never appeared in their full glow except in the circle of his dearest friends; but by singular ill fortune they who could have handed on those treasures, were satisfied with entries such as: "Pitt talked a great deal among his friends"; or, "In society he was remarkably cheerful and pleasant, full of wit and playfulness";[1] or again, "His great delight was society. There he shone with a degree of calm and steady lustre which often astonished me more than his most splendid efforts in Parliament; . . . he seemed utterly unconscious of his own superiority and much more disposed to listen than to talk; . . . his appearance dispelled all care, his brow was never clouded even in the severest public trials."[2] These are only the *hors d'œuvres* of what must have been a feast of delight; but even they suffice to refute the Whig slanders as to Pitt's austerity and selfishness. Under happier auspices he would have been known as the most lovable of English statesmen; and his exceptional fondness for children would alone suffice to expose the falsity of his alleged reply to a manufacturer who complained that he could not get enough men—"Then you must take the children."[3] Cynicism at the expense of the weak was a trait utterly alien to him. It is also incorrect to assert, with Macaulay, that "pride pervaded the whole man, was written in the harsh rigid lines of his face, was marked by the way in which he walked, in which he sat, in which he stood, and, above all, in which he bowed." The Whig historian, here following the Whig tradition, formed his estimate of the whole man from what was merely a parliamentary mannerism. Pitt, as we have seen, was a prey to shyness and *gaucherie*; and the rigid attitude which he adopted for the House was not so much the outcome of a sense of superiority (though he had an able man's consciousness of worth) as a screen to hide those defects. A curiously stilted manner has been the bane of many gifted orators and actors; but the real test is whether they could throw it off in private. That Pitt threw it off in the circle of his friends they all agree. The only defects which Wilberforce saw in him were an inadequate knowledge of human nature, a too sanguine estimate of men and of the course of events, and, in later years, occasional displays of petulance in

---

[1] "Life of Wilberforce," v, 260; "Private Papers of Wilberforce," 68.
[2] Marquis Wellesley, "Quarterly Rev." (1836).
[3] Michelet, "La Femme," Introd., ch. ii, quoted by Stanhope, iv, 405.

face of opposition.[1] The first are the defects of a noble nature, the last those of a man whose strength has long been overtaxed.

In fact, Pitt's constitution was unequal to the prolonged strain. In childhood his astonishingly precocious powers needed judicious repression. Instead, they were unduly forced by the paternal pride of Chatham. At Cambridge, at Lincoln's Inn, and in Parliament the intellectual pressure was maintained, with the result that his weakly frame was constantly overwrought and attenuated by a too active mind. Further, the pressure at Westminster was so continuous as to preclude all chance of widening his nature by foreign travel. He caught but a glimpse of the life of France in 1783; and his knowledge of other peoples and politics was therefore perforce derived from books. It is therefore surprising that the young Prime Minister displayed the sagacity and tolerance which marked his career.

But his faculties, though not transcendently great, were singularly well balanced, besides being controlled by an indomitable will and tact that rarely was at fault. In oratory he did not equal Sheridan in wit and brilliance, Burke in richness of thought and majesty of diction, or Fox in massive strength and debating facility; but, while falling little short of Fox in debate, he excelled him in elegance and conciseness, Burke in point and common sense, Sheridan in dignity and argumentative power, and all of them in the felicitous wedding of elevated thought or vigorous argument to noble diction. By the side of his serried yet persuasive periods the efforts of Fox seemed ragged, those of Burke philosophic essays, those of Sheridan rhetorical tinsel. And this harmony was not the effect of long and painful training. His maiden speech of 26th February 1781 displayed the grace and forcefulness which marked his classic utterance at the Lord Mayor's banquet ten weeks before his death.

Precocious maturity also characterized his financial plans, which displayed alike the shrewd common sense of those of Walpole and the wider aims of Adam Smith. Before his twenty-sixth year Pitt laid the basis of a system which, whatever its defects, ensured the speedy recovery of national credit and belied the spiteful croakings of foreign rivals. Four days after his death, Fox freely admitted that the establishment of the

[1] "Private Papers of Wilberforce," 67-72.

Sinking Fund had been most beneficial; and this belief, though we now see it to be ill-founded, certainly endowed the nation with courage to continue the struggle against the overgrown power of France. Scarcely less remarkable is his record of legislative achievement. His India Bill of 1784, his attempt to free Anglo-Irish trade from antiquated shackles, his effort to present to Parliament a palatable yet not ineffective scheme of Reform, raise him above the other law-givers of the eighteenth century in the grandeur of his aims if not in his actual achievements. By the India Bill of 1784 he reconciled the almost incompatible claims of eastern autocracy and western democracy. If he failed to carry fiscal and Parliamentary Reform, it was due less to tactical defects on his part than to prejudice and selfishness among those whom he sought to benefit.

On the other hand, his intense hopefulness often led him to overlook obstacles and to credit all men with his own high standard of intelligence and probity, a noble defect which not seldom marred his diplomatic and military arrangements during the Great War. At no point have I slurred over his mistakes, his diffusion of effort over too large an area of conflict, and his perhaps undue trust in doubtful allies. But, even so, as I have shown, a careful examination of all the available evidence generally reveals the reasons for his confidence; and failures due to this cause are far less disastrous, because less dispiriting to the nation, than those which are the outcome of sluggishness or cowardice. Of those unpardonable sins Pitt has never been accused even by his severest critics. After the repulse of his pacific overtures by the French Directory in September 1797 his attitude was one almost of defiance, witness his curt rejection of similar offers by Bonaparte early in 1800, which may be pronounced the gravest defect of his diplomatic career.

In that age the action of statesmen was often dilatory; and we must admit that in regard to the Act of Union with Ireland Pitt's procedure was halting and ineffective, so that finally he was driven to use corrupt means to force through the corrupt Irish Parliament a measure which in the autumn of 1798 would have been accepted thankfully by the dominant caste. His Bill of 1797 for the relief of the poor and his Land Tax Commutation Act of 1798 are examples of improvident legislation. But from a leader overburdened with the details of war and diplomacy we should not expect the keen foresight, the minute

care as to details, which distinguished Gladstone. To compare
the achievements of a statesman hard pressed by the problems
of the Revolutionary Era with those of a peaceful age when the
standard of legislative effort had been greatly raised is unfair;
and the criticism of Pitt by a distinguished historian evinces
partiality towards the Victorian statesman rather than an adequate appreciation of the difficulties besetting a Minister of
George III in those times of turmoil.[1] It is true that Pitt did
not inaugurate Factory legislation; that was the work of the
Addington Cabinet in 1802; he did not link his name with the
efforts of Romilly and others for the reform of the brutal Penal
Code; and he did little for art and literature; but neither the
personality of George nor the state of the national finances
favoured the rise of a Maecenas.

Concentration of effort on political and diplomatic questions
was the alpha and omega of Pitt's creed. The terrible pressure
of events forbade his looking far ahead or far afield; he marched
straight onward, hoping by his untiring efforts first to restore
national prosperity and thereafter to secure a peace which would
inaugurate a brighter future. His overtaxed strength collapsed
when the strain was most tense; and his life therefore figures as
a torso, which should not be criticized as if it were the perfect
statue. Yet, as moral grandeur is always inspiring, Pitt's efforts
were finally to be crowned with success by the statesmen who
had found wisdom in his teaching, inspiration in his quench-
less hope, enthusiasm in his all-absorbing love of country. An
egoist never founds a school of the prophets. But Pitt, who

Spurn'd at the sordid lust of pelf
And served his Albion for herself,

trained and inspired a band of devoted disciples such as no
other leader of the eighteenth century left behind him. Some
were unimaginative plodders, as Perceval; others were capable
administrators and shrewd diplomatists, as Castlereagh; to one
alone was vouchsafed the fire of genius, the sympathetic insight, the soaring ambition held in check by overmastering
patriotism, which were commingled in the personality of the
master; and Canning afterwards declared that he buried his
political allegiance in the grave of Pitt. It was granted to these

[1] Lord Acton, " Letters to Mary Gladstone," 45, 46, 56.

men to labour on in the cause for which he gave his life, and finally, in the years 1814-15, to bring back France to her old frontiers by arrangements which he clearly outlined in the years 1798 and 1805. Of the numerous annexations and changes of boundaries effected by Napoleon, only one, the Valtelline, was destined to survive. But Europe after Waterloo testified alike to the sagacity and the limitations of the mind of William Pitt.

STATISTICS OF THE YEARS 1792—1801

N.B.—The figures under the heading "money borrowed" are taken from the official statistics presented by the Rt. Hon. George Rose, "Brief Examination into the Increase of the Revenue, Commerce and Navigation of Great Britain" (London, 1806), p. 16. The total statistics are given in round numbers.

YEAR.	PERMANENT TAXES.	IMPORTS.	EXPORTS.	NAVY.	ARMY.	MONEY BORROWED.
1792	14,284,000	19,659,000	24,465,000	1,985,000	1,819,000	—
1793	13,941,000	19,256,000	19,676,000	3,971,000	3,993,000	4,500,000
1794	13,858,000	22,288,000	25,111,000	5,525,000	6,641,000	12,907,000
1795	13,557,000	22,736,000	25,036,000	6,315,000	11,610,000	19,490,000
1796	14,292,000	23,187,000	28,025,000	11,883,000	14,911,000	29,726,000
1797	13,332,000	21,013,000	26,315,000	13,033,000	15,488,000	44,029,000
1798	14,275,000	27,857,000	30,289,000	13,449,000	12,852,000	15,000,000
1799	15,727,000	26,837,000	33,640,000	13,642,000	11,840,000	15,500,000
1800	14,238,000	30,570,000	38,119,000	13,619,000	11,941,000	18,500,000
1801	14,641,000	32,795,000	37,786,000	15,857,000	12,117,000	25,500,000

INDEX

ABBOT, Charles (afterwards Lord Colchester), 298, 306 *n.*, 330 *n.*, 346; Speaker, 520.

Abercorn, Lord, 402.

Abercromby, Sir Ralph, 216; Commander-in-Chief in the West Indies, 226, 239, 240, 241, 246; in Ireland, 352-354; resigns, 354, 363; campaign in Holland, 381, 382; in Egypt, 387; his death, 240.

Aboukir Bay, 367-369.

"Accurate Observer," the, 466.

Acton, General, 150 *n.*

Acton, Lord, on Pitt and the execution of Louis XVI, refuted, 94 *n.*; 569.

Adair, Robert, 337 *n.*

Adams, W. D., Pitt's secretary, 531.

Addington, Henry (afterwards Viscount Sidmouth), Speaker, 180, 255, 302, 368, 436 *n.*; suggests the Patriotic Contribution, 331; at the duel between Pitt and Tierney, 334, 335; Pitt at his house, 435; tries to dissuade Pitt from Catholic Emancipation, 437; urged by the King to form a Ministry, 437; Prime Minister, 439, 445-448, 450, 451, 468, 469, 487, 488; Pitt supports him, 471, 472, 478, 479, 488, 496, 503, 504; visits Pitt at Walmer, 473, 477; his finance, 480-482; failure of his negotiations with Pitt, 483-487; plans for his overthrow, 495-499; resigns, 499; opposes abolition of the Slave Trade, 502; union with Pitt, 517; created Viscount Sidmouth, 517; Lord President, 517, 520-522; resigns, 530.

Addington, Hiley, 530.

Agriculture, Board of, instituted, 165, 293.

Agriculture, flourishing state of, 291; influence of enclosures on, 291, 292.

Alava, General, 524.

Alcudia, Duke of. *See* Godoy.

Alexander I, Czar, 487, 508, 515; his instructions to Novossiltzoff, 522, 525; his terms of alliance, 525-527; his designs on Malta, 527; at Berlin, 537; treaty of Potsdam, 539; battle of Austerlitz, 544, 560.

Aliens' Bill (1792), 94; its withdrawal demanded by France, 101, 103; renewal of (1798), 333.

Alkmaar, Convention of, 382.

All the Talents, Administration of, 496.

Alsace, 46, 53, 122, 129, 142, 197, 199, 200.

Alvanley, Lord. *See* Arden, Richard Pepper.

Amherst, Lord, Commander-in-Chief, 270.

Amiens, Treaty of, 248, 470, 472, 477, 564, 565.

Anckarström, Johann Jakob, assassinates Gustavus III, 46.

Anspach, Principality of, overrun by Napoleon, 534, 537, 560.

"Anti-Jacobin," the, 327, 336, 337, 464.

"Anti-Levelling Society," the, 68.

Antwerp, trade of, strangled by the Dutch, 72; reduction of the citadel, 76; proposed fortification of, 83; conference at (1793), 132.

Aranda, Count of, Spanish Minister, 46.

Arcola, battle of, 321.

Arden, Sir Richard Pepper (Lord Alvanley), Master of the Rolls, 34, 476; on Irish affairs, 341.

"Argus," the, 66; in the pay of the French Embassy, 66 *n.*

Armed Neutrality League, 290; collapse of, 468, 478.

Army, the, debate on the Estimates, 29, 30; state of 1793, 124, 266, 267; Pitt's measures for increasing, 278-280, 305; disaffection in, 318, 319.

Army of Reserve Act, 499, 509, 510.

Artois, Comte d' (afterwards Charles X), 2, 3, 5, 6; and the Quiberon Expedition, 259, 261-263, 287; retires to Holyrood, 263; dines with Pitt and Grenville, 377.

Assaye, battle of, 463, 505.

Assignats, royalist, manufacture of, 261.

"Associated Friends of the Constitution," the, at Glasgow, 173, 174.

Auckland, Lord (William Eden), Ambassador at The Hague, 38, 51, 68, 69, 71 *n.*, 72-74, 76, 82, 97, 99, 107, 109, 111, 126, 189; Pitt's intimacy with his daughter, 299-303; Postmaster-General, 303, 330, 331, 342, 355, 356, 394-396, 415, 421, 434; his reported intrigues, 443, 445; rupture with Pitt, 452; his "inquisitiveness," 479, 480 *n.*; 559, 560.

Augereau, P. F. C., Duc de Castiglione, 324.

Austerlitz, battle of, 536, 544, 560; reception of the news of in England, 548, 549.

Austria, alliance with Prussia (1791), 5, 43; war with France, 23, 46; her share in the partition of Poland, 53, 122; evacuates Brussels, 74; end of estrangement with England, 84; her aims in the war, 122, 123, 129; alliance with England (1793), 123, 143, 147; fails to send reinforcements to Toulon, 152, 153, 157, 158, 161, 268; disputes with Prussia, 200-202; evacuation of the Netherlands, 209, 211, 212; treaty with Russia and England (1795), 235; receives financial aid from England, 304; her struggle with Napoleon, 304, 321, 322; treaty of Campo Formio (1797), 327, 365; appeals to England, 366; schemes for expansion in Italy, 371, 378; declares War against France (1799), 374; negotiations with England (1799), 383; her defeats at Marengo, 386, 387, Ulm, 534, 542, and Austerlitz, 544, 552, 560. *See* Francis II.

Avignon, annexed by France, 220, 276.

Aylesbury, county meeting at, 188.

Baillie, Dr., 554.

Baird, Sir David, his expedition to the Cape, 532, 539.

Bank of England, crisis in 1797, 304, 308, 309.

Bankes, Sir Henry, 290, 428, 454, 520.

Bantry Bay, expedition to, 277, 308, 346.

Barère de Vieuzac, Bertrand, 83, 167.

Barham, Lord (Sir Charles Middleton), Pitt visits him at Teston, 479; appointed First Lord of the Admiralty, 521, 522, 532, 550, 551; created Lord Barham, 522.

Baring, Sir Francis, on the Cape, 251.

Barlow, Joel, 66, 70, 115, 172.

Barnard, Lady Anne, her "South Africa a Century Ago," 254.

Barras, Paul François Nicolas, Comte de, 263, 325, 328; promises help to Ireland, 348, 363.

Barrington, Sir Jonah, 411, 412.

Barthélemy, Francois, Marquis de, French envoy in Switzerland, 105, 217, 233, 236, 346.

Basle, Treaties of (1795), 217, 233, 236, 237.

Bassano, Duc de. *See* Maret.

Bath, French refugees in, 165; Pitt's stay at, 479, 547-553.

Bathurst, Bragge, 517, 518.

Bathurst, Lord, 476, 549, 550.

Bavaria, Electorate of, proposal for exchange, 122, 123, 129, 210.

Beaufoy, Henry, M.P., 10, 11.

Bedford, Duke of, 312.

Belfast, French sympathies in, 71, 78; sedition in, 181.

Belgic Provinces, French designs on, 47, 48; French conquest of, 69, 79; demand independence, 83; annexed by France, 111, 121; Austrian proposal for exchange, 122, 129, 210; reconquered, 126; Austrian evacuation of, 208-212; plans for, 371.

Belmore, Lord, 402.

Benoît, Pierre Victor, 60.

Beresford, John, Irish Chief Commissioner of the Revenue, 340, 346, 355, 356, 418, 419, 420, 424; Lord Fitzwilliam and, 341, 342; on the Irish Rebellion, 394, 395; on the Union, 401-404, 410.

Berg, Duchy of, 46.

Bergen-op-Zoom, 126, 213, failure of attack on, 382.

Bethencourt, battle of, 208.

Binns, John, 283, 286, 349, 350.

Birmingham, riots in (1791), 10, 17-19; malcontents in, 186; the "Loyal True Blues," 188, 189; riots in (1795), 287, 288.

Biron, Duc de, his mission to London, 42, 43; arrested for debt, 43.

Bischoffswerder, Baron von, Prussian Minister, 2, 5, 203.

Blankett, Commodore, expedition to the Cape, 251.

Boissy d'Anglas, François Antoine de 233.

Bolton, Lord. See Orde, Thomas.

Bonaparte, Joseph, 506, 526.

Bonaparte, Napoleon. See Napoleon.

Bond, 530.

Bone, John, 318.

Bonham, arrested, 350.

Bonney, arrested, 190; discharged, 193.

Booth, his evidence against Thomas Walker, 185.

Boyd, Sir R., 158.

Boyd, Walter, 325, 326.

Brabant. See Belgic Provinces.

Breda, captured by Dumouriez, 126.

Brest, naval preparations at, 349, 418, 420, 421; proposed attack on, 383, 386.

Bridport, Lord (Alexander Hood), 261; and the mutiny at the Nore, 311-313; blockades Brest, 420, 421.

Brissot, Jacques Pierre, 107, 223 n., 248.

British Columbia, 565.

British Convention, meets at Edinburgh, 181, 182, 184.

Brook, John, attorney and Mayor of Birmingham, 18, 186.

Brooks's Club, 20.

Brown, Matthew C., of Sheffield, 181, 182.

Brown, Colonel, 512.

Bruix, Admiral, 381 n., 420, 430.

Brunswick, Charles, Duke of, 46; his manifesto, 52, 57; his retreat through the Argonne, 62; campaign on the Rhine, 142, 200, 201; superseded, 201; opposed to continuation of the war, 207; refuses to take command in Holland, 214-216, 274.

Brunswick, Duchess of, 214, 215, 216.

Brunswick-Oels, Frederick, Duke of, 121.

Brussels, evacuated by the Austrians, 74.

Buccleugh, Duke of, 476.

Buckingham, Marquis of (George Grenville, Earl Temple), 19, 62, 158, 240, 336; on the state of Ireland, 395, 396, 412; on Lord Loughborough, 432.

Buckinghamshire, Earl of (Lord Hobart), 462, 487, 494, 495; Chancellor of the Duchy, 517, 521; resigns, 530.

Buckner, Vice-Admiral, 314.

Burdett, Sir Francis, 332.

Burges, Bland, 51, 64, 86, 259.

Burgh, Dr., 472.

Burgoing, special envoy to Madrid, 233, 235.

Burgoyne, General, 30.

Burke, Edmund, interview with Pitt and Grenville, 7, 8; fears the spread of French principles, 9, 10, 61; on Reform, 12, 24; Paine's reply to his "Reflections," 15, 16; other replies, 16; his "Appeal from the New to the Old Whigs," 16; his "Reflections," 19, 20, 70 n.; letter to Grenville after the September massacres, 60, 61; on the Treasury Bench, 89; declares the death of Louis inevitable, 91, 92; his speech on the Aliens Bill, 64, 94; his view of the war, 119, 120, 136, 137, 259, 275, 321; on the Traitorous Correspondence Bill, 164; proposes Coalition Ministry (1794), 191; his Economy Bill, 467; as an orator, compared with Pitt, 567; his death, 326.

Burke, Richard, at Coblentz, 7.

Burney, Fanny, 64.

Burton Pynsent, expenses of, 476.

Butler, Simon, 180, 181.

Bute, Earl of, sent to Madrid, 233, 235-237, 242-244.

Buzot, F. L. Nicolas, 62.

Cadusey, de, 220.

Calder, Admiral, 532, 536.

Caldiero, battle of, 321.

Calonne, Charles Alexandre de, his mission to England, 3, 5.

Calvi, capture of, 256.

Camage, W., of Sheffield, arrested, 186, 191.

Cambacérès, J. J. Régis de, 233.

Camden, Charles Pratt, 1st Earl, 33, 44.

Camden, John Jeffreys Pratt, 2nd Earl (afterwards Marquis), Lord Lieutenant of Ireland, 342-348, 352-364, 391, 392, 393, 395, 402, 406, 409, 422; his friend-

Camden, Earl—*continued.*
 ship with Pitt, 475, 476, 481, 491;
 Secretary at War, etc., 501, 507, 514;
 President of the Council, 530, 557.
Camelford, Lord (Thomas Pitt), 37; on
 Pitt's duel with Tierney, 336.
Campbell, Thomas, at the trial of Ger-
 rald, 183.
Camperdown, battle of, 328, 347.
Campo Formio, Treaty of, 327, 328, 365.
Canada, Upper, establishment of Government of, 31.
Canning, George, 39; his interview with
 Pitt, 40, 41; the "Anti-Jacobin," 327,
 336, 337, 464; on conditions of peace
 with France, 383, 384; resigns the
 Under-Secretaryship, 376, 421; strongly
 supports the Union, 421, 422; on
 Catholic Emancipation, 442; resigns
 office (1801), 451, 465; on Pitt's generosity, 457; his relations with Pitt, 459,
 464-466, 567; his marriage, 464; opposed
 to peace (1801), 469, 470; on Pitt's
 position, 471; his poems, 474, 518;
 urges Pitt to action, 481, 482; Treasurer
 of the Navy, 501; falls out with Hawkesbury, 518; defends Melville, 520; his
 sympathy with Spanish patriots, 524;
 disapproves of the expedition to Hanover, 542, 547; anxious for Pitt's health,
 547; with Pitt at Bath, 549, 550, 553;
 mentioned, 286, 325, 375, 390, 450,
 488.
Canterbury, Archbishop of. *See* Moore,
 John, and Sutton, Charles Manners.
Cape of Good Hope, the, 216, 250; British
 conquest of, 251-255, 274, 276, 323, 325,
 371, 469, 470, 478, 480, 565; Baird's
 expedition to, 532, 539.
Cape Town, capture of, 252-254; population of, 253.
Carew, 294.
Carles, John, of Birmingham, 18, 186.
Carlisle, Earl of, 322, 350; on Irish affairs,
 391, 392, 394.
Carlyle, Thomas, on the September mas-
 sacres, 61.
Carmarthen, Marquis of. *See* Leeds,
 Duke of.
Carnot, L. N. M., French general and
 Minister of War, 125, 135, 138, 141,
 208, 212, 217, 266, 272, 279, 280.

Caroline, Princess, of Brunswick, 214,
 216; as Princess of Wales, 508.
Carrington, Lord, 330, 476, 489, 557.
Carteaux, Jean Francois, 145.
Cartwright, Major John, 23; his "Com-
 monwealth in Danger," 280.
Carver, Edward, of Birmingham, 189.
Carysfort, Lord, 412, 495.
Castiglione, battle of, 243.
"Castlebar Races," the, 362.
Castlereagh, Viscount, 370, 569; account
 of, 398, 399; Irish Chief Secretary,
 399, 402, 408, 410-412, 416, 423-425,
 435-437, 441, 446, 449, 486; resigns,
 440; President of the India Board, 501;
 defends Melville, 520; Minister at War,
 530; letters to Pitt, 531, 532, 549-551;
 interview with Pitt at Bath, 551, 552; at
 Putney, 555.
Catalonia, French invasion of, 197; Republican rising in, 231, 233, 234.
Catharine II, Czarina, 4, 6, 7, 231; her
 designs on Poland, 9, 46, 122; encourages Polish malcontents, 52; invades
 Poland, 53, 54; her success, 55; offers
 alliance to England, 99; treaty with
 England and Austria (1795), 235; her
 death, 258, 321.
Cathelineau, Jacques, 136.
Catholic Emancipation, question of, 396-
 401, 414, 418, 426, 428, 431, 433, 452,
 486, 487; opposed by the King, 433-
 439; division in the Cabinet on,
 443-445; motion for, rejected, 518,
 519.
Catholics, the, in Ireland, 390, 395-401;
 in favour of the Union, 412, 417-419;
 courted by Cornwallis, 422, 423; question of promises made to them, 441-446.
Cazalès, Jacques Antoine Marie de, 43.
Ceylon, 323, 325, 371, 468-470, 565.
Chalk Farm, mass meeting at, 188, 193.
Chandermagore, 198.
Charette, François, 261-263.
Charlemont, Lord, 408.
Charleroi, surrender of, 209, 210.
Charles, Archduke of Austria, 126, 205,
 206, 377, 378.
Charles IV, of Spain, appeals to France
 on behalf of Louis, 93; his weakness
 and extravagance, 197, 230, 231, 513,
 560; his policy, 231, 233.

Charles X, 2.

Charles Emmanuel IV, King of Sardinia (1796-8), his abdication, 373, 378.

Charles Theodore, Elector of Bavaria, 122, 123.

Charlotte, Queen, her relations with the King, 506, 507.

Charmilly, de, delegate from Hayti, 220, 227, 229, 239.

Chatham, John Pitt, Earl of, First Lord of the Admiralty, 68, 125, 145, 268; his incompetence, 137, 140, 215; made Lord Privy Seal, 216, 273, 299; borrows money of Pitt, 302, 303, 476; engaged in Holland, 382; Lord President, 440, 446; letter to Pitt on his resignation, 440; Master of the Ordnance, 501, 557.

Chatham, William Pitt, 1st Lord, and Pitt compared, 320, 474, 490, 562, 565.

Chatham, Lady, 68.

Chatham, Dowager Lady, Pitt's mother, 299, 302, 476; her death, 488, 490.

Chaumont, Treaty of (1814), 523.

Chauvelin, Marquis de, French Ambassador in London, 48, 84; his cold reception, 49, 50; account of, 59, 60; tries to stir up discontent, 69; interview with Grenville, 78, 79; piqued at Pitt's interview with Maret, 80, 82, 116, 117; refused official recognition, 84, 98, 101, 115; conversation with Sheridan, 87; Lebrun's instructions to, 96; note to Grenville, 97, 98; protests against the Aliens Bill, 101, 103; interview with Grenville, 104, 105; ordered to leave England, 108-111, 117; his responsibility for the war, 115-117.

China, British embassy to, 32.

Chouans, the, 260-264, 284, 326.

Christie, William, his "Catechism of the French Constitution," 22; 175.

"Church and King Club," 13, 185.

Churchill, Charles, on Lord Loughborough, 432.

Cinque Ports Volunteers, Pitt and the, 474, 477, 488-490.

Cisalpine Republic, the, 470.

Clare, Earl of (Baron Fitzgibbon), Lord Chancellor of Ireland, 340, 342, 393, 406, 410; interviews with Pitt, 397-400; opposes Catholic Emancipation, 437.

Clarence, Duke of, 31.

Clarke, Major-General Alured, his expedition to the Cape, 251, 253.

Clarke, General, agrees to send a French expedition to Ireland, 345, 346.

Clarkson, Thomas, 502.

Clavière, Etienne, French Minister of Finance, 45, 58.

Clerfait, Field-Marshal, 209, 213-215.

Clifden, Lord, 346, 402.

Clubs, political, growth of, 12, 13, 16, 21-23; their aims, 25, 26; accused of foreign connections, 51; their rejoicings at the Revolution, 61; addresses to French National Convention, 65-67, 70, 71, 73, 76, 77, 86, 114, 115, 164, 172; growth of, in 1793, 167; their organization, 168, 169. See Chap. VII.

Coalition, the First, 123, 125, 132; weakness of, 195, 196, 278; the Second, see Chap. XVII; the Third, 529, 534 et seq.

Cobenzl, Count Ludwig, 373, 375.

Cobenzl, Count Philip, Austrian Chancellor, 75, 120 n., 560; his fall, 129.

Coblentz, Royalist leaders at, 2, 3, 20.

Coburg, Duke of, his campaign in Flanders, 121, 126, 127, 130-133, 138-141, 205, 206, 209, 210, 267.

Cochrane, Admiral, 514.

Cockburn, Lord, on the Scots, 173.

Coke of Norfolk, 188, 294.

Colchester, Lord. See Abbot, Charles.

Colpoys, Vice-Admiral, 311, 312.

Condé, captured by the Allies, 134, 136; surrendered, 210.

Conolly, Captain, 159.

Conscription, in France, 266.

Consols, great rise in (1783-1792), 31; rise in (1796), 305; fall after the Nore mutiny, 315.

Constitutional Information, London Society for, 12 n., 21, 22, 65, 66, 70, 167, 181, 184, 190.

Cooke, Edward, his letters to Auckland and Castlereagh on the Irish question, 355, 356, 362 n., 395, 396, 404, 405, 418-420, 422, 424, 425, 435-437; his pamphlet on the Union, 405, 408; his conduct during the debate on the Union, 412.

Coote, General, 379.

Copenhagen, battle of, 388, 450.

Cork, despatch of troops from, 146, 152 n., 153; sentiments of the Grand Jury on the Union, 416, 417.

Corn Laws, 288, 289.

Cornwall, representation of, 173.

Cornwallis, Admiral, 514, 532.

Cornwallis, Marquis, suggested as Commander-in-Chief in Flanders, 205, 214, 272; Master-General of the Ordnance, 273; Lord-Lieutenant of Ireland, 359, 362, 363, 389, 391-412, 417, 418, 421-426, 435, 436, 441, 443, 449; resigns, 440; Viceroy of India, 463; negotiates the Treaty of Amiens, 470, 477.

Corporation Act, the, efforts to repeal, 10, 11.

Corresponding Society for Reform of Parliamentary Representation, 21, 26, 65, 66, 167, 168, 184, 186-190, 193; monster meeting at Islington, 283, 286; supposed connection with the mutiny at the Nore, 316-318; becomes a revolutionary body, 349, 350; its papers seized, 351.

Corsica, 143, 144, 150 n., 155, 156, 158, 210, 228, 232, 233, 235, 244, 267; British occupation of, 255-257, 269; evacuated, 258, 275.

County Reform Associations, the, 23.

"Courier," the, 67.

Courtenay, John, M.P., 238.

Couthon, Georges, 134, 135.

Coutts, Thomas, 306 n., 308 n., 475-477.

Cowper, W., his pension, 455 n., 456.

Craig, Major-General Sir James, in command at the Cape, 251-254; his expedition to Malta, 368, 524, 525; Mornington's opinion of, 461.

Crancé, Dubois, 266.

Craufurd, Major-General Robert, 510.

Creevey, Thomas, 497, 521.

Crossfield, Secretary of the London Corresponding Society, 349.

Cumberland, Duke of, 448.

Curragh, affair on the, 357, 358.

Curt, delegate from Guadeloupe, 221.

Custine, General, Comte de, 73, 85, 121, 133.

Czartoryski, Prince, 522, 526.

Daer, Lord, 174.

Dalrymple, Colonel William, 173, 174.

Daly, Denis, 341.

Danton, George Jacques, Minister of Justice, 58; his alleged offer to save Louis, 94 n.; his decree annexing Belgium, 111, 112, 116, 121.

D'Arçon, 135.

Davison, Richard, of Sheffield, 189, 191, 193.

De Clifford, Lord, 420, 422.

Delacroix, Jacques Vincent, French Foreign Minister, 322.

Del Campo, Marquis, 233.

Delessart, A. de Valdec, French Foreign Minister, 43, 44; arrested, 45.

Demerara, Dutch, 241.

Democracy, new birth of, 23; progress of, 62-68; opposition to, 68.

Derby, Society for Constitutional Information at, 70.

Despard, Colonel, arrested, 350.

"Devil's Own," the, 489.

Devonshire, Duke of, 402, 497.

Devonshire, Duchess of, 497.

Dibdin, Charles, 337.

Dillon, General Theobald, murdered by his troops, 49.

Dissenters. See Nonconformists.

Dominica, revolt in, 239.

Don, General, 542, 545.

Donegal, Lord, 420, 422.

Dover Loyal Association, address to Pitt, 86.

Downes, Sir William, 395.

Downshire, Lord, 398; his opposition to the Union, 402, 418, 420, 422-424.

Doyle, General, expedition to la Vendée, 237, 262, 263.

Drake, Francis, British agent at Genoa, 155.

Drane, Mr., Mayor of Reading, 180.

Duckworth, Sir James, 532 n.

Duff, General, 357, 358.

Dumouriez, General, French Foreign Minister, 45, 46, 72; his "Reflections on Negotiations with England," 47, 48; appeals to England to prevent war with Prussia, 51; his resignation, 59; Campaign in the Low Countries, 69, 73, 74, 76, 80, 82, 83, 85, 106, 107, 267; his proposed mission to London, 109-111, 118; his self-confidence, 117; correspondence with Pache, 121; failure of his campaign in Belgium, 121, 126; his treason, 126, 131-132; Memoir on the defence of England, 509.

Duncan, Admiral Lord, 315, 328, 336, 347.

Duncombe, C. S., M.P., 12.

Dundas, Major-General Sir David, at Toulon, 157, 159, 160; in Corsica, 256, 257; his scheme of coast defence, 277, 287; and the Volunteers, 491, 492, 512.

Dundas, Henry (afterwards Lord Melville), Home Secretary, 34, 35, 63, 64, 89, 186, 190; opposes repeal of the Test Act in Scotland, 14; puts down the Birmingham riots, 18, 79; on the proclamation against seditious writings, 25; anxious for union with the Old Whigs, 36, 38; friendly to France, 44; on sedition in Scotland, 77; his scheme for rearranging the Cabinet, 124, 125; his many offices, 124, 125, 270, 271; his conduct of the war, 125, 137, 140, 147, 157, 158; ignorant of military affairs, 128; his influence in Scotland, 173, 409; and the Scottish prosecutions, 176, 178-180, 182, 184; burnt in effigy at Dundee, 177; Secretary of State for War, 191, 205, 210, 213, 216, 221, 224, 225, 238-240, 241, 243, 245-248, 257, 260, 267, 268, 325, 326, 331, 362, 363, 381, 384, 386; President of the India Board, 251, 254; letter to Pitt on the idea of a War Minister, 271, 272; his friendship with Pitt, 299, 454, 476; urges the Egyptian expedition, 387, 388; his conversations with the King on Catholic Emancipation, 433, 436, 444, 449; resigns, 440; on Pitt's resignation, 440, 441, 450; created Lord Melville, 483; his mission to Pitt at Walmer, 483, 484; on the Volunteers, 494; on the King's illness, 497; First Lord of the Admiralty, 501, 511, 514; his impeachment, 519-521; acquitted, 521; on India, 565.

Dundas, General Ralph, 357, 358, 361.

Dundas, Robert, Lord Advocate for Scotland, 14, 174, 176, 178, 179, 182-184.

Dundas, William, Secretary at War, 501.

Dundee, political agitation in, 77, 173, 174, 177, 178.

Dungannon, Ulster Volunteers in, 78.

Dunkirk, siege of, 127, 130, 131, 138-141, 147, 267; Napoleon at, 349.

Dunlop, John, Lord Provost of Glasgow, 175 n., 178.

Duroc, General, Duc de Frioul, his mission to Berlin, 535, 537.

Dutch, the, their rights over the Scheldt, 71, 72; their apathy, 213, 216, 274; at the Cape, 250-255; defeated at battle of Camperdown, 328, 347.

Dutch East India Company, 250, 252.

Dutch Republic, the, 47; treaty with England (1788), 72; threatened by France, 73-76, 80, 82, 84, 107; English assurances to, 74, 114; plots of the "Patriots," 74, 75; appeals to England for help, 77; unprepared for war, 98, 107; France declares war on, 112; French conquest of, 213-216, 250; peace with Spain, 236; alliance with France (1795), 251, 261, 274; Anglo-Russian expedition to, 379-383; remodelled by Bonaparte, 470; proposal to offer it to Prussia, 552.

East India Company, renewal of Charter, 165.

Eaton, Daniel Isaac, prosecution of, 184.

Eden, Eleanor, Pitt's relations with, 300-303, 465, 491; her marriage, 462 n.

Eden, Morton, Ambassador at Vienna, 129, 161, 199, 200, 202-204, 235, 331, 380.

Edge, Captain, 160.

Edinburgh, Conventions of Friends of the People at, 174, 179, 180; Radical club at, 178; British Convention at, 181, 182.

Egypt, Napoleon's expedition to, 255, 277 n., 278, 327, 328, 368, 377; English expedition to, 387, 388; surrender of French garrisons in, 468; to be restored to the Sultan, 468.

Ehrenthal, Swedish envoy at Madrid, 242.

El Arish, Convention of, 387.

Elba, evacuation of, 258, 275.

Eldon, Lord (Sir John Scott), 34, 35, 499, 501, 506, 514.

Eliot, Edward J., his death, 325.

Eliot, Sir Gilbert. See Minto, Earl of.

Elliot, William, Irish Under-Secretary at War, 400.

Elphinstone, Rear-Admiral Sir Keith, his expedition to the Cape, 251, 252, 254.

Ely, Lord, 393, 402.
Emmett, Addis, 394.
Enclosures, 166, 288, 291-298.
Enghien, Duc d', execution of, 516.
England, discontent in (1793), 165-167; (1795), *see* Chap. XIII; (1798), 333; fears of invasion, 277; national defence, 278-281; shortage of corn, 288-291; state of agriculture, 291; policy of enclosures, 291-298; financial crisis (1797), 304, 308, 309; increasing prosperity, 330; public opinion in (1798), 338.
" English Chronicle," the, 66, 67.
Enniskillen, Lord, 408.
Epsom, county meeting at, 188.
Erskine, Thomas, Baron, 23, 24, 89, 172, 176, 192, 488.
Euston, Lord, 412.
Evans, Thomas, Secretary of the London Corresponding Society, 349, 350; arrested, 350.

Famars evacuated by the French, 133, 134.
Farquhar, Sir Walter, 548, 553, 554, 557.
Federalism, advocated by Fox, 413.
Fellows, Henry, 318.
Ferdinand IV, King of Naples, 199, 231, 365, 366.
Ferrol, expedition to (1800), 386.
Fersen, Count, 4, 49.
Fingall, Lord, 393, 442, 449, 518, 519.
Finisterre, Cape, battle off, 532, 536.
Fitzgerald, Lord Edward, 23, 345, 346; his capture and death, 354, 355.
Fitzgerald, Pamela, 79, 345.
Fitzgibbon, Baron, *See* Clare, Earl of.
Fitzharris, Lord, 520.
Fitzwilliam, Earl, Viceroy of Ireland, 213, 339-342, 392, 432, 433, 452, 500.
Fleurus, battle of, 209, 210, 267, 270.
Flood, Henry, M.P., his motion for Reform, 11, 12.
Floridablanca, Count, his fall, 46.
Forbes, Major-General, Commander-in-Chief in Hayti, 240, 245.
Ford, Captain, 513.
Fortiquerri, Marshal, 150 *n*.
Foster, John (afterwards Baron Oriel), Irish Speaker, 393, 398; interview with Pitt, 400, 401; his opposition to the Union, 414, 418-420.

Foster, son of the Speaker, 412.
Fouché, Joseph, Duke of Otranto, 528, 529.
Fox, Charles James, gains ground with Nonconformists, 11, 12; on the Army Estimates (1792), 30; his Libel Bill, 33; opposes proclamations against seditious writings, 36; suggested coalition with Pitt, 36, 37; unpatriotic speeches, 87-89, 91, 278, 333; intimate with the French embassy, 89; opposes the Aliens Bill, 94; disapproves of the Radical Clubs, 168; opposes erection of barracks, 169; on the Scottish prosecutions, 179; in favour of peace, 198, 276, 277; on slaves in Jamaica, 238; on the massacre of royalists at Quiberon, 262; on the Treasonable Practices Bill, 285, 286; on the Bank crisis (1797), 308, 309; and the mutinies in the fleet, 312, 313, 316; his " secession," 316, 330; on the Finance Bills of 1797-8, 330, 370; his name removed from the Privy Council, 333; and Arthur O'Connor, 350; his views on the Union and Federalism, 413; on Pitt's resignation, 445; intrigues with the Prince of Wales, 449, 497; on the peace proposals, 470; on the war (1803), 488; on the Volunteers, 494; alliance with Grenville, 496; attack on Addington, 499; the King objects to his inclusion in Pitt's ministry, 499, 500; supports abolition of the Slave Trade, 502; his motion of Catholic Emancipation, 518, 519; opposes Pitt's burial in the Abbey, 559; as an orator, compared with Pitt, 567; mentioned, 24, 156, 165, 188, 191, 283, 293, 506, 517, 518, 555, 557, 562, 563.
France, the flight to Varennes, 1, 2, 4, 40; change of ministry, 45; declares war against Austria, 23, 46; first signs of friction with England, 50; the September massacres, 57, 59-62; addresses of English clubs to the Convention, 65, *et seq.*; trial of the King decreed, 74, 85; conquest of Belgium, 66, 69, 75, 83; the November decrees, 71, 72, 75, 76, 114; annexes Savoy, 72; her designs on Holland, 73-76, 80, 82; negotiations with England, 84, 95-99, 103-107; decree of 15th December, 90, 91; annexes

Belgium, 111, 121; declares war on England and Holland, 112; evacuates the Netherlands, 126; the Convention declares Pitt the enemy of the human race, 134; revolts in the South and in Brittany, 143, 144; destruction of her navy at Toulon, 160, 161; the miracle of revolutionary finance, 196; passion for unity in, 197; successes in Belgium, 208-212; conquest of Holland, 213-216; treaty of Basle, 217, 223; action in the West Indies, *see* Chaps. IX and X; peace with Spain, 236, 237, 244, 257; alliance with Holland, 251, 274; supposed connection with the mutiny at the Nore, 316; negotiations at Lille, 323-325; *coup d'état* of Fructidor 18, 1797, 324; the Directory rejects Pitt's overtures for peace, 324-327, 336, 338; intrigues with Irish rebels, 345-351, 391; preparations for the eastern expedition, 356, 357; makes offers of peace to Russia, 375; expeditions to Ireland, 362-364, 394-396; her supremacy in Europe, 365; destruction of her fleet at Aboukir, 367, 368; conquest of Naples, 372; Austria declares war on (1799), 374; her responsibility for the war, 374; defeats in Italy, 376; Peace of Amiens, 470; declares war on England (1803), 487; alliance with Spain, 513, 514.

Francis II, Emperor, his accession, 45; war with France, 46; his French policy, 120 *n.*; dismisses Cobenzl, 129; his character, 189-199, 231, 560; takes command of the army in Flanders, 206; returns to Vienna, 209; appeals to England, 366; refuses to interfere in Naples, 372; declares war against France, 374; his timid conduct, 508, 515; his truce proposals after Austerlitz, 544, 545.

Francis, Sir Philip, 23, 238, 290.

Free Trade, demand for (in corn), 289; Pitt's ideal, 427, 428.

Frederick William II, of Prussia, alliance with Austria, 5, 43; signs the Declaration of Pilnitz, 5; encourages Francis II to war, 46; his conduct of the war, 121, 129, 142, 200-204, 207, 215; difficulties of his position, 201; affects indignation with Pitt, 213; makes treaty of Basle with France, 217; his character, 231.

Frederick William III, of Prussia, refuses to join the Allies, 373, 374; his policy, 515, 523, 528, 535-537; his character, 535, 560; signs the Treaty of Potsdam, 539; his demand for Hanover, 540, 541, 552; agrees to the Convention of Schönbrunn, 553; deserts the Allies, 553, 556.

French *émigrés*, 1-3, 6, 7, 155; Pitt and, 3, 6, 259, 287, 454; in England, 63, 64, 165; and the Quiberon expedition, 259-261; hated by George III, 261.

French, Sir Thomas, 518.

Frere, Hookham, 327; Under Secretary for Foreign Affairs, 421; at Canning's wedding, 464, 465; Ambassador at Madrid, 514.

"Friends of the People," the, 23, 24, 40, 167, 168, 171.

Frost, John, 66, 70, 115, 172; his conviction, 172, 173.

Gales, of Sheffield, arrested, 186.

Game Laws, Bill for Reform of, 295.

Garat, Dominique Joseph, 111.

Garcia, Don, Spanish Governor of San Domingo, 228, 229, 235.

Gardiner, Colonel, British envoy at Warsaw, 54.

Gardner, Vice-Admiral Sir Allan, 311.

Garnier, moves that it shall be lawful to murder Pitt, 134.

General Convention of the People, proposal for, 186-189, 192, 193, 284.

Genlis, Mme. de, 79.

Genoa (the Ligurian Republic), 150 *n.*, 386, 470; annexed by Napoleon, 528, 529.

George III, his replies to Leopold II and Gustavus III on intervention in France, 3, 4; dismisses Thurlow, 34; his attitude to proposed coalition of Pitt and the Old Whigs, 36-38; his reception of Talleyrand, 43; his hostility to France, 44, 51, 115; increasing loyalty to, 86; sympathy with Louis XVI, 91; orders Chauvelin to leave the country, 108, 109 *n.*; his view of the war, 119; advocates the siege of Dunkirk, 127, 130; his influence in military affairs, 128, 205, 207, 208, 214, 215, 217; opposed to peace, 243, 276, 321-323; offered the

George III—*continued*.

crown of Corsica, 256; insists on keeping troops in Hanover, 261, 273, 274; his dislike of the *émigrés*, 261; outrage on, in the Mall, 277 *n*., 282, 283, 286; his patronage of agriculture, 291; on the peace negotiations, 324, 325; disapproves of Pitt's duel with Tierney, 336; Irish policy, 342, 358, 359, 394, 409; story of Dundas and, 388; his opposition to Catholic Emancipation, 433-439; accepts Pitt's resignation, 439, 444, 445; his madness, 447, 448, 497-499, 506, 507; extracts a pledge from Pitt, 448, 449; his neglect of literature and art, 456; objects to Fox's inclusion in the Ministry, 499, 500, 530; rejects Napoleon's peace overtures, 516; his character and relations with Pitt, 561-564.

Gerrald, Joseph, 177, 180, 181; his trial and transportation, 182, 183.

Gibbon, Edward, remark of George III to, 456.

Gibraltar, proposed cession to Spain, 277; demanded by Spain, 323, 565.

Gillray, James, 530.

Gisborne, Dr., 447.

Gladstone, W. E., his Home Rule Bill (1886), 415.

Glasgow, political agitation in, 173, 178.

Godoy, Manuel de (afterwards Duke of Alcudia and Prince of the Peace), Spanish Minister, 154, 157; his story concerning Pitt refuted, 92, 93; his relations with the Queen, 230; his character, 230, 231; Anti-British intrigues, 232, 235, 237, 242, 243, 275; makes peace with France, 233, 234, 236; protests against British action in Hayti, 234, 235; made Prince of the Peace, 237; declares war against England, 244; gives aid to France, 513, 514; 560.

Gordon, Duke of, 476.

Gordon, Duchess of, 300 *n.*; Pitt and, 459.

Gower, Earl, Ambassador at Paris, 42, 45, 47, 58; recalled, 58.

Gower, Lord Granville Leveson-, 465; Ambassador at St. Petersburg, 526, 527, 529.

Graaf-Reinet, settlement of, 252, 254.

Graham, A., and D. Williams, their report on the mutiny at the Nore, 316-318.

Granard, Lord, 402.

Grattan, Henry, 339-341, 343, 344, 398, 408, 411.

Gravina, Rear-Admiral, 148, 150, 153.

Grégoire, Henri, 72, 83, 114.

Grenada, revolt in, 239; capture of, 241.

Grenville, Thomas, special envoy at Vienna, 199, 211; his mission to Berlin (1798), 373, 374; on the peace proposals (1801), 469; negotiates the Grenville-Fox alliance, 496.

Grenville, William Wyndham, Lord, Foreign Secretary, 3, 6-9, 37, 68, 312, 421; opposes Flood's motion for Reform, 12; on the Birmingham riots, 19; his marriage, 37; his assurances to Talleyrand, 43-45; his policy regarding the Belgic Provinces, 47, 48; his treatment of Chauvelin, 50, 79, 98, 99, 104, 105, 115; assertion of neutrality, 51, 52, 61, 69, 98; policy towards Poland, 54; ignorant of events in France, 58; his concern at the November decrees, 72-74; regards war as unavoidable, 76, 77, 82; makes overtures to Austria, 84; his fears of Spanish weakness, 92; negotiations with France, 97-101, 103-108; his despatch to Whitworth on British aims, 99, 100; declines to treat with Maret, 109-112; his belief in neutrality, 113; forms the first coalition, 123; ignorant of military affairs, 128; his war policy, 129, 132, 142, 143, 150, 153 *n.*, 154-156, 161, 196, 202, 204-213, 256, 263, 266, 369, 371, 375, 377-380, 382-384; offers to resign, 213, 217, 323; West Indian policy, 224, 225, 228; negotiations with Spain, 233, 234, 243; opposed to negotiations for peace, 276, 322-326; introduces the Treasonable Practices Bill, 285; supports the Finance Bill (1797), 330; on Irish policy, 341, 342, 400, 403, 406; and the Catholic question, 432, 436, 437, 439 *n.*, 449, 519; resigns, 440; on Pitt's resignation, 445, 446; his relations with Pitt, 454, 469, 479, 480, 510, 511; on Pitt's scholarship, 458; opposed to peace (1801), 469; his plans for overthrowing Addington, 495, 496; alliance with Fox, 496; refuses to join Pitt's new ministry, 500-

502; opposes Pitt, 502-504, 510, 517, 555, 557, 559.

Grey, General Sir Charles (afterwards 1st Earl Grey), 225; letter from Pitt to, 381.

Grey, Charles (afterwards 2nd Earl Grey), 23, 188, 191, 276, 516, 519; motions for Reform, 24, 316; opposes proclamation against seditious writings, 25; supports Fox, 89; on the Scottish prosecutions, 179; opposes the Act of Union, 427, 428.

Griffith, Rev. John, of Manchester, 185.

Guadeloupe, planters appeal to England for protection, 221; captured and again recovered, 225, 237, 240, 249.

Guiana, abolition of Slave Trade in, 503.

Guipuzcoa, province of, 233, 235.

Gustavus III of Sweden, 2-4, 7; assassinated, 46.

Gustavus IV of Sweden, refuses aid against Holland, 380; makes a convention with England, 516; his hostility to Napoleon, 528.

Habeas Corpus Act, suspension of (1794), 191, 193, 285; (1798), 333, 351; in Ireland, 345.

Hague Convention (1794), 207.

Hailes, Daniel, British envoy at Warsaw, 53-55.

Hair-powder, disuse of, 290; tax on, 307.

Hameln, held by the French, 544.

Hamilton, Sir William, 150 n., 372.

Hamilton, Lady, 372.

Hammond, George, envoy to the United States, 291.

Hanover, British troops kept in, 261, 273, 274; coveted by Prussia, 535-537, 540, 541, 552; British expedition to, 542, 551, 555, 556.

Hanoverian troops, landed in England, 181, 188.

Hanriot, François, 59.

Hardenberg, Karl August, Prince von, 212; signs the Treaty of Basle, 217; Prussian Foreign Minister, 529, 536, 540, 545.

Hardwicke, Earl of, Lord-Lieutenant of Ireland, 429, 501.

Hardy, Thomas, his "Corresponding Society," 21, 23, 68, 167; letter to Dr. Adams, 65, 66; sends address from com-

bined patriotic societies to French Convention, 67, 68; circular on a General Convention, 187, 188; arrested, 190; acquitted, 192; letter from Thelwall to, 352 n.

Hare, Captain, 160.

Harington, Mr., Mayor of Bath, 165.

Harrington, Earl of, commander of the forces in London, 319; his mission to Berlin, 556.

Harris, Sir James. See Malmesbury, Lord.

Harrowby, Earl of (Dudley Ryder), 290, 294, 451; acts as Pitt's second, 334, 335; Foreign Secretary, 501, 514, 515, 517, 523; Chancellor of the Duchy, 530; his mission to Berlin, 538-547, 552 n.; breakdown of his health, 545, 546, 553, 558; recalled, 556.

Haugwitz, Count von, Prussian Foreign Minister, 202, 206, 207, 212, 515, 536, 537, 540, 543, 553, 560.

Hawkesbury, Lord, 81, 221; Foreign Secretary, 468, 479, 487; Home Secretary, 501, 507, 514, 517, 518, 521, 532, 549, 555.

Hayley, W., letter to Pitt, 455, 456.

Hayti, proposed transfer to England, 131; rising of negroes in, 220, 223; requests British protection, 220; its wealth and prosperity, 222, 223; British successes in, 223, 225-227, 232, 233; Spanish action in, 224, 227-229, 239; increasing difficulties in, 245, 246; English evacuation of, 247; 267, 274, 275.

Hébert, Jacques René, 180.

Helvoetsluys, 127, 216, 267.

Henry, Prince, of Prussia, 207.

Hermann, General, 382.

Hervilly, Comte d', 261, 274.

Hesse-Cassel, compact with England, 123.

Hessian troops, landed in England, 188.

Hobhouse, Sir Benjamin, on the Finance Bill of 1797, 329.

Hoche, General Lazare, 162, 200, 261, 262, 277, 304, 308, 346.

Hohenlohe-Kirchberg, Prince of, 121.

Holcroft, Thomas, 167, 193.

Holwood House, sale of, 473.

Holland. See Dutch Republic.

Holland, Lord, 330, 413, 481 n., 519; opposes the Act of Union, 421.

Hondschoote, battle of, 140.

Hood, Alexander. *See* Bridport, Lord.

Hood, Samuel Lord, occupies Toulon, 134, 144, 145; his difficulties and quarrels, 150-160, 232, 267; occupies Corsica, 256, 257.

Hotham, Admiral (afterwards Lord), 232.

Horsley, Samuel, Bishop of Rochester, and afterwards of St. Asaph, 286, 497.

Houchard, General, 140.

Howe, Admiral Lord, his victory of the 1st of June, 192, 225, 269; quells the mutiny at Spithead, 310-314.

Hugues, Victor, Republican leader in the West Indies, 239, 240, 248.

Humbert, General, his expedition to Ireland, 362, 394, 395.

Hutchinson, John Hely-, General (afterwards Earl of Donoughmore), at the "Castlebar Races," 362; in Egypt, 387.

Hythe military canal, 512.

Illuminati, the, 26.

Income Tax, graduated, suggested, 20, 22, 307; imposed by Pitt, 329, 370, 427, 450; abandoned by Addington, 480.

India, 387, 388, 460-464, 565.

India Bill, Pitt's (1784), 568.

Ireland, Parliament refuses franchise to Catholics, 77; grave situation in, 278, 321, 333, 336; Hoche's expedition to, 304, 308; English loan to, 308, 347; the Rebellion of 1798, 330, *and see* Chaps. XVI, XVIII; Earl Fitzwilliam's Viceroyalty, 339-342; Maynooth founded, 343; feuds and disturbances, 344, 345; Camden's policy of coercion, 345-348, 352, 355, 391; financial straits, 347; Franco-Irish plots, 349-351, 354; resignation of Abercromby, 354; progress of the Rebellion, 355-364; French invasions, 362-364, 394, 395; the Union, *see* Chaps. XVIII, XIX; policy of Cornwallis, 395, 396; corruption in Parliament, 402, 424, 425; debates on the Act of Union, 411-415, 425-428; continued danger from France, 420, 421, 425, 430; financial relations with England, 425, 427, 568; Act of Union passed, 428; pocket boroughs disfranchised, 428; Union honours, 428, 429.

Isherwood, Mr., 460.

Jackson, George, his "Diaries," 546.

Jackson, Mrs., 547.

Jackson, F. L., *chargé-d'affaires* at Madrid, 92, 229; recalled, 230.

Jacobi, Baron, Prussian Ambassador in London, 212, 213.

Jacobins Club, the, in Paris, 25, 26, 42, 168, 169.

Jamaica, sends help to Hayti, 220, 223; coffee-planting in, 222; atrocities of Maroons in, 237, 238.

Jassy, Treaty of, 29, 52.

Jay, John, American envoy to London, 291.

Jean François, negro leader, 239.

Jebb, Richard, his pamphlet against Union, 406.

Jekyll, Joseph, M.P., on the new taxes (1797), 330.

Jemappes, battle of, 57, 69, 113, 114.

Jenkinson, Charles. *See* Liverpool, Earl of.

Jermagnan, Colonel de, 160.

Jervis, Sir John. *See* St. Vincent, Earl of.

Johnstone, General, 361.

Jones, Thomas, M.P., 426.

Jourdan, Marshal, 140, 141.

Joyce, Rev. Jeremiah, letter to Horne Tooke, 190; arrested, 190; discharged, 193.

Jülich, Duchy of, 46.

June 1st, 1794, battle of, 192, 225, 269.

Kaiserslautern, battle of, 208.

Kalkreuth, General, 543.

Kaunitz, Prince, Austrian Chancellor, 5-9, 45, 50, 53, 199, 218.

Keir, Dr., of Birmingham, 17.

Keith, Sir Robert Murray, Ambassador at Vienna, 42, 46; begs for recall, 50.

Kenmare, Lord, 393.

Kent, Duke of, 447, 448.

Kenyon, Lord, 331.

Kersaint, Captain, his speech against England, 102, 103, 106.

Killala, French landing at, 362, 363.

King, Lord, opposes the Act of Union, 421.

Kinglake, A. W., 490.

Korsakoff, General, 375, 378, 379.

Kosciusko, Thaddeus, 53, 206.

Kyd, Stewart, arrested, 190; discharged, 193.

Lageard, de, witty remark of, 276.
Laharpe, F. C. de, 369.
Lake, General, 348, 357, 361, 362.
Lally-Tollendal, Comte de, 43, 93.
Lambton, John, 23.
Landrecies, surrendered, 210.
Land Tax, 30, 31; Pitt's Commutation Act, 331-333, 568.
Langara, Admiral, 144, 146, 153, 154, 157, 159, 232.
Lansdowne, Marquis of, Gillray's cartoon of, 35; intimate with Talleyrand, 51, 77 *n.*; opposes Government policy, 87; opposes the Aliens Bill, 94; on the insult to the King, 283.
Larochejaquelein, Marquis de, 136.
Las Casas, Spanish Ambassador in London, 243.
Lascelles, Mr., M.P., 559.
Lauderdale, Earl of, 23, 179, 286; opposes the Aliens Bill, 94.
Laurence, Dr. French, 427.
Lebrun, P. M. Henri, French Foreign Minister, 58, 60, 69; account of his career, 59; his instructions to Dumouriez, 73, 74; and Maret, 79-81; negotiations with England, 84, 87, 89-91, 97, 104-108, 116; his report on the negotiations, 95, 96, 101, 113, 117.
Leeds, Duke of (Marquis of Carmarthen), 35 *n.*; suggested as First Lord of the Treasury in Coalition Ministry, 36-38; interview with the King, 37; opposes the taxes of 1797, 329.
Lees, John, 355, 395, 396, 406, 418.
Leopold II, correspondence with George III on intervention in France, 2, 3; signs the Declaration of Pilnitz, 5, 6; distrusted by Pitt and Grenville, 8; anxious to avoid war with France, 42; his death, 45.
Lescure, Marquis de, 136.
Letourneur, C. L. F. Honoré, 323.
Lewins, Edward John, delegate of the United Irishmen in Paris, 346, 348.
Liancourt, Duc de, story of his flight, 63, 64.
Ligurian Republic. *See* Genoa.
Lille, 122, 123, 127, 129; peace negotiations at (1797), 247, 323-325.
Lincoln, Bishop of. *See* Tomline, George Pretyman.

Liverpool, Earl of (Charles Jenkinson), 39, 290, 322, 330, 406.
Liverpool, dock strike at, 62; press-gang at, 166, 167.
Livingston, Mr., American Envoy at Paris, 505, 506.
Lloyd, George, 169.
London, Preliminaries of, 468-470.
Long, Charles (afterwards Lord Farnborough), 415, 439, 465, 476, 557.
Longueville, Lord, letter to Pitt on the Union, 402, 403.
Lorraine, 46, 122, 142, 197, 199, 200.
Loughborough, Lord (Alexander Wedderburn), Lord Chancellor, 34, 35, 296, 297, 312, 331; his efforts to bring about a union between Pitt and the Old Whigs, 36-38, 39 *n.*; on the Scottish prosecutions, 179; interviews with Grattan, 340; on union with Ireland, 391, 399; opposes Catholic Emancipation, 431-437, 440, 443, 445; his record, 431, 432; dismissed and created Earl of Rosslyn, 451; the King's comment on his death, 451.
Louis XVI, the flight to Varennes, i, 4, 10; accepts new constitution, 7; letter to George III, 49; his trial decreed, 74, 85, 96; English sympathy for, 86; proposed appeal from England for his life, 91, 92; stories of Spanish and other efforts on his behalf, 92-94; his execution, 108, 117; his responsibility for the Revolution, 560.
Louis, Dauphin (Louis XVII), 145, 146, 156; his death, 259.
Louis XVIII. *See* Provence, Comte de.
Louisa, Queen, of Prussia, 535, 536.
Loyal Associations, growth of, 86.
Loyalty Loan, 305, 306.
Lucchesini, Marquis di, Prussian Ambassador at Vienna, 203, 207.
Lunéville, Treaty of, 470, 529.
Lyons, fall of, 147, 151.

Macartney, Earl, his embassy to Pekin, 32; Governor of the Cape, 254, 255.
MacBride, Admiral, 269 *n.*
McCullum, of Manchester, trial of, 185.
Macdonald, General, 376.
Macdonald, Sir Archibald, Attorney-General, 172.

Mack, General, 204; his plan of campaign (1794), 205; declines to serve under Coburg, 206; surrenders at Ulm, 534, 537.

Mackenzie, Sir Kenneth, 174.

Mackintosh, Sir James, his "Vindiciae Gallicae," 16, 23.

Macleod, General, M.P., 238.

McNevin, William James, delegate of the United Irishmen in Paris, 346, 348; arrested, 354, 394.

Macqueen of Braxfield, Lord Justice Clerk, his trial of Muir, 176, 178, 179; trial of Margarot and Gerrald, 183, 184.

MacRitchie, W., his "Diary of a Tour through Great Britain in 1795," 265.

Maestricht, the French demand a passage through, 82.

Mainz, siege of, 130, 134, 136, 138, 200.

Maitland, General, evacuates Hayti, 247, 248.

Mallet du Pan, 6, 135, 338, 370.

Malmesbury, Lord (Sir James Harris), furthers proposed union between Pitt and the Old Whigs, 36, 38; on the opening of the Scheldt, 75; his mission to Berlin, 200-202, 204; makes treaty with Prussia, 206-208; agreement with Hardenberg, 212; goes to Brunswick, 214, 215; his mission to Paris, 321; negotiations at Lille, 323-326; his statements controverted, 434, 445, 448, 465, 550 n.; urges Pitt to action, 481; mentioned, 90, 286, 497, 524 n., 537, 553, 559.

Malouet, Baron Pierre Victor, his "Mémoires," 92, 93; envoy from Hayti to England, 131, 221, 222, 239, 247 n.

Malt, tax on, 30, 31, 450.

Malta, Pitt's policy with regard to, 255, 277 n., 327, 468-470, 478, 480, 565; the French in, 368, 369, 373, 387, 388; Craig's expedition to, 525, 526; Russian aims in, 526-527; its value to England, 539.

Manchester, Nonconformists in, 11; political clubs founded, 12, 13, 17; disorder in, 62.

"Manchester Constitutional Society," 12, 168, 169, 185.

Mann, Admiral, 243.

Mansfield, Lord, death of, 303.

Marengo, battle of, 386, 387.

Maret, Hugues Bernard (afterwards Duc de Bassano), in London, 79, 83, 94 n., 101; interviews with Pitt, 79-82, 84; his letter to Miles, 105-107; his alleged mission to London, 108-112, 117; ordered to leave, 112; on Chauvelin, 115 n.; one of the plenipotentiaries at Lille, 323.

Margarot, Maurice, 177, 181; his trial and transportation, 182-184.

Maria Carolina, Queen of Naples, 365, 368, 372, 376.

Maria Luisa, of Parma, Queen of Spain, 230, 231, 237.

Maria Theresa, 2nd wife of the Emperor Francis II, 199.

Marie Antoinette, the flight to Varennes, 1, 4, 10; her anger, 7; her schemes, 7, 49, 85; her execution, 141.

Maritime Code, British, opposed by the Baltic powers, 388.

Markoff, Russian minister, 122.

Maroons, their atrocities in Jamaica, 237, 238.

Marseilles, the Royalists in, 144-146.

Martello towers, 512, 513.

Martinique, failure of English attack on, 221; capture of, 225; to be ceded to France, 469.

Masséna, André (Duc de Rivoli), 378, 386.

Maubeuge, siege of, 141.

Maulde, French envoy at The Hague, 76, 82, 83.

Maxwell, Colonel, 360.

Maxwell, Dr., of York, his order for daggers, 64, 65.

Maxwell, James, of York, 64, 65.

Maynooth College, founded, 343, 344.

Mealmaker, author of "An address to the People," 178.

Melas, Field-Marshal, 376.

Melvill, 324-326.

Melville, Lord. See Dundas, Henry.

Mercy d'Argenteau, Count, 4, 7, 8 n., 205.

Merry, Antony, Secretary of legation at Madrid, 242.

Merveldt, General Count, 205.

Middleton, Sir Charles. See Barham, Lord.

Miles, William Augustus, British agent at Paris, 59, 60, 79, 84, 85, 93, 94, 99, 105, 106, 109-111.

Militia, the, 509, 510.

Militia Acts, 279.

Milman, Dr., the King's physician, 506.

Mingay of Norfolk, 188.

Minto, Earl of (Sir Gilbert Elliot), his motion to repeal the Test Act in Scotland 13, 14; on Fox's conduct, 90; commissioner at Dunkirk, 138-140; commissioner at Toulon, 154, 156, 162; Viceroy of Corsica, 244, 256-258; Ambassador at Vienna, 380, 383, 384; speech on the Union, 421.

Mirabeau, Count, 2, 11, 42, 171.

Miranda, General Francesco, 103, 106, 109; ordered to prepare for invasion of Holland, 107; defeated by Coburg, 126.

Missouri River, British mercantile ports on, 244.

Mitchell, Admiral, his successes against the Dutch, 381.

Mitford, Sir John (afterwards Lord Redesdale), made Speaker, 439; letter to Pitt, 485, 486.

Moira, Earl of, 137, 158, 165, 209, 262, 268, 355, 497.

Möllendorf, Marshal, 201, 207, 208, 212, 217.

Monge, Gaspard, French Minister for the Navy, 58; his circular letter, 101-103, 106.

Montrose, Duke of, President of the Board of Trade, 501.

Moore, John, Archbishop of Canterbury, 294, 302; and Catholic Emancipation, 434, 437; death of, 477.

Moore, Sir John, on Abercromby, 240; in the West Indies, 241; in Corsica, 257, 274; in Ireland, 361; and the Volunteers, 492, 493, 510, 512, 547.

More, Hannah, 335, 337.

Moreau, General, 276, 376.

"Morning Chronicle," the, 66, 178; in the pay of the French Embassy, 66 *n*.; prosecution of, 173.

"Morning Post," the, 66.

Mornington, Earl of. *See* Wellesley, Marquis.

Morris, Gouverneur, 96 *n*.; on the state of France in 1795, 259.

Moylan, Bishop, 417, 425 *n*.

Muir, Thomas, 174, 175; goes to Paris, 175; his trial and sentence, 176, 179, 180; at Sydney, 177; his death, 177.

Mulgrave, 1st Lord, 148.

Mulgrave, Henry, 2nd Lord (afterwards Earl of Mulgrave), Chancellor of the Duchy, 501, 514; Foreign Secretary, 517, 523, 527, 538, 542, 549, 550, 552, 556.

Munro, British *chargé-d'affaires* in Paris, 64 *n*., 68.

Münster, Treaty of (1648), 71, 76.

Murphy, Father John, his barbarities in Wexford, 360-362; hanged, 362.

Murphy, Father Michael, 360; killed, 361.

Murray, Sir James, envoy at Frankfurt, 108, 122 *n*., 126 *n*.; Chief of Staff to the Duke of York, 140, 220.

Nagel, Dutch envoy in London, appeals for help, 77.

Nantes, assault of, 136.

Naples, compact with England, 123, 143, 150, 267, 268; French conquest of, 372; Nelson's vengeance on, 376; makes peace with Bonaparte, 386; 468.

Napoleon Bonaparte, 119, 120; his "Souper de Beaucaire," 146; at Toulon, 147, 148, 151, 159; his Italian campaign, 243, 257, 258, 276, 304, 308, 321, 365; his Eastern expedition, 244, 245, 255, 258, 276, 278, 328, 350, 356, 357, 363, 364, 430; disperses the royalist rising in Paris (1795), 263; peace of Campo Formio, 327; at Dunkirk, 349; First Consul, 383, 468-470, 478; proposes terms of peace to Austria and England, 383, 568; battle of Marengo, 386, 387; dupes the Czar, 388; renews peace negotiations, 468; his conquests (1802), 478; his behaviour to Whitworth, 485; declares war on England, 487; threatened invasion of England, 493, 510, 511; his position in 1804, 505; seizes Sir H. Rumbold, 515; again proposes terms of peace, 516; crowned King of Italy, 528; annexes Genoa, 528, 529; battle of Austerlitz, 544; 570.

National Debt, the (1792), 31; (1801), 451.

National Defence, 278-281.

Navy, state of the (1793), 124; causes of discontent in, 310; mutinies at Spithead and the Nore, 310-320.

Needham, General, 361.

Neerwinden, battle of, 126, 127, 267.

Nelson, Lord, in Corsica, 256; on the position of Italy, 277; at Cape St. Vincent, 276, 309; battle of the Nile, 367-369; at Naples, 372, 376; battle of Copenhagen, 388, 450; interview with Pitt, 533; battle of Trafalgar, 534, 538, 565; death of, 521, 538.

Nepean, Sir Evan, on the Scottish prosecutions, 178; Pitt at his house, 459; Irish Secretary, 501, 519.

Netherlands, Austrian, ceded to France, 327.

Netherlands, Dutch. See Dutch Republic.

New Ross, fight at, 360, 361.

New South Wales, 565.

Nicholls, Mr., 330, 472.

Nicols, General, 241.

Nile, battle of the, 368, 369.

Noël, French agent in London, 60, 69, 82, 89 n., 93, 94, 96.

Nonconformists, position of, 10, 11; no longer support Pitt, 12; riots in Birmingham, 18.

Nootka Sound dispute, the, 92, 154, 197, 235; Convention, 232.

Nore, the, mutiny at, 314-320.

Norfolk, Duke of, his seditious speech, 333; and Arthur O'Connor, 350.

Norwich, Bishop of. See Sutton, Charles Manners, 477.

Norwich, Radical Clubs at, 168, 181, 186, 284.

Novossiltzoff, Count, his mission to London, 516, 522, 525; in Berlin, 528, 529.

O'Brien, Sir Edward, 408.

O'Coigly. See Quigley.

O'Connor, Arthur, 346, 350, 351, 394.

O'Drusse, 325, 326.

O'Finn, the brothers, 351.

O'Hara, General, at Toulon, 153, 154, 156; captured, 157.

Orange, Prince of. See William V.

Orange, Wilhelmina, Princess of, 250.

Orangemen, 344, 359; oppose the Union, 425.

Orde, Thomas (afterwards Lord Bolton), 39.

Orleans, Duke of (Philippe Egalité), 59, 79.

Otto, General, 208.

Oubril, Count d', 540, 541.

Pache, Jean Nicolas, French Minister of War, 83, 121.

Paine, Thomas, his "Rights of Man," 14-16, 19-23, 25, 26, 50, 167; intimate with Talleyrand, 51; elected as deputy for Calais, 61; circulation of his works, 167, 168, 175; prosecution of, 172; story of, 180.

Palmer, T. F., transported for sedition, 178, 179.

Paoli, Pascal, 150 n., 227, 256, 257.

Paris, deputation of British residents to the National Convention, 71; activity of Britons in, 175; royalist rising in, 263.

Parker, Vice-Admiral, 311.

Parker, Richard, and the Mutiny at the Nore, 314, 315.

Parker, Theresa, on the taxes of 1797, 329.

Parliament, movement for Reform, 11, 12, 21, 23-28, 164, 171, 180, 181; evolution of the Cabinet, 34; growing power of the Prime Minister, 34; election of 1796, 295.

Parnell, Sir John, Irish Chancellor of the Exchequer, 341, 401, 411.

Parsons, Sir L., 424.

Parthenopean Republic, the, 372.

Paterson, Chairman of the British Convention, 182.

Patriotic Contribution, the (1797), 330, 331.

Paul I, Czar, 258; his indignation with France, 365, 366, 368, 369; alliance with England, 373, 376; breaks with Austria, 379; joins England in the expedition against Holland, 380; duped by Bonaparte, 388; murdered, 388.

Pays Bas. See Belgic Provinces.

Peel, Robert (senior), and the Patriotic Contribution, 331; on the Union, 428.

Peep o' Day Boys, 344.

Pelham, Thomas (afterwards Earl of Chichester), Secretary to Earl Camden, 343; Irish Chief Secretary, 359 n., 399; on Pitt's pledge to the King, 448; Home Secretary, 483, 484; omitted from Pitt's ministry, 501.

Perceval, Spencer, 466; Attorney-General 501, 569.

Perth, sedition in, 77, 174.

Pétion, Jérôme, 58.

Petty, Lord Henry, 520.

Pichegru, General Charles, 162, 200, 215, 216, 377.

Pilnitz, Declaration of, 5, 6.

Pinckard, Dr., his account of the West India expedition, 226.

Pitt, Lady Ann, marries Lord Grenville, 37.

Pitt, Thomas, of Boccanoc. *See* Camelford, Lord.

Pitt, William, his neutrality towards the French Revolution, 3-5, 6, 8; first private meeting with Burke, 7, 8; distrusts Leopold II, 8; opposes Nonconformist claims, 10-12, 24; his opposition to Reform, 12, 23, 24, 26-28; his finance, 30-32, 265, 304-309, 328-333, 369-371, 427, 450, 451; sends Lord Macartney to China, 32; insists on dismissal of Thurlow, 34; rumour of his impending fall, 35; negotiates for union with the Old Whigs, 35-39, 270; made Warden of the Cinque Ports, 39, 89; interview with Canning, 39-41; his reception of Talleyrand, 43; discussion of his policy, 46-48; assertion of neutrality, 48, 50, 52, 61, 98; cautious Polish policy, 55; ignorant of events in France, 58; life at Holwood and Walmer, 68; foresees no danger, 69; his concern at the November decrees, 72-74, 76; his assurances to Holland, 74, 114; considers war unavoidable, 76, 77; interviews with Maret, 79-80, 84; support of his policy not unanimous, 89, 90; his firm attitude, 91; Godoy's story of, 92, 93; Lebrun's charges against, 95, 113, 117; stiff reply to Chauvelin, 98, 99; declaration of policy, 100; his anger with Miles, 106; difficulties of neutrality, 112-113; faults of his policy, 114-116; harsh treatment of Radical Clubs, 114-115; his view of the war, 118-120, 219, 220; his war policy (1793), 123, 129, 131, 132, 137, 139, 144, 145, 147; his care for the navy, 124, 266; ignorant of military affairs, 128; his optimism, 131, 144, 151, 152; demands removal of Coburg, 142; Mediterranean policy, 143, 258; his intentions at Toulon, 152, 154-156; effect of Toulon on his policy, 162, 163.

His Traitorous Correspondence Bill, 164, 165; altered attitude to Reform, 164, 171, 180; policy of repression, 171, 183, 184, 190-194, 333; speech on the Scottish prosecutions, 179, 180; suspends the Habeas Corpus Act, 191; mistaken as to affairs in France, 196, 197; deprecates peace, 198; war policy in 1794, 202, 204-217; dilatoriness in ratifying Prussian Alliance, 208, 210, 269; remonstrance to Prussian Ambassador, 212, 270; insists on recall of the Duke of York, 215; policy in the West Indies, 220 *et seq.*; negotiations with Spain, 233; makes treaty with Russia and Austria, 235; speech on abolition of slavery, 238; inclines towards peace, 242, 243, 257, 276, 287; tries to avert war with Spain, 243, 244; policy at the Cape, 254, 255; attitude towards Corsica, 256-258; relations with the *émigrés*, 259, 287; the Quiberon expedition, 259-262; policy as War Minister, *see* Chap. XII.

Changes in the Cabinet, 270-272; national defence policy, 278-281; agitation against him, 282-284, 288; caricatures of, 282, 301, 335 *n.*, 337; his Sedition Bills, 285-287; action with regard to shortage of corn, 289, 290; institutes a Board of Agriculture, 293; treatment of the Enclosures question, 295-297; his Poor Bill (1797), 297, 298; his relations with Miss Eden, 300-303; his financial embarrassments, 302, 303, 473-477; issues a "Loyalty Loan," 305, 306; and the mutinies in the fleet, 312-320; compared with Chatham, 320; further efforts for peace, 321-326; hostility to his new taxes (1797), 329, 330; the "Patriotic Contribution," 330, 331; his Land Tax proposals, 331-333; his duel with Tierney, 334-336; verses in the "Anti-Jacobin," 337; Irish policy, *see* Chaps. XVI, XVIII, XIX, 566; sends a squadron to the Mediterranean, 366, 367; his Income Tax, 370, 427; his aims in Europe (1798), 371; his policy towards Switzerland, 375; the expedition to Holland, 379-383; rejects Bonaparte's offers of peace, 383-385, 473.

On commercial union with Ireland, 389, 390; his first reference to the

Pitt, William—*continued.*
Union, 393; preparations for the Union, 396-410; speeches on the Act of Union, 413-415, 426, 427; his use of bribery in Ireland, 424, 429; his proposal for Catholic Emancipation, 431; opposition of the King, 433-439; breaks down in health, 435; his resignation, 439-446, 450; his promises to the Catholics, 441, 442, 446; gives a pledge to the King during his illness, 448, 449, 518; breach with Auckland, 452; personal characteristics, 454-459, 491; his neglect of literature and art, 456; his scholarship, 458; his friendship with Wellesley and Canning, 459-466; his creations of peers, 466-468; supports Addington and the peace proposals (1801), 468-472, 478; vote of thanks to him carried, 472; at Walmer, 471, 473, 474, 477; his interest in farming and gardening, 473, 474, 479, 491; his private expenses, 474; subscription for, 476, 477; relations with Addington, 473, 477, 478, 480-482, 503, 504; at Bath, 479; negotiations with Dundas, 483, 484; his terms for return to office, 485; speech on the war with France (1803), 487, 488; death of his mother, 488; organizes the East Kent Volunteers, 489-494, 511, 512; Lady Hester Stanhope at Walmer, 490-493; refuses to join Grenville, 495, 496; agrees to accept office, 497; attack on Addington, 499; forms a ministry, 500-502; and the Slave Trade, 502, 503; difficulties of his position, 503, 504; declines Livingston's peace proposals, 505, 506; remonstrates with the Princess of Wales, 508; his measures for strengthening the army, 509, 511; constructs the Hythe Military Canal, 512; seizes Spanish treasure-ships, 514; on the restoration of the French monarchy, 515; rejects Napoleon's overtures, 516, 566; forms a junction with Addington, 517; opposes Fox's motion for Catholic Emancipation, 518, 519; on the impeachment of Lord Melville, 519-521.

His foreign policy (1805), 523-525; negotiations with Russia, 525-529; final parting with Addington, 530; fails to form a national administration, 530; multiplicity of his cares, 530, 531; interview with Nelson, 533; receives the news of Ulm, 537, 538; his speech at the Lord Mayor's banquet (1805), 538; his magnanimous offers to Prussia, 538, 539; his foresight in South Africa, 539; rejects Prussia's demand for Hanover, 541, 542; correspondence with Harrowby, 541-547; goes back to Bath, 547; story of his reception of the news of Austerlitz, 548, 549; returns home, 553, 554; last days and death, 554-558; opposition to his burial in the Abbey, 559; summary of his career and character, 560-570.

Place, Francis, 283, 284, 286, 349, 350.

Pléville, Admiral, 323.

Plunket, William C. (afterwards Baron), 399, 404, 411.

Plymouth, fortification of, 124.

Pocket Boroughs, in Ireland, disfranchised, 428.

Poland, new Constitution in, 7, 52; Russian designs on, 9, 46, 52; scheme of partition of, 53, 129; Russian invasion of, 53-56; Prussian invasion of, 122; rising in, 206; third Partition of, 218.

Polastron, Mme., 263.

Pondicherry, 198.

Ponsonby, George, 521, 559.

Ponsonby, George, and William (afterwards Baron), Fitzwilliam's overtures to, 339-342; 402.

Poor Bill, Pitt's (1797), withdrawn, 298, 568.

Portland, Duke of, proposed coalitions with Pitt, 35-38, 191, 208, 270; Canning and, 39; refuses to break with Fox, 89, 90; Home Secretary, 191, 244-247, 257, 258, 271, 285, 316, 322, 339, 341, 342, 359, 398, 404, 407, 421, 440, 446, 483; censures Abercromby, 353, 354; his letters to Shelburne on the Irish settlement of 1782, 422; Lord President, 501.

Porto Rico, failure of attack on, 246.

Portsmouth, fortification of, 124.

Portugal, Spanish designs on, 233, 234, 244; loan to, 309; defended by England, 386, 387, 468, 469; pays an annual subsidy to France, 513.

Potsdam, Treaty of (1805), 539, 540.

Press-gang, the, 166.

Pretyman, Dr. *See* Tomline, Bishop.

Price, Dr., his sermon in the Old Jewry, 12 *n.*; his death, 17.

Priestley, Dr., 10, 12, 16 *n.*; his sermon on the death of Dr. Price, 17; his chapel and house wrecked, 18.

Pringle, Admiral, his opinion of Cape Town, 254.

Prosperous, affair at, 357, 358.

Protestants, the, in Ireland, 394, 396, 397, 400, 430; their hostility to the Union, 408, 417, 423.

Provence, Comte de (afterwards Louis XVIII), 2, 129, 259; refused permission to go to Toulon, 155; at the Russian headquarters, 377.

Prussia, alliance with Austria, 5; renounces alliance with Turkey, 5 *n.*; declares war against France, 52; her betrayal of Poland, 52, 53, 129; invades Poland, 122, 123; compact with England (1793), 123; her disputes with Austria, 200-202; state of her finances, 201; English proposals to, 202, 203; treaty with England (1794), 207, 269; her breach of faith, 212; treaty with France (1795), 217, 218, 233; attitude of, in 1799, 374, 380; her conduct with regard to Hanover, 535-537, 540, 541, 552, 553, 556, 560. *See* Frederick William II *and* Frederick William III.

Puisaye, Comte de, Breton leader, 260-263, 274.

Pulteney, Sir James, failure of his attack on Ferrol, 386.

Pulteney, Sir William, 174; opposes the taxes of 1797, 329.

Putney, Bowling Green House, 554-557.

Quesnoy, siege of, 138, 141; surrendered, 210.

Quiberon Expedition, the, 227, 239, 259-262, 274; failure of landing at (1800), 385.

Quigley (O'Coigly), hanged for treason, 350, 354.

Radical, use of the term, 1 *n.*, 10, 23.

Rastadt, Congress of, 365, 374.

Redesdale, Lord. *See* Milford, Sir John.

Reeves, John, founder of the "Anti-Levelling Society," 68.

Reform, influence of the French Revolution on, in England, 11; Flood's motion for, 11, 12; Hardy's efforts for, 21; Pitt's opposition to, 23-28, 164, 171, 180; change of aims, 171, 180.

Regency, threatened, 497.

Reichenbach, Conference of, 3; Convention of, 48.

Reinhard, 108, 346.

Reuss, Prince, Austrian envoy at Berlin, 43.

Rewbell, Jean François, 325.

Reynolds, Dr., 554.

Reynolds, Sir Joshua, Pitt's neglect of, 456.

Richmond, Duke of, his charge against Paine, 50; Master-General of the Ordnance, 124, 130, 131; his incompetence, 137, 140; his Reform plan, 168, 179, 192; resigns, 273.

Richter, arrested, 190.

Rivoli, battle of, 308.

Robespierre, François Maximilien Joseph Isidore, 42, 116, 180; his fall, 192, 212.

Rochester, Bishop of. *See* Horsley, Samuel.

Roer, River, 126, 213.

Roland, J. Marie, French Minister of Home Affairs, 45, 58, 167.

Roland, Mme., 59, 86.

Rolle, Baron, French royalist agent, 5.

Rom, General, goes to San Domingo, 241.

Romilly, Sir Samuel, 61, 487 *n.*, 488, 569.

Romney, Lord, 331.

Romney, George, 167.

Rose, George, Secretary to the Treasury, 6, 38, 119*n.*, 395, 448, 450; resigns, 431, 465; 473, 475, 476, 479-482, 496, 530, 554; Paymaster of the Forces, 501, 517.

Rousseau, Jean Jacques, 72, 114, 197.

Roussillon, Spanish campaign in, 197.

Rowan, Hamilton, 180, 402.

Rumbold, Sir Horace, Ambassador at Hamburg, seized by Napoleon, 515.

Russell, Lord William, 294, 422.

Russia, her designs on Poland, 9, 46, 122, 123, 129; peace with Turkey, 29, 52; treaties with England, 123, 235, 373,

Russia—*continued.*
376, 529; successes in Italy, 376; failure of campaign in Switzerland, 378, 379; Dutch campaign, 379-383; rupture with England, 388; understanding with England, 508, 515; compact with Austria (1804), 516; treaty of Potsdam, 539. *See* Catharine II, Paul I, *and* Alexander I.
Rutland, Duke of, 456.
Ryan, James, 442, 518, 519.
Ryder, Dudley. *See* Harrowby, Earl of.

St. André, André Jeanbon, 167.
St. Asaph, Bishop of. *See* Horsley, Samuel.
St. Helen's, Lord, Ambassador at Madrid, 150, 154, 156, 228, 230.
St. Januarius, 372.
St. John, Lord, 246.
St. John, Order of, 368, 369, 373, 468, 527.
St. Lucia, 225, 237, 240, 241.
St. Vincent, Sir John Jervis, Earl of, expedition to the West Indies, 137, 225, 243; battle of St. Vincent, 244, 277, 309, 310, 336; in the Mediterranean, 366, 367, 420; First Lord of the Admiralty, 483, 495, 498, 501.
St. Vincent, revolt in, 239; relief of, 241.
St. Vincent, Cape, battle of, 244, 277, 309, 310.
Saldanha Bay, defeat of the Dutch in, 254.
San Domingo, 220, 223 *n.*, 225, 233, 235; ceded to France, 236, 237, 241, 275, 321. *See also* Hayti.
Santerre, Claude, 58.
"Sant' Iago," the, seizure of, 232, 233.
Sardinia, compact with England, 123, 143, 147, 150, 151, 267, 268; growth of Jacobinism in, 197; independence of, stipulated by Pitt, 371.
Saumur, capture of, 136.
Saurin, Capt. William, 404, 405 *n.*
Savoy, annexed by France, 68, 72, 113, 276.
Saxony, Elector of, King-elect of Poland, 54.
Scheldt, the, opening of, 47, 71, 72, 75, 79, 80, 82, 84, 86, 91, 97, 98, 105, 114, 117, 119; French gunboats in, 76, 107.

Schönbrunn, Convention of, 553.
Scotland, waking of political life in, 13, 22, 173; failure of motion to repeal the Test Act in, 13, 14; Radical movement in, 77, 173 *et seq.*
Scott, Sir John. *See* Eldon, Lord.
Scully, Denys, 442, 518, 519.
Sebastiani, Colonel, 483.
Secrecy, Parliamentary Committee of, 167, 191, 316, 351.
"Secret Committee of England," the, 349.
Seditious Meetings Bill, 285-287.
Seditious writings, proclamation against, 24, 25, 50.
Ségur, Comte de, his mission to Berlin, 42-44.
September Massacres, the, 57, 59-62.
Seringapatam, capture of, 461, 462.
Servan, Joseph, 58.
Shannon, Lord, 341, 393, 402.
Sheares, Henry and John, United Irishmen, 354; arrested, 355, 356.
Sheffield, disorder in, 62; victory of Jemappes celebrated in, 70; riots at, 166; arrests at, 185, 186; mass meeting at, 189, 193.
Sheffield Association, the, 21, 22, 25, 181.
Sheffield, Earl of, on French emissaries, 69, 70; on the Corn Trade, 290; on Pitt's redemption of Land Tax, 290, 332; on Irish affairs, 395, 404, 421.
Shepherd, John, of Faversham, his report on shortage of corn, 289.
Sheridan, Richard Brinsley, his breach with Canning, 39, 41; warns Chauvelin of Whig patriotism, 87; suggests an appeal to France to spare Louis, 91, 92, 94 *n.*; on the massacre of royalists at Quiberon, 262; and the mutinies in the fleet, 312, 313, 316, 318; on the new taxes (1797), 329; and Arthur O'Connor, 350; opposes the Act of Union, 412, 413, 421, 422, 427; on Pitt's speech on the war (1803), 488; on the danger of a standing army, 510; as an orator, compared with Pitt, 567; mentioned, 23, 24, 165, 179, 188, 191, 238, 241, 286, 290, 293, 309, 352 *n.*, 383, 497, 498, 517, 518.
Sicily, policy of defence of, 525, 526.

Sidmouth, Viscount. *See* Addington, Henry.

Sieyès, Abbé, 233.

Silesia, rising of the weavers in, 201.

Simcoe, Major-General, Governor of Hayti, 245, 246.

Sinclair, Charles, delegate to the British Convention, 181, 182; turns informer, 182.

Sinclair, Sir John, President of the Board of Agriculture, 293-295; loses his seat, 295; his correspondence with Pitt, 296; his General Enclosure Bill, 297; his financial suggestions, 305, 308 *n.*, 309, 332; withdraws amendment hostile to Pitt, 328; on Spencer Perceval, 466.

Sinking Fund, the, 31, 32, 568.

Sistova, Congress of, 3.

Skirving, William, 177; his trial and transportation, 182-184.

Slavery question, in the West Indies, 238, 239.

Slave Trade, Wilberforce's proposals for abolition of, defeated, 502-503; abolished in Guiana, 503.

Sluysken, Governor of the Cape, 251-253.

Smith, Adam, his "Wealth of Nations," 30, 567.

Smith, James, 175.

Smith, Joseph, Pitt's private secretary, 475, 476, 557.

Smith, Captain (afterwards Sir Sidney), at Toulon, 160.

Smith, General, M.P., 68; opposes erection of barracks, 169, 170.

Smith, William, M.P., 79, 457.

Smugglers, their intercourse with France, 165.

Snettisham, result of enclosures at, 292.

"Soldiers' Friend," the, 169,

Sombreuil, de, surrenders at Quiberon, 262.

Somerset, Lord Charles, Paymaster of the Forces, 501.

Somerville, Lord, President of the Board of Agriculture, 296.

Sorel, Albert, mis-statements by, refuted, 277 *n.*

Soult, Marshal, 379, 505, 508.

Spain, compact with England, 123; her co-operation at Toulon, 144, 145, 150,

151, 153, 160; disputes with the English, 153, 154, 156, 157, 197; her action in Hayti, 224, 227-229, 239, 241, 245; state of under Charles IV, 230, 231; hostility to England, 232, 233; peace with France, 236, 237, 244, 257; declares war against England, 241, 244, 275 (1804), 513, 514; Pitt and, 524, 560.

Spanish treasure-ships, seizure of, 514.

Spencer, Rev. Dr., of Birmingham, 18, 186.

Spencer, Earl, special envoy to Vienna, 211; First Lord of the Admiralty, 273, 341, 342, 366, 367, 421, 436; and the mutinies in the fleet, 311, 312, 314, 316; opposes negotiations for peace, 322; resigns, 440, 500.

Spitalfields weavers, their grievances, 166.

Spithead, mutiny at, 310-314.

Stadion, Johann Philipp Karl Joseph, Austrian Ambassador in London, 84.

Staël, Mme. de, at Juniper Hall, 64.

Stahremberg, Count, 205; Austrian Ambassador in London, 366.

Stanhope, Earl, 87, 179, 188, 490, 502.

Stanhope, Lady Hester, on Pitt and women, 299, 300, 303, 454, 455, 477, 531; at Walmer, 490-495; at Putney, 549, 554; her parting with Pitt, 557.

Stanhope, Lord Charles, 491.

Stanhope, Lord James, 557, 558.

Stanislaus, King, of Poland, 54.

"Star," the, 66.

Steele, Robert, Secretary to the Treasury, 412, 451, 454, 476, 557.

Stein, Baron vom, 392, 535, 560.

Stockport, "Friends of Universal Peace" at, 65.

Stofflet, Nicolas, 136.

Stralsund, Russians and Swedes at, 539.

Stratton, Mr., British *chargé-d'affaires* at Vienna, 75.

Stuart, General Sir Charles, in Corsica, 256, 257.

Sutton, Charles Manners, Bishop of Norwich, made Archbishop of Canterbury, 477.

Sweden, refuses to aid the expedition to Holland, 380; convention with England (1804), 516.

Swellendam, settlement of, 252.

Switzerland, 371; importance of her position, 374; Pitt's policy with regard to, 375, 377; failure of campaign in, 378, 379.
"Sun," the, 67.
Suvóroff, Prince, 376, 378, 379.
Sydney, Muir at, 177.

Tainville, French envoy at The Hague, 82.
Talleyrand, Périgord Charles Maurice de, 11; his mission to London, 41-44; second mission, 47-51; intimacy with the Opposition, 51; again in London, 60; at Juniper Hall, 64; his "Mémoire" on a Franco-British understanding, 83; doubts of his loyalty, 83; expelled from England, 103; and the peace negotiations, 325, 326.
Tallien, Jean Lambert, 262.
Talon, M., 93, 94.
Tara Hill, fight at, 357.
Targowicz, Confederation of, 53.
Tarleton, Mr., Mayor of Liverpool, 167.
Tate, Colonel, 309.
Teschen, Treaty of (1779), 365.
Test Act, the, efforts to repeal, 10, 11; in Scotland, 13, 14.
Thanet, Lord, opposes the Act of Union, 421.
Thatched House Tavern, 25.
Thelwall, John, 167, 184, 285; his trial, 193; letter to Hardy, 352 n.
Thornton, Edward, British envoy at Hamburg, 549.
Thornton, Henry, opposes the taxes of 1797, 329.
Thugut, Baron Franz von, Austrian diplomatic agent at Brussels, 46; Chancellor, 129, 143, 148, 153 n., 197 n., 203, 204, 206, 209, 211, 212, 366, 372, 373, 378, 380, 383, 560; his character and aims, 199, 200.
Thurlow, Lord, Lord Chancellor, his character, 33; dismissed, 34, 35; hostile to France, 44; on Lord Loughborough's death, 451, 452.
Tierney, George, 316, 328, 352 n., 385, 427, 520; his duel with Pitt, 334-336; satirized by Canning, 337; Treasurer of the Navy, 498; refuses to serve under Pitt, 501.
"Times," the, 67.
Tippoo Sahib, 44, 250, 336, 461.

Titchfield, Marquis of, 559.
Tobago, 49; captured by Great Britain, 198, 221.
Tomline, George Pretyman, Bishop of Lincoln, 300, 456 n., 473, 475-477, 495, 496; on Pitt's resignation, 442-444, 450, 480; on the King's illness, 447, 448; at Putney, 554-557.
Tone, Wolfe, 78, 177, 340, 344; goes to Paris, 345, 346; his capture and death, 363.
Tooke, Horne, intimate with Talleyrand, 51, 167; his speech, 190; arrested, 190; acquitted, 192, 193.
Tortuga, island of, 246.
Toulon, see Chap. VI; occupied by Hood, 134, 145, 267; British aims at, 154-156; evacuated, 160; destruction of French navy at, 160, 161, 198; Napoleon's preparations at, 336, 349.
Toussaint l'Ouverture, 221, 224, 239, 241, 247, 248.
Trafalgar, battle of, 521, 533, 534.
Traitorous Correspondence Bill, 164, 165.
Treasonable Practices Bill, 285-287.
Trevor, J. H. (afterwards Viscount Hampden), British Minister at Turin, 153 n.
Trincomalee, capture of, 254.
Trinidad, capture of, 246, 248; valued highly by Pitt, 323, 325, 468-470.
Trotter, Deputy-Treasurer of the Navy, 519, 521.
Troy, Archbishop, 412, 417, 425 n.
"True Briton," the, 67.
Turcoing, battle of, 208, 270.
Turin, captured by the allies, 376; 470.
Turkey, makes peace with Russia, 29, 52.
Tuscany, attitude of, 150 n.
Twiss, Colonel, 513.

Ulm, battle of, 524, 534, 536, 537, 556.
Union, the, with Ireland, Chs. XVIII, XIX; 568.
Unitarians, Pitt opposes removal of disabilities of, 24.
United Britons, 349.
United Constitutional Societies, meeting at Norwich (1792), 26.
United Englishmen, 349, 350.
United Irishmen, Society of, 78, 174, 175, 316, 327, 340, 344; turn to France, 345, 346, 349, 351, 357, 391.

United Provinces. *See* Dutch Republic.
United Scotsmen, 349.
United States, treaty with England (1794), 291.
Utrecht, Treaty of (1713), 48, 72.

Valdez, Don, Spanish Minister of Marine, 232.
Valenciennes, 122, 123, 127, 129; siege and fall of, 133, 134, 136; surrendered, 210, 212, 460, 461.
Valmy, battle of, 56, 57, 61, 66, 114, 200.
Vancouver, Captain, 92; ill-treated in California, 232.
Vandamme, General, 382.
Varennes, the flight to, 1, 2, 4; receipt of the news in London, 10.
Vauban, Count, 262, 263.
Vendée, la, insurrection in, 135, 136; expedition to, 237, 240, 262, 263.
Venice, suggested partition of, 129 *n.*, 200.
Vereker, Colonel, 395.
Victor Amadeus, King of Sardinia, 231.
Victor Emmanuel I, King of Sardinia, 522, 523, 539.
Villeneuve, Admiral, 532, 533.
Villiers, George, 506, 507.
Vinegar Hill, fight at, 360, 361.
Volunteer Bill (1804), 497, 498.
Volunteers, the, 124, 188, 278, 279, 337, 363; Pitt's encouragement of, 474, 477, 488-494.
Volunteers, the Ulster, 78.
Vorontzoff, Count, Russian Ambassador in London, 9, 99, 123, 315, 478, 487 *n.*, 527, 529, 541, 543, 550, 563.

Walcheren, Isle of, 547.
Wales, George, Prince of (afterwards George IV), his first speech at Westminster, 51; and the Princess Caroline, 214; and the King's illness, 448, 449, 497; interviews with Pitt, 449; Lord Mornington and, 460, 461; his relations with the King, 507, 508, and with the Princess, 508.
Wales, Princess of, her extravagant conduct, 508.
Walker, Thomas, his "Review of Political Events in Manchester," 11; founds the

Manchester Constitutional Society, 11, 12, 17; prosecution of, 185*t*
Walpole, General, acts as Tierney's second, 335.
Walpole, Horace, and the French refugees, 64.
Walter, John, of "The Times," 67.
Ward, Robert Plumer, Under-Secretary for Foreign Affairs, 550; Pitt's care for, 557.
Wardle, Colonel, 520.
Warren, Admiral Sir John, 262, 363, 532 *n.*; Ambassador at St. Petersburg, 508.
Washington, George, 291.
Watson, Dr., Bishop of Llandaff, his speech on the Union, 421.
Watt, convicted at Edinburgh, 192, 193.
Wattignies, battle of, 141, 200.
Weishaupt, Adam, 26.
Wellesley, Marquis (Earl of Mornington), 68, 313 *n.*; on Pitt's duel with Tierney, 336; his friendship with Pitt, 459-464, 554, 556, 566.
Wellesley, Sir Arthur (afterwards Duke of Wellington), in Flanders, 209, 210; battle of Assaye, 463, 505; anecdote of Pitt told by, refuted, 524; meeting with Nelson, 533; Pitt's last words on, 556.
West Indies, *see* Chaps. IX, X; British designs on, 129, 137, 155, 156, 268, 275; risings of negroes, 220, 237, 238; slavery in, 238, 239; incomes derived from, 370.
Westminster programme of 1780, 168, 171.
Westmorland, Earl of, Lord-Lieutenant of Ireland, 35, 73, 78, 151 *n.*, 152 *n.*, 282, 389, 402; Master of the Horse, 339; Lord Privy Seal, 440, 446, 501.
Wheat, shortage of (1795-6), 288-291; regulation of export and import of, 289.
Whitbread, Samuel, 18, 19, 23, 89, 291, 294; moves a vote of censure on Pitt, 312, 313; his attack on Lord Melville, 518, 519.
Whitworth, Lord, Ambassador at St. Petersburg, 99, 100, 115, 122, 369, 373; ambassador in Paris, 485, 505.
Whyte, Major-General, in the West Indies, 225, 241.
Wickham, William, envoy in Switzerland, 276, 377.

Wigan, strike of colliers at, 62.

Wigglesworth, Colonel, Commissary-General in Hayti, 245.

Wilberforce, William, opposes Flood's motion for reform, 12; his relations with Pitt, 299, 457, 458, 503; and " wicked " Williams, 318, 319; pained by Pitt's duel with Tierney, 335, 336; on the Catholic question, 417, 428; and the Slave Trade, 502, 503; and the impeachment of Melville, 520; on Lord Harrowby, 538; mentioned, 119, 238, 248, 276, 286, 420, 476, 566.

Wilkinson James, of Sheffield, 186.

William V, Prince of Orange, 47, 74, 77 *n.*, 107, 205, 216, 250, 383; his letter to the Governor of the Cape, 250-252.

Williams, " wicked," stirs up disaffection in the army, 318, 319.

Williamson, Major-General, Governor of Jamaica, 223; Governor of Hayti, 239; recalled, 239.

Willis, Dr. (jun.), 447, 448.

Wilson, Rev. Edward, 287.

Winchester, French prisoners at, 165; soldiers quartered at, 169.

Winchilsea, Lord, 412.

Windham, William, on reform, 11, 12, 24; on the war in la Vendée, 136, 137; on the erection of barracks, 170; Secretary at War, 192, 259-261, 271-273, 275, 341, 342, 379, 380, 436; opposes negotiations for peace, 322, 326; resigns, 440; opposed to peace (1801), 469, 470; on the Volunteers, 494; joins Fox and

Grenville, 500, 502, 504, 510, 517, 557; opposes motion to bury Pitt in the Abbey, 559, 560; mentioned, 89, 188, 191, 498.

" World," the, 67.

Wurmser, General, 121, 142 *n.*, 200, 243, 461.

Yarmouth, Lord, 142.

Yeu, expedition to, 263, 272, 273.

Yonge, Sir Charles, Secretary at War, 29, 128, 270.

York, Duke of, his marriage, 31; Commander-in-Chief in Flanders, 126, 127, 130, 133, 138-142, 147, 200, 201, 204, 208, 210, 213-215, 267, 269; effort to shelve him foiled, 205, 206; recalled, 215, 273; Commander-in-Chief, 273, 285, 310, 362-363, 382, 448, 507.

York, delegate to the British Convention, 181.

Yorke, Charles, Under-Secretary at War, 489, 498, 499, 509, 521, 547.

Yorke, Henry (alias Redhead), of Sheffield, 186, 189.

Young, Arthur, 291, 292; Secretary of the Board of Agriculture, 293; superintends draining works at Holwood, 296; on the new taxes (1797), 329.

Young, Admiral, 311.

Yriarte, Don Domingo d', signs the peace of Basle, 236.

Zurich, battle of, 378.

Zuype Canal, the, 382.